# Accounting
## An Introduction

A wide range of supporting resources are available online at:

# MyAccountingLab

Register to create your own personal account using the access code supplied with your copy of the book,* and access the following **student** learning resources:

- A **dynamic eText** of the book that you can search, bookmark, annotate and highlight as you please
- **Self-assessment questions** that identify your strengths before recommending a personalised study plan that points you to the resources which can help you achieve a better grade
- **Flashcards** to test your understanding of key terms
- **Links** to relevant sites on the web

*If you don't have an access code, you can still access the resources. Visit **www.myaccountinglab.com** for details.

**Sixth edition**

# Accounting
## An Introduction

**Eddie McLaney**
**and**
**Peter Atrill**

**PEARSON**

Harlow, England • London • New York • Boston • San Francisco • Toronto • Sydney
Auckland • Singapore • Hong Kong • Tokyo • Seoul • Taipei • New Delhi
Cape Town • São Paulo • Mexico City • Madrid • Amsterdam • Munich • Paris • Milan

**Pearson Education Limited**

Edinburgh Gate
Harlow
Essex CM20 2JE
England

and Associated Companies throughout the world

*Visit us on the World Wide Web at:*
www.pearson.com/uk

———————————

First published 1999 by Prentice Hall Europe
Second edition published 2002
Third edition published 2005
Fourth edition 2008
Fifth edition 2010
**Sixth edition 2012**

*The Financial Times*. With a worldwide network of highly respected journalists, *The Financial Times*
provides global business news, insightful opinion and expert analysis of business, finance and politics.
With over 500 journalists reporting from 50 countries worldwide, our in-depth coverage of international
news is objectively reported and analysed from an independent, global perspective. To find out more,
visit www.ft.com/pearsonoffer.

ISBN 978-0-273-77183-8

**British Library Cataloguing-in-Publication Data**
A catalogue record for this book is available from the British Library

**Library of Congress Cataloguing-in-Publication Data**
McLaney, E. J.
    Accounting : an introduction / Eddie McLaney and Peter Atrill. – 6th ed.
        p. cm.
    Includes bibliographical references and index.
    ISBN 978-0-273-77183-8
1. Accounting.   I. Atrill, Peter.   II. Title.
    HF5636.M44 2012
    657—dc23

                                                                    2012003953

10 9 8 7 6 5 4 3 2 1
17 16 15 14 13 12

Typeset in 9.5/12.5pt ITC Stone Serif by 35
Printed and bound by Rotolito Lombarda, Italy

# Brief contents

# Detailed contents

## Part 1 Financial accounting

## 4  Accounting for limited companies (1) — 125

## Part 2  Management accounting

## 11  Costing and performance evaluation in a competitive environment

## Part 4 Supplementary information

## *ACCOUNTING: AN INTRODUCTION*, 6th edition, ONLINE

A wide range of supporting resources are available at:

# MyAccountingLab

Register to create your own personal account using the access code supplied with your copy of the book,* and access the following teaching and learning resources:

## Resources for students

- A **dynamic eText** of the book that you can search, bookmark, annotate and highlight as you please
- **Self-assessment questions** that identify your strengths before recommending a personalised study plan that points you to the resources which can help you achieve a better grade
- **Flashcards** to test your understanding of key terms
- **Links** to relevant sites on the web

## Resources for instructors

- **Instructor's manual** with additional questions, and complete and fully worked solutions, as well as case study debriefs
- **PowerPoint slides** containing figures from the book

For more information, please contact your local Pearson Education sales representative or visit **www.myaccountinglab.com**.

*If you don't have an access code, you can still access the resources.
Visit **www.myaccountinglab.com** for details.

# Preface

This text provides a comprehensive introduction to financial accounting, management accounting and core elements of financial management. It is aimed both at students who are not majoring in accounting or finance and those who are. Those studying introductory-level accounting and/or financial management as part of their course in business, economics, hospitality management, tourism, engineering or some other area should find that the book provides complete coverage of the material at the level required. Students who are majoring in either accounting or finance should find the book useful as an introduction to the main principles, which can serve as a foundation for further study. The text does not focus on technical issues, but rather examines basic principles and underlying concepts. The primary concern throughout is the ways in which financial statements and information can be used to improve the quality of the decisions made by those who use them. To reinforce this practical emphasis, there are, throughout the text, numerous illustrative extracts with commentary from real life, including company reports, survey data and other sources.

The text is written in an 'open-learning' style. This means that there are numerous integrated activities, worked examples and questions throughout the text to help you to understand the subject fully. You are encouraged to interact with the material and to check your progress continually. Irrespective of whether you are using the book as part of a taught course or for personal study, we have found that this approach is more 'user-friendly' and makes it easier for you to learn.

We recognise that most readers will not have studied accounting or finance before, and we have therefore tried to write in a concise and accessible style, minimising the use of technical jargon. We have also tried to introduce topics gradually, explaining everything as we go. Where technical terminology is unavoidable we try to provide clear explanations. In addition, you will find all of the key terms highlighted in the text. These are then listed at the end of each chapter with a page reference. They are also listed alphabetically, with a concise definition, in the glossary given in Appendix B towards the end of the book. This should provide a convenient point of reference from which to revise.

A further important consideration in helping you to understand and absorb the topics covered is the design of the text itself. The page layout and colour scheme have been carefully considered to allow for the easy navigation and digestion of material. The layout features a large page format, an open design, and clear signposting of the various features and assessment material.

In this sixth edition, we have taken the opportunity to make improvements that have been suggested by students and lecturers who used the previous edition. We have also brought up to date and expanded the number of examples from real life. We have continued to reflect the latest developments in the international rules relating to their main financial statements. We have also made reference to changes in financing methods. We have expanded the number of student progress questions (Activities) and increased the quantity of explanatory diagrams.

More detail about the nature and use of these features is given in the 'How to use this book' section below; and the main points are also summarised, using example pages from the text, in the Guided tour on pages xxiv to xxv.

We hope that you will find the book readable and helpful.

*Eddie McLaney*
*Peter Atrill*

# How to use this book

We have organised the chapters to reflect what we consider to be a logical sequence and, for this reason, we suggest that you work through the text in the order in which it is presented. We have tried to ensure that earlier chapters do not refer to concepts or terms that are not explained until a later chapter. If you work through the chapters in the 'wrong' order, you will probably encounter concepts and terms that were explained previously.

Irrespective of whether you are using the book as part of a lecture/tutorial-based course or as the basis for a more independent mode of study, we advocate following broadly the same approach.

## Integrated assessment material

Interspersed throughout each chapter are numerous **Activities**. You are strongly advised to attempt all of these questions. They are designed to simulate the sort of quick-fire questions that your lecturer might throw at you during a lecture or tutorial. Activities serve two purposes:

- To give you the opportunity to check that you understand what has been covered so far.
- To encourage you to think about the topic just covered, either to see a link between that topic and others with which you are already familiar, or to link the topic just covered to the next.

The answer to each Activity is provided immediately after the question. This answer should be covered up until you have deduced your solution, which can then be compared with the one given.

Towards the middle/end of each chapter there is a **Self-assessment question**. This is more comprehensive and demanding than any of the Activities, and is designed to give you an opportunity to check and apply your understanding of the core coverage of the chapter. The solution to each of these questions is provided in Appendix C at the end of the book. As with the Activities, it is important that you attempt each question thoroughly before referring to the solution. If you have difficulty with a self-assessment question, you should go over the relevant chapter again.

## End-of-chapter assessment material

At the end of each chapter there are four **Review questions**. These are short questions requiring a narrative answer or discussion within a tutorial group. They are intended to help you assess how well you can recall and critically evaluate the core terms and concepts covered in each chapter. Answers to these questions are provided in the MyAccountingLab as well as Appendix D at the end of the book. At the end of each chapter, except for Chapter 1, there are eight **Exercises**. These are mostly computational and are designed to reinforce your knowledge and understanding. Exercises are graded as 'basic' and 'more advanced', according to their level of difficulty. The basic-level questions are fairly straightforward; the more advanced ones can be quite demanding but are capable of being successfully completed if you have worked conscientiously through the chapter and have attempted the basic exercises. Solutions to five of the exercises in each chapter are provided in Appendix D at the end of the book. A coloured exercise number identifies these five questions. Here, too, a thorough attempt should be made to answer each exercise before referring to the solution. Solutions to the other three exercises and to the review questions in each chapter are provided in a separate Instructors' Manual.

To familiarise yourself with the main features and how they will benefit your study from this text, an illustrated Guided tour is provided on pages xxiv–xxvii.

## Content and structure

The text comprises 16 chapters organised into three core parts: financial accounting, management accounting and financial management. A brief introductory outline of the coverage of each part and its component chapters is given in the opening pages of each part.

The market research for this text revealed a divergence of opinions, given the target market, on whether or not to include material on double-entry bookkeeping techniques. So as to not interrupt the flow and approach of the financial accounting chapters, Appendix A on recording financial transactions (including Activities and three Exercise questions) has been placed in Part 4.

## MyAccountingLab

> ## MyAccountingLab
> Visit **www.myaccountinglab.com** for practice and revision opportunities

MyAccountingLab supports this book. This banner reminds students to complete the chapter pre-test to create their personal Study Plan. The results of the test determine the Study Plan going forward.

> ## MyAccountingLab
> Go to **www.myaccountinglab.com** to check your understanding of the chapter, create a personalised study plan, and maximise your revision time

This banner reminds students to complete the chapter post-test in MyAccountingLab to track their progress and mastery of the topics included in each chapter. Their Study plan will adapt according to the results of the test.

# Guided tour of the book

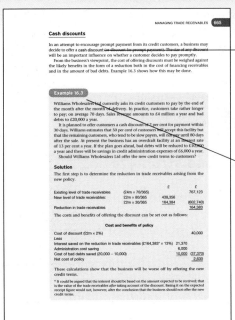

**Key terms** The key concepts and techniques in each chapter are highlighted in colour where they are first introduced.

**Examples** At frequent intervals throughout most chapters, there are numerical examples that give you step-by-step workings to follow through to the solution.

**Introductions** A brief introduction, detailing the topics covered in the chapter, and also showing how chapters are linked together.

**Learning outcomes** Bullet points at the start of each chapter show what you can expect to learn from the chapter, and provide a brief checklist of the core issues.

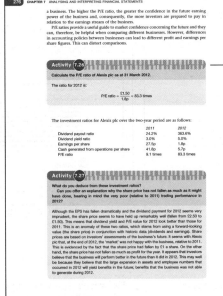

**Activities** These short questions, integrated throughout each chapter, allow you to check your understanding as you progress through the text. They comprise either a narrative question requiring you to review or critically consider topics, or a numerical problem requiring you to deduce a solution. A suggested answer is given immediately after each activity.

**'Real World' illustrations** Integrated throughout the text, these illustrative examples highlight the practical application of accounting concepts and techniques by real businesses, including extracts from company reports and financial statements, survey data and other insights from business.

**Self-assessment questions** Towards the end of most chapters you will encounter one of these questions, allowing you to attempt a comprehensive question before tackling the end-of-chapter assessment material. To check your understanding and progress, solutions are provided in Appendix C.

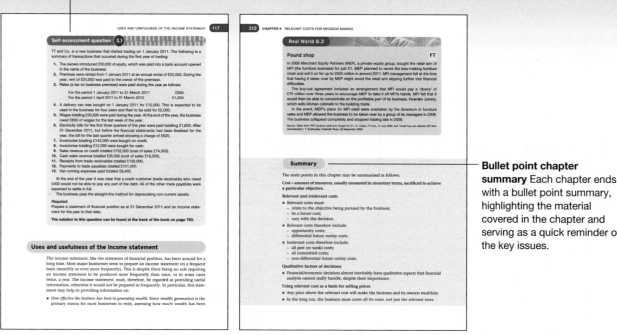

**Bullet point chapter summary** Each chapter ends with a bullet point summary, highlighting the material covered in the chapter and serving as a quick reminder of the key issues.

**Key terms summary** At the end of each chapter, there is a list (with page references) of all the key terms introduced in that chapter, allowing you to refer back easily to the essential points.

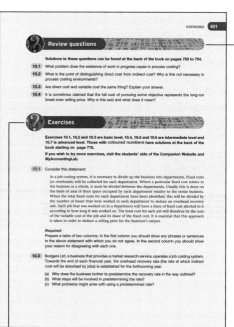

**Review questions** These short questions encourage you to review and/or critically discuss your understanding of the main topics covered in each chapter, either individually or in a group. Solutions to these questions can be found in Appendix D.

**References** Full details of the sources of information referred to in the chapter.

**Further reading** This section provides a list of relevant chapters in other textbooks that you might wish to refer to in order to pursue a topic in more depth or access an alternative perspective.

**Exercises** There are eight of these comprehensive questions at the end of most chapters. The more advanced questions are separately identified. Solutions to five questions (those with coloured numbers) are provided in Appendix E, enabling you to assess your progress. Solutions to the remaining questions are available for lecturers only. An additional exercise for each chapter can be found on the Companion Website at **www.pearsoned.co.uk/mclaney**.

# Guided tour of MyAccountingLab

**MyAccountingLab** is an online assessment and revision tool that puts you in control of your learning through a suite of study and practice tools tied to the online eText.

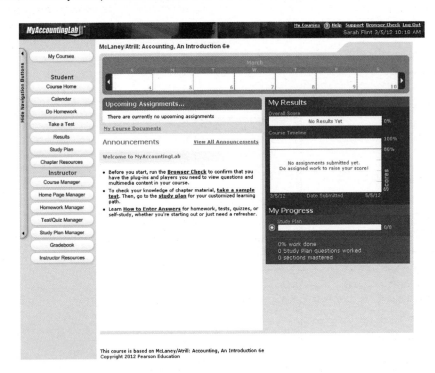

## Why should I use MyAccountingLab?

With more than 300,000 registered students using MyAccountingLab each year, you can be confident that this is the most effective and reliable learning solution for accounting available today.

We recently polled 10,000 student users of MyAccountingLab from around the globe:

- 92% of students said that MyAccountingLab learning aids helped them while completing homework and/or preparing for exams
- 89% of students said that MyAccountingLab helped them earn a higher grade.
- 92% of students would recommend MyAccountingLab for future courses.

## How do I use MyAccountingLab?

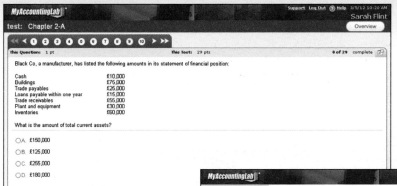

Practice tests for each chapter of the textbook enable you to check your understanding and identify the areas in which you need to do further work.

Based on your test results, we create a personalised Study Plan. This highlights areas where you still need to revise, allowing you to focus on weaker areas and study more efficiently. It also links to the eText, so you can re-read sections in topics you have not yet mastered.

We also provide step-by-step solutions to exercises, so you can see how to get the right answer.

## Lecturer training and support

Our dedicated team of Technology Specialists offer personalised training and support for **MyAccountingLab**, ensuring that you can maximise the benefits of **MyAccountingLab**. To make contact with your Technology Specialist, please email **feedback-cw@pearson.com**

For a visual walkthrough of how to make the most of **MyAccountingLab**, visit **www.myacountinglab.com**

To find details of your local sales consultant, go to **www.pearsoned.co.uk/replocater**

# Acknowledgements

We are grateful to the following for permission to reproduce copyright material:

## Figures

Figures 1.5, 9.13, 10.2, 10.12, 11.5, 13.2, 13.3, 13.5 and 14.5 from *Management Accounting for Decision Makers*, 7th ed., Pearson Education (Atrill, P. and McLaney, E.); Figures 3.8, 4.3, 5.4, 5.5, 7.8 and 15.6 from *Financial Accounting for Decision Makers*, 6th ed., Pearson Education (Atrill, P. and McLaney, E.); Figures 7.1, 15.6, 15.7, 15.11 and 16.6 from *Financial Management for Decision Makers*, 6th ed., Pearson Education (Atrill, P.) p. 69; Figure 11.1 adapted from *Activity Based Costing: A Review with Case Studies*, Chartered Institute of Management Accountants (Innes, J. and Mitchell, F., 1990), CIMA Publishing, copyright Professor John Innes; Figure 11.2 from 'A survey of factors influencing the choice of product costing systems in UK organisations', *Management Accounting Research*, December (Al-Omiri, M. and Drury, C., 2007); Figures 11.4, 11.6, 11.8, 12.7, 12.8, 12.9, 12.11, 13.14 and 14.8 from *Management Accounting Tools for Today and Tomorrow*, Chartered Institute of Management Accountants (2009); Figures 11.10 and 11.13 adapted from *Management Tools*, Bain & Company, Inc. (Rigby, D., 2009); Figure 11.11 from *The Balanced Scorecard*, Harvard Business School Press (Kaplan, R. and Norton, D., 1996); Figure 12.10 from 'Beyond budgeting', Beyond Budgeting Round Table, www.bbrt.org; Figure 15.5 from *Annual Review 2011*, Finance & Leasing Association p. 10, Asset finance provided by FLA members – new business; Figure 15.12 from *Financial Statistics*, Office for National Statistics (2010) p. 1, State Ownership Survey 2008, source: Office for National Statistics licensed under the Open Government Licence v.1.0.; Figure 15.14 from *British Enterprise: Thriving or Surviving?*, Centre for Business Research, University of Cambridge (Cosh, A. and Hughes, A., 2007).

## Tables

Table 4.11 from *Annual Report and Accounts*, Rolls-Royce plc (2010) note 14.

## Text

Real World 1.8 from 'We own Royal Bank', Robert Peston, 28/11/08, www.bbc.co.uk, BBC News; Real World 2.1 adapted from 'Balance sheets: the basics', www.businesslink.gov.uk, reproduced with permission of the copyright holder, Mr Sandeep Sud, Sanco Ltd, Hounslow; Real World 2.2 from Brandz Top 100 Most Valuable Global Brands 2011, www.millwardbrown.com, Millward Brown Optimor, 2011; Real World 3.6 from 'JJB massages results to boost profits', *Accountancy Age*, 20/10/2005, p. 3; Real World 3.8 from 'Findel shares plunge as Yorkshire home shopping firm's bad debts rise', *Yorkshire Evening Post*, 17/04/2008 (Scott, N.), reproduced by kind permission of the *Yorkshire Evening Post*; Real World 4.4 from *The UK Corporate Governance Code*, Financial Reporting Council (2010), © Financial Reporting Council (FRC), adapted and reproduced with the kind permission of the Financial Reporting Council, all rights reserved. For further information, please visit www.frc.org.uk or call +44 (0)20 7492 2300; Real World 4.5, Real World 4.6 and Real World 4.7 from *Annual Report and Accounts*, JD Wetherspoon plc (2010); Real World 5.1 from List of the International Accounting Standards and International Financial Reporting Standards, www.ifrs.org, IFRS Foundation; Real World 5.3, Real World 5.4, Real World 5.5, Real World 5.6, Real World 5.7 and Real World 5.8 from *Annual Report 2011, Business Review*, Greene King plc; Real World 5.12 from 'The rise and fall of Enron', *Journal of Accountancy*, vol. 192, no. 3 (C. William Thomas, 2002), Texas Society of Certified Public Accountants, copyright 2002,

American Institute of Certified Public Accountants, Inc. All rights reserved, used with permission; Real World 6.2 from John Timpson, The management column, *The Daily Telegraph Business*, 14/06/2010 and Real World 12.8 from John Timpson, The management column, *The Daily Telegraph Business*, 06/06/2010, copyright © Telegraph Media Group Limited 2010; Real World 7.11 from *Arnold Weinstock and the Making of GEC*, Aurum Press (Aris, S., 1998); Real World 10.9 from 'An empirical investigation of the importance of cost-plus pricing', *Managerial Auditing Journal*, vol. 20, no. 2 (Guilding, C., Drury, C. and Tayles, M., 2005), © Emerald Group Publishing Limited, all rights reserved; Real World 12.9 from *Transforming Financial Planning*, Beyond Budgeting Round Table (Bunce, P., 2007); Real World 14.9 from *A Multinational Survey of Corporate Financial Policies* (Cohen, G. and Yagil, J. 2007) exhibit 3, working paper, Haifa University; Real World 14.12 from *Positive Scoping Study at 100% owned Azuca Project in Peru*, Hochschild Mining plc (2010) table 3, © Hochschild Mining plc; Real World 16.11 and 16.13 from 'Dash for cash', *CFO Europe Magazine*, 08/07/2008 (Karaian, J.).

### The *Financial Times*

Real World 4.1 from 'Monotub Industries in a spin as founder gets Titan for £1', *Financial Times*, 23/01/2003 (Urquhart, L.); Real World 4.12 from 'Eurotunnel to pay maiden dividend', *The Financial Times*, 05/03/2009; Real World 5.2 from 'Multinationals face more tax audits', ft.com, 03/05/2011 (Cohen, N.); Real World 7.4 from Costs vibrate as VW accelerates, ft.com, 29/03/2010 (Schäfer, D.); Real World 7.6 from 'Gearing levels set to plummet', *Financial Times*, 10/02/2009 (Grant, J.); Real World 7.10 from 'New study re-writes the A to Z of value investing', ft.com, 14/08/2009 (Mathurin, P.); Real World 8.1 from 'Murdoch's MySpace dream turns to dust', ft.com, 30/06/2011 (Garrahan, M.); Real World 9.7 from 'Football League considers cut in player salaries', ft.com, 10/06/2011 (Blitz, R.); Real World 11.9 from 'It is all about the value chain', ft.com, 23/02/2004 (Bickerton, I.); Real World 11.10 from 'Hyundai prepares to relaunch brand', ft.com, 15/12/2010 (Reed, J. and Simon, B.); Real World 11.14 from 'When misuse leads to failure', *Financial Times*, 24/05/2006; Real World 15.2 from 'Man Utd's first bond suffers from lack of support', *Financial Times*, 03/02/2010 (Sakoui, A. and Blitz, R.); Real World 16.4 from 'Wal-Mart aims for further inventory cuts', *Financial Times*, 19/04/2006 (Birchall, J.).

In some instances we have been unable to trace the owners of copyright material, and we would appreciate any information that would enable us to do so.

# Introduction to accounting and finance

## Introduction

In this opening chapter we begin by considering the roles of accounting and finance. As we shall see, both can be valuable tools for decision making. We shall identify those people who are the main users of accounting and financial information and discuss the ways in which this information can improve the quality of decisions that they make. In subsequent chapters, we develop this decision-making theme by considering in some detail the kinds of financial reports and methods used to aid decision making.

Since this book is mainly concerned with accounting and financial decision making for private-sector businesses, we shall devote some time to examining the business environment. We shall, therefore, consider the purpose of a private-sector business, the main forms of business enterprise and the ways in which a business may be structured. We shall also consider what the key financial objective of a business is likely to be. These are all important considerations as they help to shape the kind of accounting and financial information that is produced.

## Learning outcomes

**When you have completed this chapter, you should be able to:**

● Explain the nature and roles of accounting and finance.

● Identify the main users of financial information and discuss their needs.

● Identify and discuss the characteristics that make accounting information useful.

● Explain the purpose of a business and describe how businesses are organised and structured.

## MyAccountingLab

Visit **www.myaccountinglab.com** for practice and revision opportunities

## What are accounting and finance?

Let us begin our study of accounting and finance by trying to understand the purpose of each of them. **Accounting** is concerned with collecting, analysing and communicating financial information. This information is useful for those people who need to make decisions and plans about businesses, including those who need to control those businesses. For example, the managers of businesses may need accounting information to decide whether to:

- develop new products or services (such as a computer manufacturer developing a new range of computers);
- increase or decrease the price or quantity of existing products or services (such as a telecommunications business changing its mobile phone call and text charges);
- borrow money to help finance the business (such as a supermarket wishing to increase the number of stores it owns);
- increase or decrease the operating capacity of the business (such as a beef-farming business reviewing the size of its herd); and
- change the methods of purchasing, production or distribution (such as a clothes retailer switching from UK to overseas suppliers).

The information provided should help in identifying and assessing the financial consequences of such decisions.

Though managers working within a business are likely to be significant users of accounting information about that particular business, they are by no means the only users. There are those outside the business (whom we shall identify later) who may need information to decide whether to:

- invest or disinvest in the ownership of the business (for example, buy or sell shares);
- lend money to the business;
- offer credit facilities (for example, a bank to grant an overdraft); and
- enter into contracts for the purchase of products or services.

Sometimes the impression is given that the purpose of accounting is simply to prepare financial reports on a regular basis. While it is true that accountants undertake this kind of work, the preparation of financial reports does not represent an end in itself. The ultimate purpose of the accountant's work is to give people better information on which to base their decisions. This decision-making perspective of accounting dictates the theme of this book and shapes the way in which we deal with each topic.

**Finance** (or **financial management**), like accounting, exists to help decision makers. It is concerned with the ways in which funds for a business are raised and invested. This lies at the very heart of what a business is about. In essence, a business exists to raise funds from investors (owners and lenders) and then to use those funds to make investments (equipment, premises, inventories and so on) in an attempt to make the business, and its owners, wealthier. It is important that funds are raised in a way that is appropriate to the particular needs of the business, and an understanding of finance should help in identifying:

- the main forms of finance available;
- the costs and benefits of each form of finance;
- the risks associated with each form of finance; and
- the role of financial markets in supplying finance.

Once the funds are raised, they must be invested in ways that will provide the business with a worthwhile return. An understanding of finance should help in evaluating:

- the returns from an investment; and
- the risks associated with an investment.

Businesses often raise and invest funds in large amounts for long periods of time. The quality of the financing and investment decisions made can, therefore, have a profound impact on the fortunes of the business.

In this book, we shall not emphasise the distinctions between accounting and finance as there is little point in doing so. We have already seen that both are concerned with the financial aspects of decision making and there are many interconnections. For example, accounting reports are a major source of information for financing and investment decision making.

## Who are the users of accounting information?

For accounting information to be useful, the accountant must be clear *for whom* the information is being prepared and *for what purpose* the information will be used. There are likely to be various groups of people (known as 'user groups') with an interest in a particular organisation, in the sense of needing to make decisions about it. For the typical private-sector business, the more important of these groups are shown in Figure 1.1. Take a look at this figure and then try Activity 1.1.

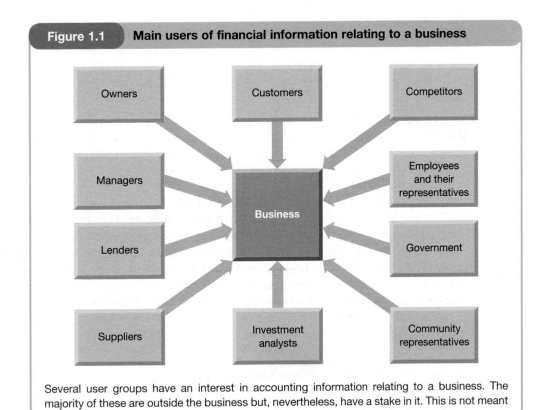

| Figure 1.1 | Main users of financial information relating to a business |

Several user groups have an interest in accounting information relating to a business. The majority of these are outside the business but, nevertheless, have a stake in it. This is not meant to be an exhaustive list of potential users; however, the groups identified are normally the most important.

**Activity (1.1)**

Ptarmigan Insurance plc (PI) is a large motor insurance business. Taking the user groups identified in Figure 1.1, suggest, for each group, the sorts of decisions likely to be made about PI and the factors to be taken into account when making these decisions.

Your answer may be along the following lines:

| User group | Decision |
|---|---|
| Customers | Whether to take further motor policies with PI. This might involve an assessment of PI's ability to continue in business and to meet their needs, particularly in respect of any insurance claims made. |
| Competitors | How best to compete against PI or, perhaps, whether to leave the market on the grounds that it is not possible to compete profitably with PI. This might involve competitors using PI's performance in various aspects as a 'benchmark' when evaluating their own performance. They might also try to assess PI's financial strength and to identify significant changes that may signal PI's future actions (for example, raising funds as a prelude to market expansion). |
| Employees | Whether to continue working for PI and, if so, whether to demand higher rewards for doing so. The future plans, profits and financial strength of the business are likely to be of particular interest when making these decisions. |
| Government | Whether PI should pay tax and, if so, how much, whether it complies with agreed pricing policies, whether financial support is needed and so on. In making these decisions an assessment of its profits, sales revenues and financial strength would be made. |
| Community representatives | Whether to allow PI to expand its premises and/or whether to provide economic support for the business. PI's ability to continue to provide employment for the community, the extent to which it is likely to use community resources and its likely willingness to help fund environmental improvements are likely to be considered when arriving at such decisions. |
| Investment analysts | Whether to advise clients to invest in PI. This would involve an assessment of the likely risks and future returns associated with PI. |
| Suppliers | Whether to continue to supply PI and, if so, whether to supply on credit. This would involve an assessment of PI's ability to pay for any goods and services supplied. |
| Lenders | Whether to lend money to PI and/or whether to require repayment of any existing loans. PI's ability to pay the interest and to repay the principal sum would be important factors in such decisions. |
| Managers | Whether the performance of the business needs to be improved. Performance to date would be compared with earlier plans or some other 'benchmark' to decide whether action needs to be taken. Managers may also wish to decide whether there should be a change in PI's future direction. This would involve looking at PI's ability to perform and at the opportunities available to it. |
| Owners | Whether to invest more in PI or to sell all, or part, of the investment currently held. This would involve an assessment of the likely risks and returns associated with PI. Owners may also be involved with decisions on rewarding senior managers. The financial performance of the business would normally be considered when making such a decision. |

Although this answer covers many of the key points, you may have identified other decisions and/or other factors to be taken into account by each group.

## The conflicting interests of users

We have seen above that each user group looks at a business from a different perspective and has its own particular interests. This means that there is always the risk that the interests of one group will collide with those of another group. Conflict between user groups is most likely to occur over the way in which the wealth of the business is generated and/or distributed. A good example is the conflict that may arise between the managers and the owners of the business. Although managers are appointed to act in the best interests of the owners, there is always a danger that they will not do so. Instead, managers may use the wealth of the business to award themselves large pay rises, to furnish large offices or to buy expensive cars for their own use. Accounting information has an important role to play in reporting the extent to which various groups have benefited from the business. Thus, owners may rely on accounting information to check whether the pay and benefits of managers are in line with agreed policy.

A further example is the potential conflict of interest between lenders and owners. There is a risk that the funds loaned to a business will not be used for purposes that have been agreed. Lenders may, therefore, rely on accounting information to check that the funds have been applied in an appropriate manner and that the terms of the loan agreement are not being broken.

### Activity 1.2

Can you think of other examples where accounting information may be used to monitor potential conflicts of interest between the various user groups identified?

Two possible examples that spring to mind are:

- employees (or their representatives) wishing to check that they are receiving a 'fair share' of the wealth created by the business and that agreed profit-sharing schemes are being adhered to;
- government wishing to check that the profits made from a contract that it has given to a business are not excessive.

You may have thought of other examples.

## How useful is accounting information?

No one would seriously claim that accounting information fully meets all of the needs of each of the various user groups. Accounting is a developing subject and we still have much to learn about user needs and the ways in which these needs should be met. Nevertheless, the information contained in accounting reports should help users make decisions relating to the business. The information should reduce uncertainty about the financial position and performance of the business. It should help to answer questions concerning the availability of funds to pay owners a return, to repay loans, to reward employees, and so on.

Typically, there is no close substitute for the information provided by the financial statements. Thus, if users cannot glean the required information from the financial statements, it is often unavailable to them. Other sources of information concerning the financial health of a business are normally much less useful.

## Activity 1.3

What other sources of information might, say, an investment analyst use in an attempt to gain an impression of the financial position and performance of a business? What kind of information might be gleaned from these sources?

Other sources of information available include:

- meetings with managers of the business;
- public announcements made by the business;
- newspaper and magazine articles;
- websites, including the website of the business;
- radio and TV reports;
- information-gathering agencies (for example, agencies that assess businesses' creditworthiness or credit ratings);
- industry reports;
- economy-wide reports.

These sources can provide information on various aspects of the business, such as new products or services being offered, management changes, new contracts offered or awarded, the competitive environment within which the business operates, the impact of new technology, changes in legislation, changes in interest rates and future levels of inflation. However, the various sources of information identified are not really substitutes for accounting reports. Rather, they are best used in conjunction with the reports in order to obtain a clearer picture of the financial health of a business.

## Evidence on the usefulness of accounting

There are arguments and convincing evidence that accounting information is at least *perceived* as being useful to users. Numerous research surveys have asked users to rank the importance of accounting information, in relation to other sources of information, for decision-making purposes. Generally, these studies have found that users rank accounting information very highly. There is also considerable evidence that businesses choose to produce accounting information that exceeds the minimum requirements imposed by accounting regulations. (For example, businesses often produce a considerable amount of accounting information for managers, which is not required by any regulations.) Presumably, the cost of producing this additional accounting information is justified on the grounds that users find it useful. Such arguments and evidence, however, leave unanswered the question of whether the information produced is actually used for decision-making purposes, that is: does it affect people's behaviour?

It is normally very difficult to assess the impact of accounting on decision making. One situation arises, however, where the impact of accounting information can be observed and measured. This is where the **shares** (portions of ownership of a business) are traded on a stock exchange. The evidence reveals that, when a business makes an announcement concerning its accounting profits, the prices at which shares are traded and the volume of shares traded often change significantly. This suggests that investors are changing their views about the future prospects of the business as a result of this new information becoming available to them and that this, in turn, leads them to make a decision either to buy or to sell shares in the business.

Although there is evidence that accounting reports are perceived as being useful and are used for decision-making purposes, it is impossible to measure just how useful accounting reports are to users. As a result we cannot say with certainty whether the cost of producing those reports represents value for money. Accounting information will usually represent only one input to a particular decision and so the precise weight attached to the accounting information by the decision maker and the benefits which flow as a result cannot be accurately assessed. It is possible, however, to identify the kinds of qualities which accounting information must possess in order to be useful. Where these qualities are lacking, the usefulness of the information will be diminished. This point is considered in the following section.

## Providing a service

One way of viewing accounting is as a form of service. The user groups identified in Figure 1.1 can be seen as the 'clients', and the accounting information produced can be seen as the service provided. The value of this service to the various 'clients' can be judged according to whether the accounting information meets their needs.

To be useful to users, the information provided must possess certain qualities. In particular, it must be relevant and it must faithfully represent what it is supposed to represent. These two qualities, which are regarded as fundamental qualities, are described below.

- **Relevance.** Accounting information should make a difference. That is, it should be capable of influencing user decisions. To do this, it must be relevant to the *prediction of future events* (such as predicting next year's profit), or to the *confirmation of past events* (such as establishing last year's profit), or to both. By confirming past events, users can check on the accuracy of their earlier predictions. This can, in turn, help them to improve the ways in which they make predictions in the future.

   To be relevant, accounting information must cross a threshold of **materiality**. A key question to be asked is whether its omission or misrepresentation would alter the decisions that users make. If the answer is no, the information is not material. This means that it should not be included within accounting reports as it will merely clutter them up and, perhaps, interfere with the users' ability to interpret them. The threshold of materiality will vary from one business to the next. What is material for one business may not be material to another. To identify the threshold, the nature of the information and the amounts involved must be considered within the context of the accounting reports of the particular business.

- **Faithful representation.** Accounting information should be capable of being relied upon to represent what it is supposed to represent. This means that it should be *complete*, that is it provides all of the information needed to understand what is being portrayed. It should also be *neutral*, which is achieved by selecting and presenting the information provided without bias. Finally, it should be *free from error*, as a result of eliminating errors and omissions in the way in which information has been selected and described. This last point does not mean that information must always be perfectly accurate; this is not really possible. Estimates may have to be made which eventually turn out to be inaccurate. It does mean, however, that there should be no errors in the way in which these estimates have been prepared and described.

## Activity 1.4

Do you think it is really feasible for all accounting information to reflect perfectly these three aspects of faithful representation (complete, neutral and free from error)?

The answer is almost certainly no. Rather, the aim should be to strive, as far as possible, towards these three aspects in the accounting information provided.

Note that accounting information must contain both fundamental qualities if it is to be useful. There is little point in producing information that is relevant, but which lacks faithful representation, or producing information that is irrelevant, but which is faithfully represented.

## Further qualities

Where accounting information is both relevant and faithfully represented, there are other qualities that, if present, can enhance its usefulness. These are comparability, verifiability, timeliness and understandability. Each of these qualities is considered below.

- **Comparability**. This quality helps users to identify similarities and differences between items of information. It may help them, for example, to identify changes in the business over time (such as, the trend in sales revenue over the past five years). It may also help them to evaluate the performance of the business in relation to similar businesses. Comparability is enhanced by treating items that are basically the same in the same manner for accounting purposes. It is also enhanced by making clear the policies that have been adopted in measuring and presenting the information.
- **Verifiability**. This quality provides assurance to users that the accounting information provided faithfully represents what it is supposed to represent. Accounting information is verifiable where different, independent experts would be able to reach a consensus that it provides a faithful portrayal. Verifiable information tends to be supported by evidence.
- **Timeliness**. Accounting information should be produced in time for users to make their decisions. A lack of timeliness will undermine the usefulness of the information. Normally, the later accounting information is produced, the less useful it becomes.
- **Understandability**. Accounting information should be set out as clearly and concisely as possible. It should also be understood by those at whom the information is aimed.

## Activity 1.5

**Do you think that accounting reports should be understandable to those who have not studied accounting?**

It would be very useful if accounting reports could be understood by everyone. This, however, is unrealistic as complex financial events and transactions cannot normally be expressed in simple terms. It is probably best that we regard accounting reports in the same way that we regard a report written in a foreign language. To understand either of these, we need to have had some preparation. When producing accounting reports, it is normally assumed that the user not only has a reasonable knowledge of business and accounting but is also prepared to invest some time in studying the reports.

Despite the answer to Activity 1.5, the onus is clearly on accountants to provide information in a way that makes it as understandable as possible to non-accountants.

It is worth emphasising that the four qualities just discussed cannot make accounting information useful. They can only enhance the usefulness of information that is already relevant and faithfully represented.

## Weighing up the costs and benefits

Even though a piece of accounting information may have all the qualities described, it does not automatically mean that it should be collected and reported to users. There is still one more hurdle to jump. Consider Activity 1.6.

## Activity 1.6

**Suppose an item of accounting information, if produced, would have all the qualities mentioned above. Can you think of a reason why, in practice, you might choose not to produce it?**

You may decide not to produce, or discover, the information if you judge the cost of doing so to be greater than the potential benefit of having the information. This cost–benefit issue will limit the extent to which accounting information is provided.

In theory, a particular item of accounting information should only be produced if the costs of providing it are less than the benefits, or value, to be derived from its use. Figure 1.2 shows the relationship between the costs and value of providing additional accounting information.

The figure shows how the value of information received by the decision maker eventually begins to decline. This is, perhaps, because additional information becomes less relevant, or because of the problems that a decision maker may have in processing the sheer quantity of information provided. The costs of providing the information,

| Figure 1.2 | Relationship between costs and the value of providing additional accounting information |

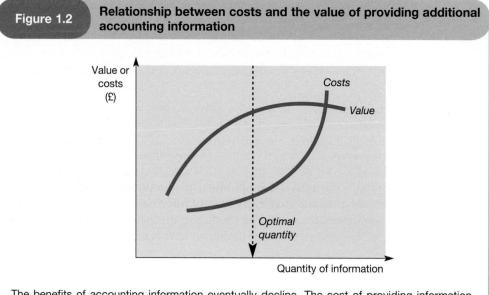

The benefits of accounting information eventually decline. The cost of providing information, however, will rise with each additional piece of information. The optimal level of information provision is where the gap between the value of the information and the cost of providing it is at its greatest.

however, will increase with each additional piece of information. The broken line indicates the point at which the gap between the value of information and the cost of providing that information is at its greatest. This represents the optimal amount of information that can be provided. This theoretical model, however, poses a number of problems in practice.

To illustrate the practical problems of establishing the value of information, let us assume that someone has collided with our car in a car park, and dented and scraped the paint from one of the doors. We wish to have the dent taken out and the door resprayed at a local garage. We know that the nearest garage would charge £350 but believe that other local garages may offer to do the job for a lower price. The only way of finding out the prices at other garages is to visit them, so that they can see the extent of the damage. Visiting the garages will involve using some petrol and will take up some of our time. Is it worth the cost of finding out the price for the job at the various local garages? The answer, as we have seen, is that if the cost of discovering the price is less than the potential benefit, it is worth having that information.

To identify the various prices for the job, there are several points to be considered, including:

- How many garages shall we visit?
- What is the cost of petrol to visit each garage?
- How long will it take to make all the garage visits?
- At what price do we value our time?

The economic benefit of having the information on the price of the job is probably even harder to assess. The following points need to be considered:

- What is the cheapest price that we might be quoted for the job?
- How likely is it that we shall be quoted a price cheaper than £350?

As we can imagine, the answers to these questions may be far from clear – remember that we have only contacted the local garage so far. When assessing the value of accounting information we are confronted with similar problems.

The provision of accounting information can be very costly; however, the costs are often difficult to quantify. The direct, out-of-pocket, costs such as salaries of accounting staff are not really a problem to identify, but these are only part of the total costs involved. There are also less direct costs, such as the cost of the user's time spent on analysing and interpreting the information contained in reports.

The economic benefit of having accounting information is even harder to assess. It is possible to apply some 'science' to the problem of weighing the costs and benefits, but a lot of subjective judgement is likely to be involved. No one would seriously advocate that the typical business should produce no accounting information. At the same time, no one would advocate that every item of information that could be seen as possessing the key characteristics should be produced, irrespective of the cost of producing it.

The qualities and constraints discussed in this section and the preceding section are summarised in Figure 1.3.

**Figure 1.3**  **The qualities that influence the usefulness of accounting information**

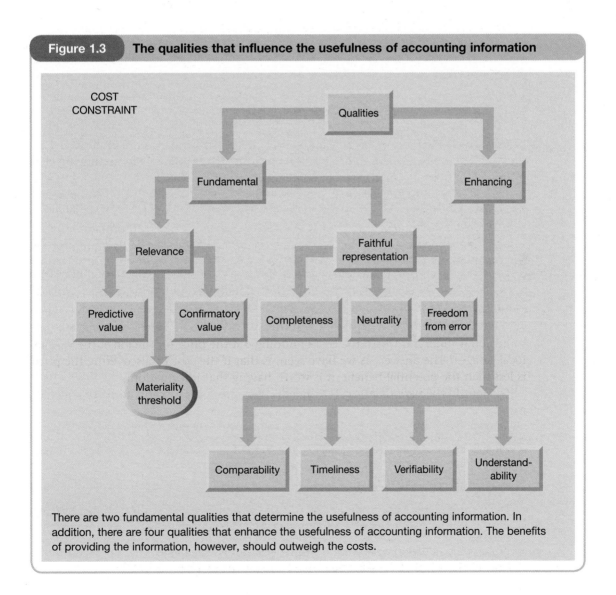

There are two fundamental qualities that determine the usefulness of accounting information. In addition, there are four qualities that enhance the usefulness of accounting information. The benefits of providing the information, however, should outweigh the costs.

## Accounting as an information system

We have already seen that accounting can be seen as the provision of a service to 'clients'. Another way of viewing accounting is as a part of the business's total information system. Users, both inside and outside the business, have to make decisions concerning the allocation of scarce economic resources. To ensure that these resources are efficiently allocated, users need economic information on which to base decisions. It is the role of the accounting system to provide that information and this will involve information gathering and communication.

The **accounting information system** should have certain features that are common to all valid information systems within a business. These are:

- identifying and capturing relevant information (in this case financial information);
- recording the information collected in a systematic manner;
- analysing and interpreting the information collected;
- reporting the information in a manner that suits the needs of users.

The relationship between these features is set out in Figure 1.4.

**Figure 1.4** **The accounting information system**

There are four sequential stages of an accounting information system. The first two stages are concerned with preparation, whereas the last two stages are concerned with using the information collected.

Given the decision-making emphasis of this book, we shall be concerned primarily with the final two elements of the process: the analysis and reporting of accounting information. We shall consider the way in which information is used by, and is useful to, users rather than the way in which it is identified and recorded.

Efficient accounting systems are an essential ingredient of an efficient business. When the accounting systems fail, the results can be disastrous. **Real World 1.1** provides an example of a systems failure when two businesses combined and then attempted to integrate their respective systems.

### Real World 1.1

#### Blaming the system                                            **FT**

When Sir Ken Morrison bought Safeway for £3.35bn in March 2004, he almost doubled the size of his supermarket chain overnight and went from being a regional operator to a national force. His plan was simple enough. He had to sell off some Safeway stores – Morrison has to date sold off 184 stores for an estimated £1.3bn – and convert the remaining

230 Safeway stores into Morrison's. Sir Ken has about another 50 to sell. But, nearly fifteen months on, and the integration process is proving harder in practice than it looked on paper. Morrison, once known for its robust performance, has issued four profit warnings in the past ten months. Each time the retailer has blamed Safeway. Last July, it was because of a faster-than-expected sales decline in Safeway stores. In March – there were two warnings that month – it was the fault of Safeway's accounting systems, which left Morrison with lower supplier incomes. This month's warning was put down to higher-than-expected costs from running parallel store systems. At the time of the first warning last July, Simon Procter, of the stockbrokers Charles Stanley, noted that the news 'has blown all profit forecasts out of the water and visibility is very poor from here on out'. But if it was difficult then to predict where Morrison's profits were heading, it is impossible now. Morrison itself cannot give guidance. 'No one envisaged this,' says Mr Procter. 'When I made that comment about visibility last July, I was thinking on a twelve-month time frame, not a two-year one.' Morrison says the complexity of the Safeway deal has put a 'significant strain' on its ability to cope with managing internal accounts. 'This is impacting the ability of the board to forecast likely trends in profitability and the directors are therefore not currently in a position to provide reliable guidance on the level of profitability as a whole,' admits the retailer.

*Source:* 'Morrison in uphill battle to integrate Safeway', Elizabeth Rigby, *Financial Times*, 26 May 2005.

As a footnote to Real World 1.1, though Morrison had its problems, these were quickly overcome and the Safeway takeover has proved to be a success.

## Financial accounting and management accounting

Accounting is usually seen as having two distinct strands. These are:

- **financial accounting**, which seeks to meet the accounting needs of all of the users identified earlier in the chapter except for managers (see Figure 1.1); and
- **management accounting**, which seeks to meet the accounting needs of managers.

The difference in their targeted user groups has led to each strand of accounting developing along different lines. The main areas of difference are as follows.

1 *Nature of the reports produced.* Financial accounting reports tend to be general purpose, that is, they contain financial information that will be useful for a broad range of users and decisions rather than being specifically designed for the needs of a particular group or set of decisions. Management accounting reports, on the other hand, are often specific-purpose reports. They are designed with a particular decision in mind and/or for a particular manager.

2 *Level of detail.* Financial accounting reports provide users with a broad overview of the performance and position of the business for a period. As a result, information is aggregated and detail is often lost. Management accounting reports, however, often provide managers with considerable detail to help them with a particular operational decision.

3 *Regulations.* Financial accounting reports, for many businesses, are subject to accounting regulations that try to ensure that they are produced with standard content and in a standard format. The law and accounting rule makers impose these regulations. As management accounting reports are for internal use only, there are

no regulations from external sources concerning the form and content of the reports. They can be designed to meet the needs of particular managers.

4 *Reporting interval.* For most businesses, financial accounting reports are produced on an annual basis, though some large businesses produce half-yearly reports and a few produce quarterly ones. Management accounting reports may be produced as frequently as required by managers. In many businesses, managers are provided with certain reports on a daily, weekly or monthly basis, which allows them to check progress frequently. In addition, special-purpose reports will be prepared when required (for example, to evaluate a proposal to purchase a piece of equipment).

5 *Time orientation.* Financial accounting reports reflect the performance and position of the business for a past period. In essence, they are backward looking. Management accounting reports, on the other hand, often provide information concerning future performance as well as past performance. It is an oversimplification, however, to suggest that financial accounting reports never incorporate expectations concerning the future. Occasionally, businesses will release projected information to other users in an attempt to raise capital or to fight off unwanted takeover bids. Even preparation of the routine financial accounting reports typically requires making some judgements about the future, as we shall see in Chapter 3.

6 *Range and quality of information.* Financial accounting reports concentrate on information that can be quantified in monetary terms. Management accounting also produces such reports, but is also more likely to produce reports that contain information of a non-financial nature, such as physical volume of inventories, number of sales orders received, number of new products launched, physical output per employee, and so on. Financial accounting places greater emphasis on the use of objective, verifiable evidence when preparing reports. Management accounting reports may use information that is less objective and verifiable, but nevertheless provide managers with the information they need.

We can see from this that financial accounting is more constrained than management accounting. Management accounting may draw from a variety of sources and use information that has varying degrees of reliability. The only real test to be applied when assessing the value of the information produced for managers is whether or not it improves the quality of the decisions made.

The differences between the two strands of accounting are summarised in Figure 1.5.

The distinctions between management and financial accounting suggest that there are differences between the information needs of managers and those of other users. While differences undoubtedly exist, there is also a good deal of overlap between these needs.

## Activity 1.7

Can you think of any areas of overlap between the information needs of managers and those of other users?

We thought of two points:

- Managers will, at times, be interested in receiving a historical overview of business operations of the sort provided to other users.
- Other users would be interested in receiving information relating to the future, such as the planned level of profits, and non-financial information such as the state of the sales order book and the extent of product innovations.

**Figure 1.5    Management and financial accounting compared**

|  | Management accounting | Financial accounting |
|---|---|---|
| Nature of the reports produced | Tend to be specific purpose | Tend to be general purpose |
| Level of detail | Often very detailed | Usually broad overview |
| Regulations | Unregulated | Usually subject to accounting regulation |
| Reporting interval | As short as required by managers | Usually annual or bi-annual |
| Time horizon | Often based on projected future information as well as past information | Almost always historical |
| Range and quality of information | Tend to contain financial and non-financial information, often use information that cannot be verified | Focus on financial information, great emphasis on objective, verifiable evidence |

Though management and financial accounting are closely linked and have broadly common objectives, they differ in emphasis in various aspects.

The distinction between the two areas of accounting reflects, to some extent, the differences in access to financial information. Managers have much more control over the form and content of information they receive. Other users have to rely on what managers are prepared to provide or what the financial reporting regulations require must be provided. Though the scope of financial accounting reports has increased over time, fears concerning loss of competitive advantage, and user ignorance concerning the reliability of forecast data, have led businesses to resist providing other users with the same detailed and wide-ranging information available to managers.

In the past it has been argued that accounting systems are biased in favour of providing information for external users. Financial accounting requirements have been the main priority and management accounting has suffered as a result. Recent survey evidence suggests, however, that this argument has lost its force. Modern management accounting systems will usually provide managers with information that is relevant to their needs rather than that determined by external reporting requirements. External reporting cycles, however, retain some influence over management accounting. Managers tend to be aware of external users' expectations (see reference 1 at the end of the chapter).

## Scope of this book

This book covers both financial accounting and management accounting topics. The next six chapters (Part 1, Chapters 2 to 7) are broadly concerned with financial accounting, and the following six (Part 2, Chapters 8 to 13) with management accounting. The final part of the book (Part 3, Chapters 14 to 16) is concerned with the financial management of the business, that is, with issues relating to the financing and investing activities of the business. As we have seen, accounting information is usually vitally important for financial management decisions.

## Has accounting become too interesting?

Over recent decades, accounting has become front-page news and has been a major talking point among those connected with the world of business. Unfortunately, the attention that accounting has attracted has been for all the wrong reasons. We have seen that investors rely on financial reports to help to keep an eye both on their investment and on the performance of the managers. What, though, if the managers provide misleading financial reports to investors? The evidence suggests that the managers of some large businesses have been doing just this.

Two of the most notorious cases have been those of:

● Enron, an energy-trading business based in Texas, which was accused of entering into complicated financial arrangements in an attempt to obscure losses and to inflate profits; and

● WorldCom, a major long-distance telephone operator in the US, which was accused of reclassifying $3.9 billion of expenses so as to falsely inflate the profit figures that the business reported to its owners (shareholders) and to others.

In the wake of these scandals, there was much closer scrutiny by investment analysts and investors of the financial reports that businesses produce. This led to further businesses, in both the US and Europe, being accused of using dubious accounting practices to bolster reported profits.

Accounting scandals can have a profound effect on all those connected with the business. The Enron scandal, for example, ultimately led to the collapse of the company, which, in turn, resulted in lost jobs and large financial losses for lenders, suppliers and investors. Confidence in the world of business can be badly shaken by such events and this can pose problems for society as a whole. Not surprisingly, therefore, the relevant authorities tend to be severe on those who perpetrate such scandals. In the US, Bernie Ebbers, the former chief executive of WorldCom, received a 25-year prison sentence for his part in the fraud.

Various reasons have been put forward to explain this spate of scandals. Some may have been caused by the pressures on managers to meet unrealistic expectations of investors for continually rising profits, others by the greed of unscrupulous executives whose pay is linked to financial performance. However, they may all reflect a particular economic environment.

**Real World 1.2** gives some comments suggesting that when all appears to be going well with a business, people can be quite gullible and over-trusting.

**Real World 1.2**

### The thoughts of Warren Buffett

Warren Buffett is one of the world's shrewdest and most successful investors. He believes that the accounting scandals mentioned above were perpetrated during the 'new economy boom' of the late 1990s when confidence was high and exaggerated predictions were being made concerning the future. He states that during that period there had been a combination of weak accounting standards and questionable behaviour by some senior managers. When investors' confidence is high, those who are tempted to take advantage of others are able to do so.

He believes that the worst is now over and that the 'dirty laundry' created during this heady period is being washed away and that the washing machine is now in the 'rinse cycle'.

*Source: The Times*, Business Section, 26 September 2002, p. 25; nisyndication.com.

Whatever the causes, the result of these accounting scandals has been to undermine the credibility of financial statements and to introduce much stricter regulations concerning the quality of financial information. We shall return to this issue in later chapters when we consider the financial statements.

## The changing face of accounting

Over the past 30 years, the environment within which businesses operate has become increasingly turbulent and competitive. Various reasons have been identified to explain these changes, including:

- increasingly sophisticated and demanding customers;
- the development of a global economy where national frontiers become less important;
- rapid changes in technology;
- the deregulation of domestic markets (for example, electricity, water and gas);
- increasing pressure from owners (shareholders) for competitive economic returns;
- the increasing volatility of financial markets.

This new, more complex, environment has brought new challenges for managers and other users of accounting information. Their needs have changed and both financial accounting and management accounting have had to respond. To meet the changing needs of users there has been a radical review of the kind of information to be reported.

The changing business environment has given added impetus to the search for a clear framework and principles upon which to base financial accounting reports. Various attempts have been made to clarify the purpose of financial accounting reports and to provide a more solid foundation for the development of accounting rules. The frameworks and principles that have been developed try to address fundamental questions such as:

- Who are the users of financial accounting information?
- What kinds of financial accounting reports should be prepared and what should they contain?
- How should items (such as profit and asset values) be measured?

In response to criticisms that the financial reports of some businesses are not clear enough to users, accounting rule makers have tried to improve reporting rules to ensure that the accounting policies of businesses are more comparable and more transparent, and that they portray economic reality more faithfully. While this has had a generally beneficial effect, the accounting scandals of recent decades have highlighted the limitations of accounting rules in protecting investors and others.

The internationalisation of businesses has created a need for accounting rules to have an international reach. It can no longer be assumed that users of accounting information relating to a particular business are based in the country in which the business has its base or are familiar with the accounting rules of that country. Thus, there has been increasing harmonisation of accounting rules across national frontiers. A more detailed review of these developments is included in Chapter 5.

Management accounting has also changed by becoming more outward looking in its focus. In the past, information provided to managers has been largely restricted to that collected within the business. However, the attitude and behaviour of customers and rival businesses have now become the object of much information gathering. Increasingly, successful businesses are those that are able to secure and maintain competitive advantage over their rivals.

To obtain this advantage, businesses have become more 'customer driven' (that is, concerned with satisfying customer needs). This has led to management accounting information that provides details of customers and the market, such as customer evaluation of services provided and market share. In addition, information about the costs and profits of rival businesses, which can be used as 'benchmarks' by which to gauge competitiveness, is gathered and reported.

To compete successfully, businesses must also find ways of managing costs. The cost base of modern businesses is under continual review and this, in turn, has led to the development of more sophisticated methods of measuring and controlling costs. These changes are considered in more detail in Chapter 11.

## Why do I need to know anything about accounting and finance?

At this point you may be asking yourself, 'Why do I need to study accounting and finance? I don't intend to become an accountant!' Well, from the explanation of what accounting and finance is about, which has broadly been the subject of this chapter so far, it should be clear that the accounting/finance function within a business is a central part of its management information system. On the basis of information provided by the system, managers make decisions concerning the allocation of resources. As we have seen, these decisions may concern whether to:

● continue with certain business operations;
● invest in particular projects; or
● sell particular products.

Such decisions can have a profound effect on all those connected with the business. It is important, therefore, that *all* those who intend to work in a business should have a fairly clear idea of certain important aspects of accounting and finance. These aspects include:

● how financial reports should be read and interpreted;
● how financial plans are made;

- how investment decisions are made;
- how businesses are financed.

Many, perhaps most, students have a career goal of being a manager within a business – perhaps a personnel manager, production manager, marketing manager or IT manager. If you are one of these students, an understanding of accounting and finance is very important. When you become a manager, even a junior one, it is almost certain that you will have to use financial reports to help you to carry out your role. It is equally certain that it is largely on the basis of financial information and reports that your performance as a manager will be judged.

As part of your management role, it is likely that you will be expected to help in forward planning for the business. This will often involve the preparation of projected financial statements and setting of financial targets. If you do not understand what the financial statements really mean and the extent to which the financial information is reliable, you will find yourself at a distinct disadvantage to others who know their way round the system. Along with other managers, you will also be expected to help decide how the limited resources available to the business should be allocated between competing options. This will require an ability to evaluate the costs and benefits of the different options available. Once again, an understanding of accounting and finance is important to carrying out this management task.

This is not to say that you cannot be an effective and successful personnel, production, marketing or IT manager unless you are also a qualified accountant. It does mean, however, that you need to become a bit 'streetwise' in accounting and finance if you are to succeed. This book should give you that street wisdom.

## Accounting for business

We have seen that the needs of the various user groups will determine the kind of accounting information to be provided; however, the forms of business ownership and the ways in which a business may be organised and structured will help to shape those needs. Thus, in the sections that follow, we consider the business environment within which accounting information is produced. A discussion of these topics should help our understanding of points that crop up in later chapters.

## What is the purpose of a business?

Peter Drucker, an eminent management thinker, has argued that '*The purpose of business is to create and keep a customer*' (see reference 2 at the end of the chapter). Drucker defined the purpose of a business in this way in 1967, at a time when most businesses did not adopt this strong customer focus. His view therefore represented a radical challenge to the accepted view of what businesses do. Forty-five years on, however, his approach has become part of the conventional wisdom. It is now widely recognised that, in order to succeed, businesses must focus on satisfying the needs of the customer.

Although the customer has always provided the main source of revenue for a business, this has often been taken for granted. In the past, too many businesses have assumed that the customer would readily accept whatever services or products were on offer. When competition was weak and customers were passive, businesses could operate under this assumption and still make a profit. However, the era of weak competition has passed. Today, customers have much greater choice and are much more assertive concerning their needs. They now demand higher quality services and goods at cheaper prices. They also require that services and goods be delivered faster with an increasing emphasis on the product being tailored to their individual needs. If a business cannot meet these needs, a competitor often can. Thus the business mantra for the current era is *'the customer is king'*; most businesses now recognise this fact and organise themselves accordingly.

**Real World 1.3** discusses how this mantra applies to business schools offering programmes for business executives.

---

### Real World 1.3

### The customer is king                    FT

For corporations, there is just one message to come out of the recession about business school executive development programmes: it is a buyers' market where the customer is king. And for most business schools, there is also only a single message: rethink your business model if you want to survive.

Customer responsiveness, total quality management and global sensitivity – all topics on which business professors can expound at length – now have to be part of what business schools practise as well as what they preach. Gone are the days when a business school could run a course because it had a professor who understood the subject; customer need has now become paramount.

With both training companies and management consultancies encroaching on the patch of the traditional business education providers, schools have seen two to three years of painful decline in revenues from executive education programmes. Now they hope that business is returning.

Where business is returning, demand has clearly changed. Companies – which pay on average $1,000 per person per day for business school programmes – are putting themselves squarely in the driving seat in the design and delivery of programmes. They are demanding the kinds of performance measures that inform other aspects of their businesses.

Business schools have talked for years about the best ways of measuring corporate return on investment for short business school programmes, and concluded that it could not really be appraised. Now some companies have decided to impose their own measurement systems, and are withholding payment for programmes until they are convinced that they have been successful.

Corporate clients are also less likely to fly their managers to overseas business schools, now requiring the professors to travel instead. In both open-enrolment and customised programmes, the schools that are proving their worth are those that are prepared to take the programmes to the clients. Even Harvard Business School, the doyen of the industry, now teaches programmes in China and India.

Technology is also much in demand, to save time and money. 'Money is an issue,' says Prof Valor (IESE Business School) 'But time is money, too.' Companies are increasingly replacing elements of classroom programmes with internet-based sessions – web seminars and online study groups or learning tools.

*Source*: Extracts from 'Business School Strategy: customer becomes king', D. Bradshaw, 9 May 2011, FT.com.

# What kinds of business ownership exist?

The particular form of business ownership has important implications for accounting purposes and so it is useful to be clear about the main forms of ownership that can arise. There are basically three arrangements:

- sole proprietorship;
- partnership; and
- limited company.

We shall now consider these.

## Sole proprietorship

**Sole proprietorship**, as the name suggests, is where an individual is the sole owner of a business. This type of business is often quite small in terms of size (as measured, for example, by sales revenue generated or number of staff employed); however, the number of such businesses is very large indeed. Examples of sole-proprietor businesses can be found in most industrial sectors but particularly within the service sector. Hence, services such as electrical repairs, picture framing, photography, driving instruction, retail shops and hotels have a large proportion of sole-proprietor businesses. The sole-proprietor business is easy to set up. No formal procedures are required and operations can often commence immediately (unless special permission is required because of the nature of the trade or service, such as running licensed premises). The owner can decide the way in which the business is to be conducted and has the flexibility to restructure or dissolve the business whenever it suits. The law does not recognise the sole-proprietor business as being separate from the owner, so the business will cease on the death of the owner.

Although the owner must produce accounting information to satisfy the taxation authorities, there is no legal requirement to produce accounting information relating to the business for other user groups. Some user groups, however, may demand accounting information about the business and may be in a position to enforce their demands (for example, a bank requiring accounting information on a regular basis as a condition of a loan). A sole proprietor has unlimited liability which means that no distinction is made between the proprietor's personal wealth and that of the business if there are business debts to be paid.

## Partnership

A **partnership** exists where two or more individuals carry on a business together with the intention of making a profit. Partnerships have much in common with sole-proprietor businesses. They are usually quite small in size (although some, such as partnerships of accountants and solicitors, can be large). Partnerships are also easy to set up as no formal procedures are required (and it is not even necessary to have a written agreement between the partners). The partners can agree whatever arrangements suit them concerning the financial and management aspects of the business. Similarly, the partnership can be restructured or dissolved by agreement between the partners.

Partnerships are not recognised in law as separate entities and so contracts with third parties must be entered into in the name of individual partners. The partners of a business usually have unlimited liability.

**Activity (1.8)**

What are the main advantages and disadvantages that should be considered when deciding between a sole proprietorship and a partnership?

The main advantages of a partnership over a sole-proprietor business are:

- sharing the burden of ownership;
- the opportunity to specialise rather than cover the whole range of services (for example, in a solicitors' practice each partner may specialise in a different aspect of the law);
- the ability to raise capital where this is beyond the capacity of a single individual.

The main disadvantages of a partnership compared with a sole proprietorship are:

- the risks of sharing ownership of a business with unsuitable individuals;
- the limits placed on individual decision making that a partnership will impose.

## Limited company

**Limited companies** can range in size from quite small to very large. The number of individuals who subscribe capital and become the owners may be unlimited, which provides the opportunity to create a very large-scale business, though many are quite small. The liability of owners, however, is limited (hence 'limited' company), which means that those individuals subscribing capital to the company are liable only for debts incurred by the company up to the amount that they have agreed to invest. This cap on the liability of the owners is designed to limit risk and to produce greater confidence to invest. Without such limits on owner liability, it is difficult to see how a modern capitalist economy could operate. In many cases, the owners of a limited company are not involved in the day-to-day running of the business and will, therefore, invest in a business only if there is a clear limit set on the level of investment risk.

The benefit of limited liability, however, imposes certain obligations on such companies. To start up a limited company, documents of incorporation must be prepared that set out, among other things, the objectives of the business. Furthermore, a framework of regulations exists that places obligations on limited companies concerning the way in which they conduct their affairs. Part of this regulatory framework requires annual financial reports to be made available to owners and lenders and usually an annual general meeting of the owners has to be held to approve the reports. In addition, a copy of the annual financial reports must be lodged with the Registrar of Companies for public inspection. In this way, the financial affairs of a limited company enter the public domain. With the exception of small companies, there is also a requirement for the annual financial reports to be subject to an audit. This involves an independent firm of accountants examining the annual reports and underlying records to see whether the reports provide a true and fair view of the financial health of the company and whether they comply with the relevant accounting rules established by law and by accounting rule makers. Limited companies are considered in more detail in Chapters 4 and 5.

All of the large household-name UK businesses (Marks and Spencer, Tesco, Shell, BSkyB, Rolls-Royce, BT, easyJet and so on) are limited companies.

> ## Activity (1.9)
>
> What are the main advantages of forming a partnership business rather than a limited liability company?
>
> The main advantages are:
>
> - the ease of setting up the business;
> - the degree of flexibility concerning the way in which the business is conducted;
> - the degree of flexibility concerning restructuring and dissolution of the business;
> - freedom from administrative burdens imposed by law (for example, the annual general meeting and the need for an independent audit).

The main disadvantage of a partnership compared with a limited company is that it is not normally possible to limit the liability of all of the partners. There is, however, a hybrid form of business ownership that is referred to as a Limited Liability Partnership (LLP). This has many of the attributes of a normal partnership but is different in so far as the LLP is responsible for any debts incurred, rather than the individual partners. This type of partnership is often used by accountants and solicitors.

This book concentrates on the accounting aspects of limited liability companies because this type of business is by far the most important in economic terms. The early chapters will introduce accounting concepts through examples that do not draw a distinction between the different types of business. Once we have dealt with the basic accounting principles, which are the same for all three types of business, we can then go on to see how they are applied to limited companies. It must be emphasised that there are no differences in the way that these three forms of business keep their day-to-day accounting records. In preparing their periodic financial statements, there are certain differences that need to be considered. These differences are not ones of principle, however, but of detail.

## How are businesses organised?

Nearly all businesses that involve more than a few owners and/or employees are set up as limited companies. Finance will come from the owners (shareholders) both in the form of a direct cash investment to buy shares (in the ownership of the business) and through the shareholders allowing past profits, which belong to them, to be reinvested in the business. Finance will also come from lenders (banks, for example), who earn interest on their loans, and from suppliers of goods and services being prepared to supply on credit, with payment occurring a month or so after the date of supply, usually on an interest-free basis.

In larger limited companies, the owners (shareholders) tend not to be involved in the daily running of the business; instead they appoint a board of directors to manage the business on their behalf. The board is charged with three major tasks:

1 setting the overall direction and strategy for the business;
2 monitoring and controlling the activities of the business; and
3 communicating with shareholders and others connected with the business.

Each board has a chairman, elected by the directors, who is responsible for running the board in an efficient manner. In addition, each board has a chief executive officer (CEO) (managing director) who is responsible for running the business on a day-to-day basis. Occasionally, the roles of chairman and CEO are combined, although it is usually considered to be a good idea to separate them in order to prevent a single individual having excessive power.

The board of directors represents the most senior level of management. Below this level, managers are employed, with each manager being given responsibility for a particular part of the business's operations.

---

**Activity 1.10**

Why are most larger businesses *not* managed as a single unit by just one manager?

Three common reasons are:

- The sheer volume of activity or number of staff employed makes it impossible for one person to manage them.
- Certain business operations may require specialised knowledge or expertise.
- Geographical remoteness of part of the business operations may make it more practical to manage each location as a separate part, or set of separate parts.

---

The operations of a business may be divided for management purposes in different ways. For smaller businesses offering a single product or service, separate departments are often created, with each department responsible for a particular function (such as marketing, personnel and finance). The managers of each department will then be accountable to the board of directors. In some cases, individual board members may also be departmental managers.

A typical departmental structure, organised along functional lines, is shown in Figure 1.6.

**Figure 1.6** A departmental structure organised according to business function

This is a typical departmental structure organised along functional lines.

The structure set out in the figure may be adapted according to the particular needs of the business. Where, for example, a business has few employees, the personnel function may not form a separate department but may form part of another department. Where business operations are specialised, separate departments may be formed to deal with each specialist area. Example 1.1 illustrates how Figure 1.6 may be modified to meet the needs of a particular business.

### Example 1.1

Supercoach Ltd owns a small fleet of coaches that it hires out with drivers for private group travel. The business employs about 50 people. It might be departmentalised as follows:

- *Marketing department*, dealing with advertising, dealing with enquiries from potential customers, maintaining good relationships with existing customers and entering into contracts with customers.
- *Routing and personnel department*, responsible for the coach drivers' routes, schedules, staff duties and rotas, and problems that arise during a particular job or contract.
- *Coach maintenance department*, looking after repair and maintenance of the coaches, buying spares, giving advice on the need to replace old or inefficient coaches.
- *Finance department*, responsible for managing the cash flows, borrowing, use of surplus funds, payment of wages and salaries, billing and collecting charges to customers, processing invoices from suppliers and paying suppliers.

For large businesses that have a diverse geographical spread and/or a wide product range, the simple departmental structure set out in Figure 1.6 will usually have to be adapted. Separate divisions are often created for each geographical area and/or major product group. Each division will be managed separately and will usually enjoy a degree of autonomy. Within each division, however, departments will often be created and organised along functional lines. Some functions providing support across the various divisions, such as personnel, may be undertaken at head office to avoid duplication. The managers of each division will be accountable to the board of directors. In some cases, individual board members may also be divisional managers.

A typical divisional organisational structure is set out in Figure 1.7. Here the main basis of the structure is geographical. North division deals with production and sales in the north and so on.

Once a particular divisional structure has been established, it need not be permanent. Successful businesses are likely to be innovative and looking to improve their operations. This may well extend to revising their divisional structure. Take for example the business whose structure is depicted in Figure 1.7. At some stage, senior management may conclude that the needs of customers and/or operational efficiency would be better served by having a structure that was based on product lines rather than on geography. This might lead to it reorganising into a structure with a separate division for each product, irrespective of where production takes place or where customers are based.

**Figure 1.7** **A divisional organisational structure**

This is a typical organisational structure for a business that has been divided into separate operating divisions.

Real World 1.4 provides an example of a reorganisation at a well-known international financial services provider. In this case, the business moved from a divisional structure based on product lines to one based on geography.

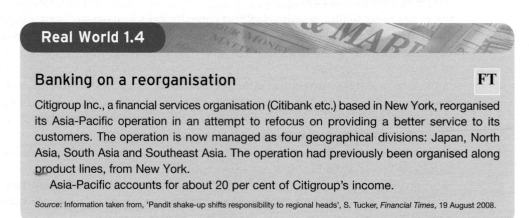

**Real World 1.4**

### Banking on a reorganisation

**FT**

Citigroup Inc., a financial services organisation (Citibank etc.) based in New York, reorganised its Asia-Pacific operation in an attempt to refocus on providing a better service to its customers. The operation is now managed as four geographical divisions: Japan, North Asia, South Asia and Southeast Asia. The operation had previously been organised along product lines, from New York.

Asia-Pacific accounts for about 20 per cent of Citigroup's income.

*Source*: Information taken from, 'Pandit shake-up shifts responsibility to regional heads', S. Tucker, *Financial Times*, 19 August 2008.

Both the divisional structure and departmental structure just described appear to be widely used, although other organisational structures may be found in practice.

## How are businesses managed?

We have already seen that the environment in which businesses operate has become increasingly turbulent and competitive. The effect of these environmental changes has been to make the role of managers more complex and demanding. It has meant that managers have had to find new ways to manage their business. This has increasingly led to the introduction of **strategic management**.

Strategic management seeks to provide a business with a clear sense of purpose and to ensure that appropriate action is taken to achieve that purpose. The action taken should link the internal resources of the business to the external environment of competitors, suppliers, customers and so on. This should be done in such a way that any business strengths, such as having a skilled workforce, are exploited and any weaknesses, such as being short of investment finance, are not exposed. To achieve this requires the development of strategies and plans that take account of the business's strengths and weaknesses, as well as the opportunities offered and threats posed by the external environment. Access to a new, expanding market is an example of an opportunity; the decision of a major competitor to reduce prices is an example of a threat. This topic will be considered in more depth in Chapter 12 when we consider business planning and budgeting.

## What is the financial objective of a business?

A business is created to enhance the wealth of its owners. Throughout this book we shall assume that this is its main objective. This may come as a surprise, as there are other objectives that a business may pursue that are related to the needs of others associated with the business. For example, a business may seek to provide good working conditions for its employees, or it may seek to conserve the environment for the local community. While a business may pursue these objectives, it is normally set up with a view to increasing the wealth of its owners. In practice, the behaviour of businesses over time appears to be consistent with this objective.

Within a market economy there are strong competitive forces at work to ensure that failure to enhance shareholder wealth will not be tolerated for long. Competition for the funds provided by shareholders and competition for managers' jobs will normally mean that shareholders' interests will prevail. If the managers do not provide the expected increase in shareholder wealth, the shareholders have the power to replace the existing management team with a new team that is more responsive to shareholders' needs. Does this mean that the needs of other groups associated with the business (employees, customers, suppliers, the community and so on) are not really important? The answer to this question is certainly no, if the business wishes to survive and prosper over the longer term.

Satisfying the needs of other groups is usually consistent with increasing the wealth of the owners over the longer term. A business with disaffected customers, for example, may find that they turn to another supplier, resulting in a loss of shareholder wealth. **Real World 1.5** reveals how satisfying customer needs in order to increase shareholder wealth is regarded by some businesses as their central purpose.

### Real World 1.5

## Cleaning up for the shareholders

Reckitt Benckiser Group plc makes a number of household, health and personal care products including Vanish, Dettol, Air Wick and Nurofen. In its 2010 annual report the business stated:

> Reckitt Benckiser's vision is to deliver better consumer solutions in household cleaning and health and personal care for the ultimate purpose of creating shareholder value.

**On a mission**

Elektron Technology plc, which operates in the fast-moving engineered products sector, states:

> Our mission is to deliver a highly competitive return to shareholders by using our technologies to create innovative solutions for our customers.

*Sources*: Reckitt and Benckiser Group plc, Annual Report 2010, p.4, and Elektron Technology plc, www.elektron-technology.com, Accessed 21 August 2011.

A dissatisfied workforce may result in low productivity, strikes and so forth, which will in turn have an adverse effect on shareholders' wealth. Similarly, a business that upsets the local community by polluting the environment may attract bad publicity, resulting in a loss of customers, and heavy fines. **Real World 1.6** provides an example of how two businesses responded to potentially damaging allegations.

### Real World 1.6

## The price of clothes                                     **FT**

US clothing and sportswear manufacturers Gap and Nike have much of their clothes produced in Asia where labour tends to be cheap. However, some of the contractors that produce clothes on behalf of the two companies have been accused of unacceptable practices.

Campaigners visited the factories and came up with damaging allegations. The factories were employing minors, they said, and managers were harassing female employees. Nike and Gap reacted by allowing independent inspectors into the factories. They promised to ensure their contractors obeyed minimum standards of employment. Earlier this year, Nike took the extraordinary step of publishing the names and addresses of all its contractors' factories on the internet. The company said it could not be sure all the abuse had stopped. It said that if campaigners visited its contractors' factories and found examples of continued malpractice, it would take action.

Nike and Gap said the approach made business sense. They needed society's approval if they were to prosper. Nike said it was concerned about the reaction of potential US recruits to the campaigners' allegations. They would not want to work for a company that was constantly in the news because of the allegedly cruel treatment of those who made its products.

*Source*: 'Fair shares?', Michael Skapinker, FT.com, 11 June 2005.

It is important to recognise that generating wealth for the owners is not the same as seeking to maximise the current year's profit. Wealth creation is a longer-term concept, which relates not only to this year's profit but to that of future years as well. In the short term, corners can be cut and risks taken that improve current profit at the expense of future profit.

**Real World 1.7** provides some examples of how emphasis on short-term profit can be damaging.

---

**Real World 1.7**

## Short-term gains, long-term problems                    **FT**

For many years, under the guise of defending capitalism, we have been allowing ourselves to degrade it. We have been poisoning the well from which we have drawn wealth. We have misunderstood the importance of values to capitalism. We have surrendered to the idea that success is pursued by making as much money as the law allowed without regard to how it was made.

Thirty years ago, retailers would be quite content to source the shoes they wanted to sell as cheaply as possible. The working conditions of those who produced them were not their concern. Then headlines and protests developed. Society started to hold them responsible for previously invisible working conditions. Companies like Nike went through a transformation. They realised they were polluting their brand. Global sourcing became visible. It was no longer viable to define success simply in terms of buying at the lowest price and selling at the highest.

Financial services and investment are today where footwear was 30 years ago. Public anger at the crisis will make visible what was previously hidden. Take the building up of huge portfolios of loans to poor people on US trailer parks. These loans were authorised without proper scrutiny of the circumstances of the borrowers. Somebody else then deemed them fit to be securitised . . . and so on through credit default swaps and the rest without anyone seeing the transaction in terms of its ultimate human origin.

Each of the decision makers thought it okay to act like the thoughtless footwear buyer of the 1970s. The price was attractive. There was money to make on the deal. Was it responsible? Irrelevant. It was legal, and others were making money that way. And the consequences for the banking system if everybody did it? Not our problem. Now we are paying the price in trillions of dollars for that imprudent attitude.

One senior investment banker whose business has survived the crisis in good shape recently confirmed this analysis to me. Again and again new product ideas had been put in front of him, without any prior thought about their ethical content.

The consumer has had a profound shock. Surely we could have expected the clever and wise people who invested our money to be better at risk management than they have shown themselves to be in the present crisis?

How could they have been so gullible in not challenging the bankers whose lending proved so flaky? How could they have believed that the levels of bonuses that were, at least in part, coming out of their savings could have been justified in 'incentivising' a better performance? How could they have believed that a 'better' performance would be one that is achieved for one bank without regard to its effect on the whole banking system? Where was the stewardship from those exercising investment on their behalf? The answer has been that very few of them do exercise that stewardship. Most have stood back and said it doesn't really pay them to do so.

→

**Real World 1.7 (*continued*)**

The failure of stewardship comes from the same mindset that created the irresponsible lending in the first place. We are back to the mindset that has allowed us to poison the well: never mind the health of the system as a whole, I'm making money out of it at the moment.

Responsibility means awareness for the system consequences of our actions. It is not a luxury. It is the cornerstone of prudence.

*Source*: M. Goyder 'How we've poisoned the well of wealth', *Financial Times*, 15 February 2009.

Though enhancing the wealth of the owners may not be a perfect description of what businesses seek to achieve, it is certainly something that businesses cannot ignore for the reasons mentioned. For the remainder of this book enhancement/maximisation of shareholders' (owners') wealth is treated as the key financial objective against which decisions will be assessed. There will usually be other non-financial/non-economic factors that will also tend to bear on decisions. The final decision may well involve some compromise.

## Balancing risk and return

All decision making involves the future. We can only make decisions about the future; no matter how much we may regret it, we cannot alter the past. Business decision making is no exception to this general rule. There is only one thing certain about the future, which is that we cannot be sure what is going to happen. Sometimes we may be able to predict with confidence that what actually occurs will be one of a limited range of possibilities. We may even feel able to ascribe statistical probabilities to the likelihood of occurrence of each possible outcome, but we can never be completely certain of the future. Risk is therefore an important factor in all financial decision making. It must be considered explicitly in all cases.

As in other aspects of life, risk and return tend to be related. Evidence shows that returns relate to risk in something like the way shown in Figure 1.8.

**Figure 1.8** **Relationship between risk and return**

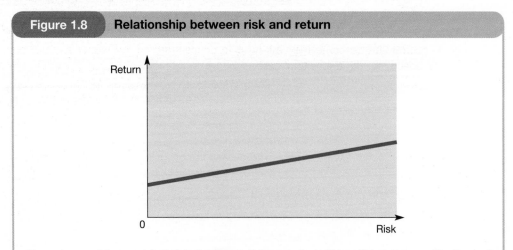

Even at zero risk a certain level of return will be required. This will increase as the level of risk increases.

This relationship between risk and return has important implications for setting financial objectives for a business. The owners (shareholders) will require a minimum return to induce them to invest at all, but will require an additional return to compensate for taking risks; the higher the risk, the higher the required return. Managers must be aware of this and must strike the appropriate balance between risk and return when setting objectives and pursuing particular courses of action.

The recent turmoil in the banking sector has shown, however, that the right balance is not always struck. Some banks have taken excessive risks in pursuit of higher returns and, as a consequence, have incurred massive losses. They are now being kept afloat with taxpayers' money. **Real World 1.8** discusses the collapse of one leading bank, in which the UK government took a majority stake, and argues that the risk appetite of banks must now change.

## Real World 1.8

### Banking on change

The taxpayer has become the majority shareholder in the Royal Bank of Scotland (RBS). This change in ownership, resulting from the huge losses sustained by the bank, will shape the future decisions made by its managers. This does not simply mean that it will affect the amount that the bank lends to homeowners and businesses. Rather it is about the amount of risk that it will be prepared to take in pursuit of higher returns.

In the past, those managing banks such as RBS saw themselves as producers of financial products that enabled banks to grow faster than the economy as a whole. They did not want to be seen as simply part of the infrastructure of the economy. It was too dull. It was far more exciting to be seen a creators of financial products that created huge profits and, at the same time, benefited us all through unlimited credit at low rates of interest. These financial products, with exotic names such as 'collateralised debt obligations' and 'credit default swaps', ultimately led to huge losses that taxpayers had to absorb in order to prevent the banks from collapse.

Now that many banks throughout the world are in taxpayers' hands, they are destined to lead a much quieter life. They will have to focus more on the basics such as taking deposits, transferring funds and making simple loans to customers. Is that such a bad thing?

The history of banking has reflected a tension between carrying out their core functions and the quest for high returns through high-risk strategies. It seems, however, that for some time to come they will have to concentrate on the former and will be unable to speculate with depositors' cash.

*Source*: Based on information in 'We own Royal Bank', Robert Peston, 28 November 2008, BBC News, www.bbc.co.uk.

## Not-for-profit organisations

Though the focus of this book is accounting as it relates to private sector businesses, there are many organisations that do not exist mainly for the pursuit of profit. Examples include:

● charities
● clubs and associations
● universities

- local government authorities
- national government departments
- churches
- trade unions.

Such organisations also need to produce accounting information for decision-making purposes. Various user groups need accounting information about these types of organisation to help them to make decisions. These groups are often the same as, or similar to, those identified for private sector businesses. They may have a stake in the future viability of the organisation and may use accounting information to check that the wealth of the organisation is being properly controlled and used in a way that is consistent with its objectives.

**Real World 1.9** provides an example of the importance of accounting to relief agencies, which are, of course, not-for-profit organisations.

---

### Real World 1.9

### Accounting for disasters                                              FT

In the aftermath of the Asian tsunami more than £400 million was raised from charitable donations. It was important that this huge amount of money for aid and reconstruction was used as efficiently and effectively as possible. That did not just mean medical staff and engineers. It also meant accountants.

The charity that exerts financial control over aid donations is Mango: Management Accounting for Non-Governmental Organisations (NGOs). It provides accountants in the field and it provides the back up, such as financial training and all the other services that should result in really robust financial management in a disaster area.

The world of aid has changed completely as a result of the tsunami. According to Mango's director, Alex Jacobs, 'Accounting is just as important as blankets. Agencies have been aware of this for years. But when you move on to a bigger scale there is more pressure to show the donations are being used appropriately.'

More recently, the earthquake in Haiti led to a call from Mango for French-speaking accountants to help support the relief programme and to help in the longer-term rebuilding of Haiti.

*Source:* Adapted from 'Tsunami: finding the right figures for disaster relief', Robert Bruce, FT.com, 7 March 2005, and 'The work of Mango: Coping with generous donations', Robert Bruce, FT.com, 27 February 2006. 'Accountants needed in Haiti', Paul Grant, *Accountancy Age*, 5 February 2010.

---

## Summary

The main points of this chapter may be summarised as follows:

**What are accounting and finance?**

- Accounting provides financial information for a range of users to help them make better judgements and decisions concerning a business.

- Finance also helps users to make better decisions and is concerned with the financing and investing activities of the business.

## Accounting and user needs

- For accounting to be useful, there must be a clear understanding of *for whom* and *for what purpose* the information will be used.

- There may be conflicts of interest between users over the ways in which the wealth of a business is generated or distributed.

- There is evidence to suggest that accounting is both used and useful for decision-making purposes.

## Providing a service

- Accounting can be viewed as a form of service as it involves providing financial information required by the various users.

- To provide a useful service, accounting must possess certain qualities, or characteristics. These are relevance, faithful representation, comparability, verifiability and understandability. In addition, accounting information must be material.

- Providing a service to users can be costly, and financial information should be produced only if the cost of providing the information is less than the benefits gained.

## Accounting information

- Accounting is part of the total information system within a business. It shares the features that are common to all information systems within a business, which are the identification, recording, analysis and reporting of information.

## Management and financial accounting

- Accounting has two main strands: management accounting and financial accounting.

- Management accounting seeks to meet the needs of the business's managers, and financial accounting seeks to meet the needs of the other user groups.

- These two strands differ in terms of the types of reports produced, the level of reporting detail, the time horizon, the degree of standardisation and the range and quality of information provided.

## Is accounting too interesting?

- In recent years, there has been a wave of accounting scandals in the US and Europe.

- This appears to reflect a particular economic environment, although other factors may also play a part.

## The changing face of accounting

- Changes in the economic environment have led to changes in the nature and scope of accounting.

- Financial accounting has improved its framework of rules and there has been greater international harmonisation of accounting rules.

- Management accounting has become more outward looking, and new methods for managing costs have emerged.

## Why study accounting?

- Everyone connected with business should be a little 'streetwise' about accounting and finance. Financial information and decisions exert an enormous influence over the ways in which a business operates.

**What is the purpose of a business?**

● To create and keep a customer.

**What kinds of business ownership exist?**

There are three main forms of business unit:

● Sole proprietorship – easy to set up and flexible to operate but the owner has unlimited liability.

● Partnership – easy to set up and spreads the burdens of ownership, but partners usually have unlimited liability and there are ownership risks if the partners are unsuitable.

● Limited company – limited liability for owners but obligations imposed on the way a company conducts its affairs.

**How are businesses organised and managed?**

● Most businesses of any size are set up as limited companies.

● A board of directors is appointed by owners (shareholders) to oversee the running of the business.

● Businesses are often divided into departments and organised along functional lines; however, larger businesses may be divisionalised along geographical and/or product lines.

● The move to strategic management has been caused by the changing and more competitive nature of business.

**What is the financial objective of a business?**

● A business may pursue a variety of objectives but the main objective for virtually all businesses is to enhance the wealth of its owners. This does not mean, however, that the needs of other groups connected with the business, such as employees, should be ignored.

● When setting financial objectives the right balance must be struck between risk and return.

## MyAccountingLab

Go to **www.myaccountinglab.com** to check your understanding of the chapter, create a personalised study plan, and maximise your revision time

## Key terms

| | |
|---|---|
| **accounting** p. 2 | **timeliness** p. 8 |
| **finance** p. 2 | **understandability** p. 8 |
| **financial management** p. 2 | **accounting information system** p. 12 |
| **shares** p. 6 | **financial accounting** p. 13 |
| **relevance** p. 7 | **management accounting** p. 13 |
| **materiality** p. 7 | **sole proprietorship** p. 21 |
| **faithful representation** p. 7 | **partnership** p. 21 |
| **comparability** p. 8 | **limited company** p. 22 |
| **verifiability** p. 8 | **strategic management** p. 27 |

## References

1  Dugdale D., Jones C. and Green S., *Contemporary Management Accounting Practices in UK Manufacturing*, CIMA Research Publication, vol. 1, no. 13, 2005.

2  Drucker P., *Effective Executive*, Heinemann, 1967.

## Further reading

If you would like to explore the topics covered in this chapter in more depth, we recommend the following books:

Drury, C., *Management and Cost Accounting*, 8th edn, Cengage Learning, 2012, chapter 1.

Elliott, B. and Elliott, J., *Financial Accounting and Reporting*, 14th edn, Financial Times Prentice Hall, 2011, chapter 7.

Horngren, C., Foster, G., Datar, S., Rajan, M. and Ittner, C., *Cost Accounting: A Managerial Emphasis*, 13th edn, Pearson International, 2010, chapter 1.

McLaney, E., *Business Finance: Theory and Practice*, 9th edn, Financial Times Prentice Hall, 2012, chapters 1 and 2.

Riahi-Belkaoui, A., *Accounting Theory*, 5th edn, Thomson Learning, 2004, chapters 1, 2 and 6.

## Review questions

**Solutions to these questions can be found at the back of the book on pages 745–6.**

**1.1** What is the purpose of producing accounting information?

**1.2** Identify the main users of accounting information for a university. For what purposes would different user groups need information? Is there a major difference in the ways in which accounting information for a university would be used compared with that of a private-sector business?

**1.3** Management accounting has been described as 'the eyes and ears of management'. What do you think this expression means?

**1.4** Financial accounting statements tend to reflect past events. In view of this, how can they be of any assistance to a user in making a decision when decisions, by their very nature, can only be made about future actions?

# PART 1

# Financial accounting

Part 1 of this book deals with the area of accounting and finance usually referred to as 'financial accounting'. Here we shall introduce three major financial statements:

- statement of financial position
- income statement
- statement of cash flows.

In Chapter 2, we provide an overview of these three statements and then go on to consider the first of these, the statement of financial position, in some detail. Included in our consideration of this statement will be an explanation of the accounting conventions used when preparing it. These 'conventions' are generally accepted rules that have evolved to help deal with practical problems experienced by preparers and users of the statement.

In Chapter 3 we examine the second of the major financial statements, the income statement. Here we shall be looking at such issues as how profit is measured and the point in time at which it is reported. Once again, there will be an explanation of the accounting conventions used when preparing this financial statement.

The limited company is the most important business form in the UK and in Chapters 4 and 5 we focus on this type of business. As far as accounting is concerned, there is nothing in essence that makes companies different from other types of private sector business, but there are some points of detail that we need to consider. Chapter 4 examines the nature of limited companies, the way in which they are financed and the accounting issues that specifically relate to this form of business. Chapter 5 considers the duty of directors of a limited company to account to its owners and to others, and the regulatory framework imposed on limited companies. Some additional reports prepared by large limited companies are also considered.

Chapter 6 deals with the last of the three financial statements, the statement of cash flows. This financial statement sets out the sources and uses of cash during an accounting period. We shall see that making profit is not enough. A business must also be able to generate cash to pay its obligations, and the statement of cash flows helps us to assess its ability to do this.

When taken together, the three financial statements provide useful information about the business's performance and position for the period concerned. It is possible, however, to gain even more helpful insights about the business by analysing these statements, using financial ratios and other techniques. Combining two figures from the financial statements in a ratio, and comparing this with a similar ratio for, say, another business, can often tell us much more than just reading the figures themselves. In Chapter 7 we consider some of the techniques for analysing financial statements.

# Measuring and reporting financial position

## Introduction

We saw in Chapter 1 that accounting has two distinct strands: financial accounting and management accounting. This chapter, along with Chapters 3, 4 and 5, examines the three major financial statements that form the core of financial accounting. We start by taking an overview of these statements to see how each contributes towards an assessment of the overall financial position and performance of a business.

Following this overview, we begin a more detailed examination by turning our attention towards one of these financial statements: the statement of financial position. We shall see how it is prepared and examine the principles underpinning it. We shall also consider its value for decision-making purposes.

## Learning outcomes

**When you have completed this chapter, you should be able to:**

- Explain the nature and purpose of the three major financial statements.

- Prepare a simple statement of financial position and interpret the information that it contains.

- Discuss the accounting conventions underpinning the statement of financial position.

- Discuss the uses and limitations of the statement of financial position for decision-making purposes.

## MyAccountingLab

Visit **www.myaccountinglab.com** for practice and revision opportunities

## Making financial decisions

We have just seen that a key purpose of this chapter is to show how the statement of financial position may help users. So, let us begin by providing an example of its value for decision making. **Real World 2.1** describes how the statement of financial position of a small business was used by a bank when considering whether to grant a loan.

### Real World 2.1

#### A sound education

Sandeep Sud is a qualified solicitor who also runs a school uniform business based in Hounslow, in partnership with his parents. The company, which has four full-time employees, uses its statement of financial position to gauge how the business is progressing. It has also been a key factor in securing a bank loan for the improvement and expansion of the company premises.

According to Sandeep:

Having a strong statement of financial position helped when it came to borrowing. When we first applied for a refurbishment loan we couldn't provide up-to-date accounts to the bank manager. This could have been a problem, but we quickly got our accounts in order and the loan was approved straight away. Because our statement of financial position was strong, the bank thought we were a good risk. Although we decided not to draw down on the loan – because we used cashflow instead – it did open our eyes to the importance of a strong statement of financial position.

*Source*: Adapted from 'Balance sheets: the basics', www.businesslink.gov.uk. Accessed 14 April 2010.

Before we consider this financial statement in detail, however, we should first gain an overview of all three major financial accounting statements. This will help us to understand the role of each as well as their interrelationships.

## The major financial statements – an overview

The major financial accounting statements aim to provide a picture of the financial position and performance of a business. To achieve this, a business's accounting system will normally produce three financial statements on a regular, recurring basis. These three statements are concerned with answering the following questions relating to a particular period:

- What cash movements took place?
- How much wealth was generated?
- What is the accumulated wealth of the business at the end of the period and what form does it take?

To address each of the above questions, there is a separate financial statement. The financial statements are:

- the **statement of cash flows**
- the **income statement** (also known as the profit and loss account)
- the **statement of financial position** (also known as the balance sheet).

Together they provide an overall picture of the financial health of the business.

Perhaps the best way to introduce these financial statements is to look at an example of a very simple business. From this we shall be able to see the sort of information that each of the statements can usefully provide. It is, however, worth pointing out that, while a simple business is our starting point, the principles for preparing the financial statements apply equally to the largest and most complex businesses. Thus, we shall frequently encounter these principles again in later chapters.

### Example 2.1

Paul was unemployed and unable to find a job. He therefore decided to embark on a business venture. With Christmas approaching, he decided to buy gift-wrapping paper from a local supplier and to sell it on the corner of his local high street. He felt that the price of wrapping paper in the high street shops was too high. This provided him with a useful business opportunity.

He began the venture with £40 of his own money, in cash. On Monday, Paul's first day of trading, he bought wrapping paper for £40 and sold three-quarters of it for £45 cash.

- **What cash movements took place in Paul's business during Monday?**

  For Monday, a *statement of cash flows* showing the cash movements (that is, cash in and cash out) for the day can be prepared as follows:

  **Statement of cash flows for Monday**

  |                                    | £      |
  | ---------------------------------- | ------ |
  |                                    |        |
  | Cash introduced (by Paul)          | 40     |
  | Cash from sales of wrapping paper  | 45     |
  | Cash paid to buy wrapping paper    | (40)   |
  | Closing balance of cash            | 45     |

  The statement shows that Paul placed £40 cash into the business. The business received £45 cash from customers, but paid £40 cash to buy the wrapping paper. This left £45 of cash by Monday evening. Note that we are taking the standard approach found in the financial statements of showing figures to be deducted (in this case the £40 paid out) in brackets. We shall take this approach consistently throughout the chapters dealing with financial statements.

- **How much wealth (that is, profit) was generated by the business during Monday?**

  An *income statement* can be prepared to show the wealth (profit) generated on Monday. The wealth generated arises from trading and will be the difference between the value of the sales made and the cost of the goods (that is, wrapping paper) sold:

  **Income statement for Monday**

  |                                      | £      |
  | ------------------------------------ | ------ |
  |                                      |        |
  | Sales revenue                        | 45     |
  | Cost of goods sold ($^3/_4$ of £40)  | (30)   |
  | Profit                               | 15     |

Note that it is only the cost of the wrapping paper *sold* that is matched against (and deducted from) the sales revenue in order to find the profit, not the whole of the cost of wrapping paper acquired. Any unsold inventories (also known as *stock*) will be charged against the future sales revenue that it generates. In this case it is $^1/_4$ of £40 = £10.

- **What is the accumulated wealth on Monday evening and what form does it take?**

  To establish the accumulated wealth at the end of Monday's trading, we can draw up a *statement of financial position* for Paul's business. This statement will also list the forms of wealth held at the end of that day:

  **Statement of financial position as at Monday evening**

  |  | £ |
  |---|---|
  | Cash (closing balance) | 45 |
  | Inventories of goods for resale ($^1/_4$ of £40) | 10 |
  | Total assets | 55 |
  | Equity | 55 |

  Note the terms 'assets' and 'equity' that appear in this statement. 'Assets' are business resources (things of value to the business) and include cash and inventories. 'Equity' is the word used in accounting to describe the investment, or stake, of the owner(s) – in this case Paul – in the business. Both of these terms will be discussed in some detail a little later in this chapter.

We can see from the financial statements in Example 2.1 that each statement provides part of a picture of the financial performance and position of the business. We begin by showing the cash movements. Cash is a vital resource that is necessary for any business to function effectively. It is required to meet debts that become due and to acquire other resources (such as inventories). Cash has been described as the 'lifeblood' of a business.

Reporting cash movements alone, however, is not enough to portray the financial health of the business. To find out how much profit was generated, we need an income statement. It is important to recognise that cash and profits rarely move in unison. During Monday, for example, the cash balance increased by £5, but the profit generated, as shown in the income statement, was £15. The cash balance did not increase in line with profit because part of the wealth generated (£10) was held in the form of inventories.

The statement of financial position that was drawn up as at the end of Monday's trading, provides an insight to the total wealth of the business. This wealth can be held in various forms. For Paul's business, wealth is held in the form of cash and inventories. Hence, when drawing up the statement of financial position, both forms will be listed. For a large business, many other forms of wealth may be held, such as property, equipment, motor vehicles and so on.

Let us now continue with our example.

**Example 2.1 (*continued*)**

On Tuesday, Paul bought more wrapping paper for £20 cash. He managed to sell all of the new inventories and all of the earlier inventories, for a total of £48.

The statement of cash flows for Tuesday will be as follows:

**Statement of cash flows for Tuesday**

|  | £ |
|---|---|
| Opening balance (from Monday evening) | 45 |
| Cash from sales of wrapping paper | 48 |
| Cash paid to buy wrapping paper | (20) |
| Closing balance | 73 |

The income statement for Tuesday will be as follows:

**Income statement for Tuesday**

|  | £ |
|---|---|
| Sales revenue | 48 |
| Cost of goods sold (£20 + £10) | (30) |
| Profit | 18 |

The statement of financial position as at Tuesday evening will be:

**Statement of financial position as at Tuesday evening**

|  | £ |
|---|---|
| Cash (closing balance) | 73 |
| Inventories | – |
| Total assets | 73 |
| Equity | 73 |

We can see that the total business wealth increased to £73 by Tuesday evening. This represents an increase of £18 (that is, £73 – £55) over Monday's figure – which, of course, is the amount of profit made during Tuesday as shown on the income statement.

**Activity 2.1**

On Wednesday, Paul bought more wrapping paper for £46 cash. However, it was raining hard for much of the day and sales were slow. After Paul had sold half of his total inventories for £32, he decided to stop trading until Thursday morning.

Have a go at drawing up the three financial statements for Paul's business for Wednesday.

**Statement of cash flows for Wednesday**

|  | £ |
|---|---|
| Opening balance (from the Tuesday evening) | 73 |
| Cash from sales of wrapping paper | 32 |
| Cash paid to buy wrapping paper | (46) |
| Closing balance | 59 |

→

**Activity 2.1 (*continued*)**

### Income statement for Wednesday

|                              | £    |
|------------------------------|-----:|
| Sales revenue                | 32   |
| Cost of goods sold (¹/₂ of £46) | (23) |
| Profit                       | 9    |

### Statement of financial position as at Wednesday evening

|                          | £   |
|--------------------------|----:|
| Cash (closing balance)   | 59  |
| Inventories (¹/₂ of £46) | 23  |
| Total assets             | 82  |
| Equity                   | 82  |

Note that the total business wealth has increased by £9 (that is, the amount of Wednesday's profit) even though the cash balance has declined. This is because the business is holding more of its wealth in the form of inventories rather than cash, compared with the position on Tuesday evening.

By Wednesday evening, the equity stood at £82. This arose from Paul's initial investment of £40, plus his profits for Monday (£15), Tuesday (£18) and Wednesday (£9). This represents Paul's total investment in his business at that time. The equity of most businesses will similarly be made up of injections of funds by the owner plus any accumulated profits.

We can see that the income statement and statement of cash flows are both concerned with measuring flows (of wealth and cash respectively) during a particular period. The statement of financial position, however, is concerned with the financial position at a particular moment in time. Figure 2.1 illustrates this point.

The three financial statements discussed are often referred to as the **final accounts** of the business.

For external users (that is virtually all users except the managers of the business concerned), these statements are normally backward looking because they are based on information concerning past events and transactions. This can be useful in providing feedback on past performance and in identifying trends that provide clues to future performance. However, the statements can also be prepared using projected data to help assess likely future profits, cash flows, and so on. The financial statements are normally prepared on a projected basis for internal decision-making and control purposes only. Managers are usually reluctant to publish these projected statements for external users, as they may reveal valuable information to competitors.

Now that we have an overview of the financial statements, we shall consider each one in detail. The remainder of this chapter is devoted to the statement of financial position. Chapter 3 looks at the income statement and Chapter 6 looks at the statement of cash flows. (Chapters 4 and 5 look at the statements of financial position and income statements of limited companies.)

**Figure 2.1**    **The relationship between the major financial statements**

The income statement and statement of cash flows are concerned with measuring flows of wealth and cash (respectively) over time. The statement of financial position, however, is concerned with measuring the amount of wealth at a particular moment in time.

## The statement of financial position

We saw a little earlier that this statement shows the forms in which the wealth of a business is held and how much wealth is held in each form. We can, however, be more specific about the nature of this statement by saying that it sets out the **assets** of a business, on the one hand, and the **claims** against the business, on the other. Before looking at the statement of financial position in more detail, we need to be clear about what these terms mean.

### Assets

An asset is essentially a resource held by a business. For a particular item to be treated as an asset for accounting purposes, it should have the following characteristics:

- *A probable future benefit must exist.* This simply means that the item must be expected to have some future monetary value. This value can arise through the asset's use within the business or through its hire or sale. Thus, an obsolete piece of equipment that could be sold for scrap would still be considered an asset, whereas an obsolete piece of equipment that has no scrap value would not be regarded as one.
- *The benefit must arise from some past transaction or event.* This means that the transaction (or other event), giving rise to a business's right to the benefit, must have already occurred and will not arise at some future date. Thus an agreement by a business to buy a piece of equipment at some future date would not mean the item is currently an asset of the business.
- *The business must have the right to control the resource.* Unless the business controls the resource, it cannot be regarded as an asset for accounting purposes. Thus, for a business offering holidays on barges, the canal system may be a very valuable resource,

but as the business will not be able to control the access of others to the canal system, it cannot be regarded as an asset of the business. (However, the barges owned by the business would be regarded as assets.)

● *The asset must be capable of measurement in monetary terms.* Unless the item can be measured in monetary terms, with a reasonable degree of reliability, it will not be regarded as an asset for inclusion on the statement of financial position. Thus, the title of a magazine (for example, *Hello!* or *Vogue*) that was created by its publisher may be extremely valuable to that publishing business, but this value is usually difficult to quantify. It will not, therefore, be treated as an asset.

Note that all four of these conditions must apply. If one of them is missing, the item will not be treated as an asset for accounting purposes, and will not, therefore, appear on the statement of financial position. Figure 2.2 summarises the above discussion in the form of a decision chart.

We can see that these conditions will strictly limit the kind of items that may be referred to as 'assets' in the statement of financial position. Certainly not all resources exploited by a business will be assets of the business for accounting purposes. Some, like the canal system or the magazine title *Hello!*, may well be assets in a broader sense, but not for accounting purposes. Once an asset has been acquired by a business, it will continue to be considered an asset until the benefits are exhausted or the business disposes of it in some way.

## Activity 2.2

Indicate which of the following items could appear as an asset on the statement of financial position of a business. Explain your reasoning in each case.

1 £1,000 owed to the business by a customer who is unable to pay.
2 A patent, bought from an inventor, that gives the business the right to produce a new product. Production of the new product is expected to increase profits over the period during which the patent is held.
3 A new marketing director, whom the business had recently hired, who is confidently expected to increase profits by over 30 per cent during the next three years.
4 A recently purchased machine that will save the business £10,000 each year. It is already being used by the business but it has been acquired on credit and is not yet paid for.

Your answer should be along the following lines.

1 Under normal circumstances, a business would expect a customer to pay the amount owed. Such an amount is therefore typically shown as an asset under the heading 'trade receivables' (or 'debtors'). However, in this particular case the customer is unable to pay. As a result, the item is incapable of providing future benefits and the £1,000 owing would not be regarded as an asset. Debts that are not paid are referred to as 'bad debts'.
2 The patent would meet all of the conditions set out above and would therefore be regarded as an asset.
3 The new marketing director would not be considered as an asset. One argument for this is that the business does not have exclusive rights of control over the director. (It may have an exclusive right to the services that the director provides, however.) Perhaps a stronger argument is that the value of the director cannot be measured in monetary terms with any degree of reliability.
4 The machine would be considered an asset even though it is not yet paid for. Once the business has agreed to buy the machine and has accepted it, the machine represents an asset even though payment is still outstanding. (The amount outstanding would be shown as a claim, as we shall see shortly.)

**Figure 2.2**    Decision chart for identifying an accounting asset

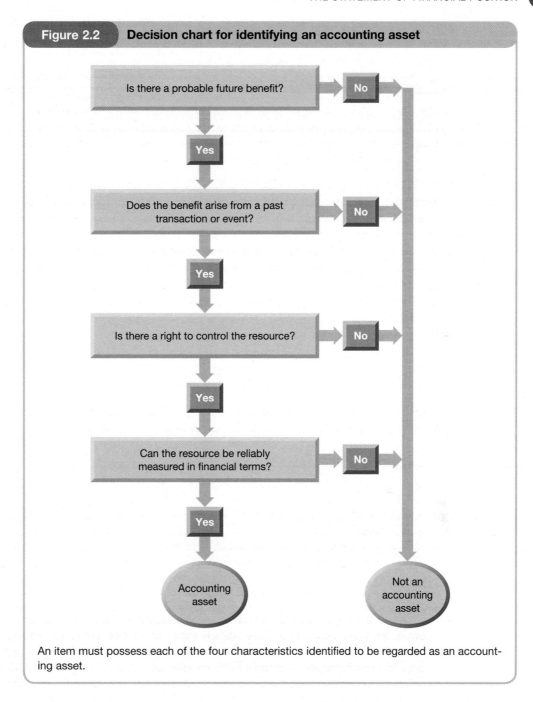

An item must possess each of the four characteristics identified to be regarded as an accounting asset.

The sorts of items that often appear as assets in the statement of financial position of a business include:

- property
- plant and equipment
- fixtures and fittings
- patents and trademarks
- trade receivables (debtors)
- investments outside the business.

**Activity (2.3)**

Can you think of two additional items that might appear as assets in the statement of financial position of a typical business?

You may be able to think of a number of other items. Two that we have met so far, because they were held by Paul's wrapping paper business (in Example 2.1), are inventories and cash.

Note that an asset does not have to be a physical item – it may be a non-physical one that gives a right to certain benefits. Assets that have a physical substance and can be touched (such as inventories) are referred to as **tangible assets**. Assets that have no physical substance but which, nevertheless, provide expected future benefits (such as patents) are referred to as **intangible assets**.

## Claims

A claim is an obligation of the business to provide cash, or some other form of benefit, to an outside party. It will normally arise as a result of the outside party providing assets for use by the business. There are essentially two types of claim against a business:

● **Equity**. This represents the claim of the owner(s) against the business. This claim is sometimes referred to as the *owner's capital*. Some find it hard to understand how the owner can have a claim against the business, particularly when we consider the example of a sole-proprietor-type business, like Paul's, where the owner *is*, in effect, the business. For accounting purposes, however, a clear distinction is made between the business and the owner(s). The business is viewed as being quite separate from the owner. It is seen as a separate entity with its own separate existence, and when financial statements are prepared, they relate to the business rather than to the owner(s). Viewed from this perspective, any funds contributed by the owner will be seen as coming from outside the business and will appear as a claim against the business in its statement of financial position.

   The equity section of the statement of financial position is broadly the same irrespective of the type of business concerned. We shall see in Chapter 4 that, with limited companies, the total equity figure must be analysed according to how each part of it first arose. For example, companies must make a distinction between that part of it that arose from retained earnings (or profits) and that part that arose from the owners putting in cash to start up the business, usually by buying shares in the company.

● **Liabilities**. Liabilities represent the claims of all individuals and organisations, apart from the owner(s). They arise from past transactions or events such as supplying goods or lending money to the business. A liability will be settled through an outflow of assets (usually cash).

Once a claim from the owners or outsiders has been incurred by a business, it will remain as an obligation until it is settled.

Now that the meaning of the terms *assets*, *equity* and *liabilities* has been established, we can consider the relationship between them. This relationship is quite straight-forward. If a business wishes to acquire assets, it must raise the necessary funds from somewhere. It may raise these funds from the owner(s), or from other outside parties, or from both. Example 2.2 illustrates this relationship.

### Example 2.2

Jerry and Company is a new business that was created by depositing £20,000 in a bank account on 1 March. This amount was raised partly from the owner (£6,000) and partly from borrowing (£14,000). Raising funds in this way will give rise to a claim on the business by both the owner (equity) and the lender (liability). If a statement of financial position of Jerry and Company is prepared following the above transactions, it will appear as follows:

**Jerry and Company**
**Statement of financial position as at 1 March**

|  | £ |
|---|---|
| **ASSETS** | |
| Cash at bank | 20,000 |
| Total assets | 20,000 |
| **EQUITY AND LIABILITIES** | |
| Equity | 6,000 |
| Liabilities – borrowing | 14,000 |
| Total equity and liabilities | 20,000 |

We can see from the statement of financial position that the total claims (equity and liabilities) are the same as the total assets. Thus:

$$Assets = Equity + Liabilities$$

This equation – which we shall refer to as the *accounting equation* – will always hold true. Whatever changes may occur to the assets of the business or the claims against it, there will be compensating changes elsewhere that will ensure that the statement of financial position always 'balances'. By way of illustration, consider the following transactions for Jerry and Company:

| | |
|---|---|
| 2 March | Bought a motor van for £5,000, paying by cheque. |
| 3 March | Bought inventories (that is, goods to be sold) on one month's credit for £3,000. (This means that the inventories were bought on 3 March, but payment will not be made to the supplier until 3 April.) |
| 4 March | Repaid £2,000 of the amount borrowed to the lender, by cheque. |
| 6 March | Owner introduced another £4,000 into the business bank account. |

A statement of financial position may be drawn up after each day in which transactions have taken place. In this way, we can see the effect of each transaction on the assets and claims of the business. The statement of financial position as at 2 March will be:

**Jerry and Company**
**Statement of financial position as at 2 March**

|  | £ |
|---|---|
| **ASSETS** | |
| Cash at bank (20,000 – 5,000) | 15,000 |
| Motor van | 5,000 |
| **Total assets** | 20,000 |
| **EQUITY AND LIABILITIES** | |
| Equity | 6,000 |
| Liabilities – borrowing | 14,000 |
| **Total equity and liabilities** | 20,000 |

As we can see, the effect of buying the motor van is to decrease the balance at the bank by £5,000 and to introduce a new asset – a motor van – to the statement of financial position. The total assets remain unchanged. It is only the 'mix' of assets that has changed. The claims against the business remain the same because there has been no change in the way in which the business has been funded.

The statement of financial position as at 3 March, following the purchase of inventories, will be:

**Jerry and Company**
**Statement of financial position as at 3 March**

|  | £ |
|---|---|
| **ASSETS** | |
| Cash at bank | 15,000 |
| Motor van | 5,000 |
| Inventories | 3,000 |
| **Total assets** | 23,000 |
| **EQUITY AND LIABILITIES** | |
| Equity | 6,000 |
| Liabilities – borrowing | 14,000 |
| Liabilities – trade payable | 3,000 |
| **Total equity and liabilities** | 23,000 |

The effect of buying inventories has been to introduce another new asset (inventories) to the statement of financial position. Furthermore, the fact that the goods have not yet been paid for means that the claims against the business will be increased by the £3,000 owed to the supplier, who is referred to as a *trade payable* (or trade creditor) on the statement of financial position.

## Activity 2.4

Try drawing up a statement of financial position for Jerry and Company as at 4 March.

The statement of financial postion as at 4 March, following the repayment of part of the borrowing, will be:

### Jerry and Company
### Statement of financial position as at 4 March

|  | £ |
|---|---|
| **ASSETS** | |
| Cash at bank (15,000 – 2,000) | 13,000 |
| Motor van | 5,000 |
| Inventories | 3,000 |
| **Total assets** | 21,000 |
| **EQUITY AND LIABILITIES** | |
| Equity | 6,000 |
| Liabilities – borrowing (14,000 – 2,000) | 12,000 |
| Liabilities – trade payable | 3,000 |
| **Total equity and liabilities** | 21,000 |

The repayment of £2,000 of the borrowing will result in a decrease in the balance at the bank of £2,000 and a decrease in the lender's claim against the business by the same amount.

## Activity 2.5

Try drawing up a statement of financial position as at 6 March for Jerry and Company.

The statement of financial position as at 6 March, following the introduction of more funds, will be:

### Jerry and Company
### Statement of financial position as at 6 March

|  | £ |
|---|---|
| **ASSETS** | |
| Cash at bank (13,000 + 4,000) | 17,000 |
| Motor van | 5,000 |
| Inventories | 3,000 |
| **Total assets** | 25,000 |
| **EQUITY AND LIABILITIES** | |
| Equity (6,000 + 4,000) | 10,000 |
| Liabilities – borrowing | 12,000 |
| Liabilities – trade payable | 3,000 |
| **Total equity and liabilities** | 25,000 |

The introduction of more funds by the owner will result in an increase in the equity of £4,000 and an increase in the cash at bank by the same amount.

This example (Jerry and Company) illustrates the point that the accounting equation (assets equals equity plus liabilities) will always hold true, because it reflects the fact that, if a business wishes to acquire more assets, it must raise funds equal to the cost of those assets. The funds raised must be provided by the owners (equity), or by others (liabilities), or by a combination of the two. Hence the total cost of assets acquired should always equal the total equity plus liabilities.

It is worth pointing out that businesses do not normally draw up a statement of financial position after each day, as shown in the example. We have done this to illustrate the effect on the statement of financial position of each transaction. In practice, a statement of financial position for a business is usually prepared at the end of a defined reporting period.

Determining the length of the reporting period will involve weighing up the costs of producing the information against the perceived benefits of the information for decision-making purposes. In practice, the reporting period will vary between businesses; it could be monthly, quarterly, half-yearly or annually. For external reporting purposes, an annual reporting period is the norm (although certain businesses, typically larger ones, report more frequently than this). For internal reporting purposes to managers, however, more frequent (perhaps monthly) financial statements may be prepared.

## The effect of trading transactions

In the example (Jerry and Company), we dealt with the effect on the statement of financial position of a number of different types of transactions that a business might undertake. These transactions covered the purchase of assets for cash and on credit, borrowing and the repayment of borrowing and the injection of equity. However, one type of transaction (trading transactions) has not yet been considered. To deal with the effect of trading transactions on the statement of financial position, let us return to Jerry and Company.

### Example 2.2 (continued)

The statement of financial position that we drew up for Jerry and Company as at 6 March was as follows:

**Jerry and Company**
**Statement of financial position as at 6 March**

|  | £ |
|---|---|
| **ASSETS** | |
| Cash at bank | 17,000 |
| Motor van | 5,000 |
| Inventories | 3,000 |
| **Total assets** | 25,000 |
| **EQUITY AND LIABILITIES** | |
| Equity | 10,000 |
| Liabilities – borrowing | 12,000 |
| Liabilities – trade payable | 3,000 |
| **Total equity and liabilities** | 25,000 |

On 7 March, the business managed to sell all of the inventories for £5,000 and received a cheque immediately from the customer for this amount. The statement of financial position on 7 March, after this transaction has taken place, will be:

**Jerry and Company**
**Statement of financial position as at 7 March**

| | £ |
|---|---|
| **ASSETS** | |
| Cash at bank (17,000 + 5,000) | 22,000 |
| Motor van | 5,000 |
| Inventories (3,000 – 3,000) | – |
| **Total assets** | 27,000 |
| **EQUITY AND LIABILITIES** | |
| Equity (10,000 + (5,000 – 3,000)) | 12,000 |
| Liabilities – borrowing | 12,000 |
| Liabilities – trade payable | 3,000 |
| **Total equity and liabilities** | 27,000 |

We can see that the inventories (£3,000) have now disappeared from the statement of financial position, but the cash at bank has increased by the selling price of the inventories (£5,000). The net effect has therefore been to increase assets by £2,000 (that is, £5,000 less £3,000). This increase represents the net increase in wealth (the profit) that has arisen from trading. Also note that the equity of the business has increased by £2,000, in line with the increase in assets. This increase in equity reflects the fact that increases in wealth, as a result of trading or other operations, will be to the benefit of the owners and will increase their stake in the business.

**Activity 2.6**

What would have been the effect on the statement of financial position if the inventories had been sold on 7 March for £1,000 rather than £5,000?

The statement of financial position on 7 March would then have been:

**Jerry and Company**
**Statement of financial position as at 7 March**

| | £ |
|---|---|
| **ASSETS** | |
| Cash at bank (17,000 + 1,000) | 18,000 |
| Motor van | 5,000 |
| Inventories (3,000 – 3,000) | – |
| **Total assets** | 23,000 |
| **EQUITY AND LIABILITIES** | |
| Equity (10,000 + (1,000 – 3,000)) | 8,000 |
| Liabilities – borrowing | 12,000 |
| Liabilities – trade payable | 3,000 |
| **Total equity and liabilities** | 23,000 |

As we can see, the inventories (£3,000) will disappear from the statement of financial position but the cash at bank will rise by only £1,000. This will mean a net reduction in assets of £2,000. This reduction represents a loss arising from trading and will be reflected in a reduction in the equity of the owners.

We can see that any decrease in wealth (that is, a loss) arising from trading or other transactions will lead to a reduction in the owner's stake in the business. If the business wished to maintain the level of assets as at 6 March, it would be necessary to obtain further funds from the owners or from borrowing, or both.

What we have just seen means that the accounting equation can be extended as follows:

> **Assets (at the end = Equity (amount at the start of the period**
> **of the period)       + profit (or – loss) for the period)**
> **                     + liabilities (at the end of the period)**

(This is assuming that the owner makes no injections or withdrawals of equity during the period.)

Any funds introduced or withdrawn by the owner for living expenses or other reasons also affect equity. If the owners withdrew £1,500 for their own use, the equity of the owners would be reduced by £1,500. If these drawings were in cash, the balance of cash would decrease by £1,500 in the statement of financial position.

Note that, like all items in the statement of financial position, the amount of equity is cumulative. This means that any profit made that is not taken out as drawings by the owner(s) remains in the business. These retained (or 'ploughed-back') earnings have the effect of expanding the business.

## Classifying assets

On the statement of financial position, assets and claims are usually grouped into categories. This is designed to help users, as a haphazard listing of these items could be confusing. Assets may be categorised as being either current or non-current.

### Current assets

**Current assets** are basically assets that are held for the short term. To be more precise, they are assets that meet any of the following conditions:

- they are held for sale or consumption during the business's normal operating cycle;
- they are expected to be sold within the next year;
- they are held principally for trading;
- they are cash, or near cash, such as easily marketable, short-term investments.

The operating cycle of a business, mentioned above, is the time between buying and/ or creating a product or service and receiving the cash on its sale. For most businesses, this will be less than a year.

The most common current assets are inventories (stock), trade receivables (customers who owe amounts for goods or services supplied on credit) and cash.

It is worth making the point here that most sales made by most businesses are made on credit. This is to say that the goods pass, or the service is rendered, to the customer at one point but the customer pays later. Retail sales are the only significant exception to this general point.

For businesses that sell goods, rather than render a service, the current assets of inventories, trade receivables and cash are interrelated. They circulate within a business as shown in Figure 2.3. We can see that cash can be used to buy inventories, which are then sold on credit. When the credit customers (trade receivables) pay, the business receives an injection of cash and so on.

**Figure 2.3    The circulating nature of current assets**

Inventories may be sold on credit to customers. When the customers pay, the trade receivables will be converted into cash, which can then be used to purchase more inventories. Then the cycle begins again.

For purely service businesses, the situation is similar, except that inventories are not involved.

## Non-current assets

**Non-current assets** (also called fixed assets) are simply assets that do not meet the definition of current assets. They tend to be held for long-term operations. Non-current assets may be either tangible or intangible. Tangible non-current assets normally consist of **property, plant and equipment**. We shall refer to them in this way from now on. This is a rather broad term that includes items such as land and buildings, motor vehicles and fixtures and fittings.

This distinction between assets that are continuously circulating within the business (current) and assets used for long-term operations (non-current) may be helpful when trying to assess the appropriateness of the mix of assets held. Most businesses will need a certain amount of both types of asset to operate effectively.

**Activity 2.7**

Can you think of two examples of assets that may be classified as non-current assets for an insurance business?

Examples of assets that may be defined as being non-current are:

- property
- furniture
- motor vehicles
- computers
- computer software
- reference books.

This is not an exhaustive list. You may have thought of others.

It is important to appreciate that how a particular asset is classified (that is, between current and non-current) may vary according to the nature of the business. This is because the *purpose* for which a particular type of asset is held may differ from business to business. For example, a motor vehicle manufacturer will normally hold inventories of the finished motor vehicles produced for resale; it would, therefore, classify them as part of the current assets. On the other hand, a business that uses motor vehicles for delivering its goods to customers (that is, as part of its long-term operations) would classify them as non-current assets.

## Activity 2.8

The assets of Kunalun and Co., a large advertising agency, are as follows:

- cash at bank
- fixtures and fittings
- office equipment
- motor vehicles
- property
- computer equipment
- work in progress (that is, partly completed work for clients).

Which of these do you think should be defined as non-current assets and which should be defined as current assets?

Your answer should be as follows:

| *Non-current assets* | *Current assets* |
| --- | --- |
| Fixtures and fittings | Cash at bank |
| Office equipment | Work in progress |
| Motor vehicles | |
| Property | |
| Computer equipment | |

## Classifying claims

As we have already seen, claims are normally classified into equity (owner's claim) and liabilities (claims of outsiders). Liabilities are further classified as either current or non-current:

### Current liabilities

**Current liabilities** are basically amounts due for settlement in the short term. To be more precise, they are liabilities that meet any of the following conditions:

- they are expected to be settled within the business's normal operating cycle;
- they are held principally for trading purposes;
- they are due to be settled within a year after the date of the relevant statement of financial position;
- there is no right to defer settlement beyond a year after the date of the relevant statement of financial position.

## Non-current liabilities

**Non-current liabilities** represent amounts due that do not meet the definition of current liabilities and so represent longer-term liabilities.

It is quite common for non-current liabilities to become current liabilities. For example, borrowings to be repaid 18 months after the date of a particular statement of financial position will appear as a non-current liability, but will appear as a current liability in the statement of financial position in the following year.

This classification of liabilities between current and non-current helps to highlight those financial obligations that must shortly be met. Users can compare the amount of current liabilities with the amount of current assets (that is, the assets that are either cash or will turn into cash within the normal operating cycle). This comparison should indicate whether a business can cover its maturing obligations.

The classification of liabilities between current and non-current should also help to indicate how long-term finance is raised. If a business relies on long-term borrowings to finance the business, the financial risks associated with the business will increase. This is because these borrowings will bring a commitment to make periodic interest payments and capital repayments. The business may be forced to stop trading if this commitment is not fulfilled. Thus, when raising long-term finance, a business must try to strike the right balance between non-current liabilities and owner's equity. We shall consider this issue in more detail in Chapter 7.

### Activity 2.9

Can you think of one example of a current liability and one of a non-current liability?

An example of a current liability would be amounts owing to suppliers for goods supplied on credit (trade payables) or a bank overdraft (a form of short-term bank borrowing that is repayable on demand). An example of a non-current liability would be long-term borrowings.

## Statement layouts

Now that we have looked at the classification of assets and liabilities, we shall consider the layout of the statement of financial position. Although there is an almost infinite number of ways in which the same information on assets and claims could be presented, we shall consider two basic layouts. The first of these follows the style that we adopted with Jerry and Company earlier (see pages 49 to 53). A more comprehensive example of this style is shown in Example 2.3.

### Example 2.3

**Brie Manufacturing**
**Statement of financial position as at 31 December 2011**

|  | £000 |
|---|---:|
| **ASSETS** | |
| **Non-current assets** | |
| Property | 45 |
| Plant and equipment | 30 |
| Motor vans | 19 |
|  | 94 |
| **Current assets** | |
| Inventories | 23 |
| Trade receivables | 18 |
| Cash at bank | 12 |
|  | 53 |
| **Total assets** | 147 |
| **EQUITY AND LIABILITIES** | |
| **Equity** | 60 |
| **Non-current liabilities** | |
| Long-term borrowings | 50 |
| **Current liabilities** | |
| Trade payables | 37 |
| **Total equity and liabilities** | 147 |

The non-current assets have a total of £94,000, which together with the current assets total of £53,000 gives a total of £147,000 for assets. Similarly, the equity totals £60,000, which together with the £50,000 for non-current liabilities and £37,000 for current liabilities gives a total for equity and liabilities of £147,000.

Within each category of asset (non-current and current) shown in Example 2.3, the items are listed in reverse order of liquidity (nearness to cash). Thus, the assets that are furthest from cash come first and the assets that are closest to cash come last. In the case of non-current assets, property is listed first as this asset is usually the most difficult to turn into cash, and motor vans are listed last as there is usually a ready market for them. In the case of current assets, we have already seen that inventories are converted to trade receivables and then trade receivables are converted to cash. Hence, under the heading of current assets, inventories are listed first, followed by trade receivables and finally cash itself. This ordering of assets is a normal practice, which is followed irrespective of the layout used.

Note that, in addition to a grand total for assets held, subtotals for non-current assets and current assets are shown. Subtotals are also used for non-current liabilities and current liabilities when more than one item appears within these categories.

This layout is the most popular in practice in the UK.

A slight variation from the standard layout illustrated in Example 2.3 is as shown in Example 2.4.

**Example 2.4**

**Brie Manufacturing**
**Statement of financial position as at 31 December 2011**

| | £000 |
|---|---:|
| **ASSETS** | |
| **Non-current assets** | |
| Property | 45 |
| Plant and equipment | 30 |
| Motor vans | 19 |
| | 94 |
| **Current assets** | |
| Inventories | 23 |
| Trade receivables | 18 |
| Cash at bank | 12 |
| | 53 |
| **Total assets** | 147 |
| **LIABILITIES** | |
| **Non-current liabilities** | |
| Long-term borrowings | (50) |
| **Current liabilities** | |
| Trade payables | (37) |
| **Total liabilities** | (87) |
| **Net assets** | 60 |
| **EQUITY** | 60 |

We can see that the total liabilities are deducted from the total assets. This derives a figure for net assets – which is equal to equity. Using this format, the basic accounting equation is rearranged so that:

$$\text{Assets} - \text{Liabilities} = \text{Equity}$$

This rearranged equation highlights the fact that equity represents the residual interest of the owner(s) after deducting all liabilities of the business.

**Self-assessment question  2.1**

The following information relates to Simonson Engineering as at 30 September 2011:

| | £ |
|---|---:|
| Plant and equipment | 25,000 |
| Trade payables | 18,000 |
| Short-term borrowing | 26,000 |
| Inventories | 45,000 |
| Property | 72,000 |
| Long-term borrowing | 51,000 |
| Trade receivables | 48,000 |
| Equity at 1 October 2010 | 117,500 |
| Cash in hand | 1,500 |
| Motor vehicles | 15,000 |
| Fixtures and fittings | 9,000 |
| Profit for the year to 30 September 2011 | 18,000 |
| Drawings for the year to 30 September 2011 | 15,000 |

→

**Self-assessment question 2.1 (*continued*)**

*Required*:
Prepare a statement of financial position for the business using the standard layout illustrated in Example 2.3.

**The solution to this question can be found at the back of the book on page 728.**

# Capturing a moment in time

As we have already seen, the statement of financial position reflects the assets, equity and liabilities of a business at *a specified point in time*. It has been compared to a photograph. A photograph 'freezes' a particular moment in time and will represent the situation only at that moment. Hence, events may be quite different immediately before and immediately after the photograph was taken. When examining a statement of financial position, therefore, it is important to establish the date for which it has been drawn up. This information should be prominently displayed in the heading to the statement, as shown above in Example 2.4. When we are trying to assess current financial position, the more recent the statement of financial position date, the better.

A business will normally prepare a statement of financial position as at the close of business on the last day of its annual reporting period. In the UK, businesses are free to choose their reporting period. When making a decision on which year-end date to choose, commercial convenience can often be a deciding factor. For example, a business operating in the retail trade may choose to have a year-end date early in the calendar year (for example, 31 January) because trade tends to be slack during that period and more staff time is available to help with the tasks involved in the preparation of the annual financial statements (such as checking the amount of inventories held). Since trade is slack, it is also a time when the amount of inventories held by the retail business is likely to be unusually low as compared with other times of the year. Thus the statement of financial position, though showing a fair view of what it purports to show, may not show a picture of what is more typically the position of the business over the rest of the year.

# The role of accounting conventions

Accounting has a number of rules or conventions that have evolved over time. They have evolved as attempts to deal with practical problems experienced by preparers and users of financial statements, rather than to reflect some theoretical ideal. In preparing the statements of financial position earlier, we have followed various **accounting conventions**, though they have not been explicitly mentioned. We shall now identify and discuss the major conventions that we have applied.

## Business entity convention

For accounting purposes, the business and its owner(s) are treated as being quite separate and distinct. This is why owners are treated as being claimants against their own business in respect of their investment. The **business entity convention** must be distinguished from the legal position that may exist between businesses and their owners. For sole proprietorships and partnerships, the law does not make any distinction between the business and its owner(s). For limited companies, on the other hand, there is a clear legal distinction between the business and its owners. (As we shall see in Chapter 4, the limited company is regarded as having a separate legal existence.) For accounting purposes, these legal distinctions are irrelevant and the business entity convention applies to all businesses.

## Historic cost convention

The **historic cost convention** holds that the value of assets shown on the statement of financial position should be based on their acquisition cost (that is, historic cost). This method of measuring asset value takes preference over other methods based on some form of current value. Many people, however, find the historic cost convention difficult to support, as outdated historic costs are unlikely to help in the assessment of current financial position. It is often argued that recording assets at their current value would provide a more realistic view of financial position and would be relevant for a wide range of decisions. However, a system of measurement based on current values can present a number of problems.

The term 'current value' can be defined in different ways. It can be defined broadly as either the current replacement cost or the current realisable value (selling price) of an asset. These two types of valuation may result in quite different figures being produced to represent the current value of an item. Furthermore, the broad terms 'replacement cost' and 'realisable value' can be defined in different ways. We must therefore be clear about what kind of current value accounting we wish to use.

Current values, however defined, are often difficult to establish with any real degree of objectivity. Activity 2.10 illustrates the practical problems associated with current value accounting.

### Activity 2.10

Plumber and Company has some motor vans that are used by staff when visiting customers' premises to carry out work. It is now the last day of the business's reporting period. If it were decided to show the vans on the statement of financial position at a current value (rather than a value based on their historic cost), how might the business arrive at a suitable value and how reliable would this figure be?

Two ways of deriving a current value are to find out:

● how much would have to be paid to buy vans of a similar type and condition (current replacement cost);
● how much a motor van dealer would pay for the vans, were the business to sell them (current realisable value).

Both options will normally rely on opinion and so a range of possible values could be produced for each. For example, both the cost to replace the vans and the proceeds of selling them is likely to vary from one dealer to another. Moreover, the range of values for each option could be significantly different from one option to the other. (The selling prices of the vans are likely to be lower than the amount required to replace them.) Thus, any value finally decided upon could arouse some debate.

The figures produced under a system of current value accounting may be heavily dependent on the opinion of managers. Unless these figures are capable of some form of independent verification, there is a danger that the financial statements will lose their credibility among users. The motor vans discussed in Activity 2.10 are less of a problem than many types of asset. There is a ready market for motor vans, which means that a value can be obtained by contacting a dealer. For a custom-built piece of equipment, however, identifying a replacement cost, or worse still a selling price, could be very difficult.

By reporting assets at their historic cost, it is argued that more reliable information is produced. Reporting in this way reduces the need for judgements, as the amount paid for a particular asset is usually a matter of demonstrable fact. Information based on past costs, however, may not always be relevant to the needs of users.

Later in the chapter, we shall consider the valuation of assets in the statement of financial position in more detail. We shall see that the historic cost convention is not always rigidly adhered to. Departures from this convention are becoming more frequent.

## Prudence convention

The **prudence convention** holds that caution should be exercised when making accounting judgements. The application of this convention normally involves recording all losses at once and in full; this refers to both actual losses and expected losses. Profits, on the other hand, are recognised only when they actually arise. Greater emphasis is, therefore, placed on expected losses than on expected profits. To illustrate the application of this convention, let us assume that certain inventories held by a business prove unpopular with customers and so a decision is made to sell them below their original cost. The prudence convention requires that the expected loss from future sales be recognised immediately rather than when the goods are eventually sold. If, however, these inventories could have been sold above their original cost, profit would only be recognised at the time of sale.

The prudence convention evolved to counteract the excessive optimism of some managers and is designed to prevent an overstatement of financial position and performance. Applying this convention, however, requires judgement. This means that the way in which it is applied by preparers of financial statements may differ over time and between businesses. Where excessive prudence is applied, it will lead to an understatement of profits and financial position. This will mean a consistent bias in the reporting of both financial performance and position.

### Activity 2.11

What might be the effect of applying excessive prudence on the quality of user decisions?

Being excessively prudent will tend to obscure the underlying financial reality and may lead to poor decisions being made. The owners, for example, may sell their stake in the business at a lower price than they would have received if a more balanced view of the financial health of the business had been presented.

In recent years, the prudence convention has weakened its grip on accounting and has become a less dominant force. Nevertheless, it remains an important convention.

## Going concern convention

The **going concern convention** holds that the financial statements should be prepared on the assumption that a business will continue operations for the foreseeable future, unless there is evidence to the contrary. In other words, it is assumed that there is no intention, or need, to sell off the non-current assets of the business.

Where a business is in financial difficulties, however, non-current assets may have to be sold in order to repay those who have enforceable claims against the business.

The realisable (sale) value of many non-current assets is often much lower than the values reported in the statement of financial position. Thus, if a forced sale of assets were to occur, significant losses would arise. This is because the value to the business of the assets, were it to continue operating, would be higher than their realisable value. These anticipated losses would need to be fully reported were a business's going concern status to be called into question. Where, however, there is no expectation that non-current assets need be sold, they can continue to be shown at their reported values.

## Dual aspect convention

The **dual aspect convention** asserts that each transaction has two aspects, both of which will affect the statement of financial position. Thus, the purchase of a motor car for cash results in an increase in one asset (motor car) and a decrease in another (cash). The repayment of borrowings results in the decrease in a liability (borrowings) and the decrease in an asset (cash).

### Activity (2.12)

What are the two aspects of each of the following transactions?

1  Purchase £1,000 of inventories on credit.
2  Owner withdraws £2,000 in cash.
3  Paying a supplier for £1,000 of inventories bought on credit a few weeks earlier.

Your answer should be as follows:

1  Inventories increase by £1,000, trade payables increase by £1,000.
2  Equity reduces by £2,000, cash reduces by £2,000.
3  Trade payables reduce by £1,000, cash reduces by £1,000.

Recording the dual aspect of each transaction ensures that the statement of financial position will continue to balance.

Figure 2.4 summarises the main accounting conventions that exert an influence on the construction of the statement of financial position.

**Figure 2.4** Accounting conventions influencing the statement of financial position

These are the key accounting conventions relating to the statement of financial position.

## Money measurement

We saw earlier that a resource will only be regarded as an asset and included on the statement of financial position if it can be measured in monetary terms, with a reasonable degree of reliability. Some resources of a business, however, do not meet this criterion and so are excluded from the statement of financial position. As a result, the scope of the statement of financial position is limited.

**Activity 2.13**

Can you think of resources of a business that cannot usually be measured reliably in monetary terms?

In answering this activity you may have thought of the following:

● the quality of the human resources of the business
● the reputation of the business's products
● the location of the business
● the relationship the business enjoys with its customers.

There have been occasional attempts to measure and report resources of a business that are normally excluded from the statement of financial position so as to provide a more complete picture of its financial position. These attempts, however, invariably fail the test of faithful representation. We saw in Chapter 1 that faithful representation is a fundamental quality of accounting information. Where this quality is missing, users of financial statements cannot be confident that the reported information represents what it is supposed to represent. The credibility of the financial statements can therefore be brought into question.

We shall now discuss some key resources of a business that normally defy faithful representation.

## Goodwill and brands

Some intangible non-current assets are similar to tangible non-current assets: they have a clear and separate identity and the cost of acquiring the asset can be reliably measured. Examples normally include patents, trademarks, copyrights and licences. Other intangible non-current assets, however, are quite different. They lack a clear and separate identity and reflect a hotchpotch of attributes, which are part of the essence of the business. Goodwill and product brands are often examples of assets that lack a clear and separate identity.

The term 'goodwill' is frequently used to cover various attributes such as the quality of the products, the skill of employees and the relationship with customers. The term 'product brands' is also used to cover various attributes, such as the brand image, the quality of the product, the trademark and so on. Where goodwill and product brands have been generated internally by the business, it is often difficult to determine their cost or to measure their current market value or even to be clear that they really exist. They are, therefore, excluded from the statement of financial position.

When they are acquired through an 'arm's-length transaction', however, the problems of uncertainty about their existence and measurement are resolved. (An arm's-length transaction is one that is undertaken between two unconnected parties.) If goodwill is acquired when taking over another business, or if a business acquires a particular product brand from another business, these items will be separately identified and a price agreed for them. Under these circumstances, they can be regarded as assets (for accounting purposes) by the business that acquired them and included on the statement of financial position.

To agree a price for acquiring goodwill or product brands means that some form of valuation must take place and this raises the question as to how it is done. Usually, the valuation will be based on estimates of future earnings from holding the asset – a process that is fraught with difficulties. Nevertheless, a number of specialist businesses now exist that are prepared to take on this challenge. **Real World 2.2** shows how one specialist business ranked and valued the top ten brands in the world for 2011.

---

**Real World 2.2**

### Brand leaders

Millward, Brown, Optimor, part of WPP marketing services group, produces an annual report which values and ranks the top world brands. For 2011, the top ten brands are as follows.

| Ranking | Brand | Value ($m) |
|---|---|---|
| 1 | Apple | 153,285 |
| 2 | Google | 111,498 |
| 3 | IBM | 100,849 |
| 4 | McDonalds | 81,016 |
| 5 | Microsoft | 78,243 |
| 6 | Coca-Cola | 73,752 |
| 7 | AT&T | 69,916 |
| 8 | Marlboro | 67,522 |
| 9 | China Mobile | 57,326 |
| 10 | General Electric | 50,318 |

We can see that the valuations placed on the brands are quite staggering.

*Source*: Brandz Top 100 Most Valuable Global Brands 2011, Millward Brown Optimor 2011, www.millwardbrown.com.

## Human resources

Attempts have been made to place a monetary measurement on the human resources of a business, but without any real success. There are, however, certain limited circumstances in which human resources are measured and reported in the statement of financial position. These circumstances normally arise with professional football clubs. While football clubs cannot own players, they can own the rights to the players' services. Where these rights are acquired by compensating other clubs for releasing the players from their contracts, an arm's-length transaction arises and the amounts paid provide a reliable basis for measurement. This means that the rights to services can be regarded as an asset of the club for accounting purposes (assuming, of course, the player will also bring benefits to the club).

**Real World 2.3** describes how one leading club reports its investment in players on the statement of financial position.

### Real World 2.3

### Spurs players appear on the pitch and on the statement of financial position

Tottenham Hotspur Football Club (Spurs) has acquired several key players as a result of paying transfer fees to other clubs. In common with most UK football clubs, Spurs reports the cost of acquiring the rights to the players' services on its statement of financial position. The club's statement as at 30 June 2010 shows the total cost of registering its squad of players at about £202 million. The club treats a proportion of each player's transfer fee as an expense each year. The exact proportion depends on the length of the particular player's contract.

The £202 million does not include 'home-grown' players such as Ledley King, because Spurs did not pay a transfer fee for them and so no clear-cut value can be placed on their services. During the year to 30 June 2010, the club was active in the transfer market and spent around £38 million on acquiring new players, including Peter Crouch, Nlko Kranjcar, and Sebastien Bassong. Some players also left the club during the year, including Darren Bent and Pascal Chimbonda, generating transfer fees of more than £24 million.

The item of players' registrations is shown as an intangible asset in the statement of financial position as it is the rights to services, not the players, that are the assets. It is shown net of depreciation (or amortisation as it is usually termed for non-current assets). The carrying amount at 30 June 2010 was £115 million and represented 40 per cent of Spurs' assets, as shown in the statement of financial position.

*Source*: Tottenham Hotspur plc Annual Report 2010.

## Monetary stability

When using money as the unit of measurement, we normally fail to recognise the fact that it will change in value over time. In the UK and throughout much of the world, however, inflation has been a persistent problem. This has meant that the value of money has declined in relation to other assets. In past years, high rates of inflation have resulted in statements of financial position, which were prepared on an historic cost basis, reflecting figures for assets that were much lower than if current values were employed. Rates of inflation have been relatively low in recent years and so the disparity between historic cost values and current values has been less pronounced. Nevertheless, it can still be significant and has added fuel to the debate concerning how to measure asset values on the statement of financial position. It is to this issue that we now turn.

## Valuing assets

As we saw earlier, when preparing the statement of financial position, the historic cost convention is normally applied for the reporting of assets. However, this point requires further explanation as, in practice, it is not simply a matter of recording each asset on the statement of financial position at its original cost. We shall see that things are a little more complex than this. Before discussing the valuation rules in some detail, however, we should point out that they are based on International Financial Reporting Standards, which are rules that are generally accepted throughout much of the world. The nature and role of financial reporting standards will be discussed in detail in Chapters 4 and 5.

### Non-current assets

Non-current assets have lives that are either *finite* or *indefinite*. Those with a finite life provide benefits to a business for a limited period of time, whereas those with an indefinite life provide benefits without a foreseeable time limit. The distinction between the two types of non-current assets applies to both tangible and intangible assets.

Initially, non-current assets are recorded at their historic cost, which will include any amounts spent on getting them ready for use.

### Non-current assets with finite lives

Benefits from assets with finite lives will be used up over time as a result of market changes, wear and tear, and so on. The amount used up, which is referred to as *depreciation* (or *amortisation*, in the case of intangible non-current assets), must be measured for each reporting period for which the assets are held. Although we shall leave a detailed examination of depreciation until Chapter 3, we need to know that when an asset has been depreciated, this must be reflected in the statement of financial position.

The total depreciation that has accumulated over the period since the asset was acquired must be deducted from its cost. This net figure (that is, the cost of the asset less the total depreciation to date) is referred to as the *carrying amount*. It is sometimes also known as *net book value* or *written down value*. The procedure just described is not really a contravention of the historic cost convention. It is simply recognition of the fact that a proportion of the historic cost of the non-current asset has been consumed in the process of generating benefits for the business.

## Activity (2.14)

Can you think of a non-current asset that has a finite life and which can be classified as:

(a) tangible
(b) intangible?

Plant, equipment, motor vehicles and computers are examples of tangible assets that are normally considered to have a finite life. A patent, which gives the owner exclusive rights to use an invention, is an example of an intangible asset that has a finite life. (Many patents are granted for a period of 20 years.)

## Non-current assets with indefinite lives

Benefits from assets with indefinite lives may, or may not, be used up over time. Property (real estate) is usually an example of a tangible non-current asset with an indefinite life. Purchased goodwill could be an example of an intangible one, though this is not always the case. These assets are not subject to routine annual depreciation over time.

## Fair values

Although initially historic cost is the standard or 'benchmark' treatment for recording non-current assets of all types (tangible and intangible, finite or indefinite lives), an alternative is allowed. Non-current assets may be recorded using **fair values** provided that these values can be measured reliably. The fair values, in this case, are the current market values (that is, the exchange values in an arm's-length transaction). The use of fair values, rather than cost figures, whether depreciated or not, can provide users with more up-to-date information, which may well be more relevant to their needs. It may also place the business in a better light, as assets such as property may have increased significantly in value over time. Of course, increasing the statement of financial position value of an asset does not make that asset more valuable. However, perceptions of the business may be altered by such a move.

One consequence of upwardly revaluing non-current assets with finite lives is that the depreciation charge will be increased. This is because the depreciation charge is based on the new (increased) value of the asset.

**Real World 2.4** shows the effect of the revaluation of non-current assets on the financial position of one large business.

## Real World 2.4

### Rising asset levels

During the year to 31 March 2010, Veolia Water UK plc, which owns Thames Water, changed its policy on the valuation of certain types of non-current assets. These assets included land and buildings, infrastructure assets, and vehicles, plant and machinery. The business switched from the use of historic cost to the use of fair values and a revaluation exercise was carried out by independent qualified valuers.

The effect of this policy change was to report a revaluation gain of more than £436 million during the year. There was a 40 per cent increase in owners' (shareholders') equity, which was largely due to this gain.

*Source*: Veolia Water UK plc, Annual report 2009/10.

## Activity (2.15)

Refer to the statement of financial position of Brie Manufacturing shown earlier in Example 2.3 (page 58). What would be the effect of revaluing the property to a figure of £110,000 on the statement of financial position?

The effect on the statement of financial position would be to increase the property to £110,000 and the gain on revaluation (that is, £110,000 − £45,000 = £65,000) would be added to equity, as it is the owner(s) who will benefit from the gain. The revised statement of financial position would therefore be as follows:

**Brie Manufacturing**
**Statement of financial position as at 31 December 2011**

|  | £000 |
|---|---|
| **ASSETS** | |
| **Non-current assets (property, plant and equipment)** | |
| Property | 110 |
| Plant and equipment | 30 |
| Motor vans | 19 |
|  | 159 |
| **Current assets** | |
| Inventories | 23 |
| Trade receivables | 18 |
| Cash at bank | 12 |
|  | 53 |
| **Total Assets** | 212 |
| **EQUITY AND LIABILITIES** | |
| **Equity** (60 + 65) | 125 |
| **Non-current liabilities** | |
| Long-term borrowings | 50 |
| **Current liabilities** | |
| Trade payables | 37 |
| **Total equity and liabilities** | 212 |

Once assets are revalued, the frequency of revaluation then becomes an important issue as assets recorded at out-of-date revaluations can mislead users. Using such figures on the statement of financial position is the worst of both worlds. It lacks the objectivity and verifiability of historic cost; it also lacks the realism of current values. Where fair values are used, revaluations should therefore be frequent enough to ensure that the carrying amount of the revalued asset does not differ materially from its true fair value at the statement of financial position date.

When an item of property, plant or equipment (a tangible asset) is revalued on the basis of fair values, all assets within that particular group must be revalued. Thus, it is not acceptable to revalue some items of property but not others. Although this provides some degree of consistency within a particular group of assets, it does not, of course, prevent the statement of financial position from containing a mixture of valuations.

Intangible assets are not often revalued to fair values. This is because revaluations can only be used where there is an active market, thereby permitting fair values to be properly determined. Such markets, however, rarely exist for intangible assets.

## The impairment of non-current assets

There is always a risk that all types of non-current asset (tangible or intangible, finite or indefinite lives) may suffer a significant fall in value. This may be due to factors such as changes in market conditions, technological obsolescence, and so on. In some cases, this fall in value may lead to the carrying amount of the asset being higher than the amount that could be recovered from the asset through its continued use or through its sale. When this occurs, the asset value is said to be impaired and the general rule is to reduce the value on the statement of financial position to the recoverable amount. Unless this is done, the asset value will be overstated. This type of impairment in value should not be confused with routine depreciation of assets with finite lives.

### Activity (2.16)

With which one of the accounting conventions that we discussed earlier is this accounting treatment of impaired assets consistent?

The answer is the prudence convention, which states that actual or anticipated losses should be recognised in full.

In many situations, a business may use either historic cost, less any depreciation, or a value-based measure when reporting its non-current assets. However, where the value-based measure is the impaired value and is smaller than the historic-cost based value, the business has no choice. The use of depreciated historic cost is not an option; the impaired value must be used.

**Real World 2.5** provides an example of where the application of the 'impairment rule', as it is called, resulted in huge write-downs (that is, reductions in the statement of financial position value of the assets) for one large business.

### Real World 2.5

#### Painting a rosy picture                                     **FT**

Akzo Nobel, the Dutch paints and chemicals company, on Tuesday defended its £8bn ($11.6bn) acquisition of ICI in 2007 after it took a €1.2bn ($1.5bn) impairment charge on the former UK industrial giant because of sharply lower paint sales.

The company saw the volume of paint sold fall by 10 per cent in the fourth quarter, with even steeper declines in Asia, one of the areas where ICI had been strong. This prompted the move to slash growth estimates and fair value for ICI.

'It's not a world of high growth any more, it's a world with completely different challenges,' said Hans Wijers, chief executive. 'We expect 2009 to be an uncertain year with a lot of volatility [and] with challenging volume circumstances.'

The €1.2bn impairment charge cuts into the €4.4bn of goodwill the company recorded when it acquired ICI and its Dulux brand name, but Akzo defended its previous assumptions as conservative.

'Could we have anticipated that the world economy would go down so much?' Mr Wijers said. 'I'm not sorry about [the ICI] transaction. It was the right thing to do at the right time and the company has become much stronger because of it.'

*Source*: 'Akzo Nobel defends ICI takeover', Michael Steen, FT.com, 24 February 2009.

There is a distinction between the treatment of different types of non-current assets in respect of the need to test as to whether impairment has taken place, as follows:

- intangible, non-current assets with indefinite lives *must be* tested annually to see whether there has been any impairment;
- all other non-current assets need only be tested where events suggest that impairment has taken place.

We should bear in mind that impairment reviews involve making judgements about the appropriate value to place on assets. Employing independent valuers to make these judgements will normally give users greater confidence in the information reported. There is always a risk that managers will manipulate impairment values to portray a picture that they would like users to see.

## Inventories

It is not only non-current assets that run the risk of a significant fall in value. The inventories of a business could also suffer this fate, which could be caused by factors such as reduced selling prices, obsolescence, deterioration, damage, and so on. Where a fall in value means that the amount likely to be recovered from the sale of the inventories will be lower than their cost, this loss must be reflected in the statement of financial position. Thus, if the net realisable value (that is, selling price less any selling costs) falls below the historic cost of inventories held, the former should be used as the basis of valuation. This reflects, once again, the influence of the prudence convention on the statement of financial position.

**Real World 2.6** reveals how one well-known business wrote down the inventories of one of its products following a sharp reduction in selling prices.

### Real World 2.6

### You're fired!

'You're fired!' is what some investors might like to tell Amstrad, run by Apprentice star Sir Alan Sugar. . . . Shares in the company fell nearly 10 per cent as it revealed that sales of its much-vaunted videophone have failed to take off.

Amstrad launched the E3, a phone allowing users to hold video calls with each other, in a blaze of publicity last year. But, after cutting the price from £99 to £49, Amstrad sold just 61,000 E3s in the year to June and has taken a £5.7m stock (inventories) write down.

*Source*: 'Amstrad(AMT)', *Investors Chronicle*, 7 October 2005.

The published financial statements of large businesses will normally show the basis on which inventories are valued. **Real World 2.7** shows how one business reports this information.

---

### Real World 2.7

## Reporting inventories

The 2010/11 annual report of Ted Baker plc, a leading designer clothes brand, includes the following explanation concerning inventories:

> Inventories and work in progress are stated at the lower of cost and net realisable value. Cost includes materials, direct labour and inward transportation costs. Net realisable value is based on estimated selling price, less further costs expected to be incurred to completion and disposal. Provision is made for obsolete, slow moving or defective items where appropriate.

*Source*: Ted Baker plc Report and Accounts 2010/11, p.51.

---

# Meeting user needs

The statement of financial position is the oldest of the three main financial statements and many businesses prepare one on a regular basis, even where they are not subject to regulations requiring it to be produced. This suggests that it is regarded as providing useful information. There are various ways in which the statement of financial position may help users, including the following:

- *It provides insights about how the business is financed and how its funds are deployed.* The statement of financial position shows how much finance is contributed by the owners and how much is contributed by outside lenders. It also shows the different kinds of assets acquired and how much is invested in each kind.
- *It can provide a basis for assessing the value of the business.* Since the statement of financial position lists, and places a value on, the various assets and claims, it can provide a starting point for assessing the value of the business. It is, however, severely limited in the extent to which it can do this. We have seen earlier that accounting rules may result in assets being shown at their historic cost and that the restrictive definition of assets may exclude certain business resources from the statement of financial position. Ultimately, the value of a business will be based on its ability to generate wealth in the future. Because of this, assets need to be valued on the basis of their wealth-generating potential. Also, other business resources that do not meet the restrictive definition of assets, such as brand values, need to be similarly valued and included.
- *Relationships between assets and claims can be assessed.* It can be useful to look at relationships between various statement of financial position items, for example the relationship between how much wealth is tied up in current assets and how much is owed in the short term (current liabilities). From this relationship, we can see whether the business has sufficient short-term assets to cover its maturing obligations. We shall look at this and other relationships between statement of financial position items in some detail in Chapter 7.

● *Performance can be assessed.* The effectiveness of a business in generating wealth can usefully be assessed against the amount of investment that was involved. Thus, the relationship between profit earned during a period and the value of the net assets invested can be helpful to many users, particularly owners and managers. This and similar relationships will also be explored in detail in Chapter 7.

## Summary

The main points of this chapter may be summarised as follows:

### The major financial statements

● There are three major financial statements: the statement of cash flows, the income statement (profit and loss account) and the statement of financial position (balance sheet).
● The statement of cash flows shows the cash movements over a particular period.
● The income statement shows the wealth (profit) generated over a particular period.
● The statement of financial position shows the accumulated wealth at a particular point in time.

### The statement of financial position

● This sets out the assets of the business, on the one hand, and the claims against those assets, on the other.
● Assets are resources of the business that have certain characteristics, such as the ability to provide future benefits.
● Claims are obligations on the part of the business to provide cash, or some other benefit, to outside parties.
● Claims are of two types: equity and liabilities.
● Equity represents the claim(s) of the owner(s) and liabilities represent the claims of others, apart from the owners.
● The statement of financial position reflects the accounting equation:

$$Assets = Equity + Liabilities$$

### Classification of assets and liabilities

● Assets are normally categorised as being current or non-current.
● Current assets are cash or near cash or are held for sale or consumption in the normal course of business, or for trading, or for the short term.
● Non-current assets are assets that are not current assets. They are normally held for the long-term operations of the business.
● Liabilities are normally categorised as being current or non-current liabilities.
● Current liabilities represent amounts due in the normal course of the business's operating cycle, or are held for trading, or are to be settled within a year of, or cannot be deferred for at least a year after, the end of the reporting period.
● Non-current liabilities represent amounts due that are not current liabilities.

### Statement of financial position layouts

- The standard layout begins with assets at the top of the statement of financial position and places equity and liabilities underneath.
- A variation of the standard layout begins with the assets at the top of the statement of financial position. From the total assets figure are deducted the non-current and current liabilities to arrive at a net assets figure. Equity is placed underneath.

### Accounting conventions

- Accounting conventions are the rules of accounting that have evolved to deal with practical problems experienced by those preparing financial statements.
- The main conventions relating to the statement of financial position include business entity, historic cost, prudence, going concern and dual aspect.

### Money measurement

- Using money as the unit of measurement limits the scope of the statement of financial position.
- Certain resources such as goodwill, product brands and human resources are difficult to measure. An 'arm's-length transaction' is normally required before such assets can be reliably measured and reported on the statement of financial position.
- Money is not a stable unit of measurement – it changes in value over time.

### Asset valuation

- The 'benchmark treatment' is to show non-current assets with finite lives at historic cost less any amounts written off for depreciation.
- The 'benchmark treatment' is to show non-current assets with indefinite lives at historic cost.
- Fair values may be used rather than historic cost, provided that they can be reliably obtained.
- Where the recoverable amount from non-current assets is below their carrying amount, this lower amount is reflected in the statement of financial position.
- Inventories are shown at the lower of cost or net realisable value.

### The usefulness of the statement of financial position

- It shows how finance has been raised and how it has been been deployed.
- It provides a basis for valuing the business, though the conventional statement of financial position can only be a starting point.
- Relationships between various statement of financial position items can usefully be explored.
- Relationships between wealth generated and wealth invested can be helpful indicators of business effectiveness.

MyAccountingLab
Go to **www.myaccountinglab.com** to check your understanding of the chapter, create a personalised study plan, and maximise your revision time

## Key terms

statement of cash flows   p. 40
income statement   p. 40
statement of financial position   p. 40
final accounts   p. 44
assets   p. 45
claims   p. 45
tangible assets   p. 48
intangible assets   p. 48
property, plant and equipment   p. 48
equity   p. 48
liabilities   p. 48

current assets   p. 54
non-current (fixed) assets   p. 55
current liabilities   p. 56
non-current liabilities   p. 57
accounting conventions   p. 60
business entity convention   p. 60
historic cost convention   p. 61
prudence convention   p. 62
going concern convention   p. 63
dual aspect convention   p. 63
fair values   p. 68

## Further reading

If you would like to explore the topics covered in this chapter in more depth, we recommend the following books:

Elliott, B. and Elliott, J., *Financial Accounting and Reporting* 15th edn, Financial Times Prentice Hall, 2012, chapters 17 and 19.

International Accounting Standards Board, *2011 International Financial Reporting Standards IFRS*, (2 volume set), 2011.

KPMG, *Insights into IFRS*, 7th edn, 2010/11, 2011, Sections 3.1, 3.2, 3.3, 3.10 and 3.13. A summarised version of this is available free at www.kpmg.com.

Melville, A. *International Financial Reporting: A Practical Guide* 3rd edn, Financial Times Prentice Hall, 2011, chapters 5 to 8.

## Review questions

Solutions to these questions can be found at the back of the book on pages 746–7.

**2.1**   An accountant prepared a statement of financial position for a business. In this statement, the equity of the owner was shown next to the liabilities. This confused the owner, who argued: 'My equity is my major asset and so should be shown as an asset on the statement of financial position.' How would you explain this misunderstanding to the owner?

**2.2**   'The statement of financial position shows how much a business is worth.' Do you agree with this statement? Explain the reasons for your response.

**2.3**   What is meant by the accounting equation? How does the form of this equation differ between the two statement of financial position layouts mentioned in the chapter?

**2.4**   In recent years there have been attempts to place a value on the 'human assets' of a business in order to derive a figure that can be included on the statement of financial position. Do you think humans should be treated as assets? Would 'human assets' meet the conventional definition of an asset for inclusion on the statement of financial position?

## Exercises

Exercises 2.1 and 2.2 are basic level, 2.3, 2.4, and 2.5 are intermediate level and 2.6 and 2.7 are advanced level. Those with **coloured numbers** have solutions at the back of the book, starting on page 760.

If you wish to try more exercises, visit the students' side of the Companion Website and MyAccountingLab.

**2.1**   On Thursday, the fourth day of his business venture, Paul, the street trader in wrapping paper (see earlier in the chapter, pages 41 to 44), bought more inventories for £53 cash. During the day he sold inventories that had cost £33 for a total of £47.

*Required*:
Draw up the three financial statements for Paul's business venture for Thursday.

**2.2**   The equity of Paul's business belongs to him because he is the sole owner of the business. Can you explain how the figure for equity by Thursday evening has arisen? You will need to look back at the events of Monday, Tuesday and Wednesday (pages 41 to 44) to do this.

**2.3**   While on holiday in Bridlington, Helen had her credit cards and purse stolen from the beach while she was swimming. She was left with only £40, which she had kept in her hotel room, but she had three days of her holiday remaining. She was determined to continue her holiday and decided to make some money to enable her to do so. She decided to sell orange juice to holidaymakers using the local beach. On the first day she bought 80 cartons of orange juice at £0.50 each for cash and sold 70 of these at £0.80 each. On the following day she bought 60 cartons at £0.50 each for cash and sold 65 at £0.80 each. On the third and final day she bought another 60 cartons at £0.50 each for cash. However, it rained and, as a result, business was poor. She managed to sell 20 at £0.80 each but sold off the rest of her inventories at £0.40 each.

*Required*:
Prepare an income statement and statement of cash flows for each day's trading and prepare a statement of financial position at the end of each day's trading.

**2.4**  On 1 March, Joe Conday started a new business. During March he carried out the following transactions:

1 March    Deposited £20,000 in a newly-opened bank account.
2 March    Bought fixtures and fittings for £6,000 cash and inventories £8,000 on credit.
3 March    Borrowed £5,000 from a relative and deposited it in the bank.
4 March    Bought a motor car for £7,000 cash and withdrew £200 in cash for his own use.
5 March    A further motor car costing £9,000 was bought. The motor car bought on 4 March was given in part exchange at a value of £6,500. The balance of purchase price for the new car was paid in cash.
6 March    Conday won £2,000 in a lottery and paid the amount into the business bank account. He also repaid £1,000 of the borrowings.

*Required*:
Draw up a statement of financial position for the business at the end of each day.

**2.5**  The following is a list of assets and claims of a manufacturing business at a particular point in time:

|  | £ |
|---|---|
| Short-term borrowing | 22,000 |
| Property | 245,000 |
| Inventories of raw materials | 18,000 |
| Trade payables | 23,000 |
| Plant and equipment | 127,000 |
| Loan from Manufacturing Finance Co. (long-term borrowing) | 100,000 |
| Inventories of finished goods | 28,000 |
| Delivery vans | 54,000 |
| Trade receivables | 34,000 |

*Required*:
Write out a statement of financial position in the standard format incorporating these figures. (*Hint*: There is a missing item that needs to be deduced and inserted.)

**2.6**  The following is a list of the assets and claims of Crafty Engineering Ltd at 30 June last year:

|  | £000 |
|---|---|
| Trade payables | 86 |
| Motor vehicles | 38 |
| Long-term borrowing from Industrial Finance Co. | 260 |
| Equipment and tools | 207 |
| Short-term borrowings | 116 |
| Inventories | 153 |
| Property | 320 |
| Trade receivables | 185 |

*Required*:
(a) Prepare the statement of financial position of the business as at 30 June last year from the above information using the standard layout. (*Hint*: There is a missing item that needs to be deduced and inserted.)
(b) Discuss the significant features revealed by this financial statement.

**2.7** The statement of financial position of a business at the start of the week is as follows:

|  | £ |
|---|---:|
| **ASSETS** | |
| Property | 145,000 |
| Furniture and fittings | 63,000 |
| Inventories | 28,000 |
| Trade receivables | 33,000 |
| **Total assets** | 269,000 |
| **EQUITY AND LIABILITIES** | |
| Equity | 203,000 |
| Short-term borrowing (bank overdraft) | 43,000 |
| Trade payables | 23,000 |
| **Total equity and liabilities** | 269,000 |

During the week the following transactions take place:

(a) Sold inventories for £11,000 cash; these inventories had cost £8,000.
(b) Sold inventories for £23,000 on credit; these inventories had cost £17,000.
(c) Received cash from trade receivables totalling £18,000.
(d) The owners of the business introduced £100,000 of their own money, which was placed in the business bank account.
(e) The owners brought a motor van, valued at £10,000, into the business.
(f) Bought inventories on credit for £14,000.
(g) Paid trade payables £13,000.

*Required*:
Show the statement of financial position after all of these transactions have been reflected.

# Measuring and reporting financial performance

## Introduction

In this chapter, we continue our examination of the major financial statements by looking at the income statement. This statement was briefly considered in Chapter 2, but we shall now look at it in some detail. We shall see how it is prepared and how it links with the statement of financial position. We shall also consider some of the key measurement problems to be faced when preparing the income statement.

## Learning outcomes

**When you have completed this chapter, you should be able to:**

● discuss the nature and purpose of the income statement;

● prepare an income statement from relevant financial information and interpret the information that it contains;

● discuss the main recognition and measurement issues that must be considered when preparing the income statement;

● explain the main accounting conventions underpinning the income statement.

## What does it mean?

Tate and Lyle plc, whose business is sweeteners, starches and sugar refining, reported sales revenue of £2,720 million and a profit of £167 million for the year ending on 31 March 2011. To understand fully the significance of these figures, we must be clear about the nature of revenue and profit. This means that we must be able to answer questions such as:

- Does the sales revenue of £2,720 million represent the cash generated from sales for the period?
- What is the relationship between the sales revenue and the profit for the period?
- Can the profit for the period of £167 million be measured with complete accuracy and certainty?
- Does the profit figure of £167 million mean that the business had £167 million *more* in the bank at the end of the year than it had at the beginning?
- How can the sales revenue and profit figures help in assessing performance?

The answers to these and other questions are covered in the chapter.

## The income statement

In Chapter 2 we considered the statement of financial position (balance sheet). We saw that it sets out the wealth of a business, and who contributed that wealth, at a particular moment in time. However, it is not usually enough for users of financial statements to have information relating only to this aspect of financial health. Businesses exist for the primary purpose of generating wealth, or profit, and it is the profit generated *during a period* that is the concern of many users. The main purpose of the income statement – or profit and loss account, as it is sometimes called – is to measure and report how much **profit** (wealth) the business has generated over a period. It also helps users to gain some impression of how that profit was made. As with the statement of financial position, which we examined in Chapter 2, the principles of preparation are the same irrespective of whether the income statement is for a sole proprietorship business or for a limited company.

The measurement of profit requires that the total revenue of the business, generated during a particular period, be identified. **Revenue** is simply a measure of the inflow of economic benefits arising from the ordinary operations of a business. These benefits will result in either an increase in assets (such as cash or amounts owed to the business by its customers) or a decrease in liabilities. Different forms of business enterprise will generate different forms of revenue. Some examples of the different forms that revenue can take are as follows:

- sales of goods (for example, by a manufacturer)
- fees for services (for example, of a solicitor)
- subscriptions (for example, of a club)
- interest received (for example, on an investment fund).

**Real World 3.1** shows the various forms of revenue generated by a leading football club.

**Real World 3.1**

## Gunning for revenue

Arsenal Football Club generated total revenue of £380 million for the year ended 31 May 2010. Like other leading clubs, it relies on various forms of revenue to sustain its success. Figure 3.1 below shows the contribution of each form of revenue for the year. The high level of revenue from property development is unusual for a football club, even for Arsenal. It arises from the fact that the club is developing its former home Highbury Stadium for residential accommodation following its move to the Emirates Stadium.

**Figure 3.1**    **Arsenal's revenue for the year ended 31 May 2010**

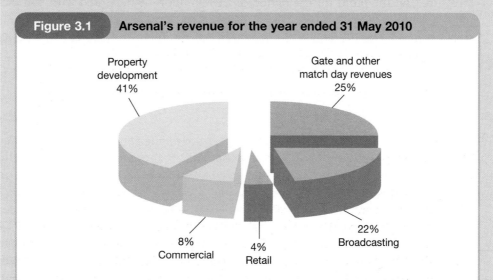

Gate receipts and broadcasting tend to be Arsenal's main forms of revenue, although commercial activities (including sponsorship and events) are also significant. During this particular year, as with 2009, there was a lot of income from property development. Revenue from player trading was negligible for 2010.

*Source*: Based on information in Arsenal Holdings plc Annual Report 2010, Financial Review.

The total expenses relating to each period must also be identified. **Expense** is really the opposite of revenue. It represents the outflow of economic benefits arising from the ordinary operations of a business. This loss of benefits will result in either a decrease in assets (such as cash) or an increase in liabilities (such as amounts owed to suppliers). Expenses are incurred in the process of generating, or attempting to generate, revenue. The nature of the business will again determine the type of expenses that will be incurred. Examples of some of the more common types of expense are:

- the cost of buying or making the goods that are sold during the period concerned – known as *cost of sales* or *cost of goods sold*
- salaries and wages
- rent and rates
- motor vehicle running expenses

- insurance
- printing and stationery
- heat and light
- telephone and postage.

The income statement simply shows the total revenue generated during a particular period and deducts from this the total expenses incurred in generating that revenue. The difference between the total revenue and total expenses will represent either profit (if revenue exceeds expenses) or loss (if expenses exceed revenue). Thus, we have:

> Profit (or loss) for the period = Total revenue for the period – Total expenses incurred in generating that revenue

The period over which profit or loss is normally measured is usually known as the **reporting period**, but it is sometimes called the 'accounting period' or 'financial period'.

## Different roles

The income statement and the statement of financial position should not be viewed in any way as substitutes for one another. Rather they should be seen as performing different roles. The statement of financial position, as we have seen, sets out the position at a single moment in time: it is a 'snapshot' of the make-up of the wealth held by the business. The income statement, on the other hand, is concerned with the *flow* of wealth over a period of time. The two statements are, however, closely related.

The income statement links the statements of financial position at the beginning and the end of a reporting period. At the start of a new reporting period, the statement of financial position shows the opening wealth position of the business. After an appropriate period, an income statement is prepared to show the wealth generated over that period. A statement of financial position is then also prepared to reveal the new wealth position at the end of the period. This statement of financial position will reflect the changes in wealth that have occurred since the previous statement of financial position was drawn up.

We saw in Chapter 2 (pages 53 to 54) that the effect on the statement of financial position of making a profit (or loss) means that the accounting equation can be extended as follows:

> Assets (at the end of the period) = Equity (amount at the start of the period + profit (or – loss) for the period)
> + Liabilities (at the end of the period)

(This is assuming that the owner makes no injections or withdrawals of equity during the period.)

The amount of profit or loss for the period affects the statement of financial position as an adjustment to equity.

The equation above can be extended to:

> Assets (at the end of the period) = Equity (amount at the start of the period)
> + (sales revenue – expenses) (for the period)
> + Liabilities (at the end of the period)

In theory, it would be possible to calculate the profit (or loss) for the period by making all adjustments for revenue and expenses through the equity section of the statement of financial position. However, this would be rather cumbersome. A better solution is to have an 'appendix' to the equity section, in the form of an income statement. By deducting expenses from revenue for the period, the income statement derives the profit (or loss) by which the equity figure in the statement of financial position needs to be adjusted. This profit (or loss) figure represents the net effect of trading for the period. By providing this 'appendix', users are presented with a detailed and more informative view of performance.

## Income statement layout

The layout of the income statement will vary according to the type of business to which it relates. To illustrate an income statement, let us consider the case of a retail business (that is, a business that buys goods in their completed state and resells them).

Example 3.1 sets out a typical layout for the income statement of a retail business.

**Example 3.1**

**Better-Price Stores**
**Income statement for the year ended 31 October 2011**

|  | £ |
|---|---:|
| Sales revenue | 232,000 |
| Cost of sales | (154,000) |
| **Gross profit** | 78,000 |
| Salaries and wages | (24,500) |
| Rent and rates | (14,200) |
| Heat and light | (7,500) |
| Telephone and postage | (1,200) |
| Insurance | (1,000) |
| Motor vehicle running expenses | (3,400) |
| Depreciation – fixtures and fittings | (1,000) |
| Depreciation – motor van | (600) |
| **Operating profit** | 24,600 |
| Interest received from investments | 2,000 |
| Interest on borrowings | (1,100) |
| **Profit for the year** | 25,500 |

We saw in Chapter 2 that brackets are used to denote when an item is to be deducted. This convention is used by accountants in preference to + or – signs and will be used throughout the text.

### Gross profit

The first part of the income statement is concerned with calculating the **gross profit** for the period. We can see that revenue, which arises from selling the goods, is the first item to appear. Deducted from this item is the cost of sales (also called cost of goods sold) during the period. This gives the gross profit, which represents the profit from buying and selling goods, without taking into account any other revenues or expenses associated with the business.

## Operating profit

From the gross profit, operating expenses (overheads) that have been incurred in operating the business (salaries and wages, rent and rates, and so on) are deducted.

The resulting figure is known as the **operating profit** for the reporting period. This represents the wealth generated during the period from the normal activities of the business. It does not take account of any income that the business may have from activities that are not included in its normal operations. Better-Price Stores in Example 3.1 is a retailer, so the interest on some spare cash that the business has invested is not part of its operating profit. Costs of financing the business are also ignored in the calculation of the operating profit.

## Profit for the period

Having established the operating profit, we add any non-operating income (such as interest receivable) and deduct any interest payable on borrowings made by the business, to arrive at the **profit for the period** (or net profit). This is the income that is attributable to the owner(s) of the business and which will be added to the equity figure in the statement of financial position. As can be seen, profit for the year is a residual: that is, the amount remaining after deducting all expenses incurred in generating the sales revenue for the period and taking account of non-operating income.

## Further issues

Having set out the main principles involved in preparing an income statement, we need to consider some further points.

## Cost of sales

The **cost of sales** (or cost of goods sold) figure for a period can be identified in different ways. In some businesses, the cost of sales amount for each individual sale is identified at the time of the transaction. Each item of sales revenue is closely matched with the relevant cost of that sale and so identifying the cost of sales figure for inclusion in the income statement is not a problem. Many large retailers (for example, supermarkets) have point-of-sale (checkout) devices that not only record each sale but also simultaneously pick up the cost of the goods that are the subject of the particular sale. Other businesses that sell a relatively small number of high-value items (for example, an engineering business that produces custom-made equipment) also tend to match sales revenue with the cost of the goods sold, at the time of the sale. However, some businesses (for example, small retailers) do not usually find it practical to match each sale to a particular cost of sales figure as the reporting period progresses. Instead, therefore, they identify the cost of sales figure at the end of the reporting period.

### Deriving the cost of sales after the end of the reporting period

To understand how this is done, we need to remember that the cost of sales figure represents the cost of goods that were *sold* by the business during the period rather than the cost of goods that were *bought* by that business during the period. Part of the goods bought during a particular period may remain in the business, as inventories, at the reporting period end. These will normally be sold in the next period. To derive the cost of sales for a period, we need to know the amount of opening and closing inventories for the period and the cost of goods bought during the period. Example 3.2 illustrates how the cost of sales is derived.

**Example 3.2**

Better-Price Stores, which we considered in Example 3.1 above, began the reporting period with unsold inventories of £40,000 and during that year bought inventories at a cost of £189,000. At the end of the year, unsold inventories of £75,000 were still held by the business.

The opening inventories at the beginning of the year *plus* the goods bought during the year will represent the total goods available for resale. Thus:

|  | £ |
|---|---:|
| Opening inventories | 40,000 |
| Purchases (goods bought) | 189,000 |
| Goods available for resale | 229,000 |

The closing inventories will represent that portion of the total goods available for resale that remains unsold at the end of the period. Thus, the cost of goods actually sold during the period must be the total goods available for resale *less* the inventories remaining at the end of the period. That is:

|  | £ |
|---|---:|
| Goods available for resale | 229,000 |
| Closing inventories | (75,000) |
| Cost of sales (or cost of goods sold) | 154,000 |

These calculations are sometimes shown on the face of the income statement as in Example 3.3.

**Example 3.3**

|  | £ | £ |
|---|---:|---:|
| Sales revenue |  | 232,000 |
| Cost of sales: |  |  |
| Opening inventories | 40,000 |  |
| Purchases (goods bought) | 189,000 |  |
| Closing inventories | (75,000) | (154,000) |
| **Gross profit** |  | 78,000 |

This is just an expanded version of the first section of the income statement for Better-Price Stores, as set out in Example 3.1. We have simply included the additional information concerning inventories balances and purchases for the year provided in Example 3.2.

## Classifying expenses

The classifications for the revenue and expense items, as with the classifications of various assets and claims in the statement of financial position, are often a matter of judgement by those who design the accounting system. Thus, the income statement set out in Example 3.1 could have included the insurance expense with the telephone and postage expense under a single heading – say, 'general expenses'. Such decisions are normally based on how useful a particular classification will be to users. This will usually mean that expense items of material size will be shown separately. For businesses that trade as limited companies, however, there are rules that dictate the classification of various items appearing in the financial statements for external reporting purposes. These rules will be discussed in Chapters 4 and 5.

### Activity 3.1

The following information relates to the activities of H & S Retailers for the year ended 30 April 2012:

|  | £ |
|---|---|
| Motor vehicle running expenses | 1,200 |
| Closing inventories | 3,000 |
| Rent and rates payable | 5,000 |
| Motor vans – cost less depreciation | 6,300 |
| Annual depreciation – motor vans | 1,500 |
| Heat and light | 900 |
| Telephone and postage | 450 |
| Sales revenue | 97,400 |
| Goods purchased | 68,350 |
| Insurance | 750 |
| Loan interest payable | 620 |
| Balance at bank | 4,780 |
| Salaries and wages | 10,400 |
| Opening inventories | 4,000 |

Prepare an income statement for the year ended 30 April 2012. (*Hint*: Not all items listed should appear on this statement.)

Your answer to this activity should be as follows:

**H & S Retailers**
**Income statement for the year ended 30 April 2012**

|  | £ | £ |
|---|---:|---:|
| Sales revenue |  | 97,400 |
| Cost of sales: |  |  |
|    Opening inventories | 4,000 |  |
|    Purchases | 68,350 |  |
|    Closing inventories | (3,000) | (69,350) |
| **Gross profit** |  | 28,050 |
| Salaries and wages |  | (10,400) |
| Rent and rates |  | (5,000) |
| Heat and light |  | (900) |
| Telephone and postage |  | (450) |
| Insurance |  | (750) |
| Motor vehicle running expenses |  | (1,200) |
| Depreciation – motor vans |  | (1,500) |
| **Operating profit** |  | 7,850 |
| Loan interest |  | (620) |
| **Profit for the year** |  | 7,230 |

Note that neither the motor vans nor the bank balance are included in this statement, because they are both assets and so neither revenues nor expenses.

Figure 3.2 shows the layout of the income statement.

## The reporting period

We have seen already that for reporting to those outside the business, a financial reporting cycle of one year is the norm, though some large businesses produce a half-yearly, or interim, financial statement to provide more frequent feedback on progress. For those who manage a business, however, it is probably essential to have much more frequent feedback on performance. Thus it is quite common for income statements to be prepared on a quarterly, monthly, weekly or even daily basis in order to show how things are progressing.

## Recognising revenue

A key issue in the measurement of profit concerns the point at which revenue is recognised. Revenue arising from the sale of goods or provision of a service could be recognised at various points. Where, for example, a motor car dealer receives an order for a new car from one of its customers, the associated revenue could be recognised by the dealer:

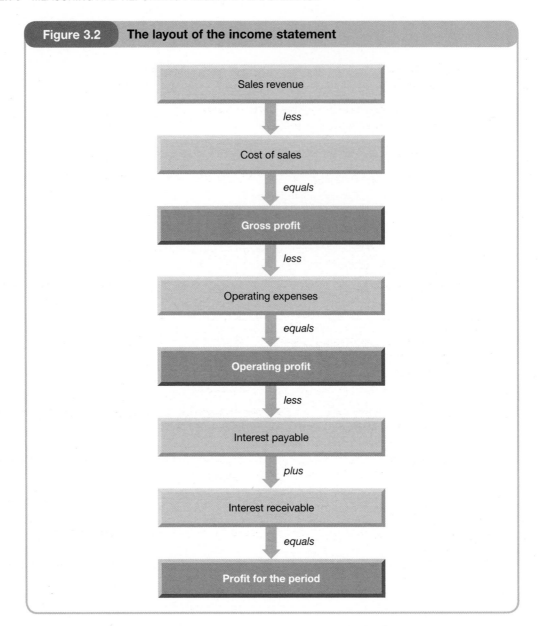

**Figure 3.2** The layout of the income statement

- at the time that the order is placed by the customer;
- at the time that the car is collected by the customer; or
- at the time that the customer pays the dealer.

These three points could well be quite far apart, particularly where the order relates to a specialist car that is sold to the customer on credit.

The point chosen is not simply a matter of academic interest: it can have a profound impact on the total revenues reported for a particular reporting period. This, in turn, could have a profound effect on profit. If the sale transaction straddled the end of a reporting period, the choice made between the three possible times for recognising the revenue could determine whether it is included as revenue of an earlier reporting period or a later one.

Irrespective of whether we are dealing with the sale of goods or the provision of services, the main criteria for recognising revenue are that:

● the amount of revenue can be measured reliably; and
● it is probable that the economic benefits will be received.

An additional criterion, however, must be applied where the revenue comes from the sale of goods, which is that

● ownership and control of the items should pass to the buyer.

Activity 3.2 provides an opportunity to apply these criteria to a practical problem.

## Activity 3.2

A manufacturing business sells goods on credit (that is, the customer pays for the goods some time after they are received). Below are four points in the production/selling cycle at which revenue might be recognised by the business:

1  when the goods are produced;
2  when an order is received from the customer;
3  when the goods are delivered to, and accepted by, the customer;
4  when the cash is received from the customer.

A significant amount of time may elapse between these different points. At what point do you think the business should recognise revenue?

All of the three criteria mentioned above will usually be fulfilled at point 3: when the goods are passed to, and accepted by, the customer. This is because

● the selling price and the settlement terms will have been agreed and therefore the amount of revenue can be reliably measured;
● delivery and acceptance of the goods leads to ownership, and control passing to the buyer;
● transferring ownership gives the seller legally enforceable rights that makes it probable that the buyer will pay.

We can see that the effect of applying these criteria is that a sale on credit is usually recognised *before* the cash is received. This means that the total sales revenue figure shown in the income statement may include sales transactions for which the cash has yet to be received. The total sales revenue figure in the income statement for a period will often, therefore, be different from the total cash received from sales during that period.

For cash sales (that is, sales where cash is paid at the same time as the goods are transferred), there will be no difference in timing between reporting sales revenue and cash received. **Real World 3.2** sets out the revenue recognition criteria for the travel business TUI Travel plc (which owns First Choice, Thomson, Exodus and many other well-known names). We can see that, although clients may pay for flights or holidays some time before they go, any money received in advance of the departure date, or use of the service, is not treated as revenue until later.

**Real World 3.2**

### Selling point

**(i) *Revenue recognition***

Revenue is recognised in the income statement when the significant risks and rewards of ownership have been transferred to the buyer.

Revenue in respect of in-house product is recognised on the date of departure. Travel agency commissions and other revenues received from the sale of third-party product are recognised when they are earned, typically on receipt of final payment. Revenue from individual travel modules directly booked by the customer with airline, hotels and incoming agencies is recognised when the customer departs or uses the respective service.

No revenue is recognised if there are significant uncertainties regarding recovery of the consideration due or associated costs.

**(ii) *Client monies received in advance (deferred income)***

Client monies received at the balance sheet [statement of financial position] date relating to holidays commencing and flights departing after the year end are deferred and included within trade and other payables.

*Source*: TUI Travel plc Annual Report and Accounts 2010, p. 76.

## Long-term contracts

Some contracts, both for goods and for services, can last for more than one reporting period. If the business providing the goods or service were to wait until the contract is completely fulfilled before recognising revenue, the income statement could give a misleading impression of the wealth generated in the various reporting periods covered by the contract. This is a particular problem for businesses that undertake major long-term contracts, where a single contract could represent a large proportion of their total activities.

### Construction contracts

Construction contracts often extend over a long period of time. Suppose that a customer enters into a contract with a builder to have a new factory built that will take three years to complete. In such a situation, it is possible to recognise revenue *before* the factory is completed provided that the building work can be broken down into a number of stages and each stage can be measured reliably. Let us assume that building the factory could be broken down into the following stages:

- Stage 1 – clearing and levelling the land and putting in the foundations.
- Stage 2 – building the walls.
- Stage 3 – putting on the roof.
- Stage 4 – putting in the windows and completing all the interior work.

Each stage can be awarded a separate price with the total for all the stages being equal to the total contract price for the factory. This means that, as each stage is completed, the builder can recognise the price for that stage as revenue and bill the customer accordingly. This is provided that the outcome of the contract as a whole can be estimated reliably.

If the builder were to wait until the factory was completed before recognising revenue, the income statement covering the final year of the contract would recognise all of the revenue on the contract and the income statements for each preceding year would recognise no revenue. This would give a misleading impression, as it would not reflect the work done during each period.

**Real World 3.3** sets out the revenue recognition criteria for one large construction business.

## Real World 3.3

### Subject to contract

AMEC plc is an international business offering consultancy, engineering and project management services. The point at which revenue on long-term contracts is recognised by the business is as follows:

> As soon as the outcome of a long-term contract can be estimated reliably, contract revenue and expenses are recognised in the income statement in proportion to the stage of completion of the contract. The stage of completion is assessed by reference to surveys of work performed. When the outcome of a contract cannot be estimated reliably, revenue is recognised only to the extent of contract costs incurred that it is probable will be recoverable, and contract costs are expensed as incurred. An expected loss on a contract is recognised immediately in the income statement.

*Source*: AMEC plc, Annual Report and Accounts 2010, Notes to Consolidated Accounts, p. 69.

## Services

Revenue from contracts for services may also be recognised in stages. Suppose a consultancy business has a contract to install a new computer system for the government, which will take several years to complete. Revenue can be recognised *before* the contract is completed as long as the contract can be broken down into stages and the particular stages of completion can be measured reliably. This is really the same approach as that used in the construction contract mentioned above.

Sometimes a continuous service is provided to a customer; for example, a telecommunications business may provide open access to the internet to those who subscribe to the service. In this case, revenue is usually recognised as the service is rendered. Benefits from providing the service are usually assumed to flow evenly over time and so revenue is recognised evenly over the subscription period.

Where it is not possible to break down a service into particular stages of completion, or to assume that benefits from providing the service accrue evenly over time, revenue will not usually be recognised until the service is fully completed. The work done by a solicitor on a house purchase for a client would normally be one such example.

**Real World 3.4** provides an example of how one major business recognises revenue from providing services.

> **Real World 3.4**
>
> ## Sky-high broadcasting revenue
>
> British Sky Broadcasting Group plc is a major satellite broadcaster that generates various forms of revenue. Here are the ways in which some of its revenues are recognised:
>
> - pay-per-view revenues – when the event (movie or football match) is viewed;
> - subscription services, including Sky TV and Sky Broadband – as the services are provided;
> - advertising revenues – when the advertising is broadcast;
> - installation, hardware and service revenue – when the goods and services are delivered.
>
> *Source*: Based on information in British Sky Broadcasting Group plc Annual Report and Accounts 2010, p. 65.

When a service is provided, there will normally be a timing difference between the recognition of revenue and the receipt of cash. Revenue for providing services is often recognised *before* the cash is received, as with the sale of goods on credit. However, there are occasions when it is the other way around, usually because the business demands payment before providing the service.

> **Activity 3.3**
>
> Can you think of any examples where cash may be demanded in advance of a service being provided? (*Hint*: Try to think of services that you may use.)
>
> Examples of cash being received in advance of the service being provided may include:
>
> - rent received from letting premises
> - telephone line rental charges
> - TV licence (BBC) or subscription fees (for example, Sky)
> - subscriptions received for the use of health clubs or golf clubs.
>
> You may have thought of others.

## Recognising expenses

Having decided on the point at which revenue is recognised, we can now turn to the issue of the recognition of expenses. The **matching convention** in accounting provides guidance on this. This convention states that expenses should be matched to the revenue that they helped to generate. In other words, the expenses associated with a particular item of revenue must be taken into account in the same reporting period as that in which the item of revenue is included. Applying this convention often means that a particular expense reported in the income statement for a period may not be the same figure as the cash paid for that item during the period. The expense reported might be either more or less than the cash paid during the period. Let us consider two examples that illustrate this point.

## When the expense for the period is more than the cash paid during the period

**Example 3.4**

Domestic Ltd, a retailer, sells household electrical appliances. It pays its sales staff a commission of 2 per cent of sales revenue generated. Total sales revenue for last year amounted to £300,000. This will mean that the commission to be paid in respect of the sales for the year will be £6,000. However, by the end of the year, the amount of sales commission that had actually been paid to staff was only £5,000. If the business reported just the amount paid, it would mean that the income statement would not reflect the full expense for the year. This would contravene the *matching convention* because not all of the expenses associated with the revenue of the year would have been matched in the income statement. This will be remedied as follows:

- Sales commission expense in the income statement will include the amount paid plus the amount outstanding (that is, £6,000 = £5,000 + £1,000).
- The amount outstanding (£1,000) represents an outstanding liability at the end of the year and will be included under the heading **accrued expenses**, or 'accruals', in the statement of financial position. As this item will have to be paid within twelve months of the year end, it will be treated as a current liability.
- The cash will already have been reduced to reflect the commission paid (£5,000) during the period.

These points are illustrated in Figure 3.3.

**Figure 3.3    Accounting for sales commission**

This illustrates the main points of Example 3.4. We can see that the sales commission expense of £6,000 (which appears in the income statement) is made up of a cash element of £5,000 and an accrued element of £1,000. The cash element appears in the statement of cash flows and the accrued element will appear as a year-end liability in the statement of financial position.

In principle, all expenses should be matched to the period in which the sales revenue to which they relate is reported. However, it is sometimes difficult to match certain expenses to sales revenue in the same precise way that we have matched sales commission to sales revenue. For example, electricity charges incurred often cannot be linked directly to particular sales in this way. As a result, the electricity charges incurred by, say, a retailer would be matched to the *period* to which they relate. Example 3.5 illustrates this.

### Example 3.5

Domestic Ltd has reached the end of its reporting period and has only paid for electricity for the first three quarters of the year (amounting to £1,900). This is simply because the electricity company has yet to send out bills for the quarter that ends on the same date as Domestic Ltd's year end. The amount of Domestic Ltd's bill for the last quarter is £500. In this situation, the amount of the electricity expense outstanding is dealt with as follows:

- Electricity expense in the income statement will include the amount paid, plus the amount of the bill for the last quarter (that is, £1,900 + £500 = £2,400) in order to cover the whole year.
- The amount of the outstanding bill (£500) represents a liability at the end of the year and will be included under the heading 'accruals' or 'accrued expenses' in the statement of financial position. This item would normally have to be paid within twelve months of the year end and will, therefore, be treated as a current liability.
- The cash will already have been reduced to reflect the amount (£1,900) paid for electricity during the period.

This treatment will mean that the correct figure for the electricity expense for the year will be included in the income statement. It will also have the effect of showing that, at the end of the reporting period, Domestic Ltd owed the amount of the last quarter's electricity bill. Dealing with the outstanding amount in this way reflects the dual aspect of the item and will ensure that the accounting equation is maintained.

Domestic Ltd may wish to draw up its income statement before it is able to discover how much it owes for the last quarter's electricity. In this case it is quite normal to make a reasonable estimate of the amount of the bill and to use this estimated amount as described above.

### Activity 3.4

How will the payment of the outstanding sales commission (Example 3.4) and the electricity bill for the last quarter (Example 3.5) be dealt with in the accounting records of Domestic Ltd?

When these amounts are eventually paid, they will be dealt with as follows:

- Reduce cash by the amounts paid.
- Reduce the amount of the accrued expense as shown on the statement of financial position by the same amounts.

If an estimated figure is used for the electricity bill and there is a slight error in the estimate, a small adjustment (either negative or positive depending on the direction of the error) can be made to the following year's expense. Dealing with the estimation error in this way is not strictly correct, but the amount is likely to be insignificant.

## Activity 3.5

Can you think of other expenses for a retailer, apart from electricity charges, that cannot be linked directly to sales revenue and for which matching will therefore be done on a time basis?

You may have thought of the following examples:

- rent and rates
- insurance
- interest payments
- licence fees payable.

This is not an exhaustive list. You may have thought of others.

## When the amount paid during the period is more than the full expense for the period

It is not unusual for a business to be in a situation where it has paid more during the year than the full expense for that year. Example 3.6 illustrates how we deal with this.

## Example 3.6

Images Ltd, an advertising agency, normally pays rent for its premises quarterly in advance (on 1 January, 1 April, 1 July and 1 October). On the last day of the last reporting period (31 December), it paid the next quarter's rent (£4,000) to the following 31 March, which was a day earlier than required. This would mean that a total of five quarters' rent was paid during the year. If Images Ltd reports all of the cash paid as an expense in the income statement, this would be more than the full expense for the year. This would contravene the matching convention because a higher figure than the expenses associated with the revenue of the year would appear in the income statement.

The problem is overcome by dealing with the rental payment as follows:

- Show the rent for four quarters as the appropriate expense in the income statement (that is, 4 × £4,000 = £16,000).
- The cash (that is, 5 × £4,000 = £20,000) would already have been paid during the year.
- Show the quarter's rent paid in advance (£4,000) as a prepaid expense under assets in the statement of financial position. (The rent paid in advance will appear as a current asset in the statement of financial position, under the heading **prepaid expenses** or 'prepayments'.)

In the next reporting period, this prepayment will cease to be an asset and will become an expense in the income statement of that period. This is because the rent prepaid relates to the next period and will be 'used up' during it.

These points are illustrated in Figure 3.4.

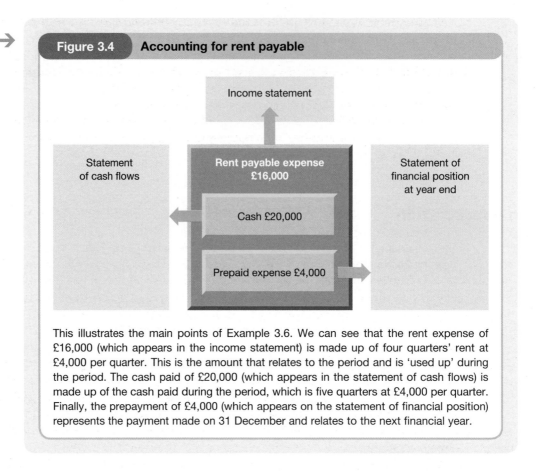

**Figure 3.4**    **Accounting for rent payable**

This illustrates the main points of Example 3.6. We can see that the rent expense of £16,000 (which appears in the income statement) is made up of four quarters' rent at £4,000 per quarter. This is the amount that relates to the period and is 'used up' during the period. The cash paid of £20,000 (which appears in the statement of cash flows) is made up of the cash paid during the period, which is five quarters at £4,000 per quarter. Finally, the prepayment of £4,000 (which appears on the statement of financial position) represents the payment made on 31 December and relates to the next financial year.

In practice, the treatment of accruals and prepayments will be subject to the **materiality convention** of accounting. This convention states that, where the amounts involved are immaterial, we should consider only what is reasonable. This may mean that an item will be treated as an expense in the period in which it is paid, rather than being strictly matched to the revenue to which it relates. For example, a business may find that, at the end of a reporting period, it has bought and paid for £5 worth of stationery that has not yet been used. No matter how small the business is, the time and effort involved in recording this as a prepayment would not be justified by the little effect that this would have on the measurement of profit or financial position. The amount would, therefore, be treated as an expense when preparing the income statement for the current period and ignored in the following period.

## Profit, cash and accruals accounting

As we have just seen, within a particular reporting period, total revenue does not usually represent total cash received, and total expenses are not the same as total cash paid. As a result, the profit figure (that is, total revenue minus total expenses) will not normally represent the net cash generated during that period. It is, therefore, important to distinguish between profit and liquidity. Profit is a measure of achievement, or productive effort, rather than a measure of cash generated. Although making a profit will increase wealth, as we have already seen in Chapter 2, cash is only one possible form in which that wealth may be held.

These points are reflected in the **accruals convention** of accounting, which asserts that profit is the excess of revenue over expenses for a period, not the excess of cash receipts over cash payments. Leading on from this, the approach to accounting that is based on the accruals convention is frequently referred to as **accruals accounting**. The statement of financial position and the income statement are both prepared on the basis of accruals accounting. The statement of cash flows, on the other hand, is not, as it simply deals with cash receipts and payments.

## Depreciation

The expense of **depreciation**, which we have met a couple of times so far in this book, requires further explanation. Most non-current assets do not have a perpetual existence, but have finite or limited lives. They are eventually 'used up' in the process of generating revenue for the business. This 'using up' may relate to physical deterioration (as with a motor vehicle). It may however be linked to obsolescence (as with a some IT software that is no longer useful) or the mere passage of time (as with a purchased patent, which has a limited period of validity).

In essence, depreciation is an attempt to measure that portion of the cost (or fair value) of a non-current asset that has been depleted in generating the revenue recognised during a particular period. Depreciation tends to be relevant both to tangible non-current assets (property, plant and equipment) and to intangible non-current assets (for example, a licence to operate a mobile phone business)). We should be clear that the principle is the same for both of these types of non-current asset.

Some non-current assets could have perpetual useful lives. These might include land and acquired goodwill. These assets are not depreciated.

In the case of intangibles, we usually refer to the expense as **amortisation**, rather than *depreciation*. In the interests of brevity, we shall use the word depreciation for both tangibles and intangibles.

### Calculating the depreciation expense

To calculate a depreciation (or amortisation) expense for a period, four factors have to be considered:

- the cost (or fair value) of the asset;
- the useful life of the asset;
- the residual value of the asset; and
- the depreciation method.

### The cost (or fair value) of the asset

The cost of an asset will include all costs incurred by the business to bring the asset to its required location and to make it ready for use. Thus, in addition to the cost of acquiring the asset, any delivery costs, installation costs (for example, setting up a new machine) and legal costs incurred in the transfer of legal title (for example, in purchasing a lease on property) will be included as part of the total cost of the asset. Similarly, any costs incurred in improving or altering an asset in order to make it suitable for its intended use within the business will also be included as part of the total cost.

## Activity 3.6

Andrew Wu (Engineering) Ltd bought a new motor car for its marketing director. The invoice received from the motor car supplier showed the following:

|  | £ |
|---|---|
| New BMW 325i | 26,350 |
| Delivery charge | 80 |
| Alloy wheels | 660 |
| Sun roof | 200 |
| Petrol | 30 |
| Number plates | 130 |
| Road fund licence | 120 |
|  | 27,570 |
| Part exchange – Reliant Robin | (1,000) |
| Amount outstanding | 26,570 |

What is the total cost of the new car that will be treated as part of the business's property, plant and equipment?

The cost of the new car will be as follows:

|  | £ |
|---|---|
| New BMW 325i | 26,350 |
| Delivery charge | 80 |
| Alloy wheels | 660 |
| Sun roof | 200 |
| Number plates | 130 |
|  | 27,420 |

This cost includes delivery charges, which are necessary to bring the asset into use, and it includes number plates, as they are a necessary and integral part of the asset. Improvements (alloy wheels and sun roof) are also regarded as part of the total cost of the motor car. The petrol and road fund licence, however, represent costs of operating the asset rather than a part of the total cost of acquiring it and making it ready for use: hence these amounts will be treated as an expense in the period incurred (although part of the cost of the licence may be regarded as a prepaid expense in the period incurred).

The part-exchange figure shown is part payment of the total amount outstanding and so is not relevant to a consideration of the total cost.

The fair value of an asset was defined in Chapter 2 as the exchange value that could be obtained in an arm's-length transaction. As we saw, assets may be revalued to fair value only if this can be measured reliably. When a revaluation is carried out, all items within the same class must be revalued and revaluations must be kept up to date. Fair values are rarely used for intangible non-current assets because there is usually no active market from which to establish fair values. If fair values have been applied, to either tangibles or intangibles, then the depreciation expense should be based on those fair values, rather than on the historic costs.

### The useful life of the asset

A non-current asset has both a *physical life* and an *economic life*. The physical life will be exhausted through the effects of wear and tear and/or the passage of time. It is possible, however, for the physical life to be extended considerably through careful maintenance, improvements, and so on. The economic life is decided by the effects of technological progress, by changes in demand or changes in the way that the business operates. After a while, the benefits of using the asset may be less than the costs involved. This may be because the asset is unable to compete with newer assets, or because it is no longer relevant to the needs of the business. The economic life of an asset may be much shorter than its physical life. For example, a computer may have a physical life of eight years and an economic life of three years.

It is the economic life that will determine the expected useful life for the purpose of calculating depreciation. Forecasting the economic life, however, may be extremely difficult in practice: both the rate at which technology progresses and shifts in consumer tastes can be swift and unpredictable.

### Residual value (disposal value)

When a business disposes of a non-current asset that may still be of value to others, some payment may be received. This payment will represent the **residual value**, or *disposal value*, of the asset. To calculate the total amount to be depreciated, the residual value must be deducted from the cost (or fair value) of the asset. The likely amount to be received on disposal can, once again, be difficult to predict. The best guide is often past experience of similar assets sold.

### Depreciation method

Once the amount to be depreciated (that is, the cost, or fair value, of the asset less any residual value) has been estimated, the business must select a method of allocating this depreciable amount between the reporting periods covering the asset's useful life. Although there are various ways in which the total depreciation may be allocated and, from this, a depreciation expense for each period derived, there are really only two methods that are commonly used in practice.

The first of these is known as the **straight-line method**. This method simply allocates the amount to be depreciated evenly over the useful life of the asset. In other words, there is an equal depreciation expense for each year that the asset is held.

---

**Example 3.7**

To illustrate this method, consider the following information:

| | |
|---|---|
| Cost of machine | £78,124 |
| Estimated residual value at the end of its useful life | £2,000 |
| Estimated useful life | 4 years |

To calculate the depreciation expense for each year, the total amount to be depreciated must be calculated. This will be the total cost less the estimated residual value: that is, £78,124 − £2,000 = £76,124. Having done this, the annual depreciation expense can be derived by dividing the amount to be depreciated by the estimated useful life of the asset of four years. The calculation is therefore:

$$\frac{£76,124}{4} = £19,031$$

Thus, the annual depreciation expense that appears in the income statement in relation to this asset will be £19,031 for each of the four years of the asset's life.

The amount of depreciation relating to the asset will be accumulated for as long as the asset continues to be owned by the business. This accumulated depreciation figure will increase each year as a result of the annual depreciation expense in the income statement. This accumulated amount will be deducted from the cost of the asset on the statement of financial position. At the end of the second year, for example, the accumulated depreciation will be £19,031 × 2 = £38,062. The asset details will appear on the statement of financial position as follows:

|  | £ |
| --- | --- |
| Machine at cost | 78,124 |
| Accumulated depreciation | (38,062) |
|  | 40,062 |

As we saw in Chapter 2, this balance of £40,062 is referred to as the **carrying amount** (sometimes also known as the **written-down value** or **net book value**) of the asset. It represents that portion of the cost (or fair value) of the asset that has still to be treated as an expense (written off) in future years. It must be emphasised that this figure does not, except by coincidence, represent the current market value, which may be quite different. The only point at which the carrying amount is intended to equal the market value of the asset is immediately before it is to be disposed of. Thus, in Example 3.7, at the end of the four-year life of the machine, the carrying amount would be £2,000 – its estimated disposal value.

The straight-line method derives its name from the fact that the carrying amount of the asset at the end of each year, when plotted against time, will result in a straight line, as shown in Figure 3.5.

| Figure 3.5 | Graph of carrying amount against time using the straight-line method |
| --- | --- |

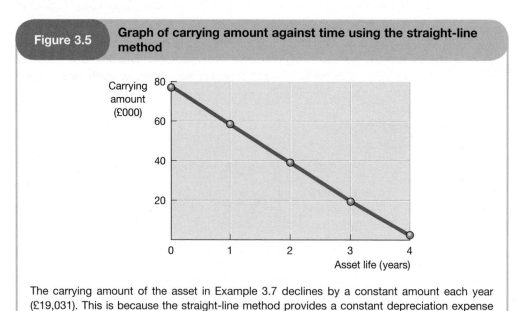

The carrying amount of the asset in Example 3.7 declines by a constant amount each year (£19,031). This is because the straight-line method provides a constant depreciation expense each year. The result, when plotted on a graph, is a straight line.

The second approach found in practice to calculating the depreciation expense for a period is referred to as the **reducing-balance method**. This method applies a fixed percentage rate of depreciation to the carrying amount of the asset each year. The effect of this will be high annual depreciation expenses in the early years and lower expenses in the later years. To illustrate this method, let us take the same information that was used in Example 3.7. By using a fixed percentage of 60 per cent of the carrying amount to determine the annual depreciation expense, the effect will be to reduce the carrying amount to £2,000 after four years.

The calculations will be as follows:

|  | £ |
|---|---|
| Cost of machine | 78,124 |
| Year 1 depreciation expense (60%* of cost) | (46,874) |
| Carrying amount | 31,250 |
| Year 2 depreciation expense (60% of carrying amount) | (18,750) |
| Carrying amount | 12,500 |
| Year 3 depreciation expense (60% of carrying amount) | (7,500) |
| Carrying amount | 5,000 |
| Year 4 depreciation expense (60% of carrying amount) | (3,000) |
| Residual value | 2,000 |

\* See the box below for an explanation of how to derive the fixed percentage.

## Deriving the fixed percentage

Deriving the fixed percentage to be applied requires the use of the following formula:

$$P = (1 - \sqrt[n]{R/C} \times 100\%)$$

where:  $P$ = the depreciation percentage
  $n$ = the useful life of the asset (in years)
  $R$ = the residual value of the asset
  $C$ = the cost, or fair value, of the asset.

The fixed percentage rate will, however, be given in all examples used in this text.

We can see that the pattern of depreciation is quite different between the two methods. If we plot the carrying amount of the asset, which has been derived using the reducing-balance method, against time, the result will be as shown in Figure 3.6.

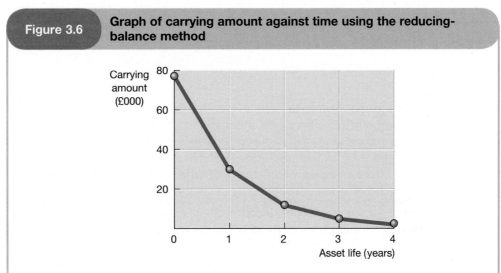

**Figure 3.6**    **Graph of carrying amount against time using the reducing-balance method**

Under the reducing-balance method, the carrying amount of the asset in Example 3.7 falls by a larger amount in the earlier years than in the later years. This is because the depreciation expense is based on a fixed-rate percentage of the carrying amount.

## Activity (3.7)

Assume that the machine used in Example 3.7 was owned by a business that made a profit before depreciation of £40,000 for each of the four years in which the asset was held.
Calculate the profit for the business for each year under each depreciation method, and comment on your findings.

Your answer should be as follows:

### Straight-line method

| | (a)<br>Profit before depreciation<br>£ | (b)<br>Depreciation<br>£ | (a – b)<br>Profit<br>£ |
|---|---|---|---|
| Year 1 | 40,000 | 19,031 | 20,969 |
| Year 2 | 40,000 | 19,031 | 20,969 |
| Year 3 | 40,000 | 19,031 | 20,969 |
| Year 4 | 40,000 | 19,031 | 20,969 |

### Reducing-balance method

| | (a)<br>Profit before depreciation<br>£ | (b)<br>Depreciation<br>£ | (a – b)<br>Profit/(loss)<br>£ |
|---|---|---|---|
| Year 1 | 40,000 | 46,874 | (6,874) |
| Year 2 | 40,000 | 18,750 | 21,250 |
| Year 3 | 40,000 | 7,500 | 32,500 |
| Year 4 | 40,000 | 3,000 | 37,000 |

The straight-line method of depreciation results in the same profit figure for each year of the four-year period. This is because both the profit before depreciation and the depreciation expense are constant over the period. The reducing-balance method, however, results in very different profit figures for the four years, despite the fact that in this example the pre-depreciation profit is the same each year. In the first year a loss is reported and, thereafter, a rising profit.

Although the *pattern* of profit over the four-year period will be quite different, depending on the depreciation method used, the *total* profit for the period (£83,876) will remain the same. This is because both methods of depreciating will allocate the same amount of total depreciation (£76,124) over the four-year period. It is only the amount allocated *between years* that will differ.

In practice, the use of different depreciation methods may not have such a dramatic effect on profits as suggested in Activity 3.7. This is because businesses typically have more than one depreciating non-current asset. Where a business replaces some of its assets each year, the total depreciation expense calculated under the reducing-balance method will reflect a range of expenses (from high through to low), as assets will be at different points in the replacement cycle. This could mean that each year's total depreciation expense may not be significantly different from that which would have been derived under the straight-line method.

## Selecting a depreciation method

How does a business choose which depreciation method to use for a particular asset? The answer is to select the one that best matches the depreciation expense to the pattern of economic benefits that the asset provides. Where these benefits are provided evenly over time (buildings, for example), the straight-line method is usually appropriate. Where assets lose their efficiency (as with certain types of machinery), the benefits provided will decline over time and so the reducing-balance method may be more appropriate. Where the pattern of economic benefits provided by the asset is uncertain, the straight-line method is normally chosen.

There is an international financial reporting standard (or international accounting standard) to deal with the depreciation of property, plant and equipment. As we shall see in Chapter 5, the purpose of accounting standards is to narrow areas of accounting difference and to try to ensure that information provided to users is transparent and comparable. The relevant standard endorses the view that the depreciation method chosen should reflect the pattern of economic benefits provided but does not specify particular methods to be used. It states that the useful life, depreciation method and residual values of non-current assets should be reviewed at least annually and adjustments made where appropriate.

**Real World 3.5** sets out the depreciation policies of Carphone Warehouse Group plc, the mobile phone and PC retailer.

---

### Real World 3.5

#### Some text about depreciation policies

Carphone Warehouse Group plc, uses the straight-line method to depreciate all its property, plant and equipment, other than land and assets in the course of construction. The financial statements for the year ended 31 March 2011 show the annual rate at which different classes of assets are depreciated as follows:

| | |
|---|---|
| Investment properties | 2 per cent |
| Short leasehold costs | 10 per cent or the lease term if less |
| Network equipment and computer hardware | 12.5 to 50 per cent |
| Fixtures and fittings | 20 to 25 per cent |
| Motor vehicles | 25 per cent |
| Software and licences | At least 12.5 per cent |

We can see that there are wide variations in the expected useful lives of the various assets held.

*Source*: Carphone Warehouse Group plc Annual Report 2011, p. 53.

---

It seems that Carphone Warehouse is typical of UK businesses in that most use the straight-line approach. The reducing-balance method is not very much used in practice in the UK.

The approach taken to calculating depreciation is summarised in Figure 3.7.

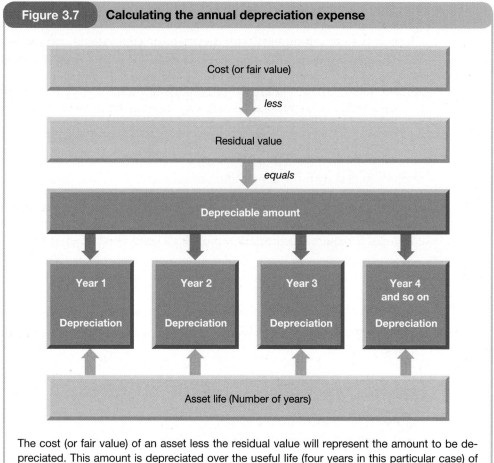

**Figure 3.7** Calculating the annual depreciation expense

The cost (or fair value) of an asset less the residual value will represent the amount to be depreciated. This amount is depreciated over the useful life (four years in this particular case) of the asset using an appropriate depreciation method.

## Impairment and depreciation

We saw in Chapter 2 that all non-current assets (tangibles and intangibles, finite and perpetual lives) could be subjected to an impairment test. Where a non-current asset with a finite life has its carrying amount reduced as a result of an impairment test, depreciation expenses for future reporting periods should be based on the impaired value of that asset.

## Depreciation and asset replacement

There seems to be a misunderstanding in the minds of some people that the purpose of depreciation is to provide the funds for the replacement of a non-current asset when it reaches the end of its useful life. However, this is not the purpose of taking account of depreciation in the financial statements. It was mentioned earlier that depreciation represents an attempt to allocate the cost or fair value (less any residual value) of a non-current asset over its expected useful life. The resulting depreciation expense for each reporting period is then used in the calculation of profit for the period. Calculating the depreciation expense for a period is therefore necessary for the proper measurement of financial performance. This must be done whether or not the business intends to replace the asset in the future.

If there is an intention to replace the asset, the depreciation expense in the income statement will not ensure that liquid funds are set aside by the business specifically for this purpose. Although the effect of a depreciation expense is to reduce profit, and therefore to reduce the amount available for withdrawal by the owners, the amounts retained within the business as a result may be invested in ways that are unrelated to the replacement of the particular asset.

## Depreciation and judgement

From what we have just seen about depreciation, it seems that accounting is not as precise and objective as it sometimes appears to be. There are areas where subjective judgement is required; depreciation provides a good illustration of this.

### Activity 3.8

What kinds of judgements must be made to calculate a depreciation expense for a period?

You may have thought of the following:

- the expected residual or disposal value of the asset
- the expected useful life of the asset
- the choice of depreciation method.

Making different judgements on these matters would result in a different pattern of depreciation expenses over the life of the asset and, therefore, in a different pattern of reported profits. However, underestimations or overestimations that are made in relation to the above will be adjusted for in the final year of an asset's life. As a result, the total depreciation expense (and total profit) over the asset's life will not be affected by estimation errors.

**Real World 3.6** describes the effect of extending the useful life of property, plant and equipment on the short-term profits of one large business.

### Real World 3.6

#### Sports massage

JJB Sports plc, a leading retailer, reported interim financial results for the six months ended 30 June 2005 that caused some disquiet among investors and analysts. The business changed the estimates for the useful life of its property, plant and equipment when calculating depreciation. It explained that this was due to new requirements to adopt International Financial Reporting Standards (IFRSs) when preparing financial statements. The article below, however, suggests that not everyone believed this.

**Real World 3.6 (*continued*)**

**JJB massages results to boost profits**

High street retailer JJB Sports massaged last week's disappointing interim results by changing its depreciation calculations, in order to boost flagging profits by £4.3 million.

Analysts admitted that they were caught on the hop, as the company reported a 35.8% drop in operating profits from £27.4 million to £17.6 million for six months ended June 2005 on revenues down 6% to £340.4 million. Operating profits would have plummeted even further [to £13.3 million] had the company not changed its accounting for depreciation. 'The company explained the change as coming out of its IFRS conversion review, but it was clearly there for other reasons,' said Teather & Greenwood retail analyst Sanjay Vidyarthi.

JJB said that an impairment review ahead of its IFRS transition had forced a rethink on the carrying value of property, plant and equipment.

It concluded that these items had useful economic lives that more closely matched the length of the short-term lease of the property, rather than the 10-year economic life, which had formed the basis of the depreciation charge in previous accounting periods.

Richard Ratner, head of equity research at Seymour Pierce, said: 'They said the way they had depreciated assets previously was not correct but I haven't seen any other companies make this kind of change.'

JJB's share price fell from 168.2p before the results to 164.7p at the end of last week.

*Source*: 'JJB massages results to boost profits', *Accountancy Age*, 20 October 2005, p. 3.

## Activity (3.9)

Sally Dalton (Packaging) Ltd bought a machine for £40,000. At the end of its useful life of four years, the amount received on sale was £4,000. When the asset was bought the business received two estimates of the likely residual value of the asset, which were: (a) £8,000 and (b) zero.

Show the pattern of annual depreciation expenses over the four years and the total depreciation expenses for the asset under each of the two estimates. The straight-line method should be used to calculate the annual depreciation expenses.

The depreciation expense, assuming estimate (a), will be £8,000 a year (that is, (£40,000 − £8,000)/4). The depreciation expense, assuming estimate (b), will be £10,000 a year (that is, £40,000/4). As the actual residual value is £4,000, estimate (a) will lead to under-depreciation of £4,000 (that is, £8,000 − £4,000) over the life of the asset and estimate (b) will lead to over-depreciation of £4,000 (that is, £0 − £4,000). These under- and overestimations will be dealt with in year 4.

The pattern of depreciation and total depreciation expenses will therefore be:

|  |  | Estimate | |
|---|---|---|---|
|  |  | (a) | (b) |
| Year |  | £ | £ |
| 1 | Annual depreciation | 8,000 | 10,000 |
| 2 | Annual depreciation | 8,000 | 10,000 |
| 3 | Annual depreciation | 8,000 | 10,000 |
| 4 | Annual depreciation | 8,000 | 10,000 |
|  |  | 32,000 | 40,000 |
| 4 | Under/(over)depreciation | 4,000 | (4,000) |
|  | Total depreciation | 36,000 | 36,000 |

The final adjustment for under-depreciation of an asset is often referred to as 'loss (or deficit) on sale of non-current asset', as the amount actually received is less than the residual value. Similarly, the adjustment for over-depreciation is often referred to as 'profit (or surplus) on sale of non-current asset'. These final adjustments are normally made as an addition to the expense (or a reduction in the expense) for depreciation in the reporting period of disposal of the asset.

**Activity (3.10)**

In practice, would you expect it to be more likely that the amount of depreciation would be overestimated or underestimated?
   Why?

We might expect there to be systematic overestimations of the annual depreciation expense.
   This is because the prudence convention tends to encourage a cautious approach to estimating the lives and residual values of assets.

## Costing inventories

The way in which we measure the cost of inventories (or stock) is important because the cost of inventories sold during a period will affect the calculation of profit and the remaining inventories held at the end of the period will affect the portrayal of wealth in the statement of financial position. In the previous chapter, we saw that historic cost is often the basis for reporting assets. It is, therefore, tempting to think that determining the cost of inventories held or used is very straightforward. However, in a period of changing prices, the costing of inventories can be a problem.

A business must determine the cost of the inventories sold during the period and the cost of the inventories remaining at the end of the period. To do this, some assumption must be made about the way in which the inventories are physically handled. The assumption made need not have anything to do with how the inventories are *actually* handled. The assumption is concerned only with providing useful accounting information.

There are three assumptions used which are:

1  **first in, first out (FIFO)** – the earliest inventories held are the first to be used;
2  **last in, first out (LIFO)** – the latest inventories held are the first to be used;
3  **weighted average cost (AVCO)** – inventories entering the business lose their separate identity and go into a 'pool'. Any issues of inventories then reflect the average cost of the inventories that are held.

Example 3.8 provides a simple illustration of the way in which each method is applied.

## Example 3.8

A business which supplies grass seed to farmers and horticulturalists has the following transactions during a period:

|  |  | Tonnes | Cost/tonne £ |
|---|---|---|---|
| 1 May | Opening inventories | 100 | 100 |
| 2 May | Bought | 500 | 110 |
| 3 May | Bought | 800 | 120 |
|  |  | 1,400 |  |
| 6 May | Sold | (900) |  |
|  | Closing inventories | 500 |  |

### First in, first out (FIFO)

Using the first in, first out approach, the first 900 tonnes of seed bought are treated as if these are the ones that are sold. This will consist of the opening inventories (100 tonnes), the purchases made on 2 May (500 tonnes) and some of the purchases made on 3 May (300 tonnes). The remainder of the 3 May purchases (500 tonnes) will comprise the closing inventories. Thus we have:

| | Cost of sales | | | Closing inventories | | |
|---|---|---|---|---|---|---|
| | Tonnes | Cost/tonne £ | Total £000 | Tonnes | Cost/tonne £ | Total £000 |
| 1 May | 100 | 100 | 10.0 | | | |
| 2 May | 500 | 110 | 55.0 | | | |
| 3 May | 300 | 120 | 36.0 | 500 | 120 | 60.0 |
| Cost of sales | | | 101.0 | Closing inventories | | 60.0 |

### Last in, first out (LIFO)

Using the last in, first out approach, the later purchases will be treated as if these were the first to be sold. This is the 3 May purchases (800 tonnes) and some of the 2 May purchases (100 tonnes). The earlier purchases (the rest of the 2 May purchase and the opening inventories) will comprise the closing inventories. Thus we have:

| | Cost of sales | | | Closing inventories | | |
|---|---|---|---|---|---|---|
| | Tonnes | Cost/tonne £ | Total £000 | Tonnes | Cost/tonne £ | Total £000 |
| 3 May | 800 | 120 | 96.0 | | | |
| 2 May | 100 | 110 | 11.0 | 400 | 110 | 44.0 |
| 1 May | | | | 100 | 100 | 10.0 |
| Cost of sales | | | 107.0 | Closing inventories | | 54.0 |

Figure 3.8 contrasts LIFO and FIFO.

**Figure 3.8**     **FIFO and LIFO treatment of the inventories in Example 3.8**

Using FIFO, the oldest purchases of inventories are treated as the first to be used leaving the later purchases in closing inventories. With LIFO it is the opposite.

## Weighted average cost (AVCO)

Using this approach, a weighted average cost will be determined that will be used to derive both the cost of goods sold and the cost of the remaining inventories held. This simply means that the total cost of the opening inventories, the 2 May and 3 May purchases, are added together and divided by the total number of tonnes to obtain the weighted average cost per tonne. Both the cost of sales and closing inventories values are based on that average cost per tonne. Thus we have:

| | Purchases | | |
|---|---|---|---|
| | Tonnes | Cost/tonne £ | Total £000 |
| 1 May | 100 | 100 | 10.0 |
| 2 May | 500 | 110 | 55.0 |
| 3 May | 800 | 120 | 96.0 |
| | 1,400 | | 161.0 |

Average cost = £161,000/1,400 = £115 per tonne.

| Cost of sales | | | Closing inventories | | |
|---|---|---|---|---|---|
| Tonnes | Cost/tonne £ | Total £000 | Tonnes | Cost/tonne £ | Total £000 |
| 900 | 115 | 103.5 | 500 | 115 | 57.5 |

## Activity 3.11

Suppose the 900 tonnes of inventories in Example 3.8 were sold for £150 per tonne.

(a) Calculate the gross profit for this sale under each of the three methods.
(b) What observations concerning the portrayal of financial position and performance can you make about each method when prices are rising?

Your answer should be along the following lines:

(a) Gross profit calculation:

|  | FIFO<br>£000 | LIFO<br>£000 | AVCO<br>£000 |
|---|---|---|---|
| Sales revenue (900 @ £150) | 135.0 | 135.0 | 135.0 |
| Cost of sales | (101.0) | (107.0) | (103.5) |
| Gross profit | 34.0 | 28.0 | 31.5 |
| Closing inventories figure | 60.0 | 54.0 | 57.5 |

(b) These figures reveal that FIFO will give the highest gross profit during a period of rising prices. This is because sales revenue is matched with the earlier (and cheaper) purchases. LIFO will give the lowest gross profit because sales revenue is matched against the more recent (and dearer) purchases. The AVCO method will normally give a figure that is between these two extremes.

The closing inventories figure in the statement of financial position will be highest with the FIFO method. This is because the cost of goods still held will be based on the more recent (and dearer) purchases. LIFO will give the lowest closing inventories figure as the goods held will be based on the earlier (and cheaper) purchases. Once again, the AVCO method will normally give a figure that is between these two extremes.

## Activity 3.12

Assume that prices in Activity 3.11 are falling rather than rising. How would your observations concerning the portrayal of financial performance and position be different for the various costing methods?

When prices are falling, the positions of FIFO and LIFO are reversed. FIFO will give the lowest gross profit as sales revenue is matched against the earlier (and dearer) goods bought. LIFO will give the highest gross profit as sales revenue is matched against the more recent (and cheaper) goods bought. AVCO will give a cost of sales figure between these two extremes. The closing inventories figure in the statement of financial position will be lowest under FIFO as the cost of inventories will be based on the more recent (and cheaper) purchases. LIFO will provide the highest closing inventories figure and AVCO will provide a figure between the two extremes.

The different costing methods will only have an effect on the reported profit from one year to the next. The figure derived for closing inventories will be carried forward and matched with sales revenue in a later period. Thus, if the cheaper purchases of inventories are matched to sales revenue in the current period, it will mean that the dearer purchases will be matched to sales revenue in a later period. Over the life of the business, therefore, the total profit will be the same whichever costing method has been used.

## Inventories – some further issues

We saw in Chapter 2 that the convention of prudence requires that inventories be valued at the lower of cost and net realisable value. (The net realisable value of inventories is the estimated selling price less any further costs that may be necessary to complete the goods and any costs involved in selling and distributing the goods.) This rule may mean that the valuation method applied to inventories (cost or net realisable value) could switch each year, depending on which of cost and net realisable value is the lower. In practice, however, the cost of the inventories held is usually below the current net realisable value – particularly during a period of rising prices. It is, therefore, the cost figure that will normally appear in the statement of financial position.

### Activity 3.13

Can you think of any circumstances where the net realisable value will be lower than the cost of inventories held, even during a period of generally rising prices?

The net realisable value may be lower where:

- goods have deteriorated or become obsolete;
- there has been a fall in the market price of the goods;
- the goods are being used as a 'loss leader';
- bad buying decisions have been made.

There is an international financial reporting standard that deals with inventories. It states that, when preparing financial statements for external reporting, the cost of inventories should normally be determined using either FIFO or AVCO. The LIFO approach is not an acceptable method to use for external reporting, but a business could use it for reports to management. The standard also requires the 'lower of cost and net realisable value' rule to be used and so endorses the application of the prudence convention.

**Real World 3.7** sets out the inventories costing methods of one well-known high street retail business.

**Real World 3.7**

### Costing inventories at leisure

Blacks Leisure Group plc, the leisure clothes and accessories business (Blacks, Millets, O'Neill, and so on), uses the weighted average basis of inventories valuation. The business reports:

> Inventories are stated at the lower of cost and net realisable value. The cost includes all costs in bringing each product into the business. Inventories are valued on a weighted average basis and this is not deemed to be materially different to that which would be calculated on a 'first in, first out' basis. Net realisable value is defined as the estimated selling price less any direct costs of disposal.

*Source*: Blacks Leisure Group plc, Annual Report 2011, p. 39.

Costing inventories and dealing with depreciation provide two examples where the **consistency convention** must be applied. This convention holds that once a particular method of accounting is selected, it should be applied consistently over time. Thus, it would not be acceptable to switch from, say, FIFO to AVCO between periods (unless exceptional circumstances make it appropriate). The purpose of this convention is to help users make valid comparisons of performance and position from one period to the next.

**Activity 3.14**

Reporting inventories in the financial statements provides a further example of the need to apply subjective judgement. For the inventories of a retail business, what are the main areas where judgement is required?

The main areas are:

- the choice of cost method (FIFO, LIFO, AVCO);
- deducing the net realisable value figure for inventories held.

## Trade receivables problems

We have seen that, when businesses sell goods or services on credit, revenue will usually be recognised before the customer pays the amounts owing. Recording the dual aspect of a credit sale will involve increasing sales revenue and increasing trade receivables by the amount of the revenue from the credit sale.

With this type of sale there is always the risk that some customers will not pay the amount due, however reliable they might have appeared to be at the time of the sale. When it becomes reasonably certain that the customer will never pay, the debt owed is considered to be a **bad debt** and this must be taken into account when preparing the financial statements.

## Activity 3.15

When preparing the financial statements, what would be the effect on the income statement and on the statement of financial position of not taking into account the fact that a debt is bad?

The effect would be to overstate the assets (trade receivables) on the statement of financial position and to overstate profit in the income statement, as the revenue (which has been recognised) will not result in any future benefit.

To provide a more realistic picture of financial performance and position, the bad debt must be 'written off'. This will involve reducing the trade receivables and increasing expenses (by creating an expense known as 'bad debts written off') by the amount of the bad debt.

The matching convention requires that the bad debt is written off in the same period as the sale that gave rise to the debt is recognised.

Note that, when a debt is bad, the accounting response is not simply to cancel the original sale. If this were done, the income statement would not be so informative. Reporting the bad debts as an expense can be extremely useful in assessing management performance.

At the end of the reporting period, it may not be possible to identify with reasonable certainty all the bad debts that have been incurred during the period. It may be that some trade receivables appear doubtful, but only at some later point in time will the true position become clear. The uncertainty that exists does not mean that, when preparing the financial statements, we should ignore the possibility that some of the trade receivables outstanding will eventually prove to be bad. It would not be prudent to do so, nor would it comply with the need to match expenses to the period in which the associated sale is recognised. As a result, the business will normally try to identify all those trade receivables that, at the end of the period, can be classified as doubtful (that is, there is a possibility that they may eventually prove to be bad). This can be done by examining individual trade receivables accounts or by taking a proportion of the total trade receivables outstanding based on past experience.

Once a figure has been derived, an expense known as an **allowance for trade receivables** can be created. This will be shown as an expense in the income statement and deducted from the total trade receivables figure in the statement of financial position.

By doing this, full account is taken, in the appropriate reporting period, of those trade receivables where there is a risk of non-payment. This accounting treatment of these 'doubtful' trade receivables will be in addition to the treatment of the 'more definite' bad debts described above.

Example 3.9 illustrates the reporting of bad debts and allowances for trade receivables.

**Example 3.9**

Desai Enterprises had trade receivables of £350,000 outstanding at the end of the reporting period to 30 June 2011. Investigation of these trade receivables revealed that £10,000 would probably be irrecoverable and that a further £30,000 were doubtful of being recoverable. Relevant extracts from the income statement for that year would be as follows:

**Income statement (extracts) for the year ended 30 June 2011**

|  | £ |
|---|---|
| Bad debts written off | 10,000 |
| Allowances for trade receivables | 30,000 |

**Statement of financial position (extracts) as at 30 June 2011**

|  | £ |
|---|---|
| Trade receivables | 340,000* |
| Allowances for trade receivables | (30,000) |
|  | 310,000 |

*That is, £350,000 – £10,000 irrecoverable trade receivables.

The allowances for trade receivables figure is, of course, an estimate; it is quite likely that the actual amount of trade receivables that prove to be bad will be different from the estimate. Let us say that, during the next reporting period, it was discovered that, in fact, £26,000 of the trade receivables considered doubtful proved to be irrecoverable. These trade receivables must now be written off as follows:

- reduce trade receivables by £26,000; and
- reduce allowances for trade receivables by £26,000.

However, allowances for trade receivables of £4,000 will remain. This amount represents an overestimate made when creating the allowance as at 30 June 2011. As the allowance is no longer needed, it should be eliminated. Remember that the allowance was made by creating an expense in the income statement for the year to 30 June 2011. As the expense was too high, the amount of the overestimate should be 'written back' in the next reporting period. In other words, it will be treated as revenue for the year to 30 June 2012. This will mean

- reducing the allowances for trade receivables by £4,000; and
- increasing revenue by £4,000.

Ideally, of course, the amount should be written back to the 2011 income statement; however, it is too late to do this. At the end of the year to 30 June 2012, not only will 2011's overestimate be written back but a new allowance should be created to take account of the trade receivables arising from 2012's credit sales that are considered doubtful.

## Activity 3.16

Clayton Conglomerates had trade receivables of £870,000 outstanding at the end of the reporting period to 31 March 2010. The chief accountant believed that £40,000 of those trade receivables were irrecoverable and that a further £60,000 were doubtful of being recoverable. In the subsequent year, it was found that an over-pessimistic estimate of those trade receivables considered doubtful had been made and that only a further £45,000 of trade receivables had actually proved to be bad.

Show the relevant income statement extracts for both 2010 and 2011 to report the bad debts written off and the allowances for trade receivables. Also show the relevant statement of financial position extract as at 31 March 2010.

Your answer should be as follows:

### Income statement (extract) for the year ended 31 March 2010

|  | £ |
|---|---|
| Bad debts written off | 40,000 |
| Allowances for trade receivables | 60,000 |

### Income statement (extract) for the year ended 31 March 2011

|  | £ |
|---|---|
| Allowances for trade receivables written back (revenue) | 15,000 |

(*Note*: This figure will usually be netted off against any allowances for trade receivables created in respect of 2011.)

### Statement of financial position (extract) as at 31 March 2010

|  | £ |
|---|---|
| Trade receivables | 830,000 |
| Allowances for trade receivables | (60,000) |
|  | 770,000 |

## Activity 3.17

The accounting treatment of bad debts and allowances for trade receivables are two further examples where judgement is needed to derive an appropriate expense figure.

What will be the effect of different judgements concerning the appropriate amount of bad debts expense and allowances for trade receivables expense on the profit for a particular period and on the total profit reported over the life of the business?

Judgement is often required in deriving a figure for bad debts incurred during a period. There may be situations where views will differ concerning whether or not a debt is irrecoverable. The decision concerning whether or not to write off a bad debt will have an effect on the expenses for the period and, hence, the reported profit. However, over the life of the business the total reported profit would not be affected, as incorrect judgements in one period will be adjusted for in a later period.

→

### Activity 3.17 (*continued*)

Suppose that a debt of £100 was written off in a period and that, in a later period, the amount owing was actually received. The increase in expenses of £100 in the period in which the bad debt was written off would be compensated for by an increase in revenue of £100 when the amount outstanding was finally received (bad debt recovered). If, on the other hand, the amount owing of £100 was never written off in the first place, the profit for the two periods would not be affected by the bad debt adjustment and would, therefore, be different – but the total profit for the two periods would be the same.

A similar situation would apply where there are differences in judgements concerning allowances for trade receivables.

**Real World 3.8** describes the rise in bad debts of one business.

### Real World 3.8

## Shopping for bad debts

Shares in Yorkshire home shopping firm Findel dived by nearly 40 per cent after profits were hit by an increase in customers slipping behind on payments. The company, which sells a range of household goods under names such as The Cotswold Company, Kitbag and Ace, said it was adding £5 million to its bad debt provision (allowances for trade receivables) for the year ended 31 March 2008, with profits hit as a result.

This came after the group experienced a 'softening' in repayments from credit customers during the past two months. Around 1.5 million customers use credit to buy goods through Findel's home shopping arm, with another one million paying by cash. The group's bad debt provision (allowances for trade receivables) before the £5 million change is understood to have been £83 million.

Findel, which is based at Burley-in-Wharfedale, West Yorkshire, said: 'In light of the deteriorating economic climate the company has conducted a further review of the Home Shopping debt book and now estimates that the bad debt provision will be £5 million higher than had previously been anticipated.'

The company warned that profits would be down as a result, but would come in higher than last year's £56 million.

*Source*: 'Findel shares plunge as Yorkshire home shopping firm's bad debts rise', Nigel Scott, *Yorkshire Evening Post*, 17 April 2008. Reproduced by kind permission of the *Yorkshire Evening Post*.

Let us now try to bring together some of the points that we have raised in this chapter through a self-assessment question.

**Self-assessment question 3.1**

TT and Co. is a new business that started trading on 1 January 2011. The following is a summary of transactions that occurred during the first year of trading:

1. The owners introduced £50,000 of equity, which was paid into a bank account opened in the name of the business.
2. Premises were rented from 1 January 2011 at an annual rental of £20,000. During the year, rent of £25,000 was paid to the owner of the premises.
3. Rates (a tax on business premises) were paid during the year as follows:

   | | |
   |---|---|
   | For the period 1 January 2011 to 31 March 2011 | £500 |
   | For the period 1 April 2011 to 31 March 2012 | £1,200 |

4. A delivery van was bought on 1 January 2011 for £12,000. This is expected to be used in the business for four years and then to be sold for £2,000.
5. Wages totalling £33,500 were paid during the year. At the end of the year, the business owed £630 of wages for the last week of the year.
6. Electricity bills for the first three quarters of the year were paid totalling £1,650. After 31 December 2011, but before the financial statements had been finalised for the year, the bill for the last quarter arrived showing a charge of £620.
7. Inventories totalling £143,000 were bought on credit.
8. Inventories totalling £12,000 were bought for cash.
9. Sales revenue on credit totalled £152,000 (cost of sales £74,000).
10. Cash sales revenue totalled £35,000 (cost of sales £16,000).
11. Receipts from trade receivables totalled £132,000.
12. Payments to trade payables totalled £121,000.
13. Van running expenses paid totalled £9,400.

At the end of the year it was clear that a credit customer (trade receivable) who owed £400 would not be able to pay any part of the debt. All of the other trade payables were expected to settle in full.

The business uses the straight-line method for depreciating non-current assets.

*Required*:
Prepare a statement of financial position as at 31 December 2011 and an income statement for the year to that date.

**The solution to this question can be found at the back of the book on page 763.**

# Uses and usefulness of the income statement

The income statement, like the statement of financial position, has been around for a long time. Most major businesses seem to prepare an income statement on a frequent basis (monthly or even more frequently). This is despite there being no rule requiring an income statement to be produced more frequently than once, or in some cases twice, a year. The income statement, must, therefore, be regarded as providing useful information, otherwise it would not be prepared so frequently. In particular, this statement may help in providing information on:

● *How effective the business has been in generating wealth.* Since wealth generation is the primary reason for most businesses to exist, assessing how much wealth has been created is an important issue. Although we have seen that different judgements concerning depreciation, inventories and bad debts may affect the calculation of profit for a period, this problem should not be overstated. For most businesses in most years, the effect of making different judgements would probably not significantly affect the final profit figure.

- *How the profit was derived.* For some users, the only item of concern may be the final profit figure, or *bottom line* as it is sometimes called. While this is a primary measure of performance, and its importance is difficult to overstate, the income statement contains other information that should also be of interest. To evaluate business performance effectively, it is important to discover how the profit figure was derived. Thus the level of sales revenue, the nature and amount of expenses incurred, and the profit in relation to sales revenue are important factors in understanding the performance of the business over a period. The analysis and interpretation of financial statements are considered in detail in Chapter 7.

## Summary

The main points of this chapter may be summarised as follows:

**The income statement (profit and loss account)**

- The income statement measures and reports how much profit (or loss) has been generated over a period.
- Profit (or loss) for the period is the difference between the total revenue and total expenses for the period.
- The income statement links the statements of financial position at the beginning and end of a reporting period.
- The income statement will normally first calculate gross profit and then deduct any overheads for the period. The final figure derived is the profit (or loss) for the period.
- Gross profit represents the difference between the sales revenue for the period and the cost of sales.

**Expenses and revenue**

- Cost of sales may be identified either by matching the cost of each sale to the particular sale or, in the case of retail and wholesaling businesses, by adjusting the goods bought during the period to take account of opening and closing inventories.
- Classifying expenses is often a matter of judgement, although there are rules for businesses that trade as limited companies.
- Revenue is recognised when the amount of revenue can be measured reliably and it is probable that the economic benefits will be received.
- Where there is a sale of goods, there is an additional criterion that ownership and control must pass to the buyer before revenue can be recognised.
- Revenue can be recognised after partial completion provided that a particular stage of completion can be measured reliably.
- The matching convention states that expenses should be matched to the revenue that they help generate.

- A particular expense reported in the income statement may not be the same as the cash paid. This will result in accruals or prepayments appearing in the statement of financial position.
- The materiality convention states that where the amounts are immaterial, we should consider only what is expedient.
- 'Accruals accounting' is preparing the income statement and statement of financial position following the accruals convention, which says that profit = revenue – expenses (not cash receipts – cash payments).

### Depreciation of non-current assets

- Depreciation requires a consideration of the cost (or fair value), useful life and residual value of an asset. It also requires a consideration of the method of depreciation.
- The straight-line method of depreciation allocates the amount to be depreciated evenly over the useful life of the asset.
- The reducing-balance method applies a fixed percentage rate of depreciation to the carrying amount of an asset each year.
- The depreciation method chosen should reflect the pattern of benefits associated with the asset.
- Depreciation is an attempt to allocate the cost (or fair value), less the residual value, of an asset over its useful life. It does not provide funds for replacement of the asset.

### Costing inventories

- The way in which we derive the cost of inventories is important in the calculation of profit and the presentation of financial position.
- The first in, first out (FIFO) method approaches matters as if the earliest inventories held are the first to be used.
- The last in, first out (LIFO) method approaches matters as if the latest inventories are the first to be used.
- The weighted average cost (AVCO) method applies an average cost to all inventories used.
- When prices are rising, FIFO gives the lowest cost of sales figure and highest closing inventories figure and LIFO gives the highest cost of sales figure and the lowest closing inventories figure. AVCO gives figures for cost of sales and closing inventories that lie between FIFO and LIFO.
- When prices are falling, the positions of FIFO and LIFO are reversed.
- Inventories are shown at the lower of cost and net realisable value.
- When a particular method of accounting, such as an inventories-costing method, is selected, it should be applied consistently over time.

### Bad debts

- Where it is reasonably certain that a credit customer will not pay, the debt is regarded as 'bad' and written off.
- Where it is doubtful that a credit customer will pay, an allowance for trade receivables expense should be created.

### Uses of the income statement

- It provides a profit figure.
- It provides information on how the profit was derived.

# MyAccountingLab

Go to **www.myaccountinglab.com** to check your understanding of the chapter, create a personalised study plan, and maximise your revision time

## Key terms

profit  p. 80
revenue  p. 80
expense  p. 81
reporting period  p. 82
gross profit  p. 83
operating profit  p. 84
profit for the period  p. 84
cost of sales  p. 84
matching convention  p. 92
accrued expenses  p. 93
prepaid expenses  p. 95
materiality convention  p. 96
accruals convention  p. 97
accruals accounting  p. 97
depreciation  p. 97

amortisation  p. 97
residual value  p. 99
straight-line method  p. 99
carrying amount  p. 100
written-down value  p. 100
net book value  p. 100
reducing-balance method  p. 100
first in, first out (FIFO)  p. 107
last in, first out (LIFO)  p. 107
weighted average cost (AVCO)
  p. 107
consistency convention  p. 112
bad debt  p. 112
allowance for trade receivables
p. 113

## Further reading

If you would like to explore the topics covered in this chapter in more depth, we recommend the following books:

Alexander, D. and Nobes, C., *Financial accounting: an international introduction,* 4th edn, Financial Times Prentice Hall, 2010, chapters 2, 9 and 10.

Elliott, B. and Elliott, J., *Financial Accounting and Reporting*, 15th edn, Financial Times Prentice Hall, 2012, chapters 2, 20 and 21.

International Accounting Standards Board, *2011 International Financial Reporting Standards IFRS* (2 volume set), 2011.

KPMG, *Insights into IFRS*, 8th edn, Sweet and Maxwell, 2011, Sections 3.2, 3.3, 3.8, 3.10 and 4.2. A summarised version of this is available free at www.kpmg.com.

## Review Questions

**Solutions to these questions can be found at the back of the book on page 747.**

**3.1**  'Although the income statement is a record of past achievement, the calculations required for certain expenses involve estimates of the future.' What does this statement mean? Can you think of examples where estimates of the future are used?

**3.2**  'Depreciation is a process of allocation and not valuation.' What do you think is meant by this statement?

**3.3**  What is the convention of consistency? Does this convention help users in making a more valid comparison between businesses?

**3.4**  'An asset is similar to an expense.' Do you agree?

## Exercises

**Exercises 3.1 to 3.3 are basic level, 3.4 and 3.5 are intermediate level and 3.6 and 3.7 are advanced level. Exercises with coloured numbers have solutions at the back of the book, starting on page 747.**

**If you wish to try more exercises, visit the students' side of the Companion Website and MyAccountingLab.**

**3.1**  You have heard the following statements made. Comment critically on them.

(a)  'Equity only increases or decreases as a result of the owners putting more cash into the business or taking some out.'
(b)  'An accrued expense is one that relates to next year.'
(c)  'Unless we depreciate this asset we shall be unable to provide for its replacement.'
(d)  'There is no point in depreciating the factory building. It is appreciating in value each year.'

**3.2**  Singh Enterprises, which started business on 1 January 2009, has a reporting period to 31 December and uses the straight-line method of depreciation. On 1 January 2009 the business bought a machine for £10,000. The machine had an expected useful life of four years and an estimated residual value of £2,000. On 1 January 2010 the business bought another machine for £15,000. This machine had an expected useful life of five years and an estimated residual value of £2,500. On 31 December 2011 the business sold the first machine bought for £3,000.

*Required*:
Show the relevant income statement extracts and statement of financial position extracts for the years 2009, 2010 and 2011.

**3.3**  The owner of a business is confused and comes to you for help. The financial statements for the business, prepared by an accountant, for the last reporting period revealed a profit of £50,000. However, during the reporting period the bank balance declined by £30,000. What reasons might explain this apparent discrepancy?

**3.4** Spratley Ltd is a builders' merchant. On 1 September the business had, as part of its inventories, 20 tonnes of sand at a cost of £18 per tonne and, therefore, at a total cost of £360. During the first week in September, the business bought the following amounts of sand:

| | Tonnes | Cost per tonne £ |
|---|---|---|
| 2 September | 48 | 20 |
| 4 September | 15 | 24 |
| 6 September | 10 | 25 |

On 7 September the business sold 60 tonnes of sand to a local builder.

*Required*:

Calculate the cost of goods sold and the cost of the remaining inventories using the following costing methods:

(a) first in, first out
(b) last in, first out
(c) weighted average cost.

**3.5** Fill in the values (a) to (f) in the following table on the assumption that there were no opening balances involved.

| | Relating to period | | At end of period | |
|---|---|---|---|---|
| | Paid/Received £ | Expense/revenue for period £ | Prepaid £ | Accruals/deferred revenues £ |
| Rent payable | 10,000 | (a) | 1,000 | |
| Rates and insurance | 5,000 | (b) | | 1,000 |
| General expenses | (c) | 6,000 | 1,000 | |
| Interest payable on borrowings | 3,000 | 2,500 | (d) | |
| Salaries | (e) | 9,000 | | 3,000 |
| Rent receivable | (f) | 1,500 | | 1,500 |

**3.6** The following is the statement of financial position of TT and Co. (see Self-assessment question 3.1 on page 117) at the end of its first year of trading:

## Statement of financial position as at 31 December 2011

|  | £ |
|---|---|
| **ASSETS** | |
| **Non-current assets** | |
| *Property, plant and equipment* | |
| Delivery van at cost | 12,000 |
| Depreciation | (2,500) |
|  | 9,500 |
| **Current assets** | |
| Inventories | 65,000 |
| Trade receivables | 19,600 |
| Prepaid expenses* | 5,300 |
| Cash | 750 |
|  | 90,650 |
| **Total assets** | 100,150 |
| **EQUITY AND LIABILITIES** | |
| **Equity** | |
| Original | 50,000 |
| Retained earnings | 26,900 |
|  | 76,900 |
| **Current liabilities** | |
| Trade payables | 22,000 |
| Accrued expenses† | 1,250 |
|  | 23,250 |
| Total equity and liabilities | 100,150 |

\* The prepaid expenses consisted of rates (£300) and rent (£5,000).
† The accrued expenses consisted of wages (£630) and electricity (£620).

During 2012, the following transactions took place:

1 The owners withdrew equity in the form of cash of £20,000.
2 Premises continued to be rented at an annual rental of £20,000. During the year, rent of £15,000 was paid to the owner of the premises.
3 Rates on the premises were paid during the year as follows: for the period 1 April 2012 to 31 March 2013 £1,300.
4 A second delivery van was bought on 1 January 2012 for £13,000. This is expected to be used in the business for four years and then to be sold for £3,000.
5 Wages totalling £36,700 were paid during the year. At the end of the year, the business owed £860 of wages for the last week of the year.
6 Electricity bills for the first three quarters of the year and £620 for the last quarter of the previous year were paid totalling £1,820. After 31 December 2012, but before the financial statements had been finalised for the year, the bill for the last quarter arrived showing a charge of £690.
7 Inventories totalling £67,000 were bought on credit.
8 Inventories totalling £8,000 were bought for cash.
9 Sales revenue on credit totalled £179,000 (cost £89,000).
10 Cash sales revenue totalled £54,000 (cost £25,000).
11 Receipts from trade receivables totalled £178,000.
12 Payments to trade payables totalled £71,000.
13 Van running expenses paid totalled £16,200.

The business uses the straight-line method for depreciating non-current assets.

*Required*:

Prepare a statement of financial position as at 31 December 2012 and an income statement for the year to that date.

**3.7** The following is the income statement for Nikov and Co. for the year ended 31 December 2011, along with information relating to the preceding year.

### Income statement for the year ended 31 December

|  | 2011 | 2010 |
|---|---|---|
|  | £000 | £000 |
| Sales revenue | 420.2 | 382.5 |
| Cost of sales | (126.1) | (114.8) |
| **Gross profit** | 294.1 | 267.7 |
| Salaries and wages | (92.6) | (86.4) |
| Selling and distribution costs | (98.9) | (75.4) |
| Rent and rates | (22.0) | (22.0) |
| Bad debts written off | (19.7) | (4.0) |
| Telephone and postage | (4.8) | (4.4) |
| Insurance | (2.9) | (2.8) |
| Motor vehicle expenses | (10.3) | (8.6) |
| Depreciation – Delivery van | (3.1) | (3.3) |
| – Fixtures and fittings | (4.3) | (4.5) |
| **Operating profit** | 35.5 | 56.3 |
| Loan interest | (4.6) | (5.4) |
| **Profit for the year** | 30.9 | 50.9 |

*Required*:

Analyse the performance of the business for the year to 31 December 2011 in so far as the information allows.

# CHAPTER 4

# Accounting for limited companies (1)

## Introduction

Most businesses in the UK, including some of the very smallest, operate in the form of limited companies. About two and a half million limited companies now exist and they account for the majority of UK business activity and employment. The economic significance of this type of business is not confined to the UK; it can be seen in many of the world's developed countries.

In this chapter we consider the nature of limited companies and how they differ from sole proprietorship businesses and partnerships. This expands the brief discussion of various business forms in Chapter 1. We examine the ways in which the owners provide finance, as well as the rules governing the way in which limited companies must account to their owners and to other interested parties. We shall also see how the financial statements, which were discussed in the previous two chapters, are prepared for this type of business.

## Learning outcomes

**When you have completed this chapter, you should be able to:**

● discuss the nature of the limited company;

● describe the main features of the equity (owners' claim) in a limited company;

● discuss the framework of rules designed to safeguard the interests of shareholders;

● explain how the income statement and statement of financial position of a limited company differ in detail from those of sole proprietorships and partnerships.

## MyAccountingLab

Visit **www.myaccountinglab.com** for practice and revision opportunities

## Why limited companies?

Although there are very many businesses in the UK that trade as sole proprietorships, as partnerships and in other forms, overwhelmingly the most important business form is the limited company. In terms of sales revenue generated, wealth created, number of people employed, exports achieved and virtually any other measure, limited companies dominate the business scene. We shall see in this chapter that limited companies are subject to a great deal of regulation. This is particularly true of those limited companies whose shares are traded on the London Stock Exchange. All of this regulation can be very tiresome for the companies and, importantly, very expensive.

In this chapter we shall be looking at a number of issues, including:

- What is a limited company?
- Why are limited companies so popular?
- What regulation must limited companies accept?
- Why do some limited companies have their shares traded on the London Stock Exchange, when this leads to even more regulation and expense?

We shall be answering these and other questions during this chapter.

## The main features of limited companies

### Legal nature

Let us begin our examination of limited companies by discussing their legal nature. A *limited company* has been described as an artificial person that has been created by law. This means that a company has many of the rights and obligations that 'real' people have. It can, for example, sue, or be sued, by others and can enter into contracts in its own name. This contrasts sharply with other types of businesses, such as sole proprietorships and partnerships (that is, unincorporated businesses). With these it is the owner(s) rather than the business that must sue, enter into contracts, and so on, because the business has no separate legal identity.

With the rare exceptions of those that are created by Act of Parliament or by Royal Charter, all UK companies are created (or *incorporated*) by registration. To create a company the person or persons wishing to create it (usually known as *promoters*) fill in a few simple forms and pay a modest registration fee. After having ensured that the necessary formalities have been met, the Registrar of Companies, a UK government official, enters the name of the new company on the Registry of Companies. Thus, in the UK, companies can be formed very easily and cheaply (for about £100).

A limited company may be owned by just one person, but most have more than one owner and some have many owners. The owners are usually known as *members* or *shareholders*. The ownership of a company is normally divided into a number, frequently a large number, of shares, each of equal size. Each owner, or shareholder, owns one or more shares in the company. Large companies typically have a very large number of shareholders. For example, at 31 March 2011, BT Group plc, the telecommunications business, had about 1.1 million different shareholders.

Since a limited company has its own legal identity, it is regarded as being quite separate from those who own and manage it. It is worth emphasising that this legal separateness of owners and the company has absolutely no connection with the business entity convention of accounting, which we discussed in Chapter 2. This accounting convention applies equally well to all business types, including sole proprietorships and partnerships where there is no legal distinction between the owner(s) and the business.

The legal separateness between the limited company and its shareholders leads to two important features of the limited company: perpetual life and limited liability. These are now explained.

## Perpetual life

A company is normally granted a perpetual existence and so will continue even where an owner of some, or even all, of the shares in the company dies. The shares of the deceased person will simply pass to the beneficiary of his or her estate. The granting of perpetual existence means that the life of a company is quite separate from the lives of those individuals who own or manage it. It is not, therefore, affected by changes in ownership that arise when individuals buy and sell shares in the company.

Though a company may be granted a perpetual existence when it is first formed, it is possible for either the shareholders or the courts to bring this existence to an end. When this is done, the assets of the company are usually sold to generate cash to meet the outstanding liabilities. Any surplus arising after all liabilities have been met will then be used to pay the shareholders. Shareholders may agree to end the life of a company where it has achieved the purpose for which it was formed or where they feel that the company has no real future. The courts may bring the life of a company to an end where creditors have applied to the courts for this to be done because they have not been paid amounts owing.

Where shareholders agree to end the life of a company, it is referred to as a 'voluntary liquidation'. **Real World 4.1** describes the demise of one company by this method.

---

**Real World 4.1**

### Monotub Industries in a spin as founder gets Titan for £1    FT

Monotub Industries, maker of the Titan washing machine, yesterday passed into corporate history with very little ceremony and with only a whimper of protest from minority shareholders.

At an extraordinary meeting held in a basement room of the group's West End headquarters, shareholders voted to put the company into voluntary liquidation and sell its assets and intellectual property to founder Martin Myerscough for £1. [The shares in the company were at one time worth 650p each.]

The only significant opposition came from Giuliano Gnagnatti who, along with other shareholders, has seen his investment shrink faster than a wool twin-set on a boil wash.

The not-so-proud owner of 100,000 Monotub shares, Mr Gnagnatti, the managing director of an online retailer, described the sale of Monotub as a 'free gift' to Mr Myerscough. This assessment was denied by Ian Green, the chairman of Monotub, who said the closest the beleaguered company had come to a sale was an offer for £60,000 that gave no guarantees against liabilities, which are thought to amount to £750,000.

The quiet passing of the washing machine, eventually dubbed the Titanic, was in strong contrast to its performance in many kitchens.

Originally touted as the 'great white goods hope' of the washing machine industry with its larger capacity and removable drum, the Titan ran into problems when it kept stopping during the spin cycle, causing it to emit a loud bang and leap into the air.

**Real World 4.1 (continued)**

Summing up the demise of the Titan, Mr Green said: 'Clearly the machine had some revolutionary aspects, but you can't get away from the fact that the machine was faulty and should not have been launched with those defects.'

The usually-vocal Mr Myerscough, who has promised to pump £250,000 into the company and give Monotub shareholders £4 for every machine sold, refused to comment on his plans for the Titan or reveal who his backers were. But . . . he did say that he intended to 'take the Titan forward'.

*Source*: 'Monotub Industries in a spin as founder gets Titan for £1', Lisa Urquhart, *Financial Times*, 23 January 2003.

## Limited liability

Since the company is a legal person in its own right, it must take responsibility for its own debts and losses. This means that, once the shareholders have paid what they have agreed to pay for the shares, their obligation to the company, and to the company's creditors, is satisfied. Thus shareholders can limit their losses to the amount that they have paid, or agreed to pay, for their shares. This is of great practical importance to potential shareholders since they know that what they can lose, as part owners of the business, is limited.

Contrast this with the position of sole proprietors or partners. They cannot 'ring-fence' assets that they do not want to put into the business. If a sole proprietorship or partnership business finds itself in a position where liabilities exceed the business assets, the law gives unsatisfied creditors the right to demand payment out of what the sole proprietor or partner may have regarded as 'non-business' assets. Thus the sole proprietor or partner could lose everything – house, car, the lot. This is because the law sees Jill the sole proprietor, as being the same as Jill the private individual. The shareholder, by contrast, can lose only the amount committed to that company. Legally, the business operating as a limited company, in which Jack owns shares, is not the same as Jack himself. This is true even if Jack were to own all of the shares in the company.

**Real World 4.2** gives an example of a well-known case where the shareholders of a particular company were able to avoid any liability to those that had lost money as a result of dealing with the company.

**Real World 4.2**

## Carlton and Granada 1 – Nationwide Football League 0

Two television broadcasting companies, Carlton and Granada, each owned 50 per cent of a separate company, ITV Digital (formerly ON Digital). ITV Digital signed a contract to pay the Nationwide Football League (in effect the three divisions of English football below the Premiership) more than £89 million on both 1 August 2002 and 1 August 2003 for the rights to broadcast football matches over three seasons. ITV Digital was unable to sell enough subscriptions for the broadcasts and collapsed because it was unable to meet its liabilities. The Nationwide Football League tried to force Carlton and Granada (ITV Digital's only shareholders) to meet ITV Digital's contractual obligations. It was unable to do so because the shareholders could not be held legally liable for the amounts owing.

Carlton and Granada subsequently merged into one business, but at the time of ITV Digital were two independent companies.

## Activity (4.1)

The fact that shareholders can limit their losses to that which they have paid, or have agreed to pay, for their shares is of great practical importance to potential shareholders.

Can you think of any practical benefit to a private-sector economy, in general, of this ability of shareholders to limit losses?

Business is a risky venture – in some cases very risky. People will usually be happier to invest money when they know the limit of their liability. If investors are given limited liability, new businesses are more likely to be formed and existing ones are likely to find it easier to raise more finance. This is good for the private-sector economy and may ultimately lead to the generation of greater wealth for society as a whole.

Although **limited liability** has this advantage to the providers of equity finance (the shareholders), it is not necessarily to the advantage of all of the others who have a stake in the business, as we saw in the case of the Nationwide Football League clubs in Real World 4.2. Limited liability is attractive to shareholders because they can, in effect, walk away from the unpaid debts of the company if their contribution has not been sufficient to meet those debts. This is likely to make any individual, or another business, wary of entering into a contract with a limited company. This can be a real problem for smaller, less established companies. Suppliers may insist on cash payment before delivery of goods or the rendering of a service. Alternatively, they may require a personal guarantee from a major shareholder that the debt will be paid, before allowing trade credit. In the latter case, the supplier circumvents the company's limited liability status by demanding the personal liability of an individual. Larger, more established companies, on the other hand, tend to have built up the confidence of suppliers.

## Legal safeguards

Various safeguards exist to protect individuals and businesses contemplating dealing with a limited company. These include the requirement to indicate limited liability status in the name of the company. By doing this, a warning is issued to prospective suppliers and lenders.

A further safeguard is the restrictions placed on the ability of shareholders to withdraw their equity from the company. These restrictions are designed to prevent shareholders from protecting their own investment and, as a result, leaving lenders and suppliers in an exposed position. We shall consider this point in more detail later in the chapter.

Finally, limited companies are required to produce annual financial statements (income statements, statements of financial position and statements of cash flows) and make these publicly available. This means that anyone interested can gain an impression of the financial performance and position of the company. The form and content of the first two of these statements are considered in some detail later in the chapter. Chapter 6 is devoted to the statement of cash flows.

## Public and private companies

When a company is registered with the Registrar of Companies, it must be registered either as a public or as a private company. The main practical difference between these is that a **public limited company** can offer its shares for sale to the general public, but a **private limited company** is restricted from doing so. A public limited company must signal its status to all interested parties by having the words 'public limited company', or its abbreviation 'plc', in its name. For a private limited company, the word 'limited' or 'Ltd' must appear as part of its name.

Private limited companies tend to be smaller businesses where the ownership is divided among relatively few shareholders who are usually fairly close to one another – for example, a family company. Numerically, there are vastly more private limited companies in the UK than there are public ones. Of the 2.49 million UK limited companies now in existence, only 7,812 (representing 0.3 per cent of the total) are public limited companies. Figure 4.2 shows the trend in the numbers of public and private limited companies in recent years.

Since individual public companies tend to be larger, they are often economically more important. In some industry sectors, such as banking, insurance, oil refining and grocery retailing, they are completely dominant. Although some large private limited companies exist, many private limited companies are little more than the vehicle through which one-person businesses operate.

**Real World 4.3** shows the extent of the market dominance of public limited companies in one particular business sector.

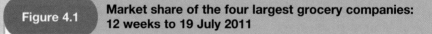

## Real World 4.3

### A big slice of the market

The grocery sector is dominated by four large players: Tesco, Sainsbury, Morrison and Asda. The first three are public limited companies and the fourth, Asda, is owned by a large US public company, Wal-Mart. Figure 4.1 shows the share of the grocery market enjoyed by each during the twelve-week period to 19 July 2011.

| Figure 4.1 | **Market share of the four largest grocery companies: 12 weeks to 19 July 2011** |

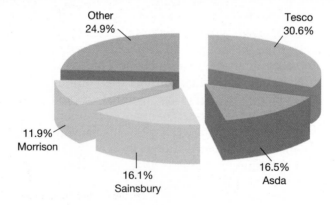

Other 24.9%

Tesco 30.6%

11.9% Morrison

16.1% Sainsbury

16.5% Asda

Tesco had by far the largest market share and the four largest grocery companies, when taken together, had more than 75 per cent of the total market during the period.

*Source*: Compiled from information in 'Discount supermarkets gain market share as shoppers scale down', Dow Jones Newswires, 19 July 2011.

**Figure 4.2**    **Numbers of public and private limited companies in the UK 2006 to 2011**

**Public limited companies**

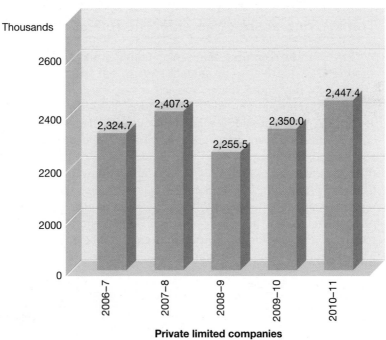

**Private limited companies**

There was broadly a rise in the number of private limited companies over the period. Over the same period there has been a gradual decline in the number of public limited companies.

*Source*: Based on information in Companies Register Activities 2011, statistical tables on companies registration activities 2010/11, www.companieshouse.gov.uk.

## Taxation

Another consequence of the legal separation of the limited company from its owners is that companies must be accountable to the tax authorities for tax on their profits and gains. This leads to the reporting of tax in the financial statements of limited companies. The charge for tax is shown in the income statement (profit and loss account). The tax charge for a particular year is based on that year's profit. Since only 50 per cent of a company's tax liability is due for payment during the year concerned, the other 50 per cent will appear on the end-of-year statement of financial position (balance sheet) as a current liability. This will be illustrated a little later in the chapter. The tax position of companies contrasts with that of sole proprietorships and partnerships, where tax is levied not on the business but on the owner(s). Thus tax does not impact on the financial statements of unincorporated businesses, but is an individual matter between the owner(s) and the tax authorities.

Companies are charged **corporation tax** on their profits and gains. The percentage rates of tax tend to vary from year to year, but have recently been 26 per cent for larger companies and 20 per cent for smaller companies. These rates of tax are levied on the company's taxable profit, which is not necessarily the same as the profit shown on the income statement. This is because tax law does not, in every respect, follow the normal accounting rules. Generally, however, the taxable profit and the company's accounting profit are pretty close to one another.

There can be tax advantages to trading as a limited company, rather than as a sole proprietor or partner. This may partly explain the rise in popularity of private limited companies over recent years.

## Transferring share ownership: the role of the Stock Exchange

We have already seen that shares in a company may be transferred from one owner to another. The desire of some shareholders to sell their shares, coupled with the desire of others to buy those shares, has led to the existence of a formal market in which shares can be bought and sold. The London Stock Exchange and similar organisations around the world provide a marketplace in which shares in public companies may be bought and sold. Share prices are determined by the laws of supply and demand, which are, in turn, determined by investors' perceptions of the future economic prospects of the companies concerned. Only the shares of certain companies (*listed* companies) may be traded on the London Stock Exchange. Just over 1,000 UK companies are listed. This represents only about 1 in 2,250 of all UK companies (public and private) and roughly one in seven public limited companies. However, many of these listed companies are massive. Nearly all of the 'household-name' UK businesses (for example, Tesco, Next, BT, Vodafone, BP, and so on) are listed companies.

**Activity (4.2)**

If, as has been pointed out earlier, the change in ownership of shares does not directly affect the particular company, why do many public companies actively seek to have their shares traded in a recognised market?

The main reason is that investors are generally very reluctant to pledge their money unless they can see some way in which they can turn their investment back into cash. In theory, the shares of a particular company may be very valuable because the company has bright prospects. However, unless this value is capable of being turned into cash, the benefit to the shareholders is dubious. After all, we cannot spend shares; we normally need cash.

This means that potential shareholders are much more likely to be prepared to buy new shares from the company (thereby providing the company with new investment finance) where they can see a way of liquidating their investment (turning it into cash) as and when they wish. Stock Exchanges provide the means of liquidation.

Although the buying and selling of 'second-hand' shares does not provide the company with cash, the fact that the buying and selling facility exists will make it easier for the company to raise new share capital when it needs to do so.

## Managing a company

A limited company may have legal personality, but it is not a human being capable of making decisions and plans about the business and exercising control over it. People must undertake these management tasks. The most senior level of management of a company is the board of directors.

The shareholders elect **directors** to manage the company on a day-to-day basis on behalf of those shareholders. By law there must be at least one director for a private limited company and two for a public limited company. In a small company, the board may be the only level of management and consist of all of the shareholders. In larger companies, the board may consist of ten or so directors out of many thousands of shareholders. Indeed, directors are not even required to be shareholders. Below the board of directors of the typical large company could be several layers of management comprising thousands of people.

In recent years, the issue of **corporate governance** has generated much debate. The term is used to describe the ways in which companies are directed and controlled. The issue of corporate governance is important because, with larger companies, those who own the company (that is, the shareholders) are usually divorced from the day-to-day control of the business. The shareholders employ the directors to manage the company for them. Given this position, it may seem reasonable to assume that the best interests of shareholders will guide the directors' decisions. However, in practice this does not always seem to be the case. The directors may be more concerned with pursuing their own interests, such as increasing their pay and 'perks' (such as expensive motor cars, overseas visits and so on) and improving their job security and status. As a result, a conflict can occur between the interests of shareholders and the interests of directors.

Where directors pursue their own interests at the expense of the shareholders, there is clearly a problem for the shareholders. However, it may also be a problem for society as a whole. If shareholders feel that their funds are likely to be mismanaged, they will be reluctant to invest. A shortage of funds will mean that companies can make fewer investments. Furthermore, the costs of finance will increase as businesses compete for what little funds are available. Thus, a lack of concern for shareholders can have a profound effect on the performance of individual companies and, with this, the health of the economy. To avoid these problems, most competitive market economies have a framework of rules to help monitor and control the behaviour of directors.

These rules are usually based around three guiding principles:

- *Disclosure.* This lies at the heart of good corporate governance. An OECD report (see reference at the end of the chapter) summed up the benefits of disclosure as follows:

  Adequate and timely information about corporate performance enables investors to make informed buy-and-sell decisions and thereby helps the market reflect the value of a corporation under present management. If the market determines that present management is not performing, a decrease in stock [share] price will sanction management's failure and open the way to management change.

- *Accountability.* This involves defining the roles and duties of the directors and establishing an adequate monitoring process. In the UK, company law requires that the directors of a business act in the best interests of the shareholders. This means, among other things, that they must not try to use their position and knowledge to make gains at the expense of the shareholders. The law also requires larger companies to have their annual financial statements independently audited. The purpose of an independent audit is to lend credibility to the financial statements prepared by the directors. We shall take a brief look at audit in Chapter 5.
- *Fairness.* Directors should not be able to benefit from access to 'inside' information that is not available to shareholders. As a result, both the law and the Stock Exchange place restrictions on the ability of directors to buy and sell the shares of the business. One example of these restrictions is that the directors cannot buy or sell shares immediately before the announcement of the annual trading results of the business or before the announcement of a significant event such as a planned merger or the loss of the chief executive.

These principles are set out in Figure 4.3 below

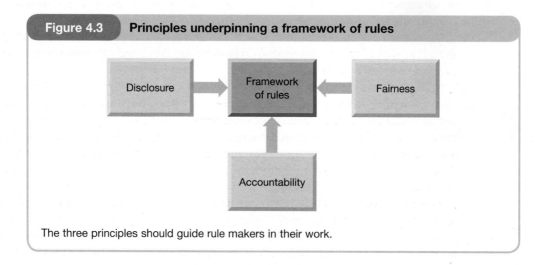

**Figure 4.3** **Principles underpinning a framework of rules**

The three principles should guide rule makers in their work.

## Strengthening the framework of rules

The number of rules designed to safeguard shareholders has increased considerably over the years. This has been in response to weaknesses in corporate governance procedures, which have been exposed through well-publicised business failures and frauds, excessive pay increases to directors and evidence that some financial reports were being 'massaged' so as to mislead shareholders. (This last point will be discussed in Chapter 5.)

Many believe, however, that the shareholders must shoulder some of the blame for any weaknesses. Not all shareholders in large companies are private individuals owning just a few shares each. In fact, ownership, by market value, of the shares listed on the London Stock Exchange is dominated by investing institutions such as insurance businesses, banks and pension funds (see Real World 15.14, page 000). These are often massive operations, owning large quantities of the shares of the companies in which they invest. These institutional investors employ specialist staff to manage their portfolios of shares in various companies. It has been argued that the large institutional shareholders, despite their size and relative expertise, have not been very active in corporate governance matters. As a result there has been little monitoring of directors. However, things seem to be changing. There is increasing evidence that institutional investors are becoming more proactive in relation to the companies in which they hold shares.

## The UK Corporate Governance Code

During the 1990s there was a real effort by the accountancy profession and the London Stock Exchange to address the problems of poor corporate governance mentioned above. A Code of Best Practice on Corporate Governance emerged in 1992. This was concerned with accountability and financial reporting. In 1995, a separate code of practice emerged. This dealt with directors' pay and conditions. These two codes were revised, 'fine-tuned' and amalgamated to produce the Combined Code, which was issued in 1998. Every few years, the impact and effectiveness of the Code has been reviewed and this resulted in revisions being made. In 2010, the Combined Code changed its name to the **UK Corporate Governance Code**.

One of the key issues covered by the Code concerns the roles of the company chairman (the senior director) and the other directors. The Code is particularly concerned with the role of 'non-executive' directors.

Non-executive directors do not work full-time in the company, but act solely in the role of director. This contrasts with 'executive' directors who are salaried employees. For example, the finance director of most large companies is a full-time employee. This person is a member of the board of directors and, as such, takes part in the key decision-making at board level. At the same time, he or she is also responsible for managing the departments of the company that act on those board decisions as far as finance is concerned.

The view reflected in the Code is that executive directors can become too embroiled in the day-to-day management of the company to be able to take a broad view. It also reflects the view that, for executive directors, conflicts can arise between their own interests and those of the shareholders. The advantage of non-executive directors can be that they are much more independent of the company than are their executive colleagues. The company remunerates non-executive directors for their work, but this would normally form only a small proportion of their total income. This gives them an independence that the executive directors may lack. Non-executive directors are often senior managers in other businesses, or people who have had good experience of such roles.

The Code sets out a number of principles relating to such matters as the role of the directors, their relations with shareholders and their accountability. **Real World 4.4** outlines some of the more important of these.

**Real World 4.4**

## The UK Corporate Governance Code

Key elements of the UK Code are as follows:

- Every listed company should have a board of directors that is collectively responsible for its success.
- There should be a clear division of responsibilities between the chairman and the chief executive officer of the company to try to ensure that a single person does not have unbridled power.
- As part of their role as members of a unitary board, non-executive directors should constructively challenge and help develop proposals on strategy.
- There should be an appropriate balance of skills, experience, independence and knowledge to enable the board to carry out its duties effectively.
- The board should receive timely information that is of sufficient quality to enable them to carry out their duties. All board members should refresh their skills regularly and new board members should receive induction.
- Appointments to the board should be the subject of rigorous, formal and transparent procedures and should be drawn from a broad talent pool.
- All directors should submit themselves for re-election at regular intervals, subject to satisfactory performance.
- Remuneration levels should be sufficient to attract, retain and motivate directors of the appropriate quality and should take account of both individual and company performance.
- There should be formal and transparent procedures for developing policy on directors' remuneration. No director should determine his or her own level of remuneration.
- The board should present a balanced and understandable assessment of the company's position and future prospects.
- The board should try to ensure that a satisfactory dialogue with shareholders occurs.
- Boards should use the annual general meeting to communicate with investors and encourage their participation.
- The board should define the company's risk appetite and tolerance and should maintain a sound risk management system.
- Formal and transparent arrangements for applying financial reporting and internal control principles and for maintaining an appropriate relationship with auditors should be in place.
- The board should undertake a formal and rigorous examination of its own performance each year, which will include its committees and individual directors.

*Source*: www.frc.org.uk.

The Code has the backing of the London Stock Exchange. This means that companies listed on the London Stock Exchange are expected to comply with the requirements of the Code or must give their shareholders good reason why they do not. Failure to do one or other of these can lead to the company's shares being suspended from listing. This is an important sanction against non-compliant companies.

## Activity 4.3

**Why might this be an important sanction against a non-compliant company?**

A major advantage of a Stock Exchange listing is that it enables investors to sell their shares whenever they wish. A company that is suspended from listing would find it hard and, therefore, expensive to raise funds from investors because there would be no ready market for the shares.

The existence of the Code has generally been agreed to have improved the quality of information available to shareholders, resulted in better checks on the powers of directors, and provided greater transparency in corporate affairs. However, rules can only be a partial answer. A balance must be struck between the need to protect shareholders and the need to encourage the entrepreneurial spirit of directors, which could be stifled under a welter of rules. This implies that rules should not be too tight, and so unscrupulous directors may still find ways around them.

## Activity 4.4

**Can you think of ways in which the shareholders themselves may try to ensure that the directors always act in the shareholders' best interests?**

Two ways are commonly used in practice:

- The shareholders may insist on monitoring closely the actions of the directors and the way in which they use the resources of the company.
- The shareholders may introduce incentive plans for directors that link their pay to the share performance of the company. In this way, the interests of the directors and shareholders will become more closely aligned.

## Implementing the Code

A detailed study of how the various principles mentioned above are implemented is beyond the scope of this book. However, it is useful to have some idea as to how companies apply the code in practice. To achieve this, we can take a look at extracts from the statement on corporate governance made by the directors of J D Wetherspoon plc, the pub operator, which is set out in its 2010 annual report and accounts.

The first extract, which is set out in **Real World 4.5**, concerns the division of responsibilities between the chairman and the chief executive.

## Real World 4.5

### Divide and rule

| Chairman's responsibility | Chief executive's responsibility |
| --- | --- |
| The chairman is responsible for the smooth running of the board and ensuring that all directors are fully informed of matters relevant to their roles | The chief executive is responsible for the smooth daily running of the business |
| Delegated responsibility of authority from the company to exchange of contracts within controlled procedures | Developing and maintaining effective management controls, planning and performance measurements |
| Providing support, advice and feedback to the chief executive | Maintaining and developing an effective organisational structure |
| Supporting the company strategy and encouraging the chief executive with development of the strategy | External and internal communications in conjunction with the chairman on any issues facing the Company |
| Chairing general meetings, board meetings, operational meetings and agreeing on board agendas and ensuring that adequate time is available for discussion of agenda items | Implementing and monitoring compliance with board policies |
| Management of chief executive's contract, appraisal and remuneration by way of making recommendations to the remuneration committee | Timely and accurate reporting of the above to the board |
| Providing support to executive directors and senior managers of the company | Recruiting and managing senior managers in the business |
| Providing the 'ethos' and 'vision' of the company | Developing and maintaining effective risk management and regulatory controls |
| Providing operational presence across the estate | Maintaining primary relationships with shareholders and investors |
| Making directors aware of shareholders' concerns | Chairing the management board responsible for implementing the Company strategy |
| Ensuring that a culture of openness exists in the Company | |
| Responsible for the leadership of the board and setting its agenda | |

*Source*: J D Wetherspoon plc, Annual Report and Accounts 2010, p. 66.

The next extract, which is set out in **Real World 4.6**, concerns the need for directors to receive timely information.

## Real World 4.6

### Time gentlemen, please!

All directors are provided with, and have full and timely access to, information which enables them to make informed decisions on corporate and business issues, including operational and financial performance. In particular, the board receives monthly information on the financial trading performance of the Company and a comprehensive finance report, including operational highlights. All directors receive sales and margin information for the Company weekly by trading unit.

*Source*: J D Wetherspoon plc, Annual Report and Accounts 2010, p. 66.

The final extract, which is set out in **Real World 4.7**, concerns the ways in which the directors seek to protect shareholder wealth through various internal controls.

## Real World 4.7

### Exercising control

During the year, the Company and the board continued to support and invest in resources to provide an internal audit and risk-management function. The system of internal control and risk mitigation is deeply embedded in the operations and of the Company culture. The board is responsible for maintaining a sound system of internal control and reviewing its effectiveness. The function can only manage, rather than entirely eliminate, the risk of failure to achieve business objectives. It can only provide reasonable and not absolute assurance against material misstatement or loss. Ongoing reviews, assessments and management took place throughout the year under review and up to the date of the approval of the annual report, and accords with the Turnbull Guidance (Guidance on Internal Control).

The Company has an internal audit function which is discharged as follows:

- Regular audits of the Company stock (inventories)
- Unannounced visits to the retail units
- Monitoring systems which control the Company cash
- Health and safety visits ensuring compliance with the Company procedures
- Reviewing and assessing the impact of legislative and regulatory change
- Annually reviewing the Company's strategy, including a review of risks facing the business
- Risk management process, identifying key risks facing the business (Company Risk Register).

The company has key controls as follows:

- Clearly defined authority limits and controls over cash-handling purchasing commitments and capital expenditure
- Comprehensive budgeting process, with a detailed 12-month operating plan and a mid-term financial plan, both approved by the board
- Business results are reported weekly (for key times), with a monthly comprehensive report in full, and compared with budget
- Forecasts are prepared regularly throughout the year for review by the board
- Complex treasury instruments are not used; decisions on treasury matters are reserved by the board

**Real World 4.7 (*continued*)**

● Regular reviews of the amount of external insurance which it obtains, bearing in mind the availability of such cover, its costs and the likelihood of the risks involved
● Regular evaluation of processes and controls in relation to the Company's financial reporting requirements.

The directors confirm that they have reviewed the effectiveness of the system of internal control. Directors insurance cover is maintained.

*Source*: J D Wetherspoon plc, Annual Report and Accounts 2010, p. 68.

## Financing limited companies

### Equity (the owners' claim)

The equity of a sole proprietorship is normally encompassed in one figure on the statement of financial position. With companies, this is usually a little more complicated, although in essence the same broad principles apply. With a company, equity is divided between shares (for example, the original investment), on the one hand, and **reserves** (that is, profits and gains subsequently made), on the other. There is also the possibility that there will be more than one type of shares and of reserves. Thus, within the basic divisions of share capital and reserves, there might well be further subdivisions. This might seem quite complicated, but we shall shortly consider the reasons for these subdivisions and all should become clearer.

### The basic division

When a company is first formed, those who take steps to form it (the promoters) will decide how much needs to be raised by the potential shareholders to set the company up with the necessary assets to operate. Example 4.1 illustrates this.

**Example 4.1**

Some friends decide to form a company to operate an office cleaning business. They estimate that the company will need £50,000 to obtain the necessary assets. Between them, they raise the cash, which they use to buy shares in the company, on 31 March 2011, with a **nominal value** (or **par value**) of £1 each.

At this point the statement of financial position of the company would be:

**Statement of financial position as at 31 March 2011**

|  | £ |
| --- | --- |
| Net assets (all in cash) | 50,000 |
| **Equity** | |
| Share capital | |
| 50,000 shares of £1 each | 50,000 |

The company now buys the necessary non-current assets (vacuum cleaners and so on) and inventories (cleaning materials) and starts to trade. During the first year, the company makes a profit of £10,000. This, by definition, means that the equity expands by £10,000. During the year, the shareholders (owners) make no drawings of their equity, so at the end of the year the summarised statement of financial position looks like this:

### Statement of financial position as at 31 March 2012

|  | £ |
|---|---|
| Net assets (various assets less liabilities*) | 60,000 |
| **Equity** | |
| Share capital | |
| 50,000 shares of £1 each | 50,000 |
| Reserves (revenue reserve) | 10,000 |
| **Total equity** | 60,000 |

* We saw in Chapter 2 that Assets = Equity + Liabilities. We also saw that this can be rearranged so that Assets − Liabilities = Equity.

The profit is shown in a reserve, known as a **revenue reserve**, because it arises from generating revenue (making sales). Note that we do not simply merge the profit with the share capital: we must keep the two amounts separate (to satisfy company law). The reason for this is that there is a legal restriction on the maximum drawings of their equity (for example, as a **dividend**) that the shareholders can make. This is defined by the amount of revenue reserves and so it is helpful to show these separately. We shall look at why there is this restriction, and how it works, a little later in the chapter.

## Share capital

### Ordinary shares

Shares represent the basic units of ownership of a business. All companies issue **ordinary shares**. Ordinary shares are often known as *equities*. The nominal value of such shares is at the discretion of the people who start up the company. For example, if the initial share capital is to be £50,000, this could be two shares of £25,000 each, 5 million shares of one penny each or any other combination that gives a total of £50,000. All shares must have equal value.

### Activity 4.5

The initial financial requirement for a new company is £50,000. There are to be two equal shareholders. Would you advise them to issue two shares of £25,000 each? Why?

Such large-denomination shares tend to be unwieldy. Suppose that one of the shareholders wanted to sell her shareholding. She would have to find one buyer. If there were shares of smaller denomination, it would be possible to sell part of the shareholding to various potential buyers. Furthermore, it would be possible to sell just part of the holding and retain a part.

In practice, £1 is the normal maximum nominal value for shares. Shares of 25 pence each and 50 pence each are probably the most common.

## Altering the nominal value of shares

As we have already seen, the promoters of a new company may make their own choice of the nominal (or par) value of the shares. This value need not be permanent. At a later date the shareholders can decide to change it.

Suppose that a company has 1 million ordinary shares of £1 each and a decision is made to change the nominal value of the shares from £1 to £0.50, in other words to halve the value. This would lead the company to issue each shareholder with a new share certificate (the shareholders' evidence of ownership of their shares) for exactly twice as many shares, each with half the nominal value. The result would be that each shareholder retains a holding of the same total nominal value. This process is known, not surprisingly, as **splitting** the shares. The opposite, reducing the number of shares and increasing their nominal value per share to compensate, is known as **consolidating**. Since each shareholder would be left, after a split or consolidation, with exactly the same proportion of ownership of the company's assets as before, the process should not increase the value of the total shares held.

Splitting is fairly common. The objective is probably to avoid individual shares becoming too valuable and therefore unwieldy, as was discussed in Activity 4.5. If the value of a company's assets increases, the value of each share should rise and, in time, could increase to a level that makes the shares less marketable. Splitting would solve this problem. Consolidating is relatively rare.

**Real World 4.8** provides an example of a share split by one business.

---

### Real World 4.8

#### Doing the splits

Premier Oil plc, the oil and gas exploration and production business, had a share split in May 2011, as announced by the business in a letter to its shareholders:

> The share split will result in shareholders holding four new ordinary shares of 12.5 pence each in the company for each existing ordinary share they held immediately prior to the share split. In recent months the price of the company's ordinary shares of 50 pence each has risen substantially to the point where the closing mid-market price on 1 April 2011 was £20.06. The board believes that the share split may improve the liquidity of the market in the company's shares and reduce the bid/offer spread of the company's shares.

*Source*: Premier Oil plc, Letter from the chairman, 15 April 2011, www.premier-oil.com.

---

### Preference shares

Some companies issue other classes of shares in addition to ordinary shares, **preference shares** being the most common. Preference shares guarantee that *if a dividend is paid*, the preference shareholders will be entitled to the first part of it up to a maximum value. This maximum is normally defined as a fixed percentage of the nominal value of the preference shares. If, for example, a company issues one million preference shares of £1 each with a dividend rate of 6 per cent, this means that the preference shareholders are entitled to receive the first £60,000 (that is, 6 per cent of £1 million) of any dividend that is paid by the company for a particular year. The excess over £60,000 goes to the ordinary shareholders. Normally, any undistributed profits and gains also accrue to the ordinary shareholders.

The ordinary shareholders are the primary risk-takers as they are entitled to share in the profits of the company only after other claims have been satisfied. There are no upper limits, however, on the amount by which they may benefit. The potential rewards available to ordinary shareholders reflect the risks that they are prepared to take. Since ordinary shareholders take most of the risks, power normally resides in their hands. Usually, only the ordinary shareholders are able to vote on issues that affect the company, such as who the directors should be.

It is open to the company to issue shares of various classes – perhaps with some having unusual and exotic conditions – but in practice it is rare to find other than straightforward ordinary and preference shares. Even preference shares are not too common. Although a company may have different classes of shares whose holders have different rights, within each class, all shares must be treated equally. The rights of the various classes of shareholders, as well as other matters relating to a particular company, are contained in that company's set of rules, known as the 'articles and memorandum of association'. A copy of these rules must be lodged with the Registrar of Companies, who makes it available for inspection by the general public.

## Reserves

As we have already seen, reserves are profits and gains that a company has made and which still form part of the shareholders' equity. One reason that past profits and gains may not continue to be part of equity is that they have been paid out to shareholders (as dividends and so on). Another reason is that reserves will be reduced by the amount of any losses that the company might suffer. In the same way that profits increase equity, losses reduce it. The shareholders' equity consists of share capital and reserves.

### Activity 4.6

**Are reserves amounts of cash? Can you think of a reason why this is an odd question?**

To deal with the second point first, it is an odd question because reserves are a claim, or part of one, on the assets of the company, whereas cash is an asset. So reserves cannot be cash.

Reserves are classified as either revenue reserves or **capital reserves**. In Example 4.1 we came across a revenue reserve. We should recall that this reserve represents the company's retained trading profits and gains on the disposal of non-current assets. It is worth mentioning that retained earnings, as they are most often called, represent overwhelmingly the largest source of new finance for UK companies. For most companies they amount to more than share issues and borrowings combined.

Capital reserves arise for two main reasons:

● issuing shares at above their nominal value (for example, issuing £1 shares at £1.50);
● revaluing (upwards) non-current assets.

Where a company issues shares at above their nominal value, UK law requires that the excess of the issue price over the nominal value be shown separately.

## Activity 4.7

Can you think why shares might be issued at above their nominal value? (*Hint*: This would not usually happen when a company is first formed and the initial shares are being issued.)

Once a company has traded and has been successful, the shares would normally be worth more than the nominal value at which they were issued. If additional shares are to be issued to new shareholders to raise finance for further expansion, unless they are issued at a value higher than the nominal value, the new shareholders will be gaining at the expense of the original ones.

Example 4.2 shows how this works.

## Example 4.2

Based on future prospects, the net assets of a company are worth £1.5 million. There are currently 1 million ordinary shares in the company, each with a nominal value of £1. The company wishes to raise an additional £0.6 million of cash for expansion and has decided to raise it by issuing new shares. If the shares are issued for £1 each (that is 600,000 shares), the total number of shares will be:

$$1.0m + 0.6m = 1.6m$$

and their total value will be the value of the existing net assets plus the new injection of cash:

$$£1.5m + £0.6m = £2.1m.$$

This means that the value of each share after the new issue will be

$$£2.1m/1.6m = £1.3125.$$

The current value of each share is

$$£1.5m/1.0m = £1.50$$

so the original shareholders will lose

$$£1.50 - £1.3125 = £0.1875 \text{ a share}$$

and the new shareholders will gain

$$£1.3125 - £1.0 = £0.3125 \text{ a share}.$$

The new shareholders will, no doubt, be delighted with this outcome; the original ones will not.

Things could be made fair between the two sets of shareholders described in Example 4.2 by issuing the new shares at £1.50 each. In this case it would be necessary to issue 400,000 shares to raise the necessary £0.6 million. £1 a share of the £1.50 is the nominal value and will be included with share capital in the statement of financial position (£400,000 in total). The remaining £0.50 is a share premium, which will be shown as a capital reserve known as the **share premium account** (£200,000 in total).

It is not clear why UK company law insists on the distinction between nominal share values and the premium. In some other countries (for example, the United States) with similar laws governing the corporate sector, there is not the necessity of distinguishing between share capital and share premium. Instead, the total value at which shares are issued is shown as one comprehensive figure on the company's statement of financial position.

**Real World 4.9** shows the equity of one very well-known business.

---

### Real World 4.9

#### Flying funds

Ryanair Holdings plc, the no-frills airline, had the following share capital and reserves as at 31 March 2011:

|  | € million |
|---|---|
| Share capital (10p ordinary shares) | 9.5 |
| Share premium | 659.3 |
| Retained earnings | 1,967.6 |
| Other reserves | 317.5 |
| Total equity | 2,953.9 |

Note how the nominal share capital figure is only a small fraction of the share premium account figure. This implies that Ryanair has issued shares at much higher prices than the 10p a share nominal value. This reflects its trading success since the company was first formed. In 2011, retained earnings (profits) made up two-thirds of the total for share capital and reserves.

*Source*: Ryanair Holdings plc, Annual Report 2011, p. 128.

---

### Bonus shares

It is always open to a company to take reserves of any kind (irrespective of whether they are capital or revenue) and turn them into share capital. This will involve transferring the desired amount from the reserve concerned to share capital and then distributing the appropriate number of new shares to the existing shareholders. New shares arising from such a conversion are known as **bonus shares**. Issues of bonus shares used to be quite frequently encountered in practice, but more recently they are much less common. Example 4.3 illustrates this aspect of share issues.

### Example 4.3

The summary statement of financial position of a company at a particular point in time is as follows:

**Statement of financial position**

| | £ |
|---|---|
| Net assets (various assets less liabilities) | 128,000 |
| **Equity** | |
| Share capital | |
| 50,000 shares of £1 each | 50,000 |
| Reserves | 78,000 |
| **Total equity** | 128,000 |

The directors decide that the company will issue existing shareholders with one new share for every share currently owned by each shareholder. The statement of financial position immediately following this will appear as follows:

**Statement of financial position**

| | £ |
|---|---|
| Net assets (various assets less liabilities) | 128,000 |
| **Equity** | |
| Share capital | |
| 100,000 shares of £1 each (50,000 + 50,000) | 100,000 |
| Reserves (78,000 − 50,000) | 28,000 |
| **Total equity** | 128,000 |

We can see that the reserves have decreased by £50,000 and share capital has increased by the same amount. Share certificates for the 50,000 ordinary shares of £1 each, which have been created from reserves, will be issued to the existing shareholders to complete the transaction.

### Activity 4.8

A shareholder of the company in Example 4.3 owned 100 shares before the bonus issue. How will things change for this shareholder as regards the number of shares owned and the value of the shareholding?

The answer should be that the number of shares would double, from 100 to 200. Now the shareholder owns one five-hundredth of the company (that is, 200/100,000). Before the bonus issue, the shareholder also owned one five-hundredth of the company (that is, 100/50,000). The company's assets and liabilities have not changed as a result of the bonus issue and so, logically, one five-hundredth of the value of the company should be identical to what it was before. Thus, each share is worth half as much as it used to be.

A bonus issue simply takes one part of the equity (a reserve) and puts it into another part (share capital). The transaction has no effect on the company's assets or liabilities, so there is no effect on shareholders' wealth.

Note that a bonus issue is not the same as a share split. A split does not affect the reserves.

---

### Activity 4.9

Can you think of any reasons why a company might want to make a bonus issue if it has no economic consequence?

We think that there are three possible reasons:

- *Share price*. To lower the value of each share without reducing the shareholders' collective or individual wealth. This has a similar effect to share splitting.
- *Shareholder confidence*. To provide the shareholders with a 'feel-good factor'. It is believed that shareholders like bonus issues because they seem to make them better off, although in practice they should not affect their wealth.
- *Lender confidence*. Where reserves arising from operating profits and/or realised gains on the sale of non-current assets (revenue reserves) are used to make the bonus issue, it has the effect of taking part of that portion of the shareholders' equity that could be withdrawn by the shareholders, and locking it up. The amount transferred becomes part of the permanent equity base of the company. (We shall see a little later in this chapter that there are severe restrictions on the extent to which shareholders may make drawings from their equity.) An individual or business contemplating lending money to the company may insist that the extent that shareholders can withdraw their funds is restricted as a condition of making the loan. This point will be explained shortly.

---

**Real World 4.10** provides an example of a bonus share issue.

---

### Real World 4.10

## It's a bonus?

Medusa Mining is a gold producer that is listed on various international stock markets. In 2010, it announced a one-for-ten bonus issue of shares to all shareholders of the company.

In a statement, the company said it had achieved several significant milestones in the last calendar year and the bonus issue was in recognition of the invaluable support the company has received from its shareholders. The bonus issue was also designed to encourage greater liquidity in Medusa shares.

Geoff Davis, managing director of Medusa, said:

> The board is extremely pleased to be in a position to reward shareholders as a result of the company having rapidly expanded its production over the last 12 months and having met all targets on time.

*Source*: Adapted from 'Medusa Mining,' www.proactiveinvestors co.uk, 8 March 2010.

---

## Share capital jargon

Before leaving our detailed discussion of share capital, it might be helpful to clarify some of the jargon relating to shares that is used in company financial statements.

Share capital that has been issued to shareholders is known as the **issued share capital** (or **allotted share capital**). Sometimes, but not very often, a company may not require shareholders to pay the whole amount that is due to be paid for the shares at the time of issue. This may happen where the company does not need the money all at once. Some money would normally be paid at the time of issue and the company would 'call' for further instalments until the shares were **fully paid shares**. That part of the total issue price that has been called is known as the **called-up share capital**. That part that has been called and paid is known as the **paid-up share capital**.

## Raising share capital

Once the company has made its initial share issue to start business (usually soon after the company is first formed) it may decide to raise additional funds by making further issues of new shares. These may be:

- *Rights issues* – issues made to existing shareholders, in proportion to their existing shareholding.
- *Public issues* – issues made to the general investing public.
- *Private placings* – issues made to selected individuals who are usually approached and asked if they would be interested in taking up new shares.

During its lifetime a company may use all three of these approaches to raising funds through issuing new shares (although only public companies can make appeals to the general public).

These approaches will be discussed in detail in Chapter 15.

## Borrowings

Most companies borrow money to supplement that raised from share issues and ploughed-back profits. Company borrowing is often on a long-term basis, perhaps on a ten-year contract. Lenders may be banks and other professional providers of loan finance. Many companies borrow in such a way that small investors, including private individuals, are able to lend small amounts. This is particularly the case with the larger, Stock Exchange listed, companies and involves them making an issue of **loan notes**, which, though large in total, can be taken up in small slices by individual investors, both private individuals and investing institutions such as pension funds and insurance companies. In some cases, these slices of loans can be bought and sold through the Stock Exchange. This means that investors do not have to wait the full term of their loan to obtain repayment, but can sell their slice of it to another would-be lender at intermediate points in the term of the loan. Loan notes are often known as *loan stock* or *debentures*.

Some of the features of financing by loan notes, particularly the possibility that the loan notes may be traded on the Stock Exchange, can lead to confusing loan notes with shares. We should be clear that shares and loan notes are not the same thing. It is the shareholders who own the company and, therefore, who share in its losses and profits. Holders of loan notes lend money to the company under a legally binding contract that normally specifies the rate of interest, the interest payment dates and the date of repayment of the loan itself.

Usually, long-term loans are secured on assets of the company. This would give the lender the right to seize the assets concerned, sell them and satisfy the repayment obligation, should the company fail to pay either its interest payments or the repayment of the loan itself, on the dates specified in the contract between the company and the lender. A mortgage granted to a private individual buying a house or a flat is a very common example of a secured loan.

Long-term financing of companies can be depicted as in Figure 4.4.

**Figure 4.4**    **Sources of long-term finance for a typical limited company**

Companies derive their long-term finance from three sources: new share issues, retained earnings and long-term borrowings. For a typical company, the sum of the first two (jointly known as 'equity finance') exceeds the third. Retained earnings usually exceed either of the other two in terms of the amount of finance raised in most years.

It is important to the prosperity and stability of a company that it strikes a suitable balance between finance provided by the shareholders (equity) and from borrowing. This topic will be explored in Chapter 7. Equity and loan notes are, of course, not the only forms of finance available to a company. In Chapter 15, we consider other sources of finance available to businesses.

**Real World 4.11** shows the long-term borrowings of Rolls-Royce plc, the engine-building business, at 31 December 2010.

### Real World 4.11

#### Borrowing at Rolls-Royce

The following extract from the annual financial statements of Rolls-Royce plc sets out the sources of the company's long-term borrowings (non-current liabilities) as at 31 December 2010.

|  | £m |
|---|---|
| **Unsecured** | |
| Bank loans | 206 |
| $7\frac{3}{8}$% Notes 2016 | 200 |
| 6.38% Notes 2013 | 162 |
| 6.55% Notes 2015 | 60 |
| 6.75% Notes 2019 | 506 |
| **Secured** | |
| Obligations under finance leases payable after five years | 1 |
| | 1,135 |

*Source*: Rolls-Royce plc Annual Report and Accounts 2010, note 14.

Note the large number of sources of the company borrowings. This is typical of most large companies and probably reflects a desire to exploit all available means of raising finance, each of which may have some advantages and disadvantages. 'Secured' in this context means that the lender would have the right, should Rolls-Royce fail to meet its interest and/or capital repayment obligations, to seize a specified asset of the business (probably some land) and use it to raise the sums involved. Normally, a lender would accept a lower rate of interest where the loan is secured as there is less risk involved. It should be said that whether a loan to a company like Rolls-Royce is secured or unsecured is usually pretty academic. It is unlikely that such a large and profitable company would fail to meet its obligations.

'Finance leases' are, in effect, arrangements where a business needs the use of a non-current asset (such as an item of machinery) and, instead of buying the asset itself, it arranges for a financier to buy the asset. The financier then leases it to the business, probably for the entire economic life of the asset. Though legally it is the financier who owns the asset, from an accounting point of view the essence of the arrangement is that, in effect, the business has borrowed cash from the financier to buy the asset. Thus, the asset appears among the business's non-current assets and the financial obligation to the financier is shown here as long-term borrowing. This is a good example of how accounting tries to report the economic *substance* of a transaction, rather than its strict legal *form*. Finance leasing is a fairly popular means of raising long-term funds.

Chapter 15 considers in some detail the factors that a business must consider when deciding how to finance its operations.

## Withdrawing equity

Companies, as we have seen, are legally obliged to distinguish, on the statement of financial position, between that part of the shareholders' equity that may be withdrawn and that part which may not. The withdrawable part consists of profits arising from trading and from the disposal of non-current assets. It is represented in the statement of financial position by *revenue reserves*. The company paying dividends to all of its shareholders is the most usual way of enabling shareholders to withdraw part of their equity. An alternative, is for the company to buy its own shares from those of its shareholders who may wish to sell them. This is usually known as a 'share repurchase'. The company would then usually cancel the shares concerned. Share repurchases usually involve only a small proportion of the shareholders, unlike a dividend which involves them all.

It is important to appreciate that the total of revenue reserves appearing in the statement of financial position is rarely the total of all trading profits and profits on disposals of non-current assets generated by the company. This total will normally have been reduced by at least one of the following three factors:

● corporation tax paid on those profits
● any dividends paid or amounts paid to purchase the company's own shares
● any losses from trading and the disposal of non-current assets.

The non-withdrawable part consists of share capital plus profits arising from shareholders buying shares in the company and from upward revaluations of assets still held. It is represented in the statement of financial position by *share capital* and *capital reserves*.

Figure 4.5 shows the important division between the part of the shareholders' equity that can be withdrawn and the part that cannot.

| Figure 4.5 | Availability for withdrawal of various parts of the shareholders' equity |

Total equity finance of limited companies consists of share capital, capital reserves and revenue reserves. Only the revenue reserves (which arise from realised profits and gains) can be used to fund a dividend or a share repurchase. In other words, the maximum legal withdrawal is the amount of the revenue reserves.

The law does not specify how large the non-withdrawable part of a particular company's shareholders' equity should be. However, when seeking to impress prospective lenders and credit suppliers, the larger this part, the better. Those considering doing business with the company must be able to see from the company's statement of financial position how large it is.

**Activity (4.10)**

Why are limited companies required to distinguish different parts of their shareholders' equity, whereas sole proprietorship and partnership businesses are not?

The reason stems from the limited liability that company shareholders enjoy but which owners of unincorporated businesses do not. If a sole proprietor or partner withdraws all of the equity, or even an amount in excess of this, the position of the lenders and credit suppliers of the business is not weakened since they can legally enforce their claims against the sole proprietor or partner as an individual. With a limited company, the business and the owners are legally separated and such a right to enforce claims against individuals does not exist. To protect the company's lenders and credit suppliers, however, the law insists that the shareholders cannot normally withdraw a specific part of their equity.

Let us now look at an example that illustrates how this protection of creditors works.

**Example 4.4**

The summary statement of financial position of a company at a particular date is as follows:

**Statement of financial position**

|  | £ |
|---|---|
| Total assets | 43,000 |
| **Equity** | |
| Share capital | |
| 20,000 shares of £1 each | 20,000 |
| Reserves (revenue) | 23,000 |
| **Total equity** | 43,000 |

A bank has been asked to make a £25,000 long-term loan to the company. If the loan were to be made, the statement of financial position immediately following would appear as follows:

**Statement of financial position (after the loan)**

|  | £ |
|---|---|
| Total assets (£43,000 + £25,000) | 68,000 |
| **Equity** | |
| Share capital | |
| 20,000 shares of £1 each | 20,000 |
| Reserves (revenue) | 23,000 |
|  | 43,000 |
| **Non-current liability** | |
| Borrowings – loan | 25,000 |
| **Total equity and liabilities** | 68,000 |

As things stand, there are assets with a total carrying amount of £68,000 to meet the bank's claim of £25,000. It would be possible and perfectly legal, however, for the shareholders to withdraw part of their equity (through a dividend or share repurchase) by an amount equal to the total revenue reserves (£23,000). The statement of financial position would then appear as follows:

**Statement of financial position**

|  | £ |
|---|---|
| Total assets (£68,000 – £23,000) | 45,000 |
| **Equity** | |
| Share capital | |
| 20,000 shares of £1 each | 20,000 |
| Reserves [revenue (£23,000 – £23,000)] | – |
|  | 20,000 |
| **Non-current liabilities** | |
| Borrowings – bank loan | 25,000 |
| **Total equity and liabilities** | 45,000 |

This leaves the bank in a very much weaker position, in that there are now total assets with a carrying amount of £45,000 to meet a claim of £25,000. Note that the difference between the amount of the borrowings (bank loan) and the total assets equals the equity (share capital and reserves) total. Thus, the equity represents a margin of safety for lenders and suppliers. The larger the amount of the equity withdrawable by the shareholders, the smaller is the potential margin of safety for lenders and suppliers.

As we have already seen, it is up to each company to decide what margin of safety is appropriate.

As a practical footnote to Example 4.4, it is worth pointing out that long-term lenders would normally seek to secure a loan against an asset of the company, such as land.

### Activity (4.11)

Would you expect a company to pay all of its revenue reserves as a dividend? What factors might be involved with a dividend decision?

It would be rare for a company to pay all of its revenue reserves as a dividend: the fact that it is legally possible does not necessarily make it a good idea. Most companies see ploughed-back profits as a major – usually *the* major – source of new finance. The factors that tend most to influence the dividend decision are likely to include:

● the availability of cash to pay a dividend: it would not be illegal to borrow to pay a dividend, but it would be unusual, and possibly imprudent;
● the needs of the business for finance for new investment;
● the expectations of shareholders concerning the amount of dividends to be paid.

You may have thought of others.

If we look back at Real World 4.9 (page 145), we can see that at 31 March 2011, Ryanair could legally have paid a dividend totalling €1,967.6 million. The company did not do this, presumably because the funds were reinvested in the business.

### Activity (4.12)

Can you remember the circumstances in which the non-withdrawable part of a company's capital could be reduced, without contravening the law? This was mentioned earlier in the chapter.

It can be reduced as a result of the company sustaining trading losses, or losses on disposal of non-current assets, which exceed the withdrawable amount of shareholders' equity. It cannot legally be reduced by shareholders making withdrawals.

## The main financial statements

As we might expect, the financial statements of a limited company are, in essence, the same as those of a sole proprietor or partnership. There are, however, some differences of detail. We shall now consider these. Example 4.5 sets out the income statement and statement of financial position of a limited company.

### Example 4.5

**Da Silva plc**
**Income statement for the year ended 31 December 2011**

|                          | £m     |
|--------------------------|--------|
| Revenue                  | 840    |
| Cost of sales            | (520)  |
| Gross profit             | 320    |
| Wages and salaries       | (98)   |
| Heat and light           | (18)   |
| Rent and rates           | (24)   |
| Motor vehicle expenses   | (20)   |
| Insurance                | (4)    |
| Printing and stationery  | (12)   |
| Depreciation             | (45)   |
| Audit fee                | (4)    |
| Operating profit         | 95     |
| Interest payable         | (10)   |
| Profit before taxation   | 85     |
| Taxation                 | (24)   |
| Profit for the year      | 61     |

**Statement of financial position as at 31 December 2011**

|                                 | £m   |
|---------------------------------|------|
| **ASSETS**                      |      |
| **Non-current assets**          |      |
| Property, plant and equipment   | 203  |
| Intangible assets               | 100  |
|                                 | 303  |
| **Current assets**              |      |
| Inventories                     | 65   |
| Trade receivables               | 112  |
| Cash                            | 36   |
|                                 | 213  |
| **Total assets**                | 516  |
| **EQUITY AND LIABILITIES**      |      |
| **Equity**                      |      |
| Ordinary shares of £0.50 each   | 200  |
| Share premium account           | 30   |
| Other reserves                  | 50   |
| Retained earnings               | 25   |
|                                 | 305  |
| **Non-current liabilities**     |      |
| Borrowings                      | 100  |
| **Current liabilities**         |      |
| Trade payables                  | 99   |
| Taxation                        | 12   |
|                                 | 111  |
| **Total equity and liabilities**| 516  |

Let us now go through these statements and pick up those aspects that are unique to limited companies.

## The income statement

The main points for consideration in the income statement are as follows:

### Profit

We can see that, following the calculation of operating profit, two further measures of profit are shown.

- The first of these is the **profit before taxation**. Interest charges are deducted from the operating profit to derive this figure. In the case of a sole proprietor or partnership business, the income statement would end here.
- The second measure of profit is the *profit for the period* (usually a year). As the company is a separate legal entity, it is liable to pay tax (known as corporation tax) on the profits generated. (This contrasts with the sole-proprietor business where it is the owner rather than the business that is liable for the tax on profits, as we saw earlier in the chapter.) This measure of profit represents the amount that is available for the shareholders.

### Audit fee

Companies beyond a certain size are required to have their financial statements audited by an independent firm of accountants, for which a fee is charged. As we shall see in Chapter 5, the purpose of the audit is to lend credibility to the financial statements. Although it is also open to sole proprietorships and partnerships to have their financial statements audited, relatively few do, so this is an expense that is most often seen in the income statement of a company.

Figure 4.6 shows an outline of the income statement for a limited company.

## The statement of financial position

The main points for consideration in the statement of financial position are as follows:

### Taxation

The amount that appears as part of the current liabilities represents 50 per cent of the tax on the profit for the year 2011. It is, therefore, 50 per cent (£12 million) of the charge that appears in the income statement (£24 million); the other 50 per cent (£12 million) will already have been paid. The unpaid 50 per cent will be paid shortly after the statement of financial position date. These payment dates are set down by law.

### Other reserves

This will include any reserves that are not separately identified on the face of the statement of financial position. It may include a *general reserve*, which normally consists of trading profits that have been transferred to this separate reserve for reinvestment ('ploughing back') into the operations of the company. It is not at all necessary to set up a separate reserve for this purpose. The trading profits could remain unallocated and still swell the retained earnings of the company. It is not entirely clear why directors decide to make transfers to general reserves, since the profits concerned remain part of

**Figure 4.6** The layout of the income statement for a limited company

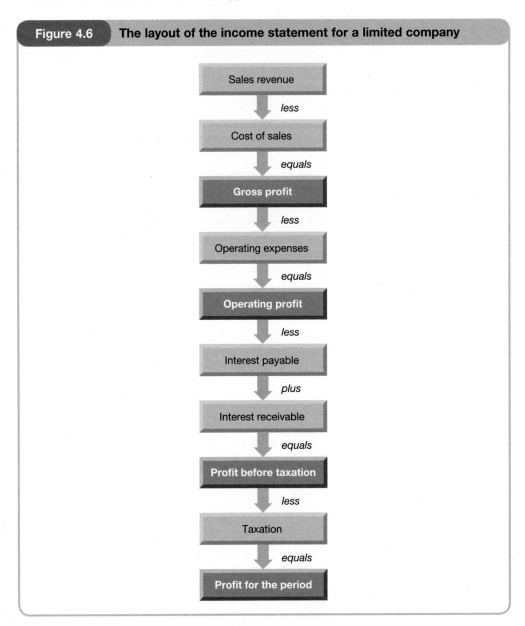

the revenue reserves, and as such they still remain available for dividend. The most plausible explanation seems to be that directors feel that placing profits in a separate reserve indicates an intention to invest the funds, represented by the reserve, permanently in the company and, therefore, not to use them to pay a dividend or to fund a share repurchase. Of course, the retained earnings appearing on the statement of financial position are also a reserve, but that fact is not indicated in its title.

## Dividends

We have already seen that dividends represent drawings by the shareholders of the company. Dividends are paid out of the revenue reserves and should be deducted from these reserves (usually retained earnings) when preparing the statement of financial position. Shareholders are often paid an annual dividend, perhaps in two parts. An 'interim' dividend may be paid part way through the year and a 'final' dividend shortly after the year end.

Dividends declared by the directors during the year but still unpaid at the year end *may* appear as a liability in the statement of financial position. To be recognised as a liability, however, they must be properly authorised before the year-end date. This normally means that the shareholders must approve the dividend.

Large companies tend to have a clear and consistent policy towards the payment of dividends. Any change in the policy provokes considerable interest and is usually interpreted by shareholders as a signal of the directors' views concerning the future. For example, an increase in dividends may be taken as a signal from the directors that future prospects are bright: a higher dividend is seen as tangible evidence of their confidence.

**Real World 4.12** provides an example of one well-known business that paid a dividend after more than twenty years of trading.

### Real World 4.12

### At last!

Groupe Eurotunnel is to pay a dividend for the first time in its two-decade history, in spite of falls in revenue from a weakening pound and last September's serious fire. However, Jacques Gounon, Eurotunnel executive chairman, warned it would take 12 to 18 months for Channel Tunnel traffic to return to levels before the fire which broke out on a truck shuttle on 11 September.

Eurotunnel will propose a dividend of €0.04 per share after declaring net profits of €40m ($50m) for the year. The figure includes a €24m arbitration award over the costs to Eurotunnel of disorder at the Sangatte detention centre, near the tunnel's French entrance, which disrupted services and forced the company to improve security. The result marks only the company's second net profit, after it made €1m, excluding the effects of a major restructuring, for 2007. Mr Gounon said the company was at a turning point: 'A clear net profit plus dividend 18 months after the restructuring is something which is not too bad'.

Eurotunnel suffered serious financial problems between its formation in 1985 and 2007, thanks to cost and time over-runs in the construction of the 50km tunnel and consistently disappointing traffic levels. Eurotunnel's 1m private shareholders, nearly all of whom are French, have long agitated for dividends.

*Source*: From Wright, R., Eurotunnel to pay maiden dividend, ft.com, 5 March 2009.

## Accounting for groups of companies

Most large businesses, including nearly all of the well-known ones, operate not as a single company but as a group of companies. In these circumstances, one company (the **parent** or **holding company**) is able to control various subsidiary companies, normally as a result of owning more than 50 per cent of their shares. Many larger businesses have numerous subsidiary companies, with each subsidiary operating some aspect of the group's activities. The reasons why many businesses operate in the form of groups include:

- a desire for each part of the business to have its own limited liability, so that financial problems in one part of a business cannot have an adverse effect on other parts;
- an attempt to make each part of the business have some sense of independence and autonomy and, perhaps, to create or perpetuate a market image of a smaller independent business.

Each company within a group will prepare its own independent annual financial statements. The law also requires, however, that the parent company prepares **consolidated** or **group financial statements**. These group financial statements amalgamate the financial statements of all of the group members. Thus, the group income statement includes the total revenue figure for all group companies, the statement of financial position includes the property, plant and equipment for all group companies, and so on. This means that the group financial statements will look like the financial statements of the parent company, had it owned and operated all of the assets of the business directly, instead of through subsidiary companies.

In view of what we have just seen, it may not be possible to detect whether the business operates through a single company or through a large number of subsidiaries, simply by looking at a set of group financial statements. Only by referring to the heading at the top of each statement, which should mention the word 'consolidated' or 'group', might we find this out. In many cases, however, one or two items will be reported that are peculiar to group financial statements. These items are:

- *Goodwill arising on consolidation.* This occurs when a parent acquires a subsidiary from previous owners and pays more for the subsidiary than the subsidiary's individual assets (net of liabilities) appear to be worth. This excess may represent such things as the value of a good reputation that the new subsidiary already has in the market, or the value of its having a loyal and skilled workforce. Goodwill arising on consolidation will appear as an intangible non-current asset on the group statement of financial position.
- *Non-controlling interests (NCI).* One of the principles followed when preparing group financial statements is that all of the revenue, expenses, assets, liabilities and cash flows of each subsidiary are reflected to their full extent in the group financial statements. This is true whether or not the parent owns all of the shares in each subsidiary, provided that the parent has control. Control normally means owning more than 50 per cent of the subsidiary's ordinary shares. Where not all of the shares are owned by the parent, the investment of those shareholders in the subsidiary, other than the parent company, appears as part of the shareholders' equity in the group statement of financial position. This shows that, although the net assets of the group are being financed mainly by the parent company's shareholders, 'outside' shareholders also finance a part. Similarly, the group income statement reflects the fact that not all of the profit of the group is attributable to the shareholders of the parent company; a part of it is attributable to the 'outside' shareholders. The interests, or claims, of outside shareholders are known as **non-controlling interests** (formerly known as *minority interests*).

Example 4.6 shows how the statement of financial position of Major plc and its subsidiary is drawn up. Note that the group statement of financial position closely resembles that of an individual company.

**Example 4.6**

Major plc has just bought, from the previous shareholders, 45 million (out of 60 million) ordinary shares in Minor plc, paying £75 million for them. The remaining 15 million Minor plc shares are owned by other shareholders. These shareholders are now referred to by Major plc as the non-controlling interests. Minor plc is now a subsidiary of Major plc and, as is clear from Major plc's statement of financial position, its only subsidiary company.

The statements of financial position of the two companies immediately following the **takeover** (that is, the acquisition of control) of Minor plc by Major plc were as follows:

**Statements of financial position**

|  | Major plc £m | Minor plc £m |
|---|---|---|
| ASSETS | | |
| Non-current assets | | |
| Property, plant and equipment | 63 | 67 |
| Intangible – 45 million shares in Minor plc | 75 | – |
|  | 138 | 67 |
| Current assets | | |
| Inventories | 37 | 21 |
| Trade receivables | 22 | 12 |
| Cash | 16 | 2 |
|  | 75 | 35 |
| Total assets | 213 | 102 |
| EQUITY AND LIABILITIES | | |
| Equity | | |
| Ordinary shares of £1 each | 100 | 60 |
| Reserves | 60 | 20 |
|  | 160 | 80 |
| Non-current liabilities | | |
| Borrowings – Loan notes | 35 | 13 |
| Current liabilities | | |
| Trade payables | 18 | 9 |
| Total equity and liabilities | 213 | 102 |

As would be normal practice, the statement of financial position of the subsidiary (Minor plc) has been revised so that the values of the individual assets are based on *fair values*, rather than what Minor plc originally paid for them. Fair values are those that would be agreed as the selling price between a buyer and a seller, both of whom are knowledgeable and willing. In this context, they probably equate to the values that Major plc would have placed on the individual tangible assets when assessing Minor plc's value.

If a statement of financial position for the group were to be drawn up immediately following the takeover, it would be as follows:

→

### Statements of financial position of Major plc and its subsidiary

|  | £m |
|---|---:|
| **ASSETS** | |
| **Non-current assets** | |
| Property, plant and equipment (63 + 67) | 130 |
| Intangible – Goodwill [75 – ($^{45}/_{60}$ × 80)] | 15 |
|  | 145 |
| **Current assets** | |
| Inventories (37 + 21) | 58 |
| Trade receivables (22 + 12) | 34 |
| Cash (16 + 2) | 18 |
|  | 110 |
| **Total assets** | 255 |
| **EQUITY AND LIABILITIES** | |
| **Equity** | |
| Ordinary shares of £1 each | 100 |
| Reserves | 60 |
| Equity attributable to equity holders of the parent | 160 |
| Non-controlling interests ($^{15}/_{60}$ × 80) | 20 |
| Total equity | 180 |
| **Non-current liabilities** | |
| Borrowings – Loan notes (35 + 13) | 48 |
| **Current liabilities** | |
| Trade payables (18 + 9) | 27 |
| **Total equity and liabilities** | 255 |

Note that all of the items, except two, in the group statement of financial position are simply the figures, for the item concerned, in each of the two statements, added together. This is despite the fact that Major plc owns only three-quarters of the shares of Minor plc. The logic of group financial statements is that if the parent owns enough shares to control its subsidiary, all of the subsidiary's assets and claims should be reflected on the group statement of financial position.

As we have seen, there are two exceptions to this approach: goodwill and non-controlling interests.

Goodwill is simply the excess of what Major paid for the shares over their fair value. Major plc bought 45 million of 60 million shares, paying £75 million. According to Minor plc's statement of financial position, there were net assets (non-current and current assets, less current and non-current liabilities) of £80 million. So Major plc paid £75 million for £60 million (that is, $^{45}/_{60}$ × £80 million) of net assets – an excess of £15 million usually referred to as 'goodwill arising on consolidation'. This asset is seen as being the value of a loyal workforce, a regular and profitable customer base and so on, that a new business setting up would not have. The relevant International Financial Reporting Standard (IFRS 3) demands that goodwill be reviewed at least annually: if its value has been impaired, it must be written down to the lower value.

The non-controlling interests (NCI) take account of the fact that, although Major plc may control all of the assets and liabilities of Minor plc, it only provides the equity finance for three-quarters of them. The other quarter, £20 million (that is, $^{15}/_{60}$ × £80 million), is still provided by shareholders in Minor plc, other than Major plc. (Note that IFRS 3 allows an alternative method of calculating goodwill on consolidation and NCI for reporting purpose, but this is beyond the scope of this chapter.)

Example 4.7 shows the income statement of Major plc and its subsidiary (Minor plc) for the first year following the takeover. As with the statement of financial position, the various revenue and expense figures are simply the individual figures for each company added together. The non-controlling interests figure (£2 million) represents $^{15}/_{60} \times$ the after-tax profit of Minor plc, which is assumed to be £8 million.

### Example 4.7

**Income statement for the first year**

|  | £m |
|---|---|
| Revenue | 123 |
| Cost of sales | (56) |
| **Gross profit** | 67 |
| Administration expenses | (28) |
| Distribution expenses | (9) |
| Profit before tax | 30 |
| Taxation | (12) |
| **Profit for the year** | 18 |
| Attributable to: |  |
| Equity holders of the parent | 16 |
| Non-controlling interests | 2 |
|  | 18 |

### Self-assessment question 4.1

The summarised statement of financial position of Dev Ltd at a particular point in time is as follows:

**Statement of financial position**

|  | £ |
|---|---|
| Net assets (various assets less liabilities) | 235,000 |
| **Equity** |  |
| Share capital: 100,000 shares of £1 each | 100,000 |
| Share premium account | 30,000 |
| Revaluation reserve | 37,000 |
| Retained earnings | 68,000 |
| **Total equity** | 235,000 |

*Required*:

(a) Without any other transactions occurring at the same time, the company made a one-for-five rights share issue at £2 per share payable in cash. This means that each shareholder was offered one share for every five already held. All shareholders took up their rights. Immediately afterwards, the company made a one-for-two bonus issue. Show the statement of financial position immediately following the bonus issue, assuming that the directors wanted to retain the maximum dividend payment potential for the future.

**Self-assessment question 4.1 (*continued*)**

(b) Explain what external influence might cause the directors to choose not to retain the maximum dividend payment possibilities.

(c) Show the statement of financial position immediately following the bonus issue, assuming that the directors wanted to retain the *minimum* dividend payment potential for the future.

(d) What is the maximum dividend that could be paid before and after the events described in (a) if the minimum dividend payment potential is achieved?

(e) Lee owns 100 shares in Dev Ltd before the events described in (a). Assuming that the net assets of the company have a value equal to their carrying amount on the statement of financial position, show how these events will affect Lee's wealth.

(f) Looking at the original statement of financial position of Dev Ltd, shown above, what four things do we know about the company's status and history that are not specifically stated on the statement of financial position?

The solution to this question can be found at the back of the book on pages 730 to 731.

## Summary

The main points of this chapter may be summarised as follows:

**Main features of a limited company**

- It is an artificial person that has been created by law.

- It has a separate life to its owners and is granted a perpetual existence.

- It must take responsibility for its own debts and losses but its owners are granted limited liability.

- A public company can offer its shares for sale to the public; a private company cannot.

- It is governed by a board of directors, which is elected by the shareholders.

- Corporate governance is a major issue; various scandals have led to the emergence of the UK Corporate Governance Code.

**Financing the limited company**

- The share capital of a company can be of two main types: ordinary shares and preference shares.

- Holders of ordinary shares (equities) are the main risk-takers and are given voting rights; they form the backbone of the company.

- Holders of preference shares are given a right to a fixed dividend before ordinary shareholders receive a dividend.

- Reserves are profits and gains made by the company and form part of the ordinary shareholders' claim.

- Borrowings provide another major source of finance.

### Share issues

- Bonus shares are issued to existing shareholders when part of the reserves of the company is converted into share capital. No funds are raised.

- Rights issues give existing shareholders the right to buy new shares in proportion to their existing holding.

- Public issues are made direct to the general investing public.

- Private placings are share issues to particular investors.

- The shares of public companies may be bought and sold on a recognised Stock Exchange.

### Reserves

- Reserves are of two types: revenue reserves and capital reserves.

- Revenue reserves arise from trading profits and from realised profits on the sale of non-current assets.

- Capital reserves arise from the issue of shares above their nominal value or from the upward revaluation of non-current assets.

- Revenue reserves can be withdrawn as dividends by the shareholders whereas capital reserves normally cannot.

### Financial statements of limited companies

- The financial statements of limited companies are based on the same principles as those of sole proprietorship and partnership businesses. However, there are some differences in detail.

- The income statement has three measures of profit displayed after the gross profit figure: operating profit, profit before taxation and profit for the period (usually a year).

- The income statement also shows audit fees and tax on profits for the period.

- Any unpaid tax and unpaid, but authorised, dividends will appear in the statement of financial position as current liabilities.

- The share capital plus the reserves make up 'equity'.

### Groups of companies

- Parent companies are required to produce group financial statements incorporating the results of all companies controlled by the parent.

- A group statement of financial position is prepared by adding like items of assets and liabilities based on 'fair values' together, as if all of the trading is undertaken through the parent company.

- A 'goodwill arising on consolidation' figure often emerges in the group statement of financial position.

- Where the parent does not own all of the shares of each subsidiary, a non-controlling interests (NCI) figure will appear in the statement of financial position, representing the outside shareholders' investment.

- A group income statement is drawn up following similar logic to that applied to the group statement of financial position.

- The group income statement will contain a non-controlling interests figure if not all subsidiaries are fully owned by the parent, which represents the outside shareholders' share of the group profit.

# MyAccountingLab

Go to **www.myaccountinglab.com** to check your understanding of the chapter, create a personalised study plan, and maximise your revision time

## Key terms

limited liability  p. 129
public limited company  p. 129
private limited company  p. 131
corporation tax  p. 132
directors  p. 133
corporate governance  p. 133
UK Corporate Governance Code  p. 135
reserves  p. 140
nominal value  p. 140
par value  p. 140
revenue reserve  p. 141
dividend  p. 141
ordinary shares  p. 141
splitting  p. 142
consolidating  p. 142
preference shares  p. 142

capital reserves  p. 143
share premium account  p. 145
bonus shares  p. 145
issued share capital  p. 147
allotted share capital  p. 147
fully paid shares  p. 148
called-up share capital  p. 148
paid-up share capital  p. 148
loan notes  p. 148
profit before taxation  p. 155
parent/holding company  p. 157
consolidated/group financial statements  p. 158
group financial statements  p. 158
non-controlling interests (NCI)  p. 158
takeover  p. 159

## Reference

Business Sector Advisory Group on Corporate Governance, *Corporate Governance: Improving Competitiveness and Access to Capital in Global Markets*, OECD, 1998, p. 14.

## Further reading

If you would like to explore the topics covered in this chapter in more depth, we recommend the following books:

Elliott, B. and Elliott, J., *Financial Accounting and Reporting*, 15th edn, Financial Times Prentice Hall, 2012, chapters 9 and 12.

Financial Reporting Council, *UK Corporate Governance Code*, FRC 2010, available free at www.frc.org.uk

Melville, A., *International Financial reporting*, 3rd edn, Financial Times Prentice Hall, 2011, chapters 1 and 18.

Thomas, A. and Ward, A. M., *Introduction to Financial Accounting*, 6th edn, McGraw Hill, 2009, chapter 29.

## Review questions

**Solutions to these questions can be found at the back of the book on page 748.**

**4.1** How does the liability of a limited company differ from the liability of a real person, in respect of amounts owed to others?

**4.2** Some people are about to form a company, as a vehicle through which to run a new business. What are the advantages to them of forming a private limited company rather than a public one?

**4.3** What is a reserve? Distinguish between a revenue reserve and a capital reserve.

**4.4** What is a preference share? Compare the main features of a preference share with those of

(a) an ordinary share; and
(b) loan notes.

## Exercises

**Exercises 4.1 to 4.3 are basic level, 4.4 and 4.5 are intermediate level and 4.6 and 4.7 are advanced level. Exercises with coloured numbers have solutions at the back of the book, starting on page 764.**

**If you wish to try more exercises, visit the students' side of the Companion Website and MyAccountingLab.**

**4.1** Comment on the following quote:
Limited companies can set a limit on the amount of debts that they will meet. They tend to have reserves of cash, as well as share capital and they can use these reserves to pay dividends to the shareholders. Many companies have preference as well as ordinary shares. The preference shares give a guaranteed dividend. The shares of many companies can be bought and sold on the Stock Exchange. Shareholders selling their shares can represent a useful source of new finance to the company.

**4.2** Comment on the following quotes:

(a) 'Bonus shares increase the shareholders' wealth because, after the issue, they have more shares, but each one of the same nominal value as they had before.'
(b) 'By law, once shares have been issued at a particular nominal value, they must always be issued at that value in any future share issues.'
(c) 'By law, companies can pay as much as they like by way of dividends on their shares, provided that they have sufficient cash to do so.'
(d) 'Companies do not have to pay tax on their profits because the shareholders have to pay tax on their dividends.'

**4.3** Briefly explain each of the following expressions that you have seen in the financial statements of a limited company:

(a) dividend
(b) audit fee
(c) share premium account.

**4.4** Iqbal Ltd started trading on 1 January 2007. During the first five years of trading, the following occurred:

| Year ended 31 December | Trading profit/(loss) £ | Profit/(loss) on sale of non-current assets £ | Upward revaluation of non-current assets £ |
|---|---|---|---|
| 2007 | (15,000) | – | – |
| 2008 | 8,000 | – | 10,000 |
| 2009 | 15,000 | 5,000 | – |
| 2010 | 20,000 | (6,000) | – |
| 2011 | 22,000 | – | – |

*Required*:
Assume that the company paid the maximum legal dividend each year. Under normal circumstances, how much would each year's dividend be?

**4.5** Hudson plc's outline statement of financial position as at a particular date was as follows:

|  | £m |
|---|---|
| Net assets (assets less liabilities) | 72 |
| **Equity** | |
| £1 ordinary shares | 40 |
| General reserve | 32 |
| **Total equity** | 72 |

The directors made a one-for-four bonus issue, immediately followed by a one-for-four rights issue at a price of £1.80 per share.

*Required*:
Show the statement of financial position of Hudson plc immediately following the two share issues.

**4.6** The following is a draft set of simplified financial statements for Pear Limited for the year ended 30 September 2011.

**Income statement for the year ended 30 September 2011**

|  | £000 |
|---|---|
| Revenue | 1,456 |
| Cost of sales | (768) |
| Gross profit | 688 |
| Salaries | (220) |
| Depreciation | (249) |
| Other operating costs | (131) |
| Operating profit | 88 |
| Interest payable | (15) |
| Profit before taxation | 73 |
| Taxation at 30% | (22) |
| Profit for the year | 51 |

## Statement of financial position as at 30 September 2011

|  | £000 |
|---|---:|
| **ASSETS** | |
| **Non-current assets** | |
| *Property, plant and equipment* | |
| Cost | 1,570 |
| Depreciation | (690) |
|  | 880 |
| **Current assets** | |
| Inventories | 207 |
| Trade receivables | 182 |
| Cash at bank | 21 |
|  | 410 |
| **Total assets** | 1,290 |
| **EQUITY AND LIABILITIES** | |
| **Equity** | |
| Share capital | 300 |
| Share premium account | 300 |
| Retained earnings at beginning of year | 104 |
| Profit for year | 51 |
|  | 755 |
| **Non-current liabilities** | |
| Borrowings (10% loan notes repayable 2014) | 300 |
| **Current liabilities** | |
| Trade payables | 88 |
| Other payables | 20 |
| Taxation | 22 |
| Borrowings (bank overdraft) | 105 |
|  | 235 |
| **Total equity and liabilities** | 1,290 |

The following information is available:

1  Depreciation has not been charged on office equipment with a carrying amount of £100,000. This class of assets is depreciated at 12 per cent a year using the reducing-balance method.

2  A new machine was purchased, on credit, for £30,000 and delivered on 29 September 2011 but has not been included in the financial statements. (Ignore depreciation.)

3  A sales invoice to the value of £18,000 for September 2011 has been omitted from the financial statements. (The cost of sales figure is stated correctly.)

4  A dividend of £25,000 had been approved by the shareholders before 30 September 2011, but was unpaid at that date. This is not reflected in the financial statements.

5  The interest payable on the loan notes for the second half-year was not paid until 1 October 2011 and has not been included in the financial statements.

6  An allowance for trade receivables is to be made at the level of 2 per cent of trade receivables.

7  An invoice for electricity to the value of £2,000 for the quarter ended 30 September 2011 arrived on 4 October and has not been included in the financial statements.

8  The charge for taxation will have to be amended to take account of the above information. Make the simplifying assumption that tax is payable shortly after the end of the year, at the rate of 30 per cent of the profit before tax.

*Required*:

Prepare a revised set of financial statements for the year ended 30 September 2011 incorporating the additional information in 1 to 8 above. (Work to the nearest £1,000.)

**4.7** Rose Limited operates a small chain of retail shops that sell high-quality teas and coffees. Approximately half of sales are on credit. Abbreviated and unaudited financial statements are as follows:

### Rose Limited
### Income statement for the year ended 31 March 2011

|  | £000 |
|---|---|
| Revenue | 12,080 |
| Cost of sales | (6,282) |
| Gross profit | 5,798 |
| Labour costs | (2,658) |
| Depreciation | (625) |
| Other operating costs | (1,003) |
| Operating profit | 1,512 |
| Interest payable | (66) |
| Profit before taxation | 1,446 |
| Taxation | (434) |
| Profit for the year | 1,012 |

### Statement of financial position as at 31 March 2011

|  | £000 |
|---|---|
| **ASSETS** | |
| **Non-current assets** | 2,728 |
| **Current assets** | |
| Inventories | 1,583 |
| Trade receivables | 996 |
| Cash | 26 |
| | 2,605 |
| **Total assets** | 5,333 |
| **EQUITY AND LIABILITIES** | |
| **Equity** | |
| Share capital (50p shares, fully paid) | 750 |
| Share premium | 250 |
| Retained earnings | 1,468 |
| | 2,468 |
| **Non-current liabilities** | |
| Borrowings – secured loan notes (2014) | 300 |
| **Current liabilities** | |
| Trade payables | 1,118 |
| Other payables | 417 |
| Tax | 434 |
| Borrowings – overdraft | 596 |
| | 2,565 |
| **Total equity and liabilities** | 5,333 |

Since the unaudited financial statements for Rose Limited were prepared, the following information has become available:

1  An additional £74,000 of depreciation should have been charged on fixtures and fittings.
2  Invoices for credit sales on 31 March 2011 amounting to £34,000 have not been included; cost of sales is not affected.
3  Trade receivables totalling £21,000 are recognised as having gone bad, but they have not yet been written off.
4  Inventories which had been purchased for £2,000 have been damaged and are unsaleable. This is not reflected in the financial statements.
5  Fixtures and fittings to the value of £16,000 were delivered just before 31 March 2011, but these assets were not included in the financial statements and the purchase invoice had not been processed.
6  Wages for Saturday-only staff, amounting to £1,000, have not been paid for the final Saturday of the year. This is not reflected in the financial statements.
7  Tax is payable at 30 per cent of profit before taxation. Assume that it is payable shortly after the year end.

*Required*:

Prepare revised financial statements for Rose Limited for the year ended 31 March 2011, incorporating the information in 1 to 7 above. (Work to the nearest £1,000.)

CHAPTER 5

# Accounting for limited companies (2)

## Introduction

This chapter continues our examination of the financial statements of limited companies. We begin by identifying the legal responsibilities of directors and then go on to discuss the main sources of accounting rules governing published financial statements. Although a detailed consideration of these accounting rules is beyond the scope of this book, the key rules that shape the form and content of the published financial statements are discussed. We also consider the efforts made to ensure that these rules are underpinned by a coherent framework of principles.

The increasing complexity of business and the added demands for information by financial report users have led to the publication of a number of additional financial reports. This chapter considers two of these, namely the segmental financial report and the business review. Both reports aim to provide users with a more complete picture of financial performance and position.

Despite the proliferation of accounting rules and the increasing supply of financial information to users of financial reports, concerns have been expressed over the quality of some published reports. This chapter ends by considering some well-publicised accounting scandals and the problem of creative accounting.

## Learning outcomes

**When you have completed this chapter, you should be able to:**

- Describe the responsibilities of directors and auditors concerning the annual financial statements provided to shareholders and others.

- Discuss both the framework of regulation and the framework of principles that help to shape the form and content of annual financial statements.

- Prepare a statement of financial position, statement of comprehensive income and statement of changes in equity, in accordance with International Financial Reporting Standards.

- Explain the purpose of two additional reports, segmental reports and the business review, and describe their main features.

- Discuss the threat posed by creative accounting and describe the main methods used to distort the fair presentation of position and performance.

# MyAccountingLab

Visit **www.myaccountinglab.com** for practice and revision opportunities

# The directors' duty to account

For large companies, it is not possible for all shareholders to be involved in the management of the company, nor do most of them wish to be involved. Instead, they appoint directors to act on their behalf. This separation of ownership from day-to-day control creates a need for directors to be accountable for their stewardship (management) of the company's assets. To fulfil this need, the directors must prepare (or have prepared on their behalf) financial statements that provide a fair representation of the financial position and performance of the business. This means that they must select appropriate accounting policies, make reasonable accounting estimates and adhere to all relevant accounting rules when preparing the statements. To avoid misstatements on the financial statements, whether from fraud or error, the directors must also maintain appropriate internal control systems.

Each of the company's shareholders has the right to be sent a copy of the financial statements produced by the directors. These statements must also be made available to the general public. This is achieved by the company submitting a copy to the Registrar of Companies (Department of Trade and Industry), which then allows anyone who wishes to do so to inspect them. In the case of listed companies, there is an additional requirement to publish the financial statements on their website.

## Activity 5.1

It can be argued that the publication of financial statements is vital to a well-functioning private sector. Why might this be the case?

There are at least two reasons:

- Unless shareholders receive regular information about the performance and position of a business they will have problems in appraising their investment. Under these circumstances, they would probably be reluctant to invest, which would adversely affect the functioning of a private enterprise economy.
- Suppliers of labour, goods, services and finance, particularly those supplying credit (loans) or goods and services on credit, need information about the financial health of a business. They would be reluctant to engage in commercial relationships where a company does not provide information. The fact that a company has limited liability increases the risks involved in dealing with it. An unwillingness to engage in commercial relationships with limited companies will, again, adversely affect the functioning of the private sector of the economy.

## The need for accounting rules

If we accept the need for directors to prepare and publish financial statements, we should also accept the need for a framework of rules concerning how these statements are prepared and presented. Without rules, there is a much greater risk that unscrupulous directors will adopt accounting policies and practices that portray an unrealistic view of financial health. There is also a much greater risk that the financial statements will not be comparable over time or with those of other businesses. Accounting rules can narrow areas of differences and reduce the variety of accounting methods. This should help ensure that businesses treat similar transactions in a similar way.

Example 5.1 illustrates the problems that may arise where businesses can exercise choice over the accounting policies used.

### Example 5.1

Rila plc and Pirin plc are both wholesalers of electrical goods. Both commenced trading on 1 March 2011 with an identical share capital. Both acquired identical property, plant and equipment on 1 March and both achieved identical trading results during the first year of trading. The following financial information relating to both businesses is available:

|  | £m |
|---|---|
| Ordinary £1 shares fully paid on 1 March 2011 | 60 |
| Non-current assets (at cost) acquired on 1 March 2011 | 40 |
| Revenue for the year to 29 February 2012 | 100 |
| Purchases of inventories during the year to 29 February 2012 | 70 |
| Expenses for the year to 29 February 2012 (excluding depreciation) | 20 |
| Trade receivables as at 29 February 2012 | 37 |
| Trade payables as at 29 February 2012 | 12 |
| Cash as at 29 February 2012 | 5 |

The non-current assets held by both businesses are leasehold buildings that have five years left to run on the lease. Inventories for both businesses have been valued at the year end at £16 million on a FIFO basis and £12 million on a LIFO basis.

When preparing their financial statements for the first year of trading:

- Rila plc decided to write off the cost of the leasehold premises at the end of the lease period. Pirin plc adopted the straight-line basis of depreciation for the leasehold buildings.
- Rila plc adopted the FIFO method of inventories valuation and Pirin plc adopted the LIFO method.

The income statements and the statements of financial position for the two businesses, ignoring taxation, will be as follows:

## Income statements for the year to 29 February 2012

|  | Rila plc £m | Pirin plc £m |
|---|---|---|
| Revenue | 100 | 100 |
| Cost of sales |  |  |
| Rila plc (£70m – £16m) | (54) |  |
| Pirin plc (£70m – £12m) |  | (58) |
| Gross profit | 46 | 42 |
| Expenses (excluding depreciation) | (20) | (20) |
| Depreciation |  |  |
| Rila plc | (–) |  |
| Pirin plc (£40m/5) |  | (8) |
| Profit for the year | 26 | 14 |

## Statements of financial position as at 29 February 2012

|  | Rila plc £m | Pirin plc £m |
|---|---|---|
| ASSETS |  |  |
| Non-current assets |  |  |
| Property, plant and equipment at cost | 40 | 40 |
| Accumulated depreciation | (–) | (8) |
|  | 40 | 32 |
| Current assets |  |  |
| Inventories | 16 | 12 |
| Trade receivables | 37 | 37 |
| Cash | 5 | 5 |
|  | 58 | 54 |
| Total assets | 98 | 86 |
| EQUITY AND LIABILITIES |  |  |
| Equity |  |  |
| Share capital | 60 | 60 |
| Retained earnings | 26 | 14 |
|  | 86 | 74 |
| Current liabilities |  |  |
| Trade payables | 12 | 12 |
| Total equity and liabilities | 98 | 86 |

Although the two businesses are identical in terms of funding and underlying trading performance, the financial statements create an impression that the financial health of each business is quite different. The accounting policies selected by Rila plc help to portray a much rosier picture. We can see that Rila plc reports a significantly higher profit for the year and higher assets at the year end.

Depreciation and inventories valuation are not the only areas where choices might be exercised. They nevertheless illustrate the potential impact of different accounting choices over the short term.

Accounting rules should help to provide greater confidence in the integrity of financial statements. This, in turn, may help a business to raise funds and to build stronger relationships with customers and suppliers. Users must be realistic, however, about what can be achieved through regulation. Problems of manipulation and of concealment can still occur even within a highly regulated environment, and examples of both will be considered later in the chapter. The scale of these problems, however, should be reduced where there is a practical set of rules.

Even with a set of rules, problems of comparability can also still occur as accounting is not a precise science. Judgements and estimates must be made when preparing financial statements and these may hinder comparisons. Furthermore, no two businesses are identical (unlike the companies in Example 5.1) and accounting policies may vary between businesses for valid reasons.

## Sources of accounting rules

In recent years, there have been increasing trends towards the internationalisation of business and the integration of financial markets. These trends have helped to strengthen the case for the international harmonisation of accounting rules. When a common set of rules is followed, users of financial statements should be better placed to compare the financial health of companies based in different countries. The existence of such rules should also relieve international companies of some of the burden of preparing financial statements. Different financial statements will no longer have to be prepared to comply with the rules of the various countries in which a particular company operates.

The International Accounting Standards Board (IASB) is an independent body that is at the forefront of the move towards harmonisation. The Board, which is based in the UK, is dedicated to developing a single set of high-quality, global accounting rules. These are designed to provide transparent and comparable information in financial statements. The rules, which are known as **International Accounting Standards** (IASs) or **International Financial Reporting Standards** (IFRSs), deal with key issues such as:

- what information should be disclosed;
- how information should be presented;
- how assets should be valued; and
- how profit should be measured.

### Activity 5.2

We have already come across some IASs and IFRSs in earlier chapters. Try to recall at least two topics where financial reporting standards were mentioned.

We came across financial reporting standards when considering:

- the valuation and impairment of assets (Chapter 2);
- depreciation and impairment of non-current assets (Chapter 3); and
- the valuation of inventories (Chapter 3).

## The growing authority of the IASB

Several important developments have greatly increased the authority of the IASB in recent years. The first major boost came when the European Commission required nearly all companies listed on the stock exchanges of EU member states to adopt IFRSs for reporting periods commencing on or after 1 January 2005. As a result, nearly 7,000 companies in 25 different countries switched to IFRSs. This was followed in 2006 by the IASB and the US Financial Accounting Standards Board agreeing a roadmap for convergence between IFRSs and US accounting rules. In that same year, China closely aligned its financial reporting standards with IFRSs. In 2007, Brazil, Canada, Chile, India, Japan and Korea all announced their intention to adopt, or converge with, IFRSs. By 2010, the point was reached where all major economies had either adopted IFRSs or had set time lines to adopt, or to converge with, IFRSs. This move towards international convergence is now supported by the Group of 20 Major Economies (G20).

Non-listed UK companies are not required to adopt IFRSs but have the option to do so. Some informed observers believe, however, that IFRSs may soon become a requirement for all UK companies.

## Adopting IFRSs

The EU requirement to adopt IFRSs, mentioned earlier, overrides any laws in force in member states that could either hinder or restrict compliance with them. The ultimate aim is to achieve a single framework of accounting rules for companies from all member states. The EU recognises that this will be achieved only if individual governments do not add to the requirements imposed by the various IFRSs. Thus, it seems that accounting rules developed within individual EU member countries will eventually disappear. For the time being, however, the EU accepts that the governments of member states may need to impose additional disclosures for some corporate governance matters and regulatory requirements.

In the UK, company law requires disclosure relating to various corporate governance issues. There is, for example, a requirement to disclose details of directors' remuneration in the published financial statements, which goes beyond anything required by IFRSs. Furthermore, the Financial Services Authority (FSA), in its role as the UK (Stock Exchange) listing authority, imposes rules on Stock Exchange listed companies. These include the requirement to publish a condensed set of interim (half-yearly) financial statements in addition to the annual financial statements. (These interim statements are not required by the IASB, although there is a standard providing guidance on their form and content.)

Figure 5.1 sets out the main sources of accounting rules for Stock Exchange listed companies. While company law and the FSA still play an important role, in the longer term IFRSs seem set to become the sole source of company accounting rules.

**Real World 5.1** provides a list of IASB standards that were in force as at 1 January 2011. It gives some idea of the range of topics that are covered.

| Figure 5.1 | Sources of external accounting rules for a UK public limited company listed on the London Stock Exchange |
| --- | --- |

International Financial Reporting Standards provide the basic framework of accounting rules for nearly all Stock Exchange listed companies. These rules are augmented by company law and by the Financial Services Authority (FSA) in its role as the UK listing authority.

## Real World 5.1

### International standards

The following is a list of the International Accounting Standards (IASs) and International Financial Reporting Standards (IFRSs) in issue as at 1 January 2011. (The latter term is used for standards issued from 2003 onwards.) Several standards have been issued and subsequently withdrawn, which explains the gaps in the numerical sequence. In addition, several have been revised and reissued.

IAS 1      Presentation of Financial Statements
IAS 2      Inventories
IAS 7      Statement of Cash Flows
IAS 8      Accounting Policies, Changes in Accounting Estimates and Errors
IAS 10     Events after the Reporting Period
IAS 11     Construction Contracts
IAS 12     Income Taxes
IAS 16     Property, Plant and Equipment
IAS 17     Leases
IAS 18     Revenue
IAS 19     Employee Benefits
IAS 20     Accounting for Government Grants and Disclosure of Government Assistance
IAS 21     The Effects of Changes in Foreign Exchange Rates
IAS 23     Borrowing Costs
IAS 24     Related Party Disclosures
IAS 26     Accounting and Reporting by Retirement Benefit Plans
IAS 27     Consolidated and Separate Financial Statements
IAS 28     Investments in Associates

| IAS 29 | Financial Reporting in Hyperinflationary Economies |
| IAS 31 | Interests in Joint Ventures |
| IAS 32 | Financial Instruments: Presentation |
| IAS 33 | Earnings per Share |
| IAS 34 | Interim Financial Reporting |
| IAS 36 | Impairment of Assets |
| IAS 37 | Provisions, Contingent Liabilities and Contingent Assets |
| IAS 38 | Intangible Assets |
| IAS 39 | Financial Instruments, Recognition and Measurement |
| IAS 40 | Investment Property |
| IAS 41 | Agriculture |
| IFRS 1 | First-time Adoption of International Financial Reporting Standards |
| IFRS 2 | Share-based Payment |
| IFRS 3 | Business Combinations |
| IFRS 4 | Insurance Contracts |
| IFRS 5 | Non-current Assets Held for Sale and Discontinued Operations |
| IFRS 6 | Exploration for and Evaluation of Mineral Resources |
| IFRS 7 | Financial Instruments: Disclosures |
| IFRS 8 | Operating Segments |
| IFRS 9 | Financial Instruments |

*Source*: IFRS Foundation, www.ifrs.org.

The IASB has an ambitious agenda and so significant changes to this list are likely to occur in the future.

# Presenting the financial statements

Now that we have gained an impression of the sources of rules affecting limited companies, let us turn our attention to the main rules to be followed in the presentation of financial statements. We shall focus on the IASB rules and, in particular, those contained in IAS 1 *Presentation of Financial Statements*. This standard is very important as it sets out the structure and content of financial statements and the principles to be followed in preparing these statements.

It might be helpful to have a set of the most recent financial statements of a Stock Exchange listed company available as you work through this section. They should all be available on the internet. Select a listed company that interests you and go to its website.

The financial statements identified in IAS 1 are as set out in Figure 5.2.

The standard states that these financial statements should normally cover a one-year period and should be accompanied by comparative information for the previous year. Thus, at the end of each reporting period companies should normally produce two of each of the statements, plus the related notes. In practice, virtually all companies satisfy this requirement by showing the equivalent figures for the previous year in a separate column in the current year's statements.

Comparative narrative information should also be provided if needed for a better grasp of current period results – for example, as background to an ongoing legal dispute.

**Figure 5.2** Financial statements required under IAS1

IAS1 *Presentation of Financial Statements* requires the preparation of the five statements shown.

## Fair representation

Before we consider the financial statements in detail, it is important to emphasise that the standard requires that they provide a fair representation of a company's financial position, financial performance and cash flows. There is a presumption that this will be achieved where they are drawn up in accordance with the various IASB standards that are currently in force. It is only in very rare circumstances that compliance with a standard would not result in a fair representation of the financial health of a company. Where the financial statements have been prepared in accordance with IASB standards, it should be clearly stated in the notes.

**Activity 5.3**

IAS 1 does not say that the requirement is for the financial statements to show a 'correct' or an 'accurate' representation of financial health. Why, in your opinion, does it not use those words? (*Hint*: Think of depreciation of non-current assets.)

Accounting can never really be said to be 'correct' or 'accurate' as these words imply that there is a precise value that an asset, claim, revenue or expense could have. This is simply not true in many, if not most, cases.

Depreciation provides a good example of where 'correct' or 'accurate' would not be appropriate. The annual depreciation expense is based on judgements about the future concerning the expected useful life and residual value of an asset. If all relevant factors are taken into account and reasonable judgements are applied, it may be possible to achieve a fair representation of the amount of the cost or fair value of the asset that is consumed for a particular period. However, a uniquely correct figure for depreciation for a period cannot be achieved.

Let us now consider each of the financial statements in turn.

## Statement of financial position

IAS 1 does not prescribe the format (or layout) for this financial statement but does set out the *minimum* information that should be presented on the face of the statement of financial position. This includes the following:

- property, plant and equipment
- investment property
- intangible assets
- financial assets (such as shares and loan notes of other companies held)
- inventories
- trade and other receivables
- cash and cash equivalents
- trade and other payables
- provisions (a provision is a liability that is of uncertain timing or amount – such as a possible obligation arising from a legal case against the company that has yet to be determined)
- financial liabilities (other than payables and provisions shown above)
- tax liabilities
- issued share capital and reserves (equity).

Additional information should be also shown where it is relevant to an understanding of the financial position of the business.

The standard requires that, on the statement of financial position, a distinction is normally made between current assets and non-current assets and between current liabilities and non-current liabilities. However, for certain types of business, such as financial institutions, the standard accepts that it may be more appropriate to order items according to their liquidity (that is, their nearness to cash).

Some of the assets and claims listed above may have to be sub-classified to comply with particular standards or because of their size or nature. Thus, sub-classifications are required for assets such as property, plant and equipment, receivables and inventories as well as for claims such as provisions and reserves. Certain details relating to share capital, such as the number of issued shares and their nominal value, must also be shown. To avoid cluttering up the statement of financial position, however, this additional information can be shown in the notes. In practice, most companies use notes for this purpose.

## Statement of comprehensive income

This statement extends the conventional income statement to include certain other gains and losses that affect shareholders' equity. It may be presented either in the form of a single statement or as two separate statements, comprising an income statement and a **statement of comprehensive income**. This choice of presentation, however, seems to be a transitional arrangement as the IASB's clear preference is for a single statement.

Again the format of the statement of comprehensive income is not prescribed, but IAS 1 sets out the *minimum* information to be presented on the face of the statement. This includes:

- revenue
- finance costs

- profits or losses arising from discontinued operations
- tax expense
- profit or loss
- each component of other comprehensive income classified by its nature
- any share of the comprehensive income of associates or joint ventures
- total comprehensive income.

The standard makes it clear that further items should be shown on the face of the income statement where they are relevant to an understanding of performance. If, for example, a business is badly affected by flooding, and inventories are destroyed as a result, the cost of the flood damage should be shown.

As a further aid to understanding, all material expenses should be separately disclosed. However, they need not be shown on the face of the income statement: they can appear in the notes to the financial statements. The kind of material items that may require separate disclosure include:

- write-down of inventories to net realisable value
- write-down of property, plant and equipment
- disposals of investments
- restructuring costs
- discontinued operations
- litigation settlements.

This is not an exhaustive list and, in practice, other material expenses may require separate disclosure.

The standard suggests two possible ways in which expenses can be presented on the face of the income statement. Expenses can be presented either:

- according to their nature, for example as depreciation, employee expenses and so on; or
- according to business functions, such as administrative activities and distribution.

The choice between the two possible ways of presenting expenses will depend on which one the directors believe will provide the more relevant and reliable information.

To understand what other information must be presented in this statement, apart from that already contained in a conventional income statement, we should remember that, broadly, the conventional income statement shows all *realised* gains and losses for the period. It also includes some unrealised losses (that is, losses relating to assets still held). However, unrealised gains, and some unrealised losses, do not pass through the income statement, but go directly to a reserve. We saw, in an earlier chapter, an example of an unrealised gain (which, therefore, would not have passed through the conventional income statement).

## Activity 5.4

**Can you think of this example?**

The example that we met earlier is where a business revalues its land and buildings. The gain arising is not shown in the conventional income statement, but is transferred to a revaluation reserve, which forms part of the equity. (We met this example in Activity 2.15 on page 69.) Land and buildings are not the only assets to which this rule relates, but these types of asset are, in practice, the most common examples of unrealised gains.

An example of an unrealised gain, or loss, that has not been mentioned so far, arises from exchange differences when the results of foreign operations are translated into UK currency. Any gain, or loss, usually bypasses the income statement and is taken directly to a currency translation reserve. A weakness of conventional accounting is that there is no robust principle that we can apply to determine precisely what should, and what should not, be included in the income statement. For example, losses arising from the impairment of non-current assets normally appear in the income statement. On the other hand, losses arising from translating the carrying amount of assets expressed in an overseas currency (because they are owned by an overseas branch) do not. There is no real difference in principle between the two types of loss, but the difference in treatment is ingrained in conventional accounting practice.

The statement of comprehensive income includes *all* gains and losses for a period and so will also take into account unrealised gains and any remaining unrealised losses. It extends the conventional income statement by including these items immediately beneath the measure of profit for the year. An illustration of this statement is shown in Example 5.2. Here, expenses are presented according to business function and comparative figures for the previous year are shown alongside the figures for the current year.

## Example 5.2

**Malik plc**
**Statement of comprehensive income for the year ended 31 December 2011**

|  | 2011 | 2010 |
| --- | --- | --- |
|  | £m | £m |
| Revenue | 100.6 | 97.2 |
| Cost of sales | (60.4) | (59.1) |
| Gross profit | 40.2 | 38.1 |
| Other income | 4.0 | 3.5 |
| Distribution expenses | (18.2) | (16.5) |
| Administration expenses | (10.3) | (11.2) |
| Other expenses | (2.1) | (2.4) |
| **Operating profit** | 13.6 | 11.5 |
| Finance charges | (2.0) | (1.8) |
| **Profit before tax** | 11.6 | 9.7 |
| Tax | (2.9) | (2.4) |
| **Profit for the year** | 8.7 | 7.3 |
| *Other comprehensive income* |  |  |
| Revaluation of property, plant and equipment | 20.3 | 6.6 |
| Foreign currency translation differences for foreign operations | 12.5 | 4.0 |
| Tax on other comprehensive income | (6.0) | (2.6) |
| Other comprehensive income for the year, net of tax | 26.8 | 8.0 |
| Total comprehensive income for the year | 35.5 | 15.3 |

This example adopts a single-statement approach to presenting comprehensive income. The alternative two-statement approach simply divides the information shown into two separate parts. The income statement, which is the first statement, begins with the revenue for the reporting period and ends with the profit for the year. The statement of comprehensive income, which is the second statement, begins with the profit for the year and ends with the total comprehensive income.

## Statement of changes in equity

The **statement of changes in equity** aims to help users to understand the changes in share capital and reserves that took place during the reporting period. It reconciles the figures for these items at the beginning of the period with those at the end. This is achieved by showing the effect on the share capital and reserves of total comprehensive income as well as the effect of share issues and purchases during the period. The effect of dividends during the period may also be shown in this statement, although dividends can be shown in the notes instead.

To see how a statement of changes in equity may be prepared, let us consider Example 5.3.

### Example 5.3

At 1 January 2011 Miro plc had the following equity:

**Miro plc**

|  | £m |
|---|---|
| Share capital (£1 ordinary shares) | 100 |
| Revaluation reserve | 20 |
| Translation reserve | 40 |
| Retained earnings | 150 |
| **Total equity** | 310 |

During 2011, the company made a profit for the year from normal business operations of £42 million and reported an upward revaluation of property, plant and equipment of £120 million (net of any tax that would be payable were the unrealised gains to be realised). A loss on exchange differences on translating the results of foreign operations of £10 million was also reported. To strengthen its financial position, the company issued 50 million ordinary shares during the year at a premium of £0.40. Dividends for the year were £27 million.

This information for 2011 can be set out in a statement of changes in equity as follows:

**Statement of changes in equity for the year ended 31 December 2011**

|  | Share capital | Share premium | Revaluation reserve | Translation reserve | Retained earnings | Total |
|---|---|---|---|---|---|---|
|  | £m | £m | £m | £m | £m | £m |
| Balance as at 1 January 2011 | 100 | – | 20 | 40 | 150 | 310 |
| Changes in equity for 2011 |  |  |  |  |  |  |
| Issue of ordinary shares (Note 1) | 50 | 20 | – | – | – | 70 |
| Dividends (Note 2) | – | – | – | – | (27) | (27) |
| Total comprehensive income for the year (Note 3) | – | – | 120 | (10) | 42 | 152 |
| Balance at 31 December 2011 | 150 | 20 | 140 | 30 | 165 | 505 |

**Notes:**
1 The premium on the share price is transferred to a specific reserve.
2 We have chosen to show dividends in the statement of changes in equity rather than in the notes. They represent an appropriation of equity and are deducted from retained earnings.
3 The effect of each component of comprehensive income on the various elements of shareholders' equity must be separately disclosed. The revaluation gain and the loss on translating foreign operations are each allocated to a specific reserve. The profit for the year is added to retained earnings.

## Statement of cash flows

The statement of cash flows should help users to assess the ability of a company to generate cash and to assess the company's need for cash. The presentation requirements for this statement are set out in IAS 7 *Statement of Cash Flows*, which we shall consider in some detail in the next chapter.

## Notes

The notes play an important role in helping users to understand the financial statements. They will normally contain the following information:

- a confirmation that the financial statements comply with relevant IFRSs;
- a summary of the measurement bases used and other significant accounting policies applied (for example, the basis of inventories valuation);
- supporting information relating to items appearing on the statement of financial position, statement of comprehensive income, statement of changes in equity and statement of cash flows; and
- other significant disclosures such as future contractual commitments that have not been recognised and financial risk management objectives and policies.

## General points

The standard provides support for three key accounting conventions when preparing the financial statements. These are:

- the going concern convention;
- the accruals convention (except for the statement of cash flows); and
- the consistency convention.

These conventions were discussed in Chapters 2 and 3.
Finally, to improve the transparency of financial statements, the standard states that:

- offsetting liabilities against assets, or expenses against income, is not allowed. Thus it is not acceptable, for example, to offset a bank overdraft against a positive bank balance (where a company has both); and
- material items must be shown separately.

## The need for a conceptual framework

In Chapters 2 and 3 we came across various accounting conventions such as the prudence, historic cost and going concern conventions. These conventions were developed as a practical response to particular problems that were confronted when preparing financial statements. They have stood the test of time and are still of value to preparers today. However, they do not provide, and were never designed to provide a **conceptual framework**, or framework of principles, to guide the development of financial statements. As we grapple with increasingly complex financial reporting problems, the need to have a sound understanding of *why* we account for things in a particular way becomes more pressing. Knowing *why* we account, rather than simply *how* we account, is vital if we are to improve the quality of financial statements.

In recent years, much effort has been expended in various countries, including the UK, to develop a clear conceptual framework that will guide us in the development of accounting. Such a framework should provide clear answers to such fundamental questions as:

- Who are the main users of financial statements?
- What is the purpose of financial statements?
- What qualities should financial information possess?
- What are the main elements of financial statements?
- How should these elements be defined, recognised and measured?

If these questions can be answered, accounting rule makers, such as the IASB, will be in a stronger position to identify best practice and to develop more coherent rules. This should, in turn, increase the credibility of financial reports in the eyes of users. It may even help reduce the possible number of rules, because some issues may be resolved by reference to the application of general principles rather than by the generation of further rules.

## The IASB framework

The quest for a conceptual framework began in earnest in the 1970s when the Financial Accounting Standards Board (FASB) in the USA devoted a large amount of time and resources to this task. It resulted in a broad framework, which other rule-making bodies, including the IASB, then drew upon to develop their own frameworks. The IASB Framework for the Preparation and Presentation of Financial Statements was produced in 1989 and has since provided guidance for the development of international accounting standards. Many of the standards that pre-dated the framework have now been replaced or revised. The IASB framework is itself, however, currently being revised.

The IASB and FASB have embarked on a joint project to produce a common conceptual framework that will underpin the accounting standards of both bodies. This project, which is ongoing, represents a major step towards convergence that will eventually lead to the replacement of the existing IASB framework. In 2010, the IASB and FASB announced completion of the first phase of the project, which deals with the objective and qualitative characteristics of financial reporting. Following this announcement, the IASB issued *A Conceptual Framework for Financial Reporting 2010*, which incorporates these revisions into its existing framework.

The revised IASB framework asserts that the objective of general purpose financial reporting is:

> to provide financial information about the reporting entity that is useful to existing and potential investors, lenders and other creditors in making decision about providing resources to the entity.

Note that it is the providers of finance that are seen as the primary users of general purpose financial reports. This is because investors, lenders and other creditors largely rely on these reports to make their investment decisions. Although other users may find general-purpose financial reports useful, the reports are not aimed at them.

The IASB framework also sets out the qualitative characteristics that make financial statements useful. The fundamental characteristics identified are relevance and faithful representation: it is these characteristics that make information useful. Characteristics that enhance the quality of financial reports are comparability, timeliness, verifiability and understandability. These are regarded as desirable, but not critical, characteristics.

In the absence of relevance and faithful representation, they cannot make information useful. All these characteristics were considered in some detail in Chapter 1. The framework acknowledges that producing financial information incurs costs, which must be justified by the benefits provided.

The IASB framework identifies two important accounting conventions: going concern and accruals. It states that financial statements should normally be prepared on the assumption that a business is a going concern. If this assumption cannot be applied, a different basis of reporting will be required. This will affect the valuation of assets held. The framework supports the accruals convention, which is seen as a better means of assessing past and future performance than reliance on cash receipts and payments. Nevertheless, information on cash flows is also considered useful for assessing financing and investing activities, liquidity and solvency.

The IASB framework goes on to identify the main elements of financial statements. Those relating to the measurement of financial position are assets, liabilities, equity, and those relating to the measurement of performance are income and expense. Each of these elements is defined and the definitions provided are similar to those discussed in Chapters 2 and 3.

The IASB framework identifies different measurement bases, such as historic cost, current cost, and realisable value. There is no attempt, however, to support a particular measurement basis. The framework simply notes that historic cost is the most widely used basis but that it is often used with other measurement bases. To determine which measurement bases should be used for a particular situation, relevant accounting standards must be consulted.

The IASB framework does not have the same legal status as the IASB standards. Nevertheless, it offers guidance for dealing with accounting issues, particularly where no relevant accounting standard exists. Managers are required to consider the framework when dealing with issues that fall outside the scope of existing standards.

Overall, the IASB framework has provoked little controversy and the principles that it contains appear to enjoy widespread acceptance. There has been some criticism, mainly from academics, that the framework is really a descriptive document and does not provide theoretical underpinning to the financial statements. It has also been suggested that the framework is too broad in nature to provide useful guidance for developing accounting standards or to deal with emerging accounting issues. These criticisms have not, however, sparked any major debates.

## The auditors' role

Shareholders are required to elect a qualified and independent person or, more usually, a firm to act as **auditors**. The auditors' main duty is to report whether, in their opinion, the financial statements do what they are supposed to do, namely to show a true and fair view of the financial performance, position and cash flows of the company. To be able to form such an opinion, auditors must carefully scrutinise the financial statements and the underlying evidence upon which they are based. In particular, they will examine the accounting principles followed, the accounting estimates made and the robustness of the company's internal control systems. The auditors' opinion must be included with the financial statements sent to the shareholders and to the Registrar of Companies.

The relationship between the shareholders, the directors and the auditors is illustrated in Figure 5.3. This shows that the shareholders elect the directors to act on their behalf, in the day-to-day running of the company. The directors are then required to 'account' to the shareholders on the performance, position and cash flows of the company, on an annual basis. The shareholders also elect auditors, whose role it is to give the shareholders an independent view of the truth and fairness of the financial statements prepared by the directors.

| Figure 5.3 | The relationship between the shareholders, the directors and the auditors |

The directors are appointed by the shareholders to manage the company on the shareholders' behalf. The directors are required to report each year to the shareholders, principally by means of financial statements, on the company's performance, position and cash flows. To give greater confidence in the statements, the shareholders also appoint auditors to investigate the reports and to express an opinion on their reliability.

## Directors' report

In addition to preparing the financial statements, UK law requires the directors to pre- pare a report to shareholders and other interested parties relating to each reporting period. The **directors' report** will contain both financial and non-financial information which goes beyond that contained in the financial statements. The information to be disclosed is diverse and will include the names of those who were directors during the reporting period, the principal activities of the company and any recommended dividend. The most important element of the report, however, is probably the **business review**. This is aimed at helping shareholders to assess how well the directors have performed. It should provide an analysis of financial performance and position and should also set out the principal risks and uncertainties facing the business. We shall consider this review in some detail later in the chapter.

In addition to disclosing the information mentioned above, the directors' report must contain a declaration that the directors are not aware of any other information that the auditors might need in preparing their audit report. Furthermore, the report must declare that the directors have taken steps to ensure that the auditors are aware of all relevant information. The auditors do not carry out an audit of the directors' report. However, they will check to see that the information in the report is consistent with that contained in the audited financial statements.

For companies listed on the Stock Exchange, the law also requires the publication of an annual directors' remuneration report. This should help shareholders to assess whether the rewards received by directors are appropriate.

# Segmental financial reports

Most large businesses are engaged in a number of different operations, with each having its own levels of risk, growth and profitability. Information relating to each type of business operation, however, is normally added together (aggregated) in the financial statements so as to provide an overall picture of financial performance and position. For example, the revenue figure in the income statement represents the sum total of the company's revenues, even though they may come from different activities. Although this aggregation of information can help to provide a broad picture, it can make it difficult to undertake comparisons over time, or between businesses. Some idea of the range and scale of the various types of operation must be gained for a proper assessment of financial health. Thus, to undertake any meaningful analysis of financial performance and position, it is usually necessary to disaggregate the information contained within the financial statements. This disaggregated information is disclosed in **segmental financial reports**.

By breaking down the financial information according to each type of business operation, or operating segment, we can evaluate the relative risks and profitability of each segment and make useful comparisons with other businesses or other business operating segments. We can also see the trend of performance for each operating segment over time and so more accurately assess the likely growth prospects for the business as a whole. We should also be able to determine more easily the impact on the overall business of changes in market conditions relating to particular operating segments.

Disclosure of information relating to the performance of each segment may also help to improve the efficiency of the business by keeping managers on their toes. Operating segments that are performing poorly will be revealed and this should put pressure on managers to take corrective action. Where an operating segment has been sold, the shareholders will be better placed to assess the wisdom of the managers' decision to sell it.

## Segmental reporting rules

An IASB standard (IFRS 8 *Operating Segments*) requires listed companies to disclose information about their various operating segments. Defining an operating segment, however, can be a tricky business. The IASB has opted for a 'management approach', which means that an operating segment is defined by reference to how management has segmented the business for internal reporting and monitoring purposes. An operating segment is, therefore, defined as a part of the business that:

● generates revenues and expenses,
● has its own separate financial statements, and
● has its results regularly reviewed for resource-allocation and assessment purposes.

Not all parts of the business will meet the criteria identified. The headquarters of the business ('head office'), for example, is unlikely to do so and will not, therefore, normally be treated as an operating segment.

**Activity 5.5**

What do you think are the main advantages of adopting the management approach?

Under the management approach, shareholders will receive similar reports to the internal reports produced for management, which means that they can assess business performance from the same viewpoint as management. It should also mean that businesses will avoid heavy reporting costs as the information will already have been produced.

There are, of course, other ways of identifying an operating segment. One approach would be to define a segment according to the industry to which it relates. This, however, may lead to endless definition and classification problems.

To be reported separately, an operating segment must be of significant size. This normally means that it must account for 10 per cent or more of the combined revenue, profits or assets of all operating segments. A segment that does not meet this size threshold may be combined with other similar segments to produce a reportable segment. Alternatively, if the directors believe it to be beneficial, it may be separately reported despite its size. If neither of these options is chosen, it should be reported with other segments under a separate category of 'all other segments'.

## Segmental disclosure

Financial information to be disclosed includes some profit (/loss) measure (for example, operating profit) for each segment along with the following income statement items:

- revenue, distinguishing between revenue from external customers and revenue from other segments of the business;
- interest revenue and interest expense;
- depreciation and other material non-cash items;
- material items of income and expense;
- any profit (loss) from associate companies or joint ventures;
- segment profit (loss); and
- income tax (where it is separately reported for a segment).

The business must also disclose the total assets for each segment and, if they are reported to management, the total liabilities. Any additions to non-current assets during the period must also be reported.

Example 5.4 provides an illustrative segmental financial report for a business.

**Example 5.4**

**Goya plc**
**Segmental report for the year ended 31 December 2011**

|  | Publishing £m | Film-making £m | All other £m | Totals £m |
|---|---|---|---|---|
| Revenue from external customers | 150 | 200 | 25 | 375 |
| Inter-segment revenue | 20 | 10 | – | 30 |
| Interest revenue | 10 | – | – | 10 |
| Interest expense | – | 15 | – | 15 |
| Depreciation | 40 | 20 | 5 | 65 |
| Reportable segment profit | 15 | 19 | 4 | 38 |
| Other material non-cash items: |  |  |  |  |
| Impairment of assets | – | 10 | – | 10 |
| Reportable segment assets | 60 | 80 | 12 | 152 |
| Expenditures for reportable segment |  |  |  |  |
| non-current assets | 12 | 18 | 2 | 32 |
| Reportable segment liabilities | 25 | 32 | 4 | 61 |

We can see that information relating to each segment, as well as a combined total for all operating segments, is shown. This information may be simply set out in the form of a table, as shown above, with no headings or totals.

Key items, which include revenues, profits, assets, and liabilities, must be reconciled with the corresponding amounts for the business as a whole. For example, Goya plc's income statement should show revenue of £375 million for the business as a whole. When carrying out a reconciliation, we should bear in mind that:

● inter-segment revenues should be eliminated as no transaction with external parties occurs;
● any profit arising from inter-segment transfers should also be eliminated;
● assets and liabilities that have not been allocated to a particular segment should be taken into account.

The last item normally refers to assets and liabilities relating to business-wide activities. Thus, head office buildings may provide an example of unallocated assets, and staff pension liabilities may provide an example of unallocated liabilities.

IFRS 8 requires certain non-financial information concerning segments to be disclosed. This includes the basis for identifying operating segments and the types of products and services that each segment provides. It also requires business-wide information to be disclosed, such as geographical areas of operations, and reliance on major customers.

## Segmental reporting problems

Various problems arise when preparing segmental reports, not least of which is that of identifying a segment. We have already seen that the relevant IFRS identifies operating segments according to the internal reporting and monitoring procedures of the business. While this may be the most sensible course of action, comparisons between segments in other businesses may be impossible because of the different ways in which they are defined.

Another problem may arise where there is a significant amount of sales between operating segments. Where this occurs, the **transfer price** of the goods or services between segments can have a substantial impact on the reported profits of each segment. (The transfer price is the price at which sales are made between different segments of the same business.) A potential risk is that revenues and profits will be manipulated for each segment through the use of particular transfer pricing policies.

### Activity 5.6

**Why might a business wish to manipulate revenues and profits in this way?**

Where a business operates in different countries, it may try to report high profits in a country that has low tax rates and to report low profits (or even losses) in a country with high tax rates.

**Real World 5.2** reveals how governments throughout the world are taking a closer look at the transfer pricing policies of multinational companies.

### Real World 5.2

#### A taxing issue                                                    **FT**

The drive by governments around the world to collect taxes from corporations as they attempt to close yawning budget deficits has sparked a rise in the number of tax authority audits of multinationals, research shows.

A survey by Taxand, a network of global tax professionals, found 82 per cent of multinational companies saw a rise in the number of government audits they were subject to, and 84 per cent said that as a result they had experienced a rise in compliance costs.

The survey interviewed the chief financial officer or tax director at 52 multinational companies. It found the single most challenging area for multinationals was transfer pricing – the price a multinational charges one part of its business for goods or services produced by another – and that this area was coming under most scrutiny from tax authorities.

'At the heart of this is the perception that multinationals may manipulate their transfer pricing strategies to create a significant tax advantage,' said Antoine Glaize, a specialist in transfer pricing at Taxand.

*Source*: 'Multinationals face more tax audits', N. Cohen, 3 May 2011, FT.com.

IFRS 8 recognises the impact of transfer pricing policies on segmental revenues and profit by stating that the basis for accounting for transactions between segments must be disclosed.

A third problem is that some expenses and assets may relate to more than one operating segment and their allocation between segments may vary between businesses. Again, this may hinder comparisons of segmental profits and profitability between businesses.

## Self-assessment question (5.1)

Segmental information relating to Turner plc for the year to 30 April 2012 is:

|  | Software £m | Electronics £m | Engineering £m | Totals £m |
|---|---|---|---|---|
| Revenues from external customers | 250 | 230 | 52 | 532 |
| Inter-segment revenues | 45 | 25 | – | 70 |
| Interest revenue | 18 | – | – | 18 |
| Interest expense | – | 25 | – | 25 |
| Depreciation | 60 | 35 | 10 | 105 |
| Reportable segment profit | 10 | 34 | 12 | 56 |
| Other material non-cash items: |  |  |  |  |
|   Impairment of assets | – | 5 | – | 5 |
| Reportable segment assets | 140 | 90 | 34 | 264 |
| Expenditures for reportable segment |  |  |  |  |
|   non-current assets | 22 | 12 | 10 | 44 |
| Reportable segment liabilities | 55 | 38 | 4 | 97 |

*Required*:

Analyse the performance of each of the three main business segments for the year and comment on your results.

**The solution to this question can be found at the back of the book on page 732.**

# Business review

A business, particularly a large business, may have extremely complex organisational arrangements, financing methods and operating characteristics. The financial statements must, however, reflect this complexity if they are to provide a faithful portrayal of financial health. As a consequence, the statements can often be lengthy, detailed and difficult to understand.

To provide a clearer picture for users, a narrative report can be provided that reviews the business and its results. UK law now requires all except the smallest companies to include a *business review* in their annual financial report. This review, which is prepared by the directors, must provide a balanced and comprehensive analysis of the performance for the reporting period and of the position at the end of the period. The review must also set out information concerning:

- the principal risks and uncertainties that are faced;
- key performance indicators;
- the main trends and factors likely to affect the future;
- the company's employees;
- environmental, social and community issues; and
- persons with whom the company has essential contractual or other arrangements, unless disclosure is prejudicial to the person or to the public interest.

**Activity 5.7**

What do you think are the main qualitative characteristics that information contained within the business review should possess? (*Hint*: Think back to Chapter 1.)

To be useful, the information should exhibit the characteristics for accounting information in general, which we identified in Chapter 1. Thus, the information should have the characteristics of relevance, faithful representation, comparability, timeliness, verifiability and understandability. The fact that we are dealing with narrative information does not alter the need for these characteristics to be present.

To achieve the quality of faithful representation, the information provided must be complete. This means that it should include all significant information that will help assess business performance. Information that places the business in an unfavourable light must not be omitted.

## The reporting framework

The particular form that a business review should take is left to the discretion of the directors. In searching for a suitable framework, the directors may look to the Reporting Standard RS 1 issued by the UK Accounting Standards Board (ASB). This statement pre-dates the legal requirement for a business review but nevertheless covers the same sort of ground. It is not mandatory; it simply aims to provide guidance on best practice.

The framework set out in RS 1 rests on the disclosure of information relating to four key elements of a business.

Figure 5.4 shows these four key elements.

We shall now discuss the information to be reported for each of these elements.

**Figure 5.4** **The key elements of the business review**

Reporting Standard RS1, issued by the UK ASB, identifies four key elements, which could be used as a basis for preparing a business review.

## The nature of the business

This part of the review should describe the environment within which the business operates. As might be imagined, this can cover a wide range and may include a commentary on key operational matters such as the products sold, business processes, business structure and competitive position. It can also include a commentary on the legal, economic and social environment.

This part should also describe the objectives of the business and the strategy adopted to achieve those objectives. **Real World 5.3** illustrates how Greene King plc, a leading brewer, which also operates a range of pubs, restaurants and hotels, uses its business review to provide an update on its growth strategy.

### Real World 5.3

#### Reviewing the situation

Greene King plc's 2011 business review states that:

> Our strategy for growth is three-fold: first, expanding the number of sites in Retail, our biggest and fastest growing division, to 1,100, and improving the overall quality of the estate; second, reducing our tenanted and leased business to around 1,200 sites, and taking more control over the offer in the core estate; and third, increasing investment and driving growth of our core ale brands. Following good progress in the year, we remain on track to meet our targets.

*Source*: Greene King plc, Annual Report 2011, Business Review, www.greenekingreports.com, p.9.

Finally, this part of the business review should include a commentary on the key performance indicators (KPIs) used to assess the success of the business strategy. KPIs will vary between businesses but will normally comprise a combination of financial and non-financial measures. Key financial measures may be based upon sales revenue growth, profit, total shareholder return, dividends, and so on. Key non-financial measures may relate to market share, employee satisfaction, product quality, supplier satisfaction, and so on.

## Business performance

This part of the review considers the development and performance of the business for the reporting period and for the future. It should include comments on anything affecting performance, such as changes in market conditions or the launch of new products or services. It should also identify trends and anything else that may affect future prospects.

**Real World 5.4** provides an extract from the 2011 business review of Greene King plc which sets out recent acquisitions by the business.

**Real World 5.4**

### Looking to expand

We acquired Cloverleaf Restaurants on 28 January 2011 for £55.7 million. Cloverleaf consists of 12 freehold, food-led sites, delivering, at the time of the acquisition, an average weekly turnover (AWT) of c.£40k and average EBITDA (earnings before interest taxation, depreciation and amortisation) per site of c.£540k. Food is 69% of sales. Cloverleaf brings us carvery expertise and another concept to expand through our new-build programme. The Cloverleaf pipeline of new sites will deliver a minimum of ten additional sites trading by the end of April 2013 and we are looking to expand the concept further south and into Scotland.

We acquired Realpubs on 27 April 2011 for £52.2 million. Realpubs consists of 14 London pubs, all but one freehold, trading a well developed premium pub dining concept. AWT is c.£25k and EBITDA per site is c.£450k. Food is currently 33% of sales and growing strongly. We are looking to work closely with the team at Realpubs to spearhead our premium growth by converting a number of Greene King London pubs to the Realpubs concept, acquiring additional sites in London and expanding the Realpubs concept outside of the M25.

*Source*: Greene King plc Annual Report 2011, Business Review, www.greenekingreports.com, p.9.

### Resources, risks and relationships

This part should comment on the resources of the business and how they are managed. The resources discussed should not be confined to items shown in the statement of financial position and may include such things as corporate reputation, patents, trademarks, brand names, market position and the quality of employees.

This part should also include comments on the main risks and uncertainties facing the business and how they are managed. **Real World 5.5** shows how Greene King plc comments on one important risk in its business review.

**Real World 5.5**

### A risky business

In its 2011 business review, Greene King plc identifies six main categories of risk to which the business is exposed. These are economic risks, regulatory risks, supply chain risks, operational risks, financial risks and people risks. The economic risks are described as follows:

> The group's business operations are sensitive to economic conditions and in particular to levels of consumer spending. Any delay in economic recovery could affect consumer expenditure and therefore our revenue. There is an on-going risk to our business of increases in the cost of key products, including food, drink, Sky and utilities.
>
> Our licensees are also affected by the economic climate, leading to the risk of more tenant defaults and business failures. Property values are also impacted by the economic uncertainty, and with it our ability to continue to make disposals at appropriate values.

*Source*: Greene King plc Annual Report 2011, Business Review, www.greenekingreports.com, p.24.

Finally, this part of the business review should include a commentary on key relationships with stakeholders, apart from shareholders, that may affect the business. The stakeholders may include customers, suppliers, employees, contractors and lenders as well as other businesses with which the business has strategic alliances. **Real World 5.6** provides an extract from Greene King plc's 2011 business review, which describes how the business obtains feedback from its employees.

### Real World 5.6

#### What are you thinking?

Our anonymous staff survey is an important tool which enables us to 'test the temperature' across the company and find out how our staff feel about being part of our team. This year around 50% of our 18,000 staff responded and shared their thoughts on roles, responsibilities, management, pay and benefits. We measure our progress in this area using an employee engagement score which we set at 3. However, this year we changed our survey provider to OCR International and with it the method of assessing employee engagement. With their help we set specific questions, with a proven link to engagement, and benchmarked the overall rating with other retail businesses. For this year our overall score was 67%, which compared reasonably well to the retail benchmark and indeed our target, both 74%.

*Source*: Greene King plc Annual Report 2011, Business Review, www.greenekingreports.com, p.28.

### Financial position

This final part of the of the business review should describe events that have influenced the financial position of the business during the reporting period and those that are likely to affect the business in the future. It should also include a discussion of the capital (financial) structure, cash flows and liquidity of the company.

**Real World 5.7** shows how, in its 2011 business review, Greene King plc comments on its cash flows.

### Real World 5.7

#### Cash is Greene King

Continuing to focus on generating strong cash flows is the key to providing options and flexibility for the group. We delivered EBITDA (earnings before interest tax, depreciation and amortisation) of £276.6 million, up 4.6% on last year, from 1.4% fewer pubs. With another year of strong working capital management delivering a cash inflow of £15.9 million, we have further improved our cash platform, allowing us to maintain investment levels in the core estate for both maintenance and expansionary purposes, to pay down debt (comfortably ahead of our normal amortisation) and to pay increasing dividends to shareholders. This remains a consistent part of our long-term financial strategy.

*Source*: Greene King plc Annual Report 2011, Business Review, www.greenekingreports.com, p.28.

This final part of the business review should also comment on the treasury policy of the business, which is concerned with managing cash, obtaining finance and managing relationships with financial institutions. Possible areas for discussion can include major financing transactions and the effects of interest charges, or interest rate changes, on the business. **Real World 5.8** shows how, in its 2011 business review, Greene King plc comments on a new financing arrangement.

---

**Real World 5.8**

### Putting it on the slate

On 4 April 2011, we announced a new five-year, £400 million, revolving, credit facility with our banking partners, starting in April 2011. This replaced the existing £400 million facility, which was due to expire in April 2012, and is fully available for five years. At the year-end, and following our recent acquisitions, this was £110 million drawn. The new facility, alongside our securitised debt, gives an expected blended average interest rate of 6.1%. This continued financial flexibility underpins the ongoing retail expansion and growth strategy.

*Source*: Greene King plc Annual Report 2011, Business Review, www.greenekingreports.com, p.23.

---

## The quality of business reviews

Business reviews are still at a fairly early stage of development, and problems concerning their quality are, perhaps, to be expected. A major risk is that these reports will paint too rosy a picture. If they are to be useful, managers must resist this temptation and must be honest about any failings. However, in a world where there is no real incentive for managers to behave in this way, and no independent scrutiny, we should not be surprised if this does not occur.

In 2006, the ASB carried out a survey of narrative reporting practice. It found that, generally, businesses provided a good account of the nature of the business and its markets as well as of their business strategy and objectives, but the reporting of principal risks, KPIs and the resources of the business needed improvement. The greatest problem area for businesses, however, was the reporting of forward-looking information. (See reference at the end of the chapter.)

---

**Activity 5.8**

Why might the reporting of forward-looking information be a problem for the directors of a business?

The directors may be concerned that the information will be of use to competitors and so damage the competitive position of the business. There is also a risk that the information may turn out to be incorrect and users may then feel that they have been misled.

## Summary financial statements

We saw earlier that the directors must provide each shareholder with a copy of the annual financial statements. For large businesses, these financial statements can be extremely detailed and complicated. Along with the accompanying notes, they may extend over many pages. It is possible, however, for the directors to provide a summarised version of the full financial statements as an alternative.

The main advantages of providing **summary financial statements** are that:

- many shareholders do not wish to receive the full version because they may not have the time, interest or skill necessary to be able to gain much from it;
- directors could improve their communication with their shareholders by providing something closer to the needs of many shareholders; and
- reproducing and posting copies of the full version is expensive and a waste of resources where particular shareholders do not wish to receive it.

It has now become common practice for large businesses to send all of their shareholders, who are private individuals, a copy of the summary financial statements. These are accompanied with a clear message that a copy of the full version is available on request. Institutional investors (insurance companies, pension funds and so on) tend to receive a full version as a matter of routine.

Critics of summary financial statements, however, argue that it is dangerous for shareholders to receive financial reports that attempt to simplify complexity. Any attempt to do so runs the risk of discarding important information and distorting the message. If a shareholder is unwilling or unable to develop the necessary accounting skills, or to spend the necessary time to examine the full version of the financial statements, the proper solution is either to seek expert advice or to invest in mutual funds managed by experts. Viewed from this perspective, the best thing that a business can do to help less sophisticated shareholders is to provide more detailed information to experts, such as investment analysts.

## Creative accounting

Despite the proliferation of accounting rules and the independent checks that are imposed, concerns over the quality of published financial statements surface from time to time. There are occasions when directors apply particular accounting policies, or structure particular transactions, in such a way as to portray a picture of financial health that is in line with what they want users to see, rather than what is a true and fair view of financial position and performance. Misrepresenting the performance and position of a business in this way is often called **creative accounting** and it poses a major problem for accounting rule makers and for society generally.

## Activity 5.9

**Why might the directors of a company engage in creative accounting?**

There are many reasons including:

- to get around restrictions (for example, to report sufficient profit to pay a dividend);
- to avoid government action (for example, the taxation of excessive profits);
- to hide poor management decisions;
- to achieve sales revenue or profit targets, thereby ensuring that performance bonuses are paid to the directors;
- to attract new share capital or long-term borrowing by showing an apparently healthy financial position; and
- to satisfy the demands of major investors concerning levels of return.

## Creative accounting methods

The ways in which unscrupulous directors can manipulate the financial statements are many and varied. However, they usually involve adopting novel or unorthodox practices for reporting key elements of the financial statements, such as revenue, expenses, assets and liabilities. They may also involve the use of complicated or obscure transactions in an attempt to hide the underlying economic reality. The manipulation carried out may be designed either to bend the rules or to break them.

We shall now consider some of the more important ways in which rules may be bent or broken.

### Misstating revenue

Some creative accounting methods are designed to overstate the revenue for a period. These methods often involve the early recognition of sales revenue or the reporting of sales transactions that have no real substance. **Real World 5.9** provides examples of both types of revenue manipulation.

## Real World 5.9

### Overstating revenue

*Early recognition of revenue* A business may report the sale of goods as soon as an order has been placed, rather than when the goods are delivered to, and accepted by, the customer. This will boost current revenues and profits and is known as 'pre-dispatching'.

*Passing goods to distributors* A business may force its distributors to accept more goods that they can sell. This will again boost current revenues and profits and is known as 'channel stuffing' or 'trade loading'.

*Artificial trading* This involves businesses in the same industry selling the same items between themselves to boost sales revenue. One example is where telecoms businesses sell unused fibre optic capacity to each other. This is known as 'hollow swaps'. Another example is where energy businesses sell energy between themselves for the same price and at the same time. This is known as 'round tripping' or 'in and out trading'.

> Note that artificial trading between similar businesses will inflate the sales revenue for a period but will not inflate reported profits. Nevertheless, this may still benefit the business. Sales revenue growth has become an important yardstick of performance for some investors and can affect the value they place on the business.
>
> *Source:* Based on information in 'Dirty laundry: how companies fudge the numbers', *The Times*, Business Section, 22 September 2002, nisyndication.com.

The manipulation of revenue has been at the heart of many of the accounting scandals recently exposed. Given its critical role in the measurement of performance, this is, perhaps, not surprising. **Real World 5.10** provides an example of how the financial results of one well-known business were distorted by the overstatement of sales revenues.

## Real World 5.10

### Recomputing the numbers     FT

In August 2007, Dell (the computer manufacturer) admitted that some unnamed 'senior executives' had been involved in a scheme to overstate sales revenue figures during the period 2003 to 2007. This was done in an attempt to make it appear that quarterly sales targets had been met, when in fact this was not the case. The overstatement of sales revenue was estimated to amount to $92 million; about 1 per cent of total profit over the period concerned.

*Source:* 'Dell to lower writedowns on restated earnings', Kevin Allison, *Financial Times*, 30 October 2007.

## Massaging expenses

Some creative accounting methods focus on the manipulation of expenses. Those expenses that rely on directors' estimates of the future or their choice of accounting policy are particularly vulnerable to manipulation.

## Activity 5.10

Can you identify the kind of expenses where the directors make estimates or choices in the ways described?

These include certain expenses that we discussed in Chapter 3, such as:

● depreciation of property, plant and equipment
● amortisation of intangible assets, such as goodwill
● inventories (cost of sales)
● allowances for trade receivables.

By changing estimates about the future (for example, the useful life or residual value of an asset), or by changing accounting policies (for example, switching from FIFO to AVCO), it may be possible to derive an expense figure, and, consequently, a profit figure, that suits the directors.

The incorrect 'capitalisation' of expenses may also be used as a means of manipulation. This involves treating expenses as if they were amounts incurred to acquire or develop non-current assets, rather than amounts consumed during the period. The net effect of this is that the expenses will be unfairly understated and profit will, therefore, be unfairly boosted. Businesses that build their own assets are often best placed to undertake this form of malpractice.

---

**Activity 5.11**

What would be the effect on the profits and total assets of a business of incorrectly capitalising expenses?

Both would be artificially inflated. Reported profits would increase because expenses would be reduced. Total assets would be increased because the expenses would be incorrectly treated as non-current assets.

---

**Real World 5.11** provides an example of one business that capitalised expenses on a huge scale.

---

**Real World 5.11**

### Sorry - wrong numbers                                                          **FT**

One particularly notorious case of capitalising expenses is alleged to have occurred in the financial statements of WorldCom (now renamed MCI). This company, which is a large US telecommunications business, is alleged to have overstated profits by treating certain operating expenses, such as basic network maintenance, as capital expenditure. This happened over a fifteen-month period during 2001 and 2002. To correct for this overstatement, profits had to be reduced by a massive $3.8 billion.

*Source*: Based on two personal views on WorldCom posted on the FT.com site, 27 June 2002.

---

### Concealing 'bad news'

Some creative accounting methods focus on the concealment of losses or liabilities. The financial statements can look much healthier if these can somehow be eliminated. One way of doing this is to create a 'separate' entity that will take over the losses or liabilities.

**Real World 5.12** describes how one large business concealed losses and liabilities.

## Real World 5.12

### For a very special purpose

Perhaps the most well-known case of concealment of losses and liabilities concerned the Enron Corporation. This was a large US energy business that used 'special purpose entities' (SPEs) as a means of concealment. SPEs were used by Enron to rid itself of problem assets that were falling in value, such as its broadband operations. In addition, liabilities were transferred to these entities to help Enron's statement of financial position look healthier. The company had to keep its gearing ratios (the relationship between borrowing and equity) within particular limits to satisfy credit-rating agencies and SPEs were used to achieve this. The SPEs used for concealment purposes were not independent of the company and should have been consolidated in the statement of financial position of Enron, along with their losses and liabilities.

When these, and other accounting irregularities, were discovered in 2001, there was a restatement of Enron's financial performance and position to reflect the consolidation of the SPEs, which had previously been omitted. As a result of this restatement, the company recognised $591 million in losses over the preceding four years and an additional $628 million worth of liabilities at the end of 2000.

The company collapsed at the end of 2001.

*Source*: 'The rise and fall of Enron', C. William Thomas, *Journal of Accountancy*, vol. 194, no. 3, 2002. This article represents the opinions of the author, which are not necessarily those of the Texas Society of Certified Public Accountants.

## Misstating assets

There are various ways in which assets may be misstated. These include:

- using asset values that are higher than their fair market values;
- capitalising costs that should have been written off as expenses, as described earlier;
- recording assets that are not owned or which do not exist.

**Real World 5.13** describes how one large business reported an asset that did not exist.

## Real World 5.13

### When things go sour

Parmalat, a large Italian dairy-and-food business, announced in December 2003 that a bank account held in the Cayman Islands with the Bank of America did not have, as had been previously reported, a balance of €3.95 billion. The fake balance turned out to be part of a web of deception: it had simply been 'invented' in order to help offset more than €16 billion of outstanding borrowings. According to Italian prosecutors, the business had borrowed heavily on the strength of fictitious sales revenues.

A Cayman Islands subsidiary, which was supposed to hold the fake bank balance, engaged in fictitious trading in an attempt to conceal the true nature of the deception. This included the supply of 300,000 tons of milk powder from a fake Singapore-based business to a Cuban business through the subsidiary.

*Source*: Based on 'How it all went so sour', Peter Gumbel, *Time Europe Magazine*, 21 November 2004.

## Inadequate disclosure

Directors may misrepresent or try to conceal certain information. This may relate to commitments made, key changes in accounting policies or estimates, significant events, and so on. The information may also relate to financial transactions between the directors and the business. **Real World 5.14** provides such an example.

### Real World 5.14

#### Banking on a loan

The chairman of Anglo Irish Bank, Mr Sean Fitzpatrick, resigned after it was discovered that he had concealed €87 million in personal loans received from the bank. This amount was more than twice that shown in the annual financial statements for personal loans received by the whole of the bank's 13 directors.

Although the annual financial statements showed that directors of Anglo Irish Bank had received personal loans totalling €41 million, the figure was actually €150 million. The loans received by Mr Fitzpatrick represented more than half of this amount. The bank revealed that Mr Fitzpatrick concealed the true extent of his personal borrowings by transferring his loans to another bank just before the end of each financial year. As a result, they did not appear in the statement of financial position at the year end. He would then transfer them back to Anglo Irish Bank once the bank's auditors had completed their annual audit. This exercise continued over an eight-year period.

A further director, Lar Bradshaw, also resigned from the board of Anglo Irish Bank. He had held a joint loan with Mr Fitzpatrick and this was also moved to another bank prior to the end of the financial year. Mr Bradshaw claimed he was unaware of this transfer of the loan but felt that it was in the bank's interests that he should go.

*Source*: Adapted from 'Anglo Irish bank chief quits over hiding €87m loan', www.belfasttelegraph.co.uk, 19 December 2008.

Figure 5.5 summarises the main methods of creative accounting.

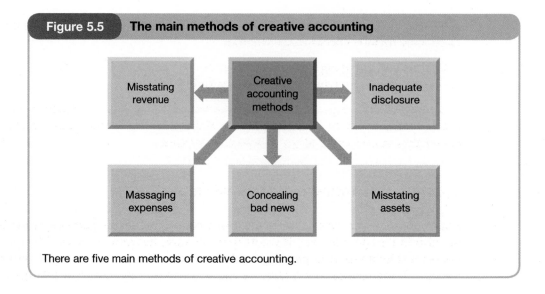

**Figure 5.5    The main methods of creative accounting**

There are five main methods of creative accounting.

## Checking for creative accounting

When examining the financial statements of a business, a number of checks may be carried out on the financial statements to help gain a feel for their reliability. These can include checks to see whether.

- the reported profits are significantly higher than the operating cash flows for the period. This may suggest that profits have been overstated;
- the tax charge is low in relation to reported profits, which may suggest, again, that profits are overstated. There may, however, be other, more innocent, explanations;
- the valuation methods used for assets held are based on historic cost or fair values. If the latter approach has been used, why and how the fair values were determined;
- there have been changes in accounting policies over the period, particularly in key areas such as revenue recognition, inventories valuation and depreciation;
- the accounting policies adopted are in line with those adopted by the rest of the industry;
- the auditors' report gives a 'clean bill of health' to the financial statements; and
- the 'small print', that is the notes to the financial statements, is being used to hide significant events or changes.

**Real World 5.15** describes the emphasis that one analyst places on this last check.

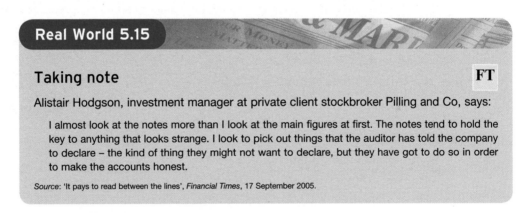

### Real World 5.15

#### Taking note                                                    FT

Alistair Hodgson, investment manager at private client stockbroker Pilling and Co, says:

> I almost look at the notes more than I look at the main figures at first. The notes tend to hold the key to anything that looks strange. I look to pick out things that the auditor has told the company to declare – the kind of thing they might not want to declare, but they have got to do so in order to make the accounts honest.

*Source*: 'It pays to read between the lines', *Financial Times*, 17 September 2005.

Checks may also be carried out to provide confirmation of positive financial health. These may include checks to see whether:

- the business is paying increased dividends;
- the directors are buying shares in the business.

Although the various checks described are useful, they cannot be used to guarantee the reliability of the financial statements. Some creative accounting practices may be very deeply seated and may go undetected for years.

## Creative accounting and economic growth

Some years ago there was a wave of creative accounting scandals, particularly in the USA but also in Europe; however, it seems that this wave has now subsided. The quality of financial statements is improving and, it is to be hoped, trust among investors and others is being restored. As a result of the actions taken by various regulatory bodies, and by accounting rule makers, creative accounting has become a more risky and difficult process for those who attempt it. However, it will never disappear completely and a further wave of creative accounting scandals may occur in the future.

The recent wave coincided with a period of strong economic growth and, during good economic times, investors and auditors become less vigilant. Thus, the opportunity to manipulate the figures becomes easier. We must not, therefore, become too complacent. Things may change again when we next experience a period of strong growth.

## Summary

The main points of this chapter may be summarised as follows.

### Directors' duty

- Separation of ownership from day-to-day control creates a need for directors to be accountable.
- To fulfil this need, the directors have a duty to prepare and publish financial statements.
- These financial statements must provide a fair representation of the financial health of the business.

### The need for accounting rules

- Accounting rules are necessary in order to avoid unacceptable accounting practices and to improve the comparability of financial statements.
- This should give greater confidence in the integrity of financial statements.

### Accounting rules

- The International Accounting Standards Board (IASB) has become an important source of rules.
- Company law and the London Stock Exchange are also sources of rules for UK companies.

### Presenting financial statements

- IAS 1 sets out the structure and content of financial statements.
- It requires preparation of a statement of financial position, statement of comprehensive income, statement of changes in equity and statement of cash flows. In addition, explanatory notes are required.
- The financial statements must provide a fair representation of the financial health of a company and this will only normally be achieved by adherence to relevant IASB standards.
- IAS 1 sets out information to be shown in the various financial statements and some of the accounting conventions and principles to be followed in preparing the statements.

### Conceptual framework

- This helps to underpin accounting standards.
- The IASB framework sets out the objective and primary users of general purpose financial reports, the qualitative characteristics and elements of financial statements and the different measurement bases that may be used.
- The IASB and FASB are working towards the development of a common conceptual framework.

### Other statutory reports

- The auditors' report provides an opinion by an independent auditor concerning whether the financial statements provide a true and fair view of the financial health of a business.

- The directors' report contains information of a financial and a non-financial nature, which goes beyond that contained in the financial statements.

- For companies listed on the Stock Exchange, an annual directors' remuneration report must also be prepared.

### Segmental reports

- Segmental reports disaggregate information on the financial statements to help users to achieve a better understanding of financial health.

- An operating segment is defined by the IASB using the 'management approach'.

- IFRS 8 requires certain information relating to each segment to be shown.

- The way in which an operating segment is defined can hinder comparisons of segments between businesses.

### Business review

- A business review is a narrative report that requires the directors to provide a balanced and comprehensive analysis of the development and performance of the business. It should also set out the principal risks.

- In the UK, the ASB has issued a Reporting Standard (RS 1) that may be used to provide a framework for a business review.

### Summary financial statements

- Summary financial statements offer a condensed version of the full financial statements.

- They aim to improve communication between the directors and those shareholders with less sophisticated information needs.

- Critics argue, however, that it is dangerous to try to simplify complexity.

### Creative accounting

- Despite the accounting rules in place there have been examples of creative accounting by directors.

- This involves using accounting practices to show what the directors would like users to see rather than what is a fair representation of reality.

- The main forms of creative accounting involve misstating revenues, massaging expenses, concealing bad news, misstating assets, and inadequate disclosure.

- There are various checks that can be carried out to the financial statements to see whether creative accounting practices may have been used.

## Key terms

International Accounting
    Standards   p. 174
International Financial Reporting
    Standards   p. 174
statement of comprehensive
    income   p. 179
statement of changes in equity
    p. 182

conceptual framework   p. 183
auditors   p. 185
directors' report   p. 186
business review   p. 186
segmental financial report   p. 187
transfer price   p. 190
summary financial statements   p. 197
creative accounting   p. 197

## Reference

1  Accounting Standards Board, *A Review of Narrative Reporting by UK Listed Companies in 2006*, January 2007.

## Further reading

If you would like to explore the topics covered in this chapter in more depth, we recommend the following books:

Alexander, D., Britton, A. and Jorissen, A. *International Financial Reporting and Analysis*, 5th edn, South Western Cengage Learning, 2011, chapters 2, 3, 8 and 9.

Elliott, B. and Elliott, J., *Financial Accounting and Reporting*, 14th edn, Financial Times Prentice Hall, 2012, chapters 10, 22 and 23.

International Accounting Standards Board, *2011 International Financial Reporting Standards* (2 volume set), 2011.

International Accounting Standards Board, *The Conceptual Framework for Financial Reporting*, September 2010.

## Review questions

Solutions to these questions can be found at the back of the book on page 749.

**5.1** 'Searching for an agreed framework of principles for accounting rules is likely to be a journey without an ending'. Discuss.

**5.2** The size of annual financial reports published by limited companies has increased steadily over the years. Can you think of any reasons, apart from the increasing volume of accounting regulation, why this has occurred?

**5.3** What problems does a user of segmental financial statements face when seeking to make comparisons between businesses?

**5.4** 'A business review should not be prepared by accountants but should be prepared by the board of directors.' Why should this be the case?

## Exercises

Exercises 5.1 and 5.2 are basic level, 5.3 and 5.4 are intermediate level and 5.5, 5.6, and 5.7 are advanced level. Those with coloured numbers have solutions at the back of the book, starting on page 766.

If you wish to try more exercises, visit the students' side of the Companion Website and MyAccountingLab.

**5.1** It has been suggested that too much information might be as bad as too little information for users of annual reports. Explain.

**5.2** What problems are likely to be encountered when preparing summary financial statements for shareholders?

**5.3** The following information was extracted from the financial statements of I. Ching (Booksellers) plc for the year to 31 December 2011:

|  | £000 |
| --- | --- |
| Finance charges | 40 |
| Cost of sales | 460 |
| Distribution expenses | 110 |
| Revenue | 943 |
| Administration expenses | 212 |
| Other expenses | 25 |
| Gain on revaluation of property, plant and equipment | 20 |
| Loss on foreign currency translations on foreign operations | 15 |
| Tax on profit for the year | 24 |
| Tax on other components of comprehensive income | 1 |

*Required*:
Prepare a statement of comprehensive income for the year ended 31 December 2011 that is set out in accordance with the requirements of IAS 1 *Presentation of Financial Statements*.

**5.4**    Manet plc had the following share capital and reserves as at 1 January 2011:

|  | £m |
|---|---|
| Share capital (£0.25 ordinary shares) | 250 |
| Share premium account | 50 |
| Revaluation reserve | 120 |
| Currency translation reserve | 15 |
| Retained earnings | 380 |
| **Total equity** | 815 |

During the year to 31 December 2011, the company revalued property, plant and equipment upwards by £30 million and made a loss on foreign exchange translation of foreign operations of £5 million. The company made a profit for the year from normal operations of £160 million during the year and paid a dividend of £80 million.

*Required*:

Prepare a statement of changes in equity in accordance with the requirements of IAS 1 *Presentation of Financial Statements*.

**5.5**    You have overheard the following statements:

(a) 'The role of independent auditors is to prepare the financial statements of the company.'
(b) 'International Accounting Standards (IASs) apply to all companies, but Stock Exchange listed companies must also adhere to International Financial Reporting Standards (IFRSs).'
(c) 'All listed companies in European Union states must follow IASs and IFRSs.'
(d) 'According to IAS 1, companies' financial statements must show an "accurate representation" of what they purport to show.'
(e) 'IAS 1 leaves it to individual companies to decide the format that they use in the statement of financial position.'
(f) 'The statement of changes in equity deals with unrealised profits and gains, for example an upward revaluation of a non-current asset.'
(g) 'If a majority of the shareholders of a listed company agree, the company need not produce a full set of financial statements, but can just produce summary financial statements.'

Critically comment on each of these statements.

**5.6**    Obtain a copy of the business review for two separate companies within the same industry. Compare the usefulness of each. In answering this question, consider the extent to which each of the two business reviews incorporate the recommendations made by the Accounting Standards Board in RS 1.

**5.7**  Segmental information relating to Dali plc for the year to 31 December 2011 is as follows:

|  | Car parts £m | Aircraft parts £m | Boat parts £m | Total £m |
|---|---|---|---|---|
| Revenues from external customers | 360 | 210 | 85 | 655 |
| Inter-segment revenues | 95 | 40 | – | 135 |
| Interest revenue | 34 | – | – | 34 |
| Interest expense | – | 28 | 8 | 36 |
| Depreciation | 80 | 55 | 15 | 150 |
| Reportable segment profit | 20 | 24 | 18 | 62 |
| Other material non-cash items | | | | |
|    Impairment of assets | – | 39 | – | 39 |
| Reportable segment assets | 170 | 125 | 44 | 339 |
| Expenditures for reportable segment | | | | |
|    non-current assets | 28 | 23 | 26 | 77 |
| Reportable segment liabilities | 85 | 67 | 22 | 174 |

*Required*:

Analyse the performance of each of the three main business segments for the year and comment on your results.

# Measuring and reporting cash flows

This chapter is devoted to the third major financial statement identified in Chapter 2: the statement of cash flows. This statement reports the movements of cash over a period and the effect of these movements on the cash position of the business. It is an important financial statement because cash is vital to the survival of a business. Without cash, a business cannot operate.

In this chapter, we shall see how the statement of cash flows is prepared and how the information that it contains may be interpreted. We shall also see why the deficiencies of the income statement, in identifying and explaining cash flows, make a separate statement necessary.

The statement of cash flows is being considered after the chapters on limited companies because the format of the statement requires an understanding of this type of business. Most limited companies are required to provide a statement of cash flows for shareholders and other users as part of their annual financial reports.

## Learning outcomes

**When you have completed this chapter, you should be able to:**

- discuss the crucial importance of cash to a business;

- explain the nature of the statement of cash flows and discuss how it can be helpful in identifying cash flow problems;

- prepare a statement of cash flows;

- interpret a statement of cash flows.

## MyAccountingLab

Visit **www.myaccountinglab.com** for practice and revision opportunities

# The statement of cash flows

The statement of cash flows is a fairly recent addition to the annual published financial statements. Companies were only required to publish an income statement and a statement of financial position (balance sheet). The prevailing view seems to have been that all the financial information needed by users would be contained within these two statements. This view may have been based partly on the assumption that if a business were profitable, it would also have plenty of cash. Although in the long run this is likely to be true, it is not necessarily true in the short to medium term.

We saw in Chapter 3 that the income statement sets out the revenue and expenses for the period, rather than the cash receipts and cash payments. This means that the profit (or loss), which represents the difference between the revenue and expenses for the period, may have little or no relation to the cash generated for the period. To illustrate this point, let us take the example of a business making a sale (generating a revenue). This may well lead to an increase in wealth that will be reflected in the income statement. However, if the sale is made on credit, no cash changes hands – at least not at the time of sale. Instead, the increase in wealth is reflected in another asset: an increase in trade receivables. Furthermore, if an item of inventories is the subject of the sale, wealth is lost to the business through the reduction in inventories. This means that an expense is incurred in making the sale, which will also be shown in the income statement. Once again, however, no cash has changed hands at the time of sale. For such reasons, the profit and the cash generated for a period will rarely go hand in hand.

Activity 6.1 should help to underline how profit and cash for a period may be affected differently by particular transactions or events.

## Activity 6.1

The following is a list of business/accounting events. In each case, state the effect (increase, decrease or none) on both profit and cash:

| | Effect | |
|---|---|---|
| | on profit | on cash |
| 1 Repayment of borrowings | ____ | ____ |
| 2 Making a profitable sale on credit | ____ | ____ |
| 3 Buying a current asset on credit | ____ | ____ |
| 4 Receiving cash from a credit customer (trade receivable) | ____ | ____ |
| 5 Depreciating a non-current asset | ____ | ____ |
| 6 Buying some inventories for cash | ____ | ____ |
| 7 Making a share issue for cash | ____ | ____ |

You should have come up with the following:

| | Effect | |
|---|---|---|
| | on profit | on cash |
| 1 Repayment of borrowings | none | decrease |
| 2 Making a profitable sale on credit | increase | none |
| 3 Buying a current asset on credit | none | none |
| 4 Receiving cash from a credit customer (trade receivable) | none | increase |
| 5 Depreciating a non-current asset | decrease | none |
| 6 Buying some inventories for cash | none | decrease |
| 7 Making a share issue for cash | none | increase |

### Activity 6.1 (*continued*)

The reasons for these answers are as follows:

1 Repaying borrowings requires that cash be paid to the lender. This means that two figures in the statement of financial position will be affected, but none in the income statement.
2 Making a profitable sale on credit will increase the sales revenue and profit figures. No cash will change hands at this point, however.
3 Buying a current asset on credit affects neither the cash balance nor the profit figure.
4 Receiving cash from a credit customer increases the cash balance and reduces the credit customer's balance. Both of these figures are on the statement of financial position. The income statement is unaffected.
5 Depreciating a non-current asset means that an expense is recognised. This causes the carrying amount of the asset, as it is recorded on the statement of financial position, to fall by an amount equal to the amount of the expense. No cash is paid or received.
6 Buying some inventories for cash means that the value of the inventories will increase and the cash balance will decrease by a similar amount. Profit is not affected.
7 Making a share issue for cash increases the shareholders' equity and increases the cash balance; profit is unaffected.

It is clear from what we have just seen that if we are to gain insights about cash movements over time, the income statement is not the place to look. Instead we need a separate financial statement. This fact has become widely recognised in recent years and in 1991 a UK financial reporting standard, FRS 1, emerged. This required all but the smallest companies to produce and publish a statement of cash flows. This standard has been superseded for listed companies from 2005 by the international standard IAS 7. The two standards have broadly similar requirements. This chapter follows the provisions of IAS 7.

## Why is cash so important?

It is worth asking why cash is so important. After all, cash is just an asset that the business needs to help it to function. In that sense, it is no different from inventories or non-current assets.

The reason for the importance of cash is that people and organisations will not normally accept anything other than cash in settlement of their claims. If a business wants to employ people, it must pay them in cash. If it wants to buy a new non-current asset to exploit a business opportunity, the seller of the asset will normally insist on being paid in cash, probably after a short period of credit. When businesses fail, it is their inability to find the cash to pay the amounts owed that really pushes them under. These factors lead to cash being the pre-eminent business asset. Cash is what analysts tend to watch most carefully when assessing the ability of businesses to survive and/or to take advantage of commercial opportunities.

During an economic downturn, the ability to generate cash takes on even greater importance. Banks become more cautious in their lending and those businesses with weak cash flows often find it difficult to obtain finance. **Real World 6.1** describes how the recent financial crisis has led banks in China to place greater emphasis on cash flows when considering loan applications.

## Real World 6.1

### Cash flow is in top three places

**FT**

'The banks are tightening the screws,' says K. B. Chan, chairman of Surface Mount Technology, which supplies consumer electronics companies. 'A lot of companies are strapped for cash.'

Stanley Wong, business development director at Man Yue Electronics, the world's fifth largest maker of aluminium capacitors, says: 'Banks don't even trust each other. They are being a lot more careful.' Mr Wong says that companies such as his, with strong cash flows, will still get working capital and other loans but bankers who used to lend to Man Yue and other manufacturers sight unseen are now tramping out to their factories for a closer look.

'The banks only look at cash flow – number one is cash flow, number two is cash flow and number three is cash flow,' says Mr Chan. 'Profit is only an accounting statement.'

*Source*: 'Rations cut for army of buyers', *Financial Times*, 20 October 2008.

Real World 6.2 is taken from a question and answer column written by John Timpson. He is the chief executive of the very successful, high street shoe repairing and key cutting business, with over 800 branches (and expanding) throughout the UK. His answer to a question highlights the importance of cash reporting in the successful management of his business. The column appeared in the *Daily Telegraph*.

## Real World 6.2

### Cash is key

*Question: You say you look at Timpson's cash position every week (or was it every day?), but what do you do with the information? What are you watching for and how do you respond when you see something? I'm swamped with analytics and data and can't see the wood for the trees.*

**Answer:** I look at our cash balance every day (not Saturdays and Sundays). It is the best way to test the financial temperature of our business. The trick is to compare with the same day last year, thus showing cash flow for the past 12 months.

It is not a perfect system (never forget that your finance department may secretly massage the cash by paying suppliers sooner or later than you anticipate) but a glance at the daily cash is more transparent than management accounts that are full of provisions and only appear once a month.

You claim to be swamped by figures – most managers have the same problem. Finance and IT take a delight in producing a deluge of data. But being in possession of too many statistics is counterproductive.

This daily cash report helps to clear the clutter created by computers – it's a simple report that helps you pose the right questions.

Why have things suddenly got worse? Are we in danger of breaking our bank borrowing limit? Why does the cash flow look so much better than in the management accounts?

→

**Real World 6.2 (*continued*)**

This cash report can also give you an early warning of changing financial circumstances. It came to my rescue in 2004 when, through a major acquisition, the business doubled in size overnight and was going through a great deal of change.

Our financial control suffered but I didn't realise how bad things were until I was waiting to board a plane to go on a Caribbean holiday. A quick look at my Blackberry (when my wife wasn't looking) showed an unexpected £500,000 deterioration in our overdraft. It wasn't a great start to the holiday and my wife was upset when I spent the first day on the telephone. However we were able to tackle the problem six weeks before it would have been revealed in the management accounts.

*Source*: John Timpson, The management column, *Daily Telegraph Business*, 14 June 2010.

# The main features of the statement of cash flows

The statement of cash flows is a summary of the cash receipts and payments over the period concerned. All payments of a particular type, for example cash payments to acquire additional non-current assets or other investments, are added together to give just one figure that appears in the statement. The net total of the statement is the net increase or decrease of the cash (and cash equivalents) of the business over the period. The statement is basically an analysis of the business's cash (and cash equivalents) movements for the period.

## A definition of cash and cash equivalents

IAS 7 defines cash as notes and coins in hand and deposits in banks and similar institutions that are accessible to the business on demand. Cash equivalents are short-term, highly liquid investments that are readily convertible to known amounts of cash and which are subject to an insignificant risk of changes of value. Cash equivalents are held for the purpose of meeting short-term cash commitments rather than for investment or other purposes.

Activity 6.2 should clarify the types of items that fall within the definition of 'cash equivalents'.

**Activity 6.2**

At the end of its reporting period, Zeneb plc's statement of financial position included the following items:

1 *A bank deposit account where one month's notice of withdrawal is required.* This deposit was made because the business has a temporary cash surplus that it will need to use in the short term for operating purposes.
2 *Ordinary shares in Jones plc (a Stock Exchange listed business).* These were acquired because Zeneb plc has a temporary cash surplus and its directors believed that the shares represent a good short-term investment. The funds invested will need to be used in the short term for operating purposes.

3 *A bank deposit account that is withdrawable instantly*. This represents an investment of surplus funds that are not seen as being needed in the short term.

4 An overdraft on the business's bank current account.

**Which (if any) of these four items would be included in the figure for cash and cash equivalents?**

Your response should have been as follows:

1 A cash equivalent because the deposit is part of the business's normal cash management activities and there is little doubt about how much cash will be obtained when the deposit is withdrawn.

2 Not a cash equivalent. Although the investment was made as part of normal cash management, there is a significant risk that the amount expected (hoped for!) when the shares are sold may not actually be forthcoming.

3 Not a cash equivalent because this represents an investment rather than a short-term surplus amount of cash.

4 This is cash itself, though a negative amount of it. The only exception to this classification would be where the business is financed in the longer term by an overdraft, when it would be part of the financing of the business, rather than negative cash.

As can be seen from the responses to Activity 6.2, whether a particular item falls within the definition of cash and cash equivalent depends on two factors:

● the nature of the item; and
● why it has arisen.

In practice, it is not usually difficult to decide whether an item is a cash equivalent.

## The relationship between the main financial statements

The statement of cash flows is now accepted, along with the income statement and the statement of financial position, as a major financial statement. The relationship between the three statements is shown in Figure 6.1. The statement of financial position reflects the combination of assets (including cash) and claims (including the shareholders' equity) of the business *at a particular point in time*. The statement of cash flows and the income statement explain the *changes over a period* to two of the items in the statement of financial position. The statement of cash flows explains the changes to cash. The income statement explains changes to equity, arising from trading operations.

## The form of the statement of cash flows

The standard layout of the statement of cash flows is summarised in Figure 6.2. We shall now explain the terms used in the statement of cash flows.

### Cash flows from operating activities

This is the net inflow or outflow from trading operations, after tax payments (or receipts) and cash paid to meet financing costs. It is equal to the sum of cash receipts from trade receivables and cash receipts from cash sales, where relevant, less the sums

**Figure 6.1** The relationship between the statement of financial position, the income statement and the statement of cash flows

The statement of financial position shows the relationship, at a particular point in time, between the business's assets and claims. The income statement explains how, over a period between two statements of financial position, the equity figure in the first statement of financial position has altered as a result of trading operations. The statement of cash flows also looks at changes over the reporting period, but this statement explains the alteration in the cash (and cash equivalent) balances from the first to the second of the two consecutive statements of financial position.

**Figure 6.2** Standard layout of the statement of cash flows

This is the standard layout for the statement of cash flows as required by IAS 7 *Statement of Cash Flows*.

paid to buy inventories, to pay rent, to pay wages and so on. From this are also deducted payments for interest on the business's borrowings, corporation tax and dividends paid.

Note that it is the amounts of cash received and paid during the period that feature in the statement of cash flows, not the revenue and expenses for that period. It is, of course, the income statement that deals with the revenue and expenses. Similarly the tax and dividend payments that appear in the statement of cash flows are those made in the period covered by the statement. Companies normally pay tax on their profits in four equal instalments. Two of these are during the year concerned and the other two are during the following year. As a result, by the end of each reporting year, half of the tax will have been paid and the remainder will be a current liability at the end of the year, to be paid off during the following year. During any particular year, therefore, the tax payment would normally equal 50 per cent of the previous year's tax charge and 50 per cent of that of the current year.

The net figure for this section is intended to indicate the net cash flows for the period that arose from normal day-to-day trading activities after taking account of the tax that has to be paid on them and the cost of servicing the finance (equity and borrowings) needed to support them.

### Cash flows from investing activities

This section of the statement is concerned with cash payments made to acquire additional non-current assets and with cash receipts from the disposal of non-current assets. These non-current assets will tend to be the usual items such as buildings and machinery. They might also be loans made by the business, or shares in another company bought by the business.

This section also includes cash receipts *arising from* financial investments (loans and equities) made outside the business. These receipts are interest on loans made by the business and dividends from shares in other companies that are owned by the business.

### Cash flows from financing activities

This part of the statement is concerned with the long-term financing of the business. So here we are considering borrowings (other than very short-term borrowings) and finance from share issues. This category is concerned with repayment/redemption of finance as well as with the raising of it. It is permissible under IAS 7 to include dividend payments made by the business here, as an alternative to including them in 'Cash flows from operating activities' (above).

This section shows the net cash flows from raising and/or paying back long-term finance.

### Net increase or decrease in cash and cash equivalents

The total of the statement must, of course, be the net increase or decrease in cash and cash equivalents over the period concerned.

The effect on a business's cash and cash equivalents of its various activities is shown in Figure 6.3. As explained, the arrows show the *normal* direction of cash flow for the typical healthy, profitable business in a typical reporting period.

## The normal direction of cash flows

Normally 'operating activities' provide positive cash flows, that is, they help to increase the business's cash resources. In fact, for most UK businesses, in most time periods, cash generated from day-to-day trading, even after deducting tax, interest and dividends, is overwhelmingly the most important source of new finance.

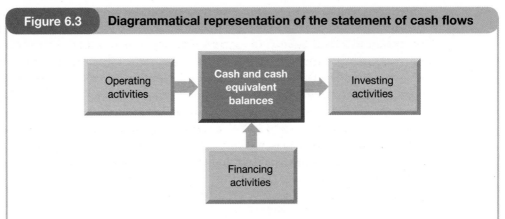

| Figure 6.3 | Diagrammatical representation of the statement of cash flows |

Various activities of the business each have their own effect on the total of the cash and cash equivalents, either positive (increasing the total) or negative (reducing it). The net increase or decrease in the cash and cash equivalents over a period will be the sum of these individual effects, taking account of the direction (cash in or cash out) of each activity.

Note that the direction of the arrow shows the *normal* direction of the cash flow in respect of each activity. In certain circumstances, each of these arrows could be reversed in direction.

## Activity 6.3

Last year's statement of cash flows for Angus plc showed a negative cash flow from operating activities. What could be the reason for this and should the business's management be alarmed by it? (*Hint*: We think that there are two broad possible reasons for a negative cash flow.)

The two reasons are:

1 The business is unprofitable. This leads to more cash being paid out to employees, to suppliers of goods and services, for interest, and so on than is received from trade receivables in respect of sales. This would be particularly alarming, because a major expense for most businesses is depreciation of non-current assets. Since depreciation does not lead to a cash flow, it is not considered in 'net cash inflows from operating activities'. This means that a negative operating cash flow might well indicate a very much larger trading loss – in other words, a significant loss of the business's wealth; something to concern management.

2 The other reason might be less alarming. A business that is expanding its activities (level of sales revenue) would tend to spend quite a lot of cash relative to the amount of cash coming in from sales. This is because it will probably be expanding its assets (non-current and current) to accommodate the increased demand. For example, a business may well need to have inventories in place before additional sales can be made. Similarly, staff have to be employed and paid. Even when the additional sales are made, those sales would normally be made on credit, with the cash inflow lagging behind the sales. All of this means that, in the first instance, in cash flow terms, the business would not necessarily benefit from the additional sales revenue. This is particularly likely to be true of a new business, which would be expanding inventories and other assets from zero. It would also need to employ and pay staff. Expansion typically causes cash flow strains for the reasons just explained. This can be a particular problem because the business's increased profitability might encourage a feeling of optimism, which could lead to lack of attention being paid to the cash flow problem.

Investing activities typically cause net negative cash flows. This is because many types of non-current asset wear out and many that do not wear out become obsolete. Also, businesses tend to seek to expand their asset base. When a business sells some non-current assets, the sale will give rise to positive cash flows, but in net terms the cash flows are normally negative with cash spent on new assets outweighing that received from disposal of old ones.

Financing can go in either direction, depending on the financing strategy at the time. Since businesses seek to expand, there is a general tendency for this area to lead to cash coming into the business rather than leaving it.

**Real World 6.3** shows the summarised statement of cash flows of Tesco plc, the UK-based supermarket company.

---

### Real World 6.3

### Cashing in

Like many larger companies, Tesco produces summary versions of its financial statements for users who do not want all of the detail. The summary statement of cash flows for the business for the year ended 26 February 2011 shows the cash flows of the business under each of the headings described above.

**Summary group statement of cash flows 52 weeks ended 26 February 2011**

|  | £m |
|---|---|
| Cash generated from operations | 5,366 |
| Interest paid | (614) |
| Corporation tax paid | (760) |
| **Net cash from operating activities** | 3,992 |
| **Net cash used in investing activities** | (1,859) |
| **Cash flows from financing activities** |  |
| Dividends paid to equity owners | (1,081) |
| Other net cash flows from financing activities | (1,955) |
| **Net cash from financing activities** | (3,036) |
| **Net decrease in cash and cash equivalents** | (903) |

*Source*: Tesco Annual Review 2011, p. 35, www.tescocorporate.com.

---

As we shall see shortly, more detailed information under each of the main headings is provided in the statement of cash flows presented to shareholders and other users.

## Preparing the statement of cash flows

### Deducing net cash flows from operating activities

As we have seen, the first section of the statement of cash flows is the 'cash flows from operating activities'. There are two approaches that can be taken to deriving this figure: the direct method and the indirect method.

## The direct method

The **direct method** involves an analysis of the cash records of the business for the period, picking out all payments and receipts relating to operating activities. These are summarised to give the total figures for inclusion in the statement of cash flows. Done on a computer, this is a simple matter, but hardly any businesses adopt the direct method.

## The indirect method

The **indirect method** is much the more popular method. It relies on the fact that, sooner or later, sales revenue gives rise to cash inflows, and expenses give rise to outflows. This means that the figure for profit for the year will be closely linked to the net cash flows from operating activities. Since businesses have to produce an income statement in any case, information from it can be used as a starting point to deduce the cash flows from operating activities.

Of course, within a particular reporting period, profit for the period will not normally equal the net cash inflows from operating activities. When sales are made on credit, the cash receipt occurs some time after the sale. This means that sales revenue made towards the end of a reporting period will be included in that reporting period's income statement. However, most of the cash from those sales will flow into the business, and should be included in the statement of cash flows, in the following period. Fortunately it is easy to deduce the cash received from sales if we have the relevant income statement and statements of financial position, as we shall see in Activity 6.4.

### Activity 6.4

How can we deduce the cash inflows from sales using the income statement and statement of financial position for the business?

The statement of financial position will tell us how much was owed in respect of credit sales at the beginning and end of the reporting period (trade receivables). The income statement tells us the sales revenue figure. If we adjust the sales revenue figure by the increase or decrease in trade receivables over the period, we deduce the cash from sales for the period.

### Example 6.1

The sales revenue figure for a business for the year was £34 million. The trade receivables totalled £4 million at the beginning of the year, but had increased to £5 million by the end of the year.

Basically, the trade receivables figure is dictated by sales revenue and cash receipts. It is increased when a sale is made and decreased when cash is received from a credit customer. If, over the year, the sales revenue and the cash receipts had been equal, the beginning-of-year and end-of-year trade receivables figures would have been equal. Since the trade receivables figure increased, it must mean that less cash was received than sales revenues were made. In fact, the cash receipts from sales must have been £33 million (that is, $34 - (5 - 4)$).

Put slightly differently, we can say that as a result of sales, assets of £34 million flowed into the business during the year. If £1 million of this went to increasing the asset of trade receivables, this leaves only £33 million that went to increase cash.

The same general point is true in respect of nearly all of the other items that are taken into account in deducing the operating profit figure. The main exception is depreciation. The depreciation expense for a reporting period is not necessarily associated with any movement in cash during that same period.

All of this means that we can take the profit before taxation (that is, the profit after interest but before taxation) for the year, add back the depreciation and interest expense charged in arriving at that profit, and adjust this total by movements in inventories, trade (and other) receivables and payables. If we then go on to deduct payments made during the reporting period for taxation, interest on borrowings and dividends, we have the net cash from operating activities.

## Example 6.2

The relevant information from the financial statements of Dido plc for last year is as follows:

|  | £m |
|---|---|
| Profit before taxation (after interest) | 122 |
| Depreciation charged in arriving at profit before taxation | 34 |
| Interest expense | 6 |
| At the beginning of the year: | |
| Inventories | 15 |
| Trade receivables | 24 |
| Trade payables | 18 |
| At the end of the year: | |
| Inventories | 17 |
| Trade receivables | 21 |
| Trade payables | 19 |

The following further information is available about payments during last year:

|  | £m |
|---|---|
| Taxation paid | 32 |
| Interest paid | 5 |
| Dividends paid | 9 |

The cash flow from operating activities is derived as follows:

|  | £m |
|---|---|
| Profit before taxation (after interest) | 122 |
| Depreciation | 34 |
| Interest expense | 6 |
| Increase in inventories (17 – 15) | (2) |
| Decrease in trade receivables (21 – 24) | 3 |
| Increase in trade payables (19 – 18) | 1 |
| **Cash generated from operating activities** | 164 |
| Interest paid | (5) |
| Taxation paid | (32) |
| Dividends paid | (9) |
| **Net cash from operating activities** | 118 |

As we can see, the net increase in **working capital*** (that is, current assets less current liabilities) as a result of trading was £162 million (that is, 122 + 34 + 6). Of this, £2 million went into increased inventories. More cash was received from

→

trade receivables than sales revenue was made. Similarly, less cash was paid to trade payables than purchases of goods and services on credit. Both of these had a favourable effect on cash. Over the year, therefore, cash increased by £164 million. When account was taken of the payments for interest, tax and dividends, the net cash from operating activities was £118 million (inflow).

Note that we needed to adjust the profit before taxation (after interest) by the depreciation and interest expenses to derive the profit before depreciation, interest and taxation.

* Working capital is a term widely used in accounting and finance, not just in the context of the statement of cash flows. We shall encounter it several times in later chapters.

## Activity 6.5

In deriving the cash generated from operating activities, we add the depreciation expense for the period to the profit before taxation. Does this mean that depreciation is a source of cash?

No, it does not mean that depreciation is a source of cash. The periodic depreciation expense is irrelevant to cash flow. Since the profit before taxation is derived *after* deducting the depreciation expense for the period, we need to eliminate the impact of depreciation by adding it back to the profit figure. This will give us the profit before tax *and before* depreciation, which is what we need.

We should be clear why it is necessary to add back an amount for interest at the start of the derivation of cash flow from operating activities only to deduct an amount for interest further down. The reason is that the first is the interest expense for the reporting period, whereas the second is the amount of cash paid out for interest during that period. These may well be different amounts, as was the case in Example 6.2.

The indirect method of deducing the net cash flow from operating activities is summarised in Figure 6.4.

## Activity 6.6

The relevant information from the financial statements of Pluto plc for last year is as follows:

|  | £m |
|---|---|
| Profit before taxation (after interest) | 165 |
| Depreciation charged in arriving at operating profit | 41 |
| Interest expense | 21 |
| At the beginning of the year: | |
| Inventories | 22 |
| Trade receivables | 18 |
| Trade payables | 15 |
| At the end of the year: | |
| Inventories | 23 |
| Trade receivables | 21 |
| Trade payables | 17 |

**Figure 6.4**    The indirect method of deducing the net cash flows from operating activities

Determining the net cash from operating activities first involves adding back the depreciation and the interest expense to the profit before taxation. Next, adjustment is made for increases or decreases in inventories, receivables and payables. Lastly, cash paid for interest, taxation and dividends is deducted.

\* Note that dividends could alternatively be included under the heading 'Cash flows from financing activities'.

**Activity 6.6 (continued)**

The following further information is available about payments during last year:

|  | £m |
|---|---|
| Taxation paid | 49 |
| Interest paid | 25 |
| Dividends paid | 28 |

What figure should appear in the statement of cash flows for 'Cash flows from operating activities'?

Net cash inflows from operating activities:

|  | £m |
|---|---|
| Profit before taxation (after interest) | 165 |
| Depreciation | 41 |
| Interest expense | 21 |
| Increase in inventories (23 – 22) | (1) |
| Increase in trade receivables (21 – 18) | (3) |
| Increase in trade payables (17 – 15) | 2 |
| Cash generated from operating activities | 225 |
| Interest paid | (25) |
| Taxation paid | (49) |
| Dividends paid | (28) |
| Net cash from operating activities | 123 |

## Deducing the other areas of the statement of cash flows

We can now go on to take a look at the preparation of a complete statement of cash flows through Example 6.3.

**Example 6.3**

Torbryan plc's income statement for the year ended 31 December 2010 and the statements of financial position as at 31 December 2010 and 2011 are as follows:

**Income statement for the year ended 31 December 2011**

|  | £m |
|---|---|
| Revenue | 576 |
| Cost of sales | (307) |
| Gross profit | 269 |
| Distribution expenses | (65) |
| Administrative expenses | (26) |
|  | 178 |
| Other operating income | 21 |
| Operating profit | 199 |
| Interest receivable | 17 |
|  | 216 |
| Interest payable | (23) |
| Profit before taxation | 193 |
| Taxation | (46) |
| Profit for the year | 147 |

### Statements of financial position as at 31 December 2010 and 2011

|  | 2010 | 2011 |
|---|---|---|
|  | £m | £m |
| **ASSETS** | | |
| **Non-current assets** | | |
| *Property, plant and equipment* | | |
| Land and buildings | 241 | 241 |
| Plant and machinery | 309 | 325 |
|  | 550 | 566 |
| **Current assets** | | |
| Inventories | 44 | 41 |
| Trade receivables | 121 | 139 |
|  | 165 | 180 |
| **Total assets** | 715 | 746 |
| **EQUITY AND LIABILITIES** | | |
| **Equity** | | |
| Called-up ordinary share capital | 150 | 200 |
| Share premium account | – | 40 |
| Retained earnings | 26 | 123 |
|  | 176 | 363 |
| **Non-current liabilities** | | |
| Borrowings – loan notes | 400 | 250 |
| **Current liabilities** | | |
| Borrowings (all bank overdraft) | 68 | 56 |
| Trade payables | 55 | 54 |
| Taxation | 16 | 23 |
|  | 139 | 133 |
| **Total equity and liabilities** | 715 | 746 |

During 2011, the business spent £95 million on additional plant and machinery. There were no other non-current-asset acquisitions or disposals. A dividend of £50 million was paid on ordinary shares during the year. The interest receivable revenue and the interest payable expense for the year were equal to the cash inflow and outflow respectively; £150,000 of loan notes were redeemed at their nominal (par) value.

The statement of cash flows would be:

### Statement of cash flows for the year ended 31 December 2011

|  | £m |
|---|---|
| ***Cash flows from operating activities*** | |
| Profit before taxation (after interest) (see Note 1 below) | 193 |
| Adjustments for: | |
| Depreciation (Note 2) | 79 |
| Interest receivable (Note 3) | (17) |
| Interest payable (Note 4) | 23 |
| Increase in trade receivables (139 – 121) | (18) |
| Decrease in trade payables (55 – 54) | (1) |
| Decrease in inventories (44 – 41) | 3 |
| **Cash generated from operations** | 262 |

|  |  |
|---|---|
| Interest paid | (23) |
| Taxation paid (Note 5) | (39) |
| Dividend paid | (50) |
| Net cash from operating activities | 150 |
| **Cash flows from investing activities** | |
| Payments to acquire tangible non-current assets | (95) |
| Interest received (Note 3) | 17 |
| Net cash used in investing activities | (78) |
| **Cash flows from financing activities** | |
| Repayments of loan notes | (150) |
| Issue of ordinary shares (Note 6) | 90 |
| Net cash used in financing activities | (60) |
| Net increase in cash and cash equivalents | 12 |
| Cash and cash equivalents at 1 January 2011 (Note 7) | (68) |
| Cash and cash equivalents at 31 December 2011 | (56) |

To see how this relates to the cash of the business at the beginning and end of the year it can be useful to provide a reconciliation as follows:

**Analysis of cash and cash equivalents during the year ended 31 December 2010**

|  | £m |
|---|---|
| Overdraft balance at 1 January 2011 | (68) |
| Net cash inflow | 12 |
| Overdraft balance at 31 December 2011 | (56) |

**Notes:**

1 This is simply taken from the income statement for the year.

2 Since there were no disposals, the depreciation charges must be the difference between the start and end of the year's plant and machinery (non-current assets) values, adjusted by the cost of any additions.

|  | £m |
|---|---|
| Carrying amount at 1 January 2011 | 309 |
| Additions | 95 |
|  | 404 |
| Depreciation (balancing figure) | (79) |
| Carrying amount at 31 December 2011 | 325 |

3 Interest receivable must be deducted to work towards what the profit would have been before it was added in the income statement, because it is not part of operations but of investing activities. The cash inflow from this source appears under the 'Cash flows from investing activities' heading.

4 The interest payable expense must be taken out, by adding it back to the profit figure. We subsequently deduct the cash paid for interest payable during the year. In this case the two figures are identical.

5 Taxation is paid by companies 50 per cent during their reporting year and 50 per cent in the following year. As a result the 2011 payment would have been half the tax on the 2010 profit (that is, the figure that would have appeared in the current liabilities at the end of 2010), plus half of the 2011 taxation charge (that is, $16 + (\frac{1}{2} \times 46) = 39$). Probably the easiest way to deduce the amount paid during the year to 31 December 2011 is by following this approach:

|  | £m |
|---|---|
| Taxation owed at start of the year (from the statement of financial position as at 31 December 2010) | 16 |
| Taxation charge for the year (from the income statement) | 46 |
|  | 62 |
|  |  |
| Taxation owed at the end of the year (from the statement of financial position as at 31 December 2011) | (23) |
| Taxation paid during the year | 39 |

This follows the logic that if we start with what the business owed at the beginning of the year, add what was owed as a result of the current year's taxation charge and then deduct what was owed at the end, the resulting figure must be what was paid during the year.

6  The share issue raised £90 million, of which £50 million went into the share capital total on the statement of financial position and £40 million into share premium.

7  There were no 'cash equivalents', just cash (though negative).

## What does the statement of cash flows tell us?

The statement of cash flows tells us how the business has generated cash during the period and where that cash has gone. Since cash is properly regarded as the lifeblood of just about any business, this is potentially very useful information.

Tracking the sources and uses of cash over several years could show financing trends that a reader of the statements could use to help to make judgements about the likely future behaviour of the business.

Looking specifically at the statement of cash flows for Torbryan plc, in Example 6.3, we can see the following:

- Net cash flow from operations seems strong, much larger than the profit-for-the-year figure, after taking account of the dividend paid. This would be expected because depreciation is deducted in arriving at profit. Working capital has absorbed some cash, which would be unsurprising if there had been an expansion of activity (sales revenue) over the year. From the information supplied, however, we do not know whether there was an expansion or not. (We have only one year's income statement.)
- There were net outflows of cash for investing activities, but this would not be unusual. Many types of non-current assets have limited lives and need to be replaced with new ones. The expenditure during the year was not out of line with the depreciation expense for the year, which is to be expected for a business with a regular replacement programme for non-current assets.
- There was a fairly major outflow of cash to redeem some borrowings, partly offset by the proceeds of a share issue. This presumably represents a change of financing strategy. Together with the ploughed-back profit from trading, there has been a significant shift in the equity/borrowings balance.

**Real World 6.4** looks at the statement of cash flows of an emerging business, LiDCO Group plc, that is experiencing negative cash flows as it seeks to establish a profitable market for its products.

## Real World 6.4

### Not losing heart

LiDCO Group plc has its shares listed on the Alternative Investment Market (AIM). AIM is a junior market of the London Stock Exchange that specialises in the shares of smaller, up-and-coming businesses.

LiDCO makes highly sophisticated equipment for monitoring the hearts of cardiac patients, typically in hospitals and clinics. The business was started by doctors and scientists. It has spent £6.8 million over ten years developing its products, obtaining registration for their use from both the UK and US authorities and creating manufacturing facilities.

LiDCO's statement of cash flows for the year to 31 January 2011 was:

|  | £000 |
|---|---|
| Net cash outflow from operating activities | 115 |
| **Cash flows from investing activities** | |
| Purchase of property, plant and equipment | (127) |
| Purchase of intangible assets | (429) |
| Interest received | 8 |
| Net cash used in investing activities | (548) |
| **Cash flows from financing activities** | |
| Repayment of finance lease | (10) |
| Issue of ordinary share capital | 1 |
| Net cash (outflow)/inflow from financing activities | (9) |
| Net (decrease)/inflow in cash and cash equivalents | (442) |

[Note that this was adapted from the statement that appeared in the business's annual report. Some more detail was supplied in the way of notes to the accounts.]

To put these figures into context, there was a loss before taxation for the year of £490,000 and the sales revenue for the year was £6.24 million. This means that the net cash inflow from operating activities was equal to 2 per cent of the revenue figure. This was an improvement, since it had been a negative (outflow) of 8 per cent in 2010, 27 per cent in 2009, 30 per cent in 2008, 40 per cent in 2007 and over 50 per cent in 2006.

2011 was the first year that the business had generated a positive net cash inflow from operating activities.

Such cash flow profiles are fairly typical of 'high-tech' businesses that have enormous start-up costs to bring their products to the market in sufficient quantities to yield a profit. Of course, not all such businesses achieve this, but LiDCO seems to be turning into a profitable business.

*Sources:* LiDCO Group plc Annual Report 2011 and AIM company profile, www.londonstockexchange.com.

## Problems with IAS 7

IAS 7 *Statement of Cash Flows* does not enjoy universal acclaim. Its critics argue that the standard is too permissive in the description and classification of important items. One example is expenditure that does not produce a recognised asset but which may benefit future periods. This might include such things as advertising, exploration activities and research and development. In practice, these may be classified as either cash flows from operating activities or as cash flows from investing activities. Not only can this be confusing to users but, by classifying this expenditure as investing activities it is possible to flatter cash flows from operating activities, which is a key measure.

Some believe that the standard would inspire greater confidence among users if it insisted that only the direct method be used to calculate cash flows from operating activities. Supporters of the direct method argue that, being cash-based, it provides greater clarity by setting out operating cash receipts and payments. No accrual-based adjustments are made, which means that it is less susceptible to manipulation than the indirect approach, which has been described as 'a gift to dodgy companies'. (See the reference at the end of the chapter.) In its defence, however, it should be said that the indirect approach may help to shed light on the quality of reported profits by reconciling profit with the net cash from operating activities for a period. A business must demonstrate an ability to convert profits into cash, and so revealing the link between profits and cash is important.

IAS 7 is also criticised for failing to require cash flows to be reconciled with movements in net debt, which may be defined as borrowings less any cash and cash equivalents. This reconciliation, so it is argued, would help users to gain a better understanding of movements in net debt and the management of cash flows. Net debt is often seen as a useful indicator of business solvency, and so linking movements in this figure to the statement of cash flows may be important. Although not required to do so, many listed UK businesses provide this reconciliation as additional information. This is, at least partly, for historical reasons: the standard that preceded IAS 7 required this information.

Example 6.4 illustrates how this reconciliation may be carried out.

## Example 6.4

Based on the information set out in the financial statements of Torbryan plc for the financial years ended 31 December 2010 and 2011 (see Example 6.3), the following reconciliation of net cash flow to movement in net debt for the year to 31 December 2011 can be carried out.

### Reconciliation of net cash flow to movement in net debt for the year to 31 December 2011

| | £m |
|---|---:|
| Net increase in cash and cash equivalents during the year | 12 |
| Repayment of loan notes | 150 |
| Decrease in net debt during the year | 162 |
| Net debt at 1 January 2011 (400 + 68*) | 468 |
| Net debt at 31 December 2011 (250 + 56) | (306) |
| Decrease in net debt during the year | 162 |

* We saw earlier that a bank overdraft is normally viewed as negative cash. An overdraft is added to other borrowings to derive the net debt, whereas a positive cash balance would be deducted.

We can see that the net debt has been reduced largely through the repayment of loan notes but partly through a reduction in the overdraft.

## Self-assessment question 6.1

Touchstone plc's income statements for the years ended 31 December 2010 and 2011 and statements of financial position as at 31 December 2010 and 2011 are as follows:

### Income statements for the years ended 2010 and 2011

|  | 2010 £m | 2011 £m |
| --- | --- | --- |
| Revenue | 173 | 207 |
| Cost of sales | (96) | (101) |
| Gross profit | 77 | 106 |
| Distribution expenses | (18) | (20) |
| Administrative expenses | (24) | (26) |
| Other operating income | 3 | 4 |
| Operating profit | 38 | 64 |
| Interest payable | (2) | (4) |
| Profit before taxation | 36 | 60 |
| Taxation | (8) | (16) |
| Profit for the year | 28 | 44 |

### Statements of financial position as at 31 December 2010 and 2011

|  | 2010 £m | 2011 £m |
| --- | --- | --- |
| ASSETS | | |
| Non-current assets | | |
| *Property, plant and equipment* | | |
| Land and buildings | 94 | 110 |
| Plant and machinery | 53 | 62 |
|  | 147 | 172 |
| Current assets | | |
| Inventories | 25 | 24 |
| Treasury bills (short-term investments) | – | 15 |
| Trade receivables | 16 | 26 |
| Cash at bank and in hand | 4 | 4 |
|  | 45 | 69 |
| Total assets | 192 | 241 |
| EQUITY AND LIABILITIES | | |
| Equity | | |
| Called-up ordinary share capital | 100 | 100 |
| Retained earnings | 30 | 56 |
|  | 130 | 156 |
| Non-current liabilities | | |
| Borrowings – loan notes (10%) | 20 | 40 |
| Current liabilities | | |
| Trade payables | 38 | 37 |
| Taxation | 4 | 8 |
|  | 42 | 45 |
| Total equity and liabilities | 192 | 241 |

Included in 'cost of sales', 'distribution expenses' and 'administrative expenses', depreciation was as follows:

|  | 2010 £m | 2011 £m |
|---|---|---|
| Land and buildings | 5 | 6 |
| Plant and machinery | 6 | 10 |

There were no non-current asset disposals in either year.

The interest payable expense equalled the cash payment made during each of the years.

The business paid dividends on ordinary shares of £14 million during 2010 and £18 million during 2011.

The Treasury bills represent a short-term investment of funds that will be used shortly in operations. There is insignificant risk that this investment will lose value.

*Required*:

Prepare a statement of cash flows for the business for 2011.

**The solution to this question can be found at the back of the book on page 768.**

## Summary

The main points of this chapter may be summarised as follows:

### The need for a statement of cash flows

- Cash is important because no business can operate without it.
- The statement of cash flows is specifically designed to reveal movements in cash over a period.
- Cash movements cannot be readily detected from the income statement, which focuses on revenue and expenses rather than on cash receipts and cash payments.
- Profit (or loss) and cash generated for the period are rarely equal.
- The statement of cash flows is a primary financial statement, along with the income statement and the statement of financial position.

### Preparing the statement of cash flows

- The layout of the statement contains three categories of cash movement: cash flows from operating activities, cash flows from investing activities, and cash flows from financing activities.
- The total of the cash movements under these three categories will provide the net increase or decrease in cash and cash equivalents for the period.
- A reconciliation can be undertaken to check that the opening balance of cash and cash equivalents plus the net increase (or decrease) for the period equals the closing balance.

### Calculating the cash generated from operations

- The net cash flows from operating activities can be derived by either the direct method or the indirect method.

- The direct method is based on an analysis of the cash records for the period, whereas the indirect method uses information contained within the income statement and statements of financial position of the business.

- The indirect method takes the net operating profit for the period, adds back any depreciation charge and then adjusts for changes in inventories, receivables and payables during the period.

**Interpreting the statement of cash flows**

- The statement of cash flows shows the main sources and uses of cash.

- Tracking the cash movements over several periods may reveal financing and investing patterns and may help predict future management action.

**Problems with IAS 7**

- IAS 7 has been criticised for being too permissive in the description and classification of important items and for allowing businesses to adopt the indirect method for determining net cash from operating activities.

- There have also been calls for movements in net debt to be reconciled with cash flows.

# MyAccountingLab

Go to **www.myaccountinglab.com** to check your understanding of the chapter, create a personalised study plan, and maximise your revision time

## Key terms

**direct method**   p. 220
**indirect method**   p. 220

**working capital**   p. 221

## Reference

'Cash flow statements', *Financial Times*, 25 August 2005, FT.com.

## Further reading

If you would like to explore the topics covered in this chapter in more depth, we recommend the following books:

Elliott, B. and Elliott, J., *Financial Accounting and Reporting*, 15th edn, Financial Times Prentice Hall, 2012, chapter 25.

Alexander, D. and Nobes, C., *Financial accounting: an international introduction,* 4th edn, Financial Times Prentice Hall, 2010, chapter 13.

International Accounting Standards Board, *2011 International Financial Reporting Standards IFRS* (2 volume set), 2011.

KPMG, *Insights into IFRS*, 8th edn, 2011, Sweet and Maxwell, Section 2.3. A summary of this book is available free at www.kpmg.com.

## Review questions

Solutions to these questions can be found at the back of the book on pages 749 to 750.

**6.1**  The typical business outside the service sector has about 50 per cent more of its resources tied up in inventories than in cash, yet there is no call for a 'statement of inventories flows' to be prepared. Why is cash regarded as more important than inventories?

**6.2**  What is the difference between the direct and indirect methods of deducing cash generated from operations?

**6.3**  Taking each of the categories of the statement of cash flows in turn, in which direction would you normally expect the cash flow to be? Explain your answer.

(a)  Cash flows from operating activities.
(b)  Cash flows from investing activities.
(c)  Cash flows from financing activities.

**6.4**  What causes the profit for the reporting period not to equal the net cash inflow?

## Exercises

Exercises 6.1 and 6.2 are basic level, 6.3 to 6.5 are intermediate level and 6.6 and 6.7 are advanced level. Exercises with coloured numbers have solutions at the back of the book, starting on page 768.

If you wish to try more exercises, visit the students' side of the Companion Website and MyAccountingLab.

**6.1**  How will each of the following events ultimately affect the amount of cash?

(a)  An increase in the level of inventories
(b)  A rights issue of ordinary shares
(c)  A bonus issue of ordinary shares
(d)  Writing off part of the value of some inventories
(e)  The disposal of a large number of the business's shares by a major shareholder
(f)  Depreciating a non-current asset.

**6.2**  The following information has been taken from the financial statements of Juno plc for last year and the year before last:

|  | Year before last £m | Last year £m |
|---|---|---|
| Operating profit | 156 | 187 |
| Depreciation charged in arriving at operating profit | 47 | 55 |
| Inventories held at end of year | 27 | 31 |
| Trade receivables at end of year | 24 | 23 |
| Trade payables at end of year | 15 | 17 |

*Required*:
What is the figure for cash generated from the operations for Juno plc for last year?

6.3 Torrent plc's income statement for the year ended 31 December 2011 and the statements of financial position as at 31 December 2010 and 2011 are as follows:

**Income statement for the year ended 31 December 2011**

| | £m |
|---|---:|
| Revenue | 623 |
| Cost of sales | (353) |
| Gross profit | 270 |
| Distribution expenses | (71) |
| Administrative expenses | (30) |
| Rental income | 27 |
| Operating profit | 196 |
| Interest payable | (26) |
| Profit before taxation | 170 |
| Taxation | (36) |
| Profit for the year | 134 |

**Statements of financial position as at 31 December 2010 and 2011**

| | 2010 £m | 2011 £m |
|---|---:|---:|
| **ASSETS** | | |
| **Non-current assets** | | |
| *Property, plant and equipment* | | |
| Land and buildings | 310 | 310 |
| Plant and machinery | 325 | 314 |
| | 635 | 624 |
| **Current assets** | | |
| Inventories | 41 | 35 |
| Trade receivables | 139 | 145 |
| | 180 | 180 |
| **Total assets** | 815 | 804 |
| **EQUITY AND LIABILITIES** | | |
| **Equity** | | |
| Called-up ordinary share capital | 200 | 300 |
| Share premium account | 40 | – |
| Revaluation reserve | 69 | 9 |
| Retained earnings | 123 | 197 |
| | 432 | 506 |
| **Non-current liabilities** | | |
| Borrowings – loan notes | 250 | 150 |
| **Current liabilities** | | |
| Borrowings (all bank overdraft) | 56 | 89 |
| Trade payables | 54 | 41 |
| Taxation | 23 | 18 |
| | 133 | 148 |
| **Total equity and liabilities** | 815 | 804 |

During 2011, the business spent £67 million on additional plant and machinery. There were no other non-current asset acquisitions or disposals.

There was no share issue for cash during the year. The interest payable expense was equal in amount to the cash outflow. A dividend of £60 million was paid.

*Required*:

Prepare the statement of cash flows for Torrent plc for the year ended 31 December 2011.

**6.4** Chen plc's income statements for the years ended 31 December 2010 and 2011 and the statements of financial position as at 31 December 2010 and 2011 are as follows:

### Income statements for the years ended 31 December 2010 and 2011

|  | 2010 £m | 2011 £m |
|---|---|---|
| Revenue | 207 | 153 |
| Cost of sales | (101) | (76) |
| Gross profit | 106 | 77 |
| Distribution expenses | (22) | (20) |
| Administrative expenses | (20) | (28) |
| Operating profit | 64 | 29 |
| Interest payable | (4) | (4) |
| Profit before taxation | 60 | 25 |
| Taxation | (16) | (6) |
| Profit for the year | 44 | 19 |

### Statements of financial position as at 31 December 2010 and 2011

|  | 2010 £m | 2011 £m |
|---|---|---|
| **ASSETS** | | |
| **Non-current assets** | | |
| *Property, plant and equipment* | | |
| Land and buildings | 110 | 130 |
| Plant and machinery | 62 | 56 |
|  | 172 | 186 |
| **Current assets** | | |
| Inventories | 24 | 25 |
| Trade receivables | 26 | 25 |
| Cash at bank and in hand | 19 | – |
|  | 69 | 50 |
| **Total assets** | 241 | 236 |
| **EQUITY AND LIABILITIES** | | |
| **Equity** | | |
| Called-up ordinary share capital | 100 | 100 |
| Retained earnings | 56 | 57 |
|  | 156 | 157 |
| **Non-current liabilities** | | |
| Borrowings – loan notes (10%) | 40 | 40 |
| **Current liabilities** | | |
| Borrowings (all bank overdraft) | – | 2 |
| Trade payables | 37 | 34 |
| Taxation | 8 | 3 |
|  | 45 | 39 |
| **Total equity and liabilities** | 241 | 236 |

Included in 'cost of sales', 'distribution expenses' and 'administrative expenses', depreciation was as follows:

|  | 2010 | 2011 |
|---|---|---|
|  | £m | £m |
| Land and buildings | 6 | 10 |
| Plant and machinery | 10 | 12 |

There were no non-current asset disposals in either year. The amount of cash paid for interest equalled the expense in each year. Dividends were paid totalling £18 million in each year.

*Required*:

Prepare a statement of cash flows for the business for 2011.

**6.5** The following are the financial statements for Nailsea plc for the years ended 30 June 2010 and 2011:

### Income statement for years ended 30 June

|  | 2010 | 2011 |
|---|---|---|
|  | £m | £m |
| Revenue | 1,230 | 2,280 |
| Operating expenses | (722) | (1,618) |
| Depreciation | (270) | (320) |
| Operating profit | 238 | 342 |
| Interest payable | – | (27) |
| Profit before taxation | 238 | 315 |
| Taxation | (110) | (140) |
| Profit for the year | 128 | 175 |

### Statements of financial position as at 30 June

|  | 2010 | 2011 |
|---|---|---|
|  | £m | £m |
| **ASSETS** | | |
| **Non-current assets** | | |
| *Property, plant and equipment (at carrying amount)* | | |
| Land and buildings | 1,500 | 1,900 |
| Plant and machinery | 810 | 740 |
|  | 2,310 | 2,640 |
| **Current assets** | | |
| Inventories | 275 | 450 |
| Trade receivables | 100 | 250 |
| Bank | – | 118 |
|  | 375 | 818 |
| **Total assets** | 2,685 | 3,458 |
| **EQUITY AND LIABILITIES** | | |
| **Equity** | | |
| Share capital (fully paid £1 shares) | 1,400 | 1,600 |
| Share premium account | 200 | 300 |
| Retained earnings | 828 | 958 |
|  | 2,428 | 2,858 |

| Non-current liabilities | | |
|---|---|---|
| Borrowings – 9% loan notes (repayable 2015) | – | 300 |
| **Current liabilities** | | |
| Borrowings (all bank overdraft) | 32 | – |
| Trade payables | 170 | 230 |
| Taxation | 55 | 70 |
| | 257 | 300 |
| **Total equity and liabilities** | 2,685 | 3,458 |

There were no disposals of non-current assets in either year. Dividends were paid in 2010 and 2011 of £40 million and £45 million, respectively.

*Required*:

Prepare a statement of cash flows for Nailsea plc for the year ended 30 June 2011.

**6.6** The following financial statements for Blackstone plc are a slightly simplified set of published accounts. Blackstone plc is an engineering business that developed a new range of products in 2007. These products now account for 60 per cent of its turnover.

**Income statement for the years ended 31 March**

| | Notes | 2010 £m | 2011 £m |
|---|---|---|---|
| Revenue | | 7,003 | 11,205 |
| Cost of sales | | (3,748) | (5,809) |
| Gross profit | | 3,255 | 5,396 |
| Operating expenses | | (2,205) | (3,087) |
| Operating profit | | 1,050 | 2,309 |
| Interest payable | 1 | (216) | (456) |
| Profit before taxation | | 834 | 1,853 |
| Taxation | | (210) | (390) |
| Profit for the year | | 624 | 1,463 |

**Statements of financial position as at 31 March**

| | Notes | 2010 £m | 2011 £m |
|---|---|---|---|
| **ASSETS** | | | |
| **Non-current assets** | | | |
| *Property, plant and equipment* | 2 | 4,300 | 7,535 |
| Intangible assets | 3 | – | 700 |
| | | 4,300 | 8,235 |
| **Current assets** | | | |
| Inventories | | 1,209 | 2,410 |
| Trade receivables | | 641 | 1,173 |
| Cash at bank | | 123 | – |
| | | 1,973 | 3,583 |
| **Total assets** | | 6,273 | 11,818 |
| **EQUITY AND LIABILITIES** | | | |
| **Equity** | | | |
| Share capital | | 1,800 | 1,800 |
| Share premium | | 600 | 600 |
| Capital reserves | | 352 | 352 |
| Retained earnings | | 685 | 1,748 |
| | | 3,437 | 4,500 |

| | | |
|---|---:|---:|
| **Non-current liabilities** | | |
| Borrowings – Bank loan (repayable 2014) | 1,800 | 3,800 |
| **Current liabilities** | | |
| Trade payables | 931 | 1,507 |
| Taxation | 105 | 195 |
| Borrowings (all bank overdraft) | – | 1,816 |
| | 1,036 | 3,518 |
| **Total equity and liabilities** | 6,273 | 11,818 |

**Notes:**

1 The expense and the cash outflow for interest payable are equal for each year.
2 The movements in property, plant and equipment during the year are:

| | Land and buildings £m | Plant and machinery £m | Fixtures and fittings £m | Total £m |
|---|---:|---:|---:|---:|
| **Cost** | | | | |
| At 1 April 2010 | 4,500 | 3,850 | 2,120 | 10,470 |
| Additions | – | 2,970 | 1,608 | 4,578 |
| Disposals | – | (365) | (216) | (581) |
| At 31 March 2011 | 4,500 | 6,455 | 3,512 | 14,467 |
| **Depreciation** | | | | |
| At 1 April 2010 | 1,275 | 3,080 | 1,815 | 6,170 |
| Charge for year | 225 | 745 | 281 | 1,251 |
| Disposals | – | (305) | (184) | (489) |
| At 31 March 2011 | 1,500 | 3,520 | 1,912 | 6,932 |
| **Carrying amount** | | | | |
| At 31 March 2011 | 3,000 | 2,935 | 1,600 | 7,535 |

3 Intangible assets represent the amounts paid for the goodwill of another engineering business acquired during the year.
4 Proceeds from the sale of non-current assets in the year ended 31 March 2011 amounted to £54 million.
5 Dividends were paid on ordinary shares of £300 million in 2009 and £400 million in 2011.

*Required*:
Prepare a statement of cash flows for Blackstone plc for the year ended 31 March 2011. (*Hint*: A loss (deficit) on disposal of non-current assets is simply an additional amount of depreciation and should be dealt with as such in preparing the statement of cash flows.)

**6.7** Simplified financial statements for York plc are:

**Income statement for the year ended 30 September 2011**

| | £m |
|---|---:|
| Revenue | 290.0 |
| Cost of sales | (215.0) |
| Gross profit | 75.0 |
| Operating expenses (Note 1) | (62.0) |
| Operating profit | 13.0 |
| Interest payable (Note 2) | (3.0) |
| Profit before taxation | 10.0 |
| Taxation | (2.6) |
| Profit for the year | 7.4 |

## Statement of financial position as at 30 September

|  | 2010 £m | 2011 £m |
|---|---|---|
| **ASSETS** | | |
| **Non-current assets** (Note 4) | 80.0 | 85.0 |
| **Current assets** | | |
| Inventories and trade receivables | 119.8 | 122.1 |
| Cash at bank | 9.2 | 16.6 |
| | 129.0 | 138.7 |
| Total assets | 209.0 | 223.7 |
| **EQUITY AND LIABILITIES** | | |
| **Equity** | | |
| Share capital | 35.0 | 40.0 |
| Share premium account | 30.0 | 30.0 |
| Reserves | 31.0 | 34.9 |
| | 96.0 | 104.9 |
| **Non-current liabilities** | | |
| Borrowings | 32.0 | 35.0 |
| **Current liabilities** | | |
| Trade payables | 80.0 | 82.5 |
| Taxation | 1.0 | 1.3 |
| | 81.0 | 83.8 |
| **Total equity and liabilities** | 209.0 | 223.7 |

Notes:

1 Operating expenses include depreciation of £13 million and a surplus of £3.2 million on the sale of non-current assets.
2 The expense and the cash outflow for interest payable are equal.
3 A dividend of £3.5 million was paid during 2011.
4 Non-current asset costs and depreciation:

| | Cost £m | Accumulated depreciation £m | Carrying amount £m |
|---|---|---|---|
| At 1 October 2010 | 120.0 | 40.0 | 80.0 |
| Disposals | (10.0) | (8.0) | (2.0) |
| Additions | 20.0 | | 20.0 |
| Depreciation | – | 13.0 | (13.0) |
| At 30 September 2011 | 130.0 | 45.0 | 85.0 |

*Required*:

Prepare a statement of cash flows for York plc for the year ended 30 September 2011.

# Analysing and interpreting financial statements

## Introduction

In this chapter we shall consider the analysis and interpretation of the financial statements that we discussed in Chapters 2, 3 and 6. We shall see how financial (or accounting) ratios can help in assessing the financial health of a business. We shall also consider the problems that are encountered when applying this technique.

Financial ratios can be used to examine various aspects of financial position and performance and are widely used for planning and control purposes. They can be very helpful to managers in a wide variety of decision areas, such as profit planning, pricing, working-capital management, financial structure and dividend policy.

## Learning outcomes

**When you have completed this chapter, you should be able to:**

- Identify the major categories of ratios that can be used for analysis purposes.

- Calculate key ratios for assessing the financial performance and position of a business and explain the significance of the ratios calculated.

- Discuss the use of ratios in helping to predict financial failure.

- Discuss the limitations of ratios as a tool of financial analysis.

MyAccountingLab

Visit **www.myaccountinglab.com** for practice and revision opportunities

# Financial ratios

Financial ratios provide a quick and relatively simple means of assessing the financial health of a business. A ratio simply relates one figure appearing in the financial statements to some other figure. This second figure might itself also appear in the financial statements (for example, operating profit in relation to the amount invested in the business (capital employed)). Alternatively the second figure may be a non-financial measure, some other factor relating to the business (for example, operating profit per employee, sales revenue per square metre of selling space, and so on).

Ratios can be very helpful when comparing the financial health of different businesses. Differences may exist between businesses in the scale of operations. This means that a direct comparison of, say, the operating profit generated by each business may be misleading. By expressing operating profit in relation to some other measure (for example, capital employed), the problem of scale is eliminated. A business with an operating profit of, say, £10,000 and capital employed of £100,000 can be compared with a much larger business with an operating profit of, say, £80,000 and capital employed of £1,000,000 by the use of a simple ratio. The operating profit to capital employed ratio for the smaller business is 10 per cent (that is, $(10,000/100,000) \times 100\%$) and the same ratio for the larger business is 8 per cent (that is, $(80,000/1,000,000) \times 100\%$). These ratios can be directly compared, whereas a comparison of the absolute operating profit figures would be much less meaningful. The need to eliminate differences in scale through the use of ratios can also apply when comparing the performance of the same business over time.

By calculating a small number of ratios it is often possible to build up a revealing picture of the position and performance of a business. It is not surprising, therefore, that ratios are widely used by those who have an interest in businesses and business performance. Although ratios are not difficult to calculate, they can be difficult to interpret. It is important to appreciate that they are really only the starting point for further analysis.

Ratios help to highlight the financial strengths and weaknesses of a business, but they cannot, by themselves, explain why those strengths or weaknesses exist or why certain changes have occurred. Only a detailed investigation will reveal these underlying reasons. Ratios tend to enable us to know which questions to ask, rather than provide the answers.

Ratios can be expressed in various forms, for example as a percentage or as a proportion. The way that a particular ratio is presented will depend on the needs of those who will use the information. Although it is possible to calculate a large number of ratios, only a few, based on key relationships, tend to be helpful to a particular user. Many ratios that could be calculated from the financial statements (for example, rent payable in relation to current assets) may not be considered because there is no clear or meaningful relationship between the two items.

There is no generally accepted list of ratios that can be applied to the financial statements, nor is there a standard method of calculating many ratios. Variations in both the choice of ratios and their calculation will be found in practice. However, it is important to be consistent in the way in which ratios are calculated for comparison purposes. The ratios that we shall discuss are very popular – presumably because they are seen as useful for decision-making purposes.

## Financial ratio classifications

Ratios can be grouped into categories, with each category relating to a particular aspect of financial performance or position. The following broad categories provide a useful basis for explaining the nature of the financial ratios to be dealt with. There are five of them:

- *Profitability*. Businesses generally exist with the primary purpose of creating wealth for their owners. Profitability ratios provide insights relating to the degree of success in achieving this purpose. They express the profit made (or figures bearing on profit, such as sales revenue or overheads) in relation to other key figures in the financial statements or to some business resource.
- *Efficiency*. Ratios may be used to measure the efficiency with which particular resources have been used within the business. These ratios are also referred to as *activity* ratios.
- *Liquidity*. It is vital to the survival of a business that there are sufficient liquid resources available to meet maturing obligations (that is, amounts owing that must be paid in the near future). Some liquidity ratios examine the relationship between liquid resources held and amounts due for payment in the near future.
- *Financial gearing*. This is the relationship between the contribution to financing the business made by the owners of the business and the amount contributed by others, in the form of loans. The level of gearing has an important effect on the degree of risk associated with a business, as we shall see. Gearing ratios tend to highlight the extent to which the business uses borrowings.
- *Investment*. Certain ratios are concerned with assessing the returns and performance of shares in a particular business from the perspective of shareholders who are not involved with the management of the business.

These five key aspects of financial health that ratios seek to examine are summarised in Figure 7.1.

The analyst must be clear *who* the target users are and *why* they need the information. Different users of financial information are likely to have different information needs, which will in turn determine the ratios that they find useful. For example, shareholders are likely to be particularly interested in their returns in relation to the level of risk associated with their investment. Profitability, investment and gearing ratios will, therefore, be of particular interest. Long-term lenders are concerned with the long-term

| Figure 7.1 | The key aspects of financial health |

Ratios can be used to examine each of the areas that we have discussed.

viability of the business and, to help them to assess this, the profitability and gearing ratios of the business are also likely to be of particular interest. Short-term lenders, such as suppliers of goods and services on credit, may be interested in the ability of the business to repay the amounts owing in the short term. As a result, the liquidity ratios should be of interest.

## The need for comparison

Merely calculating a ratio will not tell us very much about the position or performance of a business. For example, if a ratio revealed that a retail business was generating £100 in sales revenue per square metre of floor space, it would not be possible to deduce from this information alone whether this particular level of performance was good, bad or indifferent. It is only when we compare this ratio with some 'benchmark' that the information can be interpreted and evaluated.

### Activity 7.1

Can you think of any bases that could be used to compare a ratio that you have calculated from the financial statements of your business for a particular period?
*Hint*: There are three main possibilities.

You may have thought of the following bases:

- past periods for the same business
- similar businesses for the same or past periods
- planned performance for the business.

We shall now take a closer look at these three in turn.

### Past periods

By comparing the ratio that we have calculated with the same ratio, but for a previous period, it is possible to detect whether there has been an improvement or deterioration in performance. Indeed, it is often useful to track particular ratios over time (say, five or ten years) to see whether it is possible to detect trends. The comparison of ratios from different periods brings certain problems, however. In particular, there is always the possibility that trading conditions were quite different in the periods being compared. There is the further problem that, when comparing the performance of a single business over time, operating inefficiencies may not be clearly exposed. For example, the fact that sales revenue per employee has risen by 10 per cent over the previous period may at first sight appear to be satisfactory. This may not be the case, however, if similar businesses have shown an improvement of 50 per cent for the same period or had much better sales revenue per employee ratios to start with. Finally, there is the problem that inflation may have distorted the figures on which the ratios are based. Inflation can lead to an overstatement of profit and an understatement of asset values, as will be discussed later in the chapter.

## Similar businesses

In a competitive environment, a business must consider its performance in relation to that of other businesses operating in the same industry. Survival may depend on its ability to achieve comparable levels of performance. A useful basis for comparing a particular ratio, therefore, is the ratio achieved by similar businesses during the same period. This basis is not, however, without its problems. Competitors may have different year ends and so trading conditions may not be identical. They may also have different accounting policies, which can have a significant effect on reported profits and asset values (for example, different methods of calculating depreciation or valuing inventories). Finally, it may be difficult to obtain the financial statements of competitor businesses. Sole proprietorships and partnerships, for example, are not obliged to make their financial statements available to the public. In the case of limited companies, there is a legal obligation to do so. However, a diversified business may not provide a breakdown of activities that is sufficiently detailed to enable analysts to compare the activities with those of other businesses.

## Planned performance

Ratios may be compared with the targets that management developed before the start of the period under review. The comparison of planned performance with actual performance may therefore be a useful way of revealing the level of achievement attained. However, the planned levels of performance must be based on realistic assumptions if they are to be useful for comparison purposes.

Planned performance is likely to be the most valuable benchmark against which managers may assess their own business. Businesses tend to develop planned ratios for each aspect of their activities. When formulating its plans, a business may usefully take account of its own past performance and the performance of other businesses. There is no reason, however, why a particular business should seek to achieve either its own previous level of performance or that of other businesses. In some circumstances, neither of these may be seen as an appropriate target.

Analysts outside the business do not normally have access to the business's plans. For these people, past performance and the performances of other, similar, businesses may provide the only practical benchmarks.

## Calculating the ratios

Probably the best way to explain financial ratios is through an example. Example 7.1 provides a set of financial statements from which we can calculate important ratios.

## Example 7.1

The following financial statements relate to Alexis plc, which operates a wholesale carpet business:

### Statements of financial position (balance sheets) as at 31 March

|  | 2011 £m | 2012 £m |
|---|---|---|
| **ASSETS** | | |
| **Non-current assets** | | |
| *Property, plant and equipment (at cost less depreciation)* | | |
| Land and buildings | 381 | 427 |
| Fixtures and fittings | 129 | 160 |
| | 510 | 587 |
| **Current assets** | | |
| Inventories | 300 | 406 |
| Trade receivables | 240 | 273 |
| Cash at bank | 4 | – |
| | 544 | 679 |
| **Total assets** | 1,054 | 1,266 |
| **EQUITY AND LIABILITIES** | | |
| **Equity** | | |
| £0.50 ordinary shares (Note 1) | 300 | 300 |
| Retained earnings | 263 | 234 |
| | 563 | 534 |
| **Non-current liabilities** | | |
| Borrowings – 9% loan notes (secured) | 200 | 300 |
| **Current liabilities** | | |
| Trade payables | 261 | 354 |
| Taxation | 30 | 2 |
| Short-term borrowings (all bank overdraft) | – | 76 |
| | 291 | 432 |
| **Total equity and liabilities** | 1,054 | 1,266 |

### Income statements for the year ended 31 March

|  | 2011 £m | 2012 £m |
|---|---|---|
| Revenue (Note 2) | 2,240 | 2,681 |
| Cost of sales (Note 3) | (1,745) | (2,272) |
| Gross profit | 495 | 409 |
| Operating expenses | (252) | (362) |
| Operating profit | 243 | 47 |
| Interest payable | (18) | (32) |
| Profit before taxation | 225 | 15 |
| Taxation | (60) | (4) |
| Profit for the year | 165 | 11 |

**Statement of cash flows for the year ended 31 March**

|  | 2011 £m | 2011 £m | 2012 £m | 2012 £m |
|---|---:|---:|---:|---:|
| **Cash flows from operating activities** | | | | |
| Cash generated from operations | 251 | | 34 | |
| Interest paid | (18) | | (32) | |
| Taxation paid | (63) | | (32) | |
| Dividend paid | (40) | | (40) | |
| *Net cash from/(used in) operating activities* | | 130 | | (70) |
| **Cash flows from investing activities** | | | | |
| Payments to acquire property, plant and equipment | (77) | | (110) | |
| *Net cash used in investing activities* | | (77) | | (110) |
| **Cash flows from financing activities** | | | | |
| Issue of loan notes | – | | 100 | |
| *Net cash from financing activities* | | – | | 100 |
| **Net increase in cash and cash equivalents** | | 53 | | (80) |
| **Cash and cash equivalents at start of year** | | | | |
| Cash/(overdraft) | | (49) | | 4 |
| **Cash and cash equivalents at end of year** | | | | |
| Cash/(overdraft) | | 4 | | (76) |

**Notes:**

1 The market value of the shares of the business at the end of the reporting period was £2.50 for 2011 and £1.50 for 2012.
2 All sales and purchases are made on credit.
3 The cost of sales figure can be analysed as follows:

|  | 2011 £m | 2012 £m |
|---|---:|---:|
| Opening inventories | 241 | 300 |
| Purchases (Note 2) | 1,804 | 2,378 |
|  | 2,045 | 2,678 |
| Closing inventories | (300) | (406) |
| Cost of sales | 1,745 | 2,272 |

4 At 31 March 2010, the trade receivables stood at £223 million and the trade payables at £183 million.
5 A dividend of £40 million had been paid to the shareholders in respect of each of the years.
6 The business employed 13,995 staff at 31 March 2011 and 18,623 at 31 March 2012.
7 The business expanded its capacity during 2012 by setting up a new warehouse and distribution centre.
8 At 1 April 2010, the total of equity stood at £438 million and the total of equity and non-current liabilities stood at £638 million.

# A brief overview

Before we start our detailed look at the ratios for Alexis plc (in Example 7.1), it is helpful to take a quick look at what information is obvious from the financial statements. This will usually pick up some issues that ratios may not be able to identify. It may also highlight some points that could help us in our interpretation of the ratios. Starting at the top of the statement of financial position, the following points can be noted:

- *Expansion of non-current assets.* These have increased by about 15 per cent (from £510 million to £587 million). Note 7 mentions a new warehouse and distribution centre, which may account for much of the additional investment in non-current assets. We are not told when this new facility was established, but it is quite possible that it was well into the year. This could mean that not much benefit was reflected in terms of additional sales revenue or cost saving during 2012. Sales revenue, in fact, expanded by about 20 per cent (from £2,240 million to £2,681 million); greater than the expansion in non-current assets.

- *Major expansion in the elements of working capital.* Inventories increased by about 35 per cent, trade receivables by about 14 per cent and trade payables by about 36 per cent between 2011 and 2012. These are major increases, particularly in inventories and payables (which are linked because the inventories are all bought on credit – see Note 2).

- *Reduction in the cash balance.* The cash balance fell from £4 million (in funds) to a £76 million overdraft, between 2011 and 2012. The bank may be putting the business under pressure to reverse this, which could raise difficulties.

- *Apparent debt capacity.* Comparing the non-current assets with the long-term borrowings implies that the business may well be able to offer security on further borrowing. This is because potential lenders usually look at the value of assets that can be offered as security when assessing loan requests. Lenders seem particularly attracted to land and buildings as security. For example, at 31 March 2012, non-current assets had a carrying amount (the value at which they appeared in the statement of financial position) of £587 million, but long-term borrowing was only £300 million (though there was also an overdraft of £76 million). Carrying amounts are not normally, of course, market values. On the other hand, land and buildings tend to have a market value higher than their value as shown on the statement of financial position due to inflation in property values.

- *Lower operating profit.* Though sales revenue expanded by 20 per cent between 2011 and 2012, both cost of sales and operating expenses rose by a greater percentage, leaving both gross profit and, particularly, operating profit massively reduced. The level of staffing, which increased by about 33 per cent (from 13,995 to 18,623 employees – see Note 6), may have greatly affected the operating expenses. (Without knowing when the additional employees were recruited during 2012, we cannot be sure of the effect on operating expenses.) Increasing staffing by 33 per cent must put an enormous strain on management, at least in the short term. It is not surprising, therefore, that 2012 was not successful for the business – not, at least, in profit terms.

Having had a quick look at what is fairly obvious, without calculating any financial ratios, we shall now go on to calculate and interpret some.

## Profitability

The following ratios may be used to evaluate the profitability of the business:

- return on ordinary shareholders' funds
- return on capital employed
- operating profit margin
- gross profit margin.

We shall now look at each of these in turn.

## Return on ordinary shareholders' funds (ROSF)

The **return on ordinary shareholders' funds ratio** compares the amount of profit for the period available to the owners, with the owners' average stake in the business during that same period. The ratio (which is normally expressed in percentage terms) is as follows:

$$\text{ROSF} = \frac{\text{Profit for the year (less any preference dividend)}}{\text{Ordinary share capital} + \text{Reserves}} \times 100$$

The profit for the year (less any preference dividend) is used in calculating the ratio, as this figure represents the amount of profit that is attributable to the owners.

In the case of Alexis plc, the ratio for the year ended 31 March 2011 is:

$$\text{ROSF} = \frac{165}{(438 + 563)/2} \times 100 = 33.0\%$$

Note that, when calculating the ROSF, the average of the figures for ordinary shareholders' funds as at the beginning and at the end of the year has been used. This is because an average figure is normally more representative. The amount of shareholders' funds was not constant throughout the year, yet we want to compare it with the profit earned during the whole period. We know, from Note 8, that the amount of shareholders' funds at 1 April 2010 was £438 million. By a year later, however, it had risen to £563 million, according to the statement of financial position as at 31 March 2011.

The easiest approach to calculating the average amount of shareholders' funds is to take a simple average based on the opening and closing figures for the year. This is often the only information available, as is the case with Example 7.1. Averaging is normally appropriate for all ratios that combine a figure for a period (such as profit for the year) with one taken at a point in time (such as shareholders' funds).

Where not even the beginning-of-year figure is available, it will be necessary to rely on just the year-end figure. This is not ideal but, if this approach is consistently applied, it can produce ratios that are useful.

**Activity (7.2)**

Calculate the ROSF for Alexis plc for the year to 31 March 2012.

The ratio for 2012 is:

$$\text{ROSF} = \frac{11}{(563 + 534)/2} \times 100 = 2.0\%$$

Broadly, businesses seek to generate as high a value as possible for this ratio. This is provided that it is not achieved at the expense of potential future returns by, for example, taking on more risky activities. In view of this, the 2012 ratio is very poor by any standards; a bank deposit account will normally yield a better return than this. We need to try to find out why things went so badly wrong in 2012. As we look at other ratios, we should find some clues.

## Return on capital employed (ROCE)

The **return on capital employed ratio** is a fundamental measure of business performance. This ratio expresses the relationship between the operating profit generated during a period and the average long-term capital invested in the business.

The ratio is expressed in percentage terms and is as follows:

$$\text{ROCE} = \frac{\text{Operating profit}}{\text{Share capital} + \text{Reserves} + \text{Non-current liabilities}} \times 100$$

Note, in this case, that the profit figure used is the operating profit (that is, the profit *before* interest and taxation), because the ratio attempts to measure the returns to all suppliers of long-term finance before any deductions for interest payable on borrowings, or payments of dividends to shareholders, are made.

For the year to 31 March 2011, the ratio for Alexis plc is:

$$\text{ROCE} = \frac{243}{(638 + 763)/2} \times 100 = 34.7\%$$

(The capital employed figure, which is the total equity plus non-current liabilities, at 1 April 2010 is given in Note 8).

ROCE is considered by many to be a primary measure of profitability. It compares inputs (capital invested) with outputs (operating profit). This comparison is vital in assessing the effectiveness with which funds have been deployed. Once again, an average figure for capital employed should be used where the information is available.

### Activity 7.3

Calculate the ROCE for Alexis plc for the year to 31 March 2012.

The ratio for 2012 is:

$$\text{ROCE} = \frac{47}{(763 + 834)/2} \times 100 = 5.9\%$$

This ratio tells much the same story as ROSF; namely a poor performance, with the return on the assets being less than the rate that the business has to pay for most of its borrowed funds (that is, 10 per cent for the loan notes).

**Real World 7.1** shows how financial ratios are used by businesses as a basis for setting profitability targets.

### Real World 7.1

#### Targeting profitability                                    FT

The ROCE ratio is widely used by businesses when establishing targets for profitability. These targets are sometimes made public and here are some examples:

● Air France-KLM, the world's largest airline (on the basis of sales revenue) has set itself the target of achieving a ROCE of 7 per cent.

**Real World 7.1 (*continued*)**

● BMW, the car maker, has a long-term target ROCE in excess of 26 per cent.
● Marks and Spencer plc, the retailer, announced in June 2011 a target return on capital employed for new capital invested of 12 to 15 per cent over three years.
● Tesco plc, the supermarket chain, aims to increase ROCE to 14.6 per cent by 2015. So far this has not been achieved and, in 2011, ROCE was 12.9 per cent.
● EasyJet, the budget airline, has a target ROCE of 12 per cent.

*Sources*: Information taken from Air France-KLM, Press Release, 14 February 2008; 'BMW adds to carmakers' gloom', 1 August 2008, FT.com; 'M&S to shake up executive pay to reflect Bolland plan', 8 June 2011, FT.com; 'Tesco looking afar for growth', 19 April 2011, FT.com; 'Sir Stelios fires warning shot at EasyJet', 4 January 2011, FT.com.

**Real World 7.2** provides some indication of the levels of ROCE achieved by UK businesses.

**Real World 7.2**

## Achieving profitability

ROCE ratios for UK manufacturing and service companies for each of the five years ending in 2010 are shown in Figure 7.2.

**Figure 7.2** **The ROCE of UK companies**

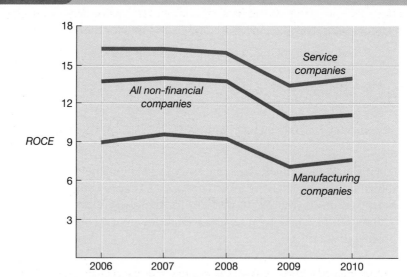

ROCE of manufacturing businesses has been consistently lower than that of service companies over the period.

According to the Office of National Statistics, the difference in ROCE between the two sectors is accounted for by the higher capital intensity of manufacturing

*Source*: Figure compiled from information taken from 'Profitability of UK companies Q1 2011', *Office of National Statistics*, www.statistics.gov.uk/, 6 July 2011.

## Operating profit margin

The **operating profit margin ratio** relates the operating profit for the period to the sales revenue. The ratio is expressed as follows:

$$\text{Operating profit margin} = \frac{\text{Operating profit}}{\text{Sales revenue}} \times 100$$

The operating profit (that is, profit before interest and taxation) is used in this ratio as it represents the profit from trading operations before the interest payable expense is taken into account. This is often regarded as the most appropriate measure of operational performance, when used as a basis of comparison, because differences arising from the way in which the business is financed will not influence the measure.

For the year ended 31 March 2011, Alexis plc's operating profit margin ratio is:

$$\text{Operating profit margin} = \frac{243}{2,240} \times 100 = 10.8\%$$

This ratio compares one output of the business (operating profit) with another output (sales revenue). The ratio can vary considerably between types of business. For example, supermarkets tend to operate on low prices and, therefore, low operating profit margins. This is done in an attempt to stimulate sales and thereby increase the total amount of operating profit generated. Jewellers, on the other hand, tend to have high operating profit margins but have much lower levels of sales volume. Factors such as the degree of competition, the type of customer, the economic climate and industry characteristics (such as the level of risk) will influence the operating profit margin of a business. This point is picked up again later in the chapter.

---

### Activity 7.4

Calculate the operating profit margin for Alexis plc for the year to 31 March 2012.

The ratio for 2012 is:

$$\text{Operating profit margin} = \frac{47}{2,681} \times 100 = 1.8\%$$

---

Once again, a very weak performance compared with that of 2011. In 2011 for every £1 of sales revenue an average of 10.8p (that is, 10.8 per cent) was left as operating profit, after paying the cost of the carpets sold and other expenses of operating the business. For 2012, however, this had fallen to only 1.8p for every £1. It seems that the reason for the poor ROSF and ROCE ratios was partially, perhaps wholly, a high level of expenses relative to sales revenue. The next ratio should provide us with a clue as to how the sharp decline in this ratio occurred.

**Real World 7.3** sets out the target operating profit margins for some well-known car manufacturers.

**Real World 7.3**

## Profit driven                                                          FT

- BMW has set a target operating profit margin for 2011 of more than 8 per cent.
- Daimler has set a target operating profit margin for its Mercedes unit of 10 per cent to be achieved by the second half of 2012.
- Nissan has a target operating profit margin of 8 per cent and a target global market share of 8 per cent to be achieved by 2017.
- Toyota announced a medium-term target operating profit margin of 5 per cent in March 2011.
- Opel, the European arm of General Motors, aims to achieve an operating profit margin of 4 to 5 per cent by 2013.
- Premium car manufacturers, such as BMW and Mercedes, appear to have higher targets for their operating profit margin than mass-market car manufacturers, although the target periods often differ.

*Source*: 'Emerging markets drive BMW profits', 4 May 2011, FT.com; 'Daimler has grand aims for small cars', 14 June 2010, FT.com; 'Nissan: Ghosn for broke', 28 June 2011, FT.com; 'Nissan: More China please', 27 June 2011, FT.com; 'Opel handed ambitious profit target', 17 December 2009, FT.com.

## Gross profit margin

The **gross profit margin ratio** relates the gross profit of the business to the sales revenue generated for the same period. Gross profit represents the difference between sales revenue and the cost of sales. The ratio is therefore a measure of profitability in buying (or producing) and selling goods or services before any other expenses are taken into account. As cost of sales represents a major expense for many businesses, a change in this ratio can have a significant effect on the 'bottom line' (that is, the profit for the year). The gross profit margin ratio is calculated as follows:

$$\text{Gross profit margin} = \frac{\text{Gross profit}}{\text{Sales revenue}} \times 100$$

For the year to 31 March 2011, the ratio for Alexis plc is:

$$\text{Gross profit margin} = \frac{495}{2,240} \times 100 = 22.1\%$$

**Activity 7.5**

Calculate the gross profit margin for Alexis plc for the year to 31 March 2012.

The ratio for 2012 is:

$$\text{Gross profit margin} = \frac{409}{2,681} \times 100 = 15.3\%$$

The decline in this ratio means that gross profit was lower *relative* to sales revenue in 2012 than it had been in 2011. Bearing in mind that:

> **Gross profit = Sales revenue – Cost of sales (or cost of goods sold)**

this means that cost of sales was higher *relative* to sales revenue in 2012, than in 2011. This could mean that sales prices were lower and/or that the purchase price of carpets had increased. It is possible that both sales prices and purchase prices had reduced, but the former at a greater rate than the latter. Similarly, they may both have increased, but with sales prices having increased at a lesser rate than purchase prices.

Clearly, part of the decline in the operating profit margin ratio is linked to the dramatic decline in the gross profit margin ratio. Whereas, after paying for the carpets sold, for each £1 of sales revenue 22.1p was left to cover other operating expenses in 2011, this was only 15.3p in 2012.

The profitability ratios for the business over the two years can be set out as follows:

|  | 2011 % | 2012 % |
|---|---|---|
| ROSF | 33.0 | 2.0 |
| ROCE | 34.7 | 5.9 |
| Operating profit margin | 10.8 | 1.8 |
| Gross profit margin | 22.1 | 15.3 |

## Activity 7.6

What do you deduce from a comparison of the declines in the operating profit and gross profit margin ratios?

We can see that the decline in the operating profit margin was 9 per cent (that is, 10.8 per cent to 1.8 per cent), whereas that of the gross profit margin was only 6.8 per cent (that is, from 22.1 per cent to 15.3 per cent). This can only mean that operating expenses were greater, compared with sales revenue in 2012, than they had been in 2011. The declines in both ROSF and ROCE were caused partly, therefore, by the business incurring higher inventories' purchasing costs relative to sales revenue and partly through higher operating expenses compared with sales revenue. We should need to compare these ratios with their planned levels before we could usefully assess the business's success.

The analyst must now carry out some investigation to discover what caused the increases in both cost of sales and operating expenses, relative to sales revenue, from 2011 to 2012. This will involve checking on what has happened with sales and inventories prices over the two years. Similarly, it will involve looking at each of the individual areas that make up operating expenses to discover which ones were responsible for the increase, relative to sales revenue. Here, further ratios, for example, staff expenses (wages and salaries) to sales revenue, could be calculated in an attempt to isolate the cause of the change from 2011 to 2012. In fact, as we discussed when we took an overview of the financial statements, the increase in staffing may well account for most of the increase in operating expenses.

**Real World 7.4** discusses how high operating costs may adversely affect the future profitability of a leading car maker.

**Real World 7.4**

### VW accelerates but costs vibrate

Volkswagen's fervent quest to overtake Japanese rival Toyota by 2018 threatens to exacerbate its already high cost structure and to hamper profitability in the coming years, analysts and industry executives have warned. The industry executives and analysts argue that VW's growth initiative – which involves a huge investment of €26.6 billion ($35.7 billion) in the next three years, the €16 billion takeovers of Porsche and its Salzburg dealership and a €1.7 billion stake in Japanese small car specialist Suzuki – will put the carmaker back on a low-(profit)margin track.

So far, Europe's largest carmaker, has been one of the most successful during the crisis. The Wolfsburg-based manufacturer posted a €911 million profit after tax and a 1.2 per cent profit margin in 2009 at a time when many others were making losses. VW is now aiming for an industry-leading, pre-tax (profit) margin of more than 8 per cent in 2018, by which time it wants to become the world's leading car producer "economically as well as ecologically", Martin Winterkorn, VW's chief executive, has said. The carmaker wants to lift its sales from 6.3 milliion cars in the past year to more than 10 million by 2018.

While few dispute that VW could overtake Toyota – which sold almost 9 million cars in 2009 – in terms of sales, the profitability target remains in doubt. "There should be more doubt in the market about the sustainability of VW's profits," says Philippe Houchois, analyst at UBS.

In spite of its success, VW's cost structure is still in dire straits, particularly in Germany. With its 370,000 global workforce, the partly state-owned carmaker trails almost all global rivals when it comes to statistics such as revenues or vehicles per employee. "People forget that despite their large scale, VW has some of the worst cost-structures in the industry. They have abysmal labour productivity and high plant costs," says Max Warburton, analyst at research firm Sanford Bernstein.

Mr Warburton says high margins have been the exception at VW. "2007 to 2008 represented a brief period of temporary profit maximisation delivered by a [now departed] temporary management team who made temporary, emergency cost cuts," he says. VW disputes that it has taken its eye off cost-cutting. Hans Dieter Pötsch, the carmaker's chief financial officer, says that "by optimising our purchasing and increasing productivity . . . we have reached cost cuts of €1 billion throughout 2009". [In addition] . . . he points to the carmaker's ongoing productivity improvement target of 10 per cent each year.

VW's profit figures for last year paint a dark picture of the carmaker's cost structures. At least three of its nine brands – Seat, Bentley and Lamborghini, and probably also Bugatti whose results are not disclosed – were lossmaking, and are not expected to return to profit this year. VW's light-truck operations only posted a profit after a one-off gain from the sale of its Brazil operations. Operating profit at the group's core brand, VW, was crimped by 79 per cent to €561 million, in spite of the marque benefiting hugely from European scrapping incentive programmes.

*Source:* Adapted from 'Costs vibrate as VW accelerates', Daniel Schäfer, FT.com, 29 March 2010.

## Efficiency

Efficiency ratios are used to try to assess how successfully the various resources of the business are managed. The following ratios consider some of the more important aspects of resource management:

- average inventories turnover period
- average settlement period for trade receivables
- average settlement period for trade payables
- sales revenue to capital employed
- sales revenue per employee.

We shall now look at each of these in turn.

## Average inventories turnover period

Inventories often represent a significant investment for a business. For some types of business (for example, manufacturers and certain retailers), inventories may account for a substantial proportion of the total assets held. **Real World 16.1** on page 646 illustrates this. The **average inventories turnover period ratio** measures the average period for which inventories are being held. The ratio is calculated as follows:

$$\text{Average inventories turnover period} = \frac{\text{Average inventories held}}{\text{Cost of sales}} \times 365$$

The average inventories for the period can be calculated as a simple average of the opening and closing inventories levels for the year. However, in the case of a highly seasonal business, where inventories levels may vary considerably over the year, a monthly average may be more appropriate, should this information be available.

In the case of Alexis plc, the inventories turnover period for the year ended 31 March 2011 is:

$$\text{Average inventories turnover period} = \frac{(241 + 300)/2}{1,745} \times 365 = 56.6 \text{ days}$$

(The opening inventories figure was taken from Note 3 to the financial statements.)

This means that, on average, the inventories held are being 'turned over' every 56.6 days. So, a carpet bought by the business on a particular day would, on average, have been sold about eight weeks later. A business will normally prefer a short inventories turnover period to a long one, because holding inventories has costs, for example the opportunity cost of the funds tied up. When judging the amount of inventories to carry, the business must consider such things as the likely demand for them, the possibility of supply shortages, the likelihood of price rises, the amount of storage space available and their perishability/susceptibility to obsolescence.

This ratio is sometimes expressed in terms of weeks or months rather than days: multiplying by 52 or 12, rather than 365, will achieve this.

### Activity 7.7

Calculate the average inventories turnover period for Alexis plc for the year ended 31 March 2012.

The ratio for 2012 is:

$$\text{Average inventories turnover period} = \frac{(300 + 406)/2}{2,272} \times 365 = 56.7 \text{ days}$$

The inventories turnover period is virtually the same in both years.

## Average settlement period for trade receivables

Selling on credit is the norm for most businesses, except for retailers. Trade receivables are a necessary evil. A business will naturally be concerned with the amount of funds tied up in trade receivables and try to keep this to a minimum. The speed of payment can have a significant effect on the business's cash flow. The **average settlement period for trade receivables ratio** calculates how long, on average, credit customers take to pay the amounts that they owe to the business. The ratio is as follows:

$$\text{Average settlement period for trade receivables} = \frac{\text{Average trade receivables}}{\text{Credit sales revenue}} \times 365$$

A business will normally prefer a shorter average settlement period to a longer one as, once again, funds are being tied up that may be used for more profitable purposes. Although this ratio can be useful, it is important to remember that it produces an *average* figure for the number of days for which debts are outstanding. This average may be badly distorted by, for example, a few large customers who are very slow or very fast payers.

Since all sales made by Alexis plc are on credit, the average settlement period for trade receivables for the year ended 31 March 2011 is:

$$\text{Average settlement period for trade receivables} = \frac{(223 + 240)/2}{2,240} \times 365 = 37.7 \text{ days}$$

(The opening trade receivables figure was taken from Note 4 to the financial statements.)

### Activity (7.8)

Calculate the average settlement period for Alexis plc's trade receivables for the year ended 31 March 2012.

The ratio for 2012 is:

$$\text{Average settlement period for trade receivables} = \frac{(240 + 273)/2}{2,681} \times 365 = 34.9 \text{ days}$$

On the face of it, this reduction in the settlement period is welcome. It means that less cash was tied up in trade receivables for each £1 of sales revenue in 2012 than in 2011. Only if the reduction were achieved at the expense of customer goodwill or a high direct financial cost might the desirability of the reduction be questioned. For example, the reduction may have been due to chasing customers too vigorously or as a result of incurring higher expenses, such as discounts allowed to customers who pay quickly.

## Average settlement period for trade payables

The **average settlement period for trade payables ratio** measures how long, on average, the business takes to pay those who have supplied goods and services on credit. The ratio is calculated as follows:

$$\text{Average settlement period for trade payables} = \frac{\text{Average trade payables}}{\text{Credit purchases}} \times 365$$

This ratio provides an average figure, which, like the average settlement period for trade receivables ratio, can be distorted by the payment period for one or two large suppliers.

As trade payables provide a free source of finance for the business, it is perhaps not surprising that some businesses attempt to increase their average settlement period for trade payables. However, such a policy can be taken too far and result in a loss of goodwill of suppliers. We shall return to the issues concerning the management of inventories, trade receivables and trade payables in Chapter 16.

For the year ended 31 March 2011, Alexis plc's average settlement period for trade payables is:

$$\text{Average settlement period for trade payables} = \frac{(183 + 261)/2}{1,804} \times 365 = 44.9 \text{ days}$$

(The opening trade payables figure was taken from Note 4 to the financial statements and the purchases figure from Note 3.)

### Activity 7.9

Calculate the average settlement period for trade payables for Alexis plc for the year ended 31 March 2012.

The ratio for 2012 is:

$$\text{Average settlement period for trade payables} = \frac{(261 + 354)/2}{2,378} \times 365 = 47.2 \text{ days}$$

There was an increase, between 2011 and 2012, in the average length of time that elapsed between buying inventories and services and paying for them. On the face of it, this is beneficial because the business is using free finance provided by suppliers. This is not necessarily advantageous, however, if it is leading to a loss of supplier goodwill that could have adverse consequences for Alexis plc.

**Real World 7.5** is an extract from an article that describes how small businesses have been affected by larger customers delaying payments during the recent recession.

**Real World 7.5**

## Taking credit where it's not due    **FT**

Late payment is a significant cause of ill will between small businesses and larger customers. By extending payment periods, usually through simple foot-dragging, debtors are able to draw on a plentiful supply of free credit. But this complicates financial planning for creditors and in extreme cases can trigger their insolvency. Successive governments have struggled to defeat the problem because small entrepreneurs are reluctant to exercise such sanctions as charging interest on late payments.

Payment periods crept up during the recession as large companies hoarded cash. The average payment period in the private sector is 52 days, according to the Federation of Small Businesses, which said that most invoices specify payment within 30 days. Companies House data show that some businesses can take six months or more to meet their debts

*Source*: Adapted from 'Small businesses hit at late Whitehall payments', Jonathan Guthrie, FT.com, 2 February 2010.

## Sales revenue to capital employed

The **sales revenue to capital employed ratio** (or net asset turnover ratio) examines how effectively the assets of the business are being used to generate sales revenue. It is calculated as follows:

$$\text{Sales revenue to capital employed ratio} = \frac{\text{Sales revenue}}{\text{Share capital} + \text{Reserves} + \text{Non-current liabilities}}$$

Generally speaking, a higher sales revenue to capital employed ratio is preferred to a lower one. A higher ratio will normally suggest that assets are being used more productively in the generation of revenue. However, a very high ratio may suggest that the business is 'overtrading on its assets', that is, it has insufficient assets to sustain the level of sales revenue achieved. (Overtrading will be considered in more detail a little later in the chapter.) When comparing this ratio for different businesses, factors such as the age and condition of assets held, the valuation bases for assets and whether assets are leased or owned outright can complicate interpretation.

A variation of this formula is to use the total assets less current liabilities (which is equivalent to long-term capital employed) in the denominator (lower part of the fraction). The identical result is obtained.

For the year ended 31 March 2011 this ratio for Alexis plc is:

$$\text{Sales revenue to capital employed} = \frac{2,240}{(638 + 763)/2} = 3.20 \text{ times}$$

## Activity 7.10

Calculate the sales revenue to capital employed ratio for Alexis plc for the year ended 31 March 2012.

The ratio for 2012 is:

$$\text{Sales revenue to capital employed} = \frac{2{,}681}{(763 + 834)/2} = 3.36 \text{ times}$$

This seems to be an improvement, since in 2012 more sales revenue was being generated for each £1 of capital employed (£3.36) than was the case in 2011 (£3.20). Provided that overtrading is not an issue, and that the additional sales are generating an acceptable profit, this is to be welcomed.

## Sales revenue per employee

The **sales revenue per employee ratio** relates sales revenue generated during a reporting period to a particular business resource, that is, labour. It provides a measure of the productivity of the workforce. The ratio is:

$$\text{Sales revenue per employee} = \frac{\text{Sales revenue}}{\text{Number of employees}}$$

Generally, businesses would prefer a high value for this ratio, implying that they are using their staff efficiently.

For the year ended 31 March 2011, the ratio for Alexis plc is:

$$\text{Sales revenue per employee} = \frac{\pounds 2{,}240m}{13{,}995} = \pounds 160{,}057$$

## Activity 7.11

Calculate the sales revenue per employee for Alexis plc for the year ended 31 March 2012.

The ratio for 2012 is:

$$\text{Sales revenue per employee} = \frac{\pounds 2{,}681m}{18{,}623} = \pounds 143{,}962$$

This represents a fairly significant decline and probably one that merits further investigation. As we discussed previously, the number of employees had increased quite notably (by about 33 per cent) during 2012 and the analyst will probably try to discover why this had not generated sufficient additional sales revenue to maintain the ratio at its 2011 level. It could be that the additional employees were not appointed until late in the year ended 31 March 2012.

The efficiency, or activity, ratios may be summarised as follows:

|  | *2011* | *2012* |
|---|---|---|
| Average inventories turnover period | 56.6 days | 56.7 days |
| Average settlement period for trade receivables | 37.7 days | 34.9 days |
| Average settlement period for trade payables | 44.9 days | 47.2 days |
| Sales revenue to capital employed (net asset turnover) | 3.20 times | 3.36 times |
| Sales revenue per employee | £160,057 | £143,962 |

## Activity (7.12)

**What do you deduce from a comparison of the efficiency ratios over the two years?**

Maintaining the inventories turnover period at the 2011 level might be reasonable, though whether this represents a satisfactory period can probably only be assessed by looking at the business's planned inventories period. The inventories turnover period for other businesses operating in carpet retailing, particularly those regarded as the market leaders, may have been helpful in formulating the plans. On the face of things, a shorter receivables collection period and a longer payables payment period are both desirable. On the other hand, these may have been achieved at the cost of a loss of the goodwill of customers and suppliers, respectively. The increased sales revenue to capital employed ratio seems beneficial, provided that the business can manage this increase. The decline in the sales revenue per employee ratio is undesirable but, as we have already seen, is probably related to the dramatic increase in the level of staffing. As with the inventories turnover period, these other ratios need to be compared with the planned standard of efficiency.

## Relationship between profitability and efficiency

In our earlier discussions concerning profitability ratios, we saw that return on capital employed (ROCE) is regarded as a key ratio by many businesses. The ratio is:

$$\text{ROCE} = \frac{\text{Operating profit}}{\text{Long-term capital employed}} \times 100$$

where long-term capital comprises share capital plus reserves plus long-term borrowings. This ratio can be broken down into two elements, as shown in Figure 7.3. The first ratio is the operating profit margin ratio and the second is the sales revenue to capital employed (net asset turnover) ratio, both of which we discussed earlier.

By breaking down the ROCE ratio in this manner, we highlight the fact that the overall return on funds employed within the business will be determined both by the profitability of sales and by efficiency in the use of capital.

Example 7.2 demonstrates that a relatively high sales revenue to capital employed ratio can compensate for a relatively low operating profit margin. Similarly, a relatively low sales revenue to capital employed ratio can be overcome by a relatively high operating profit margin. In many areas of retail and distribution (for example, supermarkets and delivery services), operating profit margins are quite low but the ROCE can be high, provided that the assets are used productively (that is, low margin, high sales revenue to capital employed).

| Figure 7.3 | The main elements of the ROCE ratio |

The ROCE ratio can be divided into two elements: operating profit to sales revenue and sales revenue to capital employed. By analysing ROCE in this way, we can see the influence of both profitability and efficiency on this important ratio.

**Example 7.2**

Consider the following information, for last year, concerning two different businesses operating in the same industry:

|  | Antler plc £m | Baker plc £m |
|---|---|---|
| Operating profit | 20 | 15 |
| Average long-term capital employed | 100 | 75 |
| Sales revenue | 200 | 300 |

The ROCE for each business is identical (20 per cent). However, the manner in which that return was achieved by each business was quite different. In the case of Antler plc, the operating profit margin is 10 per cent and the sales revenue to capital employed ratio is 2 times (so ROCE = 10% × 2 = 20%). In the case of Baker plc, the operating profit margin is 5 per cent and the sales revenue to capital employed ratio is 4 times (and so ROCE = 5% × 4 = 20%).

**Activity 7.13**

Show how the ROCE ratio for Alexis plc can be analysed into the two elements for each of the years 2011 and 2012. What conclusions can you draw from your figures?

|  | ROCE | = | Operating profit margin | × | Sales revenue to capital employed |
|---|---|---|---|---|---|
| 2011 | 34.7% | | 10.8% | | 3.20 |
| 2012 | 5.9% | | 1.8% | | 3.36 |

**Activity 7.13 (continued)**

As we can see, the relationship between the three ratios holds for Alexis plc for both years. The small apparent differences arise because the three ratios are stated here only to one or two decimal places.

Although the business was more effective at generating sales revenue (sales revenue to capital employed ratio increased) in 2012 than in 2011, in 2012 it fell well below the level necessary to compensate for the sharp decline in the effectiveness of each sale (operating profit margin). As a result, the 2012 ROCE was well below the 2011 value.

# Liquidity

Liquidity ratios are concerned with the ability of the business to meet its short-term financial obligations. The following ratios are widely used:

- current ratio
- acid test ratio
- operating cash flows to maturing obligations

These three ratios will now be considered.

## Current ratio

The **current ratio** compares the 'liquid' assets (that is, cash and those assets held that will soon be turned into cash) of the business with the current liabilities. The ratio is calculated as follows:

$$\text{Current ratio} = \frac{\text{Current assets}}{\text{Current liabilities}}$$

Some people seem to believe that there is an 'ideal' current ratio (usually 2 times or 2:1) for all businesses. However, this fails to take into account the fact that different types of business require different current ratios. For example, a manufacturing business will often have a relatively high current ratio because it has to hold inventories of finished goods, raw materials and work-in-progress. It will also normally sell goods on credit, thereby giving rise to trade receivables. A supermarket chain, on the other hand, will have a relatively low ratio, as it will hold only fast-moving inventories of finished goods, and all of its sales will be made for cash (no credit sales). **Real World 16.1** on page 646 highlights these differences.

The higher the ratio, the more liquid the business is considered to be. As liquidity is vital to the survival of a business, a higher current ratio might be thought to be preferable to a lower one. If a business has a very high ratio, however, it may be that excessive funds are tied up in cash or other liquid assets and are not, therefore, being used as productively as they might otherwise be.

As at 31 March 2011, the current ratio of Alexis plc is:

$$\text{Current ratio} = \frac{544}{291} = 1.9 \text{ times (or 1.9:1)}$$

## Activity (7.14)

Calculate the current ratio for Alexis plc as at 31 March 2012.

The ratio as at 31 March 2012 is:

$$\text{Current ratio} = \frac{679}{432} = 1.6 \text{ times (or 1.6:1)}$$

Although this is a decline from 2011 to 2012, it is not necessarily a matter of concern. The next ratio may provide a clue as to whether there seems to be a problem.

## Acid test ratio

The **acid test ratio** is very similar to the current ratio, but it represents a more stringent test of liquidity. For many businesses, inventories cannot be converted into cash quickly. (Note that, in the case of Alexis plc, the inventories turnover period was about 57 days in both years (see page 255).) As a result, it may be better to exclude this particular asset from any measure of liquidity. The acid test ratio is a variation of the current ratio, but excluding inventories.

The minimum level for this ratio is often stated as 1.0 times (or 1:1; that is, current assets (excluding inventories) equal current liabilities). In many highly successful businesses that are regarded as having adequate liquidity, however, it is not unusual for the acid test ratio to be below 1.0 without causing particular liquidity problems.

The acid test ratio is calculated as follows:

$$\text{Acid test ratio} = \frac{\text{Current assets (excluding inventories)}}{\text{Current liabilities}}$$

The acid test ratio for Alexis plc as at 31 March 2011 is:

$$\text{Acid test ratio} = \frac{544 - 300}{291} = 0.8 \text{ times (or 0.8:1)}$$

We can see that the 'liquid' current assets do not quite cover the current liabilities, so the business may be experiencing some liquidity problems.

## Activity (7.15)

Calculate the acid test ratio for Alexis plc as at 31 March 2012.

The ratio as at 31 March 2012 is:

$$\text{Acid test ratio} = \frac{679 - 406}{432} = 0.6 \text{ times}$$

The 2012 ratio is significantly below that for 2011. The 2012 level may well be a cause for concern. The rapid decline in this ratio should lead to steps being taken, at least to investigate the reason for this and, perhaps, to stop it falling further.

## Cash generated from operations to maturing obligations ratio

The **cash generated from operations to maturing obligations ratio** compares the cash generated from operations (taken from the statement of cash flows) with the current liabilities of the business. It provides a further indication of the ability of the business to meet its maturing obligations. The ratio is expressed as:

$$\text{Cash generated from operations to maturing obligations ratio} = \frac{\text{Cash generated from operations}}{\text{Current liabilities}}$$

The higher this ratio is, the better the liquidity of the business. This ratio has the advantage over the current ratio that the operating cash flows for a period usually provide a more reliable guide to the liquidity of a business than do the current assets held at the statement of financial position date. Alexis plc's ratio for the year ended 31 March 2011 is:

$$\text{Cash generated from operations to maturing obligations ratio} = \frac{251}{291} = 0.9 \text{ times}$$

This ratio indicates that the operating cash flows for the year are not quite sufficient to cover the current liabilities at the end of the year.

**Activity (7.16)**

Calculate the cash generated from operations to maturing obligations ratio for Alexis plc for the year ended 31 March 2012.

$$\text{Cash generated from operations to maturing obligations ratio} = \frac{34}{432} = 0.1 \text{ times}$$

This ratio shows an alarming decline in the ability of the business to meet its maturing obligations from its operating cash flows. It provides further evidence that liquidity should be a cause for concern.

The liquidity ratios for the two-year period may be summarised as follows:

|  | 2011 | 2012 |
|---|---|---|
| Current ratio | 1.9 | 1.6 |
| Acid test ratio | 0.8 | 0.6 |
| Cash generated from operations to maturing obligations | 0.9 | 0.1 |

## Activity (7.17)

**What do you deduce from these liquidity ratios?**

Although we cannot make a totally valid judgement without knowing the planned ratios, there appears to have been a worrying decline in liquidity. This is indicated by all three of these ratios. The most worrying is the last ratio because it shows that the ability of the business to generate cash from trading operations has declined relative to the short-term debts. The apparent liquidity problem may, however, be planned, short term and linked to the expansion in non-current assets and staffing. It may be that when the benefits of the expansion come on stream, liquidity will improve. On the other hand, short-term claimants may become anxious when they see signs of weak liquidity. This anxiety may lead them to press for payment, which could cause problems for Alexis plc.

# Financial gearing

**Financial gearing** occurs when a business is financed, at least in part, by borrowing instead of by finance provided by the owners (the shareholders) as equity. A business's level of gearing (that is, the extent to which it is financed from sources that require a fixed return) is an important factor in assessing risk. Where a business borrows, it takes on a commitment to pay interest charges and make capital repayments. Where the borrowing is heavy, this can be a significant financial burden; it can increase the risk of the business becoming insolvent. Nevertheless, most businesses are geared to some extent. (Costain Group plc, the builders and construction business, is a rare example of a UK business with no borrowings.)

Given the risks involved, we may wonder why a business would want to take on gearing (that is, to borrow). One reason may be that the owners have insufficient funds, so the only way to finance the business adequately is to borrow from others. Another reason is that gearing can be used to increase the returns to owners. This is possible provided that the returns generated from borrowed funds exceed the cost of paying interest. Example 7.3 illustrates this point.

## Example 7.3

The long-term capital structures of two new businesses, Lee Ltd and Nova Ltd, are as follows:

|                     | Lee Ltd | Nova Ltd |
|---------------------|---------|----------|
|                     | £       | £        |
| £1 ordinary shares  | 100,000 | 200,000  |
| 10% loan notes      | 200,000 | 100,000  |
|                     | 300,000 | 300,000  |

In their first year of operations, they each make an operating profit (that is, profit before interest and taxation) of £50,000. The tax rate is 30 per cent of the profit before taxation but after interest.

Lee Ltd would probably be considered relatively highly geared, as it has a high proportion of borrowed funds in its long-term capital structure. Nova Ltd is much

→

lower geared. The profit available to the shareholders of each business in the first year of operations will be:

|  | Lee Ltd £ | Nova Ltd £ |
|---|---|---|
| Operating profit | 50,000 | 50,000 |
| Interest payable | (20,000) | (10,000) |
| Profit before taxation | 30,000 | 40,000 |
| Taxation (30%) | (9,000) | (12,000) |
| Profit for the year (available to ordinary shareholders) | 21,000 | 28,000 |

The return on ordinary shareholders' funds (ROSF) for each business will be:

Lee Ltd

$$\frac{21,000}{100,000} \times 100 = 21\%$$

Nova Ltd

$$\frac{28,000}{200,000} \times 100 = 14\%$$

We can see that Lee Ltd, the more highly geared business, has generated a better ROSF than Nova Ltd. This is despite the fact that the ROCE (return on capital employed) is identical for both businesses (that is, (£50,000/£300,000) × 100 = 16.7%).

Note that at the £50,000 level of operating profit, the shareholders of both Lee Ltd and Nova Ltd benefit from gearing. Were the two businesses totally reliant on equity financing, the profit for the year (after taxation profit) would be £35,000 (that is, £50,000 less 30 per cent taxation), giving an ROSF of 11.7 per cent (that is, £35,000/£300,000). Both businesses generate higher ROSFs than this as a result of financial gearing.

An effect of gearing is that returns to shareholders become more sensitive to changes in operating profits. For a highly geared business, a change in operating profits will lead to a proportionately greater change in the ROSF ratio.

## Activity (7.18)

Assume that the operating profit was 20 per cent higher for each business than stated above (that is, an operating profit of £60,000). What would be the effect of this on ROSF?

The revised profit available to the shareholders of each business in the first year of operations will be:

|  | Lee Ltd £ | Nova Ltd £ |
|---|---|---|
| Operating profit | 60,000 | 60,000 |
| Interest payable | (20,000) | (10,000) |
| Profit before taxation | 40,000 | 50,000 |
| Taxation (30%) | (12,000) | (15,000) |
| Profit for the year (available to ordinary shareholders) | 28,000 | 35,000 |

The ROSF for each business will now be:

Lee Ltd

$$\frac{28,000}{100,000} \times 100 = 28\%$$

Nova Ltd

$$\frac{35,000}{200,000} \times 100 = 17.5\%$$

We can see that for Lee Ltd, the higher-geared business, the returns to shareholders have increased by one-third (from 21 per cent to 28 per cent), whereas for the lower-geared business, Nova Ltd, the benefits of gearing are less pronounced, increasing by only one-quarter (from 14 per cent to 17.5 per cent). The effect of gearing can, of course, work in both directions. So, for a highly geared business, a small decline in operating profit will bring about a much greater decline in the returns to shareholders.

The reason that gearing tends to be beneficial to shareholders is that interest rates for borrowings are low by comparison with the returns that the typical business can earn. On top of this, interest expenses are tax-deductible, in the way shown in Example 7.3 and Activity 7.18. This makes the effective cost of borrowing quite cheap. It is debatable whether the apparent low interest rates really are beneficial to the shareholders. Some argue that since borrowing increases the risk to shareholders, there is a hidden cost of borrowing. What are not illusory, however, are the benefits to the shareholders of the tax deductibility of interest on borrowings.

The effect of gearing is like that of two intermeshing cogwheels of unequal size (see Figure 7.4). The movement in the larger cog (operating profit) causes a more than proportionate movement in the smaller cog (returns to ordinary shareholders). The subject of gearing is discussed further in Chapter 15.

**Figure 7.4** **The effect of financial gearing**

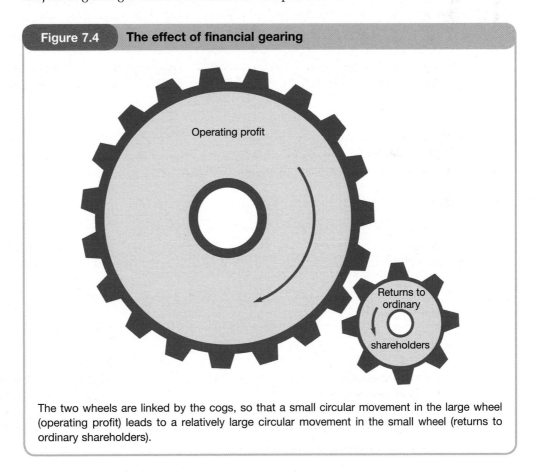

The two wheels are linked by the cogs, so that a small circular movement in the large wheel (operating profit) leads to a relatively large circular movement in the small wheel (returns to ordinary shareholders).

Two ratios are widely used to assess gearing:

- gearing ratio
- interest cover ratio.

## Gearing ratio

The **gearing ratio** measures the contribution of long-term lenders to the long-term capital structure of a business:

$$\text{Gearing ratio} = \frac{\text{Long-term (non-current) liabilities}}{\text{Share capital} + \text{Reserves} + \text{Long-term (non-current) liabilities}} \times 100$$

The gearing ratio for Alexis plc, as at 31 March 2011, is:

$$\text{Gearing ratio} = \frac{200}{(563 + 200)} \times 100 = 26.2\%$$

**Activity 7.19**

Calculate the gearing ratio of Alexis plc as at 31 March 2012.

The ratio as at 31 March 2012 is:

$$\text{Gearing ratio} = \frac{300}{(534 + 300)} \times 100 = 36.0\%$$

This is a level of gearing that would not normally be considered to be very high. This is a substantial increase in the level of gearing over the year.

## Interest cover ratio

The **interest cover ratio** measures the amount of operating profit available to cover interest payable. The ratio may be calculated as follows:

$$\text{Interest cover ratio} = \frac{\text{Operating profit}}{\text{Interest payable}}$$

The ratio for Alexis plc for the year ended 31 March 2011 is:

$$\text{Interest cover ratio} = \frac{243}{18} = 13.5 \text{ times}$$

This ratio shows that the level of operating profit is considerably higher than the level of interest payable. This means that a large fall in operating profit could occur before operating profit levels failed to cover interest payable. The lower the level of operating profit coverage, the greater the risk to lenders that interest payments will not be met. There will also be a greater risk to shareholders that the lenders will take action against the business to recover the interest due.

## Activity 7.20

Calculate the interest cover ratio of Alexis plc for the year ended 31 March 2012.

The ratio for the year ended 31 March 2012 is:

$$\text{Interest cover ratio} = \frac{47}{32} = 1.5 \text{ times}$$

Alexis plc's gearing ratios are:

|                     | 2011       | 2012     |
|---------------------|------------|----------|
| Gearing ratio       | 26.2%      | 36.0%    |
| Interest cover ratio | 13.5 times | 1.5 times |

## Activity 7.21

What do you deduce from a comparison of Alexis plc's gearing ratios over the two years?

The gearing ratio altered significantly. This is mainly due to the substantial increase in the contribution of long-term lenders to the financing of the business.

The interest cover ratio has declined dramatically from a position where operating profit covered interest 13.5 times in 2011, to one where operating profit covered interest only 1.5 times in 2012. This was partly caused by the increase in borrowings in 2012, but mainly caused by the dramatic decline in profitability in that year. The later situation looks hazardous; only a small decline in future profitability would leave the business with insufficient operating profit to cover the interest payments. The gearing ratio at 31 March 2012 would not necessarily be considered to be very high for a business that was trading successfully. It is the low profitability that is the problem.

Without knowing what the business planned these ratios to be, it is not possible to reach a valid conclusion on Alexis plc's gearing.

**Real World 7.6** is extracts from an article that discusses the likely lowering of gearing levels in the face of the recession. It explains that many businesses seem likely to issue additional ordinary shares (equity), either through making a rights issue or some public issue, and using the resulting funds to reduce borrowing as a means of reducing gearing.

**Real World 7.6**

## Changing gear

**FT**

When Stuart Siddall was corporate treasurer of Amec four years ago, analysts were critical when the engineering group swung from having substantial net debt on its balance sheet (statement of financial position) to sitting on a huge cash pile after completing disposals. "The analysts were saying 'this is inefficient balance sheet management'," says Mr Siddall.

Companies back then were expected to be highly geared, with net debt to shareholders' funds at historically high levels. How times have changed. With a wave of rights issues and other equity issuance now expected from the UK's non-financial companies – and with funds from these being used to pay down debt – the pendulum is rapidly swinging back in favour of more conservative balance sheet management. Gearing levels are set to fall dramatically, analysts say. "There is going to be an appreciable and material drop in gearing, by about a quarter or a third over the next three years", predicts Mr Siddall, now chief executive of the Association of Corporate Treasurers.

Historically, gearing levels – as measured by net debt as a proportion of shareholders funds – have run at an average of about 30 per cent over the past 20 years. Peak levels (around 45 per cent) were reached in the past few years as companies took advantage of cheap credit. Current predictions see it coming down to about 20 per cent – and staying there for a good while to come. Graham Secker, managing director of equity research at Morgan Stanley says: "This is going to be a relatively long-term phenomenon."

One of the most immediate concerns to heavily indebted companies is whether, in a recessionary environment, they will be able to generate the profit and cash flows to service their debts.

Gearing levels vary from sector to sector as well. Oil companies prefer low levels given their exposure to the volatility of oil prices. BP's net debt-shareholders' funds ratio of 21 per cent is at the low end of a 20 to 30 per cent range it considers prudent. Miners' gearing is on a clear downward trend already. Xstrata, the mining group, stressed last month that its £4.1 billion rights issue would cut gearing from 40 per cent to less than 30 per cent. A week later, BHP said its $13 billion of first-half cash flows had cut gearing to less than 10 per cent. Rio Tinto, which had gearing of 130 per cent at the last count in August 2008, is desperately trying to cut it by raising fresh equity.

Utilities tend to be highly geared because they can afford to borrow more against their typically reliable cash flows. But even here the trend is downwards. Severn Trent, the UK water group, says its appropriate long-term gearing level is 60 per cent. But "given ongoing uncertainties . . . it is prudent in the near term to retain as much liquidity and flexibility as possible". It does not expect to pursue that target until credit markets improve.

Reducing gearing is not easy, especially for the most indebted companies that need to the most: shareholders will be more reluctant to finance replacement equity in companies with highly leveraged balance sheets. The supply of fresh equity will also be constrained, not only by a glut of demand from companies but by the squeeze on investor money from a wave of government bond issuance.

Richard Jeffrey, chief investment officer at Cazenove Capital Management, says there is a risk of the government making it more difficult to raise money to improve balance sheets. "That is of extreme concern because that could become a limitation, longer term, in the capital that companies have to fund investment."

*Source*: 'Gearing levels set to plummet', Jeremy Grant, *Financial Times*, 10 February 2009.

## Self-assessment question 7.1

Both Ali plc and Bhaskar plc operate wholesale electrical stores throughout the UK. The financial statements of each business for the year ended 30 June 2012 are as follows:

### Statements of financial position as at 30 June 2012

|  | Ali plc £m | Bhaskar plc £m |
|---|---|---|
| **ASSETS** |  |  |
| **Non-current assets** |  |  |
| *Property, plant and equipment* |  |  |
| *(cost less depreciation)* |  |  |
| Land and buildings | 360.0 | 510.0 |
| Fixtures and fittings | 87.0 | 91.2 |
|  | 447.0 | 601.2 |
| **Current assets** |  |  |
| Inventories | 592.0 | 403.0 |
| Trade receivables | 176.4 | 321.9 |
| Cash at bank | 84.6 | 91.6 |
|  | 853.0 | 816.5 |
| **Total assets** | 1,300.0 | 1,417.7 |
| **EQUITY AND LIABILITIES** |  |  |
| **Equity** |  |  |
| £1 ordinary shares | 320.0 | 250.0 |
| Retained earnings | 367.6 | 624.6 |
|  | 687.6 | 874.6 |
| **Non-current liabilities** |  |  |
| Borrowings – Loan notes | 190.0 | 250.0 |
| **Current liabilities** |  |  |
| Trade payables | 406.4 | 275.7 |
| Taxation | 16.0 | 17.4 |
|  | 422.4 | 293.1 |
| **Total equity and liabilities** | 1,300.0 | 1,417.7 |

### Income statements for the year ended 30 June 2012

|  | Ali plc £m | Bhaskar plc £m |
|---|---|---|
| Revenue | 1,478.1 | 1,790.4 |
| Cost of sales | (1,018.3) | (1,214.9) |
| Gross profit | 459.8 | 575.5 |
| Operating expenses | (308.5) | (408.6) |
| Operating profit | 151.3 | 166.9 |
| Interest payable | (19.4) | (27.5) |
| Profit before taxation | 131.9 | 139.4 |
| Taxation | (32.0) | (34.8) |
| Profit for the year | 99.9 | 104.6 |

All purchases and sales were on credit. Ali plc had announced its intention to pay a dividend of £135 million and Bhaskar plc £95 million in respect of the year. The market values of a share in Ali plc and Bhaskar plc at the end of the year were £6.50 and £8.20 respectively.

**Self-assessment question 7.1 (*continued*)**

*Required*:

For each business, calculate two ratios that are concerned with each of the following aspects:

- profitability
- efficiency
- liquidity,
- gearing.

(eight ratios in total)

What can you conclude from the ratios that you have calculated?

**The solution to this question can be found at the back of the book on page 734.**

# Investment ratios

There are various ratios available that are designed to help shareholders assess the returns on their investment. The following are widely used:

- dividend payout ratio
- dividend yield ratio
- earnings per share
- operating cash flow per share
- price/earnings ratio.

## Dividend payout ratio

The **dividend payout ratio** measures the proportion of earnings that a business pays out to shareholders in the form of dividends. The ratio is calculated as follows:

$$\text{Dividend payout ratio} = \frac{\text{Dividends announced for the year}}{\text{Earnings for the year available for dividends}} \times 100$$

In the case of ordinary shares, the earnings available for dividend will normally be the profit for the year (that is, the profit after taxation) less any preference dividends relating to the year. This ratio is normally expressed as a percentage.

The dividend payout ratio for Alexis plc for the year ended 31 March 2011 is:

$$\text{Dividend payout ratio} = \frac{40}{165} \times 100 = 24.2\%$$

The information provided by this ratio is often expressed slightly differently as the **dividend cover ratio**. Here the calculation is:

$$\text{Dividend cover ratio} = \frac{\text{Earnings for the year available for dividend}}{\text{Dividend announced for the year}}$$

In the case of Alexis plc (for 2011) it would be 165/40 = 4.1 times. That is to say, the earnings available for dividend cover the actual dividend paid by just over four times.

## Activity 7.22

Calculate the dividend payout ratio of Alexis plc for the year ended 31 March 2012.

The ratio for 2012 is:

$$\text{Dividend payout ratio} = \frac{40}{11} \times 100 = 363.6\%$$

This would normally be considered to be a very alarming increase in the ratio over the two years. Paying a dividend of £40 million in 2012 may be very imprudent.

## Dividend yield ratio

The **dividend yield ratio** relates the cash return from a share to its current market value. This can help investors to assess the cash return on their investment in the business. The ratio, expressed as a percentage is:

$$\text{Dividend yield} = \frac{\text{Dividend per share}/(1-t)}{\text{Market value per share}} \times 100$$

where $t$ is the 'dividend tax credit' rate of income tax. This requires an explanation. In the UK, investors who receive a dividend from a business also receive a tax credit. As this tax credit can be offset against any tax liability arising from the dividends received, the dividends are effectively issued net of income tax, at the dividend tax credit rate.

Investors may wish to compare the returns from shares with the returns from other forms of investment. As these other forms of investment are usually quoted on a 'gross' (that is, pre-tax) basis it is useful to 'gross up' the dividend to make comparison easier. We can achieve this by dividing the **dividend per share** by $(1-t)$, where $t$ is the 'dividend tax credit' rate of income tax.

Using the 2011/12 dividend tax credit rate of 10 per cent, the dividend yield for Alexis plc for the year ended 31 March 2011 is:

$$\text{Dividend yield} = \frac{0.067^*/(1-0.10)}{2.50} \times 100 = 3.0\%$$

(The share's market value is given in Note 1 to Example 7.1 (page 246))

* Dividend proposed/number of shares = 40/(300 × 2) = £0.067 dividend per share (the 300 is multiplied by 2 because they are £0.50 shares).

**Activity (7.23)**

Calculate the dividend yield for Alexis plc for the year ended 31 March 2012.

The ratio for 2012 is:

$$\text{Dividend yield} = \frac{0.067^*/(1-0.10)}{1.50} \times 100 = 5.0\%$$

## Earnings per share

The **earnings per share (EPS)** ratio relates the earnings generated by the business, and available to shareholders, during a period, to the number of shares in issue. For equity (ordinary) shareholders, the amount available is the profit for the year (profit after taxation) less any preference dividend, where applicable. The ratio for equity shareholders is calculated as follows:

$$\text{Earnings per share} = \frac{\text{Earnings available to ordinary shareholders}}{\text{Number of ordinary shares in issue}}$$

In the case of Alexis plc, the earnings per share for the year ended 31 March 2011 is as follows:

$$\text{EPS} = \frac{£165m}{600m} = 27.5p$$

Many investment analysts regard the EPS ratio as a fundamental measure of share performance. The trend in earnings per share over time is used to help assess the investment potential of a business's shares. Although it is possible to make total profit rise through ordinary shareholders investing more in the business, this will not necessarily mean that the profitability *per share* will rise as a result.

It is not usually very helpful to compare the EPS of one business with that of another. Differences in financing arrangements (for example, in the nominal value of shares issued) can render any such comparison meaningless. However, it can be very useful to monitor the changes that occur in this ratio for a particular business over time.

**Activity (7.24)**

Calculate the earnings per share of Alexis plc for the year ended 31 March 2012.

The ratio for 2012 is:

$$\text{EPS} = \frac{£11m}{600m} = 1.8p$$

## Cash generated from operations per share

It can be argued that, in the short term at least, cash generated from operations (found in the statement of cash flows) provides a better guide to the ability of a business to pay dividends and to undertake planned expenditures than the earnings per share figure. The **cash generated from operations (CGO) per ordinary share ratio** is calculated as follows:

$$\text{Cash generated from operations per share} = \frac{\text{Cash generated from operations less preference dividend (if any)}}{\text{Number of ordinary shares in issue}}$$

The ratio for Alexis plc for the year ended 31 March 2011 is as follows:

$$\text{CGO per share} = \frac{£251\text{m}}{600\text{m}} = 41.8\text{p}$$

**Activity (7.25)**

Calculate the CGO per ordinary share for Alexis plc for the year ended 31 March 2012.

The ratio for 2012 is:

$$\text{CGO per share} = \frac{£34\text{m}}{600\text{m}} = 5.7\text{p}$$

There has been a dramatic decrease in this ratio over the two-year period.

Note that, for both years, the CGO per share for Alexis plc is higher than the earnings per share. This is not unusual. The effect of adding back depreciation to derive the CGO figures will often ensure that a higher figure is derived.

## Price/earnings (P/E) ratio

The **price/earnings ratio** relates the market value of a share to the earnings per share. This ratio can be calculated as follows:

$$\text{P/E ratio} = \frac{\text{Market value per share}}{\text{Earnings per share}}$$

The P/E ratio for Alexis plc as at 31 March 2011 is:

$$\text{P/E ratio} = \frac{£2.50}{27.5\text{p*}} = 9.1 \text{ times}$$

* The EPS figure (27.5p) was calculated on page 274.

This ratio indicates that the market value of the share is 9.1 times higher than its current level of earnings. The ratio is a measure of market confidence in the future of a business. The higher the P/E ratio, the greater the confidence in the future earning power of the business and, consequently, the more investors are prepared to pay in relation to the earnings stream of the business.

P/E ratios provide a useful guide to market confidence concerning the future and they can, therefore, be helpful when comparing different businesses. However, differences in accounting policies between businesses can lead to different profit and earnings per share figures. This can distort comparisons.

---

**Activity (7.26)**

Calculate the P/E ratio of Alexis plc as at 31 March 2012.

The ratio for 2012 is:

$$\text{P/E ratio} = \frac{£1.50}{1.8p} = 83.3 \text{ times}$$

---

The investment ratios for Alexis plc over the two-year period are as follows:

|  | 2011 | 2012 |
|---|---|---|
| Dividend payout ratio | 24.2% | 363.6% |
| Dividend yield ratio | 3.0% | 5.0% |
| Earnings per share | 27.5p | 1.8p |
| Cash generated from operations per share | 41.8p | 5.7p |
| P/E ratio | 9.1 times | 83.3 times |

---

**Activity (7.27)**

What do you deduce from these investment ratios?

Can you offer an explanation why the share price has not fallen as much as it might have done, bearing in mind the very poor (relative to 2011) trading performance in 2012?

Although the EPS has fallen dramatically and the dividend payment for 2012 seems very imprudent, the share price seems to have held up remarkably well (fallen from £2.50 to £1.50). This means that dividend yield and P/E value for 2012 look better than those for 2011. This is an anomaly of these two ratios, which stems from using a forward-looking value (the share price) in conjunction with historic data (dividends and earnings). Share prices are based on investors' assessments of the business's future. It seems with Alexis plc that, at the end of 2012, the 'market' was not happy with the business, relative to 2011. This is evidenced by the fact that the share price had fallen by £1 a share. On the other hand, the share price has not fallen as much as profit for the year. It appears that investors believe that the business will perform better in the future than it did in 2012. This may well be because they believe that the large expansion in assets and employee numbers that occurred in 2012 will yield benefits in the future; benefits that the business was not able to generate during 2012.

Real World 7.7 gives some information about the shares of several large, well-known UK businesses. This type of information is provided on a daily basis by several newspapers, notably the *Financial Times*.

---

**Real World 7.7**

## Market statistics for some well-known businesses    **FT**

The following data was extracted from the *Financial Times* of 20 July 2011, relating to the previous day's trading of the shares of some well-known businesses on the London Stock Exchange:

| Share | Price | Chng | 52-Week | | Y'ld | P/E | Volume |
| | | | High | Low | | | 000s |
|---|---|---|---|---|---|---|---|
| Marks and Spencer | 354.10 | +1.90 | 431.40 | 326.10 | 4.8 | 9.5 | 750 |
| J D Wetherspoon | 430 | +6.60 | 473 | 389.10 | 0.9 | 12.1 | 501 |
| National Express | 242 | +0.30 | 272.50 | 218 | 2.5 | 17.6 | 944 |
| Tesco | 392.05 | −2.95 | 490.50 | 280.40 | 3.7 | 13.8 | 26,566 |
| Rolls-Royce | 635.50 | +5.50 | 666.61 | 314.06 | 2.3 | 22.2 | 7,963 |
| Thomas Cook | 68.40 | +1.40 | 206.80 | 66.15 | 15.7 | 16.3 | 26,460 |

The column headings are as follows:

| | |
|---|---|
| Price | Mid-market price in pence (that is, the price midway between buying and selling price) of the shares at the end of trading on 19 July 2011. |
| Chng | Gain or loss in the mid-market price during 19 July 2011. |
| High/Low | Highest and lowest prices reached by the share during the 52 weeks ended on 19 July 2011. |
| Y'ld | Gross dividend yield, based on the most recent year's dividend and the current share price. |
| P/E | Price/earnings ratio, based on the most recent year's (after-tax) profit for the year and the current share price. |
| Volume | The number of shares (in thousands) that were bought/sold on 19 July 2011. |

So, for example for Marks and Spencer plc, the retail business:

- the shares had a mid-market price of 354.10p each at the close of Stock Exchange trading on 19 July 2011;
- the shares had increased in price by 1.90 pence during trading on 19 July 2011;
- the shares had highest and lowest prices during the previous 52 weeks of 431.40p and 326.10p, respectively;
- the shares had a dividend yield, based on the 19 July 2011 price (and the dividend for the most recent year) of 4.8 per cent;
- the shares had a P/E ratio, based on the 19 July 2011 price (and the after-taxation earnings per share for the most recent year) of 9.5;
- during 19 July 2011, 750,000 of the business's shares had changed hands from one investor to another.

*Source: Financial Times, 20 July 2011, p. 30.*

**Real World 7.8** shows how investment ratios can vary between different industry sectors.

FT

### Real World 7.8

### Yielding dividends

Investment ratios can vary significantly between businesses and between industries. To give some indication of the range of variations that occur, the average dividend yield ratios and average P/E ratios for listed businesses in twelve different industries are shown in Figure 7.5 and 7.6, respectively.

**Figure 7.5** Average dividend yield ratios for businesses in a range of industries

Average levels of dividend yield tend to vary from one industry to the next.

These dividend yield ratios are calculated from the current market value of the shares and the most recent year's dividend paid.

Some industries tend to pay out lower dividends than others, leading to lower dividend yield ratios. The average for all Stock Exchange listed businesses was 3.64 per cent (as is shown in Figure 7.5), but there is a wide variation with Software and Computer Services at 1.59 per cent and Electricity at 6.18 per cent.

Some types of businesses tend to invest heavily in developing new products, hence their tendency to pay low dividends compared with their share prices. Some of the inter-industry differences in the dividend yield ratio can be explained by the nature of the calculation of the ratio. The prices of shares at any given moment are based on expectations of their economic futures; dividends are actual past events. A business that had a good trading year recently may have paid a dividend that, in the light of investors' assessment of the business's economic future, may be high (a high dividend yield).

**Figure 7.6**    **Average price/earnings ratios for businesses in a range of industries**

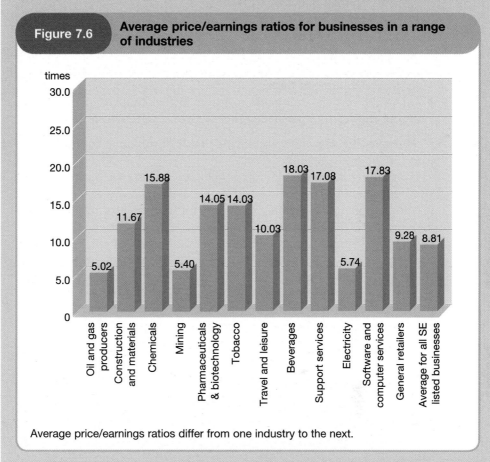

Average price/earnings ratios differ from one industry to the next.

These P/E ratios are calculated from the current market value of the shares and the most recent year's earnings per share (EPS).

Businesses that have a high share price relative to their recent historic earnings have high P/E ratios. This may be because their future is regarded as economically bright, which may be the result of investing heavily in the future at the expense of recent profits (earnings). On the other hand, high P/Es also arise where businesses have recent low earnings but investors believe that their future is brighter. The average P/E for all Stock Exchange listed businesses was 8.81 times, but Oil and Gas was as low as 5.02 times and Beverages as high as 18.03 times.

*Source*: Both figures are constructed from data appearing in the *Financial Times*, 27/28 August 2011, p. 20.

# Financial ratios and the problem of overtrading

**Overtrading** occurs where a business is operating at a level of activity that cannot be supported by the amount of finance that has been committed. For example, the business has inadequate finance to fund the level of trade receivables and inventories necessary for the level of sales revenue that it is achieving. This situation usually reflects a poor level of financial control over the business. The reasons for overtrading are varied. It may occur:

● in young, expanding businesses that fail to prepare adequately for the rapid increase in demand for their goods or services;
● in businesses where the managers may have misjudged the level of expected sales demand or have failed to control escalating project costs;
● as a result of a fall in the value of money (inflation), causing more finance to have to be committed to inventories and trade receivables, even where there is no expansion in the real volume of trade;
● where the owners are unable to inject further funds into the business themselves and/or they cannot persuade others to invest in the business.

Whatever the reason, the problems that it brings must be dealt with if the business is to survive over the longer term.

Overtrading results in liquidity problems such as exceeding borrowing limits, or slow repayment of borrowings and trade payables. It can also result in suppliers withholding supplies, thereby making it difficult to meet customer needs. The lack of cash may prevent a business from buying additional non-current assets, such as plant and equipment. This may place a strain on existing equipment leading to more frequent breakdowns and stoppages. Managers of the business might be forced to direct all of their efforts to dealing with immediate and pressing problems, such as finding cash to meet interest charges due or paying wages. Longer-term planning becomes difficult as managers spend their time lurching from crisis to crisis. Ultimately, the business may fail because it cannot meet its maturing obligations.

## Activity (7.28)

If a business is overtrading, do you think the following ratios would be higher or lower than normally expected?

1  Current ratio.
2  Average inventories turnover period.
3  Average settlement period for trade receivables.
4  Average settlement period for trade payables.

Your answer should be as follows:

1  The current ratio would be lower than normally expected. This is a measure of liquidity, and lack of liquidity is a typical symptom of overtrading.
2  The average inventories turnover period would be lower than normally expected. Where a business is overtrading, the level of inventories held will be low because of the problems of financing them. In the short term, sales revenue may not be badly affected by the low inventories levels and therefore inventories will be turned over more quickly.
3  The average settlement period for trade receivables may be lower than normally expected. Where a business is suffering from liquidity problems, it may chase credit customers more vigorously in an attempt to improve cash flows.
4  The average settlement period for trade payables may be higher than normally expected. The business may try to delay payments to its suppliers because of its liquidity problems.

To deal with the overtrading problem, a business must ensure that the finance available is consistent with the level of operations. Thus, if a business that is overtrading is unable to raise new finance, it should cut back its level of operations in line with the finance available. Although there may be lost sales and lost profits in the short term, it may be necessary to do this in an attempt to ensure survival over the longer term.

## Trend analysis

It is often helpful to see whether ratios are indicating trends. Key ratios can be plotted on a graph to provide a simple visual display of changes occurring over time. The trends occurring within a business may, for example, be plotted against trends for rival businesses or for the industry as a whole for comparison purposes. An example of trend analysis is shown in **Real World 7.9**.

### Real World 7.9

#### Trend setting

In Figure 7.7, the current ratio of three of the UK's leading supermarkets is plotted over time. We can see that the current ratios of the three businesses have tended to move closer. Tesco plc was lower than that of its main rivals, until 2005, when it overtook Morrison and 2009, when it overtook Sainsbury. Although in 2010 it resumed its position as having the lowest current ratio of the three businesses, it reverted to having the highest current ratio in 2011. The current ratio of Sainsbury shows a fairly consistent downward path (although in 2010 it increased). With well-managed businesses like Sainsbury and Tesco, it seems highly probable that these changes are the result of deliberate policy.

#### Figure 7.7    Graph plotting current ratio against time

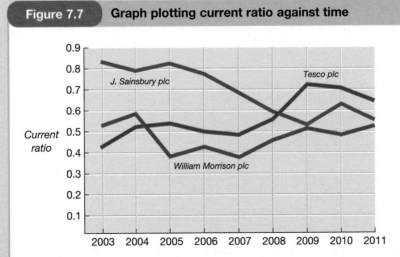

The current ratio for three leading UK supermarkets is plotted for the financial years ended during 2003 to 2011. This enables comparison to be made regarding the ratio, both for each of the three businesses over time and, between the businesses.

*Source*: Annual reports of the three businesses 2003 to 2011.

# Using ratios to predict financial failure

Financial ratios, based on current or past performance, have long been used to help predict the future. However, both the choice of ratios and the interpretation of results had normally been dependent on the judgement and opinion of the analyst. In recent years, however, attempts have been made to develop a more rigorous and systematic approach to the use of ratios for prediction purposes. In particular, researchers have shown an interest in the ability of ratios to predict the financial failure of a business.

By financial failure, we mean a business either being forced out of business or being severely adversely affected by its inability to meet its financial obligations. It is often referred to as 'going bust' or 'going bankrupt'. This, of course, is an area with which all those connected with the business are likely to be concerned.

## Using single ratios

Different ways of predicting financial failure through the use of ratios are found in the literature. Early research looked at ratios on an individual basis to assess their predictive value. A particular ratio (for example, the current ratio) for a failed business would be tracked over several years leading up to the date of the failure. The aim was to see whether the ratio displayed a trend that provided a warning sign.

Beaver (see reference 1 at the end of the chapter) carried out the first research in this area. He identified 79 businesses that had failed. He then calculated the average (mean) of various ratios for these 79 businesses, going back over the financial statements of each business for each of the ten years leading up to each business's failure. Beaver then compared these average ratios with similarly derived ratios for a sample of 79 businesses that did not fail over this period. (The research used a matched-pair design, where each failed business was matched with a non-failed business of similar size and industry type.) Beaver found that certain ratios exhibited a marked difference between the failed and non-failed businesses for up to five years prior to failure. These ratios were:

● Cash flow/Total debt
● Net income (profit)/Total assets
● Total debt/Total assets
● Working capital/Total assets
● Current ratio
● No credit interval (that is, cash generated from operations to maturing obligations)

To illustrate Beaver's findings the average current ratio of failed businesses for five years prior to failure, along with the average current ratio of non-failed businesses for the same period, is shown in Figure 7.8.

Research by Zmijewski (see reference 2), using a sample of 72 failed and 3,573 non-failed businesses over a six-year period, found that businesses that ultimately went on to fail were characterised by lower rates of return, higher levels of gearing, lower levels of coverage for their fixed interest payments and more variable returns on shares. While we may not find these results very surprising, it is interesting to note that Zmijewski, like a number of other researchers in this area, did not find liquidity ratios particularly useful in predicting financial failure. As mentioned earlier, however, Beaver found the current ratio to be a useful predictor.

| Figure 7.8 | Average (mean) current ratio of failed and non-failed businesses |

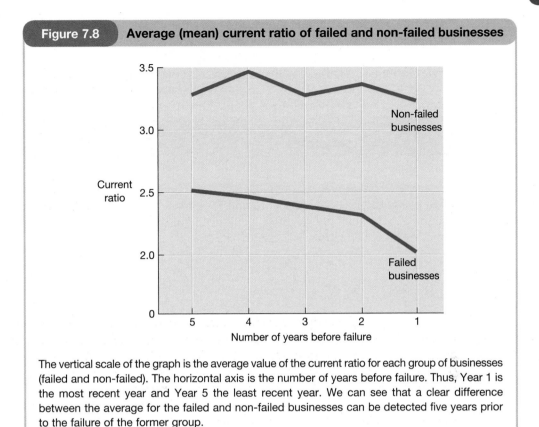

The vertical scale of the graph is the average value of the current ratio for each group of businesses (failed and non-failed). The horizontal axis is the number of years before failure. Thus, Year 1 is the most recent year and Year 5 the least recent year. We can see that a clear difference between the average for the failed and non-failed businesses can be detected five years prior to the failure of the former group.

The approach adopted by Beaver and Zmijewski is referred to as **univariate analysis** because it looks at one ratio at a time. It can produce interesting results but there are practical problems with its use. For example, past research may have identified two ratios as good predictors of financial failure. When applied to a particular business, however, one ratio predicts financial failure but the other does not. Given these conflicting signals, how should we interpret the results?

## Using combinations of ratios

The weaknesses of univariate analysis have led to the development of models that combine ratios so as to produce a single index that can be interpreted more clearly. One approach to model development, much favoured by researchers, uses **multiple discriminate analysis** (MDA). This is, in essence, a statistical technique that is similar to regression analysis and which can be used to draw a boundary between those businesses that fail and those businesses that do not. This boundary is referred to as the **discriminate function**. In this context, MDA attempts to identify those factors likely to influence financial failure. However, unlike regression analysis, MDA assumes that the observations come from two different populations (for example, failed and non-failed businesses) rather than from a single population.

To illustrate this approach, let us assume that we wish to test whether two ratios (say, the current ratio and the return on capital employed) can help to predict failure.

To do this, we can calculate these ratios, first for a sample of failed businesses and then for a matched sample of non-failed ones. From these two sets of data, we can produce a scatter diagram that plots each business according to these two ratios to produce a single coordinate. Figure 7.9 illustrates this approach.

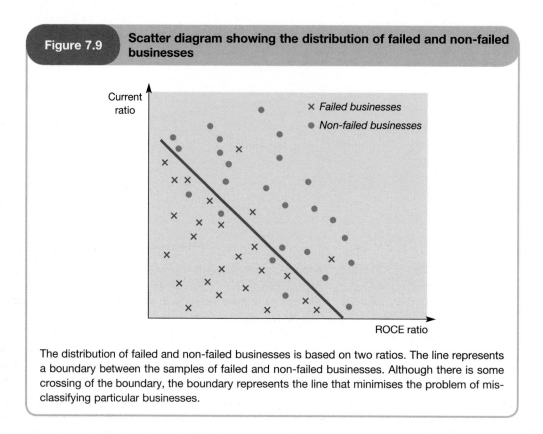

| Figure 7.9 | Scatter diagram showing the distribution of failed and non-failed businesses |

The distribution of failed and non-failed businesses is based on two ratios. The line represents a boundary between the samples of failed and non-failed businesses. Although there is some crossing of the boundary, the boundary represents the line that minimises the problem of mis-classifying particular businesses.

Using the observations plotted on the diagram, we try to identify the boundary between the failed and the non-failed businesses. This is the diagonal line in Figure 7.9.

We can see that those businesses that fall below and to the left of the line are predominantly failed and those that fall to the right are predominantly non-failed ones. Note that there is some overlap between the two populations. The boundary produced is unlikely, in practice, to eliminate all errors. Some businesses that eventually do fail may fall on the side of the boundary with non-failed businesses. The opposite also happens. However, the analysis will tend to *minimise* the misclassification errors.

The boundary shown in Figure 7.9 can be expressed in the form:

$$Z = a + (b \times \text{Current ratio}) + (c \times \text{ROCE})$$

where $a$ is a constant and $b$ and $c$ are weights to be attached to each ratio. A weighted average or total score ($Z$) is then derived. The weights given to the two ratios will depend on the slope of the line in Figure 7.9 and its absolute position. Note that this example, using the current and ROCE ratios, is purely hypothetical and only intended to illustrate the approach.

## Z-score models

Altman (see reference 3) was the first to develop a model (in 1968), using financial ratios, that was reliably able to predict financial failure. In 2000 he revised that model. The revisions needed to make the model effective for that time, however, were quite minor. Altman's revised model, the Z score model, is based on five financial ratios and is as follows:

$$Z = 0.717a + 0.847b + 3.107c + 0.420d + 0.998e$$

where

$a$ = Working capital/Total assets
$b$ = Accumulated retained profits/Total assets
$c$ = Operating profit/Total assets
$d$ = Book (statement of financial position) value of ordinary and preference shares/
　　Total liabilities at book (statement of financial position) value
$e$ = Sales revenue/Total assets

The coefficients (the numbers) in this model reflect the importance to the Z score of each of the ingredients (a to e).

In developing and revising this model, Altman carried out experiments using a paired sample of failed businesses and non-failed businesses and collected relevant data for each business for five years prior to failure. He found that the model represented by the formula shown above was able to predict failure for up to two years before it occurred. However, the predictive accuracy of the model became weaker the longer the time before the date of the actual failure.

The ratios used in this model were identified by Altman through a process of trial and error, as there is no underlying theory of financial failure to provide a guide in selecting appropriate ratios. According to Altman, those businesses with a Z score of less than 1.23 tend to fail. The lower the score, the greater is the probability of failure. Those with a Z score greater than 4.14 tend not to fail. Those businesses with a Z score between 1.23 and 4.14 occupied a 'zone of ignorance' and were difficult to classify. However, the model was able overall to classify 91 per cent of the businesses correctly; only 9 per cent fell into the 'zone of ignorance'. Altman based his model on US businesses.

In recent years, other models, using a similar approach, have been developed throughout the world. In the UK, Taffler has developed separate Z-score models for different types of business. (See reference 4 for a discussion of the work of Taffler and others.)

The prediction of financial failure is not the only area where research into the predictive ability of ratios has taken place. Researchers have also developed ratio-based models that claim to assess the vulnerability of a business to takeover by another. This is another area that is of vital importance to all those connected with the business.

**Real World 7.10** discusses some research that showed that investing in shares in businesses with very low Z scores is unsuccessful compared with investing in businesses with higher Z scores. The research did not show, however, that the higher the Z score, the more successful the investment.

## Real World 7.10

### From A to Z

**FT**

Investors looking to profit during a recession should be targeting stocks with strong fundamentals, according to research by Morgan Stanley. This "value investing" approach – buying into companies where fundamental measures, such as book value and earnings, are not yet reflected in their share prices – is not new. But Morgan Stanley's analysis has found that the ability of this approach to deliver returns in downturns depends on the financial strength of the companies – in particular, the importance attached to the balance sheet (statement of financial position) by investors.

"If a stock's balance sheet is weak, the valuation multiple will be of little importance at this stage in the economic cycle," says Graham Secker, Morgan Stanley strategy analyst. He ranked a basket of European companies by their Altman Z-score – a measure of financial strength devised by US academic Edward Altman. A Z-score can be calculated for all non-financial companies and the lower the score, the greater the risk of the company falling into financial distress. When Secker compared the companies' Z-scores with their share price movements, he discovered that the companies with weaker balance sheets underperformed the market more than two thirds of the time.

Morgan Stanley also found that a company with an Altman Z-score of less than 1 tends to underperform the wider market by more than 4 per cent over the year with an associated probability of 72 per cent. "Given the poor performance over the last year by stocks with a low Altman Z-score, the results of our backtest are now even more compelling than they were 12 months ago," argues Secker. "We calculate that the median stock with an Altman Z-score of 1 or less has underperformed the wider market by 5–6 per cent per annum between 1990 and 2008."

Secker sees this as logical. In a recession, companies with balance sheets that are perceived to be weak are deemed a higher risk by lenders and face a higher cost of capital. This turns market sentiment against them and will generally lead to their share prices falling below their peers.

In 2008, the share price performance for stocks with an Altman Z-score of less than 1 was the worst since Morgan Stanley's analysis began in 1991. Under the Morgan Stanley methodology, the 2008 score is calculated using 2007 company financials. Of all the companies with a 2008 Z-score of less than 1, the median share price performance was a loss of 49 per cent, compared with a wider market fall of 42 per cent.

When compound annual growth rates since 1991 are analysed, the results are more dramatic. On average, companies with Z-scores of less than 1 saw their shares fall 4.4 per cent, compared with an average rise of 1.3 per cent for their peers. In only five of the last 18 years has a stock with an Altman score of 1 or less outperformed the market. These were generally years of strong economic growth. However, companies with the highest Z-scores aren't necessarily the best performers. During the bear market of 2000 to 2002, companies that had a Z-score above 3 fell almost twice as much as the market.

Analysts say the 2009 Z-scores, based on 2008 balance sheets, are far lower than in previous years as companies absorb the strain of the downturn in their accounts. "There's been a lot of change between 2007 and 2008 [accounting years], tightening of credit and a vast deterioration in corporate balance sheets" says Secker. "I'd expect 2009 [Z-scores] to be much worse."

Analysis by the Financial Times and Capital IQ, the data provider, corroborates this – showing that the 2009 scores have been badly affected by the crisis. Some 8 per cent of global companies with a market capitalisation of more than $500 million have Altman scores below 1 for 2009 – based on 2008 company financials. This is the highest percentage since 2002 and the largest annual increase since 2001 – showing the impact of the recession on the balance sheets of even the largest companies. If smaller companies were included, the results would be worse – as their earnings and market capitalisations have been affected far more.

European balance sheets were hit the hardest, with companies averaging a Z-score of 2.8, compared with 4.0 for Asia and the US, according to Capital IQ. This suggests the scores are not due to chance. A similar differential was recorded in 2001 during the last recession. On this evidence, US companies appear more resilient than their global peers in a downturn. On a sector basis, healthcare and IT companies have the highest Z-scores. In 2008, their scores were more than three times higher than the average for the lowest scoring sector: utilities. A similar pattern was found in 2001 – suggesting that investors may want to think twice before buying into "defensive" utilities in a downturn.

*Source*: 'New study re-writes the A to Z of value investing', P. Mathurin, FT.com, 14 August 2009.

# Limitations of ratio analysis

Although ratios offer a quick and useful method of analysing the position and performance of a business, they are not without their problems and limitations. We shall now review some of the shortcomings of financial ratio analysis.

## Quality of financial statements

It must always be remembered that ratios are based on financial statements. The results of ratio analysis are, therefore, dependent on the quality of these underlying statements. Ratios will inherit the limitations of the financial statements on which they are based. One important limitation of financial statements is their failure to include all resources controlled by the business. Internally generated goodwill and brands, for example, are excluded from the statement of financial position because they fail to meet the strict definition of an asset. This means that, even though these resources may be of considerable value, key ratios such as ROSF, ROCE and the gearing ratio will fail to acknowledge their presence.

There is also the problem of deliberate attempts to make the financial statements misleading. We discussed this problem of *creative accounting* in Chapter 5.

## Inflation

A persistent problem, in most countries, is that the financial results of businesses can be distorted as a result of inflation. One effect of inflation is that the reported value of assets held for any length of time may bear little relation to current values. Generally speaking, the reported value of non-current assets will be understated in current terms during a period of inflation as they are usually reported at their original cost (less any amounts written off for depreciation). This means that comparisons, either between businesses or between periods, will be hindered. A difference in, say, ROCE may simply be owing to the fact that assets shown in one of the statements of financial position being compared were acquired more recently (ignoring the effect of depreciation on the asset values). Another effect of inflation is to distort the measurement of profit. In the calculation of profit, sales revenue is often matched with costs incurred at an earlier time. This is because there is often a time lag between acquiring a particular resource and using it to help generate sales revenue. For example, inventories may well be acquired several months before they are sold. During a period of inflation, this will mean that the expense does not reflect prices that are current at the time of the sale. The cost of sales figure is usually based on the historic cost of the inventories concerned. As a result, expenses will be understated in the income statement and this, in turn, means that profit will be over-stated. The longer the average inventories turnover period, the greater the distortion. One effect of this will be to distort the profitability ratios discussed earlier.

## Over-reliance on ratios

It is important not to rely exclusively on ratios, thereby losing sight of information con-tained in the underlying financial statements. As we saw earlier in the chapter, some items reported in these statements can be vital in assessing position and performance. For example, the total sales revenue, capital employed and profit figures may be useful in assessing changes in absolute size that occur over time, or in assessing differences in scale between businesses. Ratios do not provide such information. When comparing one figure with another, ratios measure relative performance and position and, therefore, provide only part of the picture. When comparing two businesses, therefore, it will often be useful to assess the absolute size of profits, as well as the relative profitability of each business. For example, Business A may generate £1 million operating profit and have a ROCE of 15 per cent and Business B may generate £100,000 operating profit and have a ROCE of 20 per cent. Although Business B has a higher level of profitability, as measured by ROCE, it generates lower total operating profits. This may well be useful information for the analyst.

## The basis for comparison

We saw earlier that if ratios are to be useful, they require a basis for comparison. Moreover, it is important that the analyst compares like with like. Where the comparison is with another business, there can be difficulties. No two businesses are identical: the greater the differences between the businesses being compared, the greater the limitations of ratio analysis. Furthermore, any differences in accounting policies, financing methods (gearing levels) and reporting period ends will add to the problems of making comparisons between businesses.

## Statement of financial position ratios

Because the statement of financial position is only a 'snapshot' of the business at a particular moment in time, any ratios based on statement of financial position figures, such as the liquidity ratios, may not be representative of the financial position of the business for the year as a whole. For example, it is common for a seasonal business to have a financial year end that coincides with a low point in business activity. As a result, inventories and trade receivables may be low at the year end. This means that the liquidity ratios may also be low. A more representative picture of liquidity can only really be gained by taking additional measurements at other points in the year.

   **Real World 7.11** points out another way in which ratios are limited.

## Real World 7.11

### Remember, it's people that really count . . .

Lord Weinstock (1924 to 2002) was an influential industrialist whose management style and philosophy helped to shape management practice in many UK businesses. During his long and successful reign at GEC plc, a major engineering business, Lord Weinstock relied heavily on financial ratios to assess performance and to exercise control. In particular, he relied on ratios relating to sales revenue, expenses, trade receivables, profit margins and inventories turnover. However, he was keenly aware of the limitations of ratios and recognised that, ultimately, people produce profits.

In a memo written to GEC managers he pointed out that ratios are an aid to good management rather than a substitute for it. He wrote:

> The operating ratios are of great value as measures of efficiency but they are only the measures and not efficiency itself. Statistics will not design a product better, make it for a lower cost or increase sales. If ill-used, they may so guide action as to diminish resources for the sake of apparent but false signs of improvement.
>
> Management remains a matter of judgement, of knowledge of products and processes and of understanding and skill in dealing with people. The ratios will indicate how well all these things are being done and will show comparison with how they are done elsewhere. But they will tell us nothing about how to do them. That is what you are meant to do.

*Source*: Extract from *Arnold Weinstock and the Making of GEC*, S. Aris, (Aurum Press, 1998), published in *The Sunday Times*, 22 February 1998, p. 3.

## Summary

The main points of this chapter may be summarised as follows.

### Ratio analysis

- Compares two related figures, usually both from the same set of financial statements.
- Is an aid to understanding what the financial statements really mean.
- Is an inexact science so results must be interpreted cautiously.
- Past periods, the performance of similar businesses and planned performance are often used to provide benchmark ratios.
- A brief overview of the financial statements can often provide insights that may not be revealed by ratios and/or may help in the interpretation of them.

### Profitability ratios

- Profitability ratios are concerned with effectiveness at generating profit.
- The profitability ratios covered are the return on ordinary shareholders' funds (ROSF), return on capital employed (ROCE), operating profit margin and gross profit margin.

### Efficiency ratios

- Efficiency ratios are concerned with efficiency of using assets/resources.
- The efficiency ratios covered are the average inventories turnover period, average settlement period for trade receivables, average settlement period for trade payables, sales revenue to capital employed and sales revenue per employee.

### Liquidity ratios

- Liquidity ratios are concerned with the ability to meet short-term obligations.
- The liquidity ratios covered are the current ratio, acid test ratio and the cash generated from operations to maturing obligations ratio.

### Gearing ratios

- Gearing ratios are concerned with relationship between equity and debt financing.
- The gearing ratios covered are the gearing ratio and interest cover ratio.

### Investment ratios

- Investment ratios are concerned with returns to shareholders.
- The investment ratios covered are the dividend payout ratio, dividend yield ratio, earnings per share, cash generated from operations per share and price/earnings ratio.

### Uses of ratios

- Ratios can be used to identify signs of overtrading.
- Individual ratios can be tracked to detect trends – for example, plotted on a graph.
- Ratios can be used to help predict financial distress. Univariate analysis does this by examining one ratio at a time, whereas multiple discriminate analysis combines several ratios within a model.

### Limitations of ratio analysis

- Ratios are only as reliable as the financial statements from which they derive.
- Inflation can distort the information.
- Ratios provide only part of the picture and there should not be over-reliance on them.
- It can be difficult to find a suitable benchmark (for example, another business) to compare with.
- Some ratios could mislead due to the 'snapshot' nature of the statement of financial position.

---

## MyAccountingLab

Go to **www.myaccountinglab.com** to check your understanding of the chapter, create a personalised study plan, and maximise your revision time

## Key terms

return on ordinary shareholders' funds ratio (ROSF)  p. 248
return on capital employed ratio (ROCE)  p. 249
operating profit margin ratio  p. 251
gross profit margin ratio  p. 252
average inventories turnover period ratio  p. 255
average settlement period for trade receivables ratio  p. 256
average settlement period for trade payables ratio  p. 257
sales revenue to capital employed ratio  p. 258
sales revenue per employee ratio  p. 259
current ratio  p. 262
acid test ratio  p. 263
cash generated from operations to maturing obligations ratio  p. 264
financial gearing  p. 265
gearing ratio  p. 268
interest cover ratio  p. 268
dividend payout ratio  p. 272
dividend cover ratio  p. 272
dividend yield ratio  p. 273
dividend per share  p. 273
earnings per share  p. 274
cash generated from operations per ordinary share  p. 275
price/earnings ratio  p. 275
overtrading  p. 279
univariate analysis  p. 283
multiple discriminate analysis  p. 283
discriminate function  p. 283

## References

1 Beaver, W. H., 'Financial Ratios as Predictors of Failure', in *Empirical Research in Accounting: Selected Studies*, Supplement, *Journal of Accounting Research*, 1966, vol. 4, pp. 71–111.

2 Zmijewski, M. E., 'Predicting Corporate Bankruptcy: An Empirical Comparison of the Extent of Financial Distress Models', Research Paper, State University of New York, 1983.

3 Altman, E. I. (2000) 'Predicting Financial Distress of Companies: Revisiting the Z-score and Zeta Models', New York University Working Paper, June.

4 Neophytou, E., Charitou, A. and Charalamnous, C. (2001) 'Predicting Corporate Failure: Empirical Evidence for the UK', University of Southampton Department of Accounting and Management Science Working Paper 01-173.

## Further reading

If you would like to explore the topics covered in this chapter in more depth, try the following books:

Elliott, B. and Elliott, J, *Financial Accounting and Reporting*, 15th edn, Financial Times Prentice Hall, 2012, chapters 28 and 29.

Schoenebeck, K. and Holtzman, M., *Interpreting and Analyzing Financial Statements*, 5th edn, Prentice Hall, 2009, chapters 2–5.

Fridson, M. and Alvarez, F., *Financial Statement Analysis: A Practitioner's Guide*, 4th edn, Wiley Finance, 2011, chapters 13 and 14.

Penman, S., *Financial Statement Analysis and Security Valuation*, 2nd edn, McGraw Hill Irwin, 2009, chapters 7–12.

## Review questions

Solutions to these questions can be found at the back of the book on page 750.

**7.1** Some businesses operate on a low operating profit margin (for example, a supermarket chain). Does this mean that the return on capital employed from the business will also be low?

**7.2** What potential problems arise for the external analyst from the use of statement of financial position figures in the calculation of financial ratios?

**7.3** Is it responsible to publish *Z*-scores of businesses that are in financial difficulties? What are the potential problems of doing this?

**7.4** Identify and discuss three reasons why the P/E ratio of two businesses operating in the same industry may differ.

## Exercises

Exercises 7.1 and 7.2 are basic level, 7.3 and 7.4 are intermediate level and 7.5, 7.6, and 7.7 are advanced level. Those with coloured numbers have solutions at the back of the book, starting on page 772.

If you wish to try more exercises, visit the students' side of the Companion Website and MyAccountingLab.

**7.1** Set out below are ratios relating to three different businesses. Each business operates within a different industrial sector.

| Ratio | A plc | B plc | C plc |
|---|---|---|---|
| Operating profit margin | 3.6% | 9.7% | 6.8% |
| Sales to capital employed | 2.4 times | 3.1 times | 1.7 times |
| Inventory turnover period | 18 days | N/A | 44 days |
| Average settlement period for trade receivables | 2 days | 12 days | 26 days |
| Current ratio | 0.8 times | 0.6 times | 1.5 times |

*Required*:
State, with reasons, which one of the three businesses is:

(a) A holiday tour operator
(b) A supermarket chain
(c) A food manufacturer.

**7.2** Amsterdam Ltd and Berlin Ltd are both engaged in retailing, but they seem to take a different approach to it according to the following information:

| Ratio | Amsterdam Ltd | Berlin Ltd |
|---|---|---|
| Return on capital employed (ROCE) | 20% | 17% |
| Return on ordinary shareholders' funds (ROSF) | 30% | 18% |
| Average settlement period for trade receivables | 63 days | 21 days |
| Average settlement period for trade payables | 50 days | 45 days |
| Gross profit margin | 40% | 15% |
| Operating profit margin | 10% | 10% |
| Average inventories' turnover period | 52 days | 25 days |

*Required*:

Describe what this information indicates about the differences in approach between the two businesses. If one of them prides itself on personal service and one of them on competitive prices, which do you think is which and why?

**7.3** Conday and Co. Ltd has been in operation for three years and produces antique reproduction furniture for the export market. The most recent set of financial statements for the business is set out as follows:

**Statement of financial position as at 30 November**

|  | £000 |
|---|---|
| **ASSETS** | |
| **Non-current assets** | |
| *Property, plant and equipment (Cost less depreciation)* | |
| Land and buildings | 228 |
| Plant and machinery | 762 |
|  | 990 |
| **Current assets** | |
| Inventories | 600 |
| Trade receivables | 820 |
|  | 1,420 |
| **Total assets** | 2,410 |
| **EQUITY AND LIABILITIES** | |
| **Equity** | |
| Ordinary shares of £1 each | 700 |
| Retained earnings | 365 |
|  | 1,065 |
| **Non-current liabilities** | |
| Borrowings – 9% loan notes (Note 1) | 200 |
| **Current liabilities** | |
| Trade payables | 665 |
| Taxation | 48 |
| Short-term borrowings (all bank overdraft) | 432 |
|  | 1,145 |
| **Total equity and liabilities** | 2,410 |

**Income statement for the year ended 30 November**

|  | £000 |
|---|---|
| Revenue | 2,600 |
| Cost of sales | (1,620) |
| Gross profit | 980 |
| Selling and distribution expenses (Note 2) | (408) |
| Administration expenses | (194) |
| Operating profit | 378 |
| Finance expenses | (58) |
| Profit before taxation | 320 |
| Taxation | (95) |
| Profit for the year | 225 |

**Notes:**

1  The loan notes are secured on the land and buildings.
2  Selling and distribution expenses include £170,000 in respect of bad debts.
3  A dividend of £160,000 was paid on the ordinary shares during the year.
4  The directors have invited an investor to take up a new issue of ordinary shares in the business at £6.40 each, making a total investment of £200,000. The directors wish to use the funds to finance a programme of further expansion.

*Required*:

(a) Analyse the financial position and performance of the business and comment on any features that you consider significant.

(b) State, with reasons, whether or not the investor should invest in the business on the terms outlined.

**7.4**  The directors of Helena Beauty Products Ltd have been presented with the following abridged financial statements:

**Helena Beauty Products Ltd Income statement for the year ended 30 September**

|  | 2011 | | 2012 | |
|---|---|---|---|---|
|  | £000 | £000 | £000 | £000 |
| Sales revenue |  | 3,600 |  | 3,840 |
| Cost of sales |  |  |  |  |
| Opening inventories | 320 |  | 400 |  |
| Purchases | 2,240 |  | 2,350 |  |
|  | 2,560 |  | 2,750 |  |
| Closing inventories | (400) | (2,160) | (500) | (2,250) |
| Gross profit |  | 1,440 |  | 1,590 |
| Expenses |  | (1,360) |  | (1,500) |
| Profit |  | 80 |  | 90 |

**Statement of financial position as at 30 September**

|  | 2011 | 2012 |
|---|---|---|
|  | £000 | £000 |
| **ASSETS** | | |
| **Non-current assets** | | |
| Property, plant and equipment | 1,900 | 1,860 |
| **Current assets** | | |
| Inventories | 400 | 500 |
| Trade receivables | 750 | 960 |
| Cash at bank | 8 | 4 |
|  | 1,158 | 1,464 |
| Total assets | 3,058 | 3,324 |
| **EQUITY AND LIABILITIES** | | |
| **Equity** | | |
| £1 ordinary shares | 1,650 | 1,766 |
| Retained earnings | 1,018 | 1,108 |
|  | 2,668 | 2,874 |
| Current liabilities | 390 | 450 |
| Total equity and liabilities | 3,058 | 3,324 |

*Required*:

Using six ratios, comment on the profitability (three ratios) and efficiency (three ratios) of the business.

**7.5** Threads Limited manufactures nuts and bolts, which are sold to industrial users. The abbreviated financial statements for 2011 and 2012 are as follows:

**Income statements for the year ended 30 June**

|  | 2011 | 2012 |
|---|---|---|
|  | £000 | £000 |
| Revenue | 1,180 | 1,200 |
| Cost of sales | (680) | (750) |
| Gross profit | 500 | 450 |
| Operating expenses | (200) | (208) |
| Depreciation | (66) | (75) |
| Operating profit | 234 | 167 |
| Interest | (–) | (8) |
| Profit before taxation | 234 | 159 |
| Taxation | (80) | (48) |
| Profit for the year | 154 | 111 |

**Statements of financial position as at 30 June**

|  | 2011 £000 | 2012 £000 |
|---|---|---|
| **ASSETS** | | |
| **Non-current assets** | | |
| Property, plant and equipment | 702 | 687 |
| **Current assets** | | |
| Inventories | 148 | 236 |
| Trade receivables | 102 | 156 |
| Cash | 3 | 4 |
| | 253 | 396 |
| Total assets | 955 | 1,083 |
| **EQUITY AND LIABILITIES** | | |
| **Equity** | | |
| Ordinary share capital (£1 shares, fully paid) | 500 | 500 |
| Retained earnings | 256 | 295 |
| | 756 | 795 |
| **Non-current liabilities** | | |
| Borrowings – Bank loan | – | 50 |
| **Current liabilities** | | |
| Trade payables | 60 | 76 |
| Other payables and accruals | 18 | 16 |
| Taxation | 40 | 24 |
| Short-term borrowings (all bank overdraft) | 81 | 122 |
| | 199 | 238 |
| Total equity and liabilities | 955 | 1,083 |

Dividends were paid on ordinary shares of £70,000 and £72,000 in respect of 2011 and 2012, respectively.

*Required*:
(a) Calculate the following financial ratios for *both* 2011 and 2012 (using year-end figures for statement of financial position items):
   1  return on capital employed
   2  operating profit margin
   3  gross profit margin
   4  current ratio
   5  acid test ratio
   6  settlement period for trade receivables
   7  settlement period for trade payables
   8  inventories turnover period.
(b) Comment on the performance of Threads Limited from the viewpoint of a business considering supplying a substantial amount of goods to Threads Limited on usual trade credit terms.

**7.6**  Refer to the financial statements for Ali plc and Bhaskar plc (see Self-assessment question 7.1 on page 271).

*Required*:
(a) Calculate the Z score for each business using the Altman model set out on page 285.
(b) Comment on the Z scores for each business and the validity of using this particular model to assess these particular businesses.

7.7   Genesis Ltd was incorporated in 2009 and has grown rapidly over the past three years. The rapid rate of growth has created problems for the business, which the directors have found difficult to deal with. Recently, a firm of management consultants has been asked to help the directors to overcome these problems.

In a preliminary report to the board of directors, the management consultants state: 'Most of the difficulties faced by the business are symptoms of an underlying problem of overtrading.'

The most recent financial statements of the business are:

### Statement of financial position as at 31 October 2012

|  | £000 |
|---|---|
| **ASSETS** | |
| **Non-current assets** | |
| *Property, plant and equipment* | |
| Land and buildings | 442 |
| Fixtures and fittings | 116 |
| Motor vans at cost | 64 |
|  | 622 |
| **Current assets** | |
| Inventories | 128 |
| Trade receivables | 104 |
|  | 232 |
| **Total assets** | 854 |
| **EQUITY AND LIABILITIES** | |
| **Equity** | |
| Ordinary £0.50 shares | 60 |
| General reserve | 50 |
| Retained earnings | 74 |
|  | 184 |
| **Non-current liabilities** | |
| Borrowings – 10% loan notes (secured) | 120 |
| **Current liabilities** | |
| Trade payables | 184 |
| Taxation | 8 |
| Short-term borrowings (all bank overdraft) | 358 |
|  | 550 |
| **Total equity and liabilities** | 854 |

**Income statement for the year ended 31 October 2012**

|  | £000 | £000 |
|---|---:|---:|
| Revenue |  | 1,640 |
| Cost of sales |  |  |
|    Opening inventories | 116 |  |
|    Purchases | 1,260 |  |
|  | 1,376 |  |
|    Closing inventories | (128) | (1,248) |
| Gross profit |  | 392 |
| Selling and distribution expenses |  | (204) |
| Administration expenses |  | (92) |
| Operating profit |  | 96 |
| Interest payable |  | (44) |
| Profit before taxation |  | 52 |
| Taxation |  | (16) |
| Profit for the year |  | 36 |

All purchases and sales were on credit.

A dividend was paid during the year on ordinary shares of £4,000.

*Required*:

(a) Explain the term 'overtrading' and state how overtrading might arise for a business.

(b) Discuss the kinds of problem that overtrading can create for a business.

(c) Calculate and discuss *five* financial ratios that might be used to establish whether the business is overtrading.

(d) State the ways in which a business may overcome the problem of overtrading.

# Management accounting

Part 2 deals with the area of accounting usually known as 'management accounting' or 'managerial accounting'. This area is concerned with providing information to help managers to manage the business. It is intended to help them to make decisions, to plan and to ensure that plans are actually achieved.

It is difficult to overestimate the extent to which management accounting, and with it the role of the management accountant, has changed over recent times. The advance of the computer has had an enormous influence. IT has released the management accountant from much of the routine work associated with preparation of management accounting reports and has provided the opportunity to take a more pro-active role within the business. This has led to the management accountant becoming part of the management team and, therefore, directly involved in planning and decision making.

At the same time, it has become increasingly obvious that businesses must be customer focused, outward looking and orientated towards value creation (as discussed in Chapter 1). This more strategic approach to management has required the management accountant to provide the types of information to managers that would have been unthought of, for the typical business, until fairly recently.

These new dimensions to the management accountant's role have implications for the kind of skills required to operate effectively. In particular, certain 'soft' skills are needed, such as interpersonal skills for working as part of an effective team and communication skills to help influence the attitudes and behaviour of others.

ugh working as part of a cross-functional team, the management accountant should gain a greater awareness of strategic and operational matters and an increased understanding of the information needs of managers. This is likely to have a positive effect on the design and development of management accounting systems. We should therefore see increasing evidence that management accounting systems are being designed to fit the particular structure and processes of the business rather than the other way round. By participating in planning, decision making and control of the business as well as providing management accounting information for these purposes, the management accountant plays a key role in achieving the objectives of the business. It is a role that should add value to the business and improve its competitive position.

Part 2 begins with a consideration of the basics of financial decision making. The first chapter in this part, Chapter 8, deals with how we identify information that is relevant to a particular decision. In practice, we may be confronted with a large volume of financial information and we must be able to discriminate between that which is relevant to a particular decision and that which can be ignored. Unless we can do this, we run the risk of making poor decisions. Chapter 9 continues our examination of the basics by considering the relationship between costs, volume of activity and profit. We shall see that an understanding of this relationship can be helpful in developing plans and in making a variety of decisions. This chapter incorporates an examination of break-even analysis, which is concerned with deducing the volume of activity at which the sales revenue equals the costs incurred so that neither profit nor loss is made by the activity. Knowledge of the break-even figure can be useful in assessing the degree of risk associated with the operations.

In Chapter 10 we look at how businesses can determine the full cost of each unit of their output. By 'full cost' we mean the figure that takes account of all of the costs of producing a product or service. This includes not just those costs that are directly caused by the unit of output, but those, like rent and administrative costs, which are indirectly involved. This topic is continued in Chapter 11, where we consider some recent developments in determining the full cost of a product or service. In this chapter we also consider how a business can set prices for its output and how costs can be controlled.

Chapter 12 deals with the way in which businesses convert their general objectives and long-term plans into workable short-term plans or budgets. Budgets are an important feature of business life and we shall be looking at the budgeting process in some detail. We shall examine the purpose of budgets and the way in which budgets are prepared. In Chapter 13 we shall consider how, after the period of the budget, the actual performance can be compared with the budgeted performance. This is done to assess performance and to help identify the reasons for any failure to meet budget targets. By finding out what has gone wrong, managers may be able to put things right for the future. The chapter concludes with a discussion of the impact of budgets on the attitudes and behaviour of managers.

# Relevant costs for decision making

## Introduction

This chapter considers the identification and use of costs in making management decisions. These decisions should be made in a way that will promote the business's achievement of its strategic objectives. We shall see that not all of the costs (and revenues) that appear to be linked to a particular business decision are relevant to it. It is important to distinguish carefully between costs (and revenues) that are relevant and those that are not. Failure to do this could well lead to bad decisions being made. The principles outlined here will provide the basis for much of the rest of the book.

## Learning outcomes

**When you have completed this chapter, you should be able to:**

- Define and distinguish between relevant costs, outlay costs and opportunity costs.

- Identify and quantify the costs that are relevant to a particular decision.

- Use relevant costs to make decisions.

- Set out relevant cost analysis in a logical form so that the conclusion may be communicated to managers.

## MyAccountingLab

Visit **www.myaccountinglab.com** for practice and revision opportunities

# What is meant by 'cost'?

**Cost** represents the amount sacrificed to achieve a particular business objective. Measuring cost may seem, at first sight, to be a straightforward process: it is simply the amount paid for the item of goods being supplied or the service being provided. When measuring cost *for decision-making purposes*, however, things are not quite that simple. The following activity illustrates why this is the case.

## Activity 8.1

You own a motor car, for which you paid a purchase price of £5,000 – much below the list price – at a recent car auction. You have just been offered £6,000 for this car.

What is the cost to you of keeping the car for your own use? *Note:* Ignore running costs and so on; just consider the 'capital' cost of the car.

By retaining the car, you are forgoing a cash receipt of £6,000. Thus, the real sacrifice, or cost, incurred by keeping the car for your own use is £6,000. Any decision that you make with respect to the car's future should logically take account of this figure. This cost is known as the 'opportunity cost' since it is the value of the opportunity forgone in order to pursue the other course of action. (In this case, the other course of action is to retain the car.)

We can see that the cost of retaining the car is not the same as the purchase price. In one sense, of course, the cost of the car in Activity 8.1 is £5,000 because that is how much was paid for it. However, this cost, which for obvious reasons is known as the **historic cost**, is only of academic interest. It cannot logically ever be used to make a decision on the car's future. If we disagree with this point, we should ask ourselves how we should assess an offer of £5,500, from another person, for the car. The answer is that we should compare the offer price of £5,500 with the **opportunity cost** of £6,000. This should lead us to reject the offer as it is less than the £6,000 opportunity cost. In these circumstances, it would not be logical to accept the offer of £5,500 on the basis that it was more than the £5,000 that we originally paid. (The only other figure that should concern us is the value to us, in terms of pleasure, usefulness and so on, of retaining the car. If we valued this more highly than the £6,000 opportunity cost, we should reject both offers.)

We may still feel, however, that the £5,000 is relevant here because it will help us in assessing the profitability of the decision. If we sold the car, we should make a profit of either £500 (£5,500 – £5,000) or £1,000 (£6,000 – £5,000) depending on which offer we accept. Since we should seek to make the higher profit, the right decision is to sell the car for £6,000. However, we do not need to know the historic cost of the car to make the right decision. What decision should we make if the car cost us £4,000 to buy? Clearly we should still sell the car for £6,000 rather than for £5,500 as the important comparison is between the offer price and the opportunity cost. We should reach the same conclusion whatever the historic cost of the car.

To emphasise the above point, let us assume that the car cost £10,000. Even in this case the historic cost would still be irrelevant. Had we just bought a car for £10,000 and found that shortly after it is only worth £6,000, we may well be fuming with rage at our mistake, but this does not make the £10,000 a **relevant cost**. The only relevant factors, in a decision on whether to sell the car or to keep it, are the £6,000 opportunity cost and the value of the benefits of keeping it. Thus, the historic cost can never be relevant to a future decision.

To say that historic cost is an **irrelevant cost** is not to say that *the effects of having incurred that cost* are always irrelevant. The fact that we own the car, and are thus in a position to exercise choice as to how to use it, is not irrelevant. It is absolutely relevant.

Opportunity costs are rarely taken into account in the routine accounting process, as they do not involve any out-of-pocket expenditure. They are normally only calculated where they are relevant to a particular management decision. Historic costs, on the other hand, do involve out-of-pocket expenditure and are recorded. They are used in preparing the annual financial statements, such as the statement of financial position (balance sheet) and the income statement. This is logical, however, since these statements are intended to be accounts of what has actually happened and are drawn up after the event.

**Real World 8.1** gives an example of how perceptions of the worth of an asset can alter as circumstances alter. When News Corp bought the social networking site, MySpace, in 2005, it judged that the benefits of ownership were worth $580 million. By 2011, this judgement had altered drastically. When the decision to sell for $35 million was being made, the fact that MySpace had an historic cost of $580 million was presumably ignored. Only the future benefits of ownership were weighed against the $35 million.

---

### Real World 8.1

## No space for MySpace
**FT**

After a drawn-out sales process and a saga that Rupert Murdoch, its chairman, would probably rather forget, News Corp has found a buyer for MySpace, agreeing to sell the loss-making social network to Specific Media in a $35 million deal.

The move, first reported by News Corp's *All Things D* website, brings to an end a turbulent episode that initially reignited Mr Murdoch's interest in the internet, with his company briefly capitalising on a website that, in its heyday, was one of the world's hottest internet properties. But years of management mistakes, the rise of Facebook and clashes between the News Corp hierarchy and MySpace managers led to Mr Murdoch's dream of a dominant global social network turning to dust.

Under the terms of the deal, News Corp will receive a small cash payment and a minority stake in Specific Media in return for MySpace, which it acquired in 2005 for $580 million. Specific Media, a California-based online advertising network founded by the Vanderhook brothers, will control the company.

MySpace had been steadily losing money in the period leading up to the sale. The News Corp division including the site is expected to post close to $500 million in operating losses this fiscal year, according to people familiar with the situation. That did not deter Specific Media, which enlisted Justin Timberlake to back its bid.

Mike Jones, MySpace chief executive, will leave the company following the sale. In a note to MySpace employees, he said there would be "a significant reduction in our workforce". At its peak, MySpace employed 1,400 people but that number has fallen to 400 through waves of cost cutting: about 200 will leave the company following the sale, according to a person close to the situation. Specific Media saw off interest from Chris DeWolfe, a former MySpace chief executive, and private equity firms, including Golden Gate Capital. But the deal's price represents a steep loss for News Corp. Its ownership of MySpace had started off so promisingly in 2005. The purchase of a fast-growing company with genuine cachet among young internet users re-invented Mr Murdoch as a 21st century news media mogul.

→

**Real World 8.1 (*continued*)**

Shortly after the acquisition, MySpace struck a $900 million three-year advertising deal with Google, which depended on strict traffic targets being met. MySpace revenues leapt from $1 million a month to $50 million a month, and Mr Murdoch confidently predicted the site would generate $1 billion in advertising revenues by the end of 2008. But then things took a turn for the worse. MySpace became cluttered with unappealing ads, Mr DeWolfe departed after clashes with News Corp management and users began to leave in droves. A move by MySpace and other News Corp digital businesses into the biggest new office development in Los Angeles was scrapped – after the $350 million, 12-year lease had been signed – leaving the company paying more than $1 million a month for an empty building.

The site shed users while Facebook was adding them in their millions. MySpace then revealed it had missed its Google targets and the management turmoil continued with two other chief executives leaving.

Mr Murdoch's frustration about the site's performance was evident. Relaunches of MySpace failed, culminating in the decision to seek a buyer. Mr Murdoch, who is spending more of his time these days looking at opportunities in the education industry, did not comment on the sale – and it is unclear whether he still has the same enthusiasm he once did for online social networking.

*Source*: 'Murdoch's MySpace dream turns to dust' M. Garrahan, FT.com, 30 June 2011.

It might be useful to end this section by stating in formal terms what we mean by cost.

## A definition of cost

Cost may be defined as the amount of resources, usually measured in monetary terms, sacrificed to achieve a particular objective. The objective might be to retain a car, to buy a particular house, to make a particular product or to render a particular service.

## Relevant costs: opportunity and outlay costs

We have just seen that, when we are making decisions concerning the future, **past costs** (that is, historic costs) are irrelevant. It is future opportunity costs and future **outlay costs** that are of concern. An opportunity cost can be defined as the value, in monetary terms, of being deprived of the next best opportunity in order to pursue the particular objective. An outlay cost is an amount of money that will have to be spent to achieve that objective. We shall shortly meet plenty of examples of both of these types of future cost.

To be relevant to a particular decision, a future outlay cost, or opportunity cost, must satisfy all three of the following criteria:

1 *It must relate to the objectives of the business*. Most businesses have enhancing owners' (shareholders') wealth as their key strategic objective. That is to say, they are seeking to become richer (see Chapter 1). Thus, to be relevant to a particular decision, a cost must have an effect on the wealth of the business.

2 *It must be a future cost.* Past costs cannot be relevant to decisions being made about the future.

3 *It must vary with the decision.* Only costs (and revenues) that are different between outcomes can be used to distinguish between them. Take, for example, a road haulage business that has decided that it will buy a new additional lorry and the decision lies between two different models. The load capacity, the fuel and maintenance costs are different for each lorry. The potential costs and revenues associated with these are relevant items. The lorry will require a driver, so the business will need to employ one, but a suitably qualified driver could drive either lorry equally well, for the same wage. The cost of employing the driver is thus irrelevant to the decision as to which lorry to buy. This is despite the fact that this cost is a future one.

If, however, the decision did not concern a choice between two models of lorry but rather whether to operate an additional lorry or not, the cost of employing the additional driver would be relevant, because it would then be a cost that would vary with the decision made.

Figure 8.1 shows a decision flow diagram for deciding which costs are relevant.

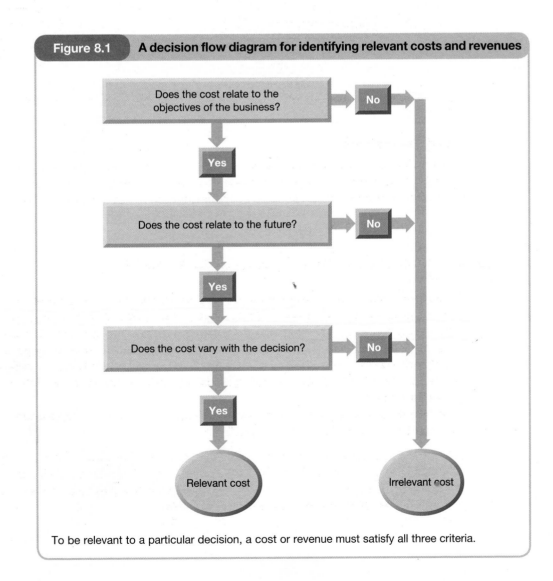

| Figure 8.1 | A decision flow diagram for identifying relevant costs and revenues |

To be relevant to a particular decision, a cost or revenue must satisfy all three criteria.

## Activity 8.2

A garage business has an old car that it bought several months ago. The car needs a replacement engine before it can be driven. It is possible to buy a reconditioned engine for £300. This would take seven hours to fit by a mechanic who is paid £15 an hour. At present the garage is short of work, but the owners are reluctant to lay off any mechanics or even to cut down their basic working week because skilled labour is difficult to find and an upturn in repair work is expected soon.

The garage paid £3,000 to buy the car. Without the engine it could be sold for an estimated £3,500. What is the minimum price at which the garage should sell the car with a reconditioned engine fitted?

The minimum price is the amount required to cover the relevant costs of the job. At this price, the business will make neither a profit nor a loss. Any price that is lower than this amount will mean that the wealth of the business is reduced. Thus, the minimum price is:

|  | £ |
|---|---|
| Opportunity cost of the car | 3,500 |
| Cost of the reconditioned engine | 300 |
| Total | 3,800 |

The original cost of the car is irrelevant for reasons that have already been discussed. It is the opportunity cost of the car that concerns us. The cost of the new engine is relevant because, if the work is done, the garage will have to pay £300 for the engine; but will pay nothing if the job is not done. The £300 is an example of a future outlay cost.

The labour cost is irrelevant because the same cost will be incurred whether the mechanic undertakes the engine-replacement work or not. This is because the mechanic is being paid to do nothing if this job is not undertaken; thus the additional labour cost arising from this job is zero.

It should be emphasised that the garage will not seek to sell the car with its reconditioned engine for £3,800; it will attempt to charge as much as possible for it. However, any price above the £3,800 will make the garage better off financially than it would be by not undertaking the engine replacement.

## Activity 8.3

Assume exactly the same circumstances as in Activity 8.2, except that the garage is quite busy at the moment. If a mechanic is to be put on the engine-replacement job, it will mean that other work that the mechanic could have done during the seven hours, all of which could be charged to a customer, will not be undertaken. The garage's labour charge is £60 an hour, though the mechanic is only paid £15 an hour.

What is the minimum price at which the garage should sell the car, with a reconditioned engine fitted, under these altered circumstances?

The minimum price is:

|  | £ |
|---|---|
| Opportunity cost of the car | 3,500 |
| Cost of the reconditioned engine | 300 |
| Labour cost (7 × £60) | 420 |
| Total | 4,220 |

We can see that the opportunity cost of the car and the cost of the engine are the same as in Activity 8.2, but now a charge for labour has been added to obtain the minimum price. The relevant labour cost here is that which the garage will have to sacrifice in making the time available to undertake the engine replacement job. While the mechanic is working on this job, the garage is losing the opportunity to do work for which a customer would pay £420. Note that the £15 an hour mechanic's wage is still not relevant. The mechanic will be paid £15 an hour irrespective of whether it is the engine-replacement work or some other job that is undertaken.

## Activity 8.4

A business is considering making a bid to undertake a contract. Fulfilment of the contract will require the use of two types of raw material. Quantities of both of these materials are held by the business. If it chose to, the business could sell the raw materials in their present state. All of the inventories of these two raw materials will need to be used on the contract. Information on the raw materials concerned is as follows:

| Inventories item | Quantity | Historic cost | Sales value | Replacement cost |
|---|---|---|---|---|
| | (units) | (£/unit) | (£/unit) | (£/unit) |
| A1 | 500 | 5 | 3 | 6 |
| B2 | 800 | 7 | 8 | 10 |

Inventories item A1 is in frequent use in the business on a variety of work.

The inventories of item B2 were bought a year ago for a contract that was abandoned. It has recently become obvious that there is no likelihood of ever using this raw material unless the contract currently being considered proceeds.

Management wishes to deduce the minimum price at which the business could undertake the contract without reducing its wealth as a result. This can be used as the baseline in deducing the bid price.

How much should be included in the minimum price in respect of the two inventories items detailed above?

The relevant costs to be included in the minimum price are:

Inventories item:  A1     £6 × 500 = £3,000
                   B2     £8 × 800 = £6,400

We are told that the item A1 is in frequent use and so, if it is used on the contract, it will need to be replaced. Sooner or later, the business will have to buy 500 units (currently costing £6 a unit) additional to those which would have been required had the contract not been undertaken.

Item B2 will never be used by the business unless the contract is undertaken. Thus, if the contract is not undertaken, the only reasonable thing for the business to do is to sell the B2. This means that if the contract is undertaken and the B2 is used, it will have an opportunity cost equal to the potential proceeds from disposal, which is £8 a unit.

Note that the historic cost information about both materials is irrelevant. This will always be the case.

## Activity 8.5

HLA Ltd is in the process of preparing a quotation for a special job for a customer. The job will have the following material requirements:

| Material | Units required | Units currently held in inventories | | | Replacement cost |
| | | Quantity held (units) | Historic cost (£/unit) | Sales value (£/unit) | (£/unit) |
| --- | --- | --- | --- | --- | --- |
| P | 400 | 0 | – | – | 40 |
| Q | 230 | 100 | 62 | 50 | 64 |
| R | 350 | 200 | 48 | 23 | 59 |
| S | 170 | 140 | 33 | 12 | 49 |
| T | 120 | 120 | 40 | 0 | 68 |

Material Q is used consistently by the business on various jobs.

The business holds materials R, S and T as the result of previous overbuying. No other use (apart from this special job) can be found for R, but the 140 units of S could be used in another job as a substitute for 225 units of material V that are about to be purchased at a price of £10 a unit. Material T has no other use, it is a dangerous material that is difficult to store and the business has been informed that it will cost £160 to dispose of the material currently held.

If it chose to, the business could sell the raw materials Q, R and S already held in their present state.

What is the relevant cost of the materials for the job specified above?

The relevant cost is as follows:

| | £ |
| --- | --- |
| **Material P** | |
| This will have to be purchased at £40 a unit (400 × £40) | 16,000 |
| **Material Q** | |
| This will have to be replaced, therefore, the relevant price is (230 × £64) | 14,720 |
| **Material R** | |
| 200 units of this are held and these could be sold. The relevant price of these is the sales revenue foregone (200 × £23) | 4,600 |
| The remaining 150 units of R would have to be purchased (150 × £59) | 8,850 |
| **Material S** | |
| This could be sold or used as a substitute for material V. | |
| The existing inventories could be sold for £1,680 (that is, 140 × £12); however, the saving on material V is higher and therefore should be taken as the relevant amount (225 × £10) | 2,250 |
| The remaining units of material S must be purchased (30 × £49) | 1,470 |
| A saving on disposal will be made if material T is used | (160) |
| **Total relevant cost** | 47,730 |

Real World 8.2 gives an example of how opportunity costs can affect a student's choice.

**Real World 8.2**

### An opportunity to take a Harvard MBA    FT

The recently appointed Dean of Harvard Business School, Professor Nitin Nohria, has identified several challenges facing elite business schools. One of these is the opportunity cost, in terms of lost salaries, for students undertaking the standard two-year MBA (master of business administration) programme. This could discourage some potential students from taking an MBA.

*Source*: 'Navigating a route for the 21st century', D. Bradshaw FT.com, 24 January 2011.

## Sunk costs and committed costs

A **sunk cost** is simply another way of referring to a past cost and so the terms 'sunk cost' and 'past cost' can be used interchangeably. A **committed cost** arises where an irrevocable decision has been made to incur the cost because, for example, a business has entered into a binding contract. As a result, it is more or less a past cost despite the fact that the cash may not be paid until some point in the future. Since the business must eventually pay, a committed cost can never be a relevant cost for decision-making purposes.

It is important to remember that, to be relevant, a cost must be capable of varying according to the decision made. If the business is already committed by a legally binding contract to a cost, that cost cannot vary with the decision.

**Activity 8.6**

Past costs are irrelevant costs. Does this mean that what happened in the past is irrelevant?

No, it does not mean this. The fact that the business has an asset that it can deploy in the future is highly relevant. What is not relevant is how much it cost to acquire that asset. This point was examined in the discussion that followed Activity 8.1.

Another reason why the past is not irrelevant is that it generally – though not always – provides us with our best guide to the future. Suppose that we need to estimate the cost of doing something in the future to help us to decide whether it is worth doing. In these circumstances our own experience, or that of others, on how much it has cost to do the thing in the past may provide us with a valuable guide to how much it is likely to cost in the future.

## Qualitative factors of decisions

Although businesses must look closely at the obvious financial effects when making decisions, they must also consider factors that are not directly economic. These are likely to be factors that have a broader, but less immediate, impact on the business. Ultimately, however, these factors are likely to have economic effect – that is, to affect the wealth of the business.

### Activity 8.7

Activity 8.3 was concerned with the cost of putting a car into a marketable condition. Apart from whether the car could be sold for more than the relevant cost of doing this, are there any other factors that should be taken into account in making a decision as to whether or not to do the work?

We can think of three points:

- Turning away another job in order to do the engine replacement may lead to customer dissatisfaction.
- Having the car available for sale may be useful commercially for the garage, beyond the profit that can be earned from that particular car sale. For example, having a good range of second-hand cars for sale may attract potential customers wanting to buy a car.
- It has been assumed that the only opportunity cost concerns labour (the charge-out rate for the seven hours concerned). In practice, most car repairs involve the use of some materials and spare parts. These are usually charged to customers at a profit to the garage. Any such profit from a job turned away would be lost to the garage. This lost profit would be an opportunity cost of the engine replacement. It should, therefore, be included in the calculation of the minimum price to be charged for the sale of the car.

You may have thought of additional points.

It is important to consider 'qualitative' factors carefully. There is a risk that they may be given less weight by managers because they are impossible to assess in terms of their ultimate economic effect. This effect can nevertheless be very significant.

## Using relevant cost as a basis for setting prices

The relevant cost of some item or activity is the minimum price for which the business can offer it for sale. This minimum price will leave the business no better off as a result of making the sale than it would have been had it pursued the next best opportunity. To profit from the sale the business would need to add a profit margin.

This relevant cost approach to pricing would normally be used only where there is not the opportunity to sell at a price that will cover all of its cost, not just the relevant part. In the long run, the business must cover all of its costs if it is to generate value and increase its owners' wealth.

## Self-assessment question 8.1

JB Limited is a small specialist manufacturer of electronic components. Makers of aircraft, for both civil and military purposes, use much of its output. One of the aircraft makers has offered a contract to JB Limited for the supply, over the next 12 months, of 400 identical components. The data relating to the production of each component are as follows:

- *Material requirements:*
  3 kg of material M1 (see Note 1 below)
  2 kg of material P2 (see Note 2 below)
  1 bought-in component (part number 678) (see Note 3 below)

  *Note 1*:  Material M1 is in continuous use by the business; 1,000 kg are currently held by the business. The original cost was £4.70/kg, but it is known that future purchases will cost £5.50/kg.

  *Note 2*:  1,200 kg of material P2 are currently held. The original cost of this material was £4.30/kg. The material has not been required for the last two years. Its scrap value is £1.50/kg. The only foreseeable alternative use is as a substitute for material P4 (in constant use) but this would involve further processing costs of £1.60/kg. The current cost of material P4 is £3.60/kg.

  *Note 3*:  It is estimated that the component (part number 678) could be bought in for £50 each.

- *Labour requirements*: Each component would require five hours of skilled labour and five hours of semi-skilled. A skilled employee is available and is currently paid £14/hour. A replacement would, however, have to be obtained at a rate of £12/hour for the work which would otherwise be done by the skilled employee. The current rate for semi-skilled work is £10/hour and an additional employee could be appointed for this work.

- *General manufacturing costs*: It is JB Limited's policy to charge a share of the general costs (rent, heating and so on) to each contract undertaken at the rate of £20 for each machine hour used on the contract. If the contract is undertaken, the general costs are expected to increase as a result of undertaking the contract by £3,200.

Spare machine capacity is available and each component would require four machine hours. A price of £200 a component has been offered by the potential customer.

*Required*:
(a)  Should the contract be accepted? Support your conclusion with appropriate figures to present to management.
(b)  What other factors ought management to consider that might influence the decision?

**The solution to this question can be found at the back of the book on page 735.**

To end the chapter, **Real World 8.3** describes another case where the decision makers, quite correctly, ignored past costs and just concentrated on future options for the business concerned.

### Real World 8.3

## Pound shop    **FT**

In 2006 Merchant Equity Partners (MEP), a private equity group, bought the retail arm of MFI (the furniture business) for just £1. MEP planned to revive the loss-making furniture chain and sell it on for up to £500 million in around 2011. MFI management felt at the time that having it taken over by MEP might avoid the retail arm slipping further into financial difficulties.

The buy-out agreement included an arrangement that MFI would pay a 'dowry' of £75 million over three years to encourage MEP to take it off MFI's hands. MFI felt that it would then be able to concentrate on the profitable part of its business, Howden Joinery, which sells kitchen cabinets to the building trade.

In the event, MEP's plans for MFI retail were overtaken by the downturn in furniture sales and MEP allowed the business to be taken over by a group of its managers in 2008. The business collapsed completely and stopped trading late in 2008.

*Source*: Taken from 'MFI furniture retail arm bought for £1', E. Callan, FT.com, 12 July 2006; and 'Favell buy-out rescues MFI from administration', T. Braithwaite, *Financial Times*, 28 September 2008.

## Summary

The main points in this chapter may be summarised as follows:

**Cost = amount of resources, usually measured in monetary terms, sacrificed to achieve a particular objective.**

**Relevant and irrelevant costs**

- Relevant costs must:
  - relate to the objective being pursued by the business;
  - be a future cost;
  - vary with the decision.
- Relevant costs therefore include:
  - opportunity costs;
  - differential future outlay costs.
- Irrelevant costs therefore include:
  - all past (or sunk) costs;
  - all committed costs;
  - non-differential future outlay costs.

**Qualitative factors of decisions**

- Financial/economic decisions almost inevitably have qualitative aspects that financial analysis cannot really handle, despite their importance.

**Using relevant cost as a basis for selling prices**

- Any price above the relevant cost will make the business and its owners wealthier.
- In the long run, the business must cover all its costs, not just the relevant ones.

# MyAccountingLab

Go to **www.myaccountinglab.com** to check your understanding of the chapter, create a personalised study plan, and maximise your revision time

## Key terms

cost  p. 302
historic cost  p. 302
opportunity cost  p. 302
relevant cost  p. 302
irrelevant cost  p. 303

past cost  p. 304
outlay cost  p. 304
sunk cost  p. 309
committed cost  p. 309

## Further reading

If you would like to explore the topics covered in this chapter in more depth, we recommend the following books:

Drury, C., *Management and Cost Accounting*, 8th edn, Cengage Learning, 2012, chapter 9.

Hilton, R., *Managerial Accounting*, 9th edn, McGraw-Hill Higher Education, 2011, chapter 14.

Horngren, C., Datar, S. and Rajan, M., *Cost Accounting: A Managerial Emphasis*, 14th edn, Prentice Hall International, 2011, chapter 11.

Kaplan, R., Atkinson, A., Matsumura, E. and Young, S. M., *Management Accounting*, 6th edn, Prentice Hall, 2011, chapter 3.

## Review questions

**Solutions to these questions can be found at the back of the book on page 751.**

**8.1** To be relevant to a particular decision, a cost must have three attributes. What are they?

**8.2** Distinguish between a sunk cost and an opportunity cost.

**8.3** Define the word 'cost' in the context of management accounting.

**8.4** What is meant by the expression 'committed cost'? How do committed costs arise?

## Exercises

**Exercises 8.1 and 8.2 are basic level, 8.3 and 8.4 are intermediate level and 8.5, 8.6 and 8.7 are advanced level. Those with coloured numbers have solutions at the back of the book, starting on page 774.**

**If you wish to try more exercises, visit the students' side of the Companion Website and MyAccountingLab.**

**8.1** Lombard Ltd has been offered a contract for which there is available production capacity. The contract is for 20,000 identical items, manufactured by an intricate assembly operation, to be produced and delivered in the next few months at a price of £80 each. The specification for one item is as follows:

| Assembly labour | 4 hours |
| Component X | 4 units |
| Component Y | 3 units |

There would also be the need to hire equipment, for the duration of the contract, at an outlay cost of £200,000.

The assembly is a highly skilled operation and the workforce is currently underutilised. It is the business's policy to retain this workforce on full pay in anticipation of high demand next year, for a new product currently being developed. There is sufficient available skilled labour to undertake the contract now under consideration. Skilled workers are paid £15 an hour.

Component X is used in a number of other sub-assemblies produced by the business. It is readily available. 50,000 units of Component X are currently held in inventories. Component Y was a special purchase in anticipation of an order that did not in the end materialise. It is, therefore, surplus to requirements and the 100,000 units that are currently held may have to be sold at a loss. An estimate of various values for Components X and Y provided by the materials planning department is as follows:

| Component | X | Y |
|---|---|---|
| | £/unit | £/unit |
| Historic cost | 4 | 10 |
| Replacement cost | 5 | 11 |
| Net realisable value | 3 | 8 |

It is estimated that any additional relevant costs associated with the contract (beyond the above) will amount to £8 an item.

*Required*:

Analyse the information and advise Lombard Ltd on the desirability of the contract.

**8.2** Andrews and Co. Ltd has been invited to tender for a contract. It is to produce 10,000 metres of an electrical cable in which the business specialises. The estimating department of the business has produced the following information relating to the contract:

- *Materials*: The cable will require a steel core, which the business buys in. The steel core is to be coated with a special plastic, also bought in, using a special process. Plastic for the covering will be required at the rate of 0.10 kg/metre of completed cable.
- *Direct labour*:

| | |
|---|---|
| Skilled: | 10 minutes/metre |
| Unskilled: | 5 minutes/metre |

The business already holds sufficient of each of the materials required, to complete the contract. Information on the cost of the inventories is as follows:

| | Steel core £/metre | Plastic £/kg |
|---|---|---|
| Historic cost | 1.50 | 0.60 |
| Current buying-in cost | 2.10 | 0.70 |
| Scrap value | 1.40 | 0.10 |

The steel core is in constant use by the business for a variety of work that it regularly undertakes. The plastic is a surplus from a previous contract where a mistake was made and an excess quantity ordered. If the current contract does not go ahead, this plastic will be scrapped.

Unskilled labour, which is paid at the rate of £7.50 an hour, will need to be taken on specifically to undertake the contract. The business is fairly quiet at the moment which means that a pool of skilled labour exists that will still be employed at full pay of £12 an hour to do nothing if the contract does not proceed. The pool of skilled labour is sufficient to complete the contract.

*Required*:

Indicate the minimum price at which the contract could be undertaken, such that the business would be neither better nor worse off as a result of doing it.

**8.3** SJ Services Ltd has been asked to quote a price for a special contract to render a service that will take the business one week to complete. Information relating to labour for the contract is as follows:

| Grade of labour | Hours required | Basic rate/hour |
|---|---|---|
| Skilled | 27 | £12 |
| Semi-skilled | 14 | £9 |
| Unskilled | 20 | £7 |

A shortage of skilled labour means that the necessary staff to undertake the contract would have to be moved from other work that is currently yielding an excess of sales revenue over labour and other costs of £8 an hour.

Semi-skilled labour is currently being paid at semi-skilled rates to undertake unskilled work. If the relevant members of staff are moved to work on the contract, unskilled labour will have to be employed for the week to replace them.

The unskilled labour actually needed to work on the contract will be specifically employed for the week of the contract.

All labour is charged to contracts at 50 per cent above the rate paid to the employees, so as to cover the contract's fair share of the business's general costs (rent, heating and so on). It is estimated that these general costs will increase by £50 as a result of undertaking the contract.

Undertaking the contract will require the use of a specialised machine for the week. The business owns such a machine, which it depreciates at the rate of £120 a week. This machine is currently being hired out to another business at a weekly rental of £175 on a week-by-week contract.

To derive the above estimates, the business has had to spend £300 on a specialised study. If the contract does not proceed, the results of the study can be sold for £250.

An estimate of the contract's fair share of the business's rent is £150 a week.

*Required*:

Deduce the minimum price at which SJ Services Ltd could undertake the contract such that it would be neither better nor worse off as a result of undertaking it.

**8.4** A business in the food industry is currently holding 2,000 tonnes of material in bulk storage. This material deteriorates with time. In the near future, it will, therefore, be necessary for it to be repackaged for sale or sold in its present form.

The material was acquired in two batches: 800 tonnes at a price of £40 a tonne and 1,200 tonnes at a price of £44 a tonne. The current market price of any additional purchases is £48 a tonne. If the business were to dispose of the material, in its present state, it could sell any quantity but for only £36 a tonne; it does not have the contacts or reputation to command a higher price.

Processing this material may be undertaken to develop either Product A or Product X. No weight loss occurs with the processing, that is, 1 tonne of the material will make 1 tonne of A or X. For Product A, there is an additional cost of £60 a tonne, after which it will sell for £105 a tonne. The marketing department estimates that a maximum of 500 tonnes could be sold in this way.

With Product X, the business incurs additional costs of £80 a tonne for processing. A market price for X is not known and no minimum price has been agreed. The management is currently engaged in discussions over the minimum price that may be charged for Product X in the current circumstances. Management wants to know the relevant cost per tonne for Product X so as to provide a basis for negotiating a profitable selling price for the product.

*Required*:

Identify the relevant cost per tonne for Product X, given sales volumes of X of:

(a) up to 1,500 tonnes
(b) over 1,500 tonnes, up to 2,000 tonnes
(c) over 2,000 tonnes.

Explain your answer.

**8.5** A local education authority is faced with a predicted decline in the demand for school places in its area. It is believed that some schools will have to close in order to remove up to 800 places from current capacity levels. The schools that may face closure are referenced as A, B, C and D. Their details are as follows:

● *School A* (capacity 200) was built 15 years ago at a cost of £1.2 million. It is situated in a 'socially disadvantaged' community area. The authority has been offered £14 million for the site by a property developer.

● *School B* (capacity 500) was built 20 years ago and cost £1 million. It was renovated only two years ago at a cost of £3 million to improve its facilities. An offer of £8 million has been made for the site by a business planning a shopping complex in this affluent part of the area.

● *School C* (capacity 600) cost £5 million to build five years ago. The land for this school is rented from a local business for an annual cost of £300,000. The land rented for School C is based on a 100-year lease. If the school closes, the property reverts immediately to the owner. If School C is not closed, it will require a £3 million investment to improve safety at the school.

- *School D* (800 capacity) cost £7 million to build eight years ago; last year £1.5 million was spent on an extension. It has a considerable amount of grounds, which is currently used for sporting events. This factor makes it popular with developers, who have recently offered £9 million for the site. If School D is closed, it will be necessary to pay £1.8 million to adapt facilities at other schools to accommodate the change.

In its accounting system, the local authority depreciates non-current assets based on 2 per cent a year on the original cost. It also differentiates between one-off, large items of capital expenditure or revenue, on the one hand, and annually recurring items, on the other.

The local authority has a central staff, which includes administrators for each school costing £200,000 a year for each school, and a chief education officer costing £80,000 a year in total.

*Required*:
(a) Prepare a summary of the relevant cash flows (costs and revenues, relative to not making any closures) under the following options:
   (1) closure of D only
   (2) closure of A and B
   (3) closure of A and C.
   Show separately the one-off effects and annually recurring items, rank the options open to the local authority and, briefly, interpret your answer. *Note*: Various approaches are acceptable provided that they are logical.
(b) Identify and comment on any two different types of irrelevant cost contained in the information given in the question.
(c) Discuss other factors that might have a bearing on the decision.

**8.6** Rob Otics Ltd, a small business that specialises in manufacturing electronic-control equipment, has just received an inquiry from a potential customer for eight identical robotic units. These would be made using Rob Otics's own labour force and factory capacity. The product specification prepared by the estimating department shows the following:

- Material and labour requirements for each robotic unit:

| | |
|---|---|
| Component X | 2 per unit |
| Component Y | 1 per unit |
| Component Z | 4 per unit |
| Assembly labour | 25 hours per unit (but see below) |
| Inspection labour | 6 hours per unit |

As part of the costing exercise, the business has collected the following information:

- *Component X.* This item is normally held by the business as it is in constant demand. There are 10 units currently held which were bought for £150 a unit. The sole supplier of Component X has announced a price rise of 20 per cent, effective immediately, for any further supplies. Rob Otics has not yet paid for the items currently held.
- *Component Y.* 25 units are currently held. This component is not normally used by Rob Otics but the units currently held are because of a cancelled order following the bankruptcy of a customer. The units originally cost the business £4,000 in total, although Rob Otics has recouped £1,500 from the liquidator of the bankrupt business. As Rob Otics can see no use for these units (apart from the possible use of some of them in the order now being considered), the finance director proposes to scrap all 25 units (zero proceeds).
- *Component Z.* This is in regular use by Rob Otics. There is none in inventories but an order is about to be sent to a supplier for 75 units, irrespective of this new proposal. The supplier charges £25 a unit on small orders but will reduce the price to £20 a unit for all units on any order over 100 units.
- *Other items.* These are expected to cost £250 in total.

Assembly labour is currently in short supply in the area and is paid at £10 an hour. If the order is accepted, all necessary labour will have to be transferred from existing work. As a result, other orders will be lost. It is estimated that for each hour transferred to this contract £38 will be lost (calculated as lost sales revenue £60, less materials £12 and labour £10). The production director suggests that, owing to a learning process, the time taken to make each unit will reduce, from 25 hours to make the first one, by one hour a unit made. (That is 25 hours to make the first one, 24 hours to make the second, 23 hours to make the third one and so on.)

Inspection labour can be provided by paying existing personnel overtime which is at a premium of 50 per cent over the standard rate of £12 an hour.

When the business is working out its contract prices, it normally adds an amount equal to £20 for each assembly labour hour to cover its general costs (such as rent and electricity). To the resulting total, 40 per cent is normally added as a profit mark-up.

*Required*:
(a) Prepare an estimate of the minimum price that you would recommend Rob Otics Ltd to charge for the proposed contract such that it would be neither better nor worse off as a result. Provide explanations for any items included.
(b) Identify any other factors that you would consider before fixing the final price.

**8.7** A business places substantial emphasis on customer satisfaction and, to this end, delivers its product in special protective containers. These containers have been made in a department within the business. Management has recently become concerned that this internal supply of containers is very expensive. As a result, outside suppliers have been invited to submit tenders for the provision of these containers. A quote of £250,000 a year has been received for a volume that compares with current internal supply.

An investigation into the internal costs of container manufacture has been undertaken and the following emerges:

(a) The annual cost of material is £120,000, according to the stores records, maintained at actual historic cost. Three-quarters (by cost) of this represents material that is regularly stocked and replenished. The remaining 25 per cent of the material cost is a special foaming chemical. This chemical is not used, by the business, for any other purpose than making the containers. There are 40 tonnes of this chemical currently held. It was bought in bulk for £750 a tonne. Today's replacement price for this material is £1,050 a tonne but it is unlikely that the business could realise more than £600 a tonne if it had to be disposed of owing to the high handling costs and special transport facilities required.

(b) The annual labour cost is £80,000 for this department. Most, however, are casual employees or recent starters. If an outside quote were accepted, therefore, little redundancy would be payable. There are, however, two long-serving employees who would each accept as a salary £15,000 a year until they reached retirement age in two years' time.

(c) The department manager has a salary of £30,000 a year. The closure of this department would release him to take over another department for which a vacancy is about to be advertised. The salary, status and prospects are similar.

(d) A rental charge of £9,750 a year, based on floor area, is allocated to the containers department. If the department were closed, the floor space released would be used for warehousing and, as a result, the business would give up the tenancy of an existing warehouse for which it is paying £15,750 a year.

(e) The plant cost £162,000 when it was bought five years ago. Its market value now is £28,000 and it could continue for another two years, at which time its market value would have fallen to zero. (The plant depreciates evenly over time.)

(f) Annual plant maintenance costs are £9,900 and allocated general administrative costs £33,750 for the coming year.

*Required*:
Calculate the annual cost of manufacturing containers for comparison with the quote using relevant figures for establishing the cost or benefit of accepting the quote. Indicate any assumptions or qualifications you wish to make.

# CHAPTER 9

# Cost-volume-profit analysis

## Introduction

This chapter is concerned with the relationship between the volume of activity, cost and profit. Broadly, cost can be analysed between an element that is fixed, relative to the volume of activity, and an element that varies according to the volume of activity. We shall consider how knowledge of this relationship can be used to make decisions and to assess risk, particularly in the context of short-term decisions.

This chapter continues the theme of Chapter 8 concerning relevant costs. We shall examine situations where a whole class of cost – fixed cost – can be treated as irrelevant for decision-making purposes.

## Learning outcomes

**When you have completed this chapter, you should be able to:**

● Distinguish between fixed cost and variable cost and use this distinction to explain the relationship between cost, volume and profit.

● Prepare a break-even chart and deduce the break-even point for some activity.

● Discuss the weaknesses of break-even analysis.

● Demonstrate the way in which marginal analysis can be used when making short-term decisions.

## MyAccountingLab

Visit **www.myaccountinglab.com** for practice and revision opportunities

## Cost behaviour

We saw in the previous chapter that cost represents the resources sacrificed to achieve a business objective. The costs incurred by a business may be classified in various ways and one useful way is according to how they behave in relation to changes in the volume of activity. Costs may be classified according to whether they:

● remain constant (fixed) when changes occur to the volume of activity; or
● vary according to the volume of activity.

These are known as **fixed costs** and **variable costs** respectively. Thus, in the case of a restaurant, the manager's salary would normally be a fixed cost while the cost of the unprepared food would be a variable cost.

As we shall see, knowing how much of each type of cost is associated with a particular activity can be of great value to the decision maker.

## Fixed cost

The way in which a fixed cost behaves can be shown by preparing a graph that plots the fixed cost of a business against the level of activity, as in Figure 9.1. The distance 0F represents the amount of fixed cost, and this stays the same irrespective of the volume of activity.

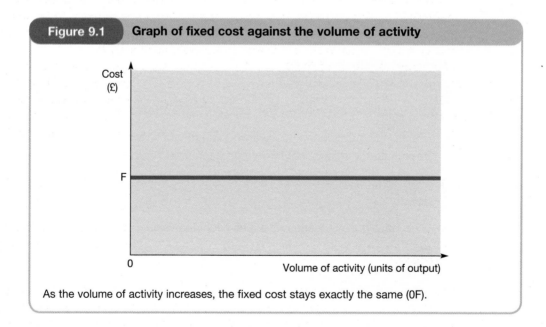

| Figure 9.1 | Graph of fixed cost against the volume of activity |

As the volume of activity increases, the fixed cost stays exactly the same (0F).

**Activity 9.1**

Can you give some examples of items of cost that are likely to be fixed for a hairdressing business?

We came up with the following:

- rent
- insurance
- cleaning cost
- staff salaries.

These items of cost are likely to be the same irrespective of the number of customers having their hair cut or styled.

Staff salaries (or wages) are often assumed to be a variable cost but in practice they tend to be fixed. Members of staff are not normally paid according to the volume of output and it is unusual to dismiss staff when there is a short-term downturn in activity. Where there is a long-term downturn, or at least it seems that way to management, redundancies may occur with fixed-cost savings. This, however, is true of all types of fixed cost. For example, management may also decide to close some branches to make rental cost savings.

There are circumstances in which the labour cost is variable (for example, where staff are paid according to how much output they produce), but this is unusual. Whether labour cost is fixed or variable depends on the circumstances in the particular case concerned.

It is important to be clear that 'fixed', in this context, means only that the cost is unaffected by changes in the volume of activity. Fixed cost is likely to be affected by inflation. If rent (a typical fixed cost) goes up because of inflation, a fixed cost will have increased, but not because of a change in the volume of activity.

Similarly, the level of fixed cost does not stay the same, irrespective of the time period involved. Fixed cost elements are almost always *time based*: that is, they vary with the length of time concerned. The rental charge for two months is normally twice that for one month. Thus, fixed cost normally varies with time, but (of course) not with the volume of output. This means that when we talk of fixed cost being, say, £1,000, we must add the period concerned, say, £1,000 a month.

**Activity 9.2**

Does fixed cost stay the same irrespective of the volume of output, even where there is a massive rise in that volume? Think in terms of the rent cost for the hairdressing business.

In fact, the rent is only fixed over a particular range (known as the 'relevant' range). If the number of people wanting to have their hair cut by the business increased, and the business wished to meet this increased demand, it would eventually have to expand its physical size. This might be achieved by opening an additional branch, or perhaps by moving the existing business to larger accommodation nearby. It may be possible to cope with relatively minor increases in activity by using existing space more efficiently, or by having longer opening hours. If activity continued to expand, however, increased rent charges would seem inevitable.

In practice, the situation described in Activity 9.2 would look something like Figure 9.2.

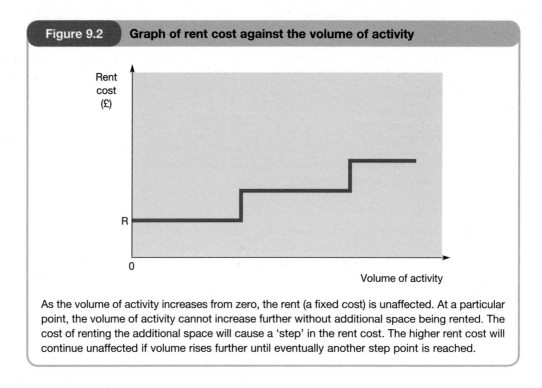

| Figure 9.2 | Graph of rent cost against the volume of activity |

As the volume of activity increases from zero, the rent (a fixed cost) is unaffected. At a particular point, the volume of activity cannot increase further without additional space being rented. The cost of renting the additional space will cause a 'step' in the rent cost. The higher rent cost will continue unaffected if volume rises further until eventually another step point is reached.

At lower volumes of activity, the rent cost shown in Figure 9.2 would be OR. As the volume of activity expands, the accommodation becomes inadequate and further expansion requires an increase in the size of the accommodation and, therefore, its cost. This higher level of accommodation provision will enable further expansion to take place. Eventually, additional cost will need to be incurred if further expansion is to occur. Elements of fixed cost that behave in this way are often referred to as **stepped fixed costs**.

## Variable cost

We saw earlier that variable cost varies with the volume of activity. In a manufacturing business, for example, this would include the cost of raw materials used.

Variable cost can be represented graphically as in Figure 9.3. At zero volume of activity, the variable cost is zero. It then increases in a straight line as activity increases.

The straight line for variable cost on this graph implies that this type of cost will be the same per unit of activity, irrespective of the volume of activity. We shall consider the practicality of this assumption a little later in this chapter.

**Activity 9.3**

Can you think of some examples of cost elements that are likely to be variable for a hairdressing business?

We can think of a couple:

- lotions, sprays and other materials used;
- laundry cost to wash towels used to dry customers' hair.

As with many types of business activity, the variable cost incurred by hairdressers tends to be low in comparison with the fixed cost: that is, fixed cost tends to make up the bulk of total cost.

---

**Figure 9.3**   **Graph of variable cost against the volume of activity**

At zero activity, there is no variable cost. However, as the volume of activity increases, so does the variable cost.

---

## Semi-fixed (semi-variable) cost

In some cases, a particular cost has an element of both fixed and variable cost. These can be described as **semi-fixed (semi-variable) costs**. An example might be the electricity cost for the hairdressing business. Some of this will be for heating and lighting, and this part is probably fixed, at least until the volume of activity expands to a point where longer opening hours or larger accommodation is necessary. The other part of the cost will vary with the volume of activity. Here we are talking about such things as power for hairdryers.

**Activity 9.4**

Can you suggest another cost for a hairdressing business that is likely to be semi-fixed (semi-variable)?

We thought of telephone charges for landlines. These tend to have a rental element, which is fixed, and there may also be certain calls that have to be made irrespective of the volume of activity involved. However, increased business would probably require more telephone calls and this would increase call charges.

## Analysing semi-fixed (semi-variable) costs

The fixed and variable elements of a particular cost may not always be clear. Past experience, however, can often provide some guidance. Let us again take the example of electricity. If we have data on what the electricity cost has been for various volumes of activity, say the relevant data over several three-month periods (electricity is usually billed by the quarter), we can estimate the fixed and variable elements. The easiest way to do this is to use the **high-low method**. This method involves taking the highest and lowest total electricity cost figures from the range of past quarterly data available. An assumption is then made that the difference between these two quarterly figures is caused entirely by the change in variable cost.

Example 9.1 demonstrates how the fixed and variable elements of electricity cost may be estimated using this method.

---

### Example 9.1

Davos Ltd collected data relating to its electricity cost and volume of activity over several quarters and found the following

|  | Lowest quarterly activity | Highest quarterly activity |
|---|---|---|
| Volume of activity | 100,000 units | 180,000 units |
| Total electricity cost | £80,000 | £120,000 |

We can see that an increase in activity of 80,000 units (that is, 180,000 – 100,000) led to an increase in total electricity cost of £40,000 (that is, £120,000 – £80,000). As it is assumed that this increase is caused by an increase in variable cost, the variable cost per unit of output must be £40,000/80,000 = £0.50 per unit.

The breakdown in total electricity cost for the highest and lowest quarters will therefore be as follows.

|  | Lowest quarterly activity 100,000 units | Highest quarterly activity 180,000 units |
|---|---|---|
| Volume of activity | £ | £ |
| Variable cost |  |  |
| 100,000 × £0.50 | 50,000 |  |
| 180,000 × £0.50 |  | 90,000 |
| Fixed cost (balancing figure) | 30,000 | 30,000 |
| Total electricity cost | 80,000 | 120,000 |

---

The weakness of this method is that it relies on only two points in a range of information relating to quarterly electricity charges. A more reliable estimate of the fixed and variable cost elements can be made if the full range of electricity cost for each quarter is used in the analysis.

By plotting total electricity cost against the volume of activity for each quarter, a graph that looks like the one shown in Figure 9.4 below may be produced.

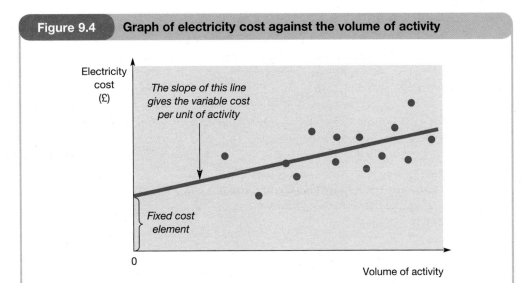

**Figure 9.4    Graph of electricity cost against the volume of activity**

*The slope of this line gives the variable cost per unit of activity*

*Fixed cost element*

Here the electricity bill for a time period (for example, three months) is plotted against the volume of activity for that same period. This is done for a series of periods. A line is then drawn that best 'fits' the various points on the graph. From this line we can then deduce both the cost at zero activity (the fixed element) and the slope of the line (the variable element).

Each of the dots in Figure 9.4 is the electricity charge for a particular quarter plotted against the volume of activity (probably measured in terms of sales revenue) for the same quarter. The diagonal line on the graph is the *line of best fit*. This means that this was the line that best seemed (to us, at least) to represent the data. A better estimate can usually be made using a statistical technique (*least squares regression*), which does not involve drawing graphs and making estimates. In terms of accuracy, however, there is probably little practical difference between the two approaches.

From the graph we can say that the fixed element of the electricity cost is the amount represented by the vertical distance from the origin at zero (bottom left-hand corner) to the point where the line of best fit crosses the vertical axis of the graph. The variable cost per unit is the amount that the graph line rises for each increase in the volume of activity.

Armed with knowledge of how much each element of cost represents for a particular product or service, it is possible to make predictions regarding total and per-unit cost at various projected levels of output. Such information can be very useful to decision makers. Much of the rest of this chapter will be devoted to seeing how it can be useful, starting with **break-even analysis**.

## Finding the break-even point

If, for a particular product or service, we know the fixed cost for a period and the variable cost per unit, we can produce a graph like the one shown in Figure 9.5. This graph shows the total cost over the possible range of volume of activity.

The bottom part of Figure 9.5 shows the fixed cost area. Added to this is the variable cost, the wedge-shaped portion at the top of the graph. The uppermost line represents the total cost over a range of volume of activity. For any particular volume, the total

| Figure 9.5 | Graph of total cost against volume of activity |
| --- | --- |

The bottom part of the graph represents the fixed cost element. To this is added the wedge-shaped top portion, which represents the variable cost. The two parts together represent total cost. At zero activity, the variable cost is zero, so total cost equals fixed cost. As activity increases so does total cost, but only because variable cost increases. We are assuming that there are no steps in the fixed cost.

cost can be measured by the vertical distance between the graph's horizontal axis and the relevant point on the uppermost line.

Logically, the total cost at zero activity is the amount of the fixed cost. This is because, even where there is nothing happening, the business will still be paying rent, salaries and so on, at least in the short term. As the volume of activity increases from zero, the fixed cost is augmented by the relevant variable cost to give the total cost.

If we take this total-cost graph in Figure 9.5, and superimpose on it a line representing total revenue over the range of volume of activity, we obtain the **break-even chart**. This is shown in Figure 9.6.

Note in Figure 9.6 that, at zero volume of activity (zero sales), there is zero sales revenue. The profit (loss), which is the difference between total sales revenue and total cost, for a particular volume of activity, is the vertical distance between the total sales revenue line and the total cost line at that volume of activity. Where there is no vertical distance between these two lines (total sales revenue equals total cost) the volume of activity is at **break-even point (BEP)**. At this point there is neither profit nor loss; that is, the activity *breaks even*. Where the volume of activity is below BEP, a loss will be incurred because total cost exceeds total sales revenue. Where the business operates at a volume of activity above BEP, there will be a profit because total sales revenue will exceed total cost. The further the volume of activity is below BEP, the higher the loss: the further above BEP it is, the higher the profit.

Deducing BEPs graphically is a laborious business. Since, however, the relationships in the graph are all linear (that is, the lines are all straight), it is easy to calculate the BEP.

We know that at BEP (but not at any other volume of activity):

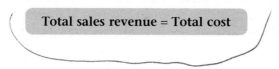

**Total sales revenue = Total cost**

| Figure 9.6 | Break-even chart |
|---|---|

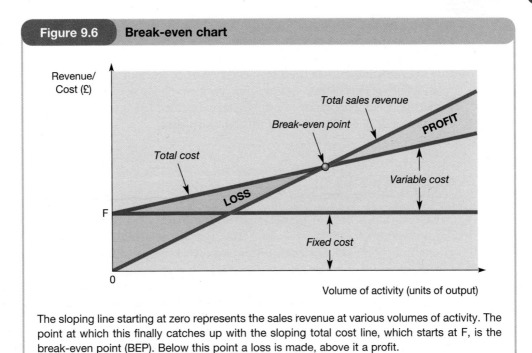

The sloping line starting at zero represents the sales revenue at various volumes of activity. The point at which this finally catches up with the sloping total cost line, which starts at F, is the break-even point (BEP). Below this point a loss is made, above it a profit.

(At all other volumes of activity except the BEP, either total sales revenue will exceed total cost or the other way round. Only at BEP are they equal.) The above formula can be expanded so that:

**Total sales revenue = Fixed cost + Variable cost**

If we call the number of units of output at BEP $b$, then

$$b \times \text{Sales revenue per unit} = \text{Fixed cost} + (b \times \text{Variable cost per unit})$$

so:

$$(b \times \text{Sales revenue per unit}) - (b \times \text{Variable cost per unit}) = \text{Fixed cost}$$

and:

$$b \times (\text{Sales revenue per unit} - \text{Variable cost per unit}) = \text{Fixed cost}$$

giving:

$$b = \frac{\text{Fixed cost}}{\text{Sales revenue per unit} - \text{Variable cost per u}}$$

If we look back at the break-even chart in Figure 9.6, this formula seems logical. The total cost line starts off at point F, higher than the starting point for the total sales revenues line (zero) by amount F (the amount of the fixed cost). Because the sales revenue per unit is greater than the variable cost per unit, the sales revenue line will gradually catch up with the total cost line. The rate at which it will catch up is dependent on the relative steepness of the two lines. Bearing in mind that the slopes of the two lines are the variable cost per unit and the selling price per unit, the above equation for calculating *b* looks perfectly logical.

Though the BEP can be calculated quickly and simply without resorting to graphs, this does not mean that the break-even chart is without value. The chart shows the relationship between cost, volume and profit over a range of activity and in a form that can easily be understood by non-financial managers. The break-even chart can therefore be a useful device for explaining this relationship.

### Example 9.2

Cottage Industries Ltd makes baskets. The fixed cost of operating the workshop for a month totals £500. Each basket requires materials that cost £2 and takes one hour to make. The business pays the basket makers £10 an hour. The basket makers are all on contracts such that if they do not work for any reason, they are not paid. The baskets are sold to a wholesaler for £14 each.

What is the BEP for basket making for the business?

#### Solution

The BEP (in number of baskets) is:

$$BEP = \frac{\text{Fixed cost}}{(\text{Sales revenue per unit} - \text{Variable cost per unit})}$$

$$= \frac{£500}{£14 - (£2 + £10)}$$

$$= 250 \text{ baskets per month}$$

Note that the BEP must be expressed with respect to a period of time.

**Real World 9.1** shows information on the BEPs of two well-known businesses.

### Real World 9.1

#### BE at Ryanair (and BA)

Commercial airlines seem to pay a lot of attention to their BEPs and their 'load factors', that is, their actual level of activity. Figure 9.7 shows the BEPs and load factors for Ryanair, the 'no frills' carrier.

We can see that Ryanair made operating profits in each of the five years considered. This is because the airline's load factor was consistently greater than its BEP.

Most airlines do not publish their break-even points. British Airways plc (BA) used to do so. In the most recent year that BA disclosed its BEP (2008) it was 64 per cent, with a load factor of 71 per cent. Those figures were quite typical of BA's results during previous recent years.

*Source:* Based on information contained in the Ryanair Holding plc Annual Report 2011 and British Airways plc Annual Report 2008.

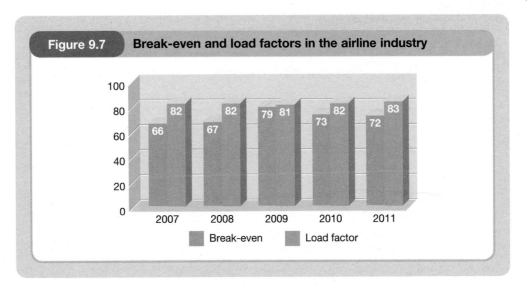

**Figure 9.7**  **Break-even and load factors in the airline industry**

Break-even   Load factor

In Real World 9.1, we saw that Ryanair's break-even point varied from one year to the next. It was as low as 66 per cent in 2007, but as high as 79 per cent in 2009. Why was it not roughly the same each year?

Break-even point depends on three broad factors. These are: sales revenue, variable cost and fixed cost. Each if these can vary quite noticeably from one year to another. Ryanair's sales revenue could be greatly affected by the level of disposable income among the travelling public and/or by levels of competition from other airlines. Costs can vary from one year to another, particularly the cost of aviation fuel.

(Interestingly, Ryanair's average fuel cost was 2.351 euros per gallon in 2009, but only 1.515 euros per gallon in 2010.)

Can you think of reasons why the managers of a business might find it useful to know the BEP of some activity that they are planning to undertake?

By knowing the BEP, it is possible to compare the expected, or planned, volume of activity with the BEP and so make a judgement about risk. If the volume of activity is expected to be only just above the break-even point, this may suggest that it is a risky venture. Only a small fall from the expected volume of activity could lead to a loss.

## Activity (9.7)

Cottage Industries Ltd (see Example 9.2) expects to sell 500 baskets a month. The business has the opportunity to rent a basket-making machine. Doing so would increase the total fixed cost of operating the workshop for a month to £3,000. Using the machine would reduce the labour time to half an hour per basket. The basket makers would still be paid £10 an hour.

(a)  How much profit would the business make each month from selling baskets
   • without the machine; and
   • with the machine?
(b)  What is the BEP if the machine is rented?
(c)  What do you notice about the figures that you calculate?

(a)  Estimated monthly profit from basket making:

|  | Without the machine | | With the machine | |
| --- | --- | --- | --- | --- |
|  | £ | £ | £ | £ |
| Sales revenue (500 × £14) |  | 7,000 |  | 7,000 |
| Materials (500 × £2) | (1,000) |  | (1,000) |  |
| Labour (500 × 1 × £10) | (5,000) |  |  |  |
| (500 × $\frac{1}{2}$ × £10) |  |  | (2,500) |  |
| Fixed cost | (500) |  | (3,000) |  |
|  |  | (6,500) |  | (6,500) |
| Profit |  | 500 |  | 500 |

(b)  The BEP (in number of baskets) with the machine:

$$\text{BEP} = \frac{\text{Fixed cost}}{\text{Sales revenue per unit} - \text{Variable cost per unit}}$$

$$= \frac{£3,000}{£14 - (£2 + £5)}$$

$$= 429 \text{ baskets a month}$$

The BEP without the machine is 250 baskets per month (see Example 9.2).

(c)  There seems to be nothing to choose between the two manufacturing strategies regarding profit, at the expected sales volume. There is, however, a distinct difference between the two strategies regarding the BEP. Without the machine, the actual volume of sales could fall by a half of that which is expected (from 500 to 250) before the business would fail to make a profit. With the machine, however, just a 14 per cent fall (from 500 to 429) would be enough to cause the business to fail to make a profit. On the other hand, for each additional basket sold above the estimated 500, an additional profit of only £2 (that is, £14 – (£2 + £10)) would be made without the machine, whereas £7 (that is, £14 – (£2 + £5)) would be made with the machine. (Note that knowledge of the BEP and the planned volume of activity gives some basis for assessing the riskiness of the activity.)

**Real World 9.2** discusses the effect of volume of activity on profit (the 'bottom line') at Halfords' Autocentres, a division of Halfords plc.

## Making the fixed costs work                                    **FT**

Analysts are relying on Halfords Autocentre division to crank up the company's total profits in 2011. As the spring MOT season looms, all 240 autocentres will have been rebranded with the Halfords name, and a marketing campaign will commence.

"Halfords can drive up customer numbers at Autocentre through national advertising and by leveraging its existing customer database," said David Jeary, retail analyst at Investec.

"The biggest fixed cost in the Autocentre business is labour, and using that labour more efficiently by increasing customer numbers means the bottom line traction is attractive."

*Source*: Adapted from 'Cycle sales push Halfords downhill', Claer Barrett, FT.com, 13 January 2011.

We shall take a closer look at the relationship between fixed cost, variable cost and profit together with any advice that we might give the management of Cottage Industries Ltd after we have briefly considered the notion of contribution.

# Contribution

The bottom part of the break-even formula (sales revenue per unit less variable cost per unit) is known as the **contribution per unit**. Thus, for the basket-making activity, without the machine the contribution per unit is £2 and with the machine it is £7. This can be quite a useful figure to know in a decision-making context. It is called 'contribution' because it contributes to meeting the fixed cost and, if there is any excess, it then contributes to profit.

We shall see, a little later in this chapter, how knowing the amount of the contribution generated by a particular activity can be valuable in making short-term decisions of various types, as well as being useful in the BEP calculation.

### Contribution margin ratio

The **contribution margin ratio** is the contribution from an activity expressed as a percentage of the sales revenue, thus:

$$\text{Contribution margin ratio} = \frac{\text{Contribution}}{\text{Sales revenue}} \times 100\%$$

Contribution and sales revenue can both be expressed in per-unit or total terms. For Cottage Industries Ltd (Example 9.2 and Activity 9.7), the contribution margin ratios are:

Without the machine, $\dfrac{14 - 12}{14} \times 100\% = 14\%$

$$\text{With the machine, } \frac{14 - 7}{14} \times 100\% = 50\%$$

The ratio can provide an impression of the extent to which sales revenue is eaten away by variable cost.

## Margin of safety

The **margin of safety** is the extent to which the planned volume of output or sales lies above the BEP. To illustrate how the margin of safety is calculated, we can use the information in Activity 9.7 relating to each option.

|  | Without the machine (number of baskets) | With the machine (number of baskets) |
|---|---|---|
| (a) Expected volume of sales | 500 | 500 |
| (b) BEP | 250 | 429 |
| Margin of safety (the difference between (a) and (b)) | 250 | 71 |
| Expressed as a percentage of expected volume of sales | 50% | 14% |

The margin of safety can be used as a partial measure of risk.

### Activity 9.8

What advice would you give Cottage Industries Ltd about renting the machine, on the basis of the values for margin of safety?

It is a matter of personal judgement, which in turn is related to individual attitudes to risk, as to which strategy to adopt. Most people, however, would prefer the strategy of not renting the machine, since the margin of safety between the expected volume of activity and the BEP is much greater. Thus, for the same level of return, the risk will be lower without renting the machine.

The relative margins of safety are directly linked to the relationship between the selling price per basket, the variable cost per basket and the fixed cost per month. Without the machine the contribution (selling price less variable cost) per basket is £2; with the machine it is £7. On the other hand, without the machine the fixed cost is £500 a month; with the machine it is £3,000. This means that, with the machine, the contributions have more fixed cost to 'overcome' before the activity becomes profitable. However, the rate at which the contributions can overcome fixed cost is higher with the machine, because variable cost is lower. Thus, one more, or one fewer, basket sold has a greater impact on profit than it does if the machine is not rented. The contrast between the two scenarios is shown graphically in Figures 9.8(a) and 9.8(b).

| Figure 9.8 | Break-even charts for Cottage Industries' basket-making activities (a) without the machine and (b) with the machine |

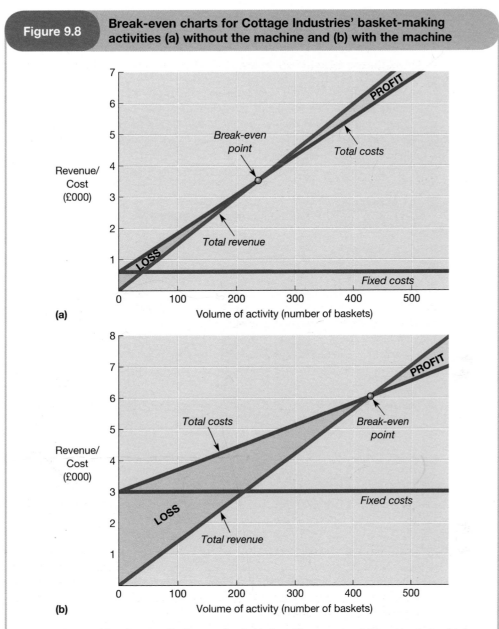

Without the machine the contribution per basket is low. Thus, each additional basket sold does not make a dramatic difference to the profit or loss. With the machine, however, the opposite is true; small increases or decreases in the sales volume will have a great effect on the profit or loss.

If we look back to Real World 9.1 (page 328), we can see that Ryanair typically had a much larger margin of safety than BA.

**Real World 9.3** goes into more detail on Ryanair's margin of safety and operating profit, over recent years.

**Real World 9.3**

## Ryanair's margin of safety

As we saw in Real World 9.1, commercial airlines pay a lot of attention to BEPs. They are also interested in their margin of safety (the difference between load factor and BEP).

Figure 9.9 shows Ryanair's margin of safety and its operating profit over a five-year period. Note that in 2009, Ryanair had a load factor that was only just above its break-even point and this led to an unusually small operating profit. In the other years, the load factors were comfortably greater than the BEP. This led to operating profits.

| Figure 9.9 | Ryanairs's margin of safety |

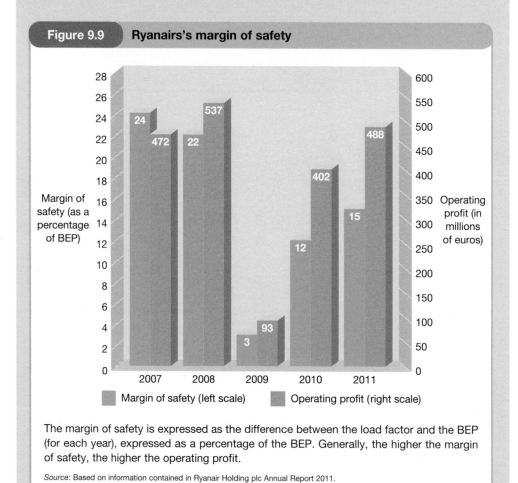

The margin of safety is expressed as the difference between the load factor and the BEP (for each year), expressed as a percentage of the BEP. Generally, the higher the margin of safety, the higher the operating profit.

*Source*: Based on information contained in Ryanair Holding plc Annual Report 2011.

## Achieving a target profit

In the same way as we can derive the volume of output necessary to break even, we can calculate the volume of output required to achieve a particular level of profit. We can expand the equation shown on page 327 so that:

Total sales revenue = Fixed cost + Total variable cost + Target profit

If we let $t$ be the required number of units of output to achieve the target profit, then

$t \times$ Sales revenue per unit = Fixed cost + ($t \times$ Variable cost per unit) + Target profit

so:

($t \times$ Sales revenue per unit) − ($t \times$ Variable cost per unit) = Fixed cost + Target profit

and:

$t \times$ (Sales revenue per unit − Variable cost per unit) = Fixed cost + Target profit

giving:

$$t = \frac{\text{Fixed cost + Target profit}}{\text{Sales revenue per unit − Variable cost per unit}}$$

### Activity 9.9

What volume of activity is required by Cottage Industries Ltd (see Example 9.2 and Activity 9.7) in order to make a profit of £4,000 a month:

(a) without the machine; and
(b) with the machine?

(a) Using the formula above, the required volume of activity without the machine:

$$\frac{\text{Fixed cost + Target profit}}{\text{Sales revenue per unit − Variable cost per unit}}$$

$$= \frac{£500 + £4,000}{£14 − (£2 + £10)}$$

$$= 2,250 \text{ baskets a month}$$

(b) The required volume of activity with the machine:

$$\frac{£3,000 + £4,000}{£14 − (£2 + £5)}$$

$$= 1,000 \text{ baskets a month}$$

## Operating gearing

The relationship between contribution and fixed cost is known as **operating gearing** (or operational gearing). An activity with a relatively high fixed cost compared with its total variable cost, at its normal level of activity, is said to have high operating gearing. Thus, Cottage Industries Ltd has higher operating gearing using the machine than it has if not using it. Renting the machine increases the level of operating gearing quite dramatically because it causes an increase in fixed cost, but at the same time it leads to a reduction in variable cost per basket.

## Operating gearing and its effect on profit

The reason why the word 'gearing' is used in this context is that, as with intermeshing gear wheels of different circumferences, a movement in one of the factors (volume of output) causes a more-than-proportionate movement in the other (profit), as illustrated by Figure 9.10.

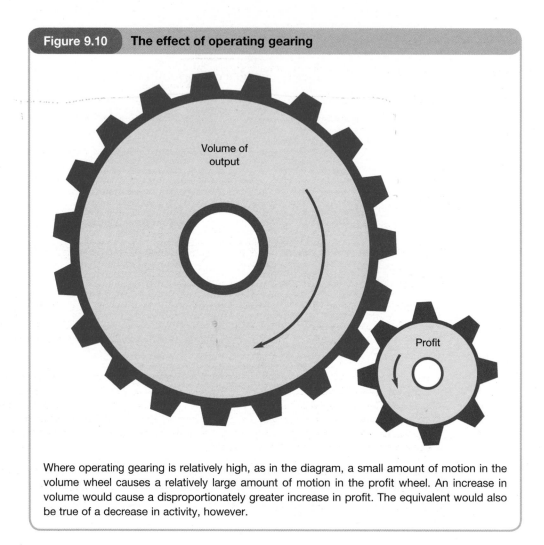

**Figure 9.10** The effect of operating gearing

Where operating gearing is relatively high, as in the diagram, a small amount of motion in the volume wheel causes a relatively large amount of motion in the profit wheel. An increase in volume would cause a disproportionately greater increase in profit. The equivalent would also be true of a decrease in activity, however.

Increasing the level of operating gearing makes profit more sensitive to changes in the volume of activity. We can demonstrate operating gearing with Cottage Industries Ltd's basket-making activities as follows:

|  | *Without the machine* | | | *With the machine* | | |
|---|---|---|---|---|---|---|
| Volume (number of baskets) | 500 | 1,000 | 1,500 | 500 | 1,000 | 1,500 |
|  | £ | £ | £ | £ | £ | £ |
| Contributions* | 1,000 | 2,000 | 3,000 | 3,500 | 7,000 | 10,500 |
| Fixed cost | (500) | (500) | (500) | (3,000) | (3,000) | (3,000) |
| Profit | 500 | 1,500 | 2,500 | 500 | 4,000 | 7,500 |

\* £2 per basket without the machine and £7 per basket with it.

Note that, without the machine (low operating gearing), a doubling of the output from 500 to 1,000 units brings a trebling of the profit. With the machine (high operating gearing), doubling output from 500 units causes profit to rise by eight times. At the same time, reductions in the volume of output tend to have a more damaging effect on profit where the operating gearing is higher.

## Activity 9.10

**What types of business activity are likely to have high operating gearing? (*Hint*: Cottage Industries Ltd might give you some idea.)**

Activities that are capital intensive tend to have high operating gearing. This is because renting or owning capital equipment gives rise to additional fixed cost, but it can also give rise to lower variable cost.

**Real World 9.4** shows how a very well-known business has benefited from high operating gearing.

## Real World 9.4

### Delivering profit through operating gearing

Domino's Pizza UK and IRL plc, the well known pizza delivery business, believes that its high level of operating gearing is causing the rate of increases in profits to be greater than the rate of the increase in sales revenue. In its preliminary financial results statement the business said:

> We have had a solid start to 2011, with like-for-like sales for the first seven weeks up 4.7% and are encouraged by the recent strength in like-for-like sales growth. This figure comes against the backdrop of exceptional comparatives from the same period in 2010 and the current difficult economic climate. We are pleased with this performance and we will be benefitting from our accelerated store openings, the recent deal with Moto motorway services, and the operational gearing which will drive our profits going forward.

Domino's is the type of business where quite a lot of its costs are fixed, such as rent, salaries, plant depreciation, motor vehicle running costs, training and advertising.

*Source*: Domino's Pizza UK and IRL plc, Preliminary results for the 52 weeks ended 26 December 2010, 15 February 2011.

## Profit-volume charts

A slight variant of the break-even chart is the **profit–volume (PV) chart**. A typical PV chart is shown in Figure 9.11.

The PV chart is obtained by plotting loss or profit against volume of activity. The slope of the graph is equal to the contribution per unit, since each additional unit sold decreases the loss, or increases the profit, by the sales revenue per unit less the variable cost per unit. At zero volume of activity there are no contributions, so there is a loss equal to the amount of the fixed cost. As the volume of activity increases, the amount of the loss gradually decreases until BEP is reached. Beyond BEP a profit is made, which increases as activity increases.

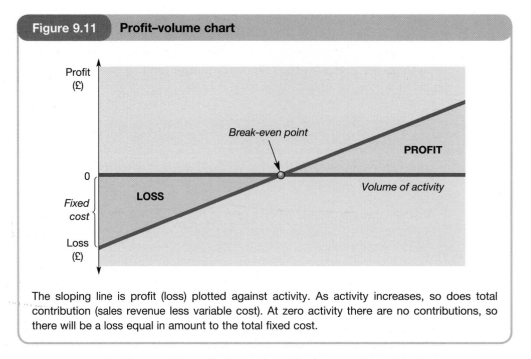

**Figure 9.11** | **Profit–volume chart**

The sloping line is profit (loss) plotted against activity. As activity increases, so does total contribution (sales revenue less variable cost). At zero activity there are no contributions, so there will be a loss equal in amount to the total fixed cost.

As we can see, the PV chart does not tell us anything not shown by the break-even chart. It does, however, highlight key information concerning the profit (loss) arising at any volume of activity. The break-even chart shows this as the vertical distance between the total cost and total sales revenue lines. The PV chart, in effect, combines the total sales revenue and total variable cost lines, which means that profit (or loss) is directly readable.

## The economist's view of the break-even chart

So far in this chapter we have treated all the relationships as linear – that is, all of the lines in the graphs have been straight. However, this may not be strictly valid.

Consider, for example, the variable cost line in the break-even chart; accountants would normally treat this as being a straight line. In reality, however, the line may not be straight because at high levels of output **economies of scale** may be available to an extent not available at lower levels. For example, a raw material (a typical variable cost) may be able to be used more efficiently with higher volumes of activity. Similarly, buying large quantities of material and services may enable the business to benefit from bulk discounts and so lower the cost.

There is also a tendency for sales revenue per unit to reduce as volume is increased. To sell more of a particular product or service, it will usually be necessary to lower the price per unit.

Economists recognise that, in real life, the relationships portrayed in the break-even chart are usually non-linear. The typical economist's view of the chart is shown in Figure 9.12.

Note, in Figure 9.12, that the total variable cost line starts to rise quite steeply with volume but, around point A, economies of scale start to take effect. With further increases in volume, total variable cost does not rise as steeply because the variable cost *for each additional unit of output* is lowered. These economies of scale continue to have a benign effect on cost until a point is reached where the business is operating towards

**Figure 9.12**    **The economist's view of the break-even chart**

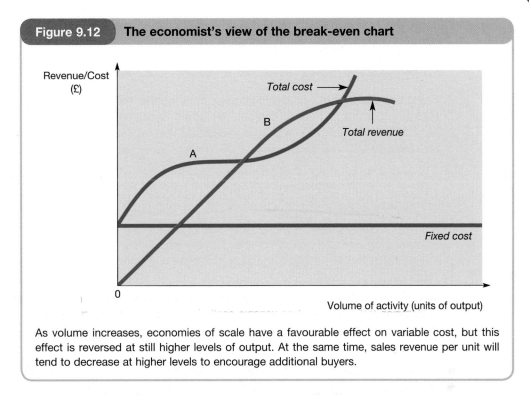

As volume increases, economies of scale have a favourable effect on variable cost, but this effect is reversed at still higher levels of output. At the same time, sales revenue per unit will tend to decrease at higher levels to encourage additional buyers.

the end of its efficient range. Beyond this range, problems will emerge that adversely affect variable cost. For example, the business may be unable to find cheap supplies of the variable cost elements or may suffer production difficulties, such as machine break-downs. As a result, the total variable cost line starts to rise more steeply.

At low levels of output, sales may be made at a relatively high price per unit. To increase sales output beyond point B, however, it may be necessary to lower the average sales price per unit. This will mean that the total revenue line will not rise as steeply, and may even curve downwards. Note how this 'curvilinear' representation of the break-even chart can easily lead to the existence of two break-even points.

Accountants justify their approach by arguing that, although the lines may not, in practice, be perfectly straight, this defect is not usually worth taking into account. This is partly because information used in the analysis is based on estimates of the future. These estimates will, inevitably, be flawed because of our inability to predict with great accuracy. It is pointless, therefore, to be concerned with the minor approximation of treating total cost and total revenue lines as straight. Only where significant economies or diseconomies of scale are involved should the non-linearity of variable cost be taken into account. Furthermore, for most businesses, the range of possible volumes of activity over which they operate (the **relevant range**) is quite narrow. When dealing with short distances, it may be perfectly reasonable to treat a curved line as being straight.

## Failing to break even

Where a business fails to reach its BEP, steps must be taken to remedy the problem: there must be an increase in sales revenue or a reduction in cost, or both. **Real World 9.5** discusses how Tesco plc, the supermarket business, failed to reach its BEP in its stores in China during 2011.

**Real World 9.5**

### Not breaking China

Tesco has stores in several countries apart from the UK. These include some European countries (particularly Eastern Europe), the United States and Asia. The Chinese stores seem to have proved more difficult for Tesco than was expected. In its preliminary results statement for 2010/11, Tesco said:

> China did not break-even during the second half of the year, which was a consequence of the slower consumer demand growth and our store roll-out being slower than planned.

It went on to say:

> Asian markets offer an exciting long-term growth opportunity and will be a key focus for our future international expansion, both in our established markets and in China. Having continued to invest through the downturn, we are now in an even stronger position as economic recovery continues.

Clearly Tesco expects break even to be achieved in China before too long, provided that it can add to its portfolio of stores and stimulate faster consumer demand growth.

*Source*: Extracts from 'Tesco plc Preliminary results 2010/11', Tesco.com, 19 April 2011.

## Weaknesses of break-even analysis

Although break-even analysis can provide useful insights concerning the relationship between cost, volume and profit, it does have its weaknesses. There are three general problems:

- *Non-linear relationships*. Break-even analysis assumes that total variable cost and total revenue lines are perfectly straight when plotted against volume of output. In real life, this is unlikely to be the case. We saw earlier, however, that, in practice, minor variations from strict linearity are unlikely to be significant and that, over the relevant range of business operations, curved lines tend to be fairly straight.
- *Stepped fixed cost*. Most types of fixed cost are not fixed over the whole range of activity. They tend to be 'stepped' in the way depicted in Figure 9.2. This means that, in practice, great care must be taken in making assumptions about fixed cost. The problem is heightened because many activities will involve various types of fixed cost (for example rent, supervisory salaries, administration cost), all of which are likely to have steps at different points.
- *Multi-product businesses*. Most businesses provide more than one product (or service). This can be a problem for break-even analysis since additional sales of one product may affect sales of another of the business's products. There is also the problem of identifying the fixed cost associated with a particular product. Fixed cost may relate to more than one product – for example, production of two products may be carried out in the same rented accommodation. There are ways of dividing the fixed cost between products, but these tend to be arbitrary, which undermines the value of the break-even analysis.

## Activity 9.11

We saw above that, in practice, relationships between costs, revenues and volumes of activity are not necessarily straight-line ones.

Can you think of at least three reasons, with examples, why this may be the case?

We thought of the following:

- *Economies of scale with labour.* A business may operate more economically at a higher volume of activity. For example, employees may be able to increase productivity by specialising in particular tasks.
- *Economies of scale with buying goods or services.* A business may find it cheaper to buy in goods and services where it is buying in bulk as discounts are often given.
- *Diseconomies of scale.* This may mean that the per-unit cost of output is higher at higher levels of activity. For example, it may be necessary to pay higher rates of pay to workers to recruit the additional staff needed at higher volumes of activity.
- *Lower sales prices at high levels of activity.* Some consumers may only be prepared to buy the particular product or service at a lower price. Thus, it may not be possible to achieve high levels of sales activity without lowering the selling price.

Despite some practical problems, break-even analysis seems to be widely used. The media frequently refer to the BEP for businesses and activities. There is seemingly constant discussion, for example, about Eurotunnel's BEP and whether it will ever be reached. Similarly, the number of people regularly needed to pay to watch a football team so that the club breaks even is often mentioned. This is illustrated in **Real World 9.6**, which is an extract from an article discussing the need for Carlisle United FC, the English Football League One club, to cut its costs.

## Real World 9.6

### Not enough coming to see the Cumbrians

The Carlisle United managing director John Nixon said that the attendance at home matches, which averages about 5,200, is well below the figure that enables the club to break even. He went on to say that the club will need to look at its costs and may need to make some cuts. He said that he did not want the club to risk going into administration.

*Source*: Information taken from 'Carlisle facing budget cuts', BBC Sport website, 25 March 2010.

**Real World 9.7** describes three different situations where breaking even is considered.

## Real World 9.7

### Breaking even is breaking out all over                    **FT**

**Southern Cross fails to break even**

Southern Cross Healthcare Group plc, a business that operated a number of residential care homes for the elderly, found itself in severe financial difficulties in July 2011. This

→

**Real World 9.7 (continued)**

resulted from failing to reach its break-even level of occupancy in its homes. According to the *Financial Times*:

> In the care home business, you can usually break even if 50 to 70 per cent of your beds are occupied. If you pay rent, you only break even when 80–85 per cent of your beds are occupied. Southern Cross' occupancy rate fell from 92 per cent in 2006 to 85 per cent in 2010 because it allowed the quality of its homes to deteriorate.

*Source*: 'Southern Cross run on a failed business model', Sarah O'Connor, FT.com, 30 May 2011.

### English universities need to charge £7,000 to break even

Fees will rise a long way at traditional universities, largely because the government is withdrawing teaching subsidies for cheaper courses. The Browne review assumed that institutions would need to charge an average of more than £7,000 to break even. Ministers say universities will need 'exceptional' reasons to want to charge more than £6,000. But top institutions are expected to push to charge nearer the £9,000 barrier. Universities that want to offer accelerated courses, teaching an honours degree within two years, might also be able to charge more.

*Source*: Taken from 'Universities may eye fees near maximum', Chris Cook, FT.com, 3 November 2010.

### Football to break even by 2013

Professional footballers would be prepared to earn less money in return for greater job security, claimed the chairman of the English Football League, after clubs agreed to find new measures to curb spiralling costs.

Greg Clarke said that with debt across the 72 clubs of the Football League growing at a compound annual rate of 15 to 20 per cent, club chairmen had no choice but to tackle football's ballooning wages, which make up the bulk of their spending.

Measures agreed by Football League chairmen at an annual two-day meeting in Cyprus will "over time" reduce the risk of clubs becoming insolvent, said Mr Clarke.

"We will end up with a similar number of players, earning maybe less money but having much better security," said Mr Clarke. He predicted that the length of player contracts would shorten or stay the same. "How much are paid out under these contracts will come down," he said.

Football's wage crisis was highlighted this week in Deloitte's annual football review, which showed that wages in the Championship, the tier below the Premier League, had grown by £129 million in the four years to 2009–10, twice the amount of revenue growth.

The wages-to-turnover ratio in the Championship was 88 per cent in 2009–10. The net debt of the 24 Championship clubs stood at £875 million.

Mr Clarke said: "I have talked to players. At the end of the day, having more financially viable football clubs that can afford to be in business is in the players' interests as well. They are not necessarily enthusiastic about reducing the amount of money [coming to them], but that is the big issues we are dealing with."

The three tiers of the Football League – the Championship, League One and League Two – agreed to adopt the framework of Financial Fair Play, the protocol set up by Uefa, the European governing body, that requires clubs to break even in order to compete in Uefa tournaments.

Clubs in the Championship, the tier below the Premier League, will adopt new regulations from the 2012–13 season aimed at creating a break-even model, even though only a handful of clubs in the Premier League are ever in contention for Uefa competitions. League One clubs will adopt the Football League's Salary Cost Management Protocol

(SCMP), which already applies to League Two clubs. The SCMP sets a threshold for the amount clubs can spend on wages as a proportion of revenue. Clubs breaking the protocol are barred from buying and selling players until they fall into line.

League One clubs will operate a shadow SCMP for the coming season, before applying it from 2012–13. The SCMP threshold for League Two will be 55 per cent for 2011–12.

Mr Clarke said it would take 6 to 9 months to draw up new regulations for the Championship clubs, involving clear definitions of revenue, costs and overheads, stress-testing a break-even model and agreeing to which sanctions would apply for breaches. He said the Football League intended to present clubs with a menu of possible sanctions, including fines, points' deductions and transfer embargoes. "The clubs will decide which ones they will support," he said.

*Source*: 'Football League considers cut in player salaries', Roger Blitz, FT.com, 10 June 2011.

**Real World 9.8** provides evidence concerning the extent to which managers use break-even analysis.

### Real World 9.8

### Break-even analysis in practice

A survey of management accounting practice in the United States was conducted in 2003. Nearly 2,000 businesses replied to the survey. These tended to be larger businesses, of which about 40 per cent were manufacturers and about 16 per cent financial services; the remainder were across a range of other industries.

The survey revealed that 62 per cent use break-even analysis extensively, with a further 22 per cent considering using the technique in the future.

Though the survey relates to the US and was undertaken several years ago, in the absence of UK evidence it provides some indication of what is likely also to be current practice in the UK and elsewhere in the developed world.

*Source*: Taken from the *2003 Survey of Management Accounting* by Ernst and Young, 2003.

## Using contribution to make decisions: marginal analysis

In the previous chapter concerning relevant costs, we saw that, when deciding between two or more possible courses of action, *only costs that vary with the decision should be included in the analysis*. This principle can be applied to the consideration of fixed cost.

For many decisions that involve:

● relatively small variations from existing practice, and/or
● relatively limited periods of time,

fixed cost is not relevant. It will be the same irrespective of the decision made. This is because fixed cost elements cannot, or will not, be altered in the short term.

**Activity 9.12**

Ali plc owns a workshop from which it provides a PC repair and maintenance service. There has recently been a downturn in demand for the service. It would be possible for Ali plc to carry on the business from smaller, cheaper accommodation.

Can you think of any reasons why the business might not immediately move to smaller, cheaper accommodation?

We thought of broadly three reasons:

1. It is not usually possible to find a buyer for the existing accommodation at very short notice and it may be difficult to find an available alternative quickly.
2. It may be difficult to move accommodation quickly where there is, say, delicate equipment to be moved.
3. Management may feel that the downturn might not be permanent, and would thus be reluctant to take such a dramatic step and deny itself the opportunity to benefit from a possible revival of trade.

We shall now consider some types of decisions where fixed cost can be regarded as irrelevant. In making these decisions, we should have as our key strategic objective the enhancement of owners' (shareholders') wealth. Since these decisions are short-term in nature, wealth will normally be increased by generating as much net cash inflow as possible.

In **marginal analysis** only costs and revenues that vary with the decision are considered. This usually means that fixed cost can be ignored. This is because marginal analysis is usually applied to minor alterations in the level of activity. It tends to be true, therefore, that the variable cost per unit will be equal to the **marginal cost,** which is the additional cost of producing one more unit of output. Whilst marginal cost normally equals variable cost, there may be times when producing one more unit will involve a step in the fixed cost. If this occurs, the marginal cost is not just the variable cost; it will include the increment, or step, in the fixed cost as well.

Marginal analysis may be used in four key areas of decision making:

- pricing/assessing opportunities to enter contracts;
- determining the most efficient use of scarce resources;
- make-or-buy decisions;
- closing or continuation decisions.

Let us consider each of these areas in turn.

## Pricing/assessing opportunities to enter contracts

To understand how marginal analysis may be used in assessing an opportunity, consider the following activity.

**Activity 9.13**

Cottage Industries Ltd (see Example 9.2, page 328) has spare capacity in that its basket makers have some spare time. An overseas retail chain has offered the business an order for 300 baskets at a price of £13 each.

Without considering any wider issues, should the business accept the order? (Assume that the business does not rent the machine.)

Since the fixed cost will be incurred in any case, it is not relevant to this decision. All we need to do is to see whether the price offered will yield a contribution. If it will, the business will be better off by accepting the contract than by refusing it.

|                                   | £     |
|-----------------------------------|-------|
| Additional revenue per unit       | 13    |
| Additional cost per unit          | (12)  |
| Additional contribution per unit  | 1     |

For 300 units, the additional contribution will be £300 (that is, 300 × £1). Since no fixed cost increase is involved, irrespective of what else is happening to the business, it will be £300 better off by taking this contract than by refusing it.

As ever with decision making, there are other factors that are either difficult or impossible to quantify. These should be taken into account before reaching a final decision. In the case of Cottage Industries Ltd's decision concerning the overseas customer, these could include the following:

- The possibility that spare capacity will have been 'sold off' cheaply when there might be another potential customer who will offer a higher price, but, by that time, the capacity will be fully committed. It is a matter of commercial judgement as to how likely this will be.
- Selling the same product, but at different prices, could lead to a loss of customer goodwill. The fact that a different price will be set for customers in different countries (that is, in different markets) may be sufficient to avoid this potential problem.
- If the business is going to suffer continually from being unable to sell its full production potential at the 'usual' price, it might be better, in the long run, to reduce capacity and make fixed cost savings. Using the spare capacity to produce marginal benefits may lead to the business failing to address this issue.
- On a more positive note, the business may see this as a way of breaking into the overseas market. This is something that might be impossible to achieve if the business charges its usual price.

The marginal cost is the minimum price at which the business can offer a product or service for sale. It will result in the business being no better off as a result of making the sale than if it had not done so. Achieving more than this minimum price will generate a profit (an increase in owners' wealth).

A marginal cost approach to pricing would only be used where there is not the opportunity to sell at a price that will cover the full cost. In the long run, the business must more than cover all of its costs, both variable and fixed, if it is to be profitable.

## Activity 9.14

A commercial aircraft is due to take off in one hour's time with 20 seats unsold. What is the minimum price at which these seats could be sold such that the airline would be no worse off as a result?

The answer is that any price above the additional cost of carrying one more passenger would represent an acceptable minimum. If there are no such costs, the minimum price is zero.

→

**Activity 9.14 (continued)**

This is not to say that the airline will seek to charge the minimum price; it will presumably seek to charge the highest price that the market will bear. The fact that the market will not bear the full cost, plus a profit margin, should not, in principle, be sufficient for the airline to refuse to sell seats, where there is spare passenger capacity.

In practice, airlines are major users of a marginal costing approach. They often offer low priced tickets for off-peak travel, where there are not sufficient customers willing to pay 'normal' prices. By insisting on a Saturday stopover for return tickets, they tend to exclude 'business' travellers, who are probably forced to travel, but for whom a Saturday stopover may be unattractive. UK train operators often offer substantial discounts for off-peak travel. Similarly, hotels often charge very low rates for rooms at off-peak times. A hotel mainly used by business travellers may well offer very low room rates for Friday and Saturday occupancy.

**Real World 9.9** provides an unusual example where humanitarian issues are the driving force for adopting marginal pricing.

---

**Real World 9.9**

### Drug prices in developing countries     **FT**

Large pharmaceutical businesses have recently been under considerable pressure to provide cheap drugs to developing countries. It has been suggested that life-saving therapeutic drugs should be sold to these countries at a price that is close to their marginal cost. Indeed the Department for International Development would like to see HIV drugs sold at marginal cost in the poorest countries. However, a number of obstacles to such a pricing policy have been identified:

1. It may lead to customer revolts in the West (the 'loss of customer goodwill' referred to above).
2. There is a concern that the drugs may not reach their intended patients and could be re-exported to western countries. A major cost of producing a new drug is the research and development costs incurred, and marginal costs of production are usually very low. Thus, a selling price based on marginal cost is likely to be considerably lower than the normal (full-cost) selling price in the West. This, it is feared, may lead to the cheap drugs provided leaking back into the West. Acquiring drugs at a price near to their marginal cost and reselling them at a figure close to the selling price in the West offers unscrupulous individuals an opportunity to make huge profits.
3. That compensation for any adverse consequences that may arise from the drugs sold will be sought in courts in the West, thereby creating the risk of huge payouts. This would make the risk to the pharmaceutical businesses of selling the drugs out of proportion to the benefits to them, in terms of the prices that would be charged.

The above problems are not insurmountable and are not the only problems surrounding this issue, but they do appear to have slowed progress towards a speedier response to a humanitarian crisis.

*Source*: Based on information from 'GSK to cut drug prices for developing countries', A. Jack, FT.com, 29 November 2009, 'Drug pricing is a social problem', R. Epstein, FT.com, 16 June 2005; 'Pressure builds to cut price of HIV medicine', FT.com, 11 March 2006; and 'Patent nonsense', *Financial Times*, 24 August 2001.

**Real World 9.10** is an extract from a *Financial Times* article concerning the rising marginal cost of oil extraction.

## The most efficient use of scarce resources

Normally, the output of a business is determined by customer demand for the particular goods or services. In some cases, however, output will be restricted by the productive capacity of the business. Limited productive capacity might stem from a shortage of any factor of production – labour, raw materials, space, machine capacity and so on. Such scarce factors are often known as *key* or *limiting* factors.

Where productive capacity acts as a brake on output, management must decide on how best to deploy the scarce resource. That is, it must decide which products, from the range available, should be produced and how many of each should be produced. Marginal analysis can be useful to management in such circumstances. The guiding principle is that the most profitable combination of products will occur where the *contribution per unit of the scarce factor* is maximised. Example 9.3 illustrates this point.

### Example 9.3

A business provides three different services, the details of which are as follows:

| Service (code name) | AX107 | AX109 | AX220 |
|---|---|---|---|
| Selling price per unit (£) | 50 | 40 | 65 |
| Variable cost per unit (£) | (25) | (20) | (35) |
| Contribution per unit (£) | 25 | 20 | 30 |
| Labour time per unit (hours) | 5 | 3 | 6 |

Within reason, the market will take as many units of each service as can be provided, but the ability to provide the service is limited by the availability of labour, all of which needs to be skilled. Fixed cost is not affected by the choice of service provided because all three services use the same facilities.

The most profitable service is AX109 because it generates a contribution of £6.67 (£20/3) an hour. The other two generate only £5.00 each an hour (£25/5 and £30/6). So, to maximise profit, priority should be given to the production that maximises the contribution per unit of limiting factor.

Our first reaction might be that the business should provide only service AX220, as this is the one that yields the highest contribution per unit sold. If so, we would have been making the mistake of thinking that it is the ability to sell that is the limiting factor. If the above analysis is not convincing, we can take a random number of available labour hours and ask ourselves what is the maximum contribution (and, therefore, profit) that could be made by providing each service exclusively. Bear in mind that there is no shortage of anything else, including market demand, just a shortage of labour.

## Activity 9.15

A business makes three different products, the details of which are as follows:

| Product (code name) | B14 | B17 | B22 |
| --- | --- | --- | --- |
| Selling price per unit (£) | 25 | 20 | 23 |
| Variable cost per unit (£) | 10 | 8 | 12 |
| Weekly demand (units) | 25 | 20 | 30 |
| Machine time per unit (hours) | 4 | 3 | 4 |

Fixed cost is not affected by the choice of product because all three products use the same machine. Machine time is limited to 148 hours a week.

Which combination of products should be manufactured if the business is to produce the highest profit?

| Product (code name) | B14 | B17 | B22 |
| --- | --- | --- | --- |
| Selling price per unit (£) | 25 | 20 | 23 |
| Variable cost per unit (£) | (10) | (8) | (12) |
| Contribution per unit (£) | 15 | 12 | 11 |
| Machine time per unit (hours) | 4 | 3 | 4 |
| Contribution per machine hour (£) | 3.75 | 4.00 | 2.75 |
| Order of priority | 2nd | 1st | 3rd |

Therefore produce:

|  |  |
| --- | --- |
| 20 units of product B17 using | 60 hours |
| 22 units of product B14 using | 88 hours |
|  | 148 hours |

This leaves unsatisfied the market demand for a further 3 units of product B14 and 30 units of product B22.

## Activity 9.16

What practical steps could be taken that might lead to a higher level of contribution for the business in Activity 9.15?

The possibilities for improving matters that occurred to us are as follows:

● Consider obtaining additional machine time. This could mean obtaining a new machine, subcontracting the machining to another business or, perhaps, squeezing a few more hours a week out of the business's own machine. Perhaps a combination of two or more of these is a possibility.

- Redesign the products in a way that requires less time per unit on the machine.
- Increase the price per unit of the three products. This might well have the effect of dampening demand, but the existing demand cannot be met at present. It may, therefore, be more profitable, in the long run, to make a greater contribution on each unit sold than to take one of the other courses of action to overcome the problem.

## Activity 9.17

Going back to Activity 9.15, what is the maximum price that the business concerned would logically be prepared to pay to have the remaining B14s machined by a subcontractor, assuming that no fixed or variable cost would be saved as a result of not doing the machining in-house?

Would there be a different maximum if we were considering the B22s?

If the remaining three B14s were subcontracted at no cost, the business would be able to earn a contribution of £15 a unit, which it would not otherwise be able to gain. Therefore, any price up to £15 a unit would be worth paying to a subcontractor to undertake the machining. Naturally, the business would prefer to pay as little as possible, but anything up to £15 would still make it worthwhile subcontracting the machining.

This would not be true of the B22s because they have a different contribution per unit; £11 would be the relevant figure in their case.

## Make-or-buy decisions

Businesses are frequently confronted by the need to decide whether themselves to produce the product or service that they sell, or to buy it in from some other business. Thus, a producer of electrical appliances might decide to subcontract the manufacture of one of its products to another business, perhaps because there is a shortage of production capacity in the producer's own factory. Alternatively, the producer may believe it to be cheaper to subcontract than to make the appliance itself. Obtaining services or products from a subcontractor is often called **outsourcing**.

In many cases whether to outsource or not is a longer term, strategic decision. In that case it needs to be assessed as such. In the present context we are considering more tactical make or buy decisions that can be taken quickly for the short term.

## Activity 9.18

Shah Ltd needs a component for one of its products. It can subcontract production of the component to a subcontractor who will provide the components for £20 each. Shah Ltd can produce the components internally for a total variable cost of £15 per component. Shah Ltd has spare capacity.

Should the component be subcontracted or produced internally?

The answer is that Shah Ltd should produce the component internally, since the variable cost of subcontracting is greater by £5 (that is, £20 – £15) than the variable cost of internal manufacture.

## Activity 9.19

Now assume that Shah Ltd (Activity 9.18) has no spare capacity, so it can only produce the component internally by reducing its output of another of its products. While it is making each component, it will lose contributions of £12 from the other product.

Should the component be subcontracted or produced internally?

The answer is to subcontract. In this case, both the variable cost of production and the opportunity cost of lost contributions must be taken into account.

Thus, the relevant cost of internal production of each component is:

|  | £ |
|---|---|
| Variable cost of production of the component | 15 |
| Opportunity cost of lost production of the other product | 12 |
|  | 27 |

This is obviously more costly than the £20 per component that will have to be paid to the subcontractor.

## Activity 9.20

What factors, other than the immediately financially quantifiable, would you consider when making a make-or-buy decision?

We feel that there are two major factors:

1 The general problems of subcontracting, particularly:
   (a) loss of control of quality;
   (b) potential unreliability of supply.
2 Expertise and specialisation. Generally, businesses should focus on their core competences. It is possible for most businesses, with sufficient determination, to do virtually everything in-house. This may, however, require a level of skill and facilities that most businesses neither have nor feel inclined to acquire. For example, though it is true that most businesses could generate their own electricity, their managements tend to take the view that this is better done by a specialist generator business. Specialists can often do things more cheaply, with less risk of things going wrong.

## Closing or continuation decisions

It is quite common for businesses to produce separate financial statements for each department or section, to try to assess their relative performance. Example 9.4 considers how marginal analysis can help decide how to respond where it is found that a particular department underperforms.

## Example 9.4

Goodsports Ltd is a retail shop that operates through three departments, all in the same accommodation. The three departments occupy roughly equal-sized areas of the accommodation. The trading results for the year just finished showed the following:

|  | Total | Sports equipment | Sports clothes | General clothes |
|---|---|---|---|---|
|  | £000 | £000 | £000 | £000 |
| Sales revenue | 534 | 254 | 183 | 97 |
| Cost | (482) | (213) | (163) | (106) |
| Profit/(loss) | 52 | 41 | 20 | (9) |

It would appear that if the general clothes department were to close, the business would be more profitable, by £9,000 a year, assuming last year's performance to be a reasonable indication of future performance.

When the cost is analysed between that part that is variable and that part that is fixed, however, the contribution of each department can be deduced and the following results obtained:

|  | Total | Sports equipment | Sports clothes | General clothes |
|---|---|---|---|---|
|  | £000 | £000 | £000 | £000 |
| Sales revenue | 534 | 254 | 183 | 97 |
| Variable cost | (344) | (167) | (117) | (60) |
| Contribution | 190 | 87 | 66 | 37 |
| Fixed cost (rent and so on) | (138) | (46) | (46) | (46) |
| Profit/(loss) | 52 | 41 | 20 | (9) |

Now it is obvious that closing the general clothes department, without any other developments, would make the business worse off by £37,000 (the department's contribution). The department should not be closed, because it makes a positive contribution. The fixed cost would continue whether the department was closed or not. As can be seen from the above analysis, distinguishing between variable and fixed cost, and deducing the contribution, can make the picture a great deal clearer.

## Activity 9.21

In considering Goodsports Ltd (in Example 9.4), we saw that the general clothes department should not be closed 'without any other developments'.

What 'other developments' could affect this decision, making continuation either more attractive or less attractive?

The things that we could think of are as follows:

● Expansion of the other departments or replacing the general clothes department with a completely new activity. This would make sense only if the space currently occupied by the general clothes department could generate contributions totalling at least £37,000 a year.

→

> **Activity 9.21 (*continued*)**
>
> ● Subletting the space occupied by the general clothes department. Once again, this would need to generate a net rent greater than £37,000 a year to make it more financially beneficial than keeping the department open.
> ● Keeping the department open, even if it generated no contribution whatsoever (assuming that there is no other use for the space), may still be beneficial. If customers are attracted into the shop because it has general clothing, they may then buy something from one of the other departments. In the same way, the activity of a sub-tenant might attract customers into the shop. (On the other hand, it might drive them away!)

Figure 9.13 summarises the four key decision-making areas where marginal analysis tends to be used.

---

**Figure 9.13** | **The four key areas of decision making using marginal analysis**

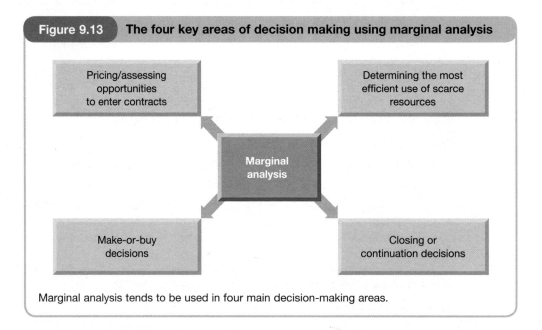

Marginal analysis tends to be used in four main decision-making areas.

---

**Self-assessment question** **9.1**

Khan Ltd can render three different types of service (Alpha, Beta and Gamma) using the same staff. Various estimates for next year have been made as follows:

| Service | Alpha | Beta | Gamma |
|---|---|---|---|
| Selling price (£/unit) | 30 | 39 | 20 |
| Variable material cost (£/unit) | 15 | 18 | 10 |
| Other variable costs (£/unit) | 6 | 10 | 5 |
| Share of fixed cost (£/unit) | 8 | 12 | 4 |
| Staff time required (hours) | 2 | 3 | 1 |

Fixed cost for next year is expected to total £40,000.

*Required*:

(a) If the business were to render only service Alpha next year, how many units of the service would it need to provide in order to break even? (Assume for this part of the question that there is no effective limit to market size and staffing level.)

(b) If the business has limited staff hours available next year, in which order of preference would the three services come?

(c) The maximum market for next year for the three services is as follows:

| | |
|---|---|
| Alpha | 3,000 units |
| Beta | 2,000 units |
| Gamma | 5,000 units |

Khan Ltd has a maximum of 10,000 staff hours available next year.

What quantities of each service should the business provide next year and how much profit would this be expected to yield?

**The solution to this question can be found at the back of the book on pages 736.**

## Summary

The main points in this chapter may be summarised as follows:

**Cost behaviour**

- Fixed cost is independent of the level of activity (for example, rent).
- Variable cost varies with the level of activity (for example, raw materials).
- Semi-fixed (semi-variable) cost is a mixture of fixed and variable costs (for example, electricity).

**Break-even analysis**

- The break-even point (BEP) is the level of activity (in units of output or sales revenue) at which total cost (fixed + variable) = total sales revenue.
- Calculation of BEP is as follows:

$$\text{BEP (in units of output)} = \frac{\text{Fixed cost for the period}}{\text{Sales revenue per unit} - \text{Variable cost per unit}}$$

- Knowledge of the BEP for a particular activity can be used to help assess risk.
- Contribution per unit = sales revenue per unit less variable cost per unit.
- Contribution margin ratio = contribution/sales revenue (×100%).
- Margin of safety = excess of planned volume (or sales revenue) of activity over volume (or sales revenue) at BEP.
- Calculation of the volume of activity ($t$) required to achieve a target profit is as follows:

$$t = \frac{\text{Fixed cost} + \text{Target profit}}{(\text{Sales revenue per unit} - \text{Variable cost per unit})}$$

- Operating gearing is the extent to which the total cost of some activity is fixed rather than variable.

- The profit–volume (PV) chart is an alternative approach to the BE chart, which is probably easier to understand.
- Economists tend to take a different approach to BE, taking account of economies (and diseconomies) of scale and of the fact that, generally, to be able to sell large volumes, price per unit tends to fall.

**Weaknesses of BE analysis**

- There are non-linear relationships between costs, revenues and volume.
- There may be stepped fixed costs. Most fixed costs are not fixed over all volumes of activity.
- Multi-product businesses have problems in allocating fixed costs to particular activities.

**Marginal analysis (ignores fixed costs where these are not affected by the decision)**

- Assessing contracts – we consider only the effect on contributions.
- Using scarce resources – the limiting factor is most effectively used by maximising its contribution per unit.
- Make-or-buy decisions – we take the action that leads to the highest total contributions.
- Closing/continuing an activity – should be assessed by net effect on total contributions.

# MyAccountingLab

Go to **www.myaccountinglab.com** to check your understanding of the chapter, create a personalised study plan, and maximise your revision time

## Key terms

fixed cost  p. 320
variable cost  p. 320
stepped fixed cost  p. 322
semi-fixed (semi-variable) cost  p. 323
high-low method  p. 324
break-even analysis  p. 325
break-even chart  p. 326
break-even point (BEP)  p. 326
contribution per unit  p. 331

contribution margin ratio  p. 331
margin of safety  p. 332
operating gearing  p. 335
profit–volume (PV) chart  p. 337
economies of scale  p. 338
relevant range  p. 339
marginal analysis  p. 344
marginal cost  p. 344
outsourcing  p. 349

## Further reading

If you would like to explore the topics covered in this chapter in more depth, we recommend the following books:

Drury, C., *Management and Cost Accounting*, 8th edn, Cengage Learning, 2012, chapter 8.

Hilton, R., *Managerial Accounting*, 9th edn, McGraw-Hill Higher Education, 2011, chapter 14.

Horngren, C., Datar, S. and Rajan, M., *Cost Accounting: A Managerial Emphasis*, 14th edn, Prentice Hall International, 2011, chapter 3.

McWatters, C., Zimmerman, J. and Morse, D., *Management Accounting: Analysis and Interpretation*, Financial Times Prentice Hall, 2008, chapter 5.

## Review questions

**Solutions to these questions can be found at the back of the book on pages 752 to 753.**

**9.1** Define the terms *fixed cost* and *variable cost*. Explain how an understanding of the distinction between fixed cost and variable cost can be useful to managers.

**9.2** What is meant by the *BEP* for an activity? How is the BEP calculated? Why is it useful to know the BEP?

**9.3** When we say that some business activity has *high operating gearing*, what do we mean? What are the implications for the business of high operating gearing?

**9.4** If there is a scarce resource that is restricting sales, how will the business maximise its profit? Explain the logic of the approach that you have identified for maximising profit.

## Exercises

**Exercises 9.1, and 9.2 are basic level, 9.3, 9.4 and 9.5 are intermediate level and 9.6 and 9.7 are advanced level. Those with coloured numbers have solutions at the back of the book, starting on page 776.**

**If you wish to try more exercises, visit the students' side of the Companion Website and MyAccountingLab.**

**9.1** Motormusic Ltd makes a standard model of car radio, which it sells to car manufacturers for £60 each. Next year the business plans to make and sell 20,000 radios. The business's costs are as follows:

*Manufacturing*

| | |
|---|---|
| Variable materials | £20 per radio |
| Variable labour | £14 per radio |
| Other variable costs | £12 per radio |
| Fixed cost | £80,000 per year |

*Administration and selling*

| | |
|---|---|
| Variable | £3 per radio |
| Fixed | £60,000 per year |

*Required*:

(a) Calculate the break-even point for next year, expressed both in quantity of radios and sales value.

(b) Calculate the margin of safety for next year, expressed both in quantity of radios and sales value.

**9.2** Lannion and Co. is engaged in providing and marketing a standard advice service. Summarised results for the past two months reveal the following:

|  | October | November |
|---|---|---|
| Sales (units of the service) | 200 | 300 |
| Sales revenue (£) | 5,000 | 7,500 |
| Operating profit (£) | 1,000 | 2,200 |

There were no price changes of any description during these two months.

*Required*:

(a) Deduce the BEP (in units of the service) for Lannion and Co.

(b) State why the business might find it useful to know its BEP.

**9.3** Gandhi Ltd renders a promotional service to small retailing businesses. There are three levels of service: the 'Basic', the 'Standard' and the 'Comprehensive'. On the basis of past experience, the business plans next year to work at absolute full capacity as follows:

| Service | Number of units of the service | Selling price | Variable cost per unit |
|---|---|---|---|
|  |  | £ | £ |
| Basic | 11,000 | 50 | 25 |
| Standard | 6,000 | 80 | 65 |
| Comprehensive | 16,000 | 120 | 90 |

The business's fixed cost totals £660,000 a year. Each service takes about the same length of time, irrespective of the level.

One of the accounts staff has just produced a report that seems to show that the Standard service is unprofitable. The relevant extract from the report is as follows:

**Standard service cost analysis**

|  | £ |  |
|---|---|---|
| Selling price per unit | 80 |  |
| Variable cost per unit | (65) |  |
| Fixed cost per unit | (20) | (£660,000/(11,000 + 6,000 + 16,000)) |
| Loss | (5) |  |

The writer of the report suggests that the business should not offer the Standard service next year.

*Required*:

(a) Should the Standard service be offered next year, assuming that the quantity of the other services could not be expanded to use the spare capacity?

(b) Should the Standard service be offered next year, assuming that the released capacity could be used to render a new service, the 'Nova', for which customers would be charged £75, and which would have variable cost of £50 and take twice as long as the other three services?

(c) What is the minimum price that could be accepted for the Basic service, assuming that the necessary capacity to expand it will come only from not offering the Standard service?

**9.4** The management of a business is concerned about its inability to obtain enough fully trained labour to enable it to meet its present budget projection.

| Service: | Alpha £000 | Beta £000 | Gamma £000 | Total £000 |
|---|---|---|---|---|
| Variable costs | | | | |
| Materials | 6 | 4 | 5 | 15 |
| Labour | 9 | 6 | 12 | 27 |
| Expenses | 3 | 2 | 2 | 7 |
| Allocated fixed costs | 6 | 15 | 12 | 33 |
| Total cost | 24 | 27 | 31 | 82 |
| Profit | 15 | 2 | 2 | 19 |
| Sales revenue | 39 | 29 | 33 | 101 |

The amount of labour likely to be available amounts to £20,000. All of the variable labour is paid at the same hourly rate. You have been asked to prepare a statement of plans, ensuring that at least 50 per cent of the budgeted sales revenues are achieved for each service and the balance of labour is used to produce the greatest profit.

*Required*:
(a) Prepare the statement, with explanations, showing the greatest profit available from the limited amount of skilled labour available, within the constraint stated. *Hint*: Remember that all labour is paid at the same rate.
(b) What steps could the business take in an attempt to improve profitability, in the light of the labour shortage?

**9.5** A hotel group prepares financial statements on a quarterly basis. The senior management is reviewing the performance of one hotel and making plans for next year.

The managers have in front of them the results for this year (based on some actual results and some forecasts to the end of this year):

| Quarter | Sales revenue £000 | Profit/(loss) £000 |
|---|---|---|
| 1 | 400 | (280) |
| 2 | 1,200 | 360 |
| 3 | 1,600 | 680 |
| 4 | 800 | 40 |
| Total | 4,000 | 800 |

The total estimated number of guests (guest nights) for this year is 50,000, with each guest night being charged at the same rate. The results follow a regular pattern; there are no unexpected cost fluctuations beyond the seasonal trading pattern shown above.

For next year, management anticipates an increase in unit variable cost of 10 per cent and a profit target for the hotel of £1 million. These will be incorporated into its plans.

*Required*:
(a) Calculate the total variable and total fixed cost of the hotel for this year. Show the provisional annual results for this year in total, showing variable and fixed cost separately. Show also the revenue and cost per guest.
(b) i If there is no increase in guests for next year, what will be the required revenue rate per hotel guest to meet the profit target?
   ii If the required revenue rate per guest is not raised above this year's level, how many guests will be required to meet the profit target?
(c) Outline and briefly discuss the assumptions that are made in typical PV or break-even analysis, and assess whether they limit its usefulness.

**9.6** A business makes three products, A, B and C. All three products require the use of two types of machine: cutting machines and assembling machines. Estimates for next year include the following:

| Product | A | B | C |
|---|---|---|---|
| Selling price (£ per unit) | 25 | 30 | 18 |
| Sales demand (units) | 2,500 | 3,400 | 5,100 |
| Material cost (£ per unit) | 12 | 13 | 10 |
| Variable production cost (£ per unit) | 7 | 4 | 3 |
| Time required per unit on cutting machines (hours) | 1.0 | 1.0 | 0.5 |
| Time required per unit on assembling machines (hours) | 0.5 | 1.0 | 0.5 |

Fixed cost for next year is expected to total £42,000.

The business has cutting machine capacity of 5,000 hours a year and assembling machine capacity of 8,000 hours a year.

*Required*:
(a) State, with supporting workings, which products in which quantities the business should plan to make next year on the basis of the above information. *Hint*: First determine which machines will be a limiting factor (scarce resource).
(b) State the maximum price per product that it would be worth the business paying to a subcontractor to carry out that part of the work that could not be done internally.

**9.7** Darmor Ltd has three products, which require the same production facilities. Information about the production cost for one unit of its products is as follows:

| Product | X | Y | Z |
|---|---|---|---|
| | £ | £ | £ |
| Labour: Skilled | 6 | 9 | 3 |
| Unskilled | 2 | 4 | 10 |
| Materials | 12 | 25 | 14 |
| Other variable costs | 3 | 7 | 7 |
| Fixed cost | 5 | 10 | 10 |

All labour and materials are variable costs. Skilled labour is paid £12 an hour and unskilled labour is paid £8 an hour. All references to labour cost above are based on basic rates of pay. Skilled labour is scarce, which means that the business could sell more than the maximum that it is able to make of any of the three products.

Product X is sold in a regulated market and the regulators have set a price of £30 per unit for it.

*Required*:
(a) State, with supporting workings, the price that must be charged for Products Y and Z, such that the business would find it equally profitable to make and sell any of the three products.
(b) State, with supporting workings, the maximum rate of overtime premium that the business would logically be prepared to pay its skilled workers to work beyond the basic time.

# Full costing

## Introduction

Full (absorption) costing is a widely used approach that takes account of all of the cost of producing a particular product or service. In this chapter, we shall see how this approach can be used to deduce the cost of some activity, such as making a unit of product (for example, a tin of baked beans), providing a unit of service (for example, a car repair), or creating a facility (for example, building an Olympic athletics stadium). The precise approach taken to deducing full cost will depend on whether each product or service is identical to the next or whether each job has its own individual characteristics. It will also depend on whether the business accounts for overheads on a segmental basis. We shall look at how full (or absorption) costing is carried out and we shall also consider its usefulness for management purposes.

This chapter considers the traditional, but still very widely used, form of full costing. In Chapter 11 we shall consider activity-based costing, which is a more recently developed approach.

## Learning outcomes

**When you have completed this chapter, you should be able to:**

- Deduce the full (absorption) cost of a cost unit in a single-product environment.

- Deduce the full (absorption) cost of a cost unit in a multi-product environment.

- Discuss the problems of deducing full (absorption) cost in practice.

- Discuss the usefulness of full (absorption) cost information to managers.

## MyAccountingLab

Visit **www.myaccountinglab.com** for practice and revision opportunities

## Why do managers want to know the full cost?

As we saw in Chapter 1, the only point in providing management accounting information is to help managers make more informed decisions. There are broadly four areas where managers use information concerning the full cost of the business's products or services. These are:

- *Pricing and output decisions.* Having full cost information can help managers to make decisions on the price to be charged to customers for the business's products or services. Linked to the pricing decisions are also decisions on the number of units of a product or service that the business should seek to provide to the market.
- *Exercising control.* Managers need information to help them make decisions that seek to ensure that the organisation's plans are met. Budgets are typically expressed in full cost terms. This means that periodic reports that compare actual performance with budgets need to be expressed in the same full cost terms.
- *Assessing relative efficiency.* Full cost information can help managers compare the cost of doing something in a particular way, or particular place, with its cost if done in a different way, or place. For example, a motor car manufacturer may find it useful to compare the cost of building a particular model of car in one of its plants, rather than another. This could help the business decide on where to locate future production.
- *Assessing performance.* The level of profit, or income, generated over a period is an important measure of business performance. To measure profit, or income, we need to compare sales revenue with the associated expenses. Where a business produces a product or renders a service, a major expense will be the cost of making the product or rendering the service. Usually, this expense is based on the full cost of whatever is sold. Measuring income provides managers (and other users) with information that can help them make a whole range of decisions.

Later in the chapter we shall consider some of the issues surrounding these four purposes.

Figure 10.1 shows the four uses of full cost information.

**Figure 10.1**    **Uses of full cost by managers**

Managers use full cost information for four main purposes.

Now let us consider **Real World 10.1**.

## Real World 10.1

### Operating cost

An interesting example of the use of full cost for pricing decisions occurs in the National Health Service (NHS). In recent years, the funding of hospitals has radically changed. A new system of Payment by Results (PBR) requires the Department of Health to produce a list of prices for an in-patient spell in hospital that covers different types of procedures. This list, which is revised annually, reflects the prices that hospitals will be paid by the government for carrying out the different procedures.

For 2011/12, the price list included the following figures:

- £5,365 for carrying out a hip replacement;
- £5,902 for carrying out a knee replacement.

These figures are based on the full cost of undertaking each type of procedure in 2009/10 (but adjusted for inflation and an efficiency discount). Full cost figures were submitted by all NHS hospitals for that year as part of their annual accounting process and an average for each type of procedure was then calculated. Figures for other procedures on the price list were derived in the same way.

*Source*: 'Payment by Results, Guidance for 2011/12', Department of Health, 18 February 2011, p. 60.

When considering the information in Real World 10.1, an important question that arises is 'what does the full cost of each type of procedure include?' Does it simply include the cost of the salaries earned by doctors and nurses during the time spent with the patient or does it also include the cost of other items? If the cost of other items is included, how is it determined? Would it include, for example, a charge for:

- the artificial hip and drugs provided for the patient;
- equipment used in the operating theatre;
- administrative and support staff within the hospital;
- heating and lighting;
- maintaining the hospital buildings;
- laundry and cleaning?

If the cost of such items is included, how can an appropriate charge for each procedure be determined? If, on the other hand, it is not included, are the figures of £5,365 and £5,902 potentially misleading?

These questions are the subject of this chapter.

## What is full costing?

**Full cost** is the total amount of resources, usually measured in monetary terms, sacrificed to achieve a given objective. It takes account of all resources sacrificed to achieve that objective. Thus, if the objective were to supply a customer with a product or service, the cost of all aspects relating to the making of the product or provision of the service would be included as part of the full cost. To derive the full cost figure, we must accumulate the elements of cost incurred and then assign them to the particular product or service.

The logic of **full costing** is that the entire cost of running a facility, say an office, is part of the cost of the output of that office. For example, the rent may be a cost that will not alter merely because we provide one more unit of the service. If the office were not rented, however, there would be nowhere for the staff to work, so rent is an important element of the cost of that service. A **cost unit** is one unit of whatever is having its cost determined. This is usually one unit of output of a particular product or service.

In the sections that follow we shall firstly see how full costing is applied to a single-product business and then for a multi-product one.

## Single-product businesses

The simplest case for which to deduce the full cost per unit is where the business has only one product or service, that is, each unit of its production is identical. Here it is simply a question of adding up all of the elements of cost of production incurred in a particular period (materials, labour, rent, fuel, power, and so on) and dividing this total by the total number of units of output for that period.

### Activity 10.1

Fruitjuice Ltd has just one product, a sparkling orange drink that is marketed as 'Orange Fizz'. During last month the business produced 7,300 litres of the drink. The cost incurred was made up as follows:

|  | £ |
|---|---|
| Ingredients (oranges and so on) | 390 |
| Fuel | 85 |
| Rent of accommodation | 350 |
| Depreciation of equipment | 75 |
| Labour | 880 |

What is the full cost per litre of producing 'Orange Fizz'?

This figure is found simply by adding together all of the elements of cost incurred and then dividing by the number of litres produced:

$$£(390 + 85 + 350 + 75 + 880)/7{,}300 = £0.24 \text{ per litre}$$

In practice, there can be problems in deciding exactly how much cost was incurred. In the case of Fruitjuice Ltd, for example, how is the cost of depreciation deduced? It is certainly an estimate and so its reliability is open to question. The cost of raw materials may also be a problem. Should we use the 'relevant' cost of the raw materials (in this case, almost certainly the replacement cost), or the actual price paid for it (historic cost)? If the cost per litre is to be used for some decision-making purpose (which it should be), the replacement cost is probably more logical. In practice, however, it seems that historic cost is more often used to deduce full cost. It is not clear why this should be the case.

There can also be problems in deciding precisely how many units of output were produced. If making Orange Fizz is not a very fast process, some of the drink will probably be in the process of being made at any given moment. This, in turn, means that some of the cost incurred last month was for some Orange Fizz that was work in progress at the end of the month, so is not included in last month's output quantity of 7,300 litres. Similarly, part of the 7,300 litres might well have been started and incurred cost in the previous month, yet all of those litres were included in the 7,300 litres that we used in our calculation of the cost per litre. Work in progress is not a serious problem, but some adjustment for the value of opening and closing work in progress for the particular period needs to be made if reliable full cost information is to be obtained.

This approach to full costing, which can be taken where all of the output consists of identical, or near identical items (of goods or services), is often referred to as **process costing**.

## Multi-product businesses

Most businesses produce more than one type of product or service. In this situation, the units of output of the product, or service, will not be identical and so the approach used with litres of 'Orange Fizz' in Activity 10.1 is inappropriate. While it is reasonable to assign an identical cost to units of output that are identical, it is not reasonable to do this where the units of output are obviously different. It would not be reasonable, for example, to assign the same cost to each car repair carried out by a garage, irrespective of the complexity and size of the repair.

### Direct and indirect cost

To provide full cost information, we need to have a systematic approach to accumulating the elements of cost and then assigning this total cost to particular cost units on some reasonable basis. Where cost units are not identical, the starting point is to separate cost into two categories: direct cost and indirect cost.

- **Direct cost**. This is the type of cost that can be identified with specific cost units. That is to say, the effect of the cost can be measured in respect of each particular cost unit. The main examples of a direct cost are direct materials and direct labour. Thus, in determining the cost of a motor car repair by a garage, both the cost of spare parts used in the repair and the cost of the mechanic's time would be part of the direct cost of that repair. Collecting elements of direct cost is a simple matter of having a cost-recording system that is capable of capturing the cost of direct materials used on each job and the cost, based on the hours worked and the rate of pay, of direct workers.
- **Indirect cost** (or **overheads**). This is all other elements of cost, that is, those items that cannot be directly measured in respect of each particular cost unit (job). Thus, the amount paid to rent the garage would be an indirect cost of a motor car repair.

We shall use the terms 'indirect cost' and 'overheads' interchangeably for the remainder of this book. Indirect cost is also sometimes known as **common cost** because it is common to all of the output of the production unit (for example, factory or department) for the period.

**Real World 10.2** gives some indication of the relative importance of direct and indirect costs in practice.

## Real World 10.2

### Counting the cost

A fairly recent survey of 176 UK businesses operating in various industries, all with an annual turnover of more than £50 million, was conducted by Al-Omiri and Drury. They discovered that the full cost of the businesses' output on average is split between direct and indirect costs as shown in Figure 10.2:

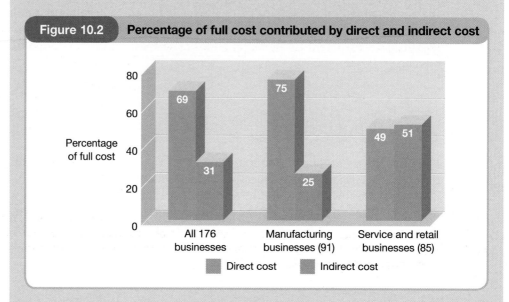

**Figure 10.2**  **Percentage of full cost contributed by direct and indirect cost**

For the manufacturers, the 75 per cent direct cost was, on average, made up as follows:

|                    | *Per cent* |
|--------------------|:----------:|
| Direct materials   | 52         |
| Direct labour      | 14         |
| Other direct costs | 9          |

*Source*: 'A survey of factors influencing the choice of product costing systems in UK organisations', M. Al-Omiri and C. Drury, *Management Accounting Research*, December 2007, p. 399–424.

## Activity (10.2)

A garage bases its prices on the direct cost of each job (car repair) that it carries out. How could the garage collect the direct cost (labour and materials) information concerning a particular job?

Usually, direct workers are required to record how long was spent on each job. Thus, the mechanic doing the job would record the length of time worked on the car by direct workers (that is the mechanic concerned and any colleagues). The stores staff would normally be required to keep a record of the cost of parts and materials used on each job.

A 'job sheet' will normally be prepared – perhaps on the computer – for each individual job. Staff would need to get into the routine of faithfully recording all elements of direct labour and materials applied to the job.

## Job costing

The term **job costing** is used to describe the way in which we identify the full cost per cost unit (unit of output or 'job') where the cost units differ. To deduce the full cost of a particular cost unit, we first identify the direct cost of the cost unit, which, by the definition of direct cost, is fairly straightforward. We then seek to 'charge' each cost unit with a fair share of indirect cost (overheads). Put another way, cost units will absorb overheads. This leads to full costing also being called **absorption costing**. The absorption process is shown graphically in Figure 10.3.

**Figure 10.3**    **The relationship between direct cost and indirect cost**

Direct cost of the unit

Fair share of indirect cost (overheads)

**Full cost of the unit**

The full cost of any particular job is the sum of those cost elements that can be measured specifically in respect of the job (direct cost) and a share of the cost of creating the environment in which production (of a product or service) can take place, but which do not relate specifically to any particular job (indirect cost).

### Activity 10.3

Sparky Ltd is a business that employs a number of electricians. The business undertakes a range of work for its customers, from replacing fuses to installing complete wiring systems in new houses.

In respect of a particular job done by Sparky Ltd, into which category (direct or indirect) would each of the following cost elements fall:

- the wages of the electrician who did the job;
- depreciation of the tools used by the electrician;
- the cost of cable and other materials used on the job;
- rent of the building where Sparky Ltd stores its inventories of cable and other materials?

The electrician's wages earned while working on the particular job and the cost of the materials used on the job are included in direct cost. This is because it is possible to measure how much time was spent on the particular job (and therefore its direct labour cost) and the amount of materials used (and therefore the direct material cost) in the job.

The others are included in the general cost of running the business and, as such, must form part of the indirect cost of doing the job. They cannot be directly measured in respect of the particular job, however.

It is important to note that whether a cost is direct or indirect depends on the item being costed – the cost objective. To refer to indirect cost without identifying the cost objective is incorrect.

Naturally, broader-reaching cost objectives, such as operating Sparky Ltd for a month, tend to include a higher proportion of direct cost than do more limited ones, such as a particular job done by Sparky Ltd. As we shall see shortly, this makes costing broader cost objectives rather more straightforward than costing narrower ones. It is generally the case that direct cost is easier to deal with than indirect cost.

## Full (absorption) costing and the behaviour of cost

We saw in Chapter 9 that the full cost of doing something (or total cost, as it is usually known in the context of marginal analysis) can be analysed between the fixed and the variable elements. This is illustrated in Figure 10.4.

**Figure 10.4    The relationship between fixed cost, variable cost and total cost**

The total cost of a job is the sum of the cost that remains the same irrespective of the level of activity (fixed cost) and that which varies according to the level of activity (variable cost).

The apparent similarity of what is shown in Figure 10.4 to that depicted in Figure 10.3 seems to lead some to believe that variable cost and direct cost are the same, and that fixed cost and indirect cost (overheads) are the same. This is incorrect.

The notions of fixed and variable are concerned with **cost behaviour** in the face of changes in the volume of activity. The notions of direct and indirect, on the other hand, are concerned with the extent to which cost elements can be measured in respect of particular cost units (jobs). The two sets of notions are entirely different. Though it may be true that there is a tendency for fixed cost elements to be indirect (overheads) and for variable cost elements to be direct, there is no link, and there are many exceptions to this tendency. Most activities, for example, have variable indirect cost. Furthermore, labour is a significant element of direct cost in most types of business activity (14 per cent of the total cost of manufacture – see Real World 10.2) but it is usually a fixed cost.

The relationship between the reaction of cost to volume changes (cost behaviour), on the one hand, and how cost elements need to be gathered to deduce the full cost (cost collection), on the other, in respect of a particular job is shown in Figure 10.5.

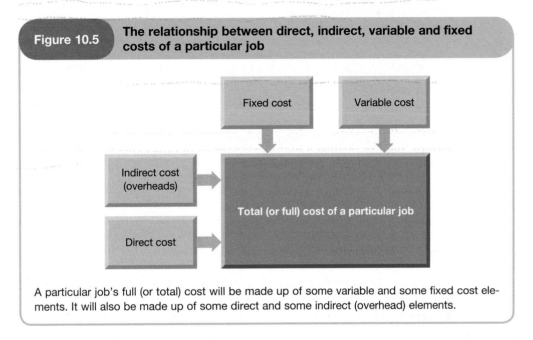

**Figure 10.5**   **The relationship between direct, indirect, variable and fixed costs of a particular job**

A particular job's full (or total) cost will be made up of some variable and some fixed cost elements. It will also be made up of some direct and some indirect (overhead) elements.

Total cost is the sum of direct and indirect costs. It is also the sum of fixed and variable costs. These two facts are independent of one another. Thus a particular element of cost may be fixed, but that tells us nothing about whether it is a direct or an indirect cost.

## The problem of indirect cost

It is worth emphasising that the distinction between direct and indirect cost is only important in a job-costing environment, that is, where units of output differ. When we were considering costing a litre of 'Orange Fizz' drink in Activity 10.1, whether particular elements of cost were direct or indirect was of no consequence, because all elements of cost were shared equally between the individual litres of 'Orange Fizz'. Where we have units of output that are not identical, however, we have to look more closely at the make-up of the cost to achieve a fair measure of the full cost of a particular job.

Although the indirect cost of any activity must form part of the cost of each cost unit, it cannot, by definition, be directly related to individual cost units. This raises a major practical issue: how is the indirect cost to be apportioned to individual cost units?

## Overheads as service renderers

It is reasonable to view the indirect cost (overheads) as rendering a service to the cost units. Take for example a legal case, undertaken by a firm of solicitors for a particular client. This job can be seen as being rendered a service by the office in which the work is done. In this sense, it is reasonable to charge each case (cost unit) with a share of the cost of running the office (rent, lighting, heating, cleaning, building maintenance, and so on). It also seems reasonable to relate the charge for the 'use' of the office to the level of service that the particular case has received from the office.

The next step is the difficult one. How might the cost of running the office, which is a cost of all work done by the firm, be divided between individual cases that are not similar in size and complexity?

One possibility is sharing this overhead cost equally between each case handled by the firm within the period. This method, however, has little to commend it unless the cases were close to being identical in terms of the extent to which they had 'benefited' from the overheads.

If we are not to propose equal shares, we must identify something observable and measurable about the cases that we feel provides a reasonable basis for distinguishing between one case and the next. In practice, time spent working on each particular cost unit by direct labour is the most popular basis. It must be stressed that this is not the 'correct' way and it certainly is not the only way.

## Job costing: a worked example

To see how job costing works, let us consider Example 10.1.

### Example 10.1

Johnson Ltd, a business that provides a personal computer maintenance and repair service, has overheads of £10,000 each month. Each month 1,000 direct labour hours are worked and charged to cost units (jobs carried out by the business). A particular PC repair undertaken by the business used direct materials costing £15. Direct labour worked on the repair was 3 hours and the wage rate is £16 an hour. Johnson Ltd charges overheads to jobs on a direct labour hour basis. What is the full (absorption) cost of the repair?

### Solution

First, let us establish the **overhead absorption (recovery) rate**, that is, the rate at which individual repairs will be charged with overheads. This is £10 (that is, £10,000/1,000) per direct labour hour.

Thus, the full cost of the repair is:

|                          |   £  |
|--------------------------|-----:|
|                          |   £  |
| Direct materials         |   15 |
| Direct labour (3 × £16)  |   48 |
|                          |   63 |
| Overheads (3 × £10)      |   30 |
| Full cost of the job     |   93 |

Note, in Example 10.1, that the number of labour hours (3 hours) appears twice in deducing the full cost: once to deduce the direct labour cost and a second time to deduce the overheads to be charged to the repair. These are really two separate issues, though they are both based on the same number of labour hours.

Note also that, if all the jobs undertaken during the month are assigned overheads in a similar manner, all £10,000 of overheads will be charged to the jobs between them. Jobs that involve a lot of direct labour will be assigned a large share of overheads. Similarly, jobs that involve little direct labour will be assigned a small share of overheads.

## Activity (10.5)

Can you think of reasons why direct labour hours tend to be regarded as the most logical basis for sharing overheads between cost units?

The reasons that occurred to us are as follows:

- Large jobs should logically attract large amounts of overheads because they are likely to have been rendered more 'service' by the overheads than small ones. The length of time that they are worked on by direct labour may be seen as a rough way of measuring relative size, though other means of doing this may be found – for example, relative physical size, where the cost unit is a physical object, like a manufactured product.
- Most overheads are related to time. Rent, heating, lighting, non-current asset depreciation, supervisors' and managers' salaries, which are all typical overheads, are all more or less time-based. That is to say that the overheads for one week tend to be about half of those for a similar two-week period. Thus, a basis of allotting overheads to jobs that takes account of the length of time that the units of output benefited from the 'service' rendered by the overheads seems logical.
- Direct labour hours are capable of being measured for each job. They will normally be measured to deduce the direct labour element of cost in any case. Thus, a direct labour hour basis of dealing with overheads is practical to apply in the real world.

It cannot be emphasised enough that there is no 'correct' way to allot overheads to jobs. Overheads, by definition, do not naturally relate to individual jobs. If, nevertheless, we wish to take account of the fact that overheads are part of the cost of all jobs, we must find some acceptable way of including a share of the total overheads in each job. If a particular means of doing this is accepted by those who use the full cost deduced, then the method is as good as any other method. Accounting is concerned only with providing useful information to decision makers. In practice, the method that seems to be regarded as being the most useful is the direct labour hour method. Real World 10.4, which we shall consider later in the chapter, provides some evidence of this.

Now let us consider **Real World 10.3**, which gives an example of one well-known organisation that does not use direct labour hours to cost its output.

## Real World 10.3

### Operating cost

As we saw in Real World 10.1 the UK National Health Service (NHS) seeks to ascertain the cost of various medical and surgical procedures that it undertakes for its patients. In determining the costs of a procedure that requires time in hospital as an 'in patient', the NHS identifies the total direct cost of the particular procedure (staff time, medication, and so on). To this it adds a share of the hospital overheads. The total overheads are absorbed by individual procedures by taking this overheads total and dividing it by the number of 'bed days' throughout the hospital for the period, to establish a 'bed-day rate'. A bed day is one patient spending one day occupying a bed in the hospital. To cost the procedure for a particular patient, the bed-day rate is applied to the cost of the procedure according to how many bed days the particular patient had.

Note that the NHS does not use the direct labour hour basis of absorption. The bed-day rate is also, however, an alternative, logical, time-based approach.

*Source: NHS Costing Manual 2010/11, Department of Health Gateway reference 15,969, 3 May 2011.*

## Activity (10.6)

Marine Suppliers Ltd undertakes a range of work, including making sails for small sailing boats on a made-to-measure basis.

The business expects the following to arise during the next month:

| | |
|---|---:|
| Direct labour cost | £60,000 |
| Direct labour time | 6,000 hours |
| Indirect labour cost | £9,000 |
| Depreciation of machinery | £3,000 |
| Rent | £5,000 |
| Heating, lighting and power | £2,000 |
| Machine time | 2,000 hours |
| Indirect materials | £500 |
| Other miscellaneous indirect production cost elements (overheads) | £200 |
| Direct materials cost | £3,000 |

The business has received an enquiry about a sail. It is estimated that the particular sail will take 12 direct labour hours to make and will require 20 square metres of sailcloth, which costs £2 per square metre.

The business normally uses a direct labour hour basis of charging indirect cost (overheads) to individual jobs.

What is the full (absorption) cost of making the sail?

The direct cost of making the sail can be identified as follows:

| | £ |
|---|---:|
| Direct materials (20 × £2) | 40.00 |
| Direct labour (12 × (£60,000/6,000)) | 120.00 |
| | 160.00 |

To deduce the indirect cost (overhead) element that must be added to derive the full cost of the sail, we first need to total these cost elements as follows:

| | £ |
|---|---:|
| Indirect labour | 9,000 |
| Depreciation | 3,000 |
| Rent | 5,000 |
| Heating, lighting and power | 2,000 |
| Indirect materials | 500 |
| Other miscellaneous indirect production cost (overhead) elements | 200 |
| Total indirect cost (overheads) | 19,700 |

Since the business uses a direct labour hour basis of charging indirect cost to jobs, we need to deduce the indirect cost (or overhead) recovery rate per direct labour hour. This is simply:

£19,700/6,000 = £3.28 per direct labour hour

Thus, the full cost of the sail would be expected to be:

| | £ |
|---|---:|
| Direct materials (20 × £2) | 40.00 |
| Direct labour (12 × (£60,000/6,000)) | 120.00 |
| Indirect cost (12 × £3.28) | 39.36 |
| Full cost | 199.36 |

Figure 10.6 shows the process for applying indirect (overhead) and direct costs to the sail that was the subject of Activity 10.6.

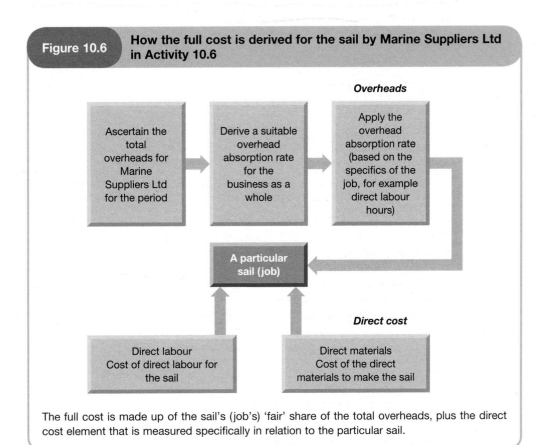

**Figure 10.6** How the full cost is derived for the sail by Marine Suppliers Ltd in Activity 10.6

The full cost is made up of the sail's (job's) 'fair' share of the total overheads, plus the direct cost element that is measured specifically in relation to the particular sail.

## Activity 10.7

Suppose that Marine Suppliers Ltd (see Activity 10.6) used a machine hour basis of charging overheads to jobs. What would be the cost of the job detailed if it was expected to take 5 machine hours (as well as 12 direct labour hours)?

The total overheads of the business will of course be the same irrespective of the method of charging them to jobs. Thus, the overhead recovery rate, on a machine hour basis, will be:

£19,700/2,000 = £9.85 per machine hour

Thus, the full cost of the sail would be expected to be:

|  | £ |
|---|---|
| Direct materials (20 × £2) | 40.00 |
| Direct labour (12 × (£60,000/6,000)) | 120.00 |
| Indirect cost (5 × £9.85) | 49.25 |
| Full cost | 209.25 |

## Selecting a basis for charging overheads

We saw earlier that there is no single correct way of charging overheads. The final choice is a matter of judgement. It seems reasonable to say, however, that the nature of the overheads should influence the choice of the basis of charging the overheads to jobs. Where production is capital-intensive and overheads are primarily machine-based (such as depreciation, machine maintenance, power, and so on), machine hours might be favoured. Otherwise direct labour hours might be preferred.

It would be irrational to choose one of these bases in preference to the other simply because it apportions either a higher or a lower amount of overheads to a particular job. The total overheads will be the same irrespective of the method of dividing that total between individual jobs and so a method that gives a higher share of overheads to one particular job must give a lower share to the remaining jobs. There is one cake of fixed size: if one person receives a relatively large slice, others must on average receive relatively small slices. To illustrate further this issue of apportioning overheads, consider Example 10.2.

### Example 10.2

A business, that provides a service, expects to incur overheads totalling £20,000 next month. The total direct labour time worked is expected to be 1,600 hours and machines are expected to operate for a total of 1,000 hours.

During the next month, the business expects to do just two large jobs. Information concerning each job is as follows:

|  | Job 1 | Job 2 |
|---|---|---|
| Direct labour hours | 800 | 800 |
| Machine hours | 700 | 300 |

How much of the total overheads will be charged to each job if overheads are to be charged on:

(a) a direct labour hour basis; and
(b) a machine hour basis?

What do you notice about the two sets of figures that you calculate?

### Solution

**(a) Direct labour hour basis**

Overhead recovery rate = £20,000/1,600 = £12.50 per direct labour hour.

Job 1    £12.50 × 800 = £10,000
Job 2    £12.50 × 800 = £10,000

**(b) Machine hour basis**

Overhead recovery rate = £20,000/1,000 = £20.00 per machine hour.

Job 1    £20.00 × 700 = £14,000
Job 2    £20.00 × 300 = £6,000

It is clear from these calculations that the total overheads charged to jobs is the same (that is, £20,000) whichever method is used. So, whereas the machine hour basis gives Job 1 a higher share than does the direct labour hour method, the opposite is true for Job 2.

It is not practical to charge overheads on one basis to one job and on the other basis to the other job. This is because either total overheads will not be fully charged to the jobs, or the jobs will be overcharged with overheads. For example, using the direct labour hour method for Job 1 (£10,000) and the machine hour basis for Job 2 (£6,000) will mean that only £16,000 of a total £20,000 of overheads will be charged to jobs. As a result, the objective of full (absorption) costing, which is to charge all overheads to jobs done, will not be achieved. In this particular case, if selling prices are based on full cost, the business may not charge high enough prices to cover all of its costs.

Figure 10.7 shows the effect of the two different bases of charging overheads to Jobs 1 and 2.

**Figure 10.7**  **The effect of different bases of charging overheads to jobs in Example 10.2**

Total overheads for month (£20,000)

Direct labour hour basis

Job 1 (£10,000)    Job 2 (£10,000)

Machine hour basis

Job 1 (£14,000)    Job 2 (£6,000)

The share of the total overheads for the month charged to jobs can differ significantly depending on the basis used.

## Activity 10.8

The point was made above that it would normally be irrational to prefer one basis of charging overheads to jobs simply because it apportions either a higher or a lower amount of overheads to a particular job. This is because the total overheads are the same irrespective of the method of charging the total to individual jobs. Can you think of any circumstances where it would not necessarily be so irrational?

This might apply where, for a particular job, a customer has agreed to pay a price based on full cost plus an agreed fixed percentage for profit. Here it would be beneficial to the producer for the total cost of the job to be as high as possible. This would be relatively unusual, but sometimes public sector organisations, particularly central and local government departments, have entered into contracts to have work done, with the price to be deduced, after the work has been completed, on a cost-plus basis. Such contracts are pretty rare these days, probably because they are open to abuse in the way described. Usually, contract prices are agreed in advance, typically in conjunction with competitive tendering.

**Real World 10.4** provides some insight into the basis of overhead recovery in practice.

## Real World 10.4

### Overhead recovery rates in practice

A survey of 129 UK manufacturing businesses, published in 2007, showed that the direct labour hour basis (or a close approximation to it) of charging indirect cost (overheads) to cost units was overwhelmingly the most popular. It was used by 72 per cent of the respondents.

The survey showed that 15 per cent of respondents used a 'production-time based overhead rate'. This is presumably something like a machine–hour rate.

Though this survey applied only to manufacturing businesses, in the absence of other information it provides some impression of what happens in practice.

*Source*: Based on information taken from 'Product costing practices in different manufacturing industries: A British survey', J. Brierley, C. Cowton and C. Drury, *International Journal of Management*, December 2007.

## Segmenting the overheads

As we have just seen, charging the same overheads to different jobs on different bases is not logical. It is perfectly reasonable, however, to charge one segment of the total overheads on one basis and another segment (or other segments) on another basis (or bases).

## Activity 10.9

Taking the same business as in Example 10.2 (page 372), on closer analysis we find that of the overheads totalling £20,000 next month, £8,000 relate to machines (depreciation, maintenance, rent of the space occupied by the machines, and so on) and the remaining £12,000 to more general overheads. The other information about the business is exactly as it was before.

How much of the total overheads will be charged to each job if the machine-related overheads are to be charged on a machine hour basis and the remaining overheads are charged on a direct labour hour basis?

*Direct labour hour basis*

> Overhead recovery rate = £12,000/1,600 = £7.50 per direct labour hour

*Machine hour basis*

> Overhead recovery rate = £8,000/1,000 = £8.00 per machine hour

*Overheads charged to jobs*

|  | Job 1 £ | Job 2 £ |
|---|---|---|
| Direct labour hour basis: |  |  |
| £7.50 × 800 | 6,000 |  |
| £7.50 × 800 |  | 6,000 |
| Machine hour basis: |  |  |
| £8.00 × 700 | 5,600 |  |
| £8.00 × 300 |  | 2,400 |
| Total | 11,600 | 8,400 |

We can see from this that the expected overheads of £20,000 are charged in total.

Segmenting the overheads in this way may well be seen as providing a better basis of charging overheads to jobs. This is quite often found in practice, usually by dividing a business into separate 'areas' (cost centres) for costing purposes, charging overheads differently from one area to the next, according to the nature of the work done in each.

## Dealing with overheads on a cost centre basis

In general, as we saw in Chapter 1, all but the smallest businesses are divided into departments. Normally, each department deals with a separate activity. The reasons for dividing a business into departments include the following:

- *Size and complexity.* Many businesses are too large and complex to be managed as a single unit. It is usually more practical to operate each business as a series of relatively independent units with each one having its own manager.
- *Expertise.* Each department normally has its own area of specialism and is managed by a specialist.
- *Accountability.* Each department can have its own accounting records that enable its performance to be assessed. This can lead to greater management control and motivation among the staff.

As is shown in Real World 10.5, which we shall consider shortly, most businesses charge overheads to cost units on a department-by-department basis. They do this because they expect that it will give rise to a more useful way of charging overheads. It is probably only in a minority of cases that it leads to any great improvement in the usefulness of the resulting full cost figures. Though it may not be of enormous benefit in many cases, applying overheads on a departmental basis it is probably not an expensive exercise. Since cost elements are collected department by department for other purposes (particularly control), to apply overheads on a department-by-department basis is a relatively simple matter.

We shall now take a look at how the departmental approach to deriving full cost works, in a service-industry context, through Example 10.3.

### Example 10.3

Autosparkle Ltd offers a motor vehicle paint-respray service. The jobs that it undertakes range from painting a small part of a saloon car, usually following a minor accident, to a complete respray of a double-decker bus.

Each job starts life in the Preparation Department, where it is prepared for the Paintshop. Here, the job is worked on by direct workers, in most cases taking some direct materials from the stores with which to treat the old paintwork and, generally, to render the vehicle ready for respraying. Thus the job will be charged with direct materials, direct labour and with a share of the Preparation Department's overheads. The job then passes into the Paintshop Department, already valued at the cost that it picked up in the Preparation Department.

In the Paintshop, the staff draw direct materials (mainly paint) from the stores and direct workers spend time respraying the job, using sophisticated spraying apparatus as well as working by hand. So, in the Paintshop, the job is charged with direct materials, direct labour and a share of that department's overheads. The job now passes into the Finishing Department, valued at the cost of the materials, labour and overheads that it accumulated in the first two departments.

→

In the Finishing Department, jobs are cleaned and polished ready to go back to the customers. Further direct labour and, in some cases, materials are added. All jobs also pick up a share of that department's overheads. The job, now complete, passes back to the customer.

Figure 10.8 shows graphically how this works for a particular job.

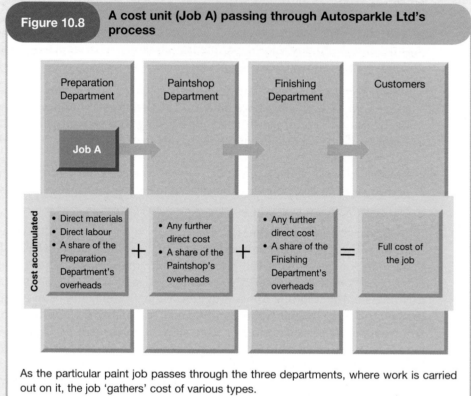

| Figure 10.8 | A cost unit (Job A) passing through Autosparkle Ltd's process |

As the particular paint job passes through the three departments, where work is carried out on it, the job 'gathers' cost of various types.

The approach to charging overheads to jobs (for example, direct labour hours) might be the same for all three departments, or it might be different from one department to another. It is possible that cost elements relating to the spraying apparatus dominate the Paintshop overhead cost, so the Paintshop's overheads might well be charged to jobs on a machine hour basis. The other two departments are probably labour intensive, so that direct labour hours may be seen as being appropriate there.

The passage of a job through the departments, picking up cost as it goes, can be compared to a snowball being rolled across snow: as it rolls, it picks up more and more snow.

Where cost determination is dealt with departmentally, each department is known as a **cost centre**. This can be defined as a particular physical area or some activity or function for which the cost is separately identified. Charging direct cost to jobs, in a departmental system, is exactly the same as where the whole business is one single cost centre. It is simply a matter of keeping a record of:

● the number of hours of direct labour worked on the particular job and the grade of labour, assuming that there are different grades with different rates of pay;

- the cost of the direct materials taken from stores and applied to the job; and
- any other direct cost elements, for example some subcontracted work, associated with the job.

This record keeping will normally be done cost centre by cost centre.

It is obviously necessary to break down the production overheads of the entire business on a cost centre basis. This means that the total overheads of the business must be divided between the cost centres, such that the sum of the overheads of all of the cost centres equals the overheads for the entire business. By charging all of their overheads to jobs, the cost centres will, between them, charge all of the overheads of the business to jobs. **Real World 10.5** provides an indication of the number of different cost centres that businesses tend to use in practice.

---

**Real World 10.5**

## Cost centres in practice

It is usual for businesses to have several cost centres. A fairly recent survey by Drury and Tayles of 186 larger UK businesses involved in various activities showed the following:

**Figure 10.9**    **Analysis of the number of cost centres within a business**

The survey of larger businesses shows, as might be expected, that they tend to have several cost centres.

---

We can see that 86 per cent of businesses surveyed had six or more cost centres and that 36 per cent of businesses had more than 20 cost centres. Though not shown on the diagram, 3 per cent of businesses surveyed had a single cost centre (that is, there was a business-wide or overall overhead rate used). Clearly, businesses that deal with overheads on a business-wide basis are relatively rare.

*Source*: Based on information taken from 'Profitability analysis in UK organisations', C. Drury and M. Tayles, *British Accounting Review*, December 2006.

For purposes of cost assignment, it is necessary to distinguish between **product cost centres** and **service cost centres.** Product cost centres are those in which jobs are worked on by direct workers and/or where direct materials are added. Here jobs can be charged with a share of their overheads. The Preparation, Paintshop and Finishing Departments, discussed above in Example 10.3, are all examples of product cost centres.

## Activity (10.10)

Can you guess what the definition of a service cost centre is?
Can you think of an example of a service cost centre?

A service cost centre is one where no direct cost is involved. It renders a service to other cost centres. Examples include:

- Cleaning
- Training
- Stores
- Maintenance
- Personnel
- Catering.

All of these render services to product cost centres and, possibly, to other service cost centres.

The service cost centre cost must be charged to product cost centres and become part of the product cost centres' overheads, so that those overheads can be recharged to jobs. This must be done so that all of the overheads of the business find their way into the cost of the jobs. If this is not achieved, the 'full' cost derived will not really be the full cost of the jobs.

Logically, the cost of a service cost centre should be charged to product cost centres on the basis of the level of service provided to the product cost centre concerned. Thus, a product cost centre that has a higher level of machine maintenance carried out should be charged with a larger share of the maintenance cost centre's (department's) cost.

The process of dividing overheads between cost centres is as follows:

- **Cost allocation.** Allocate indirect cost elements that are specific to particular cost centres. These are items that relate to, and are specifically measurable in respect of, individual cost centres, that is, they are part of the direct cost of running the cost centre. Examples include:
  - salaries of indirect workers whose activities are wholly within the cost centre, for example the salary of the cost centre manager;
  - rent, where the cost centre is housed in a building for which rent can be separately identified;
  - electricity, where it is separately metered for each cost centre.
- **Cost apportionment.** Apportion the more general overheads to the cost centres. These are overheads that relate to more than one cost centre, perhaps to them all. It would include:
  - rent, where more than one cost centre is housed in the same building;
  - electricity, where it is not separately metered;
  - salaries of cleaning staff who work in a variety of cost centres.

These overheads would be apportioned to cost centres on the basis of the extent to which each cost centre benefits from the overheads concerned. For example, the rent cost might be apportioned on the basis of the square metres of floor area occupied by each cost centre. With electricity used to power machinery, the basis of apportionment might be the level of mechanisation of each cost centre. As with charging overheads to individual jobs, there is no correct basis of apportioning general overheads to cost centres.

● Having totalled, allocated and apportioned the cost to all cost centres, it is necessary to apportion the total cost of service cost centres to product cost centres. Logically, the basis of apportionment should be the level of service rendered by the individual service cost centre to the individual production cost centre. With the personnel cost centre (department) cost, for example, the basis of apportionment might be the number of staff in each product cost centre, This is because, it could be argued that, the higher the number of staff, the more benefit the particular product cost centre would have derived from the personnel cost centre. This is, of course, rather a crude approach. A particular product cost centre may have severe personnel problems and a high staff-turnover rate, which may make it a user of the personnel service that is way out of proportion to the number of staff it employs.

The final total for each product cost centre will be charged to jobs as they pass through. The process of applying overheads to cost units on a cost centre (departmental) basis is shown in Figure 10.10.

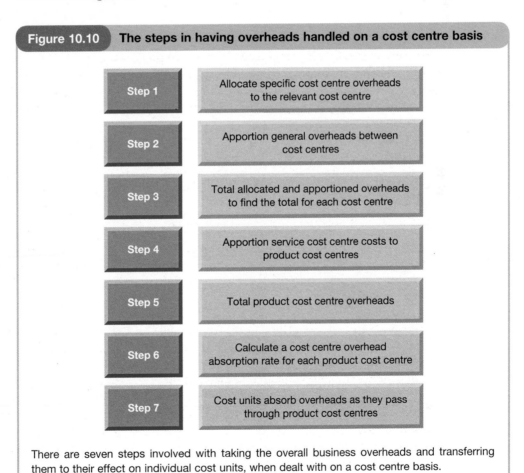

**Figure 10.10    The steps in having overheads handled on a cost centre basis**

Step 1 — Allocate specific cost centre overheads to the relevant cost centre

Step 2 — Apportion general overheads between cost centres

Step 3 — Total allocated and apportioned overheads to find the total for each cost centre

Step 4 — Apportion service cost centre costs to product cost centres

Step 5 — Total product cost centre overheads

Step 6 — Calculate a cost centre overhead absorption rate for each product cost centre

Step 7 — Cost units absorb overheads as they pass through product cost centres

There are seven steps involved with taking the overall business overheads and transferring them to their effect on individual cost units, when dealt with on a cost centre basis.

We shall now go on to consider Example 10.4, which deals with overheads on a cost centre (departmental) basis.

## Example 10.4

A business consists of four cost centres:

- Preparation department
- Machining department
- Finishing department
- Personnel and training (PT) department.

The first three are product cost centres and the last renders a service to the other three. The level of service rendered is thought to be roughly in proportion to the number of employees in each product cost centre.

Overheads, and other data, for next month are expected to be as follows:

|  | £000 |
|---|---|
| Rent | 10,000 |
| Electricity to power machines | 3,000 |
| Electricity for heating and lighting | 800 |
| Insurance of building | 200 |
| Cleaning | 600 |
| Depreciation of machines | 2,000 |
| Total monthly salaries of the indirect workers: | |
| Preparation department | 200 |
| Machining department | 240 |
| Finishing department | 180 |
| PT department | 180 |

The PT department has a staff consisting of only indirect workers (including managers). The other departments have both indirect workers (including managers) and direct workers. There are 100 indirect workers within each of the four departments and none does any 'direct' work.

Each direct worker is expected to work 160 hours next month. The number of direct workers in each department is:

| | |
|---|---|
| Preparation department | 600 |
| Machining department | 900 |
| Finishing department | 500 |

Machining department direct workers are paid £12 an hour; other direct workers are paid £10 an hour.

All of the machinery is in the machining department. Machines are expected to operate for 120,000 hours next month.

The floorspace (in square metres) occupied by the departments is as follows:

| | |
|---|---|
| Preparation department | 16,000 |
| Machining department | 20,000 |
| Finishing department | 10,000 |
| PT department | 2,000 |

Deducing the overheads, cost centre by cost centre, can be done, using a schedule, as follows:

| | Total £000 | Prep'n £000 | Mach'g £000 | Fin'g £000 | PT £000 |
|---|---|---|---|---|---|
| Allocated cost: | | | | | |
| Machine power | | 3,000 | 3,000 | | |
| Machine depreciation | | 2,000 | 2,000 | | |
| Indirect salaries | | 800 | 200 | 240 | 180 | 180 |
| Apportioned cost | | | | | |
| Rent | 10,000 | | | | |
| Heating and lighting | 800 | | | | |
| Insurance of buildings | 200 | | | | |
| Cleaning | 600 | | | | |
| Apportioned by floor area | | 11,600 | 3,867 | 4,833 | 2,417 | 483 |
| Cost centre overheads | | 17,400 | 4,067 | 10,073 | 2,597 | 663 |
| Reapportion PT cost by number of staff (including the indirect workers) | | | 202 | 288 | 173 | (663) |
| | | 17,400 | 4,269 | 10,361 | 2,770 | – |

## Activity 10.11

Assume that the machining department overheads (in Example 10.4) are to be charged to jobs on a machine hour basis, but that the direct labour hour basis is to be used for the other two departments. What will be the full (absorption) cost of a job with the following characteristics?

| | Preparation department | Machining department | Finishing department |
|---|---|---|---|
| Direct labour hours | 10 | 7 | 5 |
| Machine hours | – | 6 | – |
| Direct materials (£) | 85 | 13 | 6 |

*Hint*: This should be tackled as if each cost centre were a separate business, then departmental cost elements are added together for the job so as to arrive at the total full cost.

First, we need to deduce the indirect (overhead) recovery rates for each cost centre:

Preparation department (direct labour hour based):

$$\frac{£4,269,000}{600 \times 160} = £44.47$$

Machining department (machine hour based):

$$\frac{£10,361,000}{120,000} = £86.34$$

Finishing department (direct labour hour based):

$$\frac{£2,770,000}{500 \times 160} = £34.6\zeta$$

## Activity 10.11 (continued)

The cost of the job is as follows:

|  | £ | £ |
|---|---:|---:|
| Direct labour: |  |  |
| Preparation department (10 × £10) | 100.00 |  |
| Machining department (7 × £12) | 84.00 |  |
| Finishing department (5 × £10) | 50.00 |  |
|  |  | 234.00 |
| Direct materials: |  |  |
| Preparation department | 85.00 |  |
| Machining department | 13.00 |  |
| Finishing department | 6.00 |  |
|  |  | 104.00 |
| Overheads: |  |  |
| Preparation department (10 × £44.47) | 444.70 |  |
| Machining department (6 × £86.34) | 518.04 |  |
| Finishing department (5 × £34.63) | 173.15 |  |
|  |  | 1,135.89 |
| Full cost of the job |  | 1,473.89 |

## Activity 10.12

The manufacturing cost for Buccaneers Ltd for next year is expected to be made up as follows:

|  | £000 |
|---|---:|
| Direct materials: |  |
| Forming department | 450 |
| Machining department | 100 |
| Finishing department | 50 |
| Direct labour: |  |
| Forming department | 180 |
| Machining department | 120 |
| Finishing department | 75 |
| Indirect materials: |  |
| Forming department | 40 |
| Machining department | 30 |
| Finishing department | 10 |
| Personnel and training department | 10 |
| Indirect labour: |  |
| Forming department | 80 |
| Machining department | 70 |
| Finishing department | 60 |
| Personnel and training department | 60 |
| Maintenance cost | 50 |
| Rent | 100 |
| Heating and lighting | 20 |
| Building insurance | 10 |
| Machinery insurance | 10 |
| Depreciation of machinery | 120 |
| Total manufacturing cost | 1,645 |

The following additional information is available:

(1) Each of the four departments is treated as a separate cost centre.
(2) All direct labour is paid £6 an hour for all hours worked.
(3) The personnel and training department renders services to the production departments.
(4) The area of the building in which the business manufactures amounts to 50,000 square metres, divided as follows:

|  | Sq m |
| --- | --- |
| Forming department | 20,000 |
| Machining department | 15,000 |
| Finishing department | 10,000 |
| Personnel and training department | 5,000 |

(5) The maintenance employees are expected to divide their time between the production departments as follows:

|  | % |
| --- | --- |
| Forming department | 15 |
| Machining department | 75 |
| Finishing department | 10 |

(6) Machine hours are expected to be as follows:

|  | Hours |
| --- | --- |
| Forming department | 5,000 |
| Machining department | 15,000 |
| Finishing department | 5,000 |

On the basis of this information:

(a) Allocate and apportion overheads to the three product cost centres.
(b) Deduce overhead recovery rates for each product cost centre using two different bases for each cost centre's overheads.
(c) Calculate the full cost of a job with the following characteristics:

| Direct labour hours: | |
| --- | --- |
| Forming department | 4 hours |
| Machining department | 4 hours |
| Finishing department | 1 hour |
| Machine hours: | |
| Forming department | 1 hour |
| Machining department | 2 hours |
| Finishing department | 1 hour |
| Direct materials: | |
| Forming department | £40 |
| Machining department | £9 |
| Finishing department | £4 |

Use whichever of the two bases of overhead recovery, deduced in (b), that you consider more appropriate.

(d) Explain why you consider the basis used in (c) to be the more appropriate.

## Activity 10.12 (continued)

(a) Overheads can be allocated and apportioned as follows:

| Cost | Basis of apport't | Total £000 | Forming £000 | Machining £000 | Finishing £000 | PT £000 |
|---|---|---|---|---|---|---|
| Indirect materials | Specifically allocated | 90 | 40 | 30 | 10 | 10 |
| Indirect labour | Specifically allocated | 270 | 80 | 70 | 60 | 60 |
| Maintenance | Staff time | 50 | 7.5 | 37.5 | 5 | – |
| Rent | 100 | | | | | |
| Heat and light | 20 | | | | | |
| Buildings insurance | 10 | | | | | |
| | Area | 130 | 52 | 39 | 26 | 13 |
| Machine insurance | 10 | | | | | |
| Machine depreciation | 120 | | | | | |
| | Machine hours | 130 | 26 | 78 | 26 | – |
| | | 670 | 205.5 | 254.5 | 127 | 83 |
| PT | Direct labour | – | 39.84 | 26.56 | 16.6 | (83) |
| | | 670 | 245.34 | 281.06 | 143.6 | – |

*Note*: The direct cost is not included in the above because it is allocated *directly* to jobs

(b) Overhead recovery rates are as follows:

*Basis 1: direct labour hours*

$$\text{Forming} = \frac{£245,340}{£(180,000/6)} = £8.18 \text{ per direct labour hour}$$

$$\text{Machining} = \frac{£281,060}{£(120,000/6)} = £14.05 \text{ per direct labour hour}$$

$$\text{Finishing} = \frac{£143,600}{£(75,000/6)} = £11.49 \text{ per direct labour hour}$$

*Basis 2: machine hours*

$$\text{Forming} = \frac{£245,340}{5,000} = £49.07 \text{ per machine hour}$$

$$\text{Machining} = \frac{£281,060}{15,000} = £18.74 \text{ per machine hour}$$

$$\text{Finishing} = \frac{£143,600}{5,000} = £28.72 \text{ per machine hour}$$

(c) Full cost of job – on direct labour hour basis of overhead recovery

| | £ | £ |
|---|---|---|
| Direct labour cost (9 × £6) | | 54.00 |
| Direct materials (£40 + £9 + £4) | | 53.00 |
| Overheads: | | |
| Forming (4 × £8.18) | 32.72 | |
| Machining (4 × £14.05) | 56.20 | |
| Finishing (1 × £11.49) | 11.49 | 100.41 |
| Full cost | | 207.41 |

(d) The reason for using the direct labour hour basis rather than the machine hour basis was that labour is more important, in terms of the number of hours applied to output, than is machine time. Strong arguments could have been made for the use of the alternative basis; certainly, a machine hour basis could have been justified for the machining department.

It would be possible, and it may be reasonable, to use one basis in respect of one product cost centre's overheads and a different one for those of another. For example, machine hours could have been used for the machining department and a direct labour hours basis for the other two.

## Batch costing

The production of many types of goods and services (particularly goods) involves producing in a batch of identical, or nearly identical, units of output, but where each batch is distinctly different from other batches. For example, a theatre may put on a production whose nature (and therefore cost) is very different from that of other productions. On the other hand, ignoring differences in the desirability of the various types of seating, all of the individual units of output (tickets to see the production) are identical.

In these circumstances, the cost per ticket would normally be deduced by:

- using a job costing approach (taking account of direct and indirect costs, and so on) to find the cost of mounting the production; and then
- dividing the cost of mounting the production by the expected number of tickets to be sold to find the cost per ticket.

This is known as **batch costing**.

Figure 10.11 shows the process for deriving the cost of one cost unit (product) in a batch.

**Figure 10.11** Deriving the cost of one cost unit where production is in batches

The full cost of the batch, delivered on a 'job-costing' basis

*divided by*

The number of cost units (products) in the batch

*equals*

The full cost of one cost unit (product)

The cost for the batch is derived using a job-costing basis and this is divided by the number in the batch to determine the cost for each cost unit.

## Non-manufacturing overheads

An international accounting standard (IAS 2 *Inventories*) requires that all inventories, including work in progress, be valued at full cost for external reporting purposes. When determining full cost, only those overheads relating to the manufacturing process should be included. Non-manufacturing overheads do not form part of the full cost calculation. These overheads, which normally include costs relating to general administration, selling, marketing and distribution, should be charged to the period in which they are incurred. The rules just mentioned, however, need not be applied for internal reporting purposes.

When making management decisions, businesses sometimes include non-manufacturing overheads as part of the total cost of producing goods. To do this, a suitable basis for assigning these overheads to products must be identified. This is not an easy task and it seems that inappropriate bases are often used. One basis for assigning non-manufacturing overheads found in practice is direct labour hours, even though its relevance for this purpose is questionable. Another basis that can be found adds a percentage loading to total manufacturing costs to represent non-manufacturing overheads. This percentage is based on the percentage of total non-manufacturing overheads to total manufacturing costs. (See reference 1 at the end of the chapter.) Thus, if total non-manufacturing overheads were £2.5 million and total manufacturing costs were £10 million, a 25 per cent (£2.5m/£10m) loading would be applied. These, and other arbitrary bases for assigning non-manufacturing overheads found in practice, are unlikely to improve the quality of management decisions. Unless a fair share of non-manufacturing overheads is assigned to products, managers will make decisions based on misleading information.

Where the cost of products includes both manufacturing and non-manufacturing costs and things turn out as expected, selling the products at their full cost should cause the business to break even exactly. Thus, whatever profit (in total) is loaded onto full cost to set actual selling prices will result in that level of profit being earned for the period.

## The forward-looking nature of full (absorption) costing

Although deducing full cost can be done after the work has been completed, it is frequently predicted in advance. This is often because an idea of the full cost is needed as a basis for setting a selling price. Predictions, however, rarely turn out to be 100 per cent accurate. Where actual outcomes differ from predicted outcomes an over-recovery or under-recovery of overheads will normally occur. Example 10.5 illustrates how this over- or under-recovery is calculated.

### Example 10.5

Downham Engineering plc produces a valve. At the beginning of the year, it was planned that the valves would incur £4 million in manufacturing overheads and would require 400,000 direct labour hours for the year. The business, which uses the direct labour basis of absorbing overheads, set the overhead recovery rate at (£4.0m/400,000) = £10 per direct labour hour. At the end of the year, it was found that in producing the valves, 450,000 direct labour hours were used in the production process but that the manufacturing overheads were as planned.

As 450,000 direct labour hours were used, the amount charged for overheads would have been 450,000 × £10 = £4.5 million. This means that £0.5 million (that is, £4.5m – £4.0m) of overheads were 'over-recovered'.

For external reporting purposes, any under- or over-recovery of overheads is adjusted in the income statement. Thus, the over-recovery in Example 10.5 above will be deducted from the expenses shown in the income statement for that year.

## Activity (10.13)

Refer to Example 10.5 and assume that, at the end of the year, it was found that 380,000 direct labour hours were used during the year in making the valves and that manufacturing overheads incurred were £4.2 million.
What adjustment should be made to the income statement for the year?

The manufacturing overheads recovered will be 380,000 × £10 = £3.8 million. This means that £0.4 million (that is, £4.2m − £3.8m) has been under-recovered. This amount will be added to the expenses shown in the income statement for the year.

**Real World 10.6** is taken from the results of a survey conducted by the UK Chartered Institute of Management Accountants (CIMA) in July 2009. Broadly, the survey asked management accountants in a wide range of business types and sizes to indicate the extent to which their business used a range of management accounting techniques. A total of 439 management accountants completed the survey. The report on this survey is available online at www.cimaglobal.com/ma. We shall be making reference to this survey on a number of occasions throughout the book. When we do, we shall refer to it as the 'CIMA survey'.

## Real World 10.6

### The use of full cost information

The businesses surveyed by CIMA derived full cost information to the following extent:

**Figure 10.12    The use of full cost information**

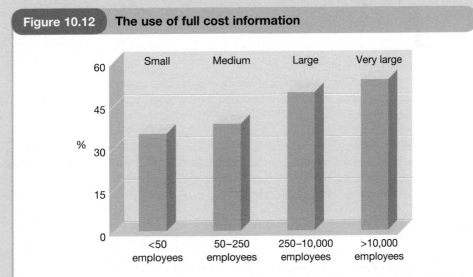

Full cost information is fairly widely used and the size of the business seems to be a factor. It is used by about 45 per cent of all of the businesses surveyed.

*Source*: Figure adapted from 'Management accounting tools for today and tomorrow', CIMA, 2009, p. 12.

It is noticeable that the level of use of full cost information, as revealed by the CIMA survey, is greater with larger businesses than with smaller ones. This also occurs with some other, but by no means all, management accounting techniques, as we shall see in later chapters. We do not know the reason for this tendency. It may be that larger businesses have greater resources and expertise than smaller ones. This may enable them to apply techniques that are not practical for smaller businesses. On the other hand, it may reflect the different types of business in each size category. For example, there is a tendency for small businesses to be engaged in service provision, rather than manufacturing.

## Self-assessment question (10.1)

Hector and Co. Ltd has been invited to tender for a contract to produce 1,000 clothes hangers. The following information relates to the contract.

- *Materials*: The clothes hangers are made of metal wire covered with a padded fabric. Each hanger requires 2 metres of wire and 0.5 square metres of fabric.
- *Direct labour*: Each hanger requires 10 minutes of skilled labour and 5 minutes of unskilled labour.

The business already holds sufficient of each of the materials required to complete the contract. Information on the cost of the materials is as follows:

|  | Metal wire £/m | Fabric £/sq m |
|---|---|---|
| Historic cost | 2.20 | 1.00 |
| Current buying-in cost | 2.50 | 1.10 |
| Scrap value | 1.70 | 0.40 |

The metal wire is in constant use by the business for a range of its products. The fabric has no other use for the business and is scheduled to be scrapped.

Unskilled labour, which is paid at the rate of £7.50 an hour, will need to be taken on specifically to undertake the contract. The business is fairly quiet at the moment, which means that a pool of skilled labour exists that will still be employed at full pay of £12.00 an hour to do nothing if the contract does not proceed. The pool of skilled labour is sufficient to complete the contract.

The business charges jobs with overheads on a direct labour hour basis. The production overheads of the entire business for the month in which the contract will be undertaken are estimated at £50,000. The estimated total direct labour hours that will be worked are 12,500. The business tends not to alter the established overhead recovery rate to reflect increases or reductions to estimated total hours arising from new contracts. The total overheads are not expected to increase as a result of undertaking the contract.

The business normally adds 12.5 per cent profit loading to the job cost to arrive at a first estimate of the tender price.

*Required:*
(a) Price this job on a traditional job-costing basis.
(b) Indicate the minimum price at which the contract could be undertaken such that the business would be neither better nor worse off as a result of doing it.

**The answer to this question can be found at the back of the book on page 778.**

## Using full (absorption) cost information

We saw at the beginning of the chapter that full (absorption) cost information may be used for four main purposes. Now that we have seen how full cost is deduced, let us consider in more detail how this information may be used. The four uses that we identified were:

- *Pricing and output decisions.* Full cost can be used as the starting point for determining prices. We shall consider this in some detail in the next section.
- *Exercising control.* Full (absorption) cost seems often to be used as the basis of budgeting and comparing actual outcomes with budgets, enabling action to be taken to exercise control. It can be useful in this context, though care needs to be taken to try to ensure that individual managers are not being held responsible for cost elements, say overheads, that they are unable to control. This point will be raised again in Chapter 11, where we consider another approach to dealing with overheads in full costing. We shall look at budgeting and control in some detail in Chapters 12 and 13.
- *Assessing relative efficiency.* Full cost seems to be used as the basis of comparing relative efficiency in terms of the comparative cost of doing similar things. For example, as we saw in Real World 10.1 on (page 361), the cost of carrying out a standard hospital in-patient procedure seems often compared on the basis of full cost between one hospital and another. The objective of this may well be to identify the cheaper hospital and encourage the other to copy its approach.

  As we saw in Chapters 8 and 9, including all aspects of cost (as full costing does) can lead to incorrect decisions. It is necessary to identify that part of the cost that is strictly relevant to a decision and to ignore the rest, be it direct or indirect in the full-costing context. Similarly, comparing the full cost of producing something, particularly when it is being produced in different organisations, can be confusing and can lead to bad decisions.
- *Assessing performance.* The conventional approach to measuring a business's income for a period requires that expenses be matched with the sales revenue to which they relate *in the same accounting period*. Thus, where a service is partially rendered in one accounting period but the revenue is recognised in the next, or where manufactured inventories are made, or partially made, in one period but sold in the next, the full cost (including an appropriate share of overheads) should be carried from the first accounting period to the second one.

  Deducing full cost is important because, unless we know the full cost of work done in one period that is sold in the next, the profit figures for each of the two periods concerned will be meaningless. Managers and others will not have a reliable means of assessing the effectiveness of the business as a whole, or the effectiveness of individual parts of it. Shortly, we shall take a quick look at an alternative approach to income measurement where full cost is not used.

The way in which full cost information is used to measure income is illustrated by Example 10.6.

## Example 10.6

During the accounting year that ended on 31 December last year, IT Modules Ltd developed a special piece of computer software for a customer, Kingsang Ltd. At the beginning of this year, after having a series of tests successfully completed by a subcontractor, the software was passed to Kingsang Ltd. IT Modules's normal practice (which is typical of most sales transactions by most businesses) is to take account of sales revenue when the product passes to the customer. The sale price of the Kingsang software was £45,000.

During last year, subcontract work costing £3,500 was used in developing the Kingsang software and 1,200 hours of direct labour, costing £24,300, were worked on it. The business uses a direct labour hour basis of charging overheads to jobs, which is believed to be fair because most of its work is labour intensive. The total production overheads for the business for last year were £77,000 and the total direct labour hours worked were 22,000. Testing the Kingsang software this year cost £1,000.

How much profit or loss did IT Modules make on the Kingsang software during last year? How much profit or loss did it make on the software during this year? At what value should IT Modules have included the software in its statement of financial position (balance sheet) at the end of last year so that the correct profit will be recorded for each of the two years?

The answers to these questions are as follows:

- No profit or loss was made during last year. This is because of IT Modules's (and the generally accepted) approach to recognising sales revenues and the need to match expenses with the revenues to which they relate in the same accounting period. The cost incurred during last year is carried forward to this year, which is the year of sale.
- As the sale is recognised this year, the cost of developing the software is treated as an expense in this year. This cost will include a reasonable share of overheads. Were IT Modules to draw up a 'mini' income statement for the Kingsang contract for this year, it would be as follows:

| Kingsang software | £ | £ |
|---|---|---|
| Sales revenue | | 45,000 |
| Cost: | | |
| Direct labour | (24,300) | |
| Subcontract | (3,500) | |
| Overheads (1,200 × (£77,000/22,000)) | (4,200) | |
| Total incurred last year | (32,000) | |
| Testing cost | (1,000) | |
| Total cost | | (33,000) |
| This year's profit from the software | | 12,000 |

- The software needs to be shown as an asset of the business (valued at £32,000) in the statement of financial position as at 31 December last year. It represents the work in progress that is carried forward to this year.

# Full cost (cost-plus) pricing

A business may seek to set its selling prices by simply adding a profit loading to the full cost of a product or service. The amount of profit is often calculated as a percentage of the full (absorption) cost figure.

## Activity 10.14

A business has just completed a service job whose full cost has been calculated at £112. For the current period, the total costs (direct and indirect) are estimated at £250,000. The profit target for the period is £100,000.

Suggest a selling price for the job.

If the profit is to be earned by jobs in proportion to their full cost, then the profit for each pound of full cost must be £0.40 (that is, £100,000/250,000). Thus, the target profit on the job must be:

£0.40 × 112 = £44.80

This means that the target price for the job must be:

£112 + £44.80 = £156.80

Other ways could be found for apportioning a share of profit to jobs – for example, direct labour or machine hours. Such bases may be preferred where it is believed that these factors are better representatives of effort and, therefore, profitworthiness. It is clearly a matter of judgement as to how profit is apportioned to units of output.

## Price makers and price takers

Despite the logic of basing selling prices on full cost, where there is a competitive market for the product or service, it is often not possible to set prices on a cost-plus basis. The problem with cost-plus pricing is that the market may not agree with the price. Businesses will usually have to accept the price that the market is prepared to pay. A business may fairly deduce the full cost of some product and then add what might be regarded as a reasonable level of profit, only to find that a rival producer is offering a similar product for a much lower price, or that the market simply will not buy at the cost-plus price.

Most suppliers are not strong enough in the market to dictate pricing. Most are *price takers* not *price makers*. They must accept the price offered by the market or they do not sell any of their products. Cost-plus pricing may be appropriate for price makers, but it has less relevance for price takers.

**Real World 10.7** illustrates how adopting a cost-plus approach to pricing may lead to a situation where falling demand leads to price rises, which, in turn lead to falling demand.

---

### Real World 10.7

#### A vicious circle in the library    **FT**

Librarians have long complained about the price rises of academic journals and Derek Haan chairman and chief executive of Elsevier Science, which publishes more than 1,600 journals, admits that journal price inflation has been a problem for the industry. He says the problem is due to falling subscription numbers as more readers make photocopies or use interlibrary lending. With fewer subscribers to share the cost of each publication, publishers have to increase prices. To stay within budgets, libraries start cancelling titles, which creates a vicious circle of dwindling subscriber numbers, soaring prices and reduced collections. Naturally, with fixed budgets, libraries will be forced to react to increasing journal prices.

*Source*: Adapted from 'Case Study: Elsevier', FT.com, 19 June 2002.

---

## Using cost-plus information by price takers

The cost-plus price is not entirely without use to price takers. When contemplating entering a market, knowing the cost-plus price will give useful information. It will tell the price taker whether or not it can profitably enter the market. As mentioned earlier, the full cost can be seen as a long-run break-even selling price. If entering a market means that this break-even price, plus an acceptable profit, cannot be achieved, then the business might be better to stay out. Having a breakdown of the full cost may put the business in a position to examine where costs might be capable of being cut. This may enable the business to bring the full cost plus profit within a figure acceptable to the market. Here, the market would be providing the target price towards which the business can work, if it wishes to compete.

It is not necessary for a business to dominate a particular market for it to be a price maker. Many small businesses are, to some extent, price makers. This tends to be where buyers find it difficult to make clear distinctions between the prices offered by various suppliers. An example of this might be a car repair undertaken by a garage, where the nature and extent of the problem is not clear. As a result, garages normally charge cost-plus prices for car repairs.

In its 'pure' sense, cost-plus pricing implies that the seller sets the price that is then accepted by the customer. Often the price will not be finalised until after the product or service has been completed; as, for example, with a motor car or work done by a firm of accountants. Sometimes, however, cost-plus is used as a basis of negotiating a price in advance, which then becomes the fixed price. This is often the case with contracts with central or local government departments. Typically, with such public contracts, the price is determined by competitive tendering. Here each potential supplier offers a price for which it will perform the subject of the contract and the department concerned selects the supplier offering the lowest price, subject to quality safeguards. In some cases, however, particularly where only one supplier is capable of doing the work, a fixed cost-plus approach is used.

Cost-plus is also often the approach taken when monopoly suppliers of public utility services are negotiating a price, which they are legally allowed to charge their customers, with the government-appointed regulator. For example, the UK mains water suppliers, when agreeing the prices that they can charge customers, argue their case with Ofwat, the water industry regulator, on the basis of cost-plus information.

**Real World 10.8** discusses how one business sees itself as partly protected from the recession that hit the UK from 2008 as a result of having contracts with its customers on a cost-plus price basis.

---

### Real World 10.8

#### Adding Spice to cost-plus pricing                          FT

Spice plc is a business that undertakes consultancy and other subcontract (outsourced) work for various UK public utilities (water and electricity suppliers). The business started when a group of managers bought Yorkshire Electricity's maintenance division to run it as a separate, independent unit.

Simon Rigby, Spice's chief executive, was very relaxed about the prospect of an economic recession. He said:

> I would not wish a recession on anybody, but if we have a recession it is going to throw Spice into very sharp focus. How do you think my 10-year cost-plus contracts are going to be affected by recession? The answer is not at all.

It must be said that Spice plc is very unusual in having so many 'cost-plus' priced contracts.

*Source*: 'Flexible business models helps Spice Holdings power ahead in outsource market', E. Jansson, *Financial Times*, 12 March 2008.

---

**Real World 10.9** considers the extent to which cost-plus pricing seems to be used in practice.

---

### Real World 10.9

#### Counting the cost plus

A fairly recent study surveyed 267 large UK and Australian businesses during the period 1999 to 2002. Their findings were broadly as follows:

- Cost plus is regarded as important in determining selling prices by most of the businesses, but many businesses only use it for a small percentage of their total sales.
- Retailers base most of their sales prices on their costs. This is not surprising; we might expect that retailers add a mark up on their cost prices to arrive at selling prices.

→

**Real World 10.9 (continued)**

- Retailers and service businesses (both financial services and others) attach more importance to cost-plus pricing than do manufacturers and others.
- Cost-plus pricing tends to be more important in industries where competition is most intense. This is, perhaps surprising because we might have expected fewer 'price makers' in more competitive markets.
- The extent of the importance of cost-plus pricing seems to have nothing to do with the size of the business. We might have imagined that larger businesses would have more power in the market and be more likely to be price makers, but the evidence does not support this. The reason could be that many larger businesses are, in effect, groups of smaller businesses. These smaller subsidiaries may not be bigger players in their markets than are small independent businesses. Also, cost-plus pricing tends to be particularly important in retailing and service businesses, where many businesses are quite small.

*Source*: 'An empirical investigation of the importance of cost-plus pricing', C. Guilding, C. Drury and M. Tayles, *Managerial Auditing Journal*, Vol. 20, No. 2, 2005.

# Criticisms of full (absorption) costing

Full costing has been criticised because, in practice, it tends to use past cost and to restrict its consideration of future cost to outlay cost. It can be argued that past cost is irrelevant, irrespective of the purpose for which the information is to be used. This is basically because it is not possible to make decisions about the past, only about the future. Similarly, it is argued that it is wrong to ignore opportunity costs. Advocates of full costing would argue, however, that it provides a useful guide to long-run average cost.

Despite the criticisms that are made of full costing, it is, according to research evidence, widely practiced (see Real World 10.6, p. 387). We saw earlier that an international accounting standard requires that all inventories, including work in progress, be valued at full cost for external reporting purposes. This means that virtually all businesses that have work in progress and/or inventories of finished goods at the end of their financial periods are obliged to apply full costing for income measurement purposes. This will include the many service providers that tend to have work in progress. The extent to which they use full cost information for other purposes is not clear.

# Full (absorption) costing versus variable costing

An alternative to full (absorption) costing is **variable (marginal) costing** – which we discussed in Chapter 9. We may recall that this approach distinguishes between fixed and variable costs and that this distinction may be helpful when making short-term decisions.

A variable costing approach will measure its income in a different way to that which we have met in this chapter. Variable costing will include only variable cost, including variable direct and variable indirect elements, as part of the cost of the goods or service produced. Any fixed cost, including fixed direct and fixed indirect elements, will be treated as a cost of the period in which it is incurred. Thus, inventories of finished products, or work in progress, carried from one accounting period to the next, will be valued only on the basis of their variable cost.

As we have seen, full costing includes in product cost not only the direct cost (whether fixed or variable) but also a 'fair' share of the indirect costs (both fixed and variable) that were incurred during the period that the product was produced.

To illustrate the difference between the two approaches, let us consider Example 10.7.

## Example 10.7

Lahore Ltd commenced operations on 1 June and makes a single product, which sells for £14 per unit. In the first two months of operations, the following results were achieved:

|  | June | July |
|---|---|---|
|  | (Number of units) | (Number of units) |
| Production output | 6,000 | 6,000 |
| Sales volume | 4,000 | 5,000 |
| Opening inventories | – | 2,000 |
| Closing inventories | 2,000 | 3,000 |

Fixed manufacturing cost is £18,000 per month and variable manufacturing cost is £5 per unit. There is also a monthly fixed non-manufacturing cost (marketing and administration) of £5,000. There was no work in progress at the end of either June or July.

The operating profit for each month is calculated below, first using a variable costing approach and then a full costing approach.

### Variable costing

In this case, only the variable costs are charged to the units produced and all the fixed cost (manufacturing and non-manufacturing) is charged to the period. Inventories will be carried forward at their variable cost.

|  | June £ | June £ | July £ | July £ |
|---|---|---|---|---|
| Sales revenue |  |  |  |  |
| (4,000 × £14) |  | 56,000 |  |  |
| (5,000 × £14) |  |  |  | 70,000 |
| Opening inventories |  |  |  |  |
| (2,000 × £5) | – |  | 10,000 |  |
| Cost of units produced |  |  |  |  |
| (6,000 × £5) | 30,000 |  | 30,000 |  |
| Closing inventories |  |  |  |  |
| (2,000 × £5) | (10,000) | (20,000) |  |  |
| (3,000 × £5) |  |  | (15,000) | (25,000) |
| Contribution margin |  | 36,000 |  | 45,000 |
| Fixed cost |  |  |  |  |
| Manufacturing | (18,000) |  | (18,000) |  |
| Non-manufacturing | (5,000) | (23,000) | (5,000) | (23,000) |
| Operating profit |  | 13,000 |  | 22,000 |

→

**Full costing**

In this case, fixed manufacturing cost becomes part of the product cost and inventories are carried forward to the next period at their full cost (that is, variable cost *plus* an appropriate fixed manufacturing cost element). There are 6,000 units produced in each period and the fixed manufacturing cost for each period is £18,000. Hence, the fixed manufacturing cost element per unit is £3 (that is, £18,000/6,000). The full cost per unit will therefore be £8 (that is, £5 + £3)

|  | June | | July | |
|---|---|---|---|---|
|  | £ | £ | £ | £ |
| Sales revenue |  |  |  |  |
| (4,000 × £14) |  | 56,000 |  |  |
| (5,000 × £14) |  |  |  | 70,000 |
| Opening inventories |  | – |  |  |
| (2,000 × £8) |  |  | 16,000 |  |
| Cost of units produced |  |  |  |  |
| (6,000 × £8) | 48,000 |  | 48,000 |  |
| Closing inventories |  |  |  |  |
| (2,000 × £8) | (16,000) | (32,000) |  |  |
| (3,000 × £8) |  |  | (24,000) | (40,000) |
| Gross profit |  | 24,000 |  | 30,000 |
| Non-manufacturing cost |  | (5,000) |  | (5,000) |
| Operating profit |  | 19,000 |  | 25,000 |

We can see that the total operating profit over the two months is £35,000 (that is, £13,000 + £22,000) when derived on a variable cost basis. On a full cost basis it is £44,000 (that is, £19,000 + £25,000). This is a difference of £9,000 (that is £44,000 – £35,000). This is accounted for by the fact that the fixed manufacturing cost element of the inventories valuation at the end of July, on the full cost basis (that is, 3,000 × £3), has yet to be treated as an expense. It has already been treated as an expense on the variable cost basis, however.

## Which method is better?

In practice, the choice of costing approach may not have such a dramatic effect on reported profit as shown in Example 10.7. Differences in operating profit revealed in this example arise from the significant changes in inventories levels between periods – from zero at the beginning of June, to 2,000 units at the end of June, to 3,000 units by the end of July. In practice, businesses do not tend to alter inventories levels so radically. Where similar amounts of inventories and work in progress are held at year ends and fixed cost remains unchanged from one reporting period to the next, reported profit will not vary much between the two approaches. This is because a similar amount of fixed cost will be treated as an expense each year; all of it originating from the current year in the case of variable costing, some of it originating from past years in the case of full costing.

It is important to note that, over the entire life of a particular business, total operating profit will be the same whichever costing method has been applied. This is because, ultimately, all fixed costs will be charged as an expense.

Variable costing proponents might argue that it is a very prudent approach to measuring profit, as all fixed production costs are charged to the period in which they are incurred. Perhaps more importantly, they would argue that only variable cost is relevant to decision makers (as we discussed in Chapters 8 and 9) and that considering fixed cost obscures the issue.

Proponents of full (absorption) costing might counter that full costing provides a fairer measure of profit, job by job. Furthermore, in the long run, all elements of cost can be avoided and so to concentrate on only those that can be avoided in the short term (the variable cost) could be misleading.

In practice, management accountants can prepare their income statements taking either, or even both, approaches. We have already seen, however, that accounting rules insist that a full costing approach is taken when preparing published financial statements.

**Real World 10.10** provides some indication of the extent to which variable costing is used in practice.

## Real World 10.10

### Variable costing in practice

A survey of 41 UK manufacturing businesses found that 68 per cent of them used a variable costing approach to management reporting.

Many would find this surprising. It seemed to be widely believed that the requirement for financial statements in published annual reports to be in full-cost terms has led those businesses to use a full-cost approach for management reporting as well. This seems not to be the case, however.

It should be added that many of those that used variable costing, quite possibly misused it. For example, three-quarters of those that used it treated labour cost as variable. Possibly in some cases the cost of labour is variable (with the level of activity), but it seems likely that this is not true for most of these businesses. At the same time, most of the 68 per cent treat all overheads as a fixed cost. It seems likely that, for most businesses, overheads would have a variable element.

*Source: Contemporary Management Accounting Practices in UK Manufacturing*, D. Dugdale, C. Jones and S. Green, CIMA Research Publication, Vol. 1, Number 13, 2005.

## Summary

The main points in this chapter may be summarised as follows:

**Full (absorption) cost = the total amount of resources sacrificed to achieve a particular objective.**

**Uses of full (absorption) cost information**

- Pricing and output decisions.
- Exercising control.
- Assessing relative efficiency.
- Income measurement.

**Single-product businesses**

- Where all the units of output are identical, the full cost can be calculated as follows:

$$\text{Cost per unit} = \frac{\text{Total cost of output}}{\text{Number of units produced}}$$

**Multi-product businesses – job costing**

- Where units of output are not identical, it is necessary to divide the cost into two categories: direct cost and indirect cost (overheads).
- Direct cost = cost that can be identified with specific cost units (for example, labour of a garage mechanic, in relation to a particular job).
- Indirect cost (overheads) = cost that cannot be directly measured in respect of a particular job (for example, the rent of a garage).
- Full (absorption) cost = direct cost + indirect cost.
- Direct/indirect is not linked to variable/fixed.
- Indirect cost is difficult to relate to individual cost units – arbitrary bases are used and there is no single correct method.
- Traditionally, indirect cost is seen as the cost of providing a 'service' to cost units.
- Direct labour hour basis of applying indirect cost to cost units is the most popular in practice.

**Dealing with indirect cost on a cost centre (departmental) basis**

- Indirect cost (overheads) can be segmented – usually on a cost centre basis – each product cost centre has its own overhead recovery rate.
- Cost centres are areas, activities or functions for which costs are separately determined.
- Overheads must be allocated or apportioned to cost centres.
- Service cost centre cost must then be apportioned to product cost centres and product cost centre overheads absorbed by cost units (jobs).

**Batch costing**

- A variation of job costing where each job consists of a number of identical (or near identical) cost units:

$$\text{Cost per unit} = \frac{\text{Cost of the batch (direct + indirect)}}{\text{Number of units in the batch}}$$

Full cost information is seen by some as not very useful because it can be backward looking: it includes information irrelevant to decision making, but excludes some relevant information.

Full (absorption) costing versus variable costing

● With full costing, both fixed and variable costs are included in product cost and treated as expenses when the product is sold.

● With variable costing, only the variable product cost is linked to the products in this way, fixed cost is treated as an expense of the period in which it was incurred.

● Variable costing tends to be more straightforward and, according to proponents, more relevant for decision making.

● Supporters of full costing argue that it gives a more complete measure of the income generated from the sale of each unit of the product.

● Such evidence as there is about the use of variable costing in practice suggests that it is widely used. The evidence implies, however, that the values tend to be miscalculated in a large proportion of cases.

# MyAccountingLab

Go to www.myaccountinglab.com to check your understanding of the chapter, create a personalised study plan, and maximise your revision time

## Key terms

full cost  p. 361
full costing  p. 362
cost unit  p. 362
process costing  p. 363
direct cost  p. 363
indirect cost  p. 363
overheads  p. 363
common cost  p. 363
job costing  p. 365
absorption costing  p. 365

cost behaviour  p. 366
overhead absorption (recovery) rate  p. 368
cost centre  p. 376
product cost centre  p. 378
service cost centre  p. 378
cost allocation  p. 378
cost apportionment  p. 378
batch costing  p. 385
variable (marginal) costing  p. 394

## Reference

1 Drury, C. and Tayles, M., 'Product costing in UK manufacturing organisations', *The European Accounting Review* 3:3, 1994, pp. 443–69.

## Further reading

If you would like to explore the topics covered in this chapter in more depth, we recommend the following books:

Drury, C., *Management and Cost Accounting*, 8th edn, Cengage Learning, 2012, chapters 3, 4 and 5.

Hilton, R., *Managerial Accounting*, 9th edn, McGraw-Hill Higher Education, 2011, chapters 2 and 3.

Horngren, C., Datar, S. and Rajan, M., *Cost Accounting: A Managerial Emphasis*, 14th edn, Prentice Hall International, 2011, chapter 4.

Kaplan, R., Atkinson, A., Matsumura, E. and Young, S. M., *Management Accounting*, 6th edn, Prentice Hall, 2011, chapter 4.

## Review questions

**Solutions to these questions can be found at the back of the book on pages 753 to 754.**

**10.1** What problem does the existence of work in progress cause in process costing?

**10.2** What is the point of distinguishing direct cost from indirect cost? Why is this not necessary in process costing environments?

**10.3** Are direct cost and variable cost the same thing? Explain your answer.

**10.4** It is sometimes claimed that the full cost of pursuing some objective represents the long-run break-even selling price. Why is this said and what does it mean?

## Exercises

**Exercises 10.1, 10.2 and 10.3 are basic level, 10.4, 10.5 and 10.6 are intermediate level and 10.7 is advanced level. Those with coloured numbers have solutions at the back of the book starting on page 778.**

**If you wish to try more exercises, visit the students' side of the Companion Website and MyAccountingLab.**

**10.1** Consider this statement:

> In a job costing system, it is necessary to divide up the business into departments. Fixed costs (or overheads) will be collected for each department. Where a particular fixed cost relates to the business as a whole, it must be divided between the departments. Usually this is done on the basis of area of floor space occupied by each department relative to the entire business. When the total fixed costs for each department have been identified, this will be divided by the number of hours that were worked in each department to deduce an overhead recovery rate. Each job that was worked on in a department will have a share of fixed cost allotted to it according to how long it was worked on. The total cost for each job will therefore be the sum of the variable cost of the job and its share of the fixed cost. It is essential that this approach is taken in order to deduce a selling price for the business's output.

*Required:*
Prepare a table of two columns. In the first column you should show any phrases or sentences in the above statement with which you do not agree. In the second column you should show your reason for disagreeing with each one.

**10.2** Bodgers Ltd, a business that provides a market research service, operates a job costing system. Towards the end of each financial year, the overhead recovery rate (the rate at which indirect cost will be absorbed by jobs) is established for the forthcoming year.

(a) Why does the business bother to predetermine the recovery rate in the way outlined?
(b) What steps will be involved in predetermining the rate?
(c) What problems might arise with using a predetermined rate?

**10.3** Pieman Products Ltd makes road trailers to the precise specifications of individual customers. The following are predicted to occur during the forthcoming year, which is about to start:

| | |
|---|---|
| Direct materials cost | £50,000 |
| Direct labour cost | £160,000 |
| Direct labour time | 16,000 hours |
| Indirect labour cost | £25,000 |
| Depreciation of machine | £8,000 |
| Rent | £10,000 |
| Heating, lighting and power | £5,000 |
| Indirect materials | £2,000 |
| Other indirect cost (overhead) elements | £1,000 |
| Machine time | 3,000 hours |

All direct labour is paid at the same hourly rate.

A customer has asked the business to build a trailer for transporting a racing motorcycle to race meetings. It is estimated that this will require materials and components that will cost £1,150. It will take 250 direct labour hours to do the job, of which 50 will involve the use of machinery.

*Required:*

Deduce a logical cost for the job and explain the basis of dealing with overheads that you propose.

**10.4** Promptprint Ltd, a printing business, has received an enquiry from a potential customer for the quotation of a price for a job. The pricing policy of the business is based on the plans for the next financial year shown below.

| | £ |
|---|---|
| Sales revenue (billings to customers) | 196,000 |
| Materials (direct) | (38,000) |
| Labour (direct) | (32,000) |
| Variable overheads | (2,400) |
| Maintenance | (3,000) |
| Depreciation | (27,600) |
| Rent | (36,000) |
| Heat and light | (8,000) |
| Profit | 49,000 |

A first estimate of the direct cost for the particular job is:

| | £ |
|---|---|
| Direct materials | 4,000 |
| Direct labour | 3,600 |

*Required:*

(a) Prepare a recommended price for the job based on the plans, commenting on your method, ignoring the information given in the Appendix (below).

(b) Comment on the validity of using financial plans in pricing and recommend any improvements you would consider desirable for the pricing policy used in (a).

(c) Incorporate the effects of the information shown in the Appendix (below) into your estimates of the direct material cost, explaining any changes you consider it necessary to make to the above direct material cost of £4,000.

**Appendix to Exercise 10.4**

Based on historic cost, direct material cost was computed as follows:

|  | £ |
|---|---|
| Paper grade 1 | 1,200 |
| Paper grade 2 | 2,000 |
| Card (zenith grade) | 500 |
| Inks and other miscellaneous items | 300 |
|  | 4,000 |

Paper grade 1 is regularly used by the business. Enough of this paper to complete the job is currently held. Because it is imported, it is estimated that if it is used for this job, a new purchase order will have to be placed shortly. Sterling has depreciated against the foreign currency by 25 per cent since the last purchase.

Paper grade 2 is purchased from the same source as grade 1. The business holds exactly enough of it for the job, but this was bought in for a special order. This order was cancelled, although the defaulting customer was required to pay £500 towards the cost of the paper. The accountant has offset this against the original cost to arrive at the figure of £2,000 shown above. This paper is rarely used and due to its special chemical coating will be unusable if it is not used on the job in question.

The card is another specialist item currently held by the business. There is no use foreseen and it would cost £750 to replace, if required. However, the inventories controller had planned to spend £130 on overprinting to use the card as a substitute for other materials costing £640. Inks and other items are in regular use in the print shop.

**10.5** Many businesses charge overheads to jobs on a cost centre basis.

*Required:*

(a) What is the advantage that is claimed for charging overheads to jobs on a cost centre basis and why is it claimed?

(b) What circumstances need to exist for it to make a difference to a particular job whether overheads are charged on a business-wide basis or on a cost centre basis? (Note that the answer to this part of the question is not specifically covered in the chapter. You should, nevertheless, be able to deduce the reason from what you know.)

**10.6** Athena Ltd is an engineering business doing work for its customers to their particular requirements and specifications. It determines the full cost of each job taking a 'job-costing' approach, accounting for overheads on a cost centre (departmental) basis. It bases its prices to customers on this full cost figure. The business has two departments (both of which are cost centres): a Machining Department, where each job starts, and a Fitting Department, which completes all of the jobs. Machining Department overheads are charged to jobs on a machine hour basis and those of the Fitting Department on a direct labour hour basis. The budgeted information for next year is as follows:

| | | |
|---|---|---|
| Heating and lighting | £25,000 | (allocated equally between the two departments) |
| Machine power | £10,000 | (all allocated to the Machining Department) |
| Direct labour | £200,000 | (£150,000 allocated to the Fitting Department and £50,000 to the Machining Department. All direct workers are paid £10 an hour) |
| Indirect labour | £50,000 | (apportioned to the departments in proportion to the direct labour cost) |
| Direct materials | £120,000 | (all applied to jobs in the Machining Department) |
| Depreciation | £30,000 | (all relates to the Machining Department) |
| Machine time | 20,000 hours | (all worked in the Machining Department) |

*Required:*

(a) Prepare a statement showing the budgeted overheads for next year, analysed between the two cost centres. This should be in the form of three columns: one for the total figure for each type of overhead and one column each for the two cost centres, where each type of overhead is analysed between the two cost centres. Each column should also show the total of overheads for the year.

(b) Derive the appropriate rate for charging the overheads of each cost centre to jobs (that is, a separate rate for each cost centre).

(c) Athena Ltd has been asked by a customer to specify the price that it will charge for a particular job that will, if the job goes ahead, be undertaken early next year. The job is expected to use direct materials costing Athena Ltd £1,200, to need 50 hours of machining time, 10 hours of Machine Department direct labour and 20 hours of Fitting Department direct labour. Athena Ltd charges a profit loading of 20 per cent to the full cost of jobs to determine the selling price.

Show workings to derive the proposed selling price for this job.

10.7 Bookdon plc manufactures three products, X, Y and Z, in two product cost centres: a machine shop and a fitting section; it also has two service cost centres: a canteen and a machine maintenance section. Shown below are next year's planned production data and manufacturing cost for the business.

|  | X | Y | Z |
|---|---|---|---|
| Production | 4,200 units | 6,900 units | 1,700 units |
| Direct materials | £11/unit | £14/unit | £17/unit |
| Direct labour |  |  |  |
| Machine shop | £6/unit | £4/unit | £2/unit |
| Fitting section | £12/unit | £3/unit | £21/unit |
| Machine hours | 6 hr/unit | 3 hr/unit | 4 hr/unit |

Planned overheads are as follows:

|  | Machine shop | Fitting section | Canteen | Machine maintenance section | Total |
|---|---|---|---|---|---|
| Allocated overheads | £27,660 | £19,470 | £16,600 | £26,650 | £90,380 |
| Rent, heat and light |  |  |  |  | £17,000 |
| Depreciation and insurance of equipment |  |  |  |  | £25,000 |

Additional data:

|  | Machine shop | Fitting section | Canteen | Machine maintenance section |
|---|---|---|---|---|
| Gross carrying amount of equipment | £150,000 | £75,000 | £30,000 | £45,000 |
| Number of employees | 18 | 14 | 4 | 4 |
| Floor space occupied | 3,600 sq m | 1,400 sq m | 1,000 sq m | 800 sq m |

All machining is carried out in the machine shop. It has been estimated that approximately 70 per cent of the machine maintenance section's cost is incurred servicing the machine shop and the remainder servicing the fitting section.

*Required:*

(a) Calculate the following planned overhead absorption rates:
   (1) A machine hour rate for the machine shop.
   (2) A rate expressed as a percentage of direct wages for the fitting section.

(b) Calculate the planned full cost per unit of Product X.

# Costing and performance evaluation in a competitive environment

## Introduction

In recent years we have seen major changes in the business world, including deregulation, privatisation, the growing expectations of shareholders and the impact of new technology. These have led to a much more fast-changing and competitive environment that has radically altered the way that businesses are managed. In this chapter, we consider some of the management accounting techniques that have been developed to help businesses maintain their competitiveness in this new era.

We begin by considering the impact of this new environment on the full-costing approach that we considered in Chapter 10. We shall see that activity-based costing, which is a development of the traditional full-costing approach, takes a much more enquiring, much less accepting attitude towards overheads. We shall also examine some recent approaches to costing that can help lower costs and, therefore, increase the ability of a business to compete on price.

Management accounting embraces both financial and non-financial measures and, in this chapter, we shall consider the increasing importance of non-financial measures in managing a business. These include the balanced scorecard approach, which seeks to integrate financial and non-financial measures into a framework for the achievement of business objectives.

Finally, we consider the idea of shareholder value, which has been a 'hot' issue among managers in recent years. Many leading businesses now claim that the quest for shareholder value is the driving force behind strategic and operational decisions. We consider what the term 'shareholder value' means and we shall look at one of the main methods of measuring shareholder value.

## Learning outcomes

**When you have completed this chapter, you should be able to:**

- Discuss the nature and usefulness of activity-based costing.

- Explain how new developments such as total life-cycle costing and target costing can be used to control costs.

→

● Discuss the importance of non-financial measures of performance in managing a business and the way in which the balanced scorecard attempts to integrate financial and non-financial measures.

● Explain the term 'shareholder value' and describe the role of EVA® in measuring and delivering shareholder value.

## MyAccountingLab

Visit **www.myaccountinglab.com** for practice and revision opportunities

# Cost determination in the changed business environment

## Costing and pricing: the traditional way

The traditional, and still widely used, approach to job costing and product pricing developed when the notion of trying to determine the cost of industrial production first emerged. This was around the time of the UK Industrial Revolution when industry displayed the following characteristics:

● *Direct-labour-intensive and direct-labour-paced production.* Labour was at the heart of production. To the extent that machinery was used, it tended to support the efforts of direct labour, and the speed of production was dictated by direct labour.

● *A low level of indirect cost relative to direct cost.* Little was spent on power, personnel services, machinery (leading to low depreciation charges) and other areas typical of the indirect cost (overheads) of modern businesses.

● *A relatively uncompetitive market.* Transport difficulties, limited industrial production worldwide and a lack of knowledge by customers of competitors' prices meant that businesses could prosper without being too scientific in costing. Typically they could simply add a margin for profit to arrive at the selling price (cost-plus pricing). Customers tended to accept those products which the supplier had to offer, rather than demanding precisely what they wanted.

Since overheads at that time represented a pretty small element of total cost, it was acceptable and practical to deal with them in a fairly arbitrary manner. Not too much effort was devoted to trying to control overheads because the potential rewards of better control were relatively small, certainly when compared with the benefits from firmer control of direct labour and material costs. It was also reasonable to charge overheads to individual jobs on a direct labour hour basis. Most of the overheads were incurred directly in support of direct labour: providing direct workers with a place to work, heating and lighting the workplace, employing people to supervise the direct workers, and so on. Direct workers, perhaps aided by machinery, carried out all production.

At that time, service industries were a relatively unimportant part of the economy and would have largely consisted of self-employed individuals. These individuals would probably have been uninterested in trying to do more than work out a rough hourly/daily rate for their time and to try to base prices on this.

## Costing and pricing: the new environment

In recent years, the world of industrial production has fundamentally changed. Most of it is now characterised by:

- *Capital-intensive and machine-paced production.* Machines are at the heart of much production, including both the manufacture of goods and the rendering of services. Most labour supports the efforts of machines, for example, technically maintaining them. Also, machines often dictate the pace of production. According to evidence provided in **Real World 10.2** on page 364, direct labour accounts on average for just 14 per cent of manufacturers' total cost.

- *A high level of indirect cost relative to direct costs.* Modern businesses tend to have very high depreciation, servicing and power costs. There are also high costs of personnel and staff welfare, which were scarcely envisaged in the early days of industrial production. At the same time, there are very low (sometimes no) direct labour costs. Although direct material cost often remains an important element of total cost, more efficient production methods lead to less waste and, therefore, to a lower total material cost, again tending to make indirect cost (overheads) more dominant. Again according to Real World 10.2, overheads account for 25 per cent of manufacturers' total cost and 51 per cent of service sector total cost.

- *A highly competitive international market.* Production, much of it highly sophisticated, is carried out worldwide. Transport, including fast airfreight, is relatively cheap. Fax, telephone and, particularly, the internet ensure that potential customers can quickly and cheaply find the prices of a range of suppliers. Markets now tend to be highly price competitive. Customers increasingly demand products custom-made to their own requirements. This means that businesses need to know their product costs with a greater degree of accuracy than historically has been the case. Businesses also need to take a considered and informed approach to pricing their output.

In the UK, as in many developed countries, service industries now dominate the economy, employing the great majority of the workforce and producing most of the value of productive output. Though there are still many self-employed individuals supplying services, many service providers are vast businesses such as banks, insurance companies and cinema operators. For most of these larger service providers, the activities very closely resemble modern manufacturing activity. They, too, are characterised by high capital intensity, overheads dominating direct costs and a competitive international market.

## Cost management systems

Changes in the competitive environment mean that businesses must now manage costs much more effectively than in the past. This, in turn, places an obligation on cost management systems to provide the information that will enable managers to do this. Traditional cost management systems have often proved inadequate for the task and, in recent years, new systems have gained in popularity. We shall take a look at some of these systems shortly but before doing so, we shall consider an important reason why the need for new systems has arisen.

## The problem of overheads

In Chapter 10 we considered the traditional approach to job costing (deriving the full cost of output where one unit of output differs from another). We may recall that this approach involves collecting, for each job, those costs that can be clearly linked to, and measured in respect of, that particular job (direct costs). All indirect costs (overheads) are allocated or apportioned to product cost centres and then charged to individual jobs according to some formula. The evidence suggests that this formula is usually based on the number of direct labour hours worked on each particular job (see Real World 10.4, page 374).

In the past, this approach has worked reasonably well, largely because overhead recovery rates (that is, rates at which overheads are absorbed by jobs) were typically of a much lower value for each direct labour hour than the rate paid to direct workers as wages or salaries. It is now, however, becoming increasingly common for overhead recovery rates to be between five and ten times the hourly rate of pay, because overheads are now much more significant. When production is dominated by direct labour paid, say, £8 an hour, it might be reasonable to have an overhead recovery rate of, say, £1 an hour. When, however, direct labour plays a relatively small part in production, to have an overhead recovery rate of, say, £50 for each direct labour hour is likely to lead to very arbitrary product costing. Even a small change in the amount of direct labour worked on a job could massively affect the total cost deduced. This is not because the direct worker is very highly paid, but because of the effect of the direct labour hours on the overhead cost loading. A further problem is that overheads are still typically charged on a direct labour hour basis even though the overheads may not be closely related to direct labour.

**Real World 11.1** provides a rather disturbing view of costing and cost control in large banks.

---

### Real World 11.1

#### Bank accounts                                          **FT**

In a study of the cost structures of 52 international banks, the German consultancy firm, Droege, found that indirect cost (overheads) could represent as much as 85 per cent of total cost. However, whilst direct costs were generally under tight management control, overheads were not. The overheads, which include such items as IT development, risk control, auditing, marketing and public relations, were often not allocated between operating divisions or were allocated in a rather arbitrary manner.

*Source:* Based on information in 'Banks have not tackled indirect costs', A. Skorecki, FT.com, 7 January 2004.

---

### Taking a closer look

The changes in the competitive environment discussed above have led to much closer attention being paid to the issue of overheads, what causes them and how they are charged to jobs. Historically, businesses have been content to accept that overheads exist and, therefore, for job (product) costing purposes they must be dealt with in as practical a way as possible. In recent years, however, there has been increasing recognition of the fact that overheads do not just happen; something must be causing them. To illustrate this point, let us consider Example 11.1.

**Example 11.1**

Modern Producers Ltd has a storage area that is set aside for its inventories of finished goods. The cost of running the stores includes a share of the factory rent and other establishment costs, such as heating and lighting. It also includes the salaries of staff employed to look after the inventories, and the cost of financing the inventories held in the stores.

The business has two product lines: A and B. Product A tends to be made in small batches and low levels of finished inventories are held. The business prides itself on its ability to supply Product B, in relatively large quantities, instantly. As a consequence, most of the space in the finished goods store is filled with finished Product Bs, ready to be despatched immediately an order is received.

Traditionally, the whole cost of operating the stores would have been treated as a part of general overheads and included in the total of overheads charged to jobs, probably on a direct labour hour basis. This means that, when assessing the cost of Products A and B, the cost of operating the stores has fallen on them according to the number of direct labour hours worked on manufacturing each one; a factor that has nothing to do with storage. In fact, most of the stores' cost should be charged to Product B, since this product causes (and benefits from) the stores' cost much more than Product A.

Failure to account more precisely for the cost of running the stores is masking the fact that Product B is not as profitable as it seems to be. It may even be leading to losses as a result of the relatively high stores-operating cost that it causes. However, much of this cost is charged to Product A, without regard to the fact that Product A causes little of it.

## Activity-based costing

**Activity-based costing (ABC)** aims to overcome the kind of problem just illustrated in, Example 11.1, by directly tracing the cost of all support activities (that is, overheads) to particular products or services. For a manufacturing business, these support activities may include materials ordering, materials handling, storage, inspection, and so on. The cost of the support activities makes up the total overheads cost. The outcome of this tracing exercise is to provide a more realistic, and more finely measured, account of the overhead cost element for a particular product or service.

To implement a system of ABC, managers must begin by carefully examining the business's operations. They will need to identify:

- each of the various support activities involved in the process of making products or providing services;
- the costs to be attributed to each support activity; and
- the factors that cause a change in the costs of each support activity, that is the **cost drivers**.

Identifying the cost drivers is a vital element of a successful ABC system. They have a cause-and-effect relationship with activity costs and so are used as a basis for attaching activity costs to a particular product or service. This point is now discussed further.

## Attributing overheads

Once the various support activities, their costs and the factors that drive these costs, have been identified, ABC requires:

- An overhead **cost pool** to be established for each activity. Thus, the business in Example 11.1 will create a cost pool for operating the finished goods store. There will be just one cost pool for each separate cost driver.
- The total cost associated with each support activity to be allocated to the relevant cost pool.
- The total cost in each pool to then be charged to output (Products A and B, in the case of Example 11.1) using the relevant cost driver.

The final step identified involves dividing the amount in each cost pool by the estimated total usage of the cost driver to derive a cost per unit of the cost driver. This unit cost figure is then multiplied by the number of units of the cost driver used by a particular product, or service, to determine the amount of overhead cost to be attached to it (or absorbed by it).

Example 11.2 should make this last step clear.

### Example 11.2

The management accountant at Modern Producers Ltd (see Example 11.1) has estimated that the cost of running the finished goods stores for next year will be £90,000. This will be the amount allocated to the 'finished goods stores cost pool'.

It is estimated that each Product A will spend an average of one week in the stores before being sold. With Product B, the equivalent period is four weeks. Both products are of roughly similar size and have very similar storage needs. It is felt, therefore, that the period spent in the stores ('product weeks') is the cost driver.

Next year, 50,000 Product As and 25,000 Product Bs are expected to pass through the stores. The estimated total usage of the cost driver will be the total number of 'product weeks' that the products will be in store. For next year, this will be:

| Product | A | 50,000 × 1 week | = | 50,000 |
|---------|---|-----------------|---|--------|
|         | B | 25,000 × 4 weeks | = | 100,000 |
|         |   |                 |   | 150,000 |

The cost per unit of cost driver is the total cost of the stores divided by the number of 'product weeks', as calculated above. This is:

$$£90,000/150,000 = £0.60$$

To determine the cost to be attached to a particular unit of product, the figure of £0.60 must be multiplied by the number of 'product weeks' that a product stays in the finished goods store. Thus, each unit of Product A will be charged with £0.60 (that is, £0.60 × 1) and each Product B with £2.40 (that is, £0.60 × 4).

## Benefits of ABC

Through the direct tracing of overheads to products in the way described, ABC seeks to establish a more accurate cost for each unit of product or service. This should help managers in assessing product profitability and in making decisions concerning pricing and the appropriate product mix. Other benefits, however, may also flow from adopting an ABC approach.

Activity **11.1**

Can you think of any other benefits that an ABC approach to costing may provide?

By identifying the various support activities' costs and analysing what causes them to change, managers should gain a better understanding of the business. This, in turn, should help them in controlling overheads and improving efficiency. It should also help them in forward planning. They may, for example, be in a better position to assess the likely effect of new products and processes on activities and costs.

## ABC versus the traditional approach

We can see that there is a basic philosophical difference between the traditional and the ABC approaches. The traditional approach views overheads as *rendering a service to cost units*, the cost of which must be charged to those units. ABC, on the other hand, views overheads as being *caused by* activities. Since it is the cost units that cause these activities, it is, therefore, the cost units that must be charged with the costs that they cause.

With the traditional approach, overheads are apportioned to product cost centres. Each product cost centre would then derive an overhead recovery rate, typically overheads per direct labour hour. Overheads would then be applied to units of output according to how many direct labour hours were worked on them.

With ABC, the overheads are analysed into cost pools, with one cost pool for each cost-driving activity. The overheads are then charged to units of output, through activity cost driver rates. These rates are an attempt to represent the extent to which each particular cost unit is believed to cause the particular part of the overheads.

Cost pools are much the same as cost centres, except that each cost pool is linked to a particular activity (operating the stores in Examples 11.1 and 11.2), rather than being more general, as is the case with cost centres in traditional job (or product) costing.

The two different approaches are illustrated in Figure 11.1.

## ABC and service industries

Much of our discussion of ABC has concentrated on the manufacturing industry, perhaps because early users of ABC were manufacturing businesses. In fact, ABC is possibly even more relevant to service industries because, in the absence of a direct material element, a service business's total cost is likely to be largely made up of overheads (see **Real World 10.2** on page 364). There is certainly evidence that ABC has been adopted more readily by businesses that sell services rather than products, as we shall see later.

Activity **11.2**

What is the difference in the way in which direct costs are accounted for when using ABC, relative to their treatment taking a traditional approach to full costing?

The answer is no difference at all. ABC is concerned only with the way in which overheads are charged to jobs to derive the full cost.

| Figure 11.1 | Traditional versus activity-based costing |
| --- | --- |

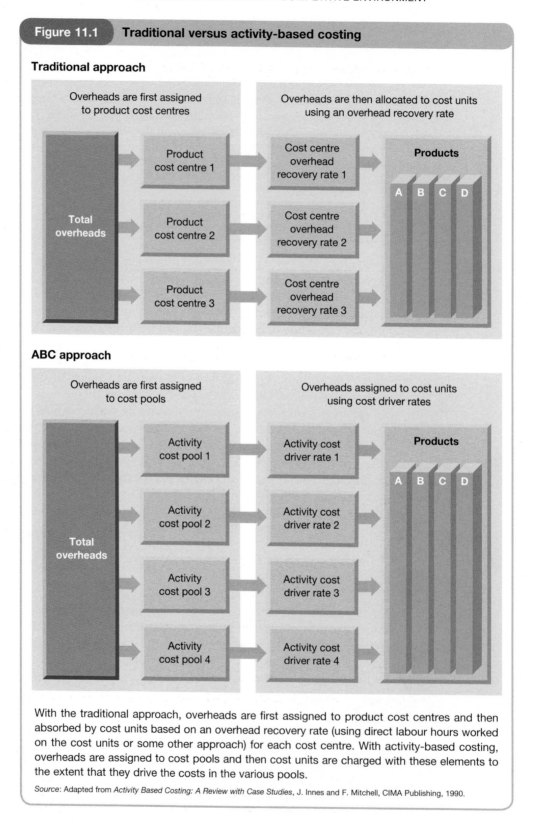

With the traditional approach, overheads are first assigned to product cost centres and then absorbed by cost units based on an overhead recovery rate (using direct labour hours worked on the cost units or some other approach) for each cost centre. With activity-based costing, overheads are assigned to cost pools and then cost units are charged with these elements to the extent that they drive the costs in the various pools.

*Source:* Adapted from *Activity Based Costing: A Review with Case Studies*, J. Innes and F. Mitchell, CIMA Publishing, 1990.

Example 11.3 provides an example of activity-based costing and brings together the points that have been raised so far.

## Example 11.3

Comma Ltd manufactures two types of Sprizzer – Standard and Deluxe. Each product requires the incorporation of a difficult-to-handle special part (one of them for a Standard and four for a Deluxe). Both of these products are made in batches (large batches for Standards and small ones for Deluxes). Each new batch requires that the production facilities are 'set up'.

Details of the two products are:

|  | Standard | Deluxe |
|---|---|---|
| Annual production and sales – units | 12,000 | 12,000 |
| Sales price per unit | £65 | £87 |
| Manufacturing batch size – units | 1,000 | 50 |
| Direct labour time per unit – hours | 2 | 2½ |
| Direct labour rate per hour | £8 | £8 |
| Direct material cost per unit | £22 | £32 |
| Number of special parts per unit | 1 | 4 |
| Number of set-ups per batch | 1 | 3 |
| Number of separate material issues from stores per batch | 1 | 1 |
| Number of sales invoices issued per year | 50 | 240 |

In recent months, Comma Ltd has been trying to persuade customers who buy the Standard to purchase the Deluxe instead. An analysis of overhead costs for Comma Ltd has provided the following information:

| Overhead cost analysis | £ | Cost driver |
|---|---|---|
| Set-up cost | 73,200 | Number of set-ups |
| Special part handling cost | 60,000 | Number of special parts |
| Customer invoicing cost | 29,000 | Number of invoices |
| Material handling cost | 63,000 | Number of batches |
| Other overheads | 108,000 | Labour hours |

**Required:**

(a) Calculate the profit per unit and the return on sales for Standard and Deluxe Sprizzers using both:
- the traditional direct-labour-hour-based absorption of overheads; and
- activity-based costing methods.

(b) Comment on the managerial implications for Comma Ltd of the results in (a) above.

## Solution

### (a) Traditional approach

Using the traditional full (absorption) costing approach that we considered in Chapter 10, the overheads are added together and an overheads recovery rate deduced as follows:

| Overheads | £ |
|---|---|
| Set-up cost | 73,200 |
| Special part handling cost | 60,000 |
| Customer invoicing cost | 29,000 |
| Material handling cost | 63,000 |
| Other overheads | 108,000 |
|  | 333,200 |

$$\text{Overhead recovery rate} = \frac{\text{Total overheads}}{\text{Number of labour hours}}$$

$$= \frac{333{,}200}{54{,}000 \,[\text{that is } (12{,}000 \times 2) + (12{,}000 \times 2\,\tfrac{1}{2})]}$$

$$= \text{£}6.17 \text{ per hour}$$

The total cost per unit of each type of Sprizzer is calculated by adding the direct cost to the overheads cost per unit. The overheads cost per unit is calculated by multiplying the number of direct labour hours spent on the product (2 hours for each Standard and $2\frac{1}{2}$ hours for each Deluxe) by the overheads recovery rate calculated above. Hence:

|  | Standard £ | Deluxe £ |
|---|---|---|
| *Direct cost* |  |  |
| Labour | 16.00 | 20.00 |
| Material | 22.00 | 32.00 |
| *Indirect cost* |  |  |
| Overheads (£6.17 per hour) | 12.34 | 15.43 |
| Total cost per unit | 50.34 | 67.43 |

The return on sales is calculated as follows:

|  | Standard £ per unit | Deluxe £ per unit |
|---|---|---|
| Sales price | 65.00 | 87.00 |
| Total cost (see above) | 50.34 | 67.43 |
| Profit | 14.66 | 19.57 |
| Return on sales [(profit/sales) × 100%] | 22.55% | 22.49% |

### ABC approach

Using the ABC costing approach, the activity cost driver rates will be calculated as follows:

| Overhead cost pool | Driver | (a) Standard driver volume | (b) Deluxe driver volume | (c) Total driver volume (a + b) | (d) Costs £ | (e) Driver rate (d/c) £ |
|---|---|---|---|---|---|---|
| Set-up | Set-ups per batch | 12 | 720 | 732 | 73,200 | 100 |
| Special part | Special parts per unit | 12,000 | 48,000 | 60,000 | 60,000 | 1 |
| Customer invoices | Invoices per year | 50 | 240 | 290 | 29,000 | 100 |
| Material handling | Number of batches | 12 | 240 | 252 | 63,000 | 250 |
| Other overheads | Labour hours | 24,000 | 30,000 | 54,000 | 108,000 | 2 |

The activity-based costs are derived as follows:

| Overhead cost pool | (f) Total costs Standard (a × e) £ | (g) Total costs Deluxe (b × e) £ | Unit costs Standard (f/12,000) £ | Unit costs Deluxe (g/12,000) £ |
|---|---|---|---|---|
| Set-up | 1,200 | 72,000 | 0.10 | 6.00 |
| Special part | 12,000 | 48,000 | 1.00 | 4.00 |
| Customer invoices | 5,000 | 24,000 | 0.42 | 2.00 |
| Material handling | 3,000 | 60,000 | 0.25 | 5.00 |
| Other overheads | 48,000 | 60,000 | 4.00 | 5.00 |
| Total overheads | | | 5.77 | 22.00 |

The total cost per unit is calculated as follows:

| | Standard £ per unit | Deluxe £ per unit |
|---|---|---|
| *Direct costs:* | | |
| Labour | 16.00 | 20.00 |
| Material | 22.00 | 32.00 |
| *Indirect costs* | | |
| See above | 5.77 | 22.00 |
| Total cost per unit | 43.77 | 74.00 |

The return on sales is calculated as follows:

| | Standard £ per unit | Deluxe £ per unit |
|---|---|---|
| Sales price | 65.00 | 87.00 |
| Total cost (see above) | 43.77 | 74.00 |
| Profit | 21.23 | 13.00 |
| Return on sales [(profit/sales) × 100%] | 32.67% | 14.94% |

(b) The figures show that under the traditional approach the returns on sales for each product are broadly equal. However, the ABC approach shows that the Standard product is far more profitable. Hence, the business should reconsider its policy of trying to persuade customers to switch to the Deluxe product.

## Criticisms of ABC

Although many businesses now adopt a system of ABC, its critics point out that ABC can be time consuming and costly. The cost of setting up the ABC system, as well as costs of running and updating it, must be incurred. These costs can be very high, particularly where the business's operations are complex and involve a large number of activities and cost drivers. Furthermore, ABC information produced under the scenario just described may be complex. If managers find ABC reports difficult to understand, there is a risk that the potential benefits of ABC will be lost.

Not all businesses are likely to benefit from ABC. Where a business sells products or services that all have similar levels of output and involve similar activities and processes, it is unlikely that the finer measurements provided by ABC will lead to strikingly different outcomes than under the traditional approach. As a result, opportunities for better pricing, planning and cost control may not be great and may not justify the cost of switching to an ABC system.

Measurement and tracing problems can arise with ABC, which may undermine any potential benefits. Not all costs can be easily identified with a particular activity and yet all overheads have to be allocated to one cost pool or another. Failure for this to happen means that not all of the overheads are taken into account. Dealing with unallocated overheads can often be done on some sensible basis. In some cases, however, a lack of data concerning a particular cost may lead to fairly arbitrary cost allocations between activities. There is also the problem that the relationship between activity costs and their cost drivers may be difficult to determine. Identifying a cause-and-effect relationship can be difficult where most activity costs are fixed and so do not vary with changes in usage.

ABC is also criticised for the same reason that full costing generally is criticised: because it does not provide very relevant information for decision making. The point was made in Chapter 10 that full costing tends to use past costs and to ignore opportunity costs. Since past costs are always irrelevant in decision making and opportunity costs can be significant, full costing information is seen as an expensive irrelevance. In contrast, advocates of full costing claim that it *is* relevant, in that it provides a long-run average cost, whereas 'relevant costing', which we considered in Chapter 8, relates only to the specific circumstances of the short term. The use of ABC, rather than the traditional approach to job (or product) costing, does not affect the validity of this irrelevance argument.

**Real World 11.2** shows how ABC came to be used at the Royal Mail.

## Real World 11.2

### Delivering ABC

Early in the 2000s the publicly-owned Royal Mail adopted ABC and used it to find the cost of making postal deliveries. Royal Mail identified 340 activities that gave rise to costs, created a cost pool and identified a cost driver for each of these.

The Royal Mail continues to use an ABC approach to deriving its costs. The volume of mail is obviously a major driver of costs.

The Royal Mail is a public sector organisation that is subject to supervision by Postcomm, the UK government appointed regulatory body. The government requires the Royal Mail to operate on a commercial basis and to make profits.

*Source*: Royal Mail Group Ltd, Regulatory Financial Statements, 2010/11.

**Real World 11.3** provides some indication of the extent to which ABC is used in practice.

## ABC in practice

A fairly recent survey of 176 UK businesses operating in various industries, all with annual sales revenue of more than £50 million, was conducted by Al-Omiri and Drury. This indicated that 29 per cent of larger UK businesses use ABC.

The adoption of ABC in the UK varies widely between industries, as is shown in Figure 11.2.

**Figure 11.2    ABC in practice**

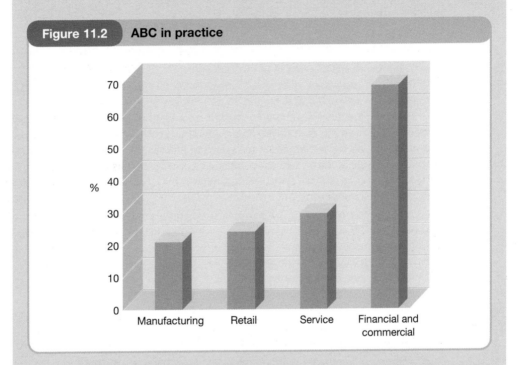

Al-Omiri and Drury took their analysis a step further by looking at the factors that lead a particular business to adopt ABC. They found that businesses that used ABC tended to be:

● large;
● sophisticated, in terms of using advanced management accounting techniques generally;
● in an intensely competitive market for their products;
● operating in a service industry, particularly in the financial services.

The 2009 CIMA survey emphatically supported the finding that larger businesses tend to use ABC more than smaller ones. It showed that only 22 per cent of businesses with fewer than 50 employees use ABC, whereas 46 per cent of businesses with more than 10,000 employees use the technique.

All of these findings are broadly in line with other recent research evidence involving businesses from around the world.

*Sources*: 'A survey of factors influencing the choice of product costing systems in UK organisations', M. Al-Omiri and C. Drury, *Management Accounting Research*, December 2007; and 'Management accounting tools for today and tomorrow', CIMA, 2009, p. 12.

## Self-assessment question 11.1

Psilis Ltd makes a product in two qualities, called 'Basic' and 'Super'. The business is able to sell these products at a price that gives a standard profit mark-up of 25 per cent of full cost. Full cost is derived using a traditional batch costing approach.

Management is concerned by the lack of profit.

To derive the full cost for each product, overheads are absorbed on the basis of direct labour hours. The costs are as follows:

|  | Basic | Super |
|---|---|---|
|  | £ | £ |
| Direct labour (all £10/hour) | 40 | 60 |
| Direct material | 15 | 20 |

The total annual overheads are £1,000,000.

Based on experience over recent years, in the forthcoming year the business expects to make and sell 40,000 Basics and 10,000 Supers.

Recently, the business's management accountant has undertaken an exercise to try to identify activities and cost drivers in an attempt to be able to deal with the overheads on a more precise basis than had been possible before. This exercise has revealed the following analysis of the annual overheads:

| Activity (and cost driver) | Cost | Annual number of activities | | |
|---|---|---|---|---|
|  | £000 | Total | Basic | Super |
| Number of machine set-ups | 280 | 100 | 20 | 80 |
| Number of quality-control inspections | 220 | 2,000 | 500 | 1,500 |
| Number of sales orders processed | 240 | 5,000 | 1,500 | 3,500 |
| General production (machine hours) | 260 | 500,000 | 350,000 | 150,000 |
| Total | 1,000 |  |  |  |

The management accountant explained the analysis of the £1,000,000 overheads as follows:

- The two products are made in relatively small batches, so that the amount of the finished product held in inventories is negligible. The Supers are made in very small batches because their demand is relatively low. Each time a new batch is produced, the machines have to be reset by skilled staff. Resetting for Basic production occurs about 20 times a year and for Supers about 80 times: about 100 times in total. The cost of employing the machine-setting staff is about £280,000 a year. It is clear that the more set-ups that occur, the higher the total set-up costs; in other words, the number of set-ups is the factor that drives set-up costs.
- All production has to be inspected for quality, and this costs about £220,000 a year. The higher specifications of the Supers mean that there is more chance that there will be quality problems. Thus the Supers are inspected in total 1,500 times annually, whereas the Basics only need about 500 inspections. The number of inspections is the factor that drives these costs.
- Sales order processing (dealing with customers' orders, from receiving the original order to dispatching the products) costs about £240,000 a year. Despite the larger amount of Basic production, there are only 1,500 sales orders each year because the Basics are sold to wholesalers in relatively large-sized orders. The Supers are sold mainly direct to the public by mail order, usually in very small-sized orders. It is believed that the number of orders drives the costs of processing orders.

*Required:*
(a) Deduce the full cost of each of the two products on the basis used at present and, from these, deduce the current selling price.
(b) Deduce the full cost of each product on an ABC basis, taking account of the management accountant's recent investigations.
(c) What conclusions do you draw? What advice would you offer the management of the business?

**The answer to this question can be found at the back of the book on pages 737 to 738.**

## Other costing approaches in the modern environment

The increasingly competitive environment in which modern businesses operate is leading to greater effort being applied in trying to manage costs. Businesses need to keep costs to a minimum so that they can supply goods and services at a price that customers will be prepared to pay and, at the same time, meet the businesses' objectives of enhancing shareholder wealth. We have just seen how ABC can help manage costs. We shall now go on to outline some other techniques that have recently emerged in an attempt to meet these goals of competitiveness and profitability. These can be used in conjunction with ABC.

### Total (or whole) life-cycle costing

This approach to costing starts from the premise that the total (or whole) life cycle of a product or service that the business provides for sale has three phases. These are:

1 The *pre-production phase*. This is the period that precedes production of the product or service. During this phase, research and development – both of the product or service and of the market – is conducted. The product or service is invented/designed and so is the means of production. The phase culminates with acquiring and setting up the necessary production facilities and with advertising and promotion.
2 The *production phase* comes next, being the one in which the product is made and sold or the service is rendered to customers.
3 The *post-production phase* comes last. During this phase, any costs necessary to correct faults that arose with products or services that have been sold (after-sales service) are incurred. There would also be the costs of closing production at the end of the product's or service's life cycle, such as the cost of decommissioning production facilities. Since after-sales service will tend to arise from as early as the first product or service being sold and probably, therefore, well before the last one is sold, this phase would typically overlap with the production phase.

Businesses often seem to consider environmental costs alongside the more obvious financial costs involved in the life of a product.

The total life cycle is shown in Figure 11.3.

In some types of business, particularly those engaged in an advanced manufacturing environment, it is estimated that a very high proportion (as much as 80 per cent) of the total costs that will be incurred over the total life of a particular product are either incurred or committed at the pre-production phase. For example, a motor car

| Figure 11.3 | The total life cycle of a product or service |
| --- | --- |

From the producer's viewpoint, the life of a product can be seen as having three distinct phases. During the first the product is developed and everything is prepared so that production and marketing can start. Next come production and sales. Lastly, dealing with post-production activities is undertaken.

manufacturer, when designing, developing and setting up production of a new model, incurs a high proportion of the total costs that will be incurred on that model during the whole of its life. Not only are pre-production costs themselves incurred during this phase, but the need to incur particular costs during the production phase is also established. This is because the design will incorporate features that will lead to particular manufacturing costs. Once the design of the car has been finalised and the manufacturing plant set up, it may be too late to 'design out' a costly feature without incurring another large cost.

### Activity 11.3

A decision taken at the design stage (during the pre-production phase) could well commit the business to costs during the post-production phase. Can you suggest a potential cost that could be built in at the design stage that will show itself *after* the manufacture of the product?

After-sales service costs could be incurred as a result of some design fault. Once the manufacturing facilities have been established, it may not be economic to revise the design but better merely to deal with the problem through after-sales service procedures.

**Total life-cycle costing** seeks to focus management's attention on the fact that it is not just during the production phase that attention needs to be paid to cost management. By the start of the production phase it may be too late to try to manage a large element of the product's or service's total life-cycle cost. Efforts need to be made to assess the costs of alternative designs.

There needs to be a review of the product or service over its entire life cycle, which could be a period of 20 or more years. Traditional management accounting, however, tends to be concerned with assessing performance over periods of just one year or less.

**Real World 11.4** provides some idea of the extent to which total life-cycle costing is used in practice.

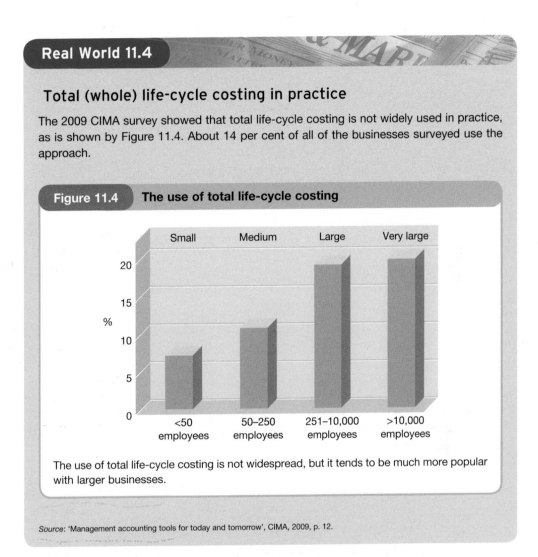

### Real World 11.4

### Total (whole) life-cycle costing in practice

The 2009 CIMA survey showed that total life-cycle costing is not widely used in practice, as is shown by Figure 11.4. About 14 per cent of all of the businesses surveyed use the approach.

**Figure 11.4    The use of total life-cycle costing**

The use of total life-cycle costing is not widespread, but it tends to be much more popular with larger businesses.

Source: 'Management accounting tools for today and tomorrow', CIMA, 2009, p. 12.

**Real World 11.5** shows how a well-known international car maker uses total life-cycle costing.

### Real World 11.5

### Total life-cycle management at Renault

According to Renault, the French motor vehicle manufacturer uses life cycle management to promote more economic and ecological vehicles.

**Real World 11.5 (*continued*)**

Renault sees the life of a particular vehicle as having a life comprising four phases:

1 **Design phase**
2 **Manufacturing phase**
3 **Use phase**
4 **End of life**

Renault links the life cycle to environmental as well as economic aspects of their business.

*Source*: www.renault.com. Renault 2011.

Note that Renault divides the *post-production phase* into two sections: use and end of life.

## Total quality management

Quality has become a major weapon that businesses deploy when competing against their rivals. As mentioned earlier, customers increasingly demand products (both of

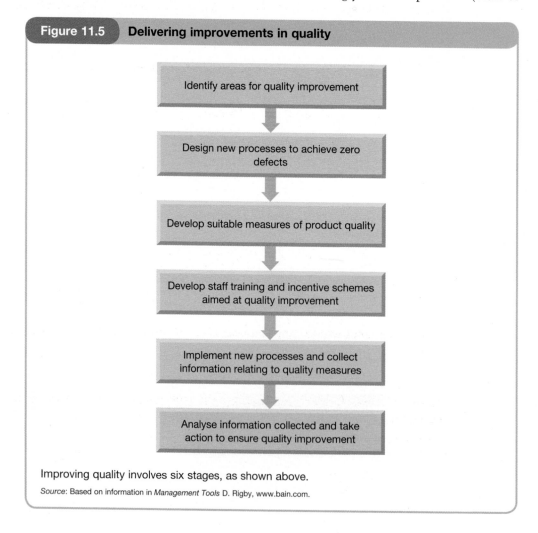

**Figure 11.5** **Delivering improvements in quality**

Identify areas for quality improvement

Design new processes to achieve zero defects

Develop suitable measures of product quality

Develop staff training and incentive schemes aimed at quality improvement

Implement new processes and collect information relating to quality measures

Analyse information collected and take action to ensure quality improvement

Improving quality involves six stages, as shown above.

*Source*: Based on information in *Management Tools* D. Rigby, www.bain.com.

goods and services) that meet their specific requirements. One of these requirements is going to be that products should be of a suitable quality. This means that the products should meet customers' needs and should be available at a price they are willing to pay.

This emphasis on creating quality products has led to **total quality management** (TQM). The TQM philosophy is concerned with providing products that meet, or exceed, customers' requirements all of the time. This implies that defective products should never reach the customer. Ideally, there should never be any defective production. TQM has been characterised as 'getting it right first time, every time'. It aims to create a virtuous sequence of events where quality improvements lead to reduced production problems, increased customer satisfaction and increased profits.

TQM requires a systematic approach to quality improvement. Figure 11.5 sets out the main steps in the process.

**Real World 11.6** provides some idea of the extent to which TQM is used in practice.

## Real World 11.6

### Quality practice

The 2009 CIMA survey showed that TQM is not widely used in practice, as is shown by Figure 11.6.

**Figure 11.6    The use of total quality management**

It is not obvious why the larger businesses do not use TQM as much as medium-size ones.

Total quality management was used by just over a quarter of all of the businesses surveyed.

*Source*: 'Management accounting tools for today and tomorrow', CIMA, 2009, p. 19.

## Costing quality procedures

Ensuring that products and services are of the right quality can only be achieved at a cost. It has been estimated that these **quality costs** can amount to up to 30 per cent of total processing costs. They tend to be incurred during the production phase of the product life cycle and fall into four main categories:

- *Prevention costs*. These are involved with procedures to try to prevent products being produced that are not up to the required quality. Such procedures might include staff training on quality issues. Some types of prevention costs might be incurred during the *Pre-production phase* of the product life cycle, where the production process could be designed in such a way as to avoid potential quality problems with the output.
- *Appraisal costs*. These are concerned with monitoring raw materials, work in progress and finished products to try to avoid substandard production from reaching the customer.
- *Internal failure costs*. These include the costs of rectifying substandard products before they pass to the customer and the costs of scrap arising from quality failures.
- *External failure costs*. These are involved with rectifying quality problems with products that have passed to the customer. There is also the cost to the business of its loss of reputation from having passed substandard products to the customer.

Figure 11.7 sets these out in diagram form.

**Figure 11.7    The main types of quality costs**

| | |
|---|---|
| Prevention costs | Procedures to avoid quality problems |
| Appraisal costs | Procedures to check quality |
| Internal failure costs | Procedures to deal with quality problems before product passes to customer |
| External failure costs | Procedures to deal with quality problems after product passes to customer |

Quality costs fall into four main categories. The first two are concerned with avoiding substandard production and the last two with dealing with it, should it arise.

## Target costing

With traditional cost-plus pricing, costs are totalled for a product or service and a percentage is added for profit to arrive at a selling price. We saw in Chapter 10 that this is not a very practical basis on which to price output for many businesses – certainly not for those operating in a price-competitive market (price takers). The cost-plus price may well be unacceptable to the market.

**Target costing** approaches the problem from the other direction. First, with the help of market research or other means, the price that buyers are prepared to pay for a product is identified, along with the estimated sales volume at the identified price. An amount for profit is then deducted from the identified price, which is in line with the business's financial objective. The resulting figure is the target cost. This target cost may well be less than the current estimated cost and so there may be a 'cost gap'. Efforts are then made to bridge this gap, that is, to make the product in a way that will enable the target cost to be met. These efforts may involve revising the design, developing more efficient means of production, or requiring suppliers of goods and services to supply more cheaply.

Target costing is seen as a part of a total life-cycle costing approach, in that cost savings are sought at a very early stage in the life cycle, during the pre-production phase.

**Real World 11.7** indicates the level of usage of target costing. This shows quite a low level of usage in the UK. In contrast, other survey evidence shows that target costing is very widely used by Japanese manufacturing businesses.

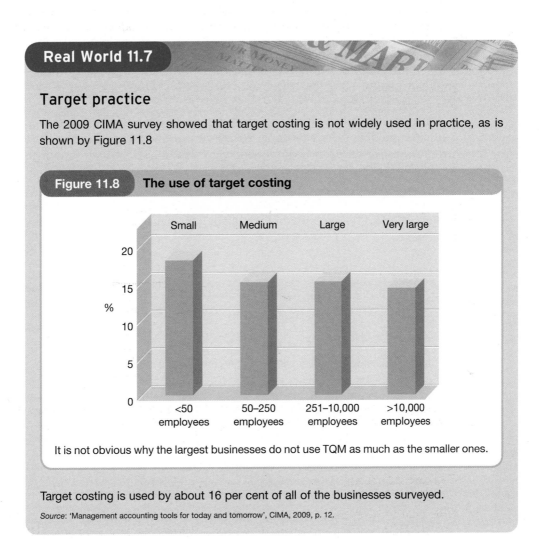

### Real World 11.7

#### Target practice

The 2009 CIMA survey showed that target costing is not widely used in practice, as is shown by Figure 11.8

##### Figure 11.8    The use of target costing

It is not obvious why the largest businesses do not use TQM as much as the smaller ones.

Target costing is used by about 16 per cent of all of the businesses surveyed.

*Source:* 'Management accounting tools for today and tomorrow', CIMA, 2009, p. 12.

**Activity (11.4)**

Although target costing has its enthusiasts, there are potential problems with its use. Can you think what these problems might be?

There seem to be three main problem areas:

● It can lead to various conflicts – for example, between the business, its suppliers and its own staff.
● It can cause a great deal of stress for employees who are trying to meet target costs that are sometimes extremely difficult to achieve.
● Although, in the end, ways may be found to meet a target cost (through product or service redesign, negotiating lower prices with suppliers, and so on), the whole process can be very expensive.

## *Kaizen* costing

*Kaizen* costing is linked to total life-cycle costing, and focuses on cost saving during the production phase. The Japanese word *kaizen* implies 'continuous changes'. The application of the *kaizen* costing approach involves continuous improvement, in terms of cost saving, throughout the production phase. Since this phase is at a relatively late stage in the life cycle (from a cost control point of view) only relatively small cost savings can usually be made. The major production-phase cost savings should already have been made through target costing.

With *kaizen* costing, efforts are made to reduce the unit manufacturing cost of the particular product or service under review, if possible taking it below the unit cost in the previous period. Percentage reduction targets can be set. Usually, production workers are encouraged to identify ways of reducing costs. This is something that the 'hands on' experience of these workers may enable them to do. Even though the scope to reduce costs is limited at the production stage, valuable savings can still be made.

**Real World 11.8** explains how a major UK manufacturer used *kaizen* costing to advantage.

**Real World 11.8**

### *Kaizen* costing is part of the package

Kappa Packaging is a major UK packaging business. It has a factory at Stalybridge where it makes, among other things, packaging (cardboard cartons) for glass bottles containing alcoholic drinks. In 2002, Kappa introduced a new approach to reducing the amount of waste paper and cardboard. Before this, the business wasted 14.6 per cent of its raw materials used. This figure was taken as the base against which improvements would be measured.

Improvements were made at Kappa as a result of:

● making staff more aware of the waste problem;
● requiring staff to monitor the amount of waste for which they were individually responsible; and
● establishing a *kaizen* team to find ways of reducing waste.

As a result of *kaizen* savings, Kappa was able to reduce waste from 14.6 per cent to 13.1 per cent in 2002 and 11 per cent in 2003. The business estimates that each 1 per cent waste saving was worth £110,000 a year. So by the end of 2003, Kappa was saving about £400,000 a year, relative to 2001: that is, over £2,000 per employee each year.

*Source:* Taken from 'Accurate measurement of process waste leads to reduced costs', www.envirowise.gov.uk, 2003.

## Value chain analysis

Another approach that seeks to manage costs, and which recognises the total life-cycle concept, is **value chain analysis**. It is useful to analyse a business into a sequence of value-creating activities. This sequence is known as the value chain, and value chain analysis examines the potential for each link in the chain to add value. For a particular product or service, the value chain is the progress of activities, through the three phases of the product life cycle from research and development to after-sales activities. In a wealth-seeking business, the objective for the product is that it should create value for the business and its owners.

Each link in the value chain represents a particular activity. All of the activities will give rise to a cost. Ideally, however, each link should add value to the product, making the product more valuable to the customer. Any links in the chain that fail to add value should be examined very critically. The objective of this examination is to assess whether the particular link could be eliminated completely or, at least, have its cost reduced.

An example of a typical non-value-added activity is inspection of the completed product or service by a quality controller. This activity does not add value to the product or service, yet it adds cost. This inspection cost might well be capable of being reduced, or even completely eliminated. The introduction of a 'quality' culture in the business could lead to all output being reliable and not needing to be inspected. This is a development that many modern businesses have achieved.

An example of a value-adding activity would be the rendering of a service to a customer for which the customer is prepared to pay more than that activity costs.

For a manufacturing business, the value-creating sequence begins with the acquisition of inputs, such as raw materials and energy, and ends with the sale of completed goods and after-sales service. Figure 11.9 sets out the main 'links' in the value chain for a manufacturing business.

Value chain analysis applies as much to service-providing businesses as it does to manufacturers. Service providers similarly have a sequence of activities leading to provision of the service to their customers. Analysing these activities in an attempt to identify and eliminate non-value added activities is very important.

**Real World 11.9** provides an example of how focusing on the value chain may help transform the performance of a business.

### Real World 11.9

#### What a sauce                                                                            **FT**

Ahold is a major Dutch retailer that has recently been recovering its fortunes, under its chief executive Anders Moberg. The business has a recovery plan that involves 're-engineering the value chain' and according to Mr Moberg, the key is a detailed analysis of the cost of goods sold. 'That is probably the single biggest opportunity [for savings] that we have.'

**Real World 11.9 (continued)**

Take a bottle of tomato ketchup. 'What are the costs of the growers of the tomatoes? What are the components of the value chain, production, marketing, packaging and distribution? Can you add a component in a different way, for example with standardised bottles? You are looking at how to re-engineer the value chain [in order] to lower the price.'

Manufacturers' brands do this, he says, 'but they keep the savings, hence they have a better return on capital'. With supermarket own-label brands on the rise – they account for 50 per cent of Ahold Dutch store sales, and 15 per cent in the US – Mr Moberg can reduce what it costs him to make products while at the same time lowering prices, attracting more shoppers to Ahold stores and thereby raising volumes.

Armed with intricate knowledge of supply chain costs, Ahold can press big brand manufacturers to cut the prices they ask of the retailer. It is a delicate balancing act. Both Grolsch, the Dutch brewer, and Peijnenburg, a bakery group, have quarrelled with Ahold about the damage inflicted on their brands by pricing policy, while Unilever, the consumer goods group, took Ahold to court, claiming it had copied its packaging.

It appears, however, to be a battle Mr Moberg is winning. Not only is customer perception of the quality of own-label products rising – a fact confirmed by independent industry research – but Ahold has a strong position with big consumer brands through its control of distribution channels, especially in the Netherlands, where its Albert Heijn chain is market leader and has 700 stores.

*Source*: 'It is all about the value chain', Ian Bickerton, FT.com, 23 February 2004.

---

**Figure 11.9** **The value chain of a manufacturing business**

The figure sets out the various links in the value chain. We can see that five primary activities are supported by four secondary activities.

*Source*: Adapted from *Competitive Advantage*, M. Porter, The Free Press, 1985, pp. 11–15.

## Benchmarking

**Benchmarking** is an activity – usually a continuing one – where a business seeks to emulate a business that is 'best in class' in order to achieve greater success. The best-in-class business provides a standard, or benchmark, against which a business can measure its own performance. It can also provide insights as to how performance can be improved. Through benchmarking, new ideas may be introduced resulting in greater operational efficiency and greater competitive advantage.

Businesses do not have to benchmark and many are understandably reluctant to divulge commercially sensitive information. Thus, a competitor business that is regarded as best in class is unlikely to put itself forward as a willing partner in the benchmarking process. Nevertheless, it may still be possible to glean a lot through an analysis of the competitor's activities using information from other sources. Where a best-in-class business is not a direct competitor, it may be prepared to share information concerning processes or functions carried out by both businesses, such as credit collection and inventories control. It may also be possible for a business to benchmark internally by using a successful division or department as the best in class.

The benchmarking process involves a series of steps, which are set out in Figure 11.10 below.

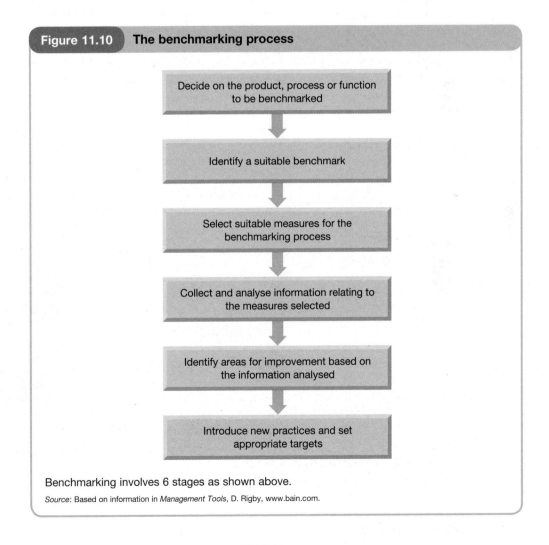

**Figure 11.10**    **The benchmarking process**

Decide on the product, process or function to be benchmarked

↓

Identify a suitable benchmark

↓

Select suitable measures for the benchmarking process

↓

Collect and analyse information relating to the measures selected

↓

Identify areas for improvement based on the information analysed

↓

Introduce new practices and set appropriate targets

Benchmarking involves 6 stages as shown above.

*Source*: Based on information in *Management Tools*, D. Rigby, www.bain.com.

**Real World 11.10** provides an example of a well-known motor car manufacturer benchmarking its cars against those of its competitors.

> ### Real World 11.10
>
> ## Tracking the best
> **FT**
>
> Hyundai Motor is preparing to relaunch its brand as "modern premium" in line with the South Korean carmaker's growing confidence and global sales. Hyundai and its sister brand Kia will this year produce more than 6 million vehicles, up about 20 per cent on 2009, and will be the industry's fifth-largest carmaking group, according to forecasts by consultancies JD Power and IHS Global Insight.
>
> Hyundai and Kia have grown faster than the overall car market during the credit crunch by building cars perceived as offering value for money. This year, they replaced Toyota as Europe's top-selling Asian carmaker, and last week Hyundai passed the 500,000 sales mark in the US for the first time.
>
> Hyundai's new brand strategy will focus on a concept dubbed modern premium, predicated on selling cars with top-end features at prices low enough to appeal to mass-market consumers. "We want to deliver premium value . . . at an affordable price," Wonhong Cho, Hyundai's head of marketing, told the *Financial Times*.
>
> The carmaker's campaign will start at next month's Detroit car show where, along with its sporty new FS coupé, Hyundai will also unveil its new corporate slogan. The company also plans a "big increase" in its marketing spending this year, Mr Cho said.
>
> Hyundai's reputation in North America was sullied in the late 1980s by models that sacrificed quality for price. The company all but withdrew from that market for much of the 1990s. Over the past decade Hyundai's chairman, Chung Mong-koo, has rebuilt the car-maker's franchise by benchmarking its vehicles against competitors' and improving their quality and reliability. With its business now growing, Hyundai is "not relying on prior industry practices to inform the way we're going to approach our business", John Krafcik, head of Hyundai America, told the *Financial Times*.
>
> *Source*: 'Hyundai prepares to relaunch brand', J. Reed, and B. Simon, FT.com, 15 December 2010.

## Non-financial measures of performance

Financial measures have long been seen as the most important ones for a business. They provide a valuable means of summarising and evaluating business achievement. There is no real doubt about the continued importance of financial measures in this role. In recent years, however, there has been increasing recognition that financial measures alone will not provide managers with sufficient information to manage a business effectively. Non-financial measures must also be used in order to gain a deeper understanding of the business and to achieve its objectives, including financial objectives.

Financial measures portray various aspects of business achievement (for example, sales revenues, profits and return on capital employed) that can help managers determine whether the business is increasing the wealth of its owners. These measures are vitally important but, in an increasingly competitive environment, managers also need to understand what *drives* the creation of wealth. These **value drivers** may be such things as employee satisfaction, customer loyalty and the level of product innovation. Often they do not lend themselves to financial measurement. Non-financial measures, however, may provide some means of assessment.

## Activity 11.5

How might we measure:

(a) employee satisfaction?
(b) customer loyalty?
(c) the level of product innovation?

(a) Employee satisfaction may be measured through the use of an employee survey. This could examine attitudes towards various aspects of the job, the degree of autonomy that is permitted, the level of recognition and reward received, the level of participation in decision making, the degree of support received in carrying out tasks, and so on. Less direct measures of satisfaction may include employee turnover rates and employee productivity. However, other factors may have a significant influence on these measures.

(b) Customer loyalty may be measured through the proportion of total sales generated from existing customers, the number of repeat sales made to customers, the percentage of customers renewing subscriptions or other contracts, and so on.

(c) The level of product innovation may be measured through the number of innovations during a period compared to those of competitors, the percentage of sales attributable to recent product innovations, the number of innovations that are brought successfully to market, and so on.

Financial measures tend to be 'lag' indicators, in that they tell us about outcomes. In other words, they measure the consequences arising from past management decisions. Non-financial measures can also act as lag indicators, of course. However, they can also be 'lead' indicators because they tend to focus on those things that drive performance. It is argued that if we measure changes in these value drivers, we may be able to predict changes in future financial performance. For example, a business may find from experience that a 10 per cent decline in the level of product innovation during one period tends to lead to a 20 per cent reduction in sales revenues over the next three periods. In this case, the level of product innovation can be regarded as a lead indicator. It can tell managers that a future decline in sales is likely, unless corrective action is taken. Thus, by using this lead indicator, managers can identify key changes at an early stage and can respond quickly.

## The balanced scorecard

One of the most impressive attempts to integrate the use of financial and non-financial measures has been the **balanced scorecard**, developed by Robert Kaplan and David Norton (see reference 1 at the end of the chapter). The balanced scorecard is both a management system and a measurement system. In essence, it provides a framework that translates the aims and objectives of a business into a series of key performance measures and targets. This framework is intended to make the strategy of the business more coherent by tightly linking it to particular targets and initiatives. As a result, managers should be able to see more clearly whether the objectives that have been set have actually been achieved.

The balanced scorecard approach involves setting objectives and developing appropriate measures and targets in four main areas:

1 *Financial.* This area will specify the financial returns required by shareholders and may involve the use of financial measures such as:
- return on capital employed;
- operating profit margin; and
- percentage sales revenue growth.

2 *Customer.* This area will specify the kind of customer and/or markets that the business wishes to service and will establish appropriate measures such as:
- customer satisfaction; and
- new customer growth levels.

3 *Internal business process.* This area will specify those business processes (for example, innovation, types of operation and after-sales service) that are important to the success of the business. It will also establish appropriate measures, such as:
- percentage of sales from new products;
- time to market for new products;
- product cycle times; and
- speed of response to customer complaints.

4 *Learning and growth.* This area will specify the kind of people, the systems and the procedures that are necessary to deliver long-term business growth. This area is often the most difficult for the development of appropriate measures. However, examples of measures may include:
- employee motivation;
- employee skills profiles; and
- information systems capabilities.

These four areas are shown in Figure 11.11.

The balanced scorecard approach does not prescribe the particular objectives, measures or targets that a business should adopt; this is a matter for the individual business to decide. There are differences between businesses in terms of technology employed, organisational structure, management philosophy and business environment, so each business should develop objectives and measures that reflect its unique circumstances. The balanced scorecard simply sets out the framework for developing a coherent set of objectives for the business and for ensuring that these objectives are then linked to specific targets and initiatives.

A balanced scorecard will be prepared for the business as a whole or, in the case of large, diverse businesses, for each major division. However, having prepared an overall scorecard, it is then possible to prepare a balanced scorecard for each sub-unit, such as a department, within the business. Thus, the balanced scorecard approach can cascade down the business and can result in a pyramid of balanced scorecards that are linked to the 'master' balanced scorecard through an alignment of the objectives and measures employed.

Though there are many measures, both financial and non-financial, that could be used in a balanced scorecard, only a handful of these should be employed. According to Kaplan and Norton, a maximum of 20 measures will normally be sufficient to enable the factors that are critical to the success of the business to be captured. (If a business has come up with more than 20 measures, it is usually because the managers have not thought hard enough about what the key measures really are.) The key measures developed should be a mix of lagging indicators (those relating to outcomes) and lead indicators (those relating to the things that drive performance).

Although the balanced scorecard employs measures across a wide range of business activity, it does not seek to dilute the importance of financial measures and objectives.

In fact, the opposite is true. Kaplan and Norton emphasise the point that a balanced scorecard must reflect a concern for the financial objectives of the business. This

**Figure 11.11**  The balanced scorecard – for translating a strategy into operational processes

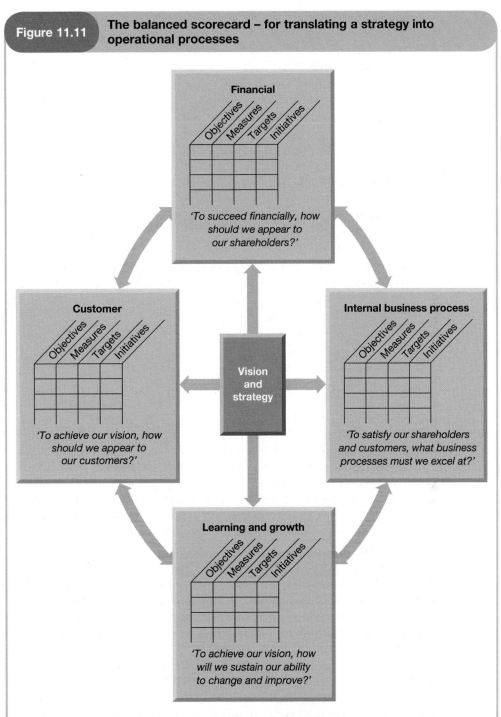

There are four main areas covered by the balanced scorecard. Note that, for each area, a fundamental question must be addressed. By answering these questions, managers should be able to develop the key objectives of the business. Once this has been done, suitable measures and targets can be developed that are relevant to those objectives. Finally, appropriate management initiatives will be developed to achieve the targets set.

*Source*: *The Balanced Scorecard* (see reference 1 at the end of the chapter).

requires that measures and objectives in the other three areas that have been identified must ultimately be related back to the financial objectives. There must be a cause-and-effect relationship. So, for example, an investment in staff development (in the learning and growth area) may lead to improved levels of after-sales service (internal business process area), which, in turn, may lead to higher levels of customer satisfaction (customer area) and, ultimately, higher sales revenues and profits (financial area). At first, cause-and-effect relationships may not be very clearly identified. However, by gathering information over time, the business can improve its understanding of the linkages and thereby improve the effectiveness of the scorecard.

Figure 11.12 shows the cause-and-effect relationship between the investment in staff development and the business's financial objectives.

**Figure 11.12** **The cause-and-effect relationship**

The investment in staff development is linked through a cause-and-effect relationship to the financial objectives of the business.

## Activity 11.6

Do you think the approach illustrated in Figure 11.12 is a rather hard-nosed way of dealing with staff development? Should staff development always have to be justified in terms of the financial results achieved?

This approach may seem rather hard-nosed. However, Kaplan and Norton argue that unless this kind of link between staff development and increased financial returns can be demonstrated, managers are likely to become cynical about the benefits of staff development and so the result may be that there will be no investment in staff.

Why is this framework referred to as a *balanced* scorecard? According to Kaplan and Norton, there are various reasons. It is because it aims to strike a balance between:

- *external* measures, relating to customers and shareholders, and *internal* measures, relating to business process, learning and growth;
- the measures that reflect *outcomes* (lag indicators) and measures that help *predict future performance* (lead indicators);
- *hard* financial measures and *soft* non-financial measures.

It is possible to adapt the balanced scorecard to fit the needs of the particular business. **Real World 11.11** shows how this has been done by Tesco plc, the large retailer.

### Real World 11.11

## Every little helps

Tesco plc has modified the balanced scorecard approach to meet its particular needs. It has added a fifth dimension, the community, to demonstrate its commitment to the communities that it serves. There is frequent monitoring of the various performance measures against the scorecard targets. The business states:

> At Tesco we use a 'balanced scorecard' approach that we call the Steering Wheel. This management tool focuses our business on the delivery of our core purpose. It is the framework for all activity linking top-line strategy to personal objectives and it ensures that we balance our priorities effectively.
>
> Community has now been introduced into that framework, sitting alongside the four other segments of the Steering Wheel: Customer, People, Finance and Operations. That is a significant step in putting both responsibility to the communities in which we operate and a commitment to environmental sustainability at the centre of our business plan. It will guarantee that the consideration of our impact on communities and on the environment becomes an integral part of our decision-making process.

*Source*: Tesco plc, 'Talking Tesco: How we compete', 2011, www.tesco.com.

**Real World 11.12** provides some impression of the extent to which the balanced scorecard is used in practice.

### Real World 11.12

## A question of balance

A 2011 survey examined the extent to which the balanced scorecard is used in practice and the level of satisfaction that it achieves. Figure 11.13 sets out the results.

### Figure 11.13    Use of the balanced scorecard

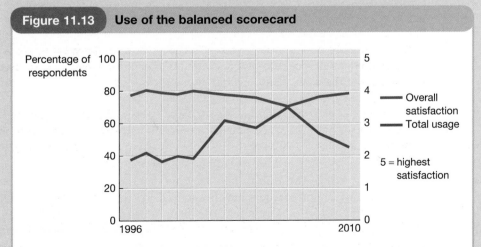

The usage level showed an increase up to about 2006, when it started to decline. There has been a high, and fairly consistent, level of satisfaction for this technique over the 15-year period.

**Real World 11.12 (*continued*)**

The survey was conducted by Bain and Company, a business consultancy business: 1,230 executives working in businesses in a broad range of industries, countries and sizes contributed to the survey.

*Source*: 'Management Tools', D. Rigby and B. Bilodeau, Bain and Co. 2011, www.bain.com.

As a footnote to our consideration of the balanced scorecard, **Real World 11.13** provides an interesting analogy with aeroplane pilots limiting themselves to just one control device.

**(un)Real World 11.13**

### Fear of flying

Kaplan and Norton invite us to imagine the following conversation between a passenger and the pilot of a jet aeroplane during a flight:

Q: I'm surprised to see you operating the plane with only a single instrument. What does it measure?
A: Airspeed. I'm really working on airspeed this flight.
Q: That's good. Airspeed certainly seems important. But what about altitude? Wouldn't an altimeter be helpful?
A: I worked on altitude for the last few flights and I've gotten pretty good on it. Now I have to concentrate on proper airspeed.
Q: But I notice you don't even have a fuel gauge. Wouldn't that be useful?
A: You're right; fuel is significant, but I can't concentrate on doing too many things well at the same time. So on this flight I'm focusing on airspeed. Once I get to be excellent at airspeed, as well as altitude, I intend to concentrate on fuel consumption on the next set of flights.

The point they are trying to make (apart from warning against flying with a pilot like this!) is that to fly an aeroplane, which is a complex activity, a wide range of navigation instruments is required. A business, however, can be even more complex to manage than an aeroplane and so a wide range of measures, both financial and non-financial, is necessary. Reliance on financial measures is not enough and so the balanced scorecard aims to provide managers with a more complete navigation system.

*Source*: *The Balanced Scorecard*, R. Kaplan and D. Norton, Harvard Business School Press, 1996.

This story makes the point that, by concentrating on only a few areas of performance, other important areas may be ignored. Too narrow a focus can adversely affect behaviour and distort performance. This may, in turn, mean that the business fails to meet its strategic objectives. Perhaps we should bear in mind another apocryphal story concerning a factory in Russia which, under the former communist regime, produced nails. The factory had its output measured according only to the weight of nails manufactured. For one financial period, it achieved its output target by producing one very large nail!

## Scorecard problems

Not all attempts to embed the balanced scorecard approach within a business are successful. Why do things go wrong? It has been suggested that often too many measures are used, thereby making the scorecard too complex and unwieldy. It has also been suggested that managers are confronted with trade-off decisions between the four different dimensions. They struggle with this because they lack a clear compass. Imagine a manager who has a limited budget and therefore has to decide whether to invest in staff training or product innovation. If both add value to the business, which choice will be optimal for the business?

Whilst such problems exist, David Norton believes that there are two main reasons why the balanced scorecard fails to take root within a business, as **Real World 11.14** explains.

---

**Real World 11.14**

### When misuse leads to failure
**FT**

There are two main reasons why companies go wrong with the widely used balanced scorecard, according to David Norton, the consultant who created the concept with Robert Kaplan, a Harvard Business School Professor.

'The number one cause of failure is that you don't have leadership at the executive levels of the organisation,' says Mr Norton. 'They don't embrace it and use it for managing their strategy.'

The second is that some companies treat it purely as a measurement tool, a problem he admits stems partly from its name. The concept has evolved since its inception, he says. The latest Kaplan–Norton thinking is that companies need a unit at corporate level – they call it an 'office of strategy management' – dedicated to ensuring that strategy is communicated to every employee and translated into plans, targets and incentives in each business unit and department.

Incentives are crucial, Mr Norton believes. Managers who have achieved breakthroughs in performance with the scorecard say they would tie it to executive compensation sooner if they were doing it again. 'There's so much change in organisations that managers don't always believe you mean what you say. The balanced scorecard may just be "flavour of the month". Tying it to compensation shows that you mean it.'

*Source:* 'When misuse leads to failure', FT.com, © The Financial Times Limited, 24 May 2006.

---

## Measuring shareholder value

Traditional measures of financial performance have been subject to much criticism in recent years. As a result, new measures that help to guide and assess strategic management decisions have been advocated. These new measures are based on the idea of increasing shareholder value. In this section, we shall consider one of the more popular of these measures. Before that, we shall first consider why increasing shareholder value is regarded as the ultimate financial objective of a business.

## The quest for shareholder value

For some years, shareholder value has been a 'hot' issue among managers. Many leading businesses now claim that the quest for shareholder value is the driving force behind their strategic and operational decisions. As a starting point, we shall consider what is meant by the term 'shareholder value'.

In simple terms, 'shareholder value' is about putting the needs of shareholders at the heart of management decisions. It is argued that shareholders invest in a business with a view to maximising their financial returns in relation to the risks that they are prepared to take. Since shareholders appoint managers to act on their behalf, management decisions and actions should reflect a concern for maximising shareholder returns. Though the business may have other 'stakeholder' groups, such as employees, customers and suppliers, it is the shareholders that should be seen as the most important group.

This, of course, is not a new idea. As we discussed in Chapter 1, maximising shareholder wealth is assumed to be the key objective of a business. However, not everyone accepts this idea. Some believe that a balance must be struck between the competing claims of the various stakeholders. A debate concerning the merits of each viewpoint is beyond the scope of this book; however, it is worth pointing out that, in recent years, the business environment has radically changed.

In the past, shareholders have been accused of being too passive and of accepting too readily the profits and dividends that managers have delivered. However, this has changed. Shareholders are now much more assertive and, as owners of the business, are in a position to insist that their needs are given priority. Since the 1980s we have witnessed the deregulation and globalisation of business, as well as enormous changes in technology. The effect has been to create a much more competitive world. This has meant not only competition for products and services but also competition for funds. Businesses must now compete more strongly for shareholder funds and so must offer competitive rates of return.

Thus, self-interest may be the most powerful reason for managers to commit themselves to maximising shareholder returns. If they do not do this, there is a real risk that shareholders will either replace them with managers who will, or allow the business to be taken over by another business that has managers who are dedicated to maximising shareholder returns.

## How can shareholder value be created?

Creating shareholder value involves a four-stage process.

- *Stage 1* Set objectives for the business that recognise the central importance of maximising shareholder returns. This will set a clear direction for the business.
- *Stage 2* Establish an appropriate means of measuring the returns, or value, that have been generated for shareholders. For reasons that we shall discuss later, the traditional methods of measuring returns to shareholders are inadequate for this purpose.
- *Stage 3* Manage the business in such a manner as to ensure that shareholder returns are maximised. This means setting demanding targets and then achieving them through the best possible use of resources, the use of incentive systems and the embedding of a shareholder value culture throughout the business.
- *Stage 4* Measure the shareholder returns over a period of time to see whether the objectives have actually been achieved.

**Figure 11.14**  **The four-stage process for creating shareholder value**

There is a four-stage process to creating shareholder value

Figure 11.14 shows the shareholder value creation process.

## The need for new measures

Given a commitment to maximise shareholder returns, we must select an appropriate measure that will help us assess the returns to shareholders over time. It is argued that the traditional methods for measuring shareholder returns are seriously flawed and so should not be used for this purpose.

**Activity 11.7**

What are the traditional methods of measuring shareholder returns?

The traditional approach is to use accounting profit or some ratio that is based on accounting profit, such as return on shareholders' funds or earnings per share.

There are broadly four problems with using accounting profit, or a ratio based on profit, to assess shareholder returns. These are:

● *Profit is measured over a relatively short period of time* (usually one year). However, when we talk about maximising shareholder returns, we are concerned with maximising returns over the *long term*. It has been suggested that using profit as the key measure will run the risk that managers will take decisions that improve performance in the short term, but which may have an adverse effect on long-term performance. For example, profits may be increased in the short term by cutting back on staff training and research expenditure. However, this type of expenditure may be vital to long-term survival.

● *Risk is ignored*. A fundamental business reality is that there is a clear relationship between the level of returns achieved and the level of risk that must be taken to achieve those returns. The higher the level of returns required, the higher the level of risk that must be taken. A management strategy that produces an increase in profits can reduce shareholder value if the increase in profits achieved is not commensurate with the increase in the level of risk. Thus, profit alone is not enough.

● *Accounting profit does not take account of all of the costs of the capital invested by the business*. The conventional approach to measuring profit will deduct the cost of borrowing (that is, interest charges) in arriving at profit for the period, but there is no similar deduction for the cost of shareholder funds. Critics of the conventional approach point out that a business will not make a profit, in an economic sense, unless it covers the cost of all capital invested, including shareholder funds. Unless the business achieves this, it will operate at a loss and so shareholder value will be reduced.

● *Accounting profit reported by a business can vary according to the particular accounting policies that have been adopted*. The way that accounting profit is measured can vary from one business to another. Some businesses adopt a very conservative approach, which would be reflected in particular accounting policies. This might include immediately treating some intangible assets (for example, research and development and goodwill) as expenses ('writing them off') rather than retaining them on the statement of financial position as assets. Similarly, the use of the reducing-balance method of depreciation (which means high depreciation charges in the early years) reduces profit in those early years.

Businesses that adopt less conservative accounting policies would report higher profits in the early years of owning depreciating assets. Writing off intangible assets over a long time period (or, perhaps, not writing off intangible assets at all) will have this effect. So will the use of the straight-line method of depreciation. As we saw in Chapter 5, there may also be some businesses that indulge in 'creative accounting'. This is adopting particular accounting policies, or carrying out particular transactions, in a way that paints a picture of financial health that is in line with what those who prepared the financial statements would like shareholders and other users to see, rather than what is a true and fair view of financial performance and position. Creative accounting has been a major problem for accounting rule makers and for society generally.

## Economic value added (EVA®)

**Economic value added (EVA®)** has been developed and trademarked by a US management consultancy firm, Stern Stewart. However, EVA® is based on the idea of economic profit; an idea that has been around for many years. The measure reflects the point made earlier that, for a business to be profitable in an economic sense, it must generate returns that exceed the required returns of investors. It is not enough simply to make an accounting profit, because this measure does not take full account of the returns required by investors.

EVA® indicates whether or not the returns generated exceed the required returns by investors. The formula is as follows:

$$EVA® = NOPAT - (R \times C)$$

where

NOPAT = net operating profit after tax

$R$ = required returns of investors

$C$ = capital invested (that is, the net assets of the business).

Only when EVA® is positive can we say that the business is increasing shareholder wealth. To maximise shareholder wealth, managers must increase EVA® by as much as possible.

## Activity 11.8

Can you suggest what managers might do in order to increase EVA®? (*Hint*: Use the formula shown above as your starting point.)

The formula suggests that in order to increase EVA® managers may try to:

- Increase NOPAT. This may be done either by reducing expenses or by increasing sales revenue.
- Reduce capital invested by using assets more efficiently. This means selling off any assets that are not generating adequate returns and investing in assets that are generating a satisfactory NOPAT.
- Reduce the required rates of return for investors. This may be achieved by changing the capital structure in favour of borrowing (which tends to be cheaper to service than share capital). However, this strategy can create problems.

EVA® relies on conventional financial statements (income statement and statement of financial position) to measure the wealth created for shareholders. However, the NOPAT and capital figures shown on these statements are used only as a starting point. They have to be adjusted because of the problems and limitations of conventional measures. According to Stern Stewart, the major problem is that both profit and capital tend to be understated because of the conservative bias in accounting measurement.

Profit is understated as a result of judgemental write-offs (such as goodwill written off or research and development expenditure written off) and as a result of excessive provisions being created (such as an allowance for trade receivables (bad debt provision)). Both of these stem from taking an unrealistically pessimistic view of the value of some of the business's assets.

Capital can also be understated because assets are reported at their original cost (less amounts written off for depreciation and so on), which can, in some cases, produce figures considerably below current market values. In addition, certain assets, such as internally generated goodwill and brand names, are omitted from the financial statements because no external transactions have occurred.

Stern Stewart has identified more than 100 adjustments that could be made to the conventional financial statements in order to eliminate the conservative bias. However, it is believed that, in practice, only a handful of adjustments will usually have to be made to the accounting figures of any particular business. Unless an adjustment is going to have a significant effect on the calculation of EVA® it is really not worth making. The adjustments made should reflect the nature of the particular business. Each business is unique and so must customise the calculation of EVA® to its particular circumstances. (This aspect of EVA® can be seen as either indicating flexibility or as being open to manipulation depending on whether or not you support this measure.)

Common adjustments that have to be made include:

1  *Research and development (R&D) costs and marketing costs*. These costs should be written off over the period that they benefit. In practice, however, they are often written off in the period in which they are incurred. This means that any amounts written off immediately should be added back to the assets on the statement of financial position. This will increase the figure for invested capital to be written off over time.

2  *Restructuring costs*. This item can be viewed as an investment in the future rather than an expense to be written off. Supporters of EVA® argue that by restructuring, the business is better placed to meet future challenges, and so any amounts incurred should be added back to assets.

3  *Marketable investments*. Investment in shares and loan notes of other businesses are not included as part of the capital invested in the business. This is because the income from marketable investments is not included in the calculation of operating profit. (Income from this source will be added in the income statement *after* operating profit has been calculated.)

In addition to these accounting adjustments, the tax charge must be adjusted so that it is based on the operating profits for the year. This means that it should not take account of the tax charge on non-operating income, such as income from investments, or the tax allowance on interest payable.

Let us now consider a simple example to show how EVA® may be calculated.

### Example 11.4

Scorpio plc was established two years ago and has produced the following statement of financial position and income statement at the end of the second year of trading.

**Statement of financial position as at the end of the second year**

|  | £m |
|---|---|
| **ASSETS** | |
| **Non-current assets** | |
| Plant and equipment | 80.0 |
| Motor vehicles | 12.4 |
| Marketable investments | 6.6 |
| | 99.0 |
| **Current assets** | |
| Inventories | 34.5 |
| Trade receivables | 29.3 |
| Cash | 2.1 |
| | 65.9 |
| **Total assets** | 164.9 |

**EQUITY AND LIABILITIES**
**Equity**

| | |
|---|---|
| Share capital | 60.0 |
| Retained earnings | 23.7 |
| | 83.7 |

**Non-current liabilities**

| | |
|---|---|
| Loan notes | 50.0 |

**Current liabilities**

| | |
|---|---|
| Trade payables | 30.3 |
| Taxation | 0.9 |
| | 31.2 |
| **Total equity and liabilities** | 164.9 |

**Income statement for the second year**

| | £m |
|---|---|
| Sales revenue | 148.6 |
| Cost of sales | (76.2) |
| Gross profit | 72.4 |
| Wages | (24.6) |
| Depreciation of plant and equipment | (12.8) |
| Marketing expenses | (22.5) |
| Allowances for trade receivables | (4.5) |
| Operating profit | 8.0 |
| Income from investments | 0.4 |
| | 8.4 |
| Interest payable | (0.5) |
| Ordinary profit before taxation | 7.9 |
| Restructuring costs | (1.9) |
| Profit before taxation | 6.0 |
| Tax | (1.5) |
| Profit for the year | 4.5 |

Discussions with the finance director reveal the following:

1 Marketing costs relate to the launch of a new product. The benefits of the marketing campaign are expected to last for three years (including this most recent year).

2 The allowance for trade receivables was created this year and the amount is considered to be very high. A more realistic figure for the allowance would be £2.0 million.

3 Restructuring costs were incurred as a result of a collapse in a particular product market. By restructuring the business, benefits are expected to flow for an infinite period.

4 The business has a 10 per cent required rate of return for investors.

5 The rate of tax on profits is 25 per cent.

The first step in calculating EVA® is to adjust the net operating profit after tax to take account of the various points revealed by the discussion with the finance director. The revised figure is calculated as follows:

→

| NOPAT adjustment | £m | £m |
|---|---|---|
| Operating profit | | 8.0 |
| Tax (Note 1) | | (2.0) |
| | | 6.0 |

**EVA® adjustments (to be added back to profit)**

| | £m | £m |
|---|---|---|
| Marketing costs ($^2/_3 \times 22.5$) | 15.0 | |
| Excess allowance | 2.5 | 17.5 |
| Adjusted NOPAT | | 23.5 |

The next step is to adjust the net assets (as represented by equity and loan notes) to take account of the points revealed.

**Adjusted net assets (or capital invested)**

| | £m | £m |
|---|---|---|
| Net assets (from the statement of financial position) | | 133.7 |
| Marketing costs (Note 2) | 15.0 | |
| Allowance for trade receivables | 2.5 | |
| Restructuring costs (Note 3) | 1.9 | 19.4 |
| | | 153.1 |
| Marketable investments (Note 4) | | (6.6) |
| **Adjusted net assets** | | 146.5 |

*Notes:*
1 Tax is based on 25% of the operating profits (£8.0m x 25% = £2.0m). (Tax complications, such as the difference between the tax allowance for non-current assets and the accounting charge for depreciation have been ignored.)
2 The marketing costs represent two years' benefits added back ($^2/_3 \times$ £22.5m).
3 The restructuring costs are added back to the net assets as they provide benefits over an infinite period. (Note that they were not added back to the operating profit as these costs were deducted after arriving at operating profit in the income statement.)
4 The marketable investments do not form part of the operating assets of the business. The income from these investments is not, therefore, part of the operating income.

**Activity (11.9)**

Can you work out the EVA® for the second year of Scorpio plc in Example 11.4?

EVA® can be calculated as follows:

$$\text{EVA}^® = \text{NOPAT} - (R \times C) = £23.5\text{m} - (10\% \times £146.5\text{m})$$
$$= £8.8\text{m (to one decimal place)}$$

We can see that EVA® is positive and so the business increased shareholder wealth during the year.

Although EVA® is used by many large businesses, both in the USA and Europe, it tends to be used for management purposes only: few businesses report this measure to shareholders. Whole Foods Market is a leading retailer of natural and organic foods, which operates more than 280 stores in the USA and the UK. **Real World 11.15** describes the way in which the business uses EVA® and the results of doing so.

## The whole picture

Whole Foods Market aims to improve its operations by achieving improvements to EVA®. To encourage managers along this path, an incentive plan, based on improvements to EVA® has been introduced. The plan embraces senior executives, regional managers and store managers (over 750 people in total) and the bonuses awarded form a significant part of their total remuneration. To make the incentive plan work, measures of EVA® based on the whole business, the regional level, the store level and the team level are calculated. Around one thousand managers are included in the incentive plan.

EVA® is used to evaluate capital investment decisions such as the acquisition of new stores and the refurbishment of existing stores. Unless there is clear evidence that value will be added, investment proposals are rejected. EVA® is also used to improve operational efficiency. It was mentioned earlier that one way in which EVA® can be increased is through an improvement in NOPAT. The business is, therefore, continually seeking ways to improve sales and profit margins and to bear down on costs.

*Source:* Based on information in www.wholefoodsmarket.com. Accessed 27 July 2011.

One often-mentioned limitation of EVA® is that it can be difficult to allocate revenues, costs and capital easily between different business units (individual stores in the case of Whole Food Markets). As a result, this technique cannot always be applied to individual business units. We have just seen, however, that Whole Food Markets seems able to do this.

The main advantage of this measure is the discipline to which managers are subjected as a result of the charge for capital that has been invested. Before any increase in shareholder wealth can be recognised, an appropriate deduction is made for the use of business resources. Thus, EVA® encourages managers to use these resources efficiently. Where managers are focused simply on increasing profits, there is a danger that the resources used to achieve any increase in profits will not be taken into proper account.

## Summary

The main points of this chapter may be summarised as follows:

**Activity-based costing is an approach to dealing with overheads (in full costing) that treats all costs as being caused or 'driven' by activities. Advocates argue that it is more relevant to the modern commercial environment than is the traditional approach.**

- It involves identifying the support activities and their costs (overheads) and then analysing these costs to see what drives them.

- The costs of each support activity (overheads) enter a cost pool and the relevant cost drivers are used to attach an amount of overheads from this pool to each unit of output.

- ABC should help provide more accurate costs for each unit of output and should help in better control of overheads.

- ABC is however time-consuming and costly, can involve measurement problems and is not likely to suit all businesses.

### Other costing methods

- Total (whole) life-cycle costing takes account of all of the costs incurred over a product's entire life.
- The life cycle of a product can be broken down into three phases: pre-production, production and post-production.
- A high proportion of cost is incurred and/or committed during the pre-production phase.
- Target costing attempts to reduce cost so that the market price covers the cost plus an acceptable profit.
- Ensuring quality output has costs, known as *quality costs*, typically divided into four aspects: prevention costs, appraisal costs, internal failure costs and external failure costs.
- *Kaizen* costing attempts to reduce costs at the production stage.
- Total quality management (TQM) is concerned with providing products that meet, or exceed, customers, requirements all of the time. This gives rise to various types of quality costs.
- Value chain analysis involves analysing the various activities in the product life cycle to identify and to try to eliminate non-value-added activities.
- Benchmarking attempts to emulate a successful aspect of, for example, another business or division.

### Non-financial measures of performance

- Non-financial measures are increasingly being used to manage the business.
- The balanced scorecard is a management tool that uses financial and non-financial measures to assess progress towards objectives.
- It has four aspects: financial, customer, internal business process, and learning and growth.
- It encourages a balanced approach to managing the business.

### Value-based management

- Shareholder value is seen as the key objective of most businesses.
- One approach used to measure shareholder value is economic value added (EVA®).
- Economic value added is a means of measuring whether the returns generated by the business exceed the required returns of investors.

$$\text{EVA}^{\circledR} = \text{NOPAT} - (R \times C)$$

where:

NOPAT = net operating profit after tax
 $R$ = required returns from investors
 $C$ = capital invested (that is, the net assets of the business).

# MyAccountingLab

Go to **www.myaccountinglab.com** to check your understanding of the chapter, create a personalised study plan, and maximise your revision time

## Key terms

activity-based costing (ABC)   p. 409
cost drivers   p. 409
cost pool   p. 410
total life-cycle costing   p. 420
total quality management (TQM)
    p. 423
quality costs   p. 424

target costing   p. 425
*Kaizen* costing   p. 426
value chain analysis   p. 427
benchmarking   p. 428
value drivers   p. 430
balanced scorecard   p. 431
economic value added (EVA®)   p. 440

## Reference

1  Kaplan, R. and Norton, D., *The Balanced Scorecard*, Harvard Business School Press, 1996.

## Further reading

If you would like to explore the topics covered in this chapter in more depth, we recommend the following books:

Drury, C., *Management and Cost Accounting,* 8th edn, Cengage Learning, 2012, chapters 10 and 11.

Hilton, R., *Managerial Accounting,* 9th edn, McGraw-Hill Higher Education, 2011, chapters 4, 5, 6 and 15.

Horngren, C., Datar, S. and Rajan, M., *Cost Accounting: A Managerial Emphasis,* 14th edn, Prentice Hall International, 2011, chapter 11.

Kaplan, R., Atkinson, A., Matsumura, E. and Young, S. M. *Management Accounting*, 6th edn, Prentice Hall, 2011, chapters 5 and 8.

## Review questions

Solutions to these questions can be found at the back of the book on pages 754 to 755.

**11.1**   How does activity-based costing differ from the traditional approach? What is the underlying difference in the philosophy of each of them?

**11.2**   The use of activity-based costing in helping to deduce full costs has been criticised. What has tended to be the basis of this criticism?

**11.3**   What are the four main areas on which the balanced scorecard is based?

**11.4**   Derry and Co. is a large computer consultancy business that has a division specialising in robotics. Can you identify three *non-financial measures* that might be used to help assess the performance of this division?

## Exercises

Exercises 11.1 and 11.2 are basic level, 11.3 and 11.4 are intermediate level and 11.5 to 11.7, are advanced level. Those with coloured numbers have solutions at the back of the book, starting on page 782.

If you wish to try more exercises, visit the students' side of the Companion Website and MyAccountingLab.

**11.1**   Aires plc was recently formed and issued 80 million £0.50 shares at nominal value and loan notes totalling £24 million. The business used the proceeds from the capital issues to purchase the remaining lease on some commercial properties. Aires plc plans to set up a wholesaling business that is expected to generate operating profits of £12 million each year. The lease will expire in four years' time. At the end of the four years, the business will be wound up and the lease will have no residual value.

The required rate of return by investors is 12 per cent.

*Required:*

Calculate the expected shareholder value generated by the business in each of the four years, using the EVA® approach.

**11.2**   Comment critically on the following statements that you have overheard:

(a)  'The balanced scorecard is another name for the statement of financial position.'
(b)  'The financial area of the balanced scorecard is, in effect, the income statement of the business and measures the profit for the period.'
(c)  'Adopting the balanced scorecard approach means accepting a particular set of targets that were set out by Kaplan and Norton.'
(d)  'The balanced scorecard approach tends to take little notice of financial objectives.'

**11.3**   Kaplan plc makes a range of suitcases of various sizes and shapes. There are 10 different models of suitcase produced by the business. To keep inventories of finished suitcases to a minimum, each model is made in a small batch. Each batch is costed as a separate job and the cost for each suitcase deduced by dividing the batch cost by the number of suitcases in the batch.

At present, the business derives the cost of each batch using a traditional job-costing approach. Recently, however, a new management accountant was appointed, who is advocating the use of activity-based costing (ABC) to deduce the cost of the batches. The management accountant claims that ABC leads to much more reliable and relevant costs and that it has other benefits.

*Required:*
(a) Explain how the business deduces the cost of each suitcase at present.
(b) Explain how ABC could be applied to costing the suitcases, highlighting the differences between ABC and the traditional approach.
(c) Explain what advantages the new management accountant probably believes ABC to have over the traditional approach.

**11.4** Comment critically on the following statements that you have overheard:

(a) 'Direct labour hours are the most appropriate basis to use to charge indirect cost (overheads) to jobs in the modern manufacturing environment where people are so important.'
(b) 'Activity-based costing is a means of more accurately accounting for direct labour cost.'
(c) 'Activity-based costing cannot really be applied to the service sector because the "activities" that it seeks to analyse tend to be related to manufacturing.'
(d) '*Kaizen* costing is an approach where great efforts are made to reduce the costs of developing a new product and setting up its production processes.'
(e) 'Benchmarking is an approach to job costing where each direct worker keeps a record of the time spent on each job on his or her workbench before it is passed on to the next direct worker or into finished inventories (stock) stores.'

**11.5** Badger Ltd (Badger) manufactures plastic building materials. After a recent analysis Badger has decided to classify its products into two varieties: Largeflo and Smallflo. There are several products in each of these two categories. Largeflo are produced on large machines by a simple process. Smallflo are manufactured on small machines by a more complex process with more production stages. The previous pricing policy has been to absorb all overheads using direct labour hours to obtain total cost. Price is then calculated as total cost plus a 35 per cent mark-up.

The recent analysis has also examined overhead costs; the results are shown below. Set-up costs are incurred during the production stage for each batch. The ordering costs for bought-in parts are incurred initially for each production type.

### Analysis of overhead costs

|  | Cost per month £ | Monthly volume |
|---|---|---|
| Large machine cost | 96,000 | 480 hours |
| Small machine cost | 44,800 | 1,280 hours |
| Set-up cost | 32,500 | 260 set-ups |
| Ordering bought-in parts | 10,800 | 120 different parts |
| Handling charges | 45,600 | 380 movements |
| Other overheads | 50,300 | (see below) |
|  | 280,000 |  |

There are 4,000 direct labour hours available each month.

Details for a typical Largeflo product (one of several Largeflo products) and a typical Smallflo product (again, one of several Smallflo products) are shown below.

|  | Largeflo | Smallflo |
|---|---|---|
| Monthly volume | 1,000 units | 500 units |
| Batch size | 1,000 units | 50 units |
| Machine time per batch |  |  |
| – large | 100 hours | – |
| – small | – | 25 hours |
| Number of bought-in parts | – | 3 per product type |
| Set-ups | 1 per batch | 2 per batch |
| Handling charges | 1 movement per batch | 5 movements per batch |
| Materials per unit | £16 | £15 |
| Direct labour per unit | $\frac{1}{2}$ hour | $\frac{1}{2}$ hour |

Direct labour is paid £16 per hour.

*Required:*

(a) Calculate the price for each of the Largeflo and Smallflo products detailed above, using traditional absorption costing based on direct labour hours.

(b) Calculate the price for the Largeflo and Smallflo products using activity-based costing. Assume that 'Other overheads' are allocated using direct labour hours.

(c) Outline the points that you would raise with the management of Badger in the light of your answers to (a) and (b).

(d) Outline the practical problems that may be encountered in implementing activity-based techniques and comment on how they may be overcome.

**11.6** Pisces plc produced the following statement of financial position and income statement at the end of the third year of trading:

### Statement of financial position (balance sheet) as at the end of the third year

| ASSETS | £m |
|---|---|
| **Non-current assets** | |
| Property | 40.0 |
| Machinery and equipment | 80.0 |
| Motor vans | 18.6 |
| Marketable investments | 9.0 |
| | 147.6 |
| **Current assets** | |
| Inventories | 45.8 |
| Trade receivables | 64.6 |
| Cash | 1.0 |
| | 111.4 |
| **Total assets** | 259.0 |
| **EQUITY AND LIABILITIES** | |
| **Equity** | |
| Share capital | 80.0 |
| Reserves | 36.5 |
| | 116.5 |
| **Non-current liabilities** | |
| Loan notes | 80.0 |
| **Current liabilities** | |
| Trade payables | 62.5 |
| | 259.0 |

### Income statement for the third year

| | £m |
|---|---|
| Sales revenue | 231.5 |
| Cost of sales | (143.2) |
| Gross profit | 88.3 |
| Wages | (43.5) |
| Depreciation of machinery and equipment | (14.8) |
| Research and development | (40.0) |
| Allowance for trade receivables | (10.5) |
| Operating loss | (20.5) |
| Income from investments | 0.6 |
| | (19.9) |
| Interest payable | (0.8) |
| Normal loss before taxation | (20.7) |
| Restructuring costs | (6.0) |
| Loss before taxation | (26.7) |
| Tax | – |
| Loss for the year | (26.7) |

An analysis of the underlying records reveals the following:

1 The research and development expense relates to the cost of developing a new product in the previous year. This cost is written off over a two-year period (starting last year). However, this is a prudent approach and the benefits are expected to last for 16 years.
2 The allowance for trade receivables (bad debts) was created this year and the amount of the provision is very high. A more realistic figure for the allowance would be £4 million.
3 Restructuring costs were incurred at the beginning of the year and are expected to provide benefits for an infinite period.
4 The business has a 7 per cent required rate of return for investors.

*Required:*
Calculate the EVA® for the business for the third year of trading.

**11.7** A business manufactures refrigerators for domestic use. There are three models: Lo, Mid and Hi. The models, their quality and their price are aimed at different markets.

Product costs are computed using a blanket (business-wide) overhead-rate. Products absorb overheads on a labour hour basis. Prices as a general rule are set based on cost plus 20 per cent. The following information is provided:

| | Lo | Mid | Hi |
|---|---|---|---|
| Material cost (£/unit) | 25 | 62.5 | 105 |
| Direct labour hours (per unit) | $^1/_2$ | 1 | 1 |
| Budget production/sales (units) | 20,000 | 1,000 | 10,000 |

The budgeted overheads for the business, for the year, amount to £4,410,000. Direct labour is costed at £8 an hour.

The business is currently facing increasing competition, especially from imported goods. As a result, the selling price of Lo has been reduced to a level that produces a very low profit margin. To address this problem, an activity-based costing approach has been suggested. The overheads have been analysed and it has been found that these are grouped around main business activities of machining (£2,780,000), logistics (£590,000) and establishment costs (£1,040,000). It is maintained that these costs could be allocated based respectively on cost drivers of machine hours, material orders and space, to reflect the use of resources in each of these areas. After analysis, the following proportionate statistics are available related to the total volume of products:

|  | Lo | Mid | Hi |
| --- | --- | --- | --- |
|  | % | % | % |
| Machine hours | 40 | 15 | 45 |
| Material orders | 47 | 6 | 47 |
| Space | 42 | 18 | 40 |

*Required:*

(a) Calculate for each product the full cost and selling price determined by:
  (1) The original (traditional) costing method.
  (2) The activity-based costing method.

(b) What are the implications of the two systems of costing in the situation given?

(c) What business/strategic options exist for the business in the light of the new information?

# Budgeting

## Introduction

In this chapter we consider the role and nature of budgets. In its 2010 annual report, BSkyB Group plc, the satellite television broadcaster, said:

> There is a comprehensive budgeting and forecasting process, and the annual budget, which is regularly reviewed and updated, is approved by the board [of directors].

The practice at BSkyB is typical of businesses of all sizes.

What is a budget? What is it for? How is it prepared? Who prepares it? Why does the board regard it as important enough to consider? We shall be looking at the answers to each of these questions in the course of this chapter.

We shall see that budgets set out short-term plans to help managers run the business. They provide the means to assess whether actual performance was as planned and, if not, the reasons for this. Budgets do not exist in a vacuum; they are an integral part of a planning framework adopted by well-run businesses. To understand fully the nature of budgets we must, therefore, understand the strategic planning framework within which they are set.

The chapter begins with a discussion of the budgeting framework and then goes on to consider detailed aspects of the budgeting process. We shall see that preparing budgets relies on an understanding of many of the issues relating to the behaviour of costs and full costing, topics that we explored in Chapters 9 and 10.

## Learning outcomes

**When you have completed this chapter, you should be able to:**

- Define a budget and show how budgets, strategic objectives and strategic plans are related.

- Explain the budgeting process and the interlinking of the various budgets within the business.

● Indicate the uses of budgeting and construct various budgets, including the cash budget, from relevant data.

● Discuss the criticisms that are made of budgeting.

# MyAccountingLab
Visit **www.myaccountinglab.com** for practice and revision opportunities

## How budgets link with strategic plans and objectives

It is vital that businesses develop plans for the future. Whatever a business is trying to achieve, it is unlikely to come about unless its managers are clear what the future direction of the business is going to be. The development of plans involves five key steps:

1 *Establish mission and objectives*
   The ultimate purpose of the business is usually set out in a **mission statement**. This is a broad statement of intent, which attempts to capture the essence of the business. The strategic objectives set out how the mission of the business can be achieved and will usually include quantifiable goals.
2 *Undertake a position analysis*
   This involves an assessment of where the business is currently placed in relation to where it wants to be, as set out in its mission and strategic objectives.
3 *Identify and assess the strategic options*
   The business must explore the various ways in which it might move from where it is now (identified in step 2) to where it wants to be (identified in step 1).
4 *Select strategic options and formulate plans*
   This involves selecting what seems to be the best of the courses of action or strategies (identified in step 3) and formulating a long-term strategic plan. This strategic plan is then normally broken down into a series of short-term plans, one for each element of the business. These plans are the budgets. Thus, a **budget** is a business plan for the short term – typically one year – and is expressed mainly in financial terms. Its role is to convert the strategic plans into actionable blueprints for the immediate future. Budgets will define precise targets concerning such things as:
   ● Cash receipts and payments.
   ● Sales volumes and revenues, broken down into amounts and prices for each of the products or services provided by the business.
   ● Detailed inventories requirements.
   ● Detailed labour requirements.
   ● Specific production requirements.
5 *Perform, review and control*
   Here the business pursues the budgets derived in step 4. By comparing the actual outcome with the budgets, managers can see if things are going according to plan or not. Action would be taken to exercise control where actual performance appears not to be matching the budgets.

**Activity (12.1)**

The approach described in step 3 above suggests that managers will systematically collect information and then carefully evaluate all the options available. Do you think this is what managers really do?

In practice, managers may not be as rational and capable as implied in the process described. They may find it difficult to handle a wealth of information relating to a wide range of options. To avoid becoming overloaded, they may restrict their range of possible options and/or discard some information. Managers may also adopt rather simple approaches to evaluating the mass of information provided. These approaches might not lead to the best decisions being made.

From the above description of the planning process, we can see that the relationship between the mission, strategic objectives, strategic plans and budgets can be summarised as follows:

- the mission sets the overall direction and, once set, is likely to last for quite a long time – perhaps throughout the life of the business;
- the strategic objectives, which are also long-term, will set out how the mission can be achieved;
- the strategic plans identify how each objective will be pursued; and
- the budgets set out, in detail, the short-term plans and targets necessary to fulfil the strategic objectives.

An analogy might be found in terms of a student enrolling on a course of study. His or her mission might be to have a happy and fulfilling life. A key strategic objective flowing from this mission might be to embark on a career that will be rewarding in various ways. He or she might have identified the particular study course as the most effective way to work towards this objective. Successfully completing the course would then be the strategic plan. In working towards this strategic plan, passing a particular stage of the course might be identified as the target for the forthcoming year. This short-term target is analogous to the budget. Having achieved the 'budget' for the first year, the budget for the second year becomes passing the second stage.

## Exercising control

However well planned the activities of a business might be, they will come to nothing unless steps are taken to try to achieve them in practice. The process of making planned events actually occur is known as **control**. This is part of step 5 (above).

Control can be defined as compelling events to conform to plan. This definition is valid in any context. For example, when we talk about controlling a motor car, we mean making the car do what we plan that it should do. In a business context, management accounting has an important role to play in the control process. This is because it is possible to state many plans in accounting terms (as budgets). Since it is also possible to state *actual* outcomes in the same terms, making comparison between actual and planned outcomes is a relatively simple matter. Where actual outcomes are at variance with budgets, this variance should be highlighted by accounting information. Managers can then take steps to get the business back on track towards the achievement of the budgets. We shall be looking quite closely at the control aspect of budgeting in Chapter 13.

| Figure 12.1 | The planning and control process |
| --- | --- |

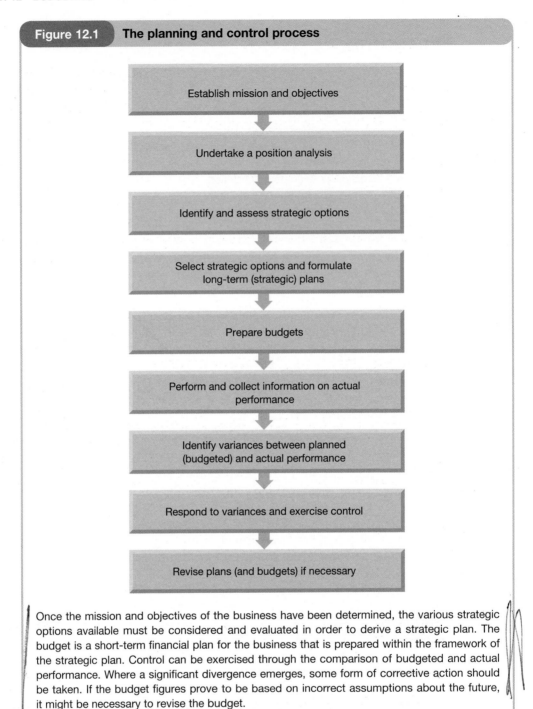

Once the mission and objectives of the business have been determined, the various strategic options available must be considered and evaluated in order to derive a strategic plan. The budget is a short-term financial plan for the business that is prepared within the framework of the strategic plan. Control can be exercised through the comparison of budgeted and actual performance. Where a significant divergence emerges, some form of corrective action should be taken. If the budget figures prove to be based on incorrect assumptions about the future, it might be necessary to revise the budget.

Figure 12.1 shows the planning and control process in diagrammatic form.

It should be emphasised that planning (including budgeting) is the responsibility of managers rather than accountants. Although accountants should play a role in the planning process, by supplying relevant information to managers and by contributing to decision making as part of the management team, they should not dominate the process. In practice, it seems that the budgeting aspect of planning is often dominated by accountants, perhaps because most budgets are expressed in financial terms. Managers are failing in their responsibilities, however, if they allow this to happen.

## Time horizon of plans and budgets

Setting strategic plans is typically a major exercise performed about every five years and budgets are usually set annually for the forthcoming year. These time horizons, however, may vary according to the needs of the particular business. Those businesses involved in certain industries – say, information technology – may feel that five years is too long a planning period since new developments can, and do, occur virtually overnight. Here, a planning horizon of two or three years may be more appropriate. Similarly, a budget need not be set for one year, although this appears to be a widely used time horizon.

One business that tends to keep its strategic planning under more frequent review is J Sainsbury plc, the supermarket business. **Real World 12.1**, which is an extract from the annual report for the business, explains how strategic planning is a regular annual event.

### Real World 12.1

#### Strategic planning at the supermarket

According to its annual report, Sainsbury has the following approach to strategic planning:

> The Board continued to focus on strategic matters during the year. We hold a two-day Strategy Conference in the autumn, with the Operating Board Directors in attendance for the first day. This enables the Board to conduct an in-depth review of the market and key opportunities and threats, consider the draft budget and corporate plan and agree the strategic goals for the short-term and longer term perspectives. The Board receives a detailed half-year update on progress against the agreed priorities and then, to complete the cycle, agrees the objectives and principal areas of focus for the next conference.

*Source*: J Sainsbury plc Annual Report 2011, p. 31.

### Activity 12.2

Can you think of any reason why most businesses prepare detailed budgets for the forthcoming year, rather than for a shorter or longer period?

The reason is probably that a year represents a long enough time for the budget preparation exercise to be worthwhile, yet short enough into the future for detailed plans to be capable of being made. As we shall see later in this chapter, the process of formulating budgets can be a time-consuming exercise, but there are economies of scale – for example, preparing the budget for the next year would not normally take twice as much time and effort as preparing the budget for the next six months.

An annual budget sets targets for the forthcoming year for all aspects of the business. It is usually broken down into monthly budgets, which define monthly targets. Indeed, in many instances, the annual budget will be built up from monthly figures. For example, the sales staff may be required to set sales targets for each month of the budget period.

In many cases the sales target will differ from month to month – many businesses experience seasonal demand variations. Other budgets will be set for each month of the budget period, as we shall explain below.

## Limiting factors

Some aspect of the business will, inevitably, stop it achieving its objectives to the maximum extent. This is often a limited ability of the business to sell its products. Sometimes, it is some production shortage (such as labour, materials or plant) that is the **limiting factor**, or, linked to these, a shortage of funds. Often, production shortages can be overcome by an increase in funds – for example, more plant can be bought or leased. This is not always a practical solution, because no amount of money will buy certain labour skills or increase the world supply of some raw material.

Easing an initial limiting factor may sometimes be possible. For example, subcontracting can eliminate a plant capacity problem. This means that some other factor, perhaps lack of sales demand, will replace the production problem, though at a higher level of output. Ultimately, however, the business will hit a ceiling; some limiting factor will prove impossible to ease.

The limiting factor must be identified. Ultimately, most, if not all, budgets will be affected by the limiting factor. If this can be identified at the outset, all managers can be informed of the restriction early in the process. When preparing the budgets, account can then be taken of the limiting factor.

## Budgets and forecasts

A budget may, as we have already seen, be defined as a business plan for the short term. Budgets are, to a great extent, expressed in financial terms. Note particularly that a budget is a *plan*, not a forecast. To talk of a plan suggests an intention or determination to achieve the targets; **forecasts** tend to be predictions of the future state of the environment.

Clearly, forecasts are very helpful to the planner/budget-setter. If, for example, a reputable forecaster has predicted the number of new cars to be purchased in the UK during next year, it will be valuable for a manager in a car manufacturing business to take account of this information when setting next year's sales budgets. However, a forecast and a budget are distinctly different.

## Periodic and continual budgets

Budgeting can be undertaken on a periodic or a continual basis. A **periodic budget** is prepared for a particular period (usually one year). Managers will agree the budget for the year and then allow the budget to run its course. Although it may be necessary to revise the budget on occasions, preparing the periodic budget is, in essence, a one-off exercise during each financial year. A **continual budget**, as the name suggests, is continually updated. We have seen that an annual budget will normally be broken down into smaller time intervals (usually monthly periods) to help control the activities of a business. A continual budget will add a new month to replace the month that has just passed, thereby ensuring that, at all times, there will be a budget for a full planning period. Continual budgets are also referred to as **rolling budgets**.

## Activity (12.3)

Which method of budgeting do you think is likely to be more costly and which method is likely to be more beneficial for forward planning?

Periodic budgeting will usually take less time and effort and will, therefore, be less costly. However, as time passes, the budget period shortens and towards the end of the financial year managers will be working to a very short planning period indeed. Continual budgeting, on the other hand, will ensure that managers always have a full year's budget to help them make decisions. It is claimed that continual budgeting ensures that managers plan throughout the year rather than just once each year. In this way it encourages a perpetual forward-looking attitude.

While continual budgeting encourages a forward-looking attitude, there is a danger that budgeting will become a mechanical exercise. Managers may not have time to step back from their other tasks each month and consider the future with sufficient care. Continually taking this future-oriented perspective may be difficult for managers to sustain.

Continual budgets do not appear to be very popular in practice. A recent study of 340 senior financial staff of small, medium and large businesses in North America revealed that only 9 per cent of businesses use them (see reference 1 at the end of the chapter).

## How budgets link to one another

A business will prepare more than one budget for a particular period. Each budget prepared will relate to a specific aspect of the business. The ideal situation is probably that there should be a separate operating budget for each person who is in a managerial position, no matter how junior. The contents of all of the individual operating budgets will be summarised in **master budgets** usually consisting of a budgeted income statement and statement of financial position (balance sheet). The cash budget is considered by some to be a third master budget.

Figure 12.2 illustrates the interrelationship and interlinking of individual operating budgets, in this particular case using a manufacturing business as an example.

The sales budget is usually the first to be prepared (at the left of Figure 12.2), as the level of sales often determines the overall level of activity for the forthcoming period. This is because it is probably the most common limiting factor (see page 458). The finished inventories requirement tends to be set by the level of sales, though it would also be dictated by the policy of the business on the level of the finished products inventories that it chooses to hold. The requirement for finished inventories will determine the required production levels, which will, in turn, dictate the requirements of the individual production departments or sections. The demands of manufacturing, in

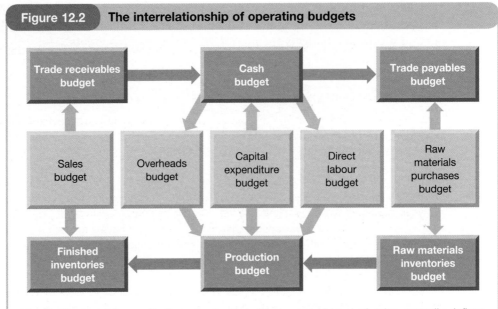

### Figure 12.2  The interrelationship of operating budgets

The starting point is usually the sales budget. The expected level of sales normally defines the overall level of activity for the business. The other operating budgets will be drawn up in accordance with this. Thus, the sales budget will largely define the finished inventories require-ments and, from this, we can define the production requirements and so on. This shows the interrelationship of operating budgets for a manufacturing business.

conjunction with the business's policy on how long it holds raw materials before they enter production, define the raw materials inventories budget. The purchases budget will be dictated by the materials inventories budget, which will, in conjunction with the policy of the business on taking credit from suppliers, dictate the trade payables budget. One of the determinants of the cash budget will be the trade payables budget; another will be the trade receivables budget, which itself derives, through the busi-ness's policy on settlement periods granted to credit customers, from the sales budget. Cash will also be affected by overheads and direct labour costs (themselves linked to production) and by capital expenditure. New finance and redemption of existing finances will also affect cash. (This is not shown in Figure 12.2 because the diagram focuses only on budgets concerned with operational matters.) The factors that affect policies on matters such as inventories holding, trade receivables collection and trade payables settlement periods will be discussed in some detail in Chapter 16.

A manufacturing business has been used as the example in Figure 12.2 simply because it has all of the types of operating budgets found in practice. Service businesses have similar arrangements of budgets, but obviously may not have inventories budgets. All of the issues relating to budgets apply equally well to all types of business.

Sales demand is not necessarily the limiting factor. Assuming that the budgeting process takes the order just described, it might be found in practice that there is some constraint other than sales demand. The production capacity of the business may, for example, be incapable of meeting the necessary levels of output to match the sales budget for one or more months. Finding a practical way of overcoming the problem may be possible. As a last resort, it might be necessary to revise the sales budget to a lower level to match the production limitation.

## Activity (12.4)

**Can you think of any ways in which a short-term shortage of production facilities of a manufacturer might be overcome?**

We thought of the following:

- Higher production in previous months and increasing inventories ('stockpiling') to meet periods of higher demand.
- Increasing production capacity, perhaps by working overtime and/or acquiring (buying or leasing) additional plant.
- Subcontracting some production.
- Encouraging potential customers to change the timing of their purchases by offering discounts or other special terms during the months that have been identified as quiet.

You might well have thought of other approaches.

There will be the horizontal relationships between budgets, which we have just looked at, but there will usually be vertical ones as well. Breaking down the sales budget into a number of subsidiary budgets, perhaps one for each regional sales manager, is a common approach. The overall sales budget will be a summary of the subsidiary ones. The same may be true of virtually all of the other budgets, most particularly the production budget.

Figure 12.3 shows the vertical relationship of the sales budgets for a business. The business has four geographical sales regions, each one the responsibility of a separate manager, who is probably located in the region concerned. Each regional manager is responsible to the overall sales manager of the business. The overall sales budget is the sum of the budgets for the four sales regions.

### Figure 12.3 The vertical relationship between a business's sales budgets

This business manages its sales through four geographical areas. The overall sales budget for the business as a whole is the sum of the four regional sales budgets.

Although sales are often managed on a geographical basis, and so their budgets reflect this, they may be managed on some other basis. For example, a business that sells a range of products may manage sales on a product-type basis, with a specialist manager responsible for each type of product. Thus, an insurance business may have separate sales managers and, therefore, separate sales budgets, for life insurance, household insurance, motor insurance and so on. Very large businesses may even have separate product-type managers for each geographical region. Each of these managers would have a separate budget, which would combine to form the overall sales budget for the business as a whole.

All of the operating budgets that we have just reviewed must mesh with the master budgets, that is, the budgeted income statement and statement of financial position.

## How budgets help managers

Budgets are generally regarded as having five areas of usefulness. These are:

1 *Budgets tend to promote forward thinking and the possible identification of short-term problems.* We saw above that a shortage of production capacity might be identified during the budgeting process. Making this discovery in good time could leave a number of means of overcoming the problem open to exploration. If the potential production problem is picked up early enough, all of the suggestions in the answer to Activity 12.4 and, possibly, other ways of overcoming the problem can be explored. Identifying the potential problem early gives managers time for calm and rational consideration of the best way of overcoming it. The best solution to the potential problem possibly may only be feasible if action can be taken well in advance. This would be true of all of the suggestions made in the answer to Activity 12.4.

2 *Budgets can be used to help co-ordination between the various sections of the business.* It is crucially important that the activities of the various departments and sections of the business are linked so that the activities of one are complementary to those of another. The activities of the purchasing/procurement department of a manufacturing business, for example, should dovetail with the raw materials needs of the production departments. If they do not, production could run out of raw materials, leading to expensive production stoppages. Possibly, just as undesirable, excessive amounts of raw materials could be bought, leading to large and unnecessary inventories holding costs. We shall see how this co-ordination tends to work in practice later in this chapter.

3 *Budgets can motivate managers to better performance.* Having a stated task can motivate managers and staff in their performance. Simply to tell managers to do their best is not very motivating, but to define a required level of achievement is more likely to be so. Managers will be better motivated by being able to relate their particular role in the business to its overall objectives. Since budgets are directly derived from strategic objectives, budgeting makes this possible. It is clearly not possible to allow managers to operate in an unconstrained environment. Having to operate in a way that matches the goals of the business is a price of working in an effective business. We shall consider the role of budgets as motivators, in more detail, in Chapter 13.

4 *Budgets can provide a basis for a system of control.* As we saw earlier in the chapter, control is concerned with ensuring that events conform to plans. If senior management wishes to control and to monitor the performance of more junior staff, it needs some yardstick against which to measure and assess performance. Current performance could possibly be compared with past performance or perhaps with what happens in another business. However, planned performance is usually the most logical yardstick. If there is information available concerning the actual performance for a period, and this can be compared with the planned performance, then a basis for control will have been established. This will enable the use of **management by exception**, an approach where senior managers can spend most of their time dealing with those staff or activities that have failed to achieve the budget (the exceptions). Thus, senior managers do not have to spend too much time on those that are performing well. It also allows junior managers to exercise self-control. By

knowing what is expected of themselves and what they have actually achieved, they can assess how well they are performing and take steps to correct matters where they are failing to achieve. We shall consider the effect of making plans and being held accountable for their achievement in Chapter 13.

5 *Budgets can provide a system of authorisation for managers to spend up to a particular limit.* Some activities (for example, staff development and research expenditure) are allocated a fixed amount of funds at the discretion of senior management. This provides the authority to spend.

Figure 12.4 shows the benefits of budgets in diagrammatic form.

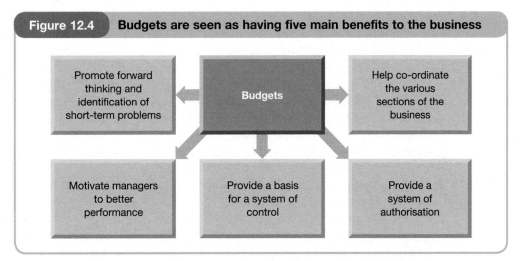

**Figure 12.4   Budgets are seen as having five main benefits to the business**

The following two activities pick up issues that relate to some of the uses of budgets.

**Activity 12.5**

The third point on the above list of the uses of budgets (motivation) implies that managers are set stated tasks. Do you think there is a danger that requiring managers to work towards such predetermined targets will stifle their skill, flair and enthusiasm?

If the budgets are set in such a way as to offer challenging yet achievable targets, the manager is still required to show skill, flair and enthusiasm. There is the danger, however, that if targets are badly set (either unreasonably demanding or too easy to achieve), they could be demotivating and have a stifling effect.

**Activity 12.6**

The fourth point on the above list of the uses of budgets (control) implies that current management performance is compared with some yardstick. What is wrong with comparing actual performance with past performance, or the performance of others, in an effort to exercise control?

What happened in the past, or is happening elsewhere, does not necessarily represent a sensible target for this year in this business. Considering what happened last year, and in other businesses, may help in the formulation of plans, but past events and the performance of others should not automatically be seen as the target.

The five identified uses of budgets can conflict with one another on occasion. Using the budget as a motivational device provides a possible example of this. Some businesses set the budget targets at a more difficult level than the managers are expected to achieve in an attempt to motivate managers to strive to reach their targets. For control purposes, however, the budget becomes less meaningful as a benchmark against which to compare actual performance. Incidentally, there is good reason to doubt the effectiveness of setting excessive targets as a motivational device, as we shall see in Chapter 13.

Conflict between the different uses will mean that managers must decide which particular uses for budgets should be given priority. Managers must be prepared, if necessary, to trade off the benefits resulting from one particular use for the benefits of another.

## The budget-setting process

Budgeting is such an important area for businesses, and other organisations, that it tends to be approached in a fairly methodical and formal way. This usually involves a number of steps, as described below.

### Step 1: Establish who will take responsibility

Those responsible for the budget-setting process must have real authority within the organisation.

**Activity 12.7**

Why would those responsible for the budget-setting process need to have real authority?

One of the crucial aspects of the process is establishing co-ordination between budgets so that the plans of one department match and are complementary to those of other departments. This usually requires compromise where adjustment of initial budgets must be undertaken. This in turn means that someone on the board of directors (or another senior manager) has to be closely involved; only people of this rank are likely to have the necessary moral and, if needed, formal managerial authority to force departmental managers to compromise.

A **budget committee** is usually formed to supervise and take responsibility for the budget-setting process. This committee usually includes a senior representative of most of the functional areas of the business – marketing, production, human resources, and so on. Often, a **budget officer** is appointed to carry out the technical tasks of the committee, or to supervise others carrying them out. Not surprisingly, given their technical expertise in the activity, accountants are often required to become budget officers.

### Step 2: Communicate budget guidelines to relevant managers

Budgets are intended to be the short-term plans that seek to work towards the achievement of strategic plans and to the overall objectives of the business. It is, therefore, important that, in drawing up budgets, managers are well aware of what the strategic plans are and how the forthcoming budget period is intended to work towards them. Managers also need to be made well aware of the commercial/economic environment in which they will be operating. This may include awareness of market trends, future rates of inflation, predicted changes in technology, and so on. It is the budget committee's responsibility to see that managers have all the necessary information.

### Step 3: Identify the key, or limiting, factor

There will be a limiting factor that will restrict the business from achieving its objectives to the maximum extent, as we saw earlier in the chapter (page 458). Identifying the limiting factor at the earliest stage in the budget-setting process will be helpful.

### Step 4: Prepare the budget for the area of the limiting factor

The limiting factor will determine the overall level of activity for the business. The limiting-factor budget will, as we have already seen, usually be the sales budget, since the ability to sell is normally the constraint on future growth. (When discussing the interrelationship of budgets earlier in the chapter, we started with the sales budget for this reason.) Sales demand, however, is not always the limiting factor.

### Step 5: Prepare draft budgets for all other areas

The other budgets are prepared, consistent with the budget for the area of the limiting factor. In all budget preparation, the computer has become an almost indispensable tool. Much of the work of preparing budgets is repetitive and tedious, yet the resultant budget has to be a reliable representation of the plans made. Computers are ideally suited to such tasks, and human beings are not. Budgets often have to be redrafted several times because of some minor alteration; computers do this without complaint.

Setting individual budgets may be approached in one of two broad ways. The *top-down approach* is where the senior management of each budget area originates the budget targets, perhaps discussing them with lower levels of management and, as a result, refining them before the final version is produced. With the *bottom-up approach*, the targets are fed upwards from the lowest level. For example, junior sales managers will be asked to set their own sales targets, which then become incorporated into the budgets of higher levels of management until the overall sales budget emerges.

Where the bottom-up approach is adopted, it is usually necessary to haggle and negotiate at different levels of authority to achieve agreement. Perhaps the plans of some departments do not fit in with those of others, or the targets set by junior managers are not acceptable to their superiors. The bottom-up approach is less popular in practice than top-down (see reference 2 at the end of the chapter).

## Activity (12.8)

What are the advantages and disadvantages of each type of budgeting approach (bottom-up and top-down)?

The bottom-up approach allows greater involvement among managers in the budgeting process and this, in turn, may increase the level of commitment to the targets set. It also allows the business to draw more fully on the local knowledge and expertise of its managers. However, this can be time-consuming and may result in some managers setting themselves undemanding targets in order to have an easy life.

The top-down approach enables senior management to communicate plans to employees and to co-ordinate the activities of the business more easily. It may also help in establishing more demanding targets for managers. However, the level of commitment to the budget may be lower as many of those responsible for achieving the budgets will have been excluded from the budget-setting process.

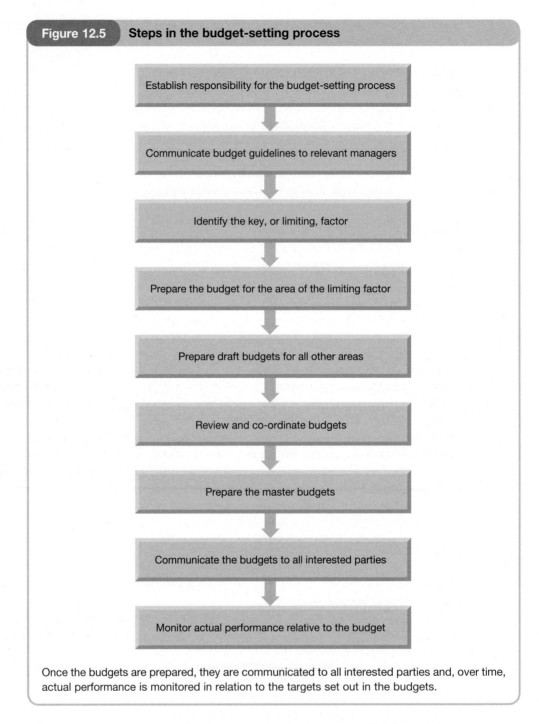

**Figure 12.5** Steps in the budget-setting process

Establish responsibility for the budget-setting process

Communicate budget guidelines to relevant managers

Identify the key, or limiting, factor

Prepare the budget for the area of the limiting factor

Prepare draft budgets for all other areas

Review and co-ordinate budgets

Prepare the master budgets

Communicate the budgets to all interested parties

Monitor actual performance relative to the budget

Once the budgets are prepared, they are communicated to all interested parties and, over time, actual performance is monitored in relation to the targets set out in the budgets.

There will be further discussion of the benefits of participation in target setting in Chapter 13.

### Step 6: Review and co-ordinate budgets

The budget committee must, at this stage, review the various budgets and satisfy itself that the budgets are consistent with one another. Where there is a lack of co-ordination, steps must be taken to ensure that the budgets mesh. Since this will require that at least one budget must be revised, this activity normally benefits from a diplomatic approach.

Ultimately, however, the committee may be forced to assert its authority and insist that alterations are made.

### Step 7: Prepare the master budgets

The master budgets are the budgeted income statement and budgeted statement of financial position – and, perhaps, a summarised cash budget. The individual operating budgets, that have already been prepared, should provide all of the information required to prepare the master budgets. The budget committee usually undertakes the task of preparing the master budgets.

### Step 8: Communicate the budgets to all interested parties

The formally agreed operating budgets are now passed to the individual managers who will be responsible for their implementation. This is, in effect, senior management formally communicating to the other managers the targets that they are expected to achieve.

### Step 9: Monitor performance relative to the budget

Much of the budget-setting activity will have been pointless unless each manager's actual performance is compared with the benchmark of planned performance, which is embodied in the budget. This issue is examined in detail in Chapter 13.

The steps in the budget-setting process are shown in diagrammatic form in Figure 12.5.

Where the established budgets are proving to be unrealistic, it is usually helpful to revise them. They may be unrealistic because certain assumptions made when the budgets were first set have turned out to be incorrect. This may occur where managers (budget-setters) have made poor judgements or where the environment has changed unexpectedly from what was, quite reasonably, assumed. Irrespective of the cause, unrealistic budgets are of little value and revising them may be the only logical approach to take. Nevertheless, revising budgets should be regarded as exceptional and only undertaken after very careful consideration.

## Using budgets in practice

This section provides a flavour of how budgets are used, the extent to which they are used and their level of accuracy.

**Real World 12.2** shows how the UK-based international engineering and support services business, Babcock International Group plc, undertakes its budgeting process.

### Real World 12.2

### Budgeting at Babcock

According to its annual report, Babcock has the following arrangements:

Comprehensive systems are in place to develop annual budgets and medium-term financial plans. The budgets are reviewed by central management before being submitted to the Board for approval. Updated forecasts for the year are prepared at least quarterly. The Board is provided with details of actual performance each month compared with budgets, forecasts and the prior year, and is given a written commentary on significant variances from approved plans.

*Source*: Babcock International Group plc, Annual Report 2010, p. 64.

There is quite a lot of recent survey evidence that reveals the extent to which budgeting is used by businesses in practice. **Real World 12.3** reviews some of this evidence, which shows that most businesses prepare and use budgets.

---

### Real World 12.3

### Budgeting in practice

A survey of 41 UK manufacturing businesses found that 40 of the 41 surveyed prepared budgets.

*Source*: *Contemporary Management Accounting Practices in UK Manufacturing*, D. Dugdale, C. Jones and S. Green, CIMA Publication, Elsevier, 2006.

Another survey of UK businesses, but this time businesses involved in the food and drink sector, found that virtually all of them used budgets.

*Source*: *An Empirical Investigation of the Evolution of Management Accounting Practices*, M. Abdel-Kader and R. Luther, Working paper No. 04/06, University of Essex, October 2004.

A survey of the opinions of senior finance staff at 340 businesses of various sizes and operating in a wide range of industries in North America revealed that 97 per cent of those businesses had a formal budgeting process.

*Source*: 'Perfect how you project', BPM Forum, 2008.

Though these three surveys relate to UK and North American businesses, they provide some idea of what is likely also to be the practice elsewhere in the developed world.

---

**Real World 12.4** below gives some insight to the accuracy of budgets.

---

### Real World 12.4

### Budget accuracy

The survey of senior finance staff of North American businesses, mentioned in Real World 12.3 above, asked them to compare the actual revenues with the budgeted revenues for 2007. Figure 12.6 shows the results:

We can see that only 66 per cent of revenue budgets were accurate within 10 per cent. The survey revealed that budgets for expenses were generally more accurate, with 74 per cent being accurate within 10 per cent.

*Source*: 'Perfect how you project', BPM Forum, 2008.

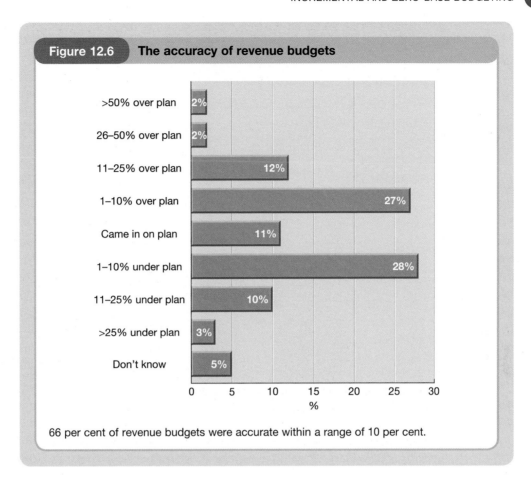

**Figure 12.6    The accuracy of revenue budgets**

66 per cent of revenue budgets were accurate within a range of 10 per cent.

## Incremental and zero-base budgeting

Budget setting is often done on the basis of what happened last year, with some adjustment for any changes in factors that are expected to affect the forthcoming budget period (for example, inflation). This approach is known as **incremental budgeting** and is often used for **discretionary budgets**, such as research and development and staff training. With this type of budget, the **budget holder** (the manager responsible for the budget) is allocated a sum of money to be spent in the area of activity concerned. Such budgets are referred to as 'discretionary' budgets because the sum allocated is normally at the discretion of senior management. These budgets are very common in local and central government (and in other public bodies), but are also used in commercial businesses to cover the types of activity that we have just referred to.

Discretionary budgets are often found in areas where there is no clear relationship between inputs (resources applied) and outputs (benefits). Compare this with, say, a raw materials usage budget in a manufacturing business, where the amount of material used and, therefore, the amount of funds involved, are clearly related to the level of production and, ultimately, to sales volumes. Discretionary budgets can easily eat up funds, with no clear benefit being derived. It is often only the proposed periodic increases in these budgets that are closely scrutinised.

**Real World 12.5** provides some idea of the extent to which incremental budgeting is used in practice.

**Real World 12.5**

## Budgeting by increments

The 2009 CIMA survey showed that incremental budgeting is quite widely used in practice, as is shown by Figure 12.7.

**Figure 12.7** The use of incremental budgeting

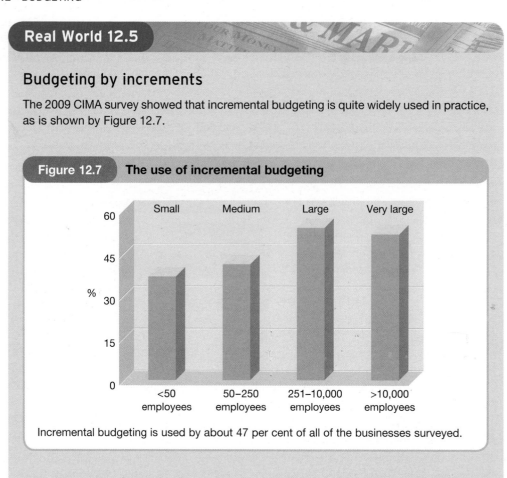

Incremental budgeting is used by about 47 per cent of all of the businesses surveyed.

It seems reasonable to presume that where businesses use an incremental approach, it is in the context of discretionary budgets.

*Source*: 'Management accounting tools for today and tomorrow', CIMA, 2009, p.15.

**Zero-base budgeting (ZBB)** rests on the philosophy that all spending needs to be justified. Thus, when establishing, say, the training budget each year, it is not automatically accepted that training courses should be financed in the future simply because they were undertaken this year. The training budget will start from a zero base (that is no resources at all) and will only be increased above zero if a good case can be made for the scarce resources of the business to be allocated to this form of activity. Top management will need to be convinced that the proposed activities represent 'value for money'.

ZBB encourages managers to adopt a more questioning approach to their areas of responsibility. To justify the allocation of resources, managers are often forced to think carefully about the particular activities and the ways in which they are undertaken. This questioning approach should result in a more efficient use of business resources. An increasing portion of the total cost of most businesses is in areas where the link between outputs and inputs is not always clear. The commitment of resources is, therefore, discretionary rather than demonstrably essential to production. Thus, ZBB is increasingly relevant.

## Activity (12.9)

Can you think of any disadvantages of using ZBB?

The principal problems with ZBB are:

● It is time-consuming and therefore expensive to undertake.
● Managers whose sphere of responsibility is subjected to ZBB can feel threatened by it.

The benefits of a ZBB approach can be gained to some extent – perhaps at not too great a cost – by using the approach on a selective basis. For example, a particular budget area could be subjected to ZBB-type scrutiny only every third or fourth year. In any case, if ZBB is used more frequently, there is the danger that managers will use the same arguments each year to justify their activities. The process will simply become a mechanical exercise and the benefits will be lost. For a typical business, some areas are likely to benefit from ZBB more than others. As mentioned earlier, the areas most likely to benefit from ZBB involve discretionary spending, such as training, advertising and research and development.

If senior management is aware that their subordinates are likely to feel threatened by the nature of this form of budgeting, care can be taken to apply ZBB with sensitivity. However, in the quest for cost control and value for money, ZBB can result in some tough decisions being made.

**Real World 12.6** gives some impression of how much ZBB is used in practice.

## Real World 12.6

### Too low for zero

A significant proportion of businesses use ZBB in practice, according to the 2009 CIMA survey. The detail is shown by Figure 12.8.

| Figure 12.8 | The use of zero-base budgeting |

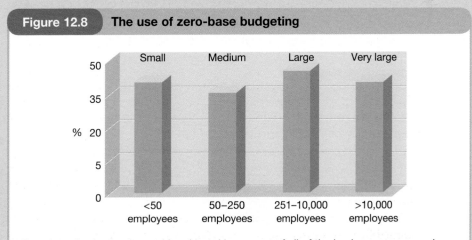

Zero-base budgeting is used by about 41 per cent of all of the businesses surveyed.

As with incremental budgeting, it is likely that ZBB is mainly used when preparing discretionary budgets.

*Source*: 'Management accounting tools for today and tomorrow', CIMA, 2009, p.15.

## Preparing the cash budget

We shall now look in some detail at how the various budgets used by the typical business are prepared, starting with the cash budget and then looking at the others. It is helpful for us to start with the cash budget because:

● It is a key budget (some people see it as a 'master budget' along with the budgeted income statement and budgeted statement of financial position); most economic aspects of a business are reflected in cash sooner or later, so that for a typical business the cash budget reflects the whole business more comprehensively than any other single budget.
● A very small, unsophisticated business (for example, a corner shop) may feel that full-scale budgeting is not appropriate to its needs, but almost certainly it should prepare a cash budget as a minimum.

Since budgets are documents that tend to be used only internally by a business, their format is a question of management choice and will vary from one business to the next. However, since all managers, irrespective of the business, are likely to be using budgets for similar purposes, some consistency of approach tends to be found. In most businesses, the cash budget will probably possess the following features:

1  The budget period would be broken down into sub-periods, typically months.
2  The budget would be in columnar form, with one column for each month.
3  Receipts of cash would be identified under various headings and a total for each month's receipts shown.
4  Payments of cash would be identified under various headings and a total for each month's payments shown.
5  The surplus of total cash receipts over payments, or of payments over receipts, for each month would be identified.
6  The running cash balance would be identified. This would be achieved by taking the balance at the end of the previous month and adjusting it for the surplus or deficit of receipts over payments for the current month.

Typically, all of the pieces of information in points 3 to 6 in this list would be useful to management for one reason or another.

Probably the best way to deal with this topic is through an example.

### Example 12.1

Vierra Popova Ltd is a wholesale business. The budgeted income statements for each of the next six months are as follows:

|  | Jan £000 | Feb £000 | Mar £000 | Apr £000 | May £000 | June £000 |
|---|---|---|---|---|---|---|
| Sales revenue | 52 | 55 | 55 | 60 | 55 | 53 |
| Cost of goods sold | (30) | (31) | (31) | (35) | (31) | (32) |
| Salaries and wages | (10) | (10) | (10) | (10) | (10) | (10) |
| Electricity | (5) | (5) | (4) | (3) | (3) | (3) |
| Depreciation | (3) | (3) | (3) | (3) | (3) | (3) |
| Other overheads | (2) | (2) | (2) | (2) | (2) | (2) |
| Total expenses | (50) | (51) | (50) | (53) | (49) | (50) |
| Profit for the month | 2 | 4 | 5 | 7 | 6 | 3 |

The business allows all of its customers one month's credit (this means, for example, that cash from January sales will be received in February). Sales revenue during December totalled £60,000.

The business plans to maintain inventories at their existing level until some time in March, when they are to be reduced by £5,000. Inventories will remain at this lower level indefinitely. Inventories purchases are made on one month's credit. December purchases totalled £30,000. Salaries, wages and 'other overheads' are paid in the month concerned. Electricity is paid quarterly in arrears in March and June. The business plans to buy and pay for a new delivery van in March. This will cost a total of £15,000, but an existing van will be traded in for £4,000 as part of the deal.

The business expects to have £12,000 in cash at the beginning of January.

The cash budget for the six months ending in June will look as follows:

|  | Jan £000 | Feb £000 | Mar £000 | Ap £000 | May £000 | June £000 |
|---|---|---|---|---|---|---|
| Receipts |  |  |  |  |  |  |
| Trade receivables (Note 1) | 60 | 52 | 55 | 55 | 60 | 55 |
| Payments |  |  |  |  |  |  |
| Trade payables (Note 2) | (30) | (30) | (31) | (26) | (35) | (31) |
| Salaries and wages | (10) | (10) | (10) | (10) | (10) | (10) |
| Electricity |  |  | (14) |  |  | (9) |
| Other overheads | (2) | (2) | (2) | (2) | (2) | (2) |
| Van purchase | – | – | (11) | – | – | – |
| Total payments | (42) | (42) | (68) | (38) | (47) | (52) |
| Cash surplus for the month | 18 | 10 | (13) | 17 | 13 | 3 |
| Opening balance (Note 3) | 12 | 30 | 40 | 27 | 44 | 57 |
| Closing balance | 30 | 40 | 27 | 44 | 57 | 60 |

Notes:

1  The cash receipts from trade receivables lag a month behind sales because customers are given a month in which to pay for their purchases. So, December sales will be paid for in January and so on.

2  In most months, the purchases of inventories will equal the cost of goods sold. This is because the business maintains a constant level of inventories. For inventories to remain constant at the end of each month, the business must replace exactly the amount that has been used. During March, however, the business plans to reduce its inventories by £5,000. This means that inventories purchases will be lower than inventories usage in that month. The payments for inventories purchases lag a month behind purchases because the business expects to be allowed a month to pay for what it buys.

3  Each month's cash balance is the previous month's figure plus the cash surplus (or minus the cash deficit) for the current month. The balance at the start of January is £12,000 according to the information provided earlier.

4  Depreciation does not give rise to a cash payment. In the context of profit measurement (in the income statement), depreciation is a very important aspect. Here, however, we are interested only in cash.

## Activity 12.10

Looking at the cash budget of Vierra Popova Ltd (Example 12.1), what conclusions do you draw and what possible course of action do you recommend regarding the cash balance over the period concerned?

Given the size of the business, there is a fairly large cash balance that seems to be increasing. Management might consider:

● putting some of the cash into an income-yielding deposit,
● increasing the investment in non-current (fixed) assets,
● paying a dividend to the owners,
● repaying borrowings.

## Activity 12.11

Vierra Popova Ltd (Example 12.1) now wishes to prepare its cash budget for the second six months of the year. The budgeted income statements for each month of the second half of the year are as follows:

|  | July £000 | Aug £000 | Sept £000 | Oct £000 | Nov £000 | Dec £000 |
|---|---|---|---|---|---|---|
| Sales revenue | 57 | 59 | 62 | 57 | 53 | 51 |
| Cost of goods sold | (32) | (33) | (35) | (32) | (30) | (29) |
| Salaries and wages | (10) | (10) | (10) | (10) | (10) | (10) |
| Electricity | (3) | (3) | (4) | (5) | (6) | (6) |
| Depreciation | (3) | (3) | (3) | (3) | (3) | (3) |
| Other overheads | (2) | (2) | (2) | (2) | (2) | (2) |
| Total expenses | (50) | (51) | (54) | (52) | (51) | (50) |
| Profit for the month | 7 | 8 | 8 | 5 | 2 | 1 |

The business will continue to allow all of its customers one month's credit.

It plans to increase inventories from the 30 June level by £1,000 each month until, and including, September. During the following three months, inventories levels will be decreased by £1,000 each month.

Inventories purchases, which had been made on one month's credit until the June payment, will, starting with the purchases made in June, be made on two months' credit.

Salaries, wages and 'other overheads' will continue to be paid in the month concerned. Electricity is paid quarterly in arrears in September and December.

At the end of December, the business intends to pay off part of some borrowings. This payment is to be such that it will leave the business with a cash balance of £5,000 with which to start next year.

Prepare the cash budget for the six months ending in December. (Remember that any information you need that relates to the first six months of the year, including the cash balance that is expected to be brought forward on 1 July, is given in Example 12.1.)

The cash budget for the six months ended 31 December is:

|  | July £000 | Aug £000 | Sept £000 | Oct £000 | Nov £000 | Dec £000 |
|---|---|---|---|---|---|---|
| *Receipts* | | | | | | |
| Trade receivables | 53 | 57 | 59 | 62 | 57 | 53 |
| *Payments* | | | | | | |
| Trade payables (Note 1) | – | (32) | (33) | (34) | (36) | (31) |
| Salaries and wages | (10) | (10) | (10) | (10) | (10) | (10) |
| Electricity | – | – | (10) | – | – | (17) |
| Other overheads | (2) | (2) | (2) | (2) | (2) | (2) |
| Borrowings repayment (Note 2) | – | – | – | – | – | (131) |
| *Total payments* | (12) | (44) | (55) | (46) | (48) | (191) |
| Cash surplus for the month | 41 | 13 | 4 | 16 | 9 | (138) |
| Opening balance | 60 | 101 | 114 | 118 | 134 | 143 |
| Closing balance | 101 | 114 | 118 | 134 | 143 | 5 |

*Notes:*

1  There will be no payment to suppliers (trade payables) in July because the June purchases will be made on two months' credit and will therefore be paid in August. The July purchases, which will equal the July cost of sales figure plus the increase in inventories made in July, will be paid for in September, and so on.

2  The borrowings repayment is simply the amount that will cause the balance at 31 December to be £5,000.

## Preparing other budgets

Though each one will have its own particular features, other budgets will tend to follow the same sort of pattern as the cash budget, that is, they will show inflows and outflows during each month and the opening and closing balances in each month.

### Example 12.2

To illustrate some of the other budgets, we shall continue to use the example of Vierra Popova Ltd that we considered in Example 12.1. To the information given there, we need to add the fact that the inventories balance at 1 January was £30,000.

**Trade receivables budget**

This would normally show the planned amount owed to the business by credit customers at the beginning and at the end of each month, the planned total credit sales revenue for each month and the planned total cash receipts from credit customers (trade receivables). The layout would be something like this:

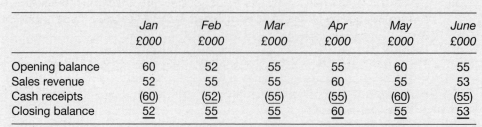

|  | Jan<br>£000 | Feb<br>£000 | Mar<br>£000 | Apr<br>£000 | May<br>£000 | June<br>£000 |
|---|---|---|---|---|---|---|
| Opening balance | 60 | 52 | 55 | 55 | 60 | 55 |
| Sales revenue | 52 | 55 | 55 | 60 | 55 | 53 |
| Cash receipts | (60) | (52) | (55) | (55) | (60) | (55) |
| Closing balance | 52 | 55 | 55 | 60 | 55 | 53 |

The opening and closing balances represent the amount that the business plans to be owed (in total) by credit customers (trade receivables) at the beginning and end of each month, respectively.

### Trade payables budget

Typically this shows the planned amount owed to suppliers by the business at the beginning and at the end of each month, the planned credit purchases for each month and the planned total cash payments to trade payables. The layout would be something like this:

|  | Jan<br>£000 | Feb<br>£000 | Mar<br>£000 | Apr<br>£000 | May<br>£000 | June<br>£000 |
|---|---|---|---|---|---|---|
| Opening balance | 30 | 30 | 31 | 26 | 35 | 31 |
| Purchases | 30 | 31 | 26 | 35 | 31 | 32 |
| Cash payment | (30) | (30) | (31) | (26) | (35) | (31) |
| Closing balance | 30 | 31 | 26 | 35 | 31 | 32 |

The opening and closing balances represent the amount planned to be owed (in total) by the business to suppliers (trade payables), at the beginning and end of each month respectively.

### Inventories budget

This would normally show the planned amount of inventories to be held by the business at the beginning and at the end of each month, the planned total inventories purchases for each month and the planned total monthly inventories usage. The layout would be something like this:

|  | Jan<br>£000 | Feb<br>£000 | Mar<br>£000 | Apr<br>£000 | May<br>£000 | June<br>£000 |
|---|---|---|---|---|---|---|
| Opening balance | 30 | 30 | 30 | 25 | 25 | 25 |
| Purchases | 30 | 31 | 26 | 35 | 31 | 32 |
| Inventories used | (30) | (31) | (31) | (35) | (31) | (32) |
| Closing balance | 30 | 30 | 25 | 25 | 25 | 25 |

The opening and closing balances represent the amount of inventories, at cost, planned to be held by the business at the beginning and end of each month respectively.

A *raw materials inventories budget*, for a manufacturing business, would follow a similar pattern, with the 'inventories usage' being the cost of the inventories put into production. A *finished inventories budget* for a manufacturer would also be similar to the above, except that 'inventories manufactured' would replace 'purchases'. A manufacturing business would normally prepare both a raw materials inventories budget and a finished inventories budget. Both of these would typically be based on the full cost of the inventories (that is, including overheads). There is no reason why the inventories should not be valued on the basis of either variable cost or direct costs, should managers feel that this would provide more useful information.

The inventories budget will normally be expressed in financial terms, but may also be expressed in physical terms (for example, kg or metres) for individual inventories items.

Note how the trade receivables, trade payables and inventories budgets in Example 12.2 link to one another, and to the cash budget, for the same business in Example 12.1. Note particularly that:

- the purchases figures in the trade payables budget and in the inventories budget are identical;
- the cash payments figures in the trade payables budget and in the cash budget are identical;
- the cash receipts figures in the trade receivables budget and in the cash budget are identical.

Other values would link different budgets in a similar way. For example, the row of sales revenue figures in the trade receivables budget would be identical to the sales revenue figures that will be found in the sales budget. This is how the linking (co-ordination), which was discussed earlier in this chapter, is achieved.

## Activity (12.12)

Have a go at preparing the trade receivables budget for Vierra Popova Ltd for the six months from July to December (see Activity 12.11).

The trade receivables budget for the six months ended 31 December is:

|  | July £000 | Aug £000 | Sep £000 | Oct £000 | Nov £000 | Dec £000 |
|---|---|---|---|---|---|---|
| Opening balance (Note 1) | 53 | 57 | 59 | 62 | 57 | 53 |
| Sales revenue (Note 2) | 57 | 59 | 62 | 57 | 53 | 51 |
| Cash receipts (Note 3) | (53) | (57) | (59) | (62) | (57) | (53) |
| Closing balance (Note 4) | 57 | 59 | 62 | 57 | 53 | 51 |

Notes:
1 The opening trade receivables figure is the previous month's sales revenue figure (sales are on one month's credit).
2 The sales revenue is the current month's figure.
3 The cash received each month is equal to the previous month's sales revenue figure.
4 The closing balance is equal to the current month's sales revenue figure.
Note that if we knew any three of the four figures each month, we could deduce the fourth.

This budget could be set out in any manner that would have given the sort of information that management would require in respect of planned levels of trade receivables and associated transactions.

## Activity (12.13)

Have a go at preparing the trade payables budget for Vierra Popova Ltd for the six months from July to December (see Activity 12.12). (*Hint*: Remember that the trade payables settlement period alters from the June purchases onwards.)

Activity 12.13 (*continued*)

The trade payables budget for the six months ended 31 December is:

|                 | July £000 | Aug £000 | Sept £000 | Oct £000 | Nov £000 | Dec £000 |
|-----------------|-----------|----------|-----------|----------|----------|----------|
| Opening balance | 32        | 65       | 67        | 70       | 67       | 60       |
| Purchases       | 33        | 34       | 36        | 31       | 29       | 28       |
| Cash payments   | –         | (32)     | (33)      | (34)     | (36)     | (31)     |
| Closing balance | 65        | 67       | 70        | 67       | 60       | 57       |

This, again, could be set out in any manner that would have given the sort of information that management would require in respect of planned levels of trade payables and associated transactions.

# Activity-based budgeting

**Activity-based budgeting (ABB)** extends, to budgeting, the principles of activity-based costing (ABC) that we discussed in Chapter 11. Under a system of ABB, once the limiting factor has been established, the sales budget is determined. Next, the activities necessary to achieve the budgeted sales are identified. Budgets for each of the various activities are prepared by multiplying the budgeted usage of the cost driver for a particular activity (as determined by the sales budget) by the budgeted rate for the relevant cost driver. The following example should help to make the process clear.

## Example 12.3

Danube Ltd produces two products, the Gamma and the Delta. The sales budget for next year shows that 60,000 units of Gamma and 80,000 units of Delta are expected to be sold. Each type of product spends time in the finished goods stores. Both products are of roughly similar size and have very similar storage needs. It is felt, therefore, that the period spent in the stores ('product weeks') is the cost driver and so a budget for this cost-driving activity is created. It is estimated that Product Gamma will spend an average of two weeks in the stores before being sold and, for Product Delta, the average period is five weeks.

To calculate the activity budget for the finished goods stores, the estimated total usage of the cost driver must be calculated. This will be the total number of 'product weeks' that the products will be in store.

The budgeted rate for the cost driver has been set at £1.50 per product week.

| Product | | Product weeks |
|---------|--------------------|---------|
| Delta   | 60,000 × 2 weeks = | 120,000 |
| Gamma   | 80,000 × 5 weeks = | 400,000 |
|         |                    | 520,000 |

The number of product weeks will then be multiplied by the budgeted rate for the cost driver to derive the activity budget figure. That is:

$$520,000 \times £1.50 = £780,000$$

The same process will be carried out for the other cost-driving activities identified.

Note that budgets are prepared according to the cost-driving activity rather than function, as is the case with the traditional approach to budgeting. In other words, there will be a separate budget for each cost pool.

Through the application of ABC principles, the factors that cause costs are known and there is a direct linking of costs with outputs. This means that ABB should provide a better understanding of future resource needs and more accurate budgets. It should also provide a better understanding of the effect on budgeted costs of changes in the usage of the cost driver, because of the explicit relationship between cost drivers, activities and costs.

Control should be improved within an ABB environment for two reasons:

- By developing more accurate budgets, managers should be provided with demanding yet achievable targets.
- ABB should ensure that costs are closely linked to responsibilities. Managers who have control over particular cost drivers will become accountable for the costs that are caused. An important principle of effective budgeting is that those responsible for meeting a particular budget (budget holders) should have control over the events that affect performance in their area.

**Real World 12.7** provides some indication of the extent to which ABB is used in practice.

### Real World 12.7

## Quite a lot of activity

The 2009 CIMA survey showed that ABB is used by a significant proportion of businesses in practice, as is shown by Figure 12.9.

| Figure 12.9 | The use of activity-based budgeting |

Activity-based budgeting is used by about 30 per cent of all of the businesses surveyed.

**Real World 12.7 (*continued*)**

Unsurprisingly, the percentages that use ABB almost precisely match the proportion of the same survey sample that use activity-based costing. It is logical that businesses that use an activity-based approach to deriving their costs should also apply the same approach to holding managers responsible for the costs that are incurred, through the budgets.

*Source:* 'Management accounting tools for today and tomorrow', CIMA, 2009, p. 15.

Self-assessment question 12.1 pulls together what we have just seen about preparing budgets.

**Self-assessment question** **12.1**

Antonio Ltd has planned production and sales for the next nine months as follows:

|  | Production Units | Sales Units |
|---|---|---|
| May | 350 | 350 |
| June | 400 | 400 |
| July | 500 | 400 |
| August | 600 | 500 |
| September | 600 | 600 |
| October | 700 | 650 |
| November | 750 | 700 |
| December | 750 | 800 |
| January | 750 | 750 |

During the period, the business plans to advertise so as to generate these increases in sales. Payments for advertising of £1,000 and £1,500 will be made in July and October respectively.

The selling price per unit will be £20 throughout the period. Forty per cent of sales are normally made on two months' credit. The other 60 per cent are settled within the month of the sale.

Raw materials will be held for one month before they are taken into production. Purchases of raw materials will be on one month's credit (buy one month, pay the next). The cost of raw materials is £8 per unit of production.

Other direct production expenses, including labour, are £6 per unit of production. These will be paid in the month concerned.

Various production overheads, which during the period to 30 June had run at £1,800 a month, are expected to rise to £2,000 each month from 1 July to 31 October. These are expected to rise again from 1 November to £2,400 a month and to remain at that level for the foreseeable future. These overheads include a steady £400 each month for depreciation. Overheads are planned to be paid 80 per cent in the month of production and 20 per cent in the following month.

To help to meet the planned increased production, a new item of plant will be bought and delivered in August. The cost of this item is £6,600; the contract with the supplier will specify that this will be paid in three equal amounts in September, October and November.

Raw materials inventories is planned to be 500 units on 1 July. The balance at the bank on the same day is planned to be £7,500.

*Required:*

(a) Draw up the following for the six months ending 31 December:
   1. A raw materials inventories budget, showing both physical quantities and financial values.
   2. A trade payables budget.
   3. A cash budget.
(b) The cash budget reveals a potential cash deficiency during October and November. Can you suggest any ways in which a modification of plans could overcome this problem?

**The answer to this question can be found at the back of the book on pages 738 to 739.**

## Non-financial measures in budgeting

The efficiency of internal operations and customer satisfaction levels have become of critical importance to businesses striving to survive in an increasingly competitive environment. As we saw in Chapter 11, non-financial performance indicators have an important role to play in assessing performance in such key areas as customer/supplier delivery times, set-up times, defect levels and customer satisfaction levels.

There is no reason why budgeting need be confined to financial targets and measures. Non-financial measures can also be used as the basis for targets and these can be brought into the budgeting process and reported alongside the financial targets for the business.

## Budgets and management behaviour

All accounting statements and reports are intended to affect the behaviour of one or more groups of people. Budgets are intended to affect the behaviour of managers, for example, to encourage them to work towards the business's objectives and to do this in a co-ordinated manner.

Whether budgets are effective and how they could be made more effective are crucial issues for managers. We shall examine this topic in detail in Chapter 13, after we have seen, in the earlier part of that chapter, how budgets can be used to help managers to exercise control.

## Who needs budgets?

Until relatively recently it would have been a heresy to suggest that budgeting was not of central importance to any business. The benefits of budgeting, mentioned earlier in this chapter, have been widely recognised and the vast majority of businesses prepare annual budgets (see Real World 12.3 on page 468). However, there is increasing concern that, in today's highly dynamic and competitive environment, budgets may actually be harmful to the achievement of business objectives. This has led a small but growing number of businesses to abandon traditional budgets as a tool of planning and control.

Various charges have been levelled against the conventional budgeting process. It is claimed that:

- Budgets cannot deal with a fast-changing environment and they are often out of date before the start of the budget period.
- They focus too much management attention on the achievement of short-term financial targets. Instead, managers should focus on the things that create value for the business (for example, innovation, building brand loyalty, responding quickly to competitive threats, and so on).
- They reinforce a 'command and control' structure that concentrates power in the hands of senior managers and prevents junior managers from exercising autonomy. This may be particularly true where a top-down approach, that allocates budgets to managers, is being used. Where managers feel constrained, attempts to retain and recruit able managers can be difficult.
- Budgeting takes up an enormous amount of management time that could be better used. In practice, budgeting can be a lengthy process that may involve much negotiation, reworking and updating. However, this may add little to the achievement of business objectives.
- Budgets are based around business functions (sales, marketing, production, and so on). To achieve the business's objectives, however, the focus should be on business processes that cut across functional boundaries and reflect the needs of the customer.
- They encourage incremental thinking by employing a 'last year plus $x$ per cent' approach to planning. This can inhibit the development of 'break out' strategies that may be necessary in a fast-changing environment.
- They can protect costs rather than lower costs, particularly in the area of discretionary budgets. In some cases, a fixed budget for an activity, such as research and development, is allocated to a manager. If the amount is not spent, the budget may be taken away and, in future periods, the budget for this activity may be either reduced or eliminated. Such a response to unused budget allocations can encourage managers to spend the whole of the budget, irrespective of need, in order to protect the allocations they receive.
- They promote 'sharp' practice among managers. In order to meet budget targets, managers may try to negotiate lower sales targets or higher cost allocations than they feel is really necessary. This helps them to build some 'slack' into the budgets and so meeting the budget becomes easier (see reference 3 at the end of the chapter).

**Real World 12.8** is taken from a question and answer column written by John Timpson. He is the chief executive of the very successful, high street shoe repairing and key cutting business, with over 800 branches (and expanding) throughout the UK. His answer to a question about budgeting echos many of the criticisms of conventional budgeting, listed above. The column appeared in the *Daily Telegraph*.

**Real World 12.8**

## Cobblers

*Question: I am interested in how you measure the financial performance of your private company. Presumably you have sales and profit targets for each of your 800 plus shops, but do you have KPIs (key performance indicators) for the group as well as cash flow, profit and sales targets? If so, how do you choose some indicators over others?*

**Answer:** A long time ago I learnt that having a lot of figures doesn't mean you are better informed – it just makes life more complicated.

In the 1980s, we set budget sales figures for every shop every week, our Finance Director insisting that individual shop numbers added up to his company budget. It was a tortuous process that took weeks of area management time and although head office hoped the plan would provide the perfect incentive, it made no difference to our performance. Sales never seemed to follow our forecast – our customers clearly didn't know how much they were expected to spend! I scrapped the budgetary process and for the last 20 years we have compared branch performance with last year – it has saved us a lot of bother.

Life at Timpson has little to do with budgets and we don't have KPIs. We have bought several loss making companies and found that every one of them was monitoring minute detail from Head Office – Sketchley, the dry cleaners, were keen on keeping a count of their 'supercrease' sales; Max Spielmann, the photo chain, kept an eye on the average price of picture frames; and shoe repairers Mr Minit was controlling costs so closely that they recorded every shop's expenditure on postage stamps. While management concentrated on the detail they seemed to miss out on the big picture. Instead of studying their computers they should have visited more shops to talk to the colleagues who met their customers.

Of the few figures I receive, the most important is the bank balance compared with the same day last year. It gives me a daily health check on our business. I get a daily report on all the new shops we have opened in the last three months and a weekly sales report for the company, in total, and by department. We revise our profit forecast every week and produce management accounts every month, but I seldom look beyond the front page summary.

The only time I ask for detail is when we are introducing a new service – like our current growth in portraits, locksmith work and complicated car keys. If you know which shops are successful you can pass their secret around the rest of the business.

With little to look at it is easy to see how the company is doing and I have plenty of time left to visit our branches and discover what is really going on.

*Source*: John Timpson, The management column, *The Daily Telegraph Business*, 6 June 2011.

Although some believe that many of the problems identified can be solved by better budgeting systems such as activity-based budgeting and zero-base budgeting and by taking a more flexible approach, others believe that a more radical solution is required.

## Beyond conventional budgeting

In recent years, a few businesses have abandoned budgeting, although they still recognise the need for forward planning. No one seriously doubts that there must be appropriate systems in place to steer a business towards its objectives. It is claimed, however, that the systems adopted should reflect a broader, more integrated approach to planning. The new systems that have been implemented are often based around a 'leaner' financial planning process that is more closely linked to other measurement and reward systems. Emphasis is placed on the use of rolling forecasts, key performance indicators (such as market share, customer satisfaction and innovations) and/or 'scorecards' (like the balanced scorecard, which we met in Chapter 11) that identify both monetary and non-monetary targets to be achieved over the long term and short term. These are often very demanding ('stretch') targets, based on benchmarks that have been set by world-class businesses.

The new 'beyond budgeting' model promotes a more decentralised, participative approach to managing the business. It is claimed that the traditional hierarchical management structure, where decision making is concentrated at the higher levels of the hierarchy, encourages a culture of dependency where meeting the budget targets set by senior managers is the key to managerial success. This traditional structure is replaced by a network structure where decision making is devolved to 'front-line' managers. A more open, questioning attitude among employees is encouraged by the new structure. There is a sharing of knowledge and best practice; protective behaviour by managers is discouraged. In addition, rewards are linked to targets based on improvement in

**Figure 12.10** **Traditional versus 'beyond budgeting' planning model**

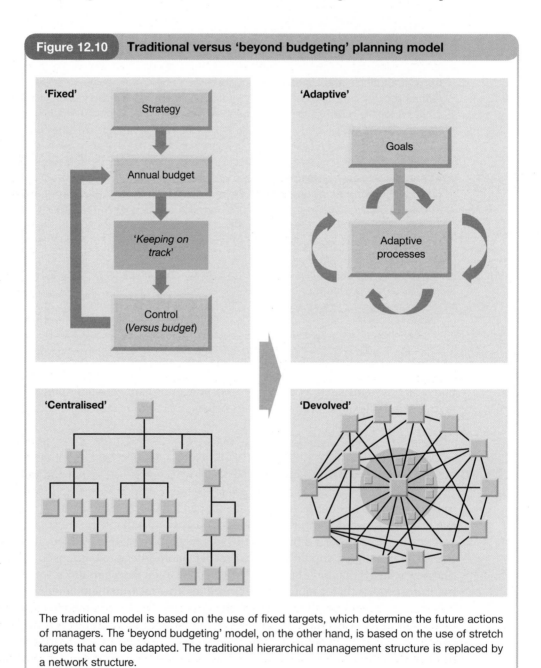

The traditional model is based on the use of fixed targets, which determine the future actions of managers. The 'beyond budgeting' model, on the other hand, is based on the use of stretch targets that can be adapted. The traditional hierarchical management structure is replaced by a network structure.

*Source*: Beyond budgeting, www.bbrt.org.

relative performance rather than to meeting the budget. It is claimed that this new approach allows greater adaptability to changing conditions, increases performance and increases motivation among staff.

Figure 12.10 sets out the main differences between the traditional and 'beyond budgeting' planning models.

**Real World 12.9** looks at the management planning systems at Toyota, the well-known Japanese motor vehicle business. Toyota does not use conventional budgets.

---

### Real World 12.9

#### Steering Toyota

Peter Bunce is at the forefront of those who argue that budgeting systems have an adverse effect on the ability of businesses to compete effectively. The following is an outline of Toyota's planning and control systems, written by him:

> Toyota is a well-known example of a sense-and-respond organisation. Instead of pushing products through rigid processes to meet sales targets, its operating systems start from the customer – it is the customer order that drives operating processes and the work that people do. The point is that in sense-and-respond companies, predetermined plans and performance contracts are an anathema and represent insurmountable barriers; which is why adaptive organisations like Toyota don't have them. However, in industries such as manufacturing, planning has a vital role to play as they have to ensure that they will have sufficient capacity for expected levels of customer orders and they have to manage and coordinate the supply chain. Every year Toyota Motor Europe develops what it calls its Original Business Plan (OBP). The OBP is just a forecast (or financial plan) for the year and provides a baseline for understanding actuals and changes, for communicating, discussion and reaching consensus (a key element of Toyota's way of working) and also for management reviews. The OBP doesn't have any of the toxic elements of a traditional budget such as agreeing and coordinating fixed targets, rewards and resources for the year ahead, and the measuring and controlling performance against such an agreement. Nor is it a reference for bonuses as it doesn't contain any targets or goals (aspirational goals are set separately by Toyota). Toyota Motors Europe also undertakes quarterly forecasts to update the OBP. These are much lighter than the OBP and don't go into much detail.

*Source*: 'Transforming financial planning', P. Bunce, www.bbrt.org, June 2007.

---

It is perhaps too early to predict whether or not the trickle of businesses that are now seeking an alternative to budgets will turn into a flood. However, it is clear that in today's highly competitive environment a business must be flexible and responsive to changing conditions. Management systems that in any way hinder these attributes will not survive.

## Long live budgets!

It is worth remembering that, despite the criticisms, budgeting remains a very widely used technique. Real World 12.3 provides evidence for this and Real World 12.10 suggests that this is unlikely to change much in the near future. Furthermore, a glance through the annual report of virtually any well-known business will reveal that budgeting is used and is not, therefore, regarded as an impediment to success. **Real World 12.10** is an account of a round table discussion at a Better Budgeting forum held in London in March 2004. This was attended by representatives of 32 large organisations, including BAA (the airport operator), the BBC, Ford Motors, Sainsbury (the supermarket business) and Unilever (the household goods group).

---

### Real World 12.10

### Alive and kicking

The report of the forum discussions said:

> If you were to believe all that has been written in recent years, you'd be forgiven for thinking that budgeting is on its way to becoming extinct. Various research reports allude to the widespread dissatisfaction with the bureaucratic exercise in cost cutting that budgeting is accused of having become. Budgets are pilloried as being out of touch with the needs of modern business and accused of taking too long, costing too much and encouraging all sorts of perverse behaviour.
>
> Yet if there was one conclusion to emerge from the day's discussions it was that budgets are in fact alive and well. Not only did all the organisations present operate a formal budget but all bar two had no interest in getting rid of it. Quite the opposite – although aware of the problems it can cause, the participants by and large regarded the budgeting system and the accompanying processes as indispensable.

Later in the report, in what could have been a reference to the use of 'rolling forecasts' among businesses that claim to have abandoned budgeting, it said:

> It quickly became obvious that, as one participant put it, 'one man's budget is another man's rolling forecast'. What people refer to when they talk about budgeting could in reality be very different things.

This presumably meant that businesses that abandon 'budgets' reintroduce them under another name.

*Source: Better Budgeting*, The Chartered Institute of Management Accountants and The Faculty of Finance and Management, Institute of Chartered Accountants in England and Wales, March 2004.

---

It can be argued, for example that Toyota's 'Original Business Plan' (see Real World 12.9) is really a budget by another name. The definition of a budget is a business plan, as we saw earlier in the chapter. Also, John Timpson, who shows no enthusiasm for budgets (see Real World 12.8) uses a 'profit forecast'. This must be some forward-looking statement.

**Real World 12.11** provides survey evidence of senior finance staff that indicates considerable support for budgets. Nevertheless, many recognised that budgeting is not always well managed and acknowledged some of the criticisms of budgets that were mentioned earlier.

---

### Real World 12.11

### Problems with budgets

The survey of the opinions of senior finance staff at 340 businesses of various sizes and operating in a wide range of industries in North America that was mentioned earlier (see Real World 12.3) showed that 86 per cent of those surveyed regarded the budget process as either 'essential' or 'very important'. However:

- 66 per cent thought that budgeting in their business was not agile or flexible enough.
- 59 per cent were not very confident that budget targets would be met in 2008.
- 67 per cent felt that their business devoted inappropriate amounts of time to budgeting (51 per cent felt it was too much and 16 per cent too little).
- 76 per cent felt that their businesses used inappropriate software in the budgeting process (generally using a spreadsheet rather than custom-designed software).

*Source*: 'Perfect how you project', BPM Forum, 2008.

Despite the undoubted problems with budgeting, and the way in which it is obviously practised in some businesses, the ideas summarised as 'beyond budgeting' (discussed above) seem not to be popular in practice, as indicated in **Real World 12.12**.

### Real World 12.12

#### Not going into the beyond

The 2009 CIMA survey showed that the beyond budgeting philosophy is little followed in practice, as is shown by Figure 12.11.

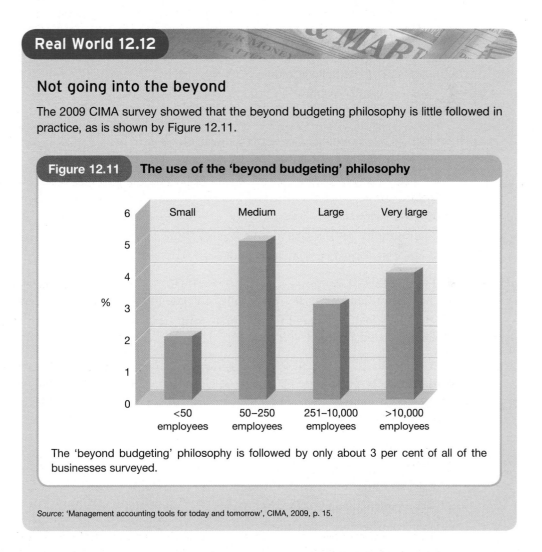

**Figure 12.11**    The use of the 'beyond budgeting' philosophy

The 'beyond budgeting' philosophy is followed by only about 3 per cent of all of the businesses surveyed.

*Source*: 'Management accounting tools for today and tomorrow', CIMA, 2009, p. 15.

In the next chapter we shall look in some detail at how budgets can be adapted for use as devices for exercising management control.

## Summary

The main points of this chapter may be summarised as follows:

**A budget is a short-term business plan, mainly expressed in financial terms.**

- Budgets are the short-term means of working towards the business's objectives.
- They are usually prepared for a one-year period with sub-periods of a month.
- There is usually a separate budget for each key area.

**Uses of budgets**

- Promote forward thinking.
- Help co-ordinate the various aspects of the business.
- Motivate performance.
- Provide the basis of a system of control.
- Provide a system of authorisation.

**The budget-setting process**

- Establish who will take responsibility.
- Communicate guidelines.
- Identify key factor.
- Prepare budget for key factor area.
- Prepare draft budgets for all other areas.
- Review and co-ordinate.
- Prepare master budgets (income statement and statement of financial position (balance sheet)).
- Communicate the budgets to interested parties.
- Monitor performance relative to budget.

**Preparing budgets**

- There is no standard style – practicality and usefulness are the key issues.
- They are usually prepared in columnar form, with a column for each month (or similarly short period).
- Each budget must link (co-ordinate) with others.

**Criticisms of budgets**

- Cannot deal with rapid change.
- Focus on short-term financial targets, rather than value creation.
- Encourage a 'top-down' management style.
- Time-consuming.
- Based around traditional business functions and do not cross boundaries.
- Encourage incremental thinking (last year's figure, plus $x$ per cent).
- Protect rather than lower costs.
- Promote 'sharp' practice among managers.
- Budgeting is very widely regarded as useful and extensively practised despite the criticisms.

# MyAccountingLab

Go to **www.myaccountinglab.com** to check your understanding of the chapter, create a personalised study plan, and maximise your revision time

## Key terms

mission statement   p. 454
budget   p. 454
control   p. 455
limiting factor   p. 458
forecast   p. 458
periodic budget   p. 458
continual budget   p. 458
rolling budget   p. 459
master budget   p. 459

management by exception   p. 462
budget committee   p. 464
budget officer   p. 464
incremental budgeting   p. 469
discretionary budget   p. 469
budget holder   p. 469
zero-base budgeting (ZBB)   p. 470
activity-based budgeting (ABB)   p. 478

## References

1  BPM Forum, *Perfect How You Project*, 2008.

2  CFO, *Alternative budgeting*, June 2006.

3  *Beyond Budgeting*, www.bbrt.org.

## Further reading

If you would like to explore the topics covered in this chapter in more depth, we recommend the following books:

1  Drury, C., *Management and Cost Accounting*, 8th edn, Cengage Learning, 2012, chapter 15.

2  Hilton, R., *Managerial Accounting*, 9th edn, McGraw-Hill Higher Education, 2011, chapter 9.

3  Horngren, C., Datar, S. and Rajan, M., *Cost Accounting: A Managerial Emphasis*, 14th edn, Prentice Hall International, 2011, chapter 6.

4  Kaplan, R., Atkinson, A., Matsumura, E. and Young, S. M., *Management Accounting*, 6th edn, Prentice Hall, 2011, chapter 10.

## Review questions

Solutions to these questions can be found at the back of the book on page 755.

**12.1**   Define a budget. How is a budget different from a forecast?

**12.2**   What were the five uses of budgets that were identified in the chapter?

**12.3**   What do budgets have to do with control?

**12.4**   What is a budget committee? What purpose does it serve?

## Exercises

Exercises 12.1 and 12.2 are basic level, 12.3 to 12.5 are intermediate level and 12.6 and 12.7 are advanced level. Those with coloured numbers have solutions at the back of the book, starting on page 784.

If you wish to try more exercises, visit the students' side of the Companion Website and MyAccountingLab.

**12.1**   Prolog Ltd is a small wholesaler of high-specification personal computers. It has in recent months been selling 50 machines a month at a price of £2,000 each. These machines cost £1,600 each. A new model has just been launched and this is expected to offer greatly enhanced performance. Its selling price and cost will be the same as for the old model. From the beginning of January, sales are planned to increase at a rate of 20 machines each month until the end of June, when sales will amount to 170 units a month. Sales are planned to continue at that level thereafter. Operating costs including depreciation of £2,000 a month are planned as follows:

|  | January | February | March | April | May | June |
|---|---|---|---|---|---|---|
| Operating costs (£000) | 6 | 8 | 10 | 12 | 12 | 12 |

Prolog expects to receive no credit for operating costs. Additional shelving for storage will be bought, installed and paid for in April, costing £12,000. Tax of £25,000 is due at the end of March. Prolog anticipates that trade receivables will amount to two months' sales revenue. To give its customers a good level of service, Prolog plans to hold enough inventories at the end of each month to fulfil anticipated demand from customers in the following month. The computer manufacturer, however, grants one month's credit to Prolog. Prolog Ltd's statement of financial position (balance sheet) appears below.

**Statement of financial position at 31 December**

| | £000 |
|---|---:|
| **ASSETS** | |
| *Non-current assets* | 80 |
| *Current assets* | |
| Inventories | 112 |
| Trade receivables | 200 |
| Cash | – |
| | 312 |
| *Total assets* | 392 |
| **EQUITY AND LIABILITIES** | |
| *Equity* | |
| Share capital (25p ordinary shares) | 10 |
| Retained profit | 177 |
| | 187 |
| *Current liabilities* | |
| Trade payables | 112 |
| Taxation | 25 |
| Overdraft | 68 |
| | 205 |
| *Total equity and liabilities* | 392 |

*Required*:
(a) Prepare a cash budget for Prolog Ltd showing the cash balance or required overdraft for the six months ending 30 June.
(b) State briefly what further information a banker would require from Prolog Ltd before granting additional overdraft facilities for the anticipated expansion of sales.

**12.2** You have overheard the following statements:

(a) 'A budget is a forecast of what is expected to happen in a business during the next year.'
(b) 'Monthly budgets must be prepared with a column for each month so that you can see the whole year at a glance, month by month.'
(c) 'Budgets are OK but they stifle all initiative. No manager worth employing would work for a business that seeks to control through budgets.'
(d) 'Activity-based budgeting is an approach that takes account of the planned volume of activity in order to deduce the figures to go into the budget.'
(e) 'Any sensible person would start with the sales budget and build up the other budgets from there.'

*Required*:
Critically discuss these statements, explaining any technical terms.

**12.3** A nursing home, which is linked to a large hospital, has been examining its budgetary control procedures, with particular reference to overhead costs.

The level of activity in the facility is measured by the number of patients treated in the budget period. For the current year, the budget stands at 6,000 patients and this is expected to be met.

For months 1 to 6 of this year (assume 12 months of equal length), 2,700 patients were treated. The actual variable overhead costs incurred during this six-month period are as follows:

| Expense | £ |
|---|---|
| Staffing | 59,400 |
| Power | 27,000 |
| Supplies | 54,000 |
| Other | 8,100 |
| Total | 148,500 |

The hospital accountant believes that the variable overhead costs will be incurred at the same rate during months 7 to 12 of the year.

Fixed overheads are budgeted for the whole year as follows:

| Expense | £ |
|---|---|
| Supervision | 120,000 |
| Depreciation/financing | 187,200 |
| Other | 64,800 |
| Total | 372,000 |

**Required:**

(a) Present an overheads budget for months 7 to 12 of the year. You should show each expense, but should not separate individual months. What is the total overhead cost for each patient that would be incorporated into any statistics?

(b) The home actually treated 3,800 patients during months 7 to 12, the actual variable overheads were £203,300 and the fixed overheads were £190,000. In summary form, examine how well the home exercised control over its overheads.

(c) Interpret your analysis and point out any limitations or assumptions.

**12.4** Linpet Ltd is to be incorporated on 1 June. The opening statement of financial position (balance sheet) of the business will then be as follows:

| | £ |
|---|---|
| *Assets* | |
| Cash at bank | 60,000 |
| *Share capital* | |
| £1 ordinary shares | 60,000 |

During June, the business intends to make payments of £40,000 for a leasehold property, £10,000 for equipment and £6,000 for a motor vehicle. The business will also purchase initial trading inventories costing £22,000 on credit.

The business has produced the following estimates:

1 Sales revenue for June will be £8,000 and will increase at the rate of £3,000 a month until September. In October, sales revenue will rise to £22,000 and in subsequent months will be maintained at this figure.

2 The gross profit percentage (that is, (gross profit/sales) × 100) on goods sold will be 25 per cent.

3 There is a risk that supplies of trading inventories will be interrupted towards the end of the accounting year. The business therefore intends to build up its initial level of inventories (£22,000) by purchasing £1,000 of inventories each month in addition to the monthly purchases necessary to satisfy monthly sales requirements. All purchases of inventories (including the initial inventories) will be on one month's credit.

4 Sales revenue will be divided equally between cash and credit sales. Credit customers are expected to pay two months after the sale is agreed.

5 Wages and salaries will be £900 a month. Other overheads will be £500 a month for the first four months and £650 thereafter. Both types of expense will be payable when incurred.

6  80 per cent of sales revenue will be generated by salespeople who will receive 5 per cent commission on sales revenue. The commission is payable one month after the sale is agreed.

7  The business intends to purchase further equipment in November for £7,000 cash.

8  Depreciation will be provided at the rate of 5 per cent a year on property and 20 per cent a year on equipment. (Depreciation has not been included in the overheads mentioned in 5 above.)

**Required:**

(a)  State why a cash budget is required for a business.

(b)  Prepare a cash budget for Linpet Ltd for the six-month period to 30 November.

**12.5**  Lewisham Ltd manufactures one product line – the Zenith. Sales of Zeniths over the next few months are planned to be as follows:

1  *Demand*

|  | Units |
|---|---|
| July | 180,000 |
| August | 240,000 |
| September | 200,000 |
| October | 180,000 |

Each Zenith sells for £3.

2  *Receipts from sales*. Credit customers are expected to pay as follows:

- 70 per cent during the month of sale
- 28 per cent during the following month.

  The remaining trade receivables are expected to go bad (that is, to be uncollectable).

  Credit customers who pay in the month of sale are entitled to deduct a 2 per cent discount from the invoice price.

3  *Finished goods inventories*. Inventories of finished goods are expected to be 40,000 units at 1 July. The business's policy is that, in future, the inventories at the end of each month should equal 20 per cent of the following month's planned sales requirements.

4  *Raw materials inventories*. Inventories of raw materials are expected to be 40,000 kg on 1 July. The business's policy is that, in future, the inventories at the end of each month should equal 50 per cent of the following month's planned production requirements. Each Zenith requires 0.5 kg of the raw material, which costs £1.50/kg. Raw materials purchases are paid in the month after purchase.

5  *Labour and overheads*. The direct labour cost of each Zenith is £0.50. The variable overhead element of each Zenith is £0.30. Fixed overheads, including depreciation of £25,000, total £47,000 a month. All labour and overheads are paid during the month in which they arise.

6  *Cash in hand*. At 1 August the business plans to have a bank balance (in funds) of £20,000.

**Required:**

Prepare the following budgets:

(a)  Finished inventories budget (expressed in units of Zenith) for each of the three months July, August and September.

(b)  Raw materials inventories budget (expressed in kilograms of the raw material) for the two months July and August.

(c)  Cash budget for August and September.

**12.6**  Daniel Chu Ltd, a new business, will start production on 1 April, but sales will not start until 1 May. Planned sales for the next nine months are as follows:

|  | Sales Units |
| --- | --- |
| May | 500 |
| June | 600 |
| July | 700 |
| August | 800 |
| September | 900 |
| October | 900 |
| November | 900 |
| December | 800 |
| January | 700 |

The selling price of a unit will be a consistent £100 and all sales will be made on one month's credit. It is planned that sufficient finished goods inventories for each month's sales should be available at the end of the previous month.

Raw materials purchases will be such that there will be sufficient raw materials inventories available at the end of each month precisely to meet the following month's planned production. This planned policy will operate from the end of April. Purchases of raw materials will be on one month's credit. The cost of raw material is £40 a unit of finished product.

The direct labour cost, which is variable with the level of production, is planned to be £20 a unit of finished production. Production overheads are planned to be £20,000 each month, including £3,000 for depreciation. Non-production overheads are planned to be £11,000 a month, of which £1,000 will be depreciation.

Various non-current (fixed) assets costing £250,000 will be bought and paid for during April.

Except where specified, assume that all payments take place in the same month as the cost is incurred.

The business will raise £300,000 in cash from a share issue in April.

*Required*:
Draw up the following for the six months ending 30 September:

(a) A finished inventories budget, showing just physical quantities.
(b) A raw materials inventories budget showing both physical quantities and financial values.
(c) A trade payables budget.
(d) A trade receivables budget.
(e) A cash budget.

12.7   Brown and Jeffreys, a West Midlands business, makes one standard product for use in the motor trade. The product, known as the Fuel Miser, for which the business holds the patent, when fitted to the fuel system of production model cars has the effect of reducing petrol consumption.

Part of the production is sold direct to a local car manufacturer, which fits the Fuel Miser as an optional extra to several of its models. The rest of the production is sold through various retail outlets, garages, and so on.

Brown and Jeffreys assemble the Fuel Miser, but all three components are manufactured by local engineering businesses. The three components are codenamed A, B and C. One Fuel Miser consists of one of each component.

The planned sales for the first seven months of the forthcoming accounting period, by channels of distribution and in terms of Fuel Miser units, are as follows:

|  | Jan | Feb | Mar | Apr | May | June | July |
|---|---|---|---|---|---|---|---|
| Manufacturers | 4,000 | 4,000 | 4,500 | 4,500 | 4,500 | 4,500 | 4,500 |
| Retail and so on | 2,000 | 2,700 | 3,200 | 3,000 | 2,700 | 2,500 | 2,400 |
|  | 6,000 | 6,700 | 7,700 | 7,500 | 7,200 | 7,000 | 6,900 |

The following further information is available:

1  There will be inventories of finished units at 1 January of 7,000 Fuel Misers.
2  The inventories of raw materials at 1 January will be:
    (a)  10,000 units
    (b)  16,500 units
    (c)  7,200 units
3  The selling price of Fuel Misers is to be £10 each to the motor manufacturer and £12 each to retail outlets.
4  The maximum production capacity of the business is 7,000 units a month. There is no possibility of increasing this output.
5  Assembly of each Fuel Miser will take 10 minutes of direct labour. Direct labour is paid at the rate of £7.20 an hour during the month of production.
6  The components are each expected to cost the following:
    (a)  £2.50
    (b)  £1.30
    (c)  £0.80
7  Indirect costs are to be paid at a regular rate of £32,000 each month.
8  The cash at the bank at 1 January will be £2,620.

The planned sales volumes must be met and the business intends to pursue the following policies for as many months as possible, consistent with meeting the sales targets:

- Finished inventories at the end of each month are to equal the following month's total sales to retail outlets and half the total of the following month's sales to the motor manufacturer.
- Raw materials at the end of each month are to be sufficient to cover production requirements for the following month. The production for July will be 6,800 units.
- Suppliers of raw materials are to be paid during the month following purchase. The payment for January will be £21,250.
- Customers will pay in the month of sale, in the case of sales to the motor manufacturer, and the month after sale, in the case of retail sales. Retail sales during December were 2,000 units at £12 each.

*Required*:
Prepare the following budgets in monthly columnar form, both in terms of money and units (where relevant), for the six months of January to June inclusive:

(a)  Sales budget.*
(b)  Finished inventories budget (valued at direct cost).[†]
(c)  Raw materials inventories budget (one budget for each component).[†]
(d)  Production budget (direct costs only).*
(e)  Trade receivables budget.[†]
(f)  Trade payables budget.[†]
(g)  Cash budget.[†]

*    The sales and production budgets should merely state each month's sales or production in units and in money terms.
[†]    The other budgets should all seek to reconcile the opening balance of inventories, trade receivables, trade payables or cash with the closing balance through movements of the relevant factors over the month.

# Accounting for control

Associated British Foods Group plc, the food processor, states in its 2010 annual report (p. 41):

> Performance against budget is monitored at operational level and centrally, with variances being reported promptly.

This raises important issues such as the way in which performance is monitored, the nature of variances, why the business should identify them, how they should be reported and what action the business should take where variances occur. These issues provide the focus for the chapter. We shall see that the procedures at Associated British Foods are widely adopted throughout the business world.

This chapter develops some of the themes that were discussed in Chapter 12. We shall see how a budget can be used to help control a business and how, by collecting information on actual performance and comparing it with a revised budget, it is possible to identify those activities that are in control and those that are not.

Budgets are designed to influence the behaviour of managers and so we shall explore their value as a motivational device. We shall also consider the ways in which managers may use budgets in practice. Finally, we shall take a look at standard costing and its relationship with budgeting. We shall see that standards can provide the building blocks for budgets.

## Learning outcomes

**When you have completed this chapter, you should be able to:**

● Discuss the role and limitations of budgets for performance evaluation and control.

● Undertake variance analysis and discuss possible reasons for the variances calculated.

● Discuss the issues that should be taken into account when designing an effective system of budgetary control.

● Explain the nature, role and limitations of standard costing.

# MyAccountingLab

Visit **www.myaccountinglab.com** for practice and revision opportunities

# Budgeting for control

In Chapter 12, we saw that budgets provide a useful basis for exercising control over a business. Control involves making events conform to a plan and, since the budget is a short-term plan, making events conform to it is an obvious way to try to control the business. We also saw that, for most businesses, the routine is as shown in Figure 13.1.

**Figure 13.1    The budgetary control process**

Budgets, once set, provide the yardstick for assessing whether things are going to plan. Variances between budgeted and actual performance can be identified and reacted to.

If plans are drawn up sensibly, we have a basis for exercising control over the business. We must, however, measure actual performance in the same terms as those in which the budget is stated. If they are not in the same terms, proper comparison will not be possible.

Exercising control involves finding out where and why things did not go according to plan and then seeking ways to put them right for the future. One reason why things may not have gone according to plan is that the budget targets were unachievable. In this case, it may be necessary to revise the budgets for future periods so that targets become achievable.

This last point should not be taken to mean that budget targets can simply be ignored if the going gets tough; rather, that they should be adaptable. Unrealistic budgets cannot form a basis for exercising control and little can be gained by sticking with them.

**Real World 13.1** reveals how one important budget had to be dramatically revised because it had become unrealistic.

**Real World 13.1**

## No medals for budgeting FT

The government's dramatic increase this spring in the budget for the 2012 Olympic games, almost tripling the £3.3 billion cost to the taxpayer estimated at the time of winning the 2005 bid, has put the event on a 'firmer financial footing', says a report by the National Audit Office (NAO).

Nevertheless, the revised £9.3 billion London Olympics budget contains 'significant areas of uncertainty' that could drive costs up, unless effective controls are exercised. Sir John Bourn, head of the NAO, warned the government it still had to 'work to contain funding and achieve value for money'. He highlighted areas of uncertainty affecting costs, including the design specifications and future use of the Olympic venues, the level of price inflation in the construction sector and the contracts negotiated by suppliers.

The NAO, in effect, gives the revised budget its seal of approval, saying it 'should be sufficient' to cover the estimated costs of the games, provided – a 'most important pro-viso' – the assumptions on which the budget is based hold good. But its report calls for action by the government to ensure proper controls over the huge project.

*Source:* Adapted from 'Watchdog warns on Olympic costs', Jean Eaglesham, FT.com, 20 July 2007.

Provided that there is an adequate system of budgetary control, decision making and responsibility can be delegated to junior management, yet senior management can still retain control. This is because senior managers can use the system to discover which junior managers are meeting budget targets and therefore working towards achieving the objectives of the business. (We should remember that budgets are the short-term plans for achieving the business's objectives.) This enables a *management-by-exception* environment to be created where senior management can focus on areas where things are *not* going according to plan (the exceptions – it is to be hoped). Junior managers who are performing to budget can be left to get on with their jobs.

## Types of control

The control process just outlined is known as **feedback control.** Its main feature is that steps are taken to get operations back on track as soon as there is a signal that they have gone wrong. This is similar to the thermostatic control that is a feature of most central heating systems. The thermostat incorporates a thermometer that senses when the temperature has fallen below a preset level (analogous to the budget). The thermostat then takes action to correct matters by activating the heating device that restores the required minimum temperature. Figure 13.2 depicts the stages in a feedback control system using budgets.

There is an alternative type of control, known as **feedforward control**. Here predictions are made as to what can go wrong and steps are then taken to avoid any undesirable outcome. Budgets can also be used to exert this type of control. It involves preparing a budget and then comparing it with a forecast of actual outcomes in order to identify potential problems. For example, a cash budget may be compared with a forecast of

**Figure 13.2    Feedback control**

When a comparison of budgeted and actual performance shows a divergence, steps can be taken to get performance back on track. If the budget needs revising, this can be done.

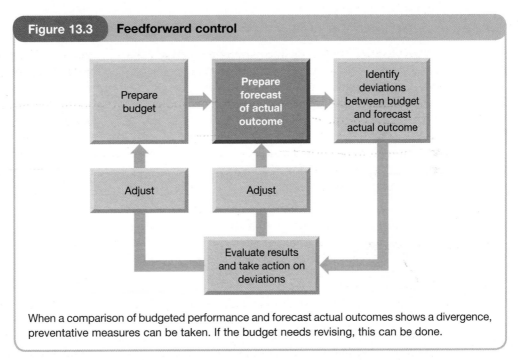

**Figure 13.3    Feedforward control**

When a comparison of budgeted performance and forecast actual outcomes shows a divergence, preventative measures can be taken. If the budget needs revising, this can be done.

actual cash flows. Where significant deviations from budget are revealed, corrective action may be taken before the problems arise. Figure 13.3 depicts the stages in a feedforward control system using budgets.

Feedforward controls are proactive and try to anticipate problems beforehand, whereas feedback controls react to existing problems. To put it another way, feedforward controls are preventative, whereas feedback controls are remedial. As it is better to avoid problems rather than have to solve them, feedforward controls are preferable.

However, they require timely and accurate predictions of actual outcomes, which is not always available.

# Variances from budget

We saw in Chapter 1 that the key financial objective of a business is to increase the wealth of its owners (shareholders). Since profit is the net increase in wealth from business operations, the most important budget target to meet is the profit target. We shall therefore take this as our starting point when comparing the budget with the actual results. Example 13.1 shows the budgeted and actual income statements for Baxter Ltd for the month of May.

## Example 13.1

The following are the budgeted and actual income statements for Baxter Ltd, a manufacturing business, for the month of May:

|  | Budget | Actual |
|---|---|---|
| Output (production and sales) | 1,000 units | 900 units |
|  | £ | £ |
| Sales revenue | 100,000 | 92,000 |
| Raw materials | (40,000) (40,000 metres) | (36,900) (37,000 metres) |
| Labour | (20,000) (2,500 hours) | (17,500) (2,150 hours) |
| Fixed overheads | (20,000) | (20,700) |
| Operating profit | 20,000 | 16,900 |

From these figures, it is clear that the budgeted profit was not achieved. As far as May is concerned, this is a matter of history. However, the business (or one or more aspects of it) is out of control. Senior management must discover where things went wrong during May and try to ensure that these mistakes are not repeated in later months. It is not enough to know that things went wrong overall. We need to know where and why. To achieve this we must compare the budgeted and actual figures for the various items (sales revenue, raw materials, and so on) in the statement shown above.

## Activity 13.1

Can you see any problems in comparing the various items (sales revenue, raw materials, and so on) for the budget with the actual performance of Baxter Ltd in an attempt to draw conclusions as to which aspects were out of control?

The problem is that the actual level of output was not as budgeted. In fact it was 10 per cent lower than budget. This means that we cannot, for example, say that there was a labour cost saving of £2,500 (that is, £20,000 – £17,500) and conclude that all is well in that area.

## Flexing the budget

One practical way to overcome our difficulty is to 'flex' the budget to what it would have been had the planned level of output been 900 units rather than 1,000 units. Flexing the budget simply means revising it, assuming a different volume of output.

To flex the budget, we need to know which revenues and costs are fixed and which are variable relative to the volume of output. Once we know this, flexing is a simple operation. We shall assume that sales revenue, material cost and labour cost vary strictly with volume. Fixed overheads, by definition, will not. Whether, in real life, labour cost does vary with the volume of output is not so certain, but it will serve well enough as an assumption for our purposes. If labour cost is actually fixed, we can simply take this into account in the flexing process.

On the basis of our assumptions regarding the behaviour of revenues and costs, the flexed budget would be as follows:

|  | Flexed budget |
|---|---|
| Output (production and sales) | 900 units |
|  | £ |
| Sales revenue | 90,000 |
| Raw materials | (36,000) (36,000 metres) |
| Labour | (18,000) (2,250 hours) |
| Fixed overheads | (20,000) |
| Operating profit | 16,000 |

This is simply the original budget, with the sales revenue, raw materials and labour cost figures scaled down by 10 per cent (the same factor as the actual output fell short of the budgeted one).

Putting the original budget, the flexed budget and the actual for May together gives us the following:

|  | Original budget | Flexed budget | Actual |
|---|---|---|---|
| Output (production and sales) | 1,000 units | 900 units | 900 units |
|  | £ | £ | £ |
| Sales revenue | 100,000 | 90,000 | 92,000 |
| Raw materials | (40,000) | (36,000) (36,000 m) | (36,900) (37,000 m) |
| Labour | (20,000) | (18,000) (2,250 hr) | (17,500) (2,150 hr) |
| Fixed overheads | (20,000) | (20,000) | (20,700) |
| Operating profit | 20,000 | 16,000 | 16,900 |

Flexible budgets allow us to make a more valid comparison between the budget (using the flexed figures) and the actual results. Key differences, or variances, between budgeted and actual results for each aspect of the business's activities can then be calculated. In the rest of this section we consider some of the variances that may be calculated.

## Sales volume variance

Let us begin by dealing with the shortfall in sales volume. It may seem as if we are saying that this does not matter, because we just revise the budget and carry on as if all is well. It is clearly not true that losing sales volume does not matter because a sales volume shortfall normally means losing profit. The first point we must pick up, therefore, is the profit shortfall arising from the loss of sales of 100 units of the product.

**Activity (13.2)**

What will be the loss of profit arising from the sales volume shortfall, assuming that everything except sales volume was as planned?

The answer is simply the difference between the original and flexed budget profit figures. The only difference between these two profit figures is the volume of sales; everything else was the same. (That is to say that the flexing was carried out assuming that the per-unit sales revenue, raw material cost and labour cost were all as originally budgeted.) This means that the figure for the loss of profit due to the volume shortfall, taken alone, is £4,000 (that is, £20,000 – £16,000).

When we considered the relationship between cost, volume and profit in Chapter 3, we saw that selling one unit fewer will result in one fewer contribution to profit. The contribution is sales revenue less variable cost. We can see from the original budget that the unit sales revenue is £100 (that is, £100,000/1,000), raw material cost is £40 a unit (that is, £40,000/1,000) and labour cost is £20 a unit (that is, £20,000/1,000). Thus the contribution is £40 a unit (that is, £100 – (£40 + £20)).

If 100 units of sales are lost, £4,000 (that is, 100 × £40) of contributions and therefore profit are forgone. Incidentally, this would be an alternative means of finding the sales volume variance, instead of taking the difference between the original and flexed budget profit figures. Once we have produced the flexed budget, however, it is generally easier to compare the two profit figures.

The difference between the original and flexed budget profit figures is called the sales volume variance.

In this case, it is an **adverse variance** because, taken alone, it has the effect of making the actual profit lower than the budgeted profit. A variance that has the effect of increasing profit beyond the budgeted profit is known as a **favourable variance**. We can therefore say that a **variance** is the effect of that factor (taken alone) on the budgeted profit. Later we shall consider other forms of variance, some of which may be favourable and some adverse. The difference between the sum of all the various favourable and adverse variances will represent the difference between the budgeted and actual profit. This is shown in Figure 13.4.

When calculating a particular variance, such as sales volume, we assume that all other factors went according to plan.

**Activity (13.3)**

What else do the relevant managers of Baxter Ltd need to know about the May sales volume variance?

They need to know why the volume of sales fell below the budgeted figure. Only by discovering this information will they be in a position to try to ensure that it does not occur again.

| Figure 13.4 | Relationship between the budgeted and actual profit |

The variances represent the differences between the budgeted and actual profit and so can be used to reconcile the two profit figures.

Who should be held accountable for this sales volume variance? The answer is probably the sales manager, who should know precisely why this has occurred. This is not the same as saying, however, that it was the sales manager's fault. The problem may have been that the business failed to produce the budgeted quantities so that not enough items were available to sell. Nevertheless, the sales manager should know the reason for the problem.

The budget and actual figures for Baxter Ltd for *June* are given in Activity 13.4 and will be used as the basis for a series of activities that provide an opportunity to calculate and assess the variances. We shall continue to use the *May* figures for explaining the variances.

Note that the business had budgeted for a higher level of output for *June* than it did for *May*.

## Activity 13.4

| | Budget for June | Actual for June |
|---|---|---|
| Output (production and sales) | 1,100 units | 1,150 units |
| | £ | £ |
| Sales revenue | 110,000 | 113,500 |
| Raw materials | (44,000) (44,000 metres) | (46,300) (46,300 metres) |
| Labour | (22,000) (2,750 hours) | (23,200) (2,960 hours) |
| Fixed overheads | (20,000) | (19,300) |
| Operating profit | 24,000 | 24,700 |

Try flexing the June budget, comparing it with the original June budget and so find the sales volume variance.

**Activity 13.4 (continued)**

|  | Flexed budget |
|---|---|
| Output (production and sales) | 1,150 units |
|  | £ |
| Sales revenue | 115,000 |
| Raw materials | (46,000) (46,000 metres) |
| Labour | (23,000) (2,875 hours) |
| Fixed overheads | (20,000) |
| Operating profit | 26,000 |

The sales volume variance is £2,000 (favourable) (that is, £26,000 – £24,000). It is favourable because the original budget profit was lower than the flexed budget profit. This arises from more sales actually being made than were budgeted.

For the month of May, we have already identified one reason why the budgeted profit of £20,000 was not achieved and that the actual profit was only £16,900. This was the £4,000 loss of profit (adverse variance) that arose from the sales volume shortfall. Now that the budget is flexed, we can compare like with like and reach further conclusions about May's trading.

The fact that the sales revenue, raw materials, labour and fixed overheads figures differ between the flexed budget and the actual results (see page 501) suggests that the adverse sales volume variance was not the only problem area. To identify those relating to each of the revenue and cost items mentioned, we need to calculate further variances. We shall now do this.

## Sales price variance

Starting with the sales revenue figure, we can see that, for *May*, there is a difference of £2,000 (favourable) between the flexed budget and the actual figures. This can only arise from higher prices being charged than were envisaged in the original budget, because any variance arising from the volume difference has already been 'stripped out' in the flexing process. This price difference is known as the **sales price variance**. Higher sales prices will, all other things being equal, mean more profit. So there is a favourable variance.

When senior management is trying to identify the reason for a sales price variance, it would normally be the sales manager who should be able to offer an explanation. As we shall see later in the chapter, favourable variances of significant size will normally be investigated.

**Activity (13.5)**

Using the figures in Activity 13.4, what is the sales price variance for June?

The sales price variance for *June* is £1,500 (adverse) (that is, £115,000 – £113,500). Actual sales prices, on average, must have been lower than those budgeted. The actual price averaged £98.70 (that is, £113,500/1,150) whereas the budgeted price was £100. Selling output at a lower price than that budgeted will have an adverse effect on profit, hence an adverse variance.

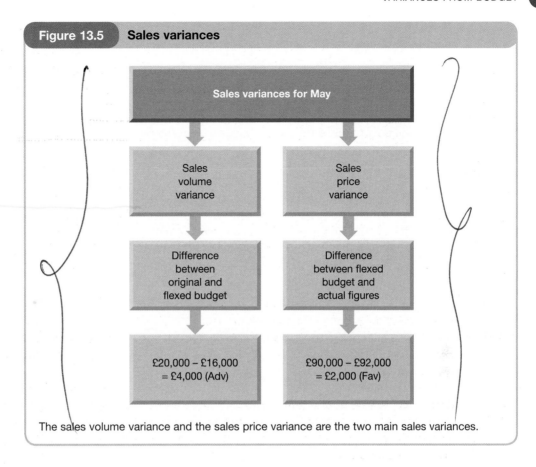

**Figure 13.5    Sales variances**

Sales variances for May

Sales volume variance

Sales price variance

Difference between original and flexed budget

Difference between flexed budget and actual figures

£20,000 – £16,000 = £4,000 (Adv)

£90,000 – £92,000 = £2,000 (Fav)

The sales volume variance and the sales price variance are the two main sales variances.

The sales variances are summarised in Figure 13.5.

Let us now move on to look at the cost variances, starting with materials variances.

## Materials variances

In *May*, there was an overall or **total direct materials variance** of £900 (adverse) (that is, £36,900 – £36,000). It is adverse because the actual material cost was higher than the budgeted one, which has an adverse effect on operating profit.

Who should be held accountable for this variance? The answer depends on whether the difference arises from excess usage of the raw material, in which case it is the production manager, or whether it is a higher-than-budgeted cost per metre being paid, in which case it is the responsibility of the buying manager. Fortunately, we can go beyond this total variance to examine the effect of changes in both usage and cost. We can see from the figures that in *May* there was a 1,000 metre excess usage of the raw material (that is, 37,000 metres – 36,000 metres). All other things being equal, this alone would have led to a profit shortfall of £1,000, since clearly the budgeted cost per metre is £1. The £1,000 (adverse) variance is known as the **direct materials usage variance**. Normally, this variance would be the responsibility of the production manager.

## Activity 13.6

Using the figures in Activity 13.4, what was the direct material usage variance for June?

The direct material usage variance for *June* was £300 (adverse) (that is, (46,300 metres – 46,000 metres) × £1). It is adverse because more material was used than was budgeted, for an output of 1,150 units. Excess usage of material will tend to reduce profit.

The other aspect of direct materials is their cost. The **direct materials price variance** simply takes the actual cost of materials used and compares it with the cost that was allowed, given the quantity used. In *May* the actual cost of direct materials used was £36,900, whereas the allowed cost of the 37,000 metres was £37,000. Thus we have a favourable variance of £100. Paying less than the budgeted cost will have a favourable effect on profit, hence a favourable variance.

## Activity 13.7

Using the figures in Activity 13.4, what was the direct materials price variance for June?

The direct materials price variance for *June* was zero (that is, £46,300 – (46,300 × £1)).

## Figure 13.6 Total, usage and price variances for direct materials for May

The total direct materials variance is the sum of the direct materials usage variance and the price variance. It can be analysed into those two.

As we have just seen, the total direct materials variance is the sum of the usage variance and the price variance. The relationship between the direct materials variances for May is shown in Figure 13.6.

## Labour variances

Direct labour variances are similar in form to those for direct materials. The **total direct labour variance** for *May* was £500 (favourable) (that is, £18,000 – £17,500). It is favourable because £500 less was spent on labour than was budgeted for the actual level of output achieved.

Again, this total variance is not particularly helpful and needs to be analysed further into its usage and cost elements. We should bear in mind that the number of hours used to complete a particular quantity of output is the responsibility of the production manager, whereas the responsibility for the rate of pay lies primarily with the human resources manager.

The **direct labour efficiency variance** compares the number of hours that would be allowed for the achieved level of production with the actual number of hours taken. It then costs this difference at the allowed hourly rate. Thus, for *May*, it was (2,250 hours – 2,150 hours) × £8 = £800 (favourable). We know that the budgeted hourly rate is £8 because the original budget shows that 2,500 hours were budgeted to cost £20,000. The variance is favourable because fewer hours were used than would have been allowed for the actual level of output. Working more quickly would tend to lead to higher profit.

### Activity 13.8

**Using the figures in Activity 13.4, what was the direct labour efficiency variance for June?**

The direct labour efficiency variance for *June* was £680 (adverse) (that is, (2,960 hours – 2,875 hours) × £8). It is adverse because the work took longer than the budget allowed and so will have an adverse effect on profit.

The **direct labour rate variance** compares the actual cost of the hours worked with the allowed cost. For 2,150 hours worked in *May*, the allowed cost would be £17,200 (that is, 2,150 × £8). So, the direct labour rate variance is £300 (adverse) (that is, £17,500 – £17,200).

The relationship between the direct labour variances for May is shown in Figure 13.7.

### Activity 13.9

**Using the figures in Activity 13.4, what was the direct labour rate variance for June?**

The direct labour rate variance for *June* was £480 (favourable) (that is, (2,960 × £8) – £23,200). It is favourable because a lower rate was paid than the budgeted one. Paying a lower wage rate will have a favourable effect on profit.

| Figure 13.7 | **Total, efficiency and rate variances for direct labour for May** |

The total direct labour variance is the sum of the direct labour efficiency variance and the rate variance. It can be analysed into those two.

## Fixed overhead variance

The final area is that of overheads. In our example, we have assumed that all of the overheads are fixed. Variable overheads certainly exist in practice, but they have been omitted here simply to restrict the amount of detail. Variances involving variable overheads are similar in style to labour and material variances.

The **fixed overhead spending variance** is simply the difference between the flexed (or original – they will be the same) budget and the actual figures. For *May*, this was £700 (adverse) (that is, £20,700 – £20,000). It is adverse because more overheads cost was actually incurred than was budgeted. This would tend to lead to less profit. In theory, this is the responsibility of whoever controls overheads expenditure.

In practice, overheads tend to be a very slippery area. It is one that is notoriously difficult to control. Of course fixed overheads (and variable ones) are usually made up of more than one type of cost. Typically, they would include such things as rent, administrative costs, management salaries, cleaning, electricity, and so on. These items could be separately budgeted and the actual figures recorded. Individual spending variances could then be identified for each overhead item. This should reveal any problem areas.

### Activity 13.10

Using the figures in Activity 13.4, what was the fixed overhead spending variance for June?

The fixed overhead spending variance for *June* was £700 (favourable) (that is, £20,000 – £19,300). It was favourable because less was spent on overheads than was budgeted, thereby having a favourable effect on profit.

We are now in a position to reconcile the original *May* budgeted operating profit with the actual operating profit, as follows:

|  | £ | £ |
|---|---|---|
| Budgeted operating profit |  | 20,000 |
| **Favourable variances** |  |  |
| Sales price | 2,000 |  |
| Direct materials price | 100 |  |
| Direct labour efficiency | 800 | 2,900 |
| **Adverse variances** |  |  |
| Sales volume | (4,000) |  |
| Direct materials usage | (1,000) |  |
| Direct labour rate | (300) |  |
| Fixed overhead spending | (700) | (6,000) |
| Actual operating profit |  | 16,900 |

## Activity (13.11)

If you were the chief executive of Baxter Ltd, what attitude would you take to the overall difference between the budgeted profit and the actual one?

How would you react to the individual variances that are the outcome of the analysis shown above?

You would probably be concerned about how large the variances are and their direction (favourable or adverse). In particular you may have thought of the following:

- The overall adverse profit variance is £3,100 (that is £20,000 − £16,900). This represents 15.5 per cent of the budgeted profit (that is £3,100/£20,000 × 100%) and you (as chief executive) would almost certainly see it as significant and worrying.
- The £4,000 adverse sales volume variance represents 20 per cent of budgeted profit and would be a particular cause of concern.
- The £2,000 favourable sales price variance represents 10 per cent of budgeted profit. Since this is favourable it might be seen as a cause for celebration rather than concern. On the other hand it means that Baxter Ltd's output was, on average, sold at prices 10 per cent above the planned price. This could have been the cause of the worrying adverse sales volume variance. The business may have sold fewer units because it charged higher prices.
- The £100 favourable direct materials price variance is very small in relation to budgeted profit – only 0.5 per cent. It would be unrealistic to expect the actual figures to hit the precise budgeted figures each month and so this is unlikely to be regarded as significant. The direct materials usage variance, however, represents 5 per cent of the budgeted profit. The chief executive may feel this is cause for concern.
- The £800 favourable direct labour efficiency variance represents 4 per cent of budgeted profit. Although it is a favourable variance, the reasons for it may be worth investigating. The £300 adverse direct labour rate variance represents only 1.5 per cent of the budgeted profit and may not be regarded as significant.
- The £700 fixed overhead adverse variance represents 3.5 per cent of budgeted profit. The chief executive may feel that this is too low to cause real concern.

The chief executive will now need to ask some questions as to why things went so badly wrong in several areas and what can be done to improve future performance.

We shall shortly come back to the dilemma as to which variances to investigate and which to accept.

## Activity (13.12)

Using the figures in Activity 13.4, try reconciling the original operating profit figure for June with the actual June figure.

|  | £ | £ |
|---|---|---|
| Budgeted operating profit |  | 24,000 |
| **Favourable variances** |  |  |
| Sales volume | 2,000 |  |
| Direct labour rate | 480 |  |
| Fixed overhead spending | 700 | 3,180 |
| **Adverse variances** |  |  |
| Sales price | (1,500) |  |
| Direct materials usage | (300) |  |
| Direct labour efficiency | (680) | (2,480) |
| Actual operating profit |  | 24,700 |

## Activity (13.13)

The following are the budgeted and actual income statements for Baxter Ltd for the month of July:

|  | Budget | Actual |
|---|---|---|
| Output (production and sales) | 1,000 units | 1,050 units |
|  | £ | £ |
| Sales revenue | 100,000 | 104,300 |
| Raw materials | (40,000) (40,000 metres) | (41,200) (40,500 metres) |
| Labour | (20,000) (2,500 hours) | (21,300) (2,600 hours) |
| Fixed overheads | (20,000) | (19,400) |
| Operating profit | 20,000 | 22,400 |

Produce a reconciliation of the budgeted and actual operating profit, going into as much detail as possible with the variance analysis.

The original budget, the flexed budget and the actual are as follows:

|  | Original budget | Flexed budget | Actual |
|---|---|---|---|
| Output |  |  |  |
| (production and sales) | 1,000 units | 1,050 units | 1,050 units |
|  | £ | £ | £ |
| Sales revenue | 100,000 | 105,000 | 104,300 |
| Raw materials | (40,000) | (42,000) (42,000 m) | (41,200) (40,500 m) |
| Labour | (20,000) | (21,000) (2,625 hrs) | (21,300) (2,600 hrs) |
| Fixed overheads | (20,000) | (20,000) | (19,400) |
| Operating profit | 20,000 | 22,000 | 22,400 |

**Reconciliation of the budgeted and actual operating profits for July**

|  | £ | £ |
|---|---|---|
| Budgeted operating profit |  | 20,000 |
| **Favourable variances:** |  |  |
| Sales volume (22,000 − 20,000) | 2,000 |  |
| Direct materials usage [(42,000 − 40,500) × £1] | 1,500 |  |
| Direct labour efficiency [(2,625 − 2,600) × £8] | 200 |  |
| Fixed overhead spending (20,000 − 19,400) | 600 | 4,300 |
| **Adverse variances:** |  |  |
| Sales price (105,000 − 104,300) | (700) |  |
| Direct materials price [(40,500 × £1) − 41,200] | (700) |  |
| Direct labour rate [(2,600 × £8) − 21,300] | (500) | (1,900) |
| Actual operating profit |  | 22,400 |

**Real World 13.2** shows how two UK-based businesses, Next plc, the retailer, and Tate and Lyle plc, the food ingredients business, use variance analysis to exercise control over their operations. Many businesses explain in their annual reports how they operate systems of budgetary control.

### Real World 13.2

## Variance analysis in practice

**What Next?**

In its 2011 annual report, Next plc states:

> The Board is responsible for approving semi-annual Group budgets. Performance against budget is reported to the Board monthly and any substantial variances are explained.

**Refined controls**

Tate and Lyle plc makes it clear that it too uses budgets and variance analysis to help keep control over its activities. The 2011 annual report states:

> There is a comprehensive budgeting and planning system for all items of expenditure with an annual budget approved by the Board. Results are reported against budget on a monthly basis, with significant variances investigated.

The board of directors of neither of these businesses will seek explanations of variances arising at each branch/department, but they will be looking at figures for the businesses as a whole, or the results for major divisions of them.

Equally certainly, branch/department managers will receive a monthly (or perhaps more frequent) report of variances arising within their area of responsibility alone.

*Sources: Next plc Annual Report 2011 (p. 25) and Tate and Lyle plc Annual Report 2011 (p. 39).*

**Real World 13.3** gives some indication of the importance of flexible budgeting in practice.

**Real World 13.3**

## Flexing the budgets

A study of the UK food and drinks industry by Abdel-Kader and Luther provides us with an indication of the importance attached by management accountants to flexible budgeting. The study asked those in charge of the management accounting function to rate the importance of flexible budgeting by selecting one of three possible categories – 'not important', 'moderately important' or 'important'. Figure 13.8 sets out the results, from the sample of 117 respondents.

**Figure 13.8** **Degree of importance attached to flexible budgeting**

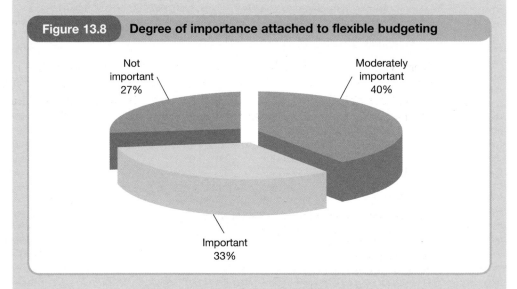

Not important 27%

Moderately important 40%

Important 33%

**Figure 13.9** **Frequency of use of flexible budgets**

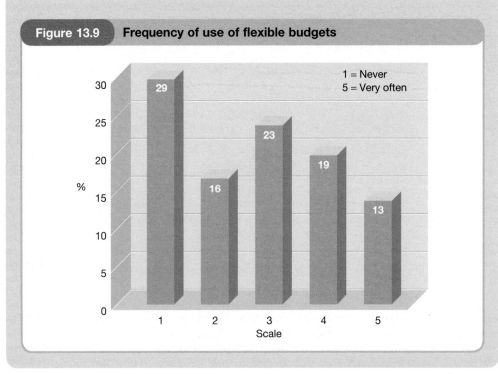

1 = Never
5 = Very often

Respondents were also asked to state the frequency with which flexible budgeting was used within the business, using a five-point scale ranging from 1 (never) through to 5 (very often). Figure 13.9 sets out the results.

We can see that, whilst flexible budgeting is regarded as important by a significant proportion of management accountants and is being used in practice, not all businesses use it.

*Source*: Taken from information appearing in *An Empirical Investigation of the Evolution of Management Accounting Practices*, M. Abdel-Kader and R. Luther, Working paper No. 04/06, University of Essex, October 2004.

# Reasons for adverse variances

Adverse variances may occur simply because the budgets against which performance is being measured are unachievable. If this is the case, budgets will not provide a useful means of exercising control. There are other reasons, however, that may lead to actual performance deviating from budgeted performance.

## Activity (13.14)

The variances that we have considered are:

- sales volume
- sales price
- direct materials usage
- direct materials price
- direct labour efficiency
- direct labour rate
- fixed overhead spending.

Assuming that the budget targets are reasonable, jot down some possible reasons for *adverse* variances for each of the above occurring.

The reasons that we thought of included the following:

*Sales volume*
- Poor performance by sales staff.
- Deterioration in market conditions between the time that the budget was set and the actual event.
- Lack of goods or services to sell as a result of some production problem.

*Sales price*
- Poor performance by sales staff.
- Deterioration in market conditions between the time of setting the budget and the actual event.

*Direct materials usage*
- Poor performance by production department staff, leading to high rates of scrap.
- Substandard materials, leading to high rates of scrap.
- Faulty machinery, causing high rates of scrap.

→

**Activity 13.14** (*continued*)

*Direct materials price*
● Poor performance by the buying department staff.
● Using higher quality material than was planned.
● Change in market conditions between the time that the budget was set and the actual event.

*Labour efficiency*
● Poor supervision.
● A low-skill grade of worker taking longer to do the work than was envisaged for the correct skill grade.
● Low-grade materials, leading to high levels of scrap and wasted labour time.
● Problems with a customer for whom a service is being rendered.
● Problems with machinery, leading to labour time being wasted.
● Dislocation of materials supply, leading to workers being unable to proceed with production.

*Labour rate*
● Poor performance by the human resources department.
● Using a higher grade of worker than was planned.
● Change in labour market conditions between the time of setting the budget and the actual event.

*Fixed overheads*
● Poor supervision of overheads.
● General increase in costs of overheads not taken into account in the budget.

Note that different variances may have the same underlying cause. For example, the purchase of low quality, cheaper materials may result in an unfavourable direct materials usage variance, a favourable direct materials price variance and an unfavourable direct labour efficiency variance.

## Variance analysis in service industries

Although we have tended to use the example of a manufacturing business to explain variance analysis, this should not be taken to imply that variance analysis is not relevant and useful to service sector businesses. It is simply that manufacturing businesses tend to have all of the variances found in practice. Service businesses, for example, may not have material variances.

Real World 13.2, which we met earlier in the chapter, revealed that Next plc, a well-known retailer, uses budgets and variance analysis to help manage its complex business.

## Non-operating-profit variances

There are many areas of business that have a budget but where a failure to meet it will not have a direct effect on operating profit. It will often, however, have an indirect effect and, sometimes, a profound one. The cash budget, for example, sets out planned receipts, payments and the resultant cash balance for the period. If this budget turns out to be wrong, for example, because of unforeseen expenditures, there may be unplanned cash shortages and accompanying costs. These costs may be limited to interest incurred on borrowing. If, however, the cash shortage cannot be covered by borrowing, the consequences could be more serious, such as lost profits from projects that were abandoned because of a lack of funds.

Control must, therefore, be exercised over areas such as cash management, to try to avoid adverse **non-operating profit variances**.

## Investigating variances

It is unreasonable to expect budget targets to be met precisely each month and so variances will usually arise. Discovering the reasons for these variances can be costly. Information will usually have to be produced and examined and discussions with employees carried out. Sometimes, activities may have to be stopped to discover what went wrong. Since small variances are almost inevitable, and investigating variances can be expensive, managers need some guiding principle concerning which variances to investigate and which to accept.

### Activity (13.15)

What principle do you feel should guide managers when deciding whether to spend money investigating a particular variance? (Hint: Think back to Chapter 1)

When deciding whether to produce accounting information, there should be a consideration of both benefit and cost. The benefit likely to be gained from knowing why a variance arose needs to be weighed against the cost of obtaining that knowledge.

There are difficulties in implementing this principle, however, as both the value of the benefit and the cost of investigation may be difficult to assess in advance of the investigation.

The following practical guidelines for investigating variances, which try to take some account of benefit and cost, may be adopted by managers:

- Significant *adverse* variances should normally be investigated as a continuation of the underlying problem could be very costly. Managers must decide what 'significant' means and, ultimately, this will be a matter of managerial judgement. It may be decided, for example, that variances above a threshold of a percentage of the budgeted figure (say, 5 per cent) or a fixed financial amount (say, £1,000) are considered significant.
- Significant *favourable* variances should probably be investigated. Although they may not cause such immediate concern as adverse variances, they still indicate that things are not going according to plan. If actual performance is significantly better than planned, it may mean that the budget target is unrealistically low.
- Insignificant variances, though not triggering immediate investigation, should be kept under review. For each aspect of operations, the cumulative sum of variances,

over a series of control periods, should be zero, with small adverse variances in some periods being compensated for by small favourable ones in others. This is because small variances caused by random factors will not necessarily recur.

While these guidelines may be of some help, managers must be flexible. They may, for example, decide against investigating a significant variance where the cost of correcting the potential causes is expected to be very high. They may calculate that it would be cheaper to live with the problem and so adjust the budget.

Where a variance is caused by systemic (non-random) factors, which will recur over time, the cumulative sum of the periodic variances will not be zero but an increasing figure. Even though the individual variances may be insignificant, the cumulative effect of these variances may not. Thus, an investigation may well be worthwhile, particularly if the variances are adverse.

To illustrate the cumulative effect of relatively small systemic variances, let us consider Example 13.2.

---

**Example 13.2**

Indisurers Ltd finds that the variances for direct labour efficiency for processing motor insurance claims, since the beginning of the year, are as follows:

|          | £              |           | £              |
|----------|----------------|-----------|----------------|
| January  | 25 (adverse)   | July      | 20 (adverse)   |
| February | 15 (favourable)| August    | 15 (favourable)|
| March    | 5 (favourable) | September | 23 (adverse)   |
| April    | 20 (adverse)   | October   | 15 (favourable)|
| May      | 22 (adverse)   | November  | 5 (favourable) |
| June     | 8 (favourable) | December  | 26 (adverse)   |

The average total cost of labour performing this task is about £1,200 a month. Management believes that none of these variances, taken alone, is significant given the monthly labour cost. The question is, are they significant when taken together? If we add them together, taking account of the signs, we find that we have a net adverse variance for the year of £73. Of itself this, too, is probably not significant, but we should expect the cumulative total to be close to zero where the variances are random. We might feel that a pattern is developing and, given long enough, a net adverse variance of significant size might build up.

Investigating the labour efficiency might be worth doing. Finding the cause of the variance would put management in a position to correct a systemic fault, which could lead to future cost savings. (Note that 12 periods are probably not enough to reach a statistically sound conclusion on whether the variances are random or not, but it provides an illustration of the point.)

---

Plotting the cumulative variances, from month to month, as in Figure 13.10, makes it clear what is happening as time proceeds.

| Figure 13.10 | The cumulative variances for labour efficiency in motor insurance claim handling at Indisurers Ltd |
| --- | --- |

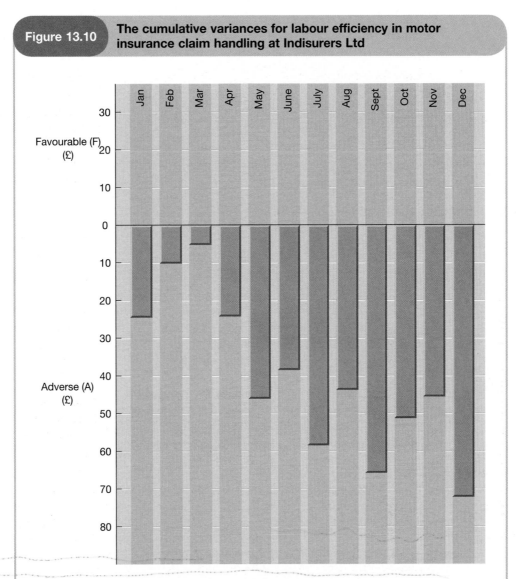

Starting at zero at the beginning of January, each month the cumulative variance is plotted. This is the sum taking account of positive and negative signs. The January figure is £25 (A). The February one is £10 (A) (that is £25 (A) plus £15 (F)), and so on. The graph seems to show an overall trend of adverse variances, but with several favourable variances involved.

**Real World 13.4** provides some evidence concerning the use of variance analysis.

## Real World 13.4

### Using variance analysis

The CIMA survey, mentioned in previous chapters, examined the extent to which the use of variance analysis varies with business size. Figure 13.11 reveals the results.

**Real World 13.4 (continued)**

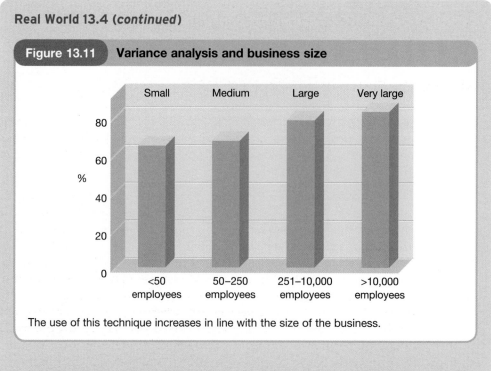

Figure 13.11 Variance analysis and business size

The use of this technique increases in line with the size of the business.

The survey also revealed that variance analysis was the most widely used of a variety of costing tools examined (which included the techniques covered in previous chapters). Overall, more than 70 per cent of respondents used this technique.

*Source*: Figure adapted from 'Management accounting tools for today and tomorrow', CIMA, 2009, p. 12.

## Compensating variances

There may be superficial appeal in the idea of **compensating variances**. These are favourable and adverse variances which are linked and which are traded off against each other. A sales manager, for example, may suggest that more of a particular service could be sold if prices were lowered, as this would result in increased profits. This suggestion would lead to a favourable sales volume variance, but also to an adverse sales price variance. On the face of it, provided that the former is greater than the latter, all would be well.

**Activity (13.16)**

Can you think of a reason why the sales manager should not go ahead with the price reduction?

The change in policy will have ramifications for other areas of the business, including:

● The need to supply more of the service. Staff and other resources may not be available to accommodate this increase.
● The need to provide more finance. Increased levels of activity will lead to an increased need for funds to pay, for example, additional staff costs.

Trading off variances in this way is, therefore, not normally acceptable without a more far-reaching consultation and revision of plans.

## Making budgetary control effective

It should be clear from what we have seen of **budgetary control** that a system, or a set of routines, must be put in place to enable the potential benefits to be gained. Most businesses that operate successful budgetary control systems tend to share some common features. These include the following:

- *A serious attitude taken to the system*. This should apply to all levels of management, right from the very top. For example, senior managers need to make clear to junior managers that they take notice of the monthly variance reports and base some of their actions and decisions upon them.
- *Clear demarcation between areas of managerial responsibility*. It needs to be clear which manager is responsible for each business area so that accountability can more easily be ascribed for any area that seems to be going out of control.
- *Budget targets that are challenging yet achievable*. Setting unachievable targets is likely to have a demotivating effect. Managers may be invited to participate in establishing their own targets to help create a sense of ownership. This, in turn, may increase levels of commitment and motivation. We shall consider this in more detail shortly.
- *Established data collection, analysis and reporting routines*. These should take the actual results and the budget figures and use them to calculate and report the variances. This should be part of the business's regular accounting information system, so that the required reports are automatically produced each month.
- *Reports aimed at individual managers, rather than general-purpose documents*. This avoids managers having to read through many pages of reports to find the part that is relevant to them.
- *Fairly short reporting periods*. These would typically be one month long, so that things cannot go too far wrong before they are picked up.
- *Timely variance reports*. Reports should be produced and made available to managers shortly after the end of the relevant reporting period. If it is not until the end of June that a manager is informed that the performance in May was below the budgeted level, it is quite likely that the performance for June will be below target as well. Reports on the performance in May ideally need to emerge in early June.
- *Action being taken to get operations back under control if they are shown to be out of control*. The report will not change things by itself. Managers need to take action to try to ensure that the reporting of significant adverse variances leads to action to put things right for the future.

## Behavioural issues

Budgets are prepared with the objective of affecting the attitudes and behaviour of managers. The point was made in Chapter 12 that budgets are intended to motivate managers; research evidence generally shows that budgets can be effective in achieving this. More specifically, the research shows:

- The existence of budgets can improve job satisfaction and performance. Where a manager's role might otherwise be ill-defined or ambiguous, budgets can bring structure and certainty. Budgets provide clear, quantifiable, targets that must be pursued. This can be reassuring to managers and can increase their level of commitment.
- Demanding, yet achievable, budget targets tend to motivate better than less demanding targets. It seems that setting the most demanding targets that are acceptable to managers is a very effective way to motivate them.
- Unrealistically demanding targets tend to have an adverse effect on managers' performance. Once managers begin to view the budget targets as being too difficult to achieve, their level of motivation and performance declines. The relationship between the level of performance and the perceived degree of budget difficulty is shown in Figure 13.12.
- The participation of managers in setting their targets tends to improve motivation and performance. This is probably because those managers feel a sense of commitment to the targets and a moral obligation to achieve them.

| Figure 13.12 | Relationship between the level of performance and the perceived degree of budget difficulty |
| --- | --- |

At a low level of budget difficulty, performance also tends to be low as managers do not find the targets sufficiently motivating. However, as the degree of difficulty starts to increase, managers rise to the challenge and improve their performance. Beyond a certain point, the budgets are seen by managers as being too difficult to achieve and so motivation and performance decline.

It has been suggested that allowing managers to set their own targets will lead to slack (that is, easily achievable) targets being introduced. This would make achievement of the target that much easier. On the other hand, in an effort to impress, a manager may select a target that is not really achievable. These points imply that care must be taken in the extent to which managers have unfettered choice of their own targets.

Conflict can occur in the budget-setting process, as different groups may well have different agendas. For example, junior managers may be keen to build slack into their budgets while their senior managers may seek to impose unrealistically demanding budget targets. Sometimes, such conflict can be constructive and can result in better decisions being made. To resolve the conflict over budget targets, negotiations may have to take place and other options may have to be explored. This may lead to a better understanding by all parties of the issues involved, and final agreement may result in demanding, yet achievable, targets.

## The impact of management style

There has been a great deal of discussion among experts on the way in which managers use information generated by the budgeting system and the impact of its use on the attitudes and behaviour of subordinates (that is, the staff). A pioneering study by Hopwood (see reference 1 at the end of the chapter) examined the way that managers, working within a manufacturing environment, used budget information to evaluate the performance of subordinates. He argued that three distinct styles of management could be observed. These are:

- *Budget-constrained style*. This management style focuses rigidly on the ability of subordinates to meet the budget. Other factors relating to the performance of subordinates are not given serious consideration even though they might include improving the long-term effectiveness of the area for which the subordinate has responsibility.
- *Profit-conscious style*. This management style uses budget information in a more flexible way and often in conjunction with other data. The main focus is on the ability of each subordinate to improve long-term effectiveness.
- *Non-accounting style*. In this case, budget information plays no significant role in the evaluation of a subordinate's performance.

### Activity 13.17

How might a manager respond to information that indicates a subordinate has not met the budget targets for the period, assuming the manager adopts:

(a) a budget-constrained style?
(b) a profit-conscious style?
(c) a non-accounting style?

(a) A manager adopting a budget-constrained style is likely to take the budget information very seriously. This may result in criticism of the subordinate and, perhaps, some form of sanction.
(b) A manager adopting a profit-conscious style is likely to take a broader view when examining the budget information and so will take other factors into consideration (for example, factors that could not have been anticipated at the time of preparing the budgets), before deciding whether criticism or punishment is justified.
(c) A manager adopting a non-accounting style will regard the failure to meet the budget as being relatively unimportant and so no action may be taken.

Hopwood found that subordinates working for a manager who adopts a budget-constrained style had unfortunate experiences. They suffered higher levels of job-related stress and had poorer working relationships, with both their colleagues and their manager, than those subordinates whose manager adopted one of the other two styles. Hopwood also found that the subordinates of a budget-constrained style of manager were more likely to manipulate the budget figures, or to take other undesirable actions, to ensure the budgets were met.

### Reservations about the Hopwood study

Though Hopwood's findings are interesting, subsequent studies have cast doubt on their universal applicability. Later studies confirm that human attitudes and behaviour are complex and can vary according to the particular situation. For example, it has been found that the impact of different management styles on such factors as job-related stress and the manipulation of budget figures seems to vary. The impact is likely to depend on such factors as the level of independence enjoyed by the subordinates and the level of uncertainty associated with the tasks to be undertaken.

It seems that where there is a high level of interdependence between business divisions, subordinate managers are more likely to feel that they have less control over their performance. This is because the performance of staff in other divisions could be an important influence on the final outcome. In such a situation, rigid application of the budget could be viewed as being unfair and may lead to undesirable behaviour. However, where managers have a high degree of independence, the application of budgets as a measure of performance is likely to be more acceptable. In this case, the managers are likely to feel that the final outcome is much less dependent on the performance of others.

Later studies have also shown that where a subordinate is undertaking a task that has a high degree of uncertainty concerning the outcome (for example, developing a new product), budget targets are unlikely to be an adequate measure of performance. In such a situation, other factors and measures should be taken into account in order to derive a more complete assessment of performance. However, where a task has a low degree of uncertainty concerning the outcome (for example, producing a standard product using standard equipment and an experienced workforce), budget measures may be regarded as more reliable indicators of performance. Thus, it appears that a budget-constrained style is more likely to work where subordinates enjoy a fair amount of independence and where the tasks set have a low level of uncertainty concerning their outcomes.

## Failing to meet the budget

The existence of budgets gives senior managers a ready means to assess the performance of their subordinates (that is, junior managers). If a junior manager fails to meet a budget, this must be handled carefully by the relevant senior manager. Adverse variances may imply that the manager needs help. If this is the case, a harsh, critical approach would have a demotivating effect and would be counterproductive.

**Real World 13.5** gives some indication of the effects of the **behavioural aspects of budgetary control** in practice.

### Real World 13.5

### Behavioural problems

A survey carried out by Drury and others indicates that there is a large degree of participation in setting budgets by those who will be expected to perform to the budget (the budget holders).

The survey also indicates that senior managers have greater influence in setting the targets than their junior manager budget holders. Where there is a conflict between the cost estimates submitted by the budget holders and their senior managers, in 40 per cent of respondent businesses the senior manager's view would prevail without negotiation. In nearly 60 per cent of cases, however, a reduction would be negotiated between the budget holder and the senior manager. The general philosophy of the businesses that responded to the survey, regarding budget holders influencing the setting of their own budgets, is:

- 23 per cent of respondents believe that budget holders should not have too much influence since they will seek to obtain easy budgets (build in slack) if they do;
- 69 per cent of respondents take an opposite view.

The general view on how senior managers should judge their subordinates is:

- 46 per cent of respondent businesses think that senior managers should judge junior managers mainly on their ability to achieve the budget;
- 40 per cent think otherwise.

Though this research is not very recent (1993), in the absence of more recent evidence it provides some feel for budget setting in practice.

*Source: A Survey of Management Accounting Practices in UK Manufacturing Companies, C. Drury, S. Braund, P. Osborne and M. Tayles, Chartered Association of Certified Accountants, 1993.*

## Budgets and innovation

We saw in the previous chapter that budgets are often criticised for reinforcing a 'command and control' structure that concentrates power in the hands of senior managers and prevents junior managers from exercising autonomy. It has been argued that this can deter innovation and can leave junior managers feeling constrained and frustrated. There is not compelling evidence, however, to support this view. **Real World 13.6** discusses some research that explored the possible tension between budgetary control and innovative behaviour.

### Real World 13.6

### Not guilty

A research project was carried out within a large multinational business, which is referred to as 'Astoria' by researchers to preserve its anonymity. The business employs a broadly traditional budgeting system even though it is subject to rapid technological change and operates within a highly competitive environment. Interviews with 25 managers, drawn from different functional areas, were conducted to see whether the budgeting process stifled innovation in any way. The researchers concluded:

. . . we found little evidence to suggest that managers at Astoria were deterred from engaging in innovative activities simply because they had budget responsibilities. Of course, the amount of resources available to them may have presented a sort of boundary, but they didn't see the presence of budgetary targets as a constraint. The closest we came to finding any suggestion that budgets might inhibit innovation was a comment from one manager who remarked that 'everybody has a sandpit to play in. My sandpit financially is my control plan. If I stay within it, I'm free to play.' More generally, managers considered that, if they felt restricted in pursuing innovation, it was the degree of general empowerment they had that mattered. One manager went so far as to say that he felt 'constrained in some ways by not having enough hours in the day'. Our findings suggest that, although much of the accounting literature argues that budgets may deter innovation, this seems far from the truth.

*Source: 'Budgeting and innovation', D. Marginson and S. Ogden, Financial Management, April 2005, pp. 29–31.*

## Self-assessment question (13.1)

Toscanini Ltd makes a standard product, which is budgeted to sell at £4.00 a unit, in a competitive market. It is made by taking a budgeted 0.4 kg of material, budgeted to cost £2.40/kg and having it worked on by hand by an employee, paid a budgeted £8.00/hour, for a budgeted 6 minutes. Monthly fixed overheads are budgeted at £4,800. The output for May was budgeted at 4,000 units.

The actual results for May were as follows:

|  | £ |
|---|---|
| Sales revenue (3,500 units) | 13,820 |
| Materials (1,425 kg) | (3,420) |
| Labour (345 hours) | (2,690) |
| Fixed overheads | (4,900) |
| Actual operating profit | 2,810 |

No inventories of any description existed at the beginning or end of the month.

*Required*:

(a) Deduce the budgeted profit for May and reconcile it, through variances, with the actual profit in as much detail as the information provided will allow.

(b) State which manager should be held accountable, in the first instance, for each variance calculated.

(c) Assuming that the budget was well set and achievable, suggest at least one feasible reason for each of the variances that you identified in (a), given what you know about the business's performance for May.

(d) If it were discovered that the actual total world market demand for the business's product was 10 per cent lower than estimated when the May budget was set, explain how and why the variances that you identified in (a) could be revised to provide information that would be potentially more useful.

**The solution to this question appears at the back of the book on pages 740–741.**

## Standard quantities and costs

We have already seen that a budget is a business plan for the short term – typically one year – that is expressed mainly in financial terms. A budget is often constructed from standards. **Standard quantities and costs** (or revenues) are those planned for an individual unit of input or output and provide the building blocks for budgets.

We can say about Baxter Ltd's operations (see Example 13.1 on page 500) that:

- the standard selling price is £100 for one unit of output;
- the standard marginal cost for one manufactured unit is £60;
- the standard raw materials cost is £40 for one unit of output;
- the standard raw materials usage is 40 metres for one unit of output;
- the standard raw materials price is £1 a metre (that is, for one unit of input);
- the standard labour cost is £20 for one unit of output;
- the standard labour time is 2.50 hours for one unit of output;
- the standard labour rate is £8 an hour (that is, for one unit of input).

Standards, like the budgets to which they are linked, represent targets against which actual performance is measured. They also provide the basis for variance analysis, which, as we have seen, helps managers to identify where deviations from planned, or standard, performance have occurred and the extent of those deviations. To maintain their usefulness for planning and control purposes, they should be subject to frequent review and, where necessary, revision. **Real World 13.7** provides some evidence on the frequency of updating standards in practice.

### Real World 13.7

#### Keeping up to date

KPMG, the accountancy firm, conducted interviews with senior financial officers of 12 large international manufacturing businesses covering pharmaceuticals, industrials and consumer goods. A key finding was that increasing economic volatility was leading to more frequent updates of standards. Most of the businesses updated standards annually. However, one updated on a quarterly basis and one had not updated for two years because of the costs and time involved.

*Source*: 'Standard costing: Insights from leading companies', KPMG, February 2010.

Standards may be applied to a wide variety of products or services. A firm of accountants, for example, may set standard costs per hour for each grade of staff (audit manager, audit senior, trainee, and so on). When planning a particular audit of a client business, it can decide the standard hours that each grade of staff should spend on the audit and, using the standard cost per hour for each grade, it can derive a standard cost or 'budget' for the job as a whole. These standards can subsequently be compared with the actual hours and hourly rates.

## Setting standards

When setting standards various points have to be considered. We shall now explore some of the more important of these.

### Who sets the standards?

Standards often result from the collective effort of various individuals including management accountants, industrial engineers, human resource managers, production managers and other employees. The manager responsible for achieving a particular standard will usually have some involvement and may provide specialised knowledge. This provides the opportunity to influence the final decision, with the consequent risk that 'slack' may be built into the standard in order to make it easier to achieve. The same problem was mentioned earlier in relation to budgets.

### How is information gathered?

Setting standards involves gathering information concerning how much material should be used, how much machine time should be required, how much direct labour time should be spent, and so on. Two possible ways of collecting information for standard setting are available.

## Activity (13.18)

**Can you think what these two methods might be?**

The first is to examine the particular processes and tasks involved in producing the product or service and to develop suitable estimates. Standards concerning material usage, machine time and direct labour hours may be established by carrying out dummy production runs, time-and-motion studies and so on. This will require close collaboration between the management accountant, industrial engineers and those involved in the production process.

The second approach is to collect information relating to past costs, times and usage for the same, or similar, products and to use this information as a basis for predicting the future. This information may have to be adjusted to reflect changes in price, changes in the production process, and so on.

Where the product or service is entirely new or involves entirely new processes, the first approach will probably have to be used, even though it is usually more costly.

## What kind of standards should be used?

There are basically two types of standards that may be used: **ideal standards** and **practical standards**. Ideal standards, as the name suggests, assume perfect operating conditions where there is no inefficiency due to lost production time, defects and so on. The objective of setting ideal standards, which are attainable in theory at least, is to encourage employees to strive towards excellence. Practical standards, also as the name suggests, do not assume ideal operating conditions. Although they demand a high level of efficiency, account is taken of possible lost production time, defects and so on. They are designed to be challenging yet achievable.

There are two major difficulties with using the ideal standards.

● They do not provide a useful basis for exercising control. Unless the standards set are realistic, any variances computed are extremely difficult to interpret.
● They may not achieve their intended purpose of motivating managers: indeed, the opposite may occur. We saw earlier that the evidence suggests that where managers regard a target as beyond their grasp, it is likely to have a demotivating effect.

Given these problems, it is not surprising that practical standards seem to enjoy more widespread support than ideal standards. Nevertheless, by taking account of wastage, lost production time and so on, there is a risk that they will entrench operating inefficiencies.

## The learning-curve effect

Where an activity undertaken by direct workers has been unchanged for some time, and the workers are experienced at performing it, the standard labour time will normally stay unchanged. However, where a new activity is introduced, or new workers are involved with performing an existing activity, a **learning-curve** effect will normally occur. This is shown in Figure 13.13.

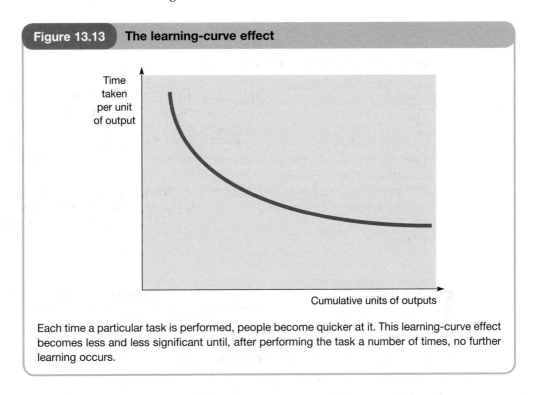

| Figure 13.13 | The learning-curve effect |

Each time a particular task is performed, people become quicker at it. This learning-curve effect becomes less and less significant until, after performing the task a number of times, no further learning occurs.

The first unit of output takes a relatively long time to produce. As experience is gained, the worker takes less time to produce each successive unit of output. The rate of reduction in the time taken will, however, decrease as experience is gained. Thus, for example, the reduction in time taken between the first and second unit produced will be much bigger than the reduction between, say, the ninth and the tenth. Eventually, the rate of reduction in time taken will reduce to zero so that each unit will take as long as the preceding one. At this point, the point where the curve in Figure 13.13 becomes horizontal (the bottom right of the graph), the learning-curve effect will have been eliminated and a steady, long-term standard time for the activity will have been established.

The learning-curve effect seems to have little to do with whether workers are skilled or unskilled; if they are unfamiliar with the task, the learning-curve effect will arise. Practical experience shows that learning curves show remarkable regularity and, therefore, predictability from one activity to another.

The learning-curve effect applies equally well to activities involved with providing a service (such as dealing with an insurance claim, in an insurance business) as to manufacturing-type activities (like upholstering an armchair by hand, in a furniture-making business).

Clearly, the learning-curve effect must be taken into account when setting standards, and when interpreting any adverse labour efficiency variances, where a new process and/or new staff are involved.

## Other uses for standard costing

We have already seen that standards can play a valuable role in performance evaluation and control. However, standards relating to costs, usages, selling prices and so on, may also be used for other purposes such as:

- measuring operating efficiency,
- product sourcing decisions,
- determining the cost of inventories and work in progress for income measurement purposes,
- determining the cost of items for use in pricing decisions.

This does not mean that standards should be seen as the primary measure in all cases. When making decisions about operating efficiency, product sourcing or pricing, they may be used as a secondary measure.

**Real World 13.8** provides some information on the use of standards for decision making.

### Real World 13.8

#### Standard practice

The KPMG survey, mentioned in Real World 13.7 (page 525), found that some of the twelve manufacturing businesses in the study had moved away from using standard costing as the key measure of operating effectiveness and for product sourcing decisions. Instead, they relied on other operating and financial measures.

*Source*: 'Standard costing: Insights from leading companies', KPMG, February 2010.

## Some problems . . .

Although standards and variances may be useful for decision-making purposes, they have limited application. Many business and commercial activities do not have direct relationships between inputs and outputs, as is the case with, say, the number of direct labour hours worked and the number of products manufactured. Many expenses of modern business are in areas such as human resource development and advertising, where the expense is discretionary and there is no direct link to the level of output.

There are also potential problems when applying standard costing techniques. These include the following:

- Standards can quickly become out of date as a result of both changes in the production process and price changes. When standards become outdated, performance can be adversely affected. For example, a human resources manager who recognises that it is impossible to meet targets on rates of pay for labour, because of general labour cost rises, may have less incentive to minimise costs.
- Factors may affect a variance for which a particular manager is accountable but over which the manager has no control. When assessing the manager's performance,

these uncontrollable factors should be taken into account but there is always a risk that they will not.

- In practice, creating clear lines of demarcation between the areas of responsibility of various managers may be difficult. In this case, one of the prerequisites of effective standard costing is lost.
- Once a standard has been met, there is no incentive for employees to improve the quality or quantity of output further. There are usually no additional rewards for doing so; only additional work. Indeed, employees may have a disincentive for exceeding a standard as it may then be viewed by managers as too loose and therefore in need of tightening. However, simply achieving a standard, and no more, may not be enough in highly competitive and fast-changing markets. To compete effectively, a business may need to strive for continuous improvement, and standard costing techniques may impede this *kaizen* process.
- Standard costing may create incentives for managers and employees to act in undesirable ways. It may, for example, encourage the build-up of excess inventories, leading to significant storage and financing costs. This problem can arise where there are opportunities for discounts on bulk purchases of materials, which the purchasing manager then exploits to achieve a favourable direct materials price variance. One way to avoid this problem might be to impose limits on the level of inventories held.

## Activity (13.19)

Can you think of another example of how a manager may achieve a favourable direct materials price variance but in doing so would create problems for a business?

A manager may buy cheaper, but lower quality, materials. Although this may lead to a favourable price variance, it may also lead to additional inspection and re-working costs and, perhaps, lost sales.

To avoid this problem, the manager may be required to buy material of a particular quality or from particular sources.

A final example of the perverse incentives created by standard costing relates to labour efficiency variances. Where these variances are calculated for individual employees, and form the basis for their rewards, there is little incentive for them to work cooperatively. Cooperative working may be in the best interests of the business, however. To avoid this problem, some businesses calculate labour efficiency variances for groups of employees rather than individual employees. This, however, creates the risk that some individuals will become 'free riders' and will rely on the more conscientious employees to carry the load.

## Activity (13.20)

How might the business try to eliminate the 'free-rider' problem just mentioned?

One way would be to carry out an evaluation, perhaps by the group members themselves, of individual contributions to group output, as well as evaluating group output as a whole.

**Real World 13.9** indicates that, despite the problems mentioned above, standard costing is used by businesses.

---

### Real World 13.9

#### Using variance analysis

The CIMA survey, mentioned previously, examined the extent to which the use of standard costing varies with business size. Figure 13.14 reveals the results.

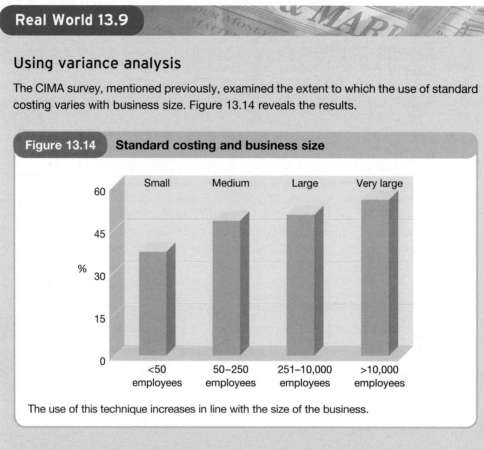

**Figure 13.14** **Standard costing and business size**

The use of this technique increases in line with the size of the business.

Once again, we should be careful not to assume from this information that business size determines the extent of usage.

*Source*: Figure adapted from 'Management accounting tools for today and tomorrow', CIMA, 2009, p. 12.

---

## The new business environment

The traditional standard costing approach was developed during an era when business operations were characterised by few product lines, long production runs and heavy reliance on direct labour. More recently, the increasingly competitive environment and the onward march of technology have changed the business landscape. Now, many business operations are characterised by a wide range of different products, shorter product life cycles (leading to shorter production runs) and automated production processes. The effect of these changes has resulted in:

- more frequent development of standards to deal with frequent changes to the product range;
- a change in the focus for control – where manufacturing systems are automated, for example, direct labour becomes less important than direct materials;

- a decline in the importance of monitoring from cost and usage variances – where manufacturing systems are automated, deviations from standards relating to costs and usage become less frequent and less significant.

Thus, where a business has highly automated production systems, traditional standard costing, with its emphasis on costs and usage, is likely to take on less importance. Other elements of the production process such as quality, production levels, product cycle times, delivery times and the need for continuous improvement become the focus of attention. This does not mean, however, that a standards-based approach is not useful for the new manufacturing environment. It can still provide valuable control information and there is no reason why standard costing systems cannot be redesigned to reflect a concern for some of the elements mentioned earlier. Nevertheless, other measures, including non-financial ones, may help to augment the information provided by the standard costing system.

**Real World 13.10** reveals the extent to which particular standard costing variances are calculated.

## Real World 13.10

### Standard use

Senior financial managers of 33 UK businesses were asked about their costing systems. It emerged that standard costing was used by 30 of the businesses concerned, which represented most of the businesses that might be expected to use this method. The popularity among these businesses of standards for each of the main cost items is set out in Figure 13.15.

**Figure 13.15    The popularity of standards in practice**

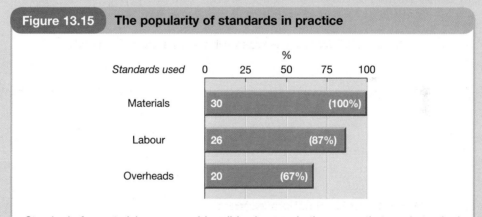

Standards for materials were used by all businesses in the survey that used standard costing. Standards for labour were used by nearly all businesses.

Despite the popularity of materials standards, the study found that four businesses calculated the total direct materials variance only and that only two thirds of businesses calculated both the direct materials price and usage variances. For labour standards, the variance analysis is even less complete. The study found that 15 businesses calculated the total direct labour variance only and only one third of businesses calculated both the direct labour and efficiency variances. It seems, therefore, that standard costing was not extensively employed by the businesses.

Source: Figure based on information in *Contemporary Management Accounting Practices in UK Manufacturing*, D. Dugdale, C. Jones and S. Green, CIMA Publication, Elsevier, 2006.

## Summary

The main points of this chapter may be summarised as follows:

### Controlling through budgets

- Budgets act as a system of both feedback and feedforward control.
- To exercise control, budgets can be flexed to match actual volume of output.

### Variance analysis

- Variances may be favourable or adverse according to whether they result in an increase to, or a decrease from, the budgeted profit figure.
- Budgeted profit plus all favourable variances less all adverse variances equals actual profit.
- Commonly calculated variances:
  - Sales volume variance = difference between the original budget and the flexed budget profit figures.
  - Sales price variance = difference between actual sales revenue and actual volume at the standard sales price.
  - Total direct materials variance = difference between the actual direct materials cost and the direct materials cost according to the flexed budget.
  - Direct materials usage variance = difference between actual usage and budgeted usage, for the actual volume of output, multiplied by the standard materials cost.
  - Direct materials price variance = difference between the actual materials cost and the actual usage multiplied by the standard materials cost.
  - Total direct labour variance = difference between the actual direct labour cost and the direct labour cost according to the flexed budget.
  - Direct labour efficiency variance = difference between actual labour time and budgeted time, for the actual volume of output, multiplied by the standard labour rate.
  - Direct labour rate variance = difference between the actual labour cost and the actual labour time multiplied by the standard labour rate.
  - Fixed overhead spending variance = difference between the actual and budgeted spending on fixed overheads.
- Significant and/or persistent variances should normally be investigated to establish their cause. However, the costs and benefits of investigating variances must be considered.
- Trading off favourable variances against linked adverse variances should not be automatically acceptable.
- Not all activities can usefully be controlled through traditional variance analysis.

### Effective budgetary control

- Good budgetary control requires establishing systems and routines to ensure such things as a clear distinction between individual managers' areas of responsibility; prompt, frequent and relevant variance reporting; and senior management commitment.
- There are behavioural aspects of control relating to management style, participation in budget setting and the failure to meet budget targets that should be taken into account by senior managers.
- The view that budgetary control stifles initiative is not well supported by the evidence.

### Standard costing

- Standards = budgeted physical quantities and financial values for one unit of inputs and outputs.
- Two types of standards: ideal standards and practical standards.
- Information necessary for developing standards can be gathered by analysing the task or by using past data.
- There tends to be a learning-curve effect: routine tasks are performed more quickly with experience.
- Standards can be useful in providing data for income measurement, pricing decisions, product sourcing and efficiency measurement.
- Standards have their limitations, particularly in modern manufacturing environments; however, they are still widely used.

## MyAccountingLab

Go to **www.myaccountinglab.com** to check your understanding of the chapter, create a personalised study plan, and maximise your revision time

## Key terms

**feedback control**  p. 498
**feedforward control**  p. 498
**flexing the budget**  p. 501
**flexible budgets**  p. 501
**sales volume variance**  p. 502
**adverse variance**  p. 502
**favourable variance**  p. 502
**variance**  p. 502
**sales price variance**  p. 504
**total direct materials variance**  p. 505
**direct materials usage variance**  p. 505
**direct materials price variance**  p. 506
**total direct labour variance**  p. 507

**direct labour efficiency variance**  p. 507
**direct labour rate variance**  p. 507
**fixed overhead spending variance**  p. 508
**non-operating-profit variances**  p. 515
**compensating variances**  p. 518
**budgetary control**  p. 519
**behavioural aspects of budgetary control**  p. 522
**standard quantities and costs**  p. 524
**ideal standards**  p. 526
**practical standards**  p. 526
**learning curve**  p. 527

## Reference

1  Hopwood, A. G., 'An empirical study of the role of accounting data in performance evaluation', *Empirical Research in Accounting: A supplement to the Journal of Accounting Research*, 1972, pp. 156–82.

## Further reading

If you would like to explore the topics covered in this chapter in more depth, we recommend the following books:

Bhimani, A., Horngren, C., Datar, S. and Rajan, M., *Management and Cost Accounting,* 4th edn, Financial Times Prentice Hall, 2012, chapters 14 to 16.

Drury, C., *Management and Cost Accounting*, 8th edn, Cengage Learning, 2012, chapters 16 to 18.

Hilton, R., *Managerial Accounting*, 9th edn., McGraw-Hill Higher Education, 2011, chapter 10.

Kaplan, R., Atkinson, A., Matsumura, E. and Young, S.M., *Management Accounting*, 6th edn, Pearson, 2011, chapter 12.

## Review questions

Solutions to these questions can be found at the back of the book on page 756.

**13.1** Explain what is meant by feedforward control and distinguish it from feedback control.

**13.2** What is meant by a variance? What is the point in analysing variances?

**13.3** What is the point in flexing the budget in the context of variance analysis? Does flexing imply that differences between budget and actual in the volume of output are ignored in variance analysis?

**13.4** Should all variances be investigated to find their cause? Explain your answer.

## Exercises

Exercises 13.1 and 13.2 are basic level, 13.3 and 13.4 are intermediate level and 13.5, 13.6, and 13.7 are advanced level. Those with **coloured numbers** have solutions at the back of the book, starting on page 788.

If you wish to try more exercises, visit the students' side of the Companion Website and MyAccountingLab.

**13.1** You have recently overheard the following remarks:

(a) 'A favourable direct labour rate variance can only be caused by staff working more efficiently than budgeted.'
(b) 'Selling more units than budgeted, because the units were sold at less than standard price, automatically leads to a favourable sales volume variance.'
(c) 'Using below-standard materials will tend to lead to adverse materials usage variances but cannot affect labour variances.'
(d) 'Higher-than-budgeted sales could not possibly affect the labour rate variance.'
(e) 'An adverse sales price variance can only arise from selling a product at less than standard price.'

*Required*:
Critically assess these remarks, explaining any technical terms.

**13.2** You have recently overheard the following remarks:

(a) 'When calculating variances, we in effect ignore differences of volume of output, between original budget and actual, by flexing the budget. If there were a volume difference, it is water under the bridge by the time that the variances come to be calculated.'
(b) 'It is very valuable to calculate variances because they will tell you what went wrong.'
(c) 'All variances should be investigated to find their cause.'
(d) 'Research evidence shows that the more demanding the target, the more motivated the manager.'
(e) 'Most businesses do not have feedforward controls of any type, just feedback controls through budgets.'

*Required*:
Critically assess these remarks, explaining any technical terms.

**13.3** Pilot Ltd makes a standard product, which is budgeted to sell at £5.00 a unit. It is made by taking a budgeted 0.5 kg of material, budgeted to cost £3.00 a kilogram and working on it by hand by an employee, paid a budgeted £10.00 an hour, for a budgeted $7^1/_2$ minutes. Monthly fixed overheads are budgeted at £6,000. The output for March was budgeted at 5,000 units.

The actual results for March were as follows:

|  | £ |
|---|---|
| Sales revenue (5,400 units) | 26,460 |
| Materials (2,830 kg) | (8,770) |
| Labour (650 hours) | (6,885) |
| Fixed overheads | (6,350) |
| Actual operating profit | 4,455 |

No inventories existed at the start or end of March.

*Required*:
(a) Deduce the budgeted profit for March and reconcile it with the actual profit in as much detail as the information provided will allow.
(b) State which manager should be held accountable, in the first instance, for each variance calculated.

**13.4** Antonio plc makes Product X, the standard costs of which are:

|  | £ |
|---|---|
| Sales revenue | 31 |
| Direct labour (1 hour) | (11) |
| Direct materials (1 kg) | (10) |
| Fixed overheads | (3) |
| Standard profit | 7 |

The budgeted output for March was 1,000 units of Product X; the actual output was 1,100 units, which was sold for £34,950. There were no inventories at the start or end of March.

The actual production costs were:

|  | £ |
|---|---|
| Direct labour (1,075 hours) | 12,210 |
| Direct materials (1,170 kg) | 11,630 |
| Fixed overheads | 3,200 |

*Required*:
Calculate the variances for March as fully as you are able from the available information and use them to reconcile the budgeted and actual profit figures.

**13.5** Bradley-Allen Ltd makes one standard product. Its budgeted operating statement for May is as follows:

|  |  | £ | £ |
|---|---|---|---|
| Sales (volume and revenue): | 800 units |  | 64,000 |
| Direct materials: | Type A | (12,000) |  |
|  | Type B | (16,000) |  |
| Direct labour: | Skilled | (4,000) |  |
|  | Unskilled | (10,000) |  |
| Fixed overheads: | (All fixed) | (12,000) |  |
|  |  |  | (54,000) |
| Budgeted operating profit |  |  | 10,000 |

The standard costs were as follows:

| | | |
|---|---|---|
| Direct materials: | Type A | £50/kg |
| | Type B | £20/m |
| Direct labour: | Skilled | £10/hour |
| | Unskilled | £8/hour |

During May, the following occurred:

1  950 units were sold for a total of £73,000.
2  310 kilos (costing £15,200) of type A material were used in production.
3  920 metres (costing £18,900) of type B material were used in production.
4  Skilled workers were paid £4,628 for 445 hours.
5  Unskilled workers were paid £11,275 for 1,375 hours.
6  Fixed overheads cost £11,960.

There were no inventories of finished production or of work in progress at either the beginning or end of May.

*Required*:
(a)  Prepare a statement that reconciles the budgeted to the actual profit of the business for May, through variances. Your statement should analyse the difference between the two profit figures in as much detail as you are able.
(b)  Explain how the statement in (a) might be helpful to managers.

**13.6**  Mowbray Ltd makes and sells one product, the standard costs of which are as follows:

| | £ |
|---|---|
| Direct materials (3 kg at £2.50/kg) | (7.50) |
| Direct labour (15 minutes at £9.00/hr) | (2.25) |
| Fixed overheads | (3.60) |
| | (13.35) |
| Selling price | 20.00 |
| Standard profit margin | 6.65 |

The monthly production and sales are planned to be 1,200 units.
The actual results for May were as follows:

| | £ | |
|---|---|---|
| Sales revenue | 18,000 | |
| Direct materials | (7,400) | (2,800 kg) |
| Direct labour | (2,300) | (255 hr) |
| Fixed overheads | (4,100) | |
| Operating profit | 4,200 | |

There were no inventories at the start or end of May. As a result of poor sales demand during May, the business reduced the price of all sales by 10 per cent.

*Required*:
Calculate the budgeted profit for May and reconcile it to the actual profit through variances, going into as much detail as is possible from the information available.

**13.7**  Brive plc has the following standards for its only product:

| | |
|---|---|
| Selling price: | £110/unit |
| Direct labour: | 1 hour at £10.50/hour |
| Direct material: | 3 kg at £14.00/kg |
| Fixed overheads: | £27.00/unit, based on a budgeted output of 800 units/month |

During May, there was an actual output of 850 units and the operating statement for the month was as follows:

|  | £ |
| --- | --- |
| Sales revenue | 92,930 |
| Direct labour (890 hours) | (9,665) |
| Direct materials (2,410 kg) | (33,258) |
| Fixed overheads | (21,365) |
| Operating profit | 28,642 |

There were no inventories of any description at the beginning and end of May.

*Required*:

Prepare the original budget and a budget flexed to the actual volume. Use these to compare the budgeted and actual profits of the business for the month, going into as much detail with your analysis as the information given will allow.

# PART 3

# Financial management

Part 3 is concerned with the area of accounting and finance usually known as 'business finance' or 'financial management'. Broadly, we shall be looking at decisions concerning the raising and investment of finance. Businesses can be seen, from a purely economic perspective, as organisations that raise money from investors and others (broadly, shareholders and lenders) and that use those funds to make investments (typically in plant and other assets) that will make the business and its owners wealthier. Clearly, these are important decision-making areas typically involving large amounts of money and relatively long-term commitments.

Chapter 14 considers how businesses make decisions about what represents a worthwhile investment. We shall be looking particularly at investments in such things as factories, offices and plant, which might enable businesses to provide some product or service for which a profitable market is seen. The decision-making techniques that we shall consider could equally well be applied to making investments in the shares of a business, or any other type of 'financial' investment, which individuals might make using their own money.

Chapter 15 deals with the other side of the investment: where the investment finance comes from. Here we shall be reviewing the various types of funding used by businesses of various sizes, including raising funds from the owners of the business (the shareholders in the case of limited companies).

Chapter 16 looks at a particular area of fundraising and investment: the management of working capital. Working capital consists of the short-term assets and claims of the business: inventories, trade receivables, cash and trade payables. These items typically involve large amounts of finance and need to be managed carefully. The chapter considers how working capital can be managed effectively.

# Making capital investment decisions

## Introduction

This chapter looks at how businesses should assess proposed investments in new plant, machinery, buildings and other long-term assets. This is a very important area; expensive and far-reaching consequences can flow from bad investment decisions.

We shall also consider the problem of risk and how this may be taken into account when evaluating investment proposals. Finally, we shall discuss the ways that managers can oversee capital investment projects and how control may be exercised throughout the life of a project.

## Learning outcomes

**When you have completed this chapter, you should be able to:**

- Explain the nature and importance of investment decision making.

- Identify the four main investment appraisal methods found in practice.

- Discuss the strengths and weaknesses of various techniques for dealing with risk in investment appraisal.

- Explain the methods used to monitor and control investment projects.

## MyAccountingLab

Visit **www.myaccountinglab.com** for practice and revision opportunities

# The nature of investment decisions

The essential feature of investment decisions is *time*. Investment involves making an outlay of something of economic value, usually cash, at one point in time, which is expected to yield economic benefits to the investor at some other point in time. Usually, the outlay precedes the benefits. Furthermore, the outlay is typically a single large amount while the benefits arrive as a series of smaller amounts over a fairly protracted period.

Investment decisions tend to be of profound importance to the business because:

- *Large amounts of resources are often involved.* Many investments made by businesses involve laying out a significant proportion of their total resources (see Real World 14.2). If mistakes are made with the decision, the effects on the businesses could be significant, if not catastrophic.
- *It is often difficult and/or expensive to bail out of an investment once it has been undertaken.* Investments made by a business are often specific to its needs. A hotel business, for example, may invest in a new, custom-designed hotel complex. If the business found, after having made the investment, that room occupancy rates were too low, the only course of action might be to sell the complex. The specialist nature of the complex may, however, lead to it having a rather limited resale value. This could mean that the amount recouped from the investment is much less than it had originally cost.

**Real World 14.1** gives an illustration of a major investment decision by a well-known airline business.

### Real World 14.1

#### Plane common sense?

In July 2011, American Airlines announced the purchase of 200 Boeing 737s and 260 Airbus 320 aircraft. This represents the largest order in aviation history, and the new aircraft will be delivered to the company over the period 2013 to 2022. Although the precise cost of the new aircraft was not revealed, it has been estimated to be more than £12 billion.

This level of investment is quite extraordinary, even though American Airlines is the fourth largest airline in the world. The business clearly believes that acquiring the new aircraft will be a profitable move, but how would it have reached this conclusion? Presumably, the likely future benefits from passenger fares and likely future operating costs will have been major inputs to the decision.

*Source*: Based on information in www.bbc.co.uk, 20 July 2011, and www.telegraph.co.uk, 20 July 2011.

The issues raised by American Airlines' investment will be the main subject of this chapter.

**Real World 14.2** indicates the level of annual net investment for a number of randomly selected, well-known UK businesses. We can see that the scale of investment varies from one business to another. (It also tends to vary from one year to the next for a particular business.) In nearly all of these businesses the scale of investment was significant, despite the fact that many businesses were cutting back on investment during the economic recession.

**Real World 14.2**

## The scale of investment by UK businesses

| | Expenditure on additional non-current assets as a percentage of: | |
| --- | --- | --- |
| | Annual sales revenue | End-of-year non-current assets |
| British Airways plc (airline) | 6.4 | 6.4 |
| British Sky Broadcasting plc (television) | 7.5 | 15.8 |
| Go-Ahead Group plc (transport) | 4.4 | 17.2 |
| Marks and Spencer plc (stores) | 5.8 | 9.8 |
| Wm Morrison Supermarkets plc (supermarkets) | 5.9 | 11.8 |
| J D Wetherspoon (pub operator) | 8.2 | 9.7 |
| Severn Trent Water Ltd (water and sewerage) | 30.9 | 7.9 |
| Tate and Lyle plc (sugar and allied products) | 3.8 | 7.5 |

*Source*: Annual reports of the businesses concerned for the financial year ending in 2010.

**Real World 14.2** considers only expenditure on non-current assets, but this type of investment often requires a significant outlay on current assets to support it (additional inventories, for example). This suggests that the real scale of investment is even greater than indicated above.

**Activity (14.1)**

When managers are making decisions involving capital investments, what should the decision seek to achieve?

Investment decisions must be consistent with the objectives of the particular organisation. For a private-sector business, maximising the wealth of the owners (shareholders) is normally assumed to be the key financial objective.

## Investment appraisal methods

Given the importance of investment decisions, it is essential that proper screening of investment proposals takes place. An important part of this screening process is to ensure that appropriate methods of evaluation are used.

Research shows that there are basically four methods used by businesses to evaluate investment opportunities. They are:

- accounting rate of return (ARR)
- payback period (PP)

- net present value (NPV)
- internal rate of return (IRR).

It is possible to find businesses that use variants of these four methods. It is also possible to find businesses, particularly smaller ones, that do not use any formal appraisal method but rely instead on the 'gut feeling' of their managers. Most businesses, however, seem to use one (or more) of these four methods.

We are going to assess the effectiveness of each of these methods, but we shall see that only one of them (NPV) is a wholly logical approach. The other three all have flaws. To help in examining each of the methods, it might be useful to see how each of them would cope with a particular investment opportunity. Let us consider the following example.

### Example 14.1

Billingsgate Battery Company has carried out some research that shows that there is a market for a standard service that it has recently developed.

Provision of the service would require investment in a machine that would cost £100,000, payable immediately. Sales of the service would take place throughout the next five years. At the end of that time, it is estimated that the machine could be sold for £20,000.

Inflows and outflows from sales of the service would be expected to be:

| Time | | £000 |
| --- | --- | --- |
| Immediately | Cost of machine | (100) |
| 1 year's time | Operating profit before depreciation | 20 |
| 2 years' time | Operating profit before depreciation | 40 |
| 3 years' time | Operating profit before depreciation | 60 |
| 4 years' time | Operating profit before depreciation | 60 |
| 5 years' time | Operating profit before depreciation | 20 |
| 5 years' time | Disposal proceeds from the machine | 20 |

Note that, broadly speaking, the operating profit before deducting depreciation (that is, before non-cash items) equals the net amount of cash flowing into the business. Broadly, apart from depreciation, all of this business's expenses cause cash to flow out of the business. Sales revenues tend to lead to cash flowing in. Expenses tend to lead to it flowing out. For the time being, we shall assume that working capital – which is made up of inventories, trade receivables and trade payables – remains constant. This means that operating profit before depreciation will tend to equal the net cash inflow.

To simplify matters, we shall assume that the cash from sales and for the expenses of providing the service are received and paid, respectively, at the end of each year. This is clearly unlikely to be true in real life. Money will have to be paid to employees (for salaries and wages) on a weekly or a monthly basis. Customers will pay within a month or two of buying the service. On the other hand, making the assumption probably does not lead to a serious distortion. It is a simplifying assumption, that is often made in real life, and it will make things more straightforward for us now. We should be clear, however, that there is nothing about any of the four methods that *demands* that this assumption is made.

Having set up the example, we shall now go on to consider how each of the appraisal methods works.

## Accounting rate of return (ARR)

The first of the four methods that we shall consider is the **accounting rate of return (ARR)**. This method takes the average accounting operating profit that the investment will generate and expresses it as a percentage of the average investment made over the life of the project. In other words:

$$\text{ARR} = \frac{\text{Average annual operating profit}}{\text{Average investment to earn that profit}} \times 100\%$$

We can see from the equation that, to calculate the ARR, we need to deduce two pieces of information about the particular project:

- the annual average operating profit; and
- the average investment.

In our example, the average annual operating profit *before depreciation* over the five years is £40,000 (that is, £000(20 + 40 + 60 + 60 + 20)/5). Assuming 'straight-line' depreciation (that is, equal annual amounts), the annual depreciation charge will be £16,000 (that is, £(100,000 – 20,000)/5). Therefore, the average annual operating profit *after depreciation* is £24,000 (that is, £40,000 – £16,000).

The average investment over the five years can be calculated as follows:

$$\text{Average investment} = \frac{\text{Cost of machine} + \text{Disposal value*}}{2}$$
$$= \frac{£100,000 + £20,000}{2}$$
$$= £60,000$$

(*Note: To find the average investment we are simply adding the value of the amount invested at the beginning and end of the investment period together and dividing by two.)

The ARR of the investment, therefore, is:

$$\text{ARR} = \frac{£24,000}{£60,000} \times 100\% = 40\%$$

The following decision rules apply when using ARR:

- For any project to be acceptable, it must achieve a target ARR as a minimum.
- Where there are competing projects that all seem capable of exceeding this minimum rate (that is, where the business must choose between more than one project), the one with the higher (or highest) ARR should be selected.

To decide whether the 40 per cent return is acceptable, we need to compare this percentage return with the minimum rate required by the business.

## Activity (14.2)

Chaotic Industries is considering an investment in a fleet of ten delivery vans to take its products to customers. The vans will cost £15,000 each to buy, payable immediately. The annual running costs are expected to total £50,000 for each van (including the driver's salary). The vans are expected to operate successfully for six years, at the end of which period they will all have to be sold, with disposal proceeds expected to be about £3,000 a van. At present, the business outsources transport, for all of its deliveries, to a commercial carrier. It is expected that this carrier will charge a total of £530,000 each year for the next six years to undertake the deliveries.

What is the ARR of buying the vans? (Note that cost savings are as relevant a benefit from an investment as are net cash inflows.)

The vans will save the business £30,000 a year (that is, £530,000 − (£50,000 × 10)), before depreciation, in total. Therefore, the inflows and outflows will be:

| Time | | £000 |
|---|---|---|
| Immediately | Cost of vans (10 × £15,000) | (150) |
| 1 year's time | Saving before depreciation | 30 |
| 2 years' time | Saving before depreciation | 30 |
| 3 years' time | Saving before depreciation | 30 |
| 4 years' time | Saving before depreciation | 30 |
| 5 years' time | Saving before depreciation | 30 |
| 6 years' time | Saving before depreciation | 30 |
| 6 years' time | Disposal proceeds from the vans (10 × £3,000) | 30 |

The total annual depreciation expense (assuming a straight-line method) will be £20,000 (that is, (£150,000 − £30,000)/6). Therefore, the average annual saving, *after depreciation*, is £10,000 (that is, £30,000 − £20,000).

The average investment will be

$$\text{Average investment} = \frac{£150,000 + £30,000}{2}$$

$$= £90,000$$

and the ARR of the investment is

$$\text{ARR} = \frac{£10,000}{£90,000} \times 100\%$$

$$= 11.1\%$$

## ARR and ROCE

In essence, ARR and the return on capital employed (ROCE) ratio take the same approach to measuring business performance. Both relate operating profit to the cost of assets used to generate that profit. ROCE, however, assesses the performance of the overall business *after* it has performed, while ARR assesses the potential performance of a particular investment *before* it has performed.

We saw that investments are required to achieve a minimum target ARR. Given the link between ARR and ROCE, this target could be based on overall rates of returns previously achieved – as measured by ROCE. It could also be based on the industry-average ROCE.

The link between ARR and ROCE strengthens the case for adopting ARR as the appropriate method of investment appraisal. ROCE is a widely-used measure of profitability and some businesses express their financial objective in terms of a target ROCE. It therefore seems sensible to use a method of investment appraisal that is consistent with this overall measure of business performance. A secondary point in favour of ARR is that it provides a result expressed in percentage terms, which many managers seem to prefer.

## Problems with ARR

### Activity 14.3

ARR suffers from a major defect as a means of assessing investment opportunities. Can you reason out what this is? Consider the three competing projects whose profits are shown below. All three involve investment in a machine that is expected to have no residual value at the end of the five years. Note that all of the projects have the same total operating profits after depreciation over the five years.

| Time | | Project A £000 | Project B £000 | Project C £000 |
|---|---|---|---|---|
| Immediately | Cost of machine | (160) | (160) | (160) |
| 1 year's time | Operating profit after depreciation | 20 | 10 | 160 |
| 2 years' time | Operating profit after depreciation | 40 | 10 | 10 |
| 3 years' time | Operating profit after depreciation | 60 | 10 | 10 |
| 4 years' time | Operating profit after depreciation | 60 | 10 | 10 |
| 5 years' time | Operating profit after depreciation | 20 | 160 | 10 |

(*Hint*: The defect is not concerned with the ability of the decision maker to forecast future events, though this too can be a problem. Try to remember the essential feature of investment decisions, which we identified at the beginning of this chapter.)

The problem with ARR is that it ignores the time factor. In this example, exactly the same ARR would have been computed for each of the three projects.

Since the same total operating profit over the five years (£200,000) arises in all three of these projects, and the average investment in each project is £80,000 (that is, £160,000/2), each project will give rise to the same ARR of 50 per cent (that is, £40,000/£80,000).

To maximise the wealth of the owners, a manager faced with a choice between the three projects set out in Activity 14.3 should select Project C. This is because most of the benefits arise within twelve months of making the initial investment. Project A would rank second and Project B would come a poor third. Any appraisal technique that is not capable of distinguishing between these three situations is seriously flawed. We shall look at why timing is so important later in the chapter.

There are further problems associated with the ARR method, which we shall now discuss.

### Use of average investment

Using the average investment in calculating ARR can lead to daft results. Example 14.2 illustrates the kind of problem that can arise.

---

**Example 14.2**

George put forward an investment proposal to his boss. The business uses ARR to assess investment proposals using a minimum 'hurdle' rate of 27 per cent. Details of the proposal were:

| | |
|---|---|
| Cost of equipment | £200,000 |
| Estimated residual value of equipment | £40,000 |
| Average annual operating profit before depreciation | £48,000 |
| Estimated life of project | 10 years |
| Annual straight-line depreciation charge | £16,000 (that is, (£200,000 – £40,000)/10) |

The ARR of the project will be:

$$ARR = \frac{48,000 - 16,000}{(200,000 + 40,000)/2} \times 100\% = 26.7\%$$

The boss rejected George's proposal because it failed to achieve an ARR of at least 27 per cent. Although George was disappointed, he realised that there was still hope. In fact, all that the business had to do was to give away the piece of equipment at the end of its useful life rather than sell it. The residual value of the equipment then became zero and the annual depreciation charge became ([£200,000 – £0]/10) = £20,000 a year. The revised ARR calculation was then:

$$ARR = \frac{48,000 - 20,000}{(200,000 + 0)/2} \times 100\% = 28\%$$

---

### Use of accounting profit

We have seen that ARR is based on the use of accounting profit. When measuring performance over the whole life of a project, however, it is cash flows rather than accounting profits that are important. Cash is the ultimate measure of the economic wealth generated by an investment. This is because it is cash that is used to acquire resources and for distribution to owners. Accounting profit is more appropriate for reporting achievement on a periodic basis. It is a useful measure of productive effort for a relatively short period, such as a year or half year. It is really a question of 'horses for courses'. Accounting profit is fine for measuring performance over short period, but cash is the appropriate measure when considering performance over the life of a project.

### Competing investments

The ARR method can create problems when considering competing investments of different size. Consider Activity 14.4.

## Activity (14.4)

Sinclair Wholesalers plc is currently considering opening a new sales outlet in Coventry. Two possible sites have been identified for the new outlet. Site A has an area of 30,000 sq m. It will require an average investment of £6m and will produce an average operating profit of £600,000 a year. Site B has an area of 20,000 sq m. It will require an average investment of £4m and will produce an average operating profit of £500,000 a year.

What is the ARR of each investment opportunity? Which site would you select and why?

The ARR of Site A is £600,000/£6m = 10 per cent. The ARR of Site B is £500,000/£4m = 12.5 per cent. Site B, therefore has the higher ARR. In terms of the absolute operating profit generated, however, Site A is the more attractive. If the ultimate objective is to increase the wealth of the shareholders of Sinclair Wholesalers plc, it would be better to choose Site A even though the percentage return is lower. It is the absolute size of the return rather than the relative (percentage) size that is important. This is a general problem of using comparative measures, such as percentages, when the objective is measured in absolute terms, like an amount of money.

**Real World 14.3** illustrates how using percentage measures can lead to confusion.

## Real World 14.3

### Increasing road capacity by sleight of hand

During the 1970s, the Mexican government wanted to increase the capacity of a major four-lane road. It came up with the idea of repainting the lane markings so that there were six narrower lanes occupying the same space as four wider ones had previously done. This increased the capacity of the road by 50 per cent (that is, $^2/_4 \times 100$). A tragic outcome of the narrower lanes was an increase in deaths from road accidents. A year later the Mexican government had the six narrower lanes changed back to the original four wider ones. This reduced the capacity of the road by 33 per cent (that is, $^2/_6 \times 100$). The Mexican government reported that, overall, it had increased the capacity of the road by 17 per cent (that is, 50% − 33%), despite the fact that its real capacity was identical to that which it had been originally. The confusion arose because each of the two percentages (50 per cent and 33 per cent) is based on different bases (four and six).

*Source: Reckoning with Risk, G. Gigerenzer, Penguin, 2002.*

## Payback period (PP)

The second approach to appraising possible investments is the **payback period (PP)**. This is the time taken for an initial investment to be repaid out of the net cash inflows from a project. As the PP method takes time into account, it appears at first glance to overcome a key weakness of the ARR method.

Let us consider PP in the context of the Billingsgate Battery example. We should recall that the project's cash flows are:

| Time | | £000 |
|---|---|---|
| Immediately | Cost of machine | (100) |
| 1 year's time | Operating profit before depreciation | 20 |
| 2 years' time | Operating profit before depreciation | 40 |
| 3 years' time | Operating profit before depreciation | 60 |
| 4 years' time | Operating profit before depreciation | 60 |
| 5 years' time | Operating profit before depreciation | 20 |
| 5 years' time | Disposal proceeds | 20 |

Note that all of these figures are amounts of cash to be paid or received (we saw earlier that operating profit before depreciation is a rough measure of the cash flows from the project).

We can see that this investment will take three years before the £100,000 outlay is covered by the inflows. (This is still assuming that the cash flows occur at year ends.) Derivation of the payback period can be shown by calculating the cumulative cash flows as follows:

| Time | | Net cash flows £000 | Cumulative cash flows £000 | |
|---|---|---|---|---|
| Immediately | Cost of machine | (100) | (100) | |
| 1 year's time | Operating profit before depreciation | 20 | (80) | (−100 + 20) |
| 2 years' time | Operating profit before depreciation | 40 | (40) | (−80 + 40) |
| 3 years' time | Operating profit before depreciation | 60 | 20 | (−40 + 60) |
| 4 years' time | Operating profit before depreciation | 60 | 80 | (20 + 60) |
| 5 years' time | Operating profit before depreciation | 20 | 100 | (80 + 20) |
| 5 years' time | Disposal proceeds | 20 | 120 | (100 + 20) |

We can see that the cumulative cash flows become positive at the end of the third year. Had we assumed that the cash flows arise evenly over the year, the precise payback period would be:

$$2 \text{ years} + (^{40}/_{60}) \text{ years} = 2^2/_3 \text{ years}$$

where 40 represents the cash flow still required at the beginning of the third year to repay the initial outlay and 60 is the projected cash flow during the third year.

The following decision rules apply when using PP:

- For a project to be acceptable it should have a payback period no longer than a maximum payback period set by the business.
- If there were two (or more) competing projects whose payback periods were all shorter than the maximum payback period requirement, the project with the shorter (or shortest) payback period should be selected.

If, for example, Billingsgate Battery had a maximum acceptable payback period of four years, the project would be undertaken. A project with a longer payback period would not be acceptable.

## Activity 14.5

What is the payback period of the Chaotic Industries project from Activity 14.2?

The inflows and outflows are expected to be:

| Time | | Net cash flows £000 | Cumulative net cash flows £000 | |
|---|---|---|---|---|
| Immediately | Cost of vans | (150) | (150) | |
| 1 year's time | Saving before depreciation | 30 | (120) | (−150 + 30) |
| 2 years' time | Saving before depreciation | 30 | (90) | (−120 + 30) |
| 3 years' time | Saving before depreciation | 30 | (60) | (−90 + 30) |
| 4 years' time | Saving before depreciation | 30 | (30) | (−60 + 30) |
| 5 years' time | Saving before depreciation | 30 | 0 | (−30 + 30) |
| 6 years' time | Saving before depreciation | 30 | 30 | (0 + 30) |
| 6 years' time | Disposal proceeds from the vans | 30 | 60 | (30 + 30) |

The payback period here is five years; that is, it is not until the end of the fifth year that the vans will pay for themselves out of the savings that they are expected to generate.

The logic of using PP is that projects that can recoup their cost quickly are economically more attractive than those with longer payback periods. In other words, it emphasises liquidity.

The PP method has certain advantages. It is quick and easy to calculate. It can, also, be easily understood by managers. PP is an improvement on ARR in respect of the timing of the cash flows. It is not, however, a complete answer to the problem.

## Problems with PP

## Activity 14.6

In what respect is PP not a complete answer as a means of assessing investment opportunities? Consider the cash flows arising from three competing projects:

| Time | | Project 1 £000 | Project 2 £000 | Project 3 £000 |
|---|---|---|---|---|
| Immediately | Cost of machine | (200) | (200) | (200) |
| 1 year's time | Operating profit before depreciation | 70 | 20 | 70 |
| 2 years' time | Operating profit before depreciation | 60 | 20 | 100 |
| 3 years' time | Operating profit before depreciation | 70 | 160 | 30 |
| 4 years' time | Operating profit before depreciation | 80 | 30 | 200 |
| 5 years' time | Operating profit before depreciation | 50 | 20 | 440 |
| 5 years' time | Disposal proceeds | 40 | 10 | 20 |

(*Hint*: Again, the defect is not concerned with the ability of the manager to forecast future events. This is a problem, but it is a problem whatever approach we take.)

### Activity 14.6 (*continued*)

The PP for each project is three years and so the PP method would regard the projects as being equally acceptable. It cannot distinguish between those projects that pay back a significant amount early within the three-year payback period and those that do not.

In addition, this method ignores cash flows after the payback period. A decision maker concerned with increasing owners' wealth would greatly prefer Project 3 because the cash inflows are received earlier. In fact, most of the initial cost of making the investment has been repaid by the end of the second year. Furthermore, the cash inflows are greater in total.

The cumulative cash flows of each project in Activity 14.6 are set out in Figure 14.1.

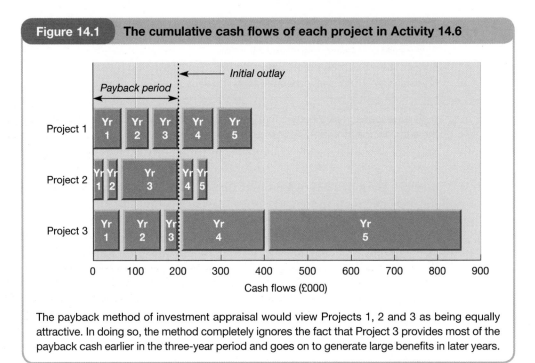

**Figure 14.1** **The cumulative cash flows of each project in Activity 14.6**

The payback method of investment appraisal would view Projects 1, 2 and 3 as being equally attractive. In doing so, the method completely ignores the fact that Project 3 provides most of the payback cash earlier in the three-year period and goes on to generate large benefits in later years.

We shall now consider some additional points concerning the PP method.

### Relevant information

We saw earlier that the PP method is simply concerned with how quickly the initial investment can be recouped. Cash flows arising beyond the payback period are ignored. While this neatly avoids the practical problems of forecasting cash flows over a long period, it means that not all relevant information may be taken into account.

### Risk

By favouring projects with a short payback period, the PP method appears to provide a means of dealing with the problem of risk. This is, however, a fairly crude approach to the problem. It looks only at the risk that the project will end earlier than expected. This is only one of many risk areas. What, for example, about the risk that the demand for the product may be less than expected? There are more systematic approaches to dealing with risk that can be used, which we shall look at later in the chapter.

## Wealth maximisation

Although the PP method takes some note of the timing of project costs and benefits, it is not concerned with maximising the wealth of the business owners. Instead, it favours projects that pay for themselves quickly.

## Required payback period

Managers must select a maximum acceptable payback period. As this cannot be objectively determined, it is really a matter of judgement. The maximum period can, therefore, vary from one business to the next.

**Real World 14.4** looks at a power saving device used by Tesco plc, the supermarket chain, and the payback period involved.

---

**Real World 14.4**

### It's payback time at Tesco    FT

According to the Confederation of British Industry, £8.5 billion a year is wasted on energy just in the UK. That adds up to about 22 million tonnes of $CO_2$ – or the equivalent of Scotland's total commercial carbon emissions in a year. There are a number of reasons why so much energy is wasted. But one is a mismatch between the electricity required to run equipment in organisations and the power that is delivered to their premises. That is where voltage power optimisation comes in – a technology that one company, power-Perfector, has a licence to sell in the UK.

Angus Robertson, its chief executive, points out that all electrical equipment intended for use on commercial three-phase circuits in Europe is designed to run on 380 volts – the equivalent of 220V in domestic, single-phase circuits. Yet the average voltage supplied in the UK is 419V (242 in single phase), a figure which cannot be changed without a whole-sale revamp of the grid, which is out on cost grounds. Mr Robertson explains the problem: 'Take an electric motor. If you put 419V into a motor rated at 380V it doesn't go faster or more efficiently. But it does have to dissipate the extra energy – mostly in the form of heat, which is wasted. If you go into a Tesco with one of our VPO units, the compressors for the refrigerators are not running so hot, so the air conditioning doesn't have to work so hard – so there's a compounding of benefits.'

There are further bonuses. 'We expect light bulbs to last twice as long,' says Mr Robertson. 'And when we installed a unit at Buxton Press, the decibel level dropped drastically. The electric motors were less hot, so making less noise. Maintenance intervals increased too.' The maintenance-free unit, which is fitted at the point where a three-phase power supply enters the building, can save up to 20 per cent in energy costs, says powerPerfector, depending on the quality of the supply and the types of electrical equipment in use.

Nationwide, the company says, it can provide an average 13 per cent kWh reduction, which, it says, means the approximate payback period for a supermarket is 18 months, an office two years and a school three years.

Tesco is putting in about 500 powerPerfector units this year, at a cost of about £25 million, as part of a rolling programme that will see the equipment in most of its 2,300 stores and distribution centres across the UK. 'We expect to save 5 to 8 per cent of each store's total energy usage,' says Bukky Adegbeyeni, head of the environmental team at the store chain. 'We expect our return on investment to be about 20 per cent, so we will achieve payback in five years.'

*Source:* Extracts from: 'Case study: power efficiency', R. Jaggi, FT.com, 25 November 2009.

# Net present value (NPV)

From what we have seen so far, it seems that to make sensible investment decisions, we need a method of appraisal that both:

● considers *all* of the costs and benefits of each investment opportunity; and
● makes a logical allowance for the *timing* of those costs and benefits.

The third of the four methods of investment appraisal, the **net present value (NPV)** method provides us with this.

Consider the Billingsgate Battery example's cash flows, which we should recall are:

| Time | | £000 |
|------|------|------|
| Immediately | Cost of machine | (100) |
| 1 year's time | Operating profit before depreciation | 20 |
| 2 years' time | Operating profit before depreciation | 40 |
| 3 years' time | Operating profit before depreciation | 60 |
| 4 years' time | Operating profit before depreciation | 60 |
| 5 years' time | Operating profit before depreciation | 20 |
| 5 years' time | Disposal proceeds | 20 |

Given a financial objective of maximising owners' wealth, it would be easy to assess this investment if all cash inflows and outflows were to occur immediately. It would then simply be a matter of adding up the cash inflows (total £220,000) and comparing them with the cash outflows (£100,000). This would lead us to conclude that the project should go ahead because the owners would be better off by £120,000. Of course, it is not as easy as this because time is involved. The cash outflow will occur immediately, whereas the cash inflows will arise at different times.

Time is an important issue because people do not normally see an amount paid out now as equivalent in value to the same amount being received in a year's time. Therefore, if we were offered £100 in one year's time in exchange for paying out £100 now, we would not be interested, unless we wished to do someone a favour.

## Activity (14.7)

Why would you see £100 to be received in a year's time as not equal in value to £100 to be paid immediately? (There are basically three reasons.)

The reasons are:

● interest lost
● risk
● inflation.

We shall now take a closer look at these three reasons in turn.

## Interest lost

If we are to be deprived of the opportunity to spend our money for a year, we could equally well be deprived of its use by placing it on deposit in a bank or building society.

By doing this, we could have our money back at the end of the year along with some interest earned. This interest, which is foregone if we do not place our money on deposit, represents an *opportunity cost*. As we saw in Chapter 8, an opportunity cost occurs where one course of action deprives us of the opportunity to derive some benefit from an alternative action.

An investment must exceed the opportunity cost of the funds invested if it is to be worthwhile. Therefore, if Billingsgate Battery Company sees putting the money in the bank on deposit as the alternative to investment in the machine, the return from investing in the machine must be better than that from investing in the bank. If this is not the case, there is no reason to buy the machine.

## Risk

All investments expose their investors to **risk**. Hence buying a machine, on the strength of estimates made before its purchase, exposes a business to risk. Things may not turn out as expected.

### Activity 14.8

Can you suggest some areas where things could go other than according to plan in the Billingsgate Battery Company example (basically, buying a machine and using it to render a service for five years)?

We have come up with the following:

- The machine might not work as well as expected; it might break down, leading to loss of the business's ability to provide the service.
- Sales of the service may not be as buoyant as expected.
- Labour costs may prove to be higher than expected.
- The sale proceeds of the machine could prove to be less than were estimated.

It is important to remember that the purchase decision must be taken *before* any of these things are known. It is only after the machine has been purchased that we find out whether, say, the forecast level of sales is going to be achieved. We can study reports and analyses of the market. We can commission sophisticated market surveys and advertise widely to promote sales. All these may give us more confidence in the likely outcome. Ultimately, however, we must decide whether to accept the risk that things will not turn out as expected in exchange for the opportunity to generate wealth.

We saw in Chapter 1 that people normally expect greater returns in exchange for taking on greater risk. Examples of this in real life are not difficult to find. One such example is that banks tend to charge higher rates of interest to borrowers whom the bank perceives as more risky. Those who can offer good security for a loan and who can point to a regular source of income, tend to be charged lower rates of interest.

Going back to Billingsgate Battery Company's investment opportunity, it is not enough to say that we should buy the machine providing the expected returns are higher than those from investing in a bank deposit. We should expect much greater returns than the bank deposit interest rate because of the much greater risk involved. The logical equivalent of investing in the machine would be an investment that is of similar risk. Determining how risky a particular project is and, therefore, how large the **risk premium** should be, is a difficult task. We shall consider this in more detail later in the chapter.

## Inflation

If we are to be deprived of £100 for a year, when we come to spend that money it will not buy the same amount of goods and services as it would have done a year earlier. Generally, we shall not be able to buy as many tins of baked beans or loaves of bread or bus tickets as before. This is because of the loss in the purchasing power of money, or **inflation**, which occurs over time. Investors will expect to be compensated for this loss of purchasing power. This will be on top of a return that takes account of what could be gained from an alternative investment of similar risk.

In practice, interest rates observable in the market tend to take inflation into account. This means that, rates offered to building society and bank depositors include an allowance for the expected rate of inflation.

## What will logical investors do?

To summarise, logical investors seeking to increase their wealth will only invest when they believe they will be adequately compensated for the loss of interest, for the loss in the purchasing power of money invested and for the risk that the expected returns may not materialise. This normally involves checking to see whether the proposed investment will yield a return greater than the basic rate of interest (which will include an allowance for inflation) plus an appropriate risk premium.

These three factors (interest lost, risk and inflation) are set out in Figure 14.2.

**Figure 14.2** **Factors influencing the return required by investors from a project**

There are three factors that influence the required return to investors (opportunity cost of finance).

Let us now return to the Billingsgate Battery Company example. We should recall that the cash flows expected from this investment are:

| Time | | £000 |
|------|------|------|
| Immediately | Cost of machine | (100) |
| 1 year's time | Operating profit before depreciation | 20 |
| 2 years' time | Operating profit before depreciation | 40 |
| 3 years' time | Operating profit before depreciation | 60 |
| 4 years' time | Operating profit before depreciation | 60 |
| 5 years' time | Operating profit before depreciation | 20 |
| 5 years' time | Disposal proceeds | 20 |

We have already seen that it is not enough simply to compare the basic cash inflows and outflows for the investment. Each of these cash flows must be expressed in similar terms, so that a direct comparison can be made between the sum of the inflows over time and the immediate £100,000 investment. Fortunately, we can do this.

Let us assume that, instead of making this investment, the business could make an alternative investment with similar risk and obtain a return of 20 per cent a year.

## Activity (14.9)

We know that Billingsgate Battery Company could alternatively invest its money at a rate of 20 per cent a year. How much do you judge the present (immediate) value of the expected first year receipt of £20,000 to be? In other words, if instead of having to wait a year for the £20,000, and being deprived of the opportunity to invest it at 20 per cent, you could have some money now, what sum to be received now would you regard as exactly equivalent to getting £20,000 but having to wait a year for it?

We should obviously be happy to accept a lower amount if we could get it immediately than if we had to wait a year. This is because we could invest it at 20 per cent (in the alternative project). Logically, we should be prepared to accept the amount that, with a year's income, will grow to £20,000. If we call this amount PV (for present value) we can say:

$$PV + (PV \times 20\%) = £20,000$$

that is, the amount plus income from investing the amount for the year equals the £20,000.

If we rearrange this equation we find:

$$PV \times (1 + 0.2) = £20,000$$

(Note that 0.2 is the same as 20 per cent, but expressed as a decimal.) Further rearranging gives:

$$PV = £20,000/(1 + 0.2) = £16.667$$

Therefore, logical investors who have the opportunity to invest at 20 per cent a year would not mind whether they have £16,667 now or £20,000 in a year's time. In this sense we can say that, given a 20 per cent alternative investment opportunity, the present value of £20,000 to be received in one year's time is £16,667.

If we derive the present value (PV) of each of the cash flows associated with Billingsgate's machine investment, we could easily make the direct comparison between the cost of making the investment (£100,000) and the various benefits that will derive from it in years 1 to 5.

Using the same logic as was used to derive the PV of a cash flow expected after one year, it can be shown that the PV of a particular cash flow is:

**PV of the cash flow of year $n$ = actual cash flow of year $n$ divided by $(1 + r)^n$**

where $n$ is the year of the cash flow (that is, how many years into the future) and $r$ is the opportunity financing cost expressed as a decimal (instead of as a percentage).

We have already seen how this works for the £20,000 inflow for year 1 for the Billingsgate project. For year 2 the calculation would be:

PV of year 2 cash flow (that is, £40,000) = £40,000/$(1 + 0.2)^2$ = £40,000/$(1.2)^2$
= £40,000/1.44 = £27,778

This means that the present value of the £40,000 to be received in two years' time is £27,778.

## Activity 14.10

See if you can show that an investor would find £27,778, receivable now, as equally acceptable to receiving £40,000 in two years' time, assuming that there is a 20 per cent investment opportunity.

The reasoning goes like this:

|  | £ |
|---|---|
| Amount available for immediate investment | 27,778 |
| Income for year 1 (20% × 27,778) | 5,556 |
|  | 33,334 |
| Income for year 2 (20% × 33,334) | 6,667 |
|  | 40,001 |

(The extra £1 is only a rounding error.)

This is to say that since the investor can turn £27,778 into £40,000 in two years, these amounts are equivalent. We can say that £27,778 is the present value of £40,000 receivable after two years (given a 20 per cent cost of finance).

Now let us calculate the present values of all of the cash flows associated with the Billingsgate machine project and, from them, the *net present value (NPV)* of the project as a whole.

The relevant cash flows and calculations are:

| Time | Cash flow £000 | Calculation of PV | PV £000 |
|---|---|---|---|
| Immediately (time 0) | (100) | (100)/$(1 + 0.2)^0$ | (100.00) |
| 1 year's time | 20 | 20/$(1 + 0.2)^1$ | 16.67 |
| 2 years' time | 40 | 40/$(1 + 0.2)^2$ | 27.78 |
| 3 years' time | 60 | 60/$(1 + 0.2)^3$ | 34.72 |
| 4 years' time | 60 | 60/$(1 + 0.2)^4$ | 28.94 |
| 5 years' time | 20 | 20/$(1 + 0.2)^5$ | 8.04 |
| 5 years' time | 20 | 20/$(1 + 0.2)^5$ | 8.04 |
| Net present value (NPV) |  |  | 24.19 |

Note that $(1 + 0.2)^0 = 1$.

Once again, we must decide whether the machine project is acceptable to the business. To help us, the following decision rules for NPV should be applied:

- If the NPV is positive the project should be accepted; if it is negative the project should be rejected.
- If there are two (or more) competing projects that have positive NPVs, the project with the higher (or highest) NPV should be selected.

In this case, the NPV is positive, so we should accept the project and buy the machine. The reasoning behind this decision rule is quite straightforward. Investing in the machine will make the business, and its owners, £24,190 better off than they would be by taking up the next best available opportunity. The gross benefits from investing in this machine are worth a total of £124,190 today. Since the business can 'buy' these benefits for just £100,000 today, the investment should be made. If, however, the present value of the gross benefits were below £100,000, it would be less than the cost of 'buying' those benefits and the opportunity should, therefore, be rejected.

## Activity (14.11)

What is the *maximum* the Billingsgate Battery Company would be prepared to pay for the machine, given the potential benefits of owning it?

The business would logically be prepared to pay up to £124,190 since the wealth of the owners of the business would be increased up to this price – although the business would prefer to pay as little as possible.

## Using present value tables

To deduce each PV in the Billingsgate Battery Company project, we took the relevant cash flow and multiplied it by $1/(1 + r)^n$. There is a slightly different way to do this. Tables exist that show values of this **discount factor** for a range of values of $r$ and $n$. Such a table appears at the end of this book, in Appendix F on page 810. Take a look at it.

Look at the column for 20 per cent and the row for one year. We find that the factor is 0.833. This means that the PV of a cash flow of £1 receivable in one year is £0.833. So the present value of a cash flow of £20,000 receivable in one year's time is £16,660 (that is, $0.833 \times £20,000$). This is the same result, ignoring rounding errors, as we found earlier by using the equation.

## Activity (14.12)

What is the NPV of the Chaotic Industries project from Activity 14.2, assuming a 15 per cent opportunity cost of finance (discount rate)? (Use the present value table in Appendix F, page 809)

Remember that the inflows and outflow are expected to be:

| Time | | £000 |
|---|---|---|
| Immediately | Cost of vans | (150) |
| 1 year's time | Saving before depreciation | 30 |
| 2 years' time | Saving before depreciation | 30 |
| 3 years' time | Saving before depreciation | 30 |
| 4 years' time | Saving before depreciation | 30 |
| 5 years' time | Saving before depreciation | 30 |
| 6 years' time | Saving before depreciation | 30 |
| 6 years' time | Disposal proceeds from the vans | 30 |

### Activity 14.12 (continued)

The calculation of the NPV of the project is as follows:

| Time | Cash flows £000 | Discount factor (15%) | Present value £000 |
|---|---|---|---|
| Immediately | (150) | 1.000 | (150.00) |
| 1 year's time | 30 | 0.870 | 26.10 |
| 2 years' time | 30 | 0.756 | 22.68 |
| 3 years' time | 30 | 0.658 | 19.74 |
| 4 years' time | 30 | 0.572 | 17.16 |
| 5 years' time | 30 | 0.497 | 14.91 |
| 6 years' time | 30 | 0.432 | 12.96 |
| 6 years' time | 30 | 0.432 | 12.96 |
| | | NPV | (23.49) |

## Activity 14.13

How would you interpret this result?

The fact that the project has a negative NPV means that the present values of the benefits from the investment are worth less than they cost. Any cost up to £126,510 (the present value of the benefits) would be worth paying, but not £150,000.

The present value table in Appendix F shows how the value of £1 diminishes as its receipt goes further into the future. Assuming an opportunity cost of finance of 20 per cent a year, £1 to be received immediately, obviously, has a present value of £1. However, as the time before it is to be received increases, the present value diminishes significantly, as is shown in Figure 14.3.

### The discount rate and the cost of capital

We have seen that the appropriate discount rate to use in NPV assessments is the opportunity cost of finance. This is, in effect, the cost to the business of the finance needed to fund the investment. It will normally be the cost of a mixture of funds (shareholders' funds and borrowings) employed by the business and is often referred to as the **cost of capital**. We shall refer to it as the cost of capital from now on.

## Why NPV is better

From what we have seen, NPV offers a better approach to appraising investment opportunities than either ARR or PP. This is because it fully takes account of each of the following:

- *The timing of the cash flows.* By discounting the various cash flows associated with each project according to when they are expected to arise, NPV takes account of the time value of money. Furthermore, as the discounting process incorporates the

| Figure 14.3 | Present value of £1 receivable at various times in the future, assuming an annual financing cost of 20 per cent |
| --- | --- |

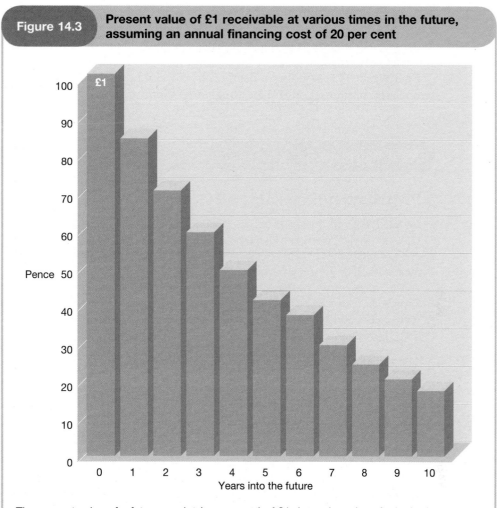

The present value of a future receipt (or payment) of £1 depends on how far in the future it will occur. Those that occur in the near future will have a larger present value than those occurring at a more distant point in time.

opportunity cost of capital, the net benefit *after* financing costs have been met is identified (as the NPV of the project).
- *The whole of the relevant cash flows*. NPV includes *all* of the relevant cash flows. They are treated differently according to their date of occurrence, but they are all taken into account. In this way, they all have an influence on the decision.
- *The objectives of the business*. NPV is the only method of appraisal in which the output of the analysis has a direct bearing on the wealth of the owners of the business. Positive NPVs enhance wealth; negative ones reduce it. Since we assume that private sector businesses seek to increase owners' wealth, NPV is superior to the other two methods (ARR and PP) that we have discussed so far.

## NPV's wider application

NPV is the most logical approach to making business decisions about investments in productive assets. It also provides the basis for valuing any economic asset, that is, any asset capable of yielding financial benefits. This definition will include such things as equity shares and loans. In fact, when we talk of *economic value*, we mean the value derived by adding together the discounted (present) values of all future cash flows from the asset concerned.

**Real World 14.5** describes a decision by a well-known business to invest further in two related businesses, and the estimated NPV of the savings that would result.

---

### Real World 14.5

#### Pepsi bottles it                                                  **FT**

PepsiCo, the soft drinks group, on Monday offered about $6 billion to buy the shares it does not already own in its two largest bottlers, Pepsi Bottling Group and PepsiAmericas. The US company's plan to consolidate its bottling business would give it control of 80 per cent of its North America beverage distribution volume.

The move comes as PepsiCo targets cost savings over the next three years to be re-invested in its beverages business. Although the company's US foods business is producing strong sales and profits, its US soft drinks business is struggling as sales of fizzy drinks and sports drinks have declined.

The move should allow Pepsi to find $200 million of annual cost savings, with a net present value of some $1.5 billion.

*Source:* Adapted from, 'Pepsi bottles it', Lex Column, FT.com, 20 April 2009.

---

## Internal rate of return (IRR)

This is the last of the four major methods of investment appraisal found in practice. It is closely related to the NPV method in that both involve discounting future cash flows. The **internal rate of return (IRR)** of an investment is the discount rate that, when applied to its future cash flows, will produce an NPV of precisely zero. In essence, it represents the yield from an investment opportunity.

---

### Activity (14.14)

We should recall that, when we discounted the cash flows of the Billingsgate Battery Company machine project at 20 per cent, we found that the NPV was a positive figure of £24,190 (see page 559). What does the NPV of the machine project tell us about the rate of return that the investment will yield for the business (that is, the project's IRR)?

The fact that the NPV is positive when discounting at 20 per cent implies that the rate of return that the project generates is more than 20 per cent. The fact that the NPV is a pretty large figure implies that the actual rate of return is quite a lot above 20 per cent. We should expect increasing the size of the discount rate to reduce NPV, because a higher discount rate gives a lower discounted figure.

---

IRR cannot usually be calculated directly. Iteration (trial and error) is the approach normally adopted. Doing this manually, however, is fairly laborious. Fortunately, computer spreadsheet packages can do this with ease.

Despite it being laborious, we shall now go on and derive the IRR for the Billingsgate project manually, to show how it works.

Let us try a higher rate, say 30 per cent and see what happens.

| Time | Cash flow £000 | Discount factor 30% | PV £000 |
|------|------|------|------|
| Immediately (time 0) | (100) | 1.000 | (100.00) |
| 1 year's time | 20 | 0.769 | 15.38 |
| 2 years' time | 40 | 0.592 | 23.68 |
| 3 years' time | 60 | 0.455 | 27.30 |
| 4 years' time | 60 | 0.350 | 21.00 |
| 5 years' time | 20 | 0.269 | 5.38 |
| 5 years' time | 20 | 0.269 | 5.38 |
| | | NPV | (1.88) |

By increasing the discount rate from 20 per cent to 30 per cent, we have reduced the NPV from £24,190 (positive) to £1,880 (negative). Since the IRR is the discount rate that will give us an NPV of exactly zero, we can conclude that the IRR of Billingsgate Battery Company's machine project is very slightly below 30 per cent. Further trials could lead us to the exact rate, but there is probably not much point, given the likely inaccuracy of the cash flow estimates. For most practical purposes, it is good enough to say that the IRR is about 30 per cent.

The relationship between the NPV method discussed earlier and the IRR is shown graphically in Figure 14.4 using the information relating to the Billingsgate Battery Company.

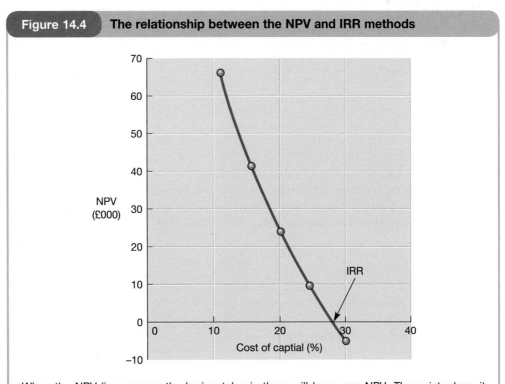

**Figure 14.4** The relationship between the NPV and IRR methods

When the NPV line crosses the horizontal axis there will be a zero NPV. The point where it crosses is the IRR.

In Figure 14.4, if the discount rate is equal to zero, the NPV will be the sum of the net cash flows. In other words, no account is taken of the time value of money. However, as the discount rate increases there is a corresponding decrease in the NPV of the project. When the NPV line crosses the horizontal axis there will be a zero NPV. That point represents the IRR.

## Activity (14.15)

What is the internal rate of return of the Chaotic Industries project from Activity 14.2? (*Hint*: Remember that you already know the NPV of this project at 15 per cent (from Activity 14.12).)

Since we know that, at a 15 per cent discount rate, the NPV is a relatively large negative figure, our next trial is using a lower discount rate, say 10 per cent:

| Time | Cash flows £000 | Discount factor (10% – from the table) | Present value £000 |
|---|---|---|---|
| Immediately | (150) | 1.000 | (150.00) |
| 1 year's time | 30 | 0.909 | 27.27 |
| 2 years' time | 30 | 0.826 | 24.78 |
| 3 years' time | 30 | 0.751 | 22.53 |
| 4 years' time | 30 | 0.683 | 20.49 |
| 5 years' time | 30 | 0.621 | 18.63 |
| 6 years' time | 30 | 0.564 | 16.92 |
| 7 years' time | 30 | 0.564 | 16.92 |
| | | NPV | (2.46) |

This figure is close to zero NPV. However, the NPV is still negative and so the precise IRR will be a little below 10 per cent.

We could undertake further trials to derive the precise IRR. If, however, we have to do this manually, further trials can be time consuming.

We can get an acceptable approximation to the answer fairly quickly by first calculating the change in NPV arising from a 1 per cent change in the discount rate. This can be done by taking the difference between the two trials (that is, 15 per cent and 10 per cent) that have already been carried out (in Activities 14.12 and 14.15):

| Trial | Discount factor % | Net present value £000 |
|---|---|---|
| 1 | 15 | (23.49) |
| 2 | 10 | (2.46) |
| Difference | 5 | 21.03 |

The change in NPV for every 1 per cent change in the discount rate will be:

$$(21.03/5) = 4.21$$

The amount by which the IRR would need to fall below the 10% discount rate, in order to achieve a zero NPV would therefore be:

$$[2.46/4.21] \times 1\% = 0.58\%$$

The IRR is therefore:

$$(10.00 - 0.58) = 9.42\%$$

To say that the IRR is about 9 or 10 per cent, however, is near enough for most purposes.

Note that this approach to obtaining a more accurate figure for IRR assumes a straight-line relationship between the discount rate and NPV. We can see from Figure 14.4 that this assumption is not strictly correct. Over a relatively short range, however, this simplifying assumption is not usually a problem and so we can still arrive at a reasonable approximation using the approach that we took.

In practice, most businesses have computer software packages that will derive a project's IRR very quickly. In practice, therefore, it is not usually necessary either to make a series of trial discount rates or to make the approximation just described.

The following decision rules are applied when using IRR:

- For any project to be acceptable, it must meet a minimum IRR requirement. This is often referred to as the *hurdle rate* and, logically, this should be the opportunity cost of capital.
- Where there are competing projects, the one with the higher (or highest) IRR should be selected.

**Real World 14.6** illustrates how the IRR from oil projects are sensitive to oil price changes.

---

### Real World 14.6

#### Oil businesses over a barrel                    FT

Total, the French oil company, said yesterday that oil prices had slipped to within sight of the threshold below which some of its most expensive projects will no longer be commercially viable. Total's extra heavy oil sands project in Canada requires an oil price of just below $90 a barrel to achieve a 12.5 per cent internal rate of return, while Total's developments in the deep waters off Angola need about $70 a barrel, the company revealed in a mid-year presentation. International oil prices yesterday traded at $102.10 on the New York Mercantile Exchange.

Chistophe de Margerie, Total's chief executive, warned there was no space for a windfall tax: He said that whatever the price, taxes were not a solution, but noted: "At $100 a barrel we need the money to train people and develop new energies, new discoveries, renewable energy and to tackle climate change." However, Richard Lines, head of petroleum economics at Wood Mackenzie, the industry consultants, said companies were making the same internal rate of return on big, capital intensive projects at $100 a barrel as they were four to five years ago at $40 because costs had risen so dramatically and fiscal terms deteriorated.

*Source*: 'Oil prices put projects at risk', C. Hoyos, FT.com, 12 September 2008.

**Real World 14.7** gives some examples of IRRs sought in practice.

## Problems with IRR

IRR has certain key attributes in common with NPV. All cash flows are taken into account and their timing is logically handled. The main problem of IRR, however, is that it does not directly address the question of wealth generation. It can therefore lead to the wrong decision being made. This is because the IRR approach will always rank a project with, for example, an IRR of 25 per cent above that of a project with an IRR of 20 per cent. Although accepting the project with the higher percentage return will often generate more wealth, this may not always be the case. This is because IRR completely ignores the *scale of investment*.

With a 15 per cent cost of capital, £15 million invested at 20 per cent for one year, will make us wealthier by £0.75 million (that is, $15 \times (20 - 15)\% = 0.75$). With the same cost of capital, £5 million invested at 25 per cent for one year will make us only £0.5 million (that is, $5 \times (25 - 15)\% = 0.50$). IRR does not recognise this.

**Activity (14.16)**

Which other investment appraisal method ignores the scale of investment?

We saw earlier that the ARR method suffers from this problem

Competing projects do not usually possess such large differences in scale and so IRR and NPV normally give the same signal. However, as NPV will always give the correct signal, it is difficult to see why any other method should be used.

A further problem with the IRR method is that it has difficulty handling projects with unconventional cash flows. In the examples studied so far, each project has a negative cash flow arising at the start of its life and then positive cash flows thereafter. In practice, however, a project may have both positive and negative cash flows at future points in its life. Such a pattern of cash flows can result in there being more than one IRR, or even no IRR at all. This would make the IRR method difficult to use, although it should be said that this problem is also quite rare in practice. This is never a problem for NPV, however.

## Some practical points

When undertaking an investment appraisal, there are several practical points to bear in mind:

- *Past costs*. As with all decisions, we should take account only of **relevant costs** in our analysis. This means that only costs that vary with the decision should be considered, as we discussed at length in Chapter 8. In other words, all past costs should be ignored as they cannot vary with the decision. A business may incur costs (such as development costs and market research costs) *before* the evaluation of an opportunity to launch a new product. As those costs have already been incurred, they should be disregarded, even though the amounts may be substantial. Costs that have already been committed but not yet paid should also be disregarded. Where a business has entered into a binding contract to incur a particular cost, it becomes in effect a past cost even though payment may not be due until some point in the future.
- *Common future costs*. It is not only past costs that do not vary with the decision; some future costs may also be the same. For example, the cost of raw materials may not vary with the decision whether to invest in a new piece of manufacturing plant or to continue to use existing plant.
- *Opportunity costs*. Opportunity costs arising from benefits forgone must be taken into account. For example, when considering a decision concerning whether or not to continue to use a machine already owned by the business, the realisable value of the machine might be an important **opportunity cost**.
- *Taxation*. Owners will be interested in the after-tax returns generated from the business. As a result, taxation will usually be an important consideration when making an investment decision. The profits from the project will be taxed, the capital investment may attract tax relief and so on. Tax is levied on these at significant rates. This means that, in real life, unless tax is formally taken into account, the wrong decision could easily be made. The timing of the tax outflow should also be taken into account when preparing the cash flows for the project.

- *Cash flows not profit flows*. We have seen that for the NPV, IRR and PP methods, it is cash flows rather than profit flows that are relevant to the assessment of investment projects. In an investment appraisal requiring the application of any of these methods, details of the profits for the investment period may be given. These need to be adjusted in order to derive the cash flows. We should remember that the operating profit *before* non-cash items (such as depreciation) is an approximation to the cash flows for the period. We should, therefore, work back to this figure.

    When the data are expressed in profit rather than cash flow terms, an adjustment in respect of working capital may also be necessary. Some adjustment should be made to take account of changes in working capital. For example, launching a new product may give rise to an increase in the net investment made in trade receivables and inventories less trade payables. This working capital investment would normally require an immediate outlay of cash. This outlay for additional working capital should be shown in the NPV calculations as an initial cash outflow. However, at the end of the life of the project, the additional working capital will be released. This divestment results in an effective inflow of cash at the end of the project. It should also be taken into account at the point at which it is received.

- *Year-end assumption*. In the examples and activities considered so far, we have assumed that cash flows arise at the end of the relevant year. This simplifying assumption is used to make the calculations easier. (It is perfectly possible, however, to deal more precisely with the timing of the cash flows.) As we saw earlier, this assumption is clearly unrealistic, as money will have to be paid to employees on a weekly or monthly basis, credit customers will pay within a month or two of buying the product or service and so on. It is probably not a serious distortion, however. We should be clear that there is nothing about any of the four appraisal methods that demands that this assumption be made.

- *Interest payments*. When using discounted cash flow techniques (NPV and IRR), interest payments should not be taken into account in deriving cash flows for the period. Discounting already takes account of the costs of financing. To include interest charges in deriving cash flows for the period would therefore be double counting.

- *Other factors*. Investment decision making must not be viewed as simply a mechanical exercise. The results derived from a particular investment appraisal method will be only one input to the decision-making process. There may be broader issues connected to the decision that have to be taken into account but which may be difficult or impossible to quantify.

The reliability of the forecasts and the validity of the assumptions used in the evaluation will also have a bearing on the final decision.

## Activity (14.17)

The directors of Manuff (Steel) Ltd are considering closing one of the business's factories. There has been a reduction in the demand for the products made at the factory in recent years. The directors are not optimistic about the long-term prospects for these products. The factory is situated in an area where unemployment is high.

The factory is leased with four years of the lease remaining. The directors are uncertain whether the factory should be closed immediately or at the end of the period of the lease. Another business has offered to sublease the premises from Manuff (Steel) Ltd at a rental of £40,000 a year for the remainder of the lease period.

The machinery and equipment at the factory cost £1,500,000. The value at which they appear in the statement of financial position is £400,000. In the event of immediate closure, the machinery and equipment could be sold for £220,000. The working capital at the factory is £420,000. It could be liquidated for that amount immediately, if required. Alternatively, the working capital can be liquidated in full at the end of the lease period. Immediate closure would result in redundancy payments to employees of £180,000.

If the factory continues in operation until the end of the lease period, the following operating profits (losses) are expected:

|  | Year 1 £000 | Year 2 £000 | Year 3 £000 | Year 4 £000 |
|---|---|---|---|---|
| Operating profit (loss) | 160 | (40) | 30 | 20 |

These figures are derived after deducting a charge of £90,000 a year for depreciation of machinery and equipment. The residual value of the machinery and equipment at the end of the lease period is estimated at £40,000.

Redundancy payments are expected to be £150,000 at the end of the lease period if the factory continues in operation. The business has an annual cost of capital of 12 per cent. Ignore taxation.

*Required:*
(a) Determine the relevant cash flows arising from a decision to continue operations until the end of the lease period rather than to close immediately.
(b) Calculate the net present value of continuing operations until the end of the lease period, rather than closing immediately.
(c) What other factors might the directors take into account before making a final decision on the timing of the factory closure?
(d) State, with reasons, whether or not the business should continue to operate the factory until the end of the lease period.

Your answer should be:

(a) Relevant cash flows

|  | Years | | | | |
|---|---|---|---|---|---|
|  | *0* £000 | *1* £000 | *2* £000 | *3* £000 | *4* £000 |
| Operating cash flows (Note 1) |  | 250 | 50 | 120 | 110 |
| Sale of machinery (Note 2) | (220) |  |  |  | 40 |
| Redundancy costs (Note 3) | 180 |  |  |  | (150) |
| Sublease rentals (Note 4) |  | (40) | (40) | (40) | (40) |
| Working capital invested (Note 5) | (420) |  |  |  | 420 |
|  | (460) | 210 | 10 | 80 | 380 |

*Notes:*

1. Each year's operating cash flows are calculated by adding back the depreciation charge for the year to the operating profit for the year. In the case of the operating loss, the depreciation charge is deducted.
2. In the event of closure, machinery could be sold immediately. As a result, an opportunity cost of £220,000 is incurred if operations continue.
3. By continuing operations, there will be a saving in immediate redundancy costs of £180,000. However, redundancy costs of £150,000 will be paid in four years' time.
4. By continuing operations, the opportunity to sublease the factory will be foregone.
5. Immediate closure would mean that working capital could be liquidated. By continuing operations this opportunity is foregone. However, working capital can be liquidated in four years' time.

→

**Activity 14.17 (continued)**

(b)

| | Years | | | | |
|---|---|---|---|---|---|
| | 0 | 1 | 2 | 3 | 4 |
| Discount factors (12 per cent) | 1.000 | 0.893 | 0.797 | 0.712 | 0.636 |
| Present value | (460) | 187.5 | 8.0 | 57.0 | 241.7 |
| Net present value | 34.2 | | | | |

(c) Other factors that may influence the decision include:
- *The overall strategy of the business.* The business may need to set the decision within a broader context. It may be necessary to manufacture the products at the factory because they are an integral part of the business's product range. The business may wish to avoid redundancies in an area of high unemployment for as long as possible.
- *Flexibility.* A decision to close the factory is probably irreversible. If the factory continues, however, there may be a chance that the prospects for the factory will brighten in the future.
- *Creditworthiness of sub-lessee.* The business should investigate the creditworthiness of the sub-lessee. Failure to receive the expected sublease payments would make the closure option far less attractive.
- *Accuracy of forecasts.* The forecasts made by the business should be examined carefully. Inaccuracies in the forecasts or any underlying assumptions may change the expected outcomes.

(d) The NPV of the decision to continue operations rather than close immediately is positive. Hence, shareholders would be better off if the directors took this course of action. The factory should therefore continue in operation rather than close down. This decision is likely to be welcomed by employees and would allow the business to maintain its flexibility.

The main methods of investment appraisal are summarised in Figure 14.5.

**Figure 14.5** **The main investment appraisal methods**

The figure shows the four investment appraisal methods discussed in the chapter.

# Investment appraisal in practice

Many surveys have been conducted in the UK, and elsewhere in the world, into the methods of investment appraisal used by businesses. They have shown the following features:

- Businesses tend to use more than one method to assess each investment decision.
- The discounting methods (NPV and IRR) have become increasingly popular over time. NPV and IRR are now the most popular of the four methods.
- PP continues to be popular and, to a lesser extent, so does ARR. This is despite the theoretical shortcomings of both of these methods.
- Larger businesses tend to rely more heavily on discounting methods than smaller businesses.

**Real World 14.8** shows the results of a survey of a number of UK manufacturing businesses concerning their use of investment appraisal methods.

---

**Real World 14.8**

### A survey of UK business practice

Senior financial managers at 83 of the UK's largest manufacturing businesses were asked about the investment appraisal methods used to evaluate both strategic and non-strategic projects. Strategic projects usually aim to increase or change the competitive capabilities of a business, such as introducing a new manufacturing process.

| Method | Non-strategic projects Mean score | Strategic projects Mean score |
|---|---|---|
| Net present value | 3.6829 | 3.9759 |
| Payback | 3.4268 | 3.6098 |
| Internal rate of return | 3.3293 | 3.7073 |
| Accounting rate of return | 1.9867 | 2.2667 |

Response scale 1 = never, 2 = rarely, 3 = often, 4 = mostly, 5 = always

We can see that, for both non-strategic and for strategic investments, the NPV method is the most popular. As the sample consists of large businesses (nearly all with annual total sales revenue in excess of £100 million), a fairly sophisticated approach to evaluation might be expected. Nevertheless, for non-strategic investments, the payback method comes second in popularity. It drops to third place for strategic projects.

The survey also found that 98 per cent of respondents used more than one method and 88 per cent used more than three methods of investment appraisal.

*Source:* Based on information in, 'Strategic capital investment decision-making: A role for emergent analysis tools? A study of practice in large UK manufacturing companies', F. Alkaraan, and D. Northcott, *The British Accounting Review* 38, 2006, p. 159.

---

A survey of large businesses in five leading industrialised countries, including the UK, also shows considerable support for the NPV and IRR methods. There is less support for the payback method but, nevertheless, it still seems to be fairly widely used. **Real World 14.9** sets out some key findings.

## Real World 14.9

### A multinational survey of business practice

A survey of investment and financing practices in five different countries was carried out by Cohen and Yagil. This survey, based on a sample of the largest 300 businesses in each country, revealed the following concerning the popularity of three of the investment appraisal methods discussed in this chapter.

**Frequency of the use of investment appraisal techniques**

| Average | Japan | Canada | Germany | UK | US | |
|---------|-------|--------|---------|------|------|----------------|
| 3.93 | 3.29 | 4.15 | 4.08 | 4.16 | 4.00 | IRR |
| 3.80 | 3.57 | 4.09 | 3.50 | 4.00 | 3.88 | NPV |
| 3.55 | 3.52 | 3.57 | 3.33 | 3.89 | 3.46 | Payback period |

Response scale 1 = Never 5 = Always

Key findings of the survey include the following:

- IRR is more popular than NPV in all countries, except Japan. The difference between the popularity of the two methods, however, is not statistically significant.
- Managers of UK businesses use investment appraisal techniques the most, while managers of Japanese businesses use them the least. This may be related to business traditions within each country.
- There is a positive relationship between business size and the popularity of the IRR and NPV methods. This may be related to the greater experience and understanding of financial theory of managers of larger businesses.

Source: 'A multinational survey of corporate financial policies', G. Cohen, and J. Yagil, Working Paper, Haifa University, 2007.

## Activity (14.18)

Earlier in the chapter, we discussed the limitations of the PP method. Can you suggest reasons that might explain why it is still a reasonably popular method of investment appraisal among managers?

There seem to be several possible reasons:

- PP is easy to understand and use.
- It can avoid the problems of forecasting far into the future.
- It gives emphasis to the early cash flows when there is greater certainty concerning the accuracy of their predicted value.
- It emphasises the importance of liquidity. Where a business has liquidity problems, a short payback period for a project is likely to appear attractive.

The popularity of PP may suggest a lack of sophistication by managers, concerning investment appraisal. This criticism is most often made against managers of smaller businesses. This point is borne out by both of the surveys discussed in Real Worlds 14.9

and 14.10, which have found that smaller businesses are much less likely to use discounted cash flow methods (NPV and IRR) than are larger ones. Other surveys have tended to reach a similar conclusion.

IRR may be popular because it expresses outcomes in percentage terms rather than in absolute terms. This form of expression seems to be preferred by managers, despite the problems of percentage measures that we discussed earlier. This may be because managers are used to using percentage figures as targets (for example, return on capital employed).

**Real World 14.10** shows extracts from the 2010 annual report of a well-known business: Rolls-Royce plc, the builder of engines for aircraft and other purposes.

---

### Real World 14.10

## The use of NPV at Rolls-Royce

In its 2010 annual report and accounts, Rolls-Royce plc stated that:

> The Group continues to subject all investments to rigorous examination of risks and future cash flows to ensure that they create shareholder value. All major investments require Board approval.
> The Group has a portfolio of projects at different stages of their life cycles. Discounted cash flow analysis of the remaining life of projects is performed on a regular basis.

*Source*: Rolls-Royce plc Annual Report 2010, p. 51.

---

Rolls-Royce makes clear that it uses NPV (the report refers to creating shareholder value and to discounted cash flow, which strongly imply NPV). It is interesting to note that Rolls-Royce not only assesses new projects but also reassesses existing ones. This must be a sensible commercial approach. Businesses should not continue with existing projects unless those projects have a positive NPV based on future cash flows. Just because a project seemed to have a positive NPV before it started does not mean that this will persist, in the light of changing circumstances. Activity 14.17 (page 568) considered a decision to close down a project.

---

### Self-assessment question 14.1

Beacon Chemicals plc is considering buying some equipment to produce a chemical named X14. The new equipment's capital cost is estimated at £100 million. If its purchase is approved now, the equipment can be bought and production can commence by the end of this year. £50 million has already been spent on research and development work. Estimates of revenues and costs arising from the operation of the new equipment are:

|  | Year 1 | Year 2 | Year 3 | Year 4 | Year 5 |
|---|---|---|---|---|---|
| Sales price (£/litre) | 100 | 120 | 120 | 100 | 80 |
| Sales volume (million litres) | 0.8 | 1.0 | 1.2 | 1.0 | 0.8 |
| Variable cost (£/litre) | 50 | 50 | 40 | 30 | 40 |
| Fixed cost (£000) | 30 | 30 | 30 | 30 | 30 |

**Self-assessment question 14.1 (*continued*)**

If the equipment is bought, sales of some existing products will be lost resulting in a loss of contribution of £15 million a year, over the life of the equipment.

The accountant has informed you that the fixed cost includes depreciation of £20 million a year on the new equipment. It also includes an allocation of £10 million for fixed overheads. A separate study has indicated that if the new equipment were bought, additional overheads, excluding depreciation, arising from producing the chemical would be £8 million a year. Production would require additional working capital of £30 million.

For the purposes of your initial calculations ignore taxation.

*Required:*

(a) Deduce the relevant annual cash flows associated with buying the equipment.

(b) Deduce the payback period.

(c) Calculate the net present value using a discount rate of 8 per cent.

(*Hint*: You should deal with the investment in working capital by treating it as a cash outflow at the start of the project and an inflow at the end.)

**The answer to this question can be found at the back of the book on page 741.**

# Investment appraisal and strategic planning

So far, we have tended to view investment opportunities as unconnected, independent, events. In practice, however, successful businesses are those that set out a clear strategic framework for the selection of investment projects in the way that was described in Chapter 1. Unless this framework is in place, it may be difficult to identify those projects that are likely to generate a positive NPV. The best investment projects are usually those that match the business's internal strengths (for example, skills, experience, access to finance) with the opportunities available. In areas where this match does not exist, other businesses, for which the match does exist, are likely to have a distinct competitive advantage. This means that they will be able to provide the product or service at a better price and/or quality.

Setting out the framework just described is an essential part of *strategic planning*. In practice, strategic plans often have a time span of around five years. It involves asking 'where do we want our business to be in five years' time and how can we get there?' It will set the appropriate direction in terms of products, markets, financing and so on, to ensure that the business is best placed to generate profitable investment opportunities.

**Real World 14.11** shows how easyJet made an investment that fitted its strategic objectives.

**Real World 14.11**

**easyFit**                                                                                           **FT**

easyJet, the UK budget airline, bought a small rival airline, GB Airways Ltd (GB) in late 2007 for £103m. According to an article in the *Financial Times*:

GB is a good strategic fit for easyJet. It operates under a British Airways franchise from Gatwick, which happens to be easyJet's biggest base. The deal makes easyJet the single largest passenger carrier at the UK airport. There is plenty of scope for scale economies in purchasing and back office functions. Moreover, easyJet should be able to boost GB's profitability by switching the carrier to its low-cost business model . . . easyJet makes an estimated £4 a passenger, against GB's £1. Assuming easyJet can drag up GB to its own levels of profitability, the company's value to the low-cost carrier is roughly four times its standalone worth.

The article makes the point that this looks like a good investment for easyJet, because of the strategic fit. For a business other than easyJet, the lack of strategic fit may well have meant that buying GB for exactly the same price of £103 million would not have been a good investment.

*Source*: 'Easy ride', Chris Hughes, 26 October 2007, FT. com.

# Dealing with risk

As already mentioned, all investment projects are risky: there is a chance that what is forecast to happen will not actually occur. Risk can be particularly important in the context of investment decisions because of the timescales and amounts involved. Investment projects may be carried out over long periods and may involve very large sums. If things go wrong, therefore, the impact can be both significant and lasting.

There are various approaches to dealing with risk. We shall now consider one of the most popular of these.

## Sensitivity analysis

**Sensitivity analysis** involves an examination of the key input values affecting an investment project to see how changes in each input might influence its viability.

First, the investment project is appraised, using the best estimates for each of the input factors (for example, labour cost, material cost, discount rate, and so on). Assuming that the NPV is positive, the estimate used for each input factor is then examined to see how far it could be changed before the project becomes no longer viable for that reason alone.

Let us suppose that the NPV for an investment in a machine to provide a particular service is a positive value. To carry out a sensitivity analysis on this project, we would consider each of the key input factors, in turn. These may include

- initial outlay for the machine;
- sales volume and selling price;
- relevant operating costs;
- life of the project; and
- financing costs (to be used as the discount rate).

We try to find the value that each factor could have before the NPV figure becomes negative (that is, the value for the factor at which the NPV is zero). The difference between the value for each factor at which the NPV equals zero and its estimated value represents the 'margin of safety' for that factor. The factors affecting the sensitivity of a particular NPV analysis are set out in Figure 14.6.

**Figure 14.6** Factors affecting the sensitivity of NPV calculations

Sensitivity analysis involves identifying the key factors that affect the project. In the figure, six factors have been identified for the particular project. (In practice, the key factors are likely to vary between projects.) Once identified, each factor will be examined in turn to find the value it should have for the project to have a zero NPV.

As a result of carrying out a sensitivity analysis, the decision maker is able to get a 'feel' for the project, which otherwise might not be possible. A computer spreadsheet model of the project can be very helpful in carrying out sensitivity analysis as it then becomes easy to try various values for the input factors and to see the effect of each.

Example 14.3 illustrates a sensitivity analysis and is straightforward enough to be undertaken without recourse to a spreadsheet model.

**Example 14.3**

S. Saluja (Property Developers) Ltd intends to bid at an auction, to be held today, for a manor house that has fallen into disrepair. The auctioneer believes that the house will be sold for about £450,000. The business wishes to renovate the property and to divide it into flats, to be sold for £150,000 each. The renovation will be in two stages and will cover a two-year period. Stage 1 will cover the first year of the project. It will cost £500,000 and the six flats completed during this stage are expected to be sold for a total of £900,000 at the end of the first year. Stage 2 will cover the second year of the project. It will cost £300,000 and the three remaining flats are expected to be sold at the end of the second year for a total of £450,000. If the business buys the property, the cost of renovation will be the subject of a binding contract with local builders. There is, however, some uncertainty over the remaining input values. The business estimates its cost of capital at 12 per cent a year.

**Required:**
(a) What is the NPV of the proposed project?
(b) Assuming none of the other inputs deviates from the best estimates provided:
  (1) What auction price would have to be paid for the manor house to cause the project to have a zero NPV?

(2) What cost of capital would cause the project to have a zero NPV?

(3) What is the sale price of each of the flats that would cause the project to have a zero NPV? (Each flat is projected to be sold for the same price: £150,000.)

(c) Comment on your calculations carried out in answering (b).

## Solution

(a) The NPV of the proposed project is:

|  | Cash flows £ | Discount factor 12% | Present value £ |
|---|---|---|---|
| Year 1 (£900,000 – £500,000) | 400,000 | 0.893 | 357,200 |
| Year 2 (£450,000 – £300,000) | 150,000 | 0.797 | 119,550 |
| Initial outlay |  |  | (450,000) |
| Net present value |  |  | 26,750 |

(b) (1)  To obtain a zero NPV, the auction price would have to be £26,750 higher than the current estimate – that is, a total price of £476,750. This is about 6 per cent above the current estimated price.

(2)  As there is a positive NPV, the cost of capital that would cause the project to have a zero NPV must be higher than 12 per cent. Let us try 20 per cent.

|  | Cash flows £ | Discount factor 20% | Present value £ |
|---|---|---|---|
| Year 1 (£900,000 – £500,000) | 400,000 | 0.833 | 333,200 |
| Year 2 (£450,000 – £300,000) | 150,000 | 0.694 | 104,100 |
| Initial outlay |  |  | (450,000) |
| Net present value |  |  | (12,700) |

As the NPV using a 20 per cent discount rate is negative, the 'break-even' cost of capital lies somewhere between 12 per cent and 20 per cent. A reasonable approximation is obtained as follows:

|  | Discount rate % | Net present value £ |
|---|---|---|
|  | 12 | 26,750 |
|  | 20 | (12,700) |
| Difference | 8 | 39,450 |

The change in NPV for every 1 per cent change in the discount rate will be:

$$39,450/8 = £4,931$$

The amount by which the discount rate would need to fall below 20%, in order to achieve a zero NPV, would therefore be:

$$12,700/4,931 = 2.6\%$$

The cost of capital (that is, the discount rate) would, therefore, have to be 17.4 per cent (20.0 – 2.6) for the project to have a zero NPV.

→

This calculation is, of course, the same as that used earlier in the chapter, when calculating the IRR of the project. In other words, 17.4 per cent is the IRR of the project.

(3) To obtain a zero NPV, the sale price of each flat must be reduced so that the NPV is reduced by £26,750. In year 1, six flats are sold and in year 2, three flats. The discount factor at the 12 per cent rate for year 1 is 0.893 and for year 2 is 0.797. We can derive the fall in price per flat (Y) to give a zero NPV by using the equation:

$$(6Y \times 0.893) + (3Y \times 0.797) = £26,750$$
$$Y = £3,452$$

The sale price of each flat necessary to obtain a zero NPV is therefore:

$$£150,000 - £3,452 = £146,548$$

This represents a fall in the estimated price of 2.3 per cent.

(c) These calculations indicate that the auction price would have to be about 6 per cent above the estimated price before a zero NPV is obtained. The margin of safety is, therefore, not very high for this factor. In practice this should not represent a real risk because the business could withdraw from the bidding if the price rises to an unacceptable level.

The other two factors represent more real risks.

Only after the project is at a very late stage can the business be sure as to what actual price per flat will prevail. It would be unusual to be able to have fixed contracts for sale of all of the flats before the auction. The calculations reveal that the price of the flats would only have to fall by 2.3 per cent from the estimated price before the NPV is reduced to zero. Hence, the margin of safety for this factor is very small.

The cost of capital is less sensitive to changes. There would have to be an increase from 12 per cent to 17.4 per cent before the project produced a zero NPV. It may be possible to raise finance for the project at a rate fixed before the auction of the house. However, even if the funding cost cannot be fixed in advance, the cost of capital seems not a very sensitive factor.

It seems from the calculations that the sale price of the flats is the key sensitive factor to consider. A careful re-examination of the market value of the flats seems appropriate before a final decision is made.

A slightly different form of sensitivity analysis from that just described is to pose a series of 'what if?' questions. This can help to see how possible changes to each input factor will affect the viability of the investment project. When considering sales, for example, the following 'what if?' questions may be asked:

- What if sales volume is 5 per cent higher than expected?
- What if sales volume is 10 per cent lower than expected?
- What if sales price is reduced by 15 per cent?
- What if sales price could be increased by 20 per cent?

While this form of sensitivity analysis also examines the effect of changes in each key factor, it does not seek to find the point at which a change makes the project no longer viable.

There are three major drawbacks with the use of sensitivity analysis:

● It does not give managers clear decision rules concerning acceptance or rejection of the project and so they must rely on their own judgement.
● It does not provide any indication of the likelihood that a particular change to an input factor will actually occur.
● It is a static form of analysis. Only one input is considered at a time, while the rest are held constant. In practice, however, it is likely that more than one input value will differ from the best estimates provided. Even so, it would be possible to deal with changes in various inputs simultaneously, were the project data put onto a spreadsheet model. This approach, where more than one variable is altered at a time, is known as **scenario building**.

**Real World 14.12** describes the evaluation of a mining project that incorporated sensitivity analysis to test the robustness of the findings.

### Real World 14.12

#### Golden opportunity

In a news release, Hochschild Mining plc announced positive results from an independent study of the profitability of its Azuca project in southern Peru. The project involves mining for gold and silver. The business provided calculations based on the most likely outcome (the base case) along with sensitivity analysis of key variables. These variables were the estimated prices for gold and silver and the discount rate to be applied.

The base case is shown in the first column of figures. The other three columns show the position if other assumptions are made about the prices of gold and silver.

The following results were obtained:

**Azuca project sensitivity analysis**

| | | | | |
|---|---|---|---|---|
| Gold price ($/ounce) | $1,000 | $1,100 | $1,200 | $1,300 |
| Silver price ($/ounce) | $17.00 | $18.70 | $20.40 | $21.90 |
| IRR (%) | 21% | 30% | 38% | 46% |
| Cash flow ($m) | $107m | $155m | $204m | $247m |
| NPV (5% discount rate) | $61m | $97m | $133m | $165m |
| NPV (10% discount rate) | $32m | $60m | $87m | $112m |

Source: 'Positive scoping study at 100% owned Azuca project in Peru', News release, Hochschild Mining plc, 30 September 2010 (www.hochschildmining).

## Managing investment projects

So far, we have been concerned with the process of carrying out the necessary calculations that enable managers to select among already identified investment opportunities. Though the assessment of projects is undoubtedly important, we must bear in mind that it is only *part* of the process of investment decision making. There are other important aspects that managers must also consider.

It is possible to see the investment process as a sequence of five stages, each of which managers must consider. The five stages are set out in Figure 14.7. We shall now consider these.

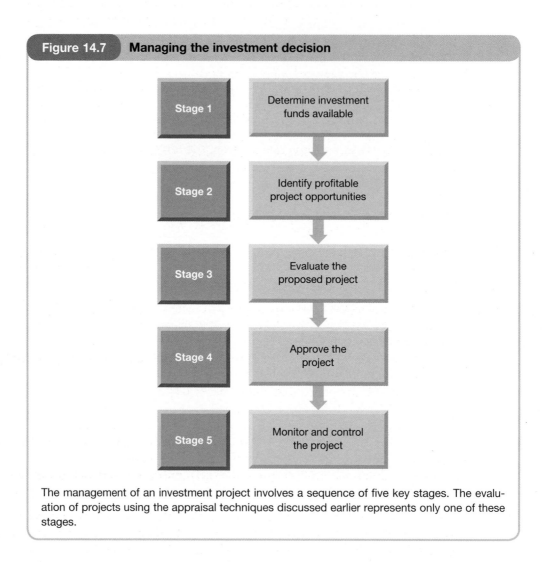

**Figure 14.7** **Managing the investment decision**

Stage 1 — Determine investment funds available

Stage 2 — Identify profitable project opportunities

Stage 3 — Evaluate the proposed project

Stage 4 — Approve the project

Stage 5 — Monitor and control the project

The management of an investment project involves a sequence of five key stages. The evaluation of projects using the appraisal techniques discussed earlier represents only one of these stages.

## Stage 1: Determine investment funds available

The amount of funds available for investment may be limited by the external market for funds or by internal management. In practice, it is often the business's own senior managers that restrict the amount available, perhaps because they lack confidence in the business's ability to handle higher levels of investment. In either case, it may mean that the funds will not be sufficient to finance all of the apparently profitable investment opportunities available. This shortage of investment funds is known as **capital rationing**. When it arises, managers are faced with the task of deciding on the most profitable use of those funds available.

## Stage 2: Identify profitable project opportunities

A vital part of the investment process is the search for profitable investment opportunities. The business should carry out methodical routines for identifying feasible projects. This may be done through a research and development department or by some other means. Failure to do so will inevitably lead to the business losing its competitive position with respect to product development, production methods or market penetration. To help identify good investment opportunities, some businesses provide financial incentives to members of staff who come forward with good investment proposals. The search process will, however, usually involve looking outside the business to identify changes in technology, customer demand, market conditions, and so on. Information will need to be gathered and this may take some time, particularly for unusual or non-routine investment opportunities.

It has been argued that Stages 1 and 2 should be reversed. This is because, in theory, finance can always be found for any profitable investment opportunities.

## Stage 3: Evaluate the proposed project

If management is to agree to the investment of funds in a project, that project's proposal must be rigorously screened. For larger projects, this will involve providing answers to a number of questions, including:

- What are the nature and purpose of the project?
- Does the project align with the overall strategy and objectives of the business?
- How much finance is required?
- What other resources (such as expertise, work space, and so on) are required for successful completion of the project?
- How long will the project last and what are its key stages?
- What is the expected pattern of cash flows?
- What are the major problems associated with the project and how can they be overcome?
- What is the NPV of the project? If capital is rationed, how does the NPV of this project compare with that of other opportunities available?
- Have risk and inflation been taken into account in the appraisal process and, if so, what are the results?

The ability and commitment of those responsible for proposing and managing the project will be vital to its success. This means that, when evaluating a new project, one consideration will be the quality of those proposing it. Senior managers may decide not to support a project that appears profitable on paper if they lack confidence in the ability of key managers to see it through to completion.

## Stage 4: Approve the project

Once the managers responsible for investment decision making are satisfied that the project should be undertaken, formal approval can be given. However, a decision on a project may be postponed if senior managers need more information from those proposing the project, or if revisions are required to the proposal. Proposals may be rejected if they are considered unprofitable or likely to fail. Before rejecting a proposal, however, the implications of not pursuing the project for such areas as market share, staff morale and existing business operations must be carefully considered.

## Stage 5: Monitor and control the project

Making a decision to invest in, say, the plant needed to provide a new service does not automatically cause the investment to be made and provision of the service to go smoothly ahead. Managers will need to manage the project actively through to completion. This, in turn, will require further information-gathering exercises.

Much of the control of a project would be through the routine budgetary control procedures that we met in Chapter 13. Management should also receive progress reports at regular intervals concerning the project. These reports should provide information relating to the actual cash flows for each stage of the project, which can then be compared against the forecast figures provided when the proposal was submitted for approval. The reasons for significant variations should be ascertained and corrective action taken where possible. Any changes in the expected completion date of the project or any expected variations in future cash flows from budget should be reported immediately; in extreme cases, managers may even abandon the project if circumstances appear to have changed dramatically for the worse.

Project management techniques (for example, critical path analysis) should be employed wherever possible and their effectiveness reported to senior management.

An important part of the control process is a **post-completion audit** of the project. This is, in essence, a review of the project performance to see if it lived up to expectations and whether any lessons can be learned from the way that the investment process was carried out. In addition to an evaluation of financial costs and benefits, non-financial measures of performance, such as the ability to meet deadlines and levels of quality achieved, should also be reported. We should recall that total life-cycle costing, which we discussed in Chapter 11, is based on similar principles.

The fact that a post-completion audit is an integral part of the management of the project should also encourage those who submit projects to use realistic estimates.

**Real World 14.13** provides some evidence of a need for greater realism.

---

**Real World 14.13**

### Looking on the bright side

McKinsey and Co, the management consultants, surveyed 2,500 senior managers worldwide during the spring of 2007. The managers were asked their opinions on investments made by their businesses in the previous three years. The general opinion is that estimates for the investment decision inputs had been too optimistic. For example sales levels had been overestimated in about 50 per cent of cases, but underestimated in less than 20 per cent of cases. It is not clear whether the estimates were sufficiently inaccurate to call into question the decision that had been made.

The survey goes on to ask about the extent that investments made seemed, in the light of the actual outcomes, to have been mistakes. Managers felt that 19 per cent of investments that had been made should not have gone ahead. On the other hand, they felt that 31 per cent of rejected projects should have been taken up. Managers also felt that 'good money was thrown after bad' in that existing investments that were not performing well were continuing to be supported in a significant number of cases.

*Source*: Based on information in 'How companies spend their money', A McKinsey Global Survey, www.theglobalmarketer.com, 2007.

Other studies confirm a tendency among managers to use over-optimistic estimates when preparing investment proposals. (See reference 1 at the end of the chapter.) It seems that sometimes this is done deliberately in an attempt to secure project approval. Where over-optimistic estimates are used, the managers responsible may well find themselves accountable at the post-completion audit stage. Such audits, however, can be difficult and time-consuming to carry out. The likely benefits must, therefore, be weighed against the costs involved. Senior management may feel, therefore, that only projects above a certain size should be subject to a post-completion audit.

**Real World 14.14** provides some indication of the extent to whch post-completion audits are used by businesses.

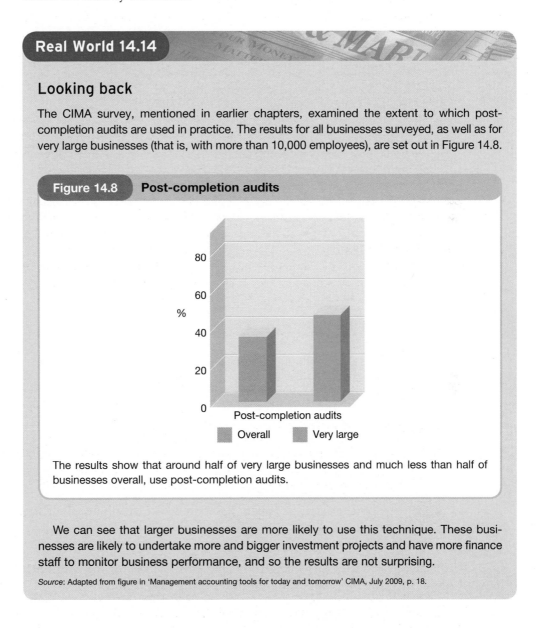

**Real World 14.14**

### Looking back

The CIMA survey, mentioned in earlier chapters, examined the extent to which post-completion audits are used in practice. The results for all businesses surveyed, as well as for very large businesses (that is, with more than 10,000 employees), are set out in Figure 14.8.

**Figure 14.8    Post-completion audits**

The results show that around half of very large businesses and much less than half of businesses overall, use post-completion audits.

We can see that larger businesses are more likely to use this technique. These businesses are likely to undertake more and bigger investment projects and have more finance staff to monitor business performance, and so the results are not surprising.

*Source*: Adapted from figure in 'Management accounting tools for today and tomorrow' CIMA, July 2009, p. 18.

**Real World 14.15** describes how one large retailer, Kingfisher plc, goes about monitoring and controlling its investment projects. Kingfisher sells do-it-yourself goods notably through the B and Q chain of stores.

## Real World 14.15

### Getting a grip

The 2011 annual report of Kingfisher plc reveals that the business invested £310 million during the year 2010/11 in continuing operations. To monitor and control this vast level of expenditure, the following procedures are adopted:

- An annual strategic planning process based on detailed plans for all divisions for the next three years. This process drives the key strategic capital allocation decisions and the output is reviewed by the Board, twice a year.
- A capital approval process through a Capital Expenditure committee, which includes the Group Chief Executive, Group Finance Director, Group Property Director and the three regional Chief Executive Officers, as required. The committee is delegated to review all projects between £0.75 million and £15.0 million.
- Projects above this level are approved by the Board, although all projects above £0.75 million are notified to the Board.
- Clear investment criteria with challenging hurdle rates for IRR (Internal Rate of Return) and discounted payback.
- An annual post-investment review process to undertake a full review of all projects above £0.75 million which were completed in the last four years, together with a review of recent performance on all other existing stores. The findings of this exercise are considered by both the Retail Board and the Board and directly influence the Regional and Group Development Strategy and the assumptions for similar project proposals going forward.

*Sources*: Kingfisher plc, Annual Report 2010/11, p. 24, (www.kingfisher co.uk).

## Summary

The main points of this chapter may be summarised as follows:

**Accounting rate of return (ARR) is the average accounting profit from the project expressed as a percentage of the average investment.**

- Decision rule – projects with an ARR above a defined minimum are acceptable; the greater the ARR, the more attractive the project becomes.
- Conclusion on ARR:
  - does not relate directly to shareholders' wealth – can lead to illogical conclusions;
  - takes almost no account of the timing of cash flows;
  - ignores some relevant information and may take account of some irrelevant;
  - relatively simple to use;
  - much inferior to NPV.

**Payback period (PP) is the length of time that it takes for the cash outflow for the initial investment to be repaid out of resulting cash inflows.**

- Decision rule – projects with a PP up to a defined maximum period are acceptable; the shorter the PP, the more attractive the project.
- Conclusion on PP:
  - does not relate to shareholders' wealth;
  - ignores inflows after the payback date;

- takes little account of the timing of cash flows;
- ignores much relevant information;
- does not always provide clear signals and can be impractical to use;
- much inferior to NPV, but it is easy to understand and can offer a liquidity insight, which might be the reason for its widespread use.

**Net present value (NPV) is the sum of the discounted values of the net cash flows from the investment.**

- Money has a time value.
- Decision rule – all positive NPV investments enhance shareholders' wealth; the greater the NPV, the greater the enhancement and the greater the attractiveness of the project.
- PV of a cash flow = cash flow $\times 1/(1 + r)^n$, assuming a constant discount rate.
- Discounting brings cash flows at different points in time to a common valuation basis (their present value), which enables them to be directly compared.
- Conclusion on NPV:
  - relates directly to shareholders' wealth objective;
  - takes account of the timing of cash flows;
  - takes all relevant information into account;
  - provides clear signals and is practical to use.

**Internal rate of return (IRR) is the discount rate that, when applied to the cash flows of a project, causes it to have a zero NPV.**

- Represents the average percentage return on the investment, taking account of the fact that cash may be flowing in and out of the project at various points in its life.
- Decision rule – projects that have an IRR greater than the cost of capital are acceptable; the greater the IRR, the more attractive the project.
- Cannot normally be calculated directly; a trial and error approach is often necessary.
- Conclusion on IRR:
  - does not relate directly to shareholders' wealth. Usually gives the same signals as NPV but can mislead where there are competing projects of different size;
  - takes account of the timing of cash flows;
  - takes all relevant information into account;
  - problems of multiple IRRs when there are unconventional cash flows;
  - inferior to NPV.

**Use of appraisal methods in practice:**

- all four methods identified are widely used;
- the discounting methods (NPV and IRR) show a steady increase in usage over time;
- many businesses use more than one method;
- larger businesses seem to be more sophisticated in their choice and use of appraisal methods than smaller ones.

**Investment appraisal and strategic planning**

- It is important that businesses invest in a strategic way so as to play to their strengths.

**Dealing with risk**

- Sensitivity analysis is an assessment, taking each input factor in turn, of how much each one can vary from estimate before a project is not viable.
  - Provides useful insights to projects.
  - Does not give a clear decision rule, but provides an impression.

– Does not indicate the likelihood of changes made to an input factor actually occurring.

– Can be rather static, but scenario building solves this problem.

**Managing investment projects**

- Determine investment funds available – dealing, if necessary, with capital rationing problems.

- Identify profitable project opportunities.

- Evaluate the proposed project.

- Approve the project.

- Monitor and control the project – using a post-completion audit approach.

# MyAccountingLab

Go to **www.myaccountinglab.com** to check your understanding of the chapter, create a personalised study plan, and maximise your revision time

## Key terms

accounting rate of return (ARR) p. 545
payback period (PP) p. 549
net present value (NPV) p. 554
risk p. 555
risk premium p. 555
inflation p. 556
discount factor p. 559

cost of capital p. 560
internal rate of return (IRR) p. 562
relevant costs p. 567
opportunity cost p. 567
sensitivity analysis p. 575
scenario building p. 579
capital rationing p. 580
post-completion audit p. 582

## Reference

1 Linder S., *Fifty Years of Research on Accuracy of Capital Expenditure Project Estimates: A Review of the Findings and Their Validity*, Otto Beisham Graduate School of Management, April 2005.

## Further reading

If you would like to explore the topics covered in this chapter in more depth, we recommend the following books:

Arnold, G., *Corporate Financial Management*, 4th edn, Financial Times Prentice Hall, 2008, chapters 2, 3 and 4.

Drury, C., *Management and Cost Accounting*, 8th edn, South Western Cengage Learning, 2012, chapters 13 and 14.

McLaney, E., *Business Finance: Theory and Practice*, 9th edn, Financial Times Prentice Hall, 2012, chapters 4, 5 and 6.

Pike, R., Neale, B. and Lindsley, P. *Corporate Finance and Investment*, 6th edn, Prentice Hall, 2009, chapters 5, 6 and 7.

## Review questions

Solutions to these questions can be found at the back of the book on pages 756–757.

**14.1** Why is the net present value method of investment appraisal considered to be theoretically superior to other methods that are found in practice?

**14.2** The payback method has been criticised for not taking the time value of money into account. Could this limitation be overcome? If so, would this method then be preferable to the NPV method?

**14.3** Research indicates that the IRR method is extremely popular even though it has shortcomings when compared to the NPV method. Why might managers prefer to use IRR rather than NPV when carrying out discounted cash flow evaluations?

**14.4** Why are cash flows rather than profit flows used in the IRR, NPV and PP methods of investment appraisal?

## Exercises

Exercises 14.1 and 14.2 are basic level, 14.3 and 14.4 are intermediate level and 14.5, 14.6, and 14.7 are advanced level. Those with **coloured numbers** have solutions at the back of the book starting on page 791.

If you wish to try more exercises, visit the students' side of the Companion Website and MyAccountingLab.

**14.1** The directors of Mylo Ltd are currently considering two mutually exclusive investment projects. Both projects are concerned with the purchase of new plant. The following data are available for each project:

|  | Project | |
|---|---|---|
|  | 1 | 2 |
|  | £000 | £000 |
| Cost (immediate outlay) | 100 | 60 |
| Expected annual operating profit (loss): | | |
| Year 1 | 29 | 18 |
| 2 | (1) | (2) |
| 3 | 2 | 4 |
| Estimated residual value of the plant after 3 years | 7 | 6 |

The business has an estimated cost of capital of 10 per cent. It uses the straight-line method of depreciation for all non-current (fixed) assets when calculating operating profit. Neither project would increase the working capital of the business. The business has sufficient funds to meet all investment expenditure requirements.

*Required:*

(a) Calculate for each project:
   (1) The net present value.
   (2) The approximate internal rate of return.
   (3) The payback period.

(b) State, with reasons, which, if any, of the two investment projects the directors of Mylo Ltd should accept.

**14.2** Arkwright Mills plc is considering expanding its production of a new yarn, code name X15. The plant is expected to cost £1 million and have a life of five years and a nil residual value. It will be bought, paid for and ready for operation on 31 December Year 0. £500,000 has already been spent on development costs of the product; this has been charged in the income statement in the year it was incurred.

The following results are projected for the new yarn:

|  | Year 1 | Year 2 | Year 3 | Year 4 | Year 5 |
|---|---|---|---|---|---|
|  | £m | £m | £m | £m | £m |
| Sales revenue | 1.2 | 1.4 | 1.4 | 1.4 | 1.4 |
| Costs, including depreciation | (1.0) | (1.1) | (1.1) | (1.1) | (1.1) |
| Profit before tax | 0.2 | 0.3 | 0.3 | 0.3 | 0.3 |

Tax is charged at 50 per cent on annual profits (before tax and after depreciation) and paid one year in arrears. Depreciation of the plant has been calculated on a straight-line basis. Additional working capital of £0.6 million will be required at the beginning of the project and released at the end of Year 5. You should assume that all cash flows occur at the end of the year in which they arise.

*Required:*
(a) Prepare a statement showing the incremental cash flows of the project relevant to a decision concerning whether or not to proceed with the construction of the new plant.
(b) Compute the net present value of the project using a 10 per cent discount rate.
(c) Compute the payback period to the nearest year. Explain the meaning of this term.

**14.3** Dirk plc has recently created a new male fragrance 'Sirocco' at a total cost of £0.4 million. The company is now considering producing the fragrance, which will require an immediate outlay for new equipment of £10.5 million. Estimates relating to production of the fragrance are:

|  | Year 1 | Year 2 | Year 3 | Year 4 |
|---|---|---|---|---|
| Sales price (£/per bottle) | 9.0 | 8.0 | 6.0 | 6.0 |
| Sales volume (bottles) | 1.0m | 1.2m | 1.2m | 0.5m |
| Variable cost (£/per bottle) | 1.0 | 1.0 | 1.0 | 1.4 |
| Fixed cost (£) | 4.5m | 4.5m | 4.5m | 4.5m |

The fixed cost includes depreciation of £2.5 million a year for the new equipment that is needed. This equipment will be sold at the end of the four years of production and the sales proceeds will reflect the residual value. Fixed cost also includes an allocation of £0.3 million to represent a 'fair share' of general business overheads.

If the project goes ahead, sales of an existing male fragrance 'Mistral' will decline, resulting in a loss of contribution of £0.8 million per year for the next three years.

Producing the new fragrance will require an immediate outlay for working capital of £1.8 million, which can be released at the end of the production period.

Dirk plc has a cost of capital of 8 per cent.

*Required:*
(a) Calculate for the investment project:
    (1) the net present value
    (2) the approximate internal rate of return.
(b) Briefly comment on the results of your calculations in (a).

**14.4** Newton Electronics Ltd has incurred expenditure of £5 million over the past three years researching and developing a miniature hearing aid. The hearing aid is now fully developed. The directors are considering which of three mutually exclusive options should be taken to exploit the potential of the new product. The options are:

1   The business could manufacture the hearing aid itself. This would be a new departure, since the business has so far concentrated on research and development projects. However, the business has manufacturing space available that it currently rents to another business for £100,000 a year. The business would have to purchase plant and equipment costing £9 million and invest £3 million in working capital immediately for production to begin.

   A market research report, for which the business paid £50,000, indicates that the new product has an expected life of five years. Sales of the product during this period are predicted as:

**Predicted sales for the year ended 30 November**

|  | Year 1 | Year 2 | Year 3 | Year 4 | Year 5 |
|---|---|---|---|---|---|
| Number of units (000s) | 800 | 1,400 | 1,800 | 1,200 | 500 |

   The selling price per unit will be £30 in the first year but will fall to £22 in the following three years. In the final year of the product's life, the selling price will fall to £20. Variable production costs are predicted to be £14 a unit. Fixed production costs (including depreciation) will be £2.4 million a year. Marketing costs will be £2 million a year.

   The business intends to depreciate the plant and equipment using the straight-line method and based on an estimated residual value at the end of the five years of £1 million. The business has a cost of capital of 10 per cent a year.

2   Newton Electronics Ltd could agree to another business manufacturing and marketing the product under licence. A multinational business, Faraday Electricals plc, has offered to undertake the manufacture and marketing of the product. In return it will make a royalty payment to Newton Electronics Ltd of £5 per unit. It has been estimated that the annual number of sales of the hearing aid will be 10 per cent higher if the multinational business, rather than if Newton Electronics Ltd, manufactures and markets the product.

3   Newton Electronics Ltd could sell the patent rights to Faraday Electricals plc for £24 million, payable in two equal instalments. The first instalment would be payable immediately and the second at the end of two years. This option would give Faraday Electricals the exclusive right to manufacture and market the new product.

Ignore taxation.

*Required:*

(a)  Calculate the net present value (as at the beginning of Year 1) of each of the options available to Newton Electronics Ltd.

(b)  Identify and discuss any other factors that Newton Electronics Ltd should consider before arriving at a decision.

(c)  State, with reasons, what you consider to be the most suitable option.

**14.5**   C. George (Controls) Ltd manufactures a thermostat that can be used in a range of kitchen appliances. The manufacturing process is, at present, semi-automated. The equipment used cost £540,000 and has a carrying amount (as shown on the statement of financial position) of £300,000. Demand for the product has been fairly stable at 50,000 units a year in recent years.

   The following data, based on the current level of output, have been prepared in respect of the product:

|  | Per unit | |
|---|---|---|
|  | £ | £ |
| Selling price |  | 12.40 |
| Labour | (3.30) |  |
| Materials | (3.65) |  |
| Overheads: Variable | (1.58) |  |
| Fixed | (1.60) |  |
|  |  | (10.13) |
| Operating profit |  | 2.27 |

Although the existing equipment is expected to last for a further four years before it is sold for an estimated £40,000, the business has recently been considering purchasing new equipment that would completely automate much of the production process. The new equipment would cost £670,000 and would have an expected life of four years, at the end of which it would be sold for an estimated £70,000. If the new equipment is purchased, the old equipment could be sold for £150,000 immediately.

The assistant to the business's accountant has prepared a report to help assess the viability of the proposed change, which includes the following data:

|  | Per unit | |
| --- | --- | --- |
|  | £ | £ |
| Selling price | | 12.40 |
| Labour | (1.20) | |
| Materials | (3.20) | |
| Overheads: Variable | (1.40) | |
| Fixed | (3.30) | |
|  | | (9.10) |
| Operating profit | | 3.30 |

Depreciation charges will increase by £85,000 a year as a result of purchasing the new machinery; however, other fixed costs are not expected to change.

In the report the assistant wrote:

> The figures shown above that relate to the proposed change are based on the current level of output and take account of a depreciation charge of £150,000 a year in respect of the new equipment. The effect of purchasing the new equipment will be to increase the operating profit to sales revenue ratio from 18.3 per cent to 26.6 per cent. In addition, the purchase of the new equipment will enable us to reduce our inventories level immediately by £130,000.
>
> In view of these facts, I recommend purchase of the new equipment.

The business has a cost of capital of 12 per cent. Ignore taxation.

*Required:*

(a) Prepare a statement of the incremental cash flows arising from the purchase of the new equipment.
(b) Calculate the net present value of the proposed purchase of new equipment.
(c) State, with reasons, whether the business should purchase the new equipment.
(d) Explain why cash flow forecasts are used rather than profit forecasts to assess the viability of proposed capital expenditure projects.

**14.6** The accountant of your business has recently been taken ill through overwork. In his absence his assistant has prepared some calculations of the profitability of a project, which are to be discussed soon at the board meeting of your business. His workings, which are set out below, include some errors of principle. You can assume that there are no arithmetical errors.

|  | Year 0 £000 | Year 1 £000 | Year 2 £000 | Year 3 £000 | Year 4 £000 | Year 5 £000 |
| --- | --- | --- | --- | --- | --- | --- |
| Sales revenue | | 450 | 470 | 470 | 470 | 470 |
| *Less Costs* | | | | | | |
| Materials | | 126 | 132 | 132 | 132 | 132 |
| Labour | | 90 | 94 | 94 | 94 | 94 |
| Overheads | | 45 | 47 | 47 | 47 | 47 |
| Depreciation | | 120 | 120 | 120 | 120 | 120 |
| Working capital | 180 | | | | | |
| Interest on working capital | | 27 | 27 | 27 | 27 | 27 |
| Write-off of development costs | – | 30 | 30 | 30 | – | – |
| Total costs | 180 | 438 | 450 | 450 | 420 | 420 |
| Operating profit/(loss) | (180) | 12 | 20 | 20 | 50 | 50 |

$$\frac{\text{Total profit (loss)}}{\text{Cost of equipment}} = \frac{(£28,000)}{£600,000} = \text{Return on investment (4.7\%)}$$

You ascertain the following additional information:

1  The cost of equipment includes £100,000, being the carrying value of an old machine. If it were not used for this project it would be scrapped with a zero net realisable value. New equipment costing £500,000 will be purchased on 31 December Year 0. You should assume that all other cash flows occur at the end of the year to which they relate.
2  The development costs of £90,000 have already been spent.
3  Overheads have been costed at 50 per cent of direct labour, which is the business's normal practice. An independent assessment has suggested that incremental overheads are likely to amount to £30,000 a year.
4  The business's cost of capital is 12 per cent.

Ignore taxation in your answer.

*Required:*
(a)  Prepare a corrected statement of the incremental cash flows arising from the project. Where you have altered the assistant's figures you should attach a brief note explaining your alterations.
(b)  Calculate:
    (1)  The project's payback period.
    (2)  The project's net present value as at 31 December Year 0.
(c)  Write a memo to the board advising on the acceptance or rejection of the project.

**14.7**  Simtex Ltd has invested £120,000 to date in developing a new type of shaving foam. The shaving foam is now ready for production and it has been estimated that the new product will sell 160,000 cans a year over the next four years. At the end of four years, the product will be discontinued and replaced by a new product.

The shaving foam is expected to sell at £6 a can and the variable cost is estimated at £4 per can. Fixed cost (excluding depreciation) is expected to be £300,000 a year. (This figure includes £130,000 in fixed cost incurred by the existing business that will be apportioned to this new product.)

To manufacture and package the new product, equipment costing £480,000 must be acquired immediately. The estimated value of this equipment in four years' time is £100,000. The business calculates depreciation using the straight-line method (equal amounts each year). It has an estimated cost of capital of 12 per cent.

*Required:*
(a)  Deduce the net present value of the new product.
(b)  Calculate by how much each of the following must change before the new product is no longer profitable:
    (1)  the discount rate;
    (2)  the initial outlay on new equipment;
    (3)  the net operating cash flows;
    (4)  the residual value of the equipment.
(c)  Should the business produce the new product?

# Financing a business

## Introduction

In this chapter we shall examine various aspects of financing a business. We begin by considering the main sources of finance available. Some of these sources have already been touched upon when we discussed the financing of limited companies in Chapter 4. We shall now look at these in more detail as well as discuss other sources of finance that have not yet been mentioned. The factors to be taken into account when choosing an appropriate source of finance are also considered.

Following our consideration of the main sources of finance, we shall examine how long-term finance may be raised. We shall take a look at various aspects of the capital markets, including the ways in which share capital may be issued, the role of the Stock Exchange and the financing of smaller businesses.

## Learning outcomes

**When you have completed this chapter, you should be able to:**

● Identify the main sources of finance available to a business and explain the advantages and disadvantages of each.

● Outline the ways in which share capital may be issued.

● Explain the role and nature of the Stock Exchange.

● Discuss the ways in which smaller businesses may seek to raise finance.

MyAccountingLab
Visit **www.myaccountinglab.com** for practice and revision opportunities

## Sources of finance

When considering the various sources of finance available to a business, it is useful to distinguish between *internal* and *external* sources of finance. By internal sources we mean sources that do not require the agreement of anyone beyond the directors and managers of the business. Thus, retained profits are considered an internal source because the directors of the business have power to retain profits without the agreement of the shareholders, whose profits they are. Finance from an issue of new shares, on the other hand, is an external source because it requires the compliance of potential shareholders.

Within each of the two categories just described, we can further distinguish between *long-term* and *short-term* sources of finance. There is no agreed definition concerning each of these terms but, for the purpose of this chapter, long-term sources are defined as those that provide finance for at least one year. Short-term sources are therefore defined as those that provide finance for up to one year. As we shall see, sources that are regarded as short-term when first used, often end up being used by the business for quite long periods.

We shall begin the chapter by considering the various sources of internal finance available. We shall then go on to consider the various sources of external finance. This is probably an appropriate order since, in practice, businesses tend to look first to internal sources before going outside for new funds.

## Internal sources of finance

Internal sources of finance usually have the advantage that they are flexible. They may also be obtained quickly – particularly working capital sources – and do not require the compliance of other parties. We shall now describe the main internal sources of funds. These are summarised in Figure 15.1.

**Figure 15.1    Major internal sources of finance**

The major internal source of long-term finance is the earnings that are retained rather than distributed to shareholders. The major internal sources of short-term finance involve reducing the level of trade receivables and inventories and increasing the level of trade payables.

## Internal sources of long-term finance

### Retained earnings

Retained earnings are the major source of finance for most businesses. They represent much the most important source of new finance for UK businesses in terms of value of funds raised. Funds are increased by retaining earnings within the business rather than distributing them to shareholders in the form of dividends.

---

**Activity (15.1)**

**Are retained earnings a free source of finance for the business?**

It is tempting to think that retained earnings are a cost-free source of funds for a business. However, this is not the case. If earnings are reinvested rather than distributed in cash to shareholders, those shareholders cannot reinvest this cash in other forms of investment. They will therefore expect a rate of return from the earnings reinvested which is equivalent to what they would receive if the funds had been invested in another opportunity with the same level of risk.

---

The reinvestment of earnings, rather than the issue of new shares, can be a useful way of raising finance from equity (ordinary share) investors. No issue costs are incurred and the amount raised is certain once the earnings are secure. When new shares are issued, on the other hand, issue costs may be substantial, as we shall see later in the chapter. Also, there may be uncertainty over the success of the issue. Where new shares are issued to outside investors, some dilution of control may also be suffered by existing shareholders.

The decision to retain earnings, rather than pay them out as dividends, is made by the directors. They may find it easier simply to retain earnings rather than to ask investors to subscribe to a new share issue. Retained earnings are already held by the business and so there is no delay in receiving the funds. Moreover, there is often less scrutiny when earnings are being retained for reinvestment purposes than when new shares are being issued. Investors will examine closely the reasons for any new share issue. A problem with the use of earnings as a source of finance, however, is that their timing and future level cannot always be reliably determined.

Some shareholders may prefer earnings to be retained by the business rather than distributed in the form of dividends. If the business ploughs back its earnings, it may be expected that business expansion and share values increases will result. An important reason for preferring earnings to be retained is the effect of taxation on the shareholder. In the UK, dividends are treated as income for tax purposes and therefore attract income tax. Gains on the sale of shares attract capital gains tax. Generally speaking, capital gains tax bites less hard than income tax. A further advantage of capital gains over dividends is that the shareholder has a choice as to when to sell the shares and realise the gain. In the UK, it is only when the gain is realised that capital gains tax comes into play. It is claimed that investors may be attracted to particular businesses according to the dividend/retention policies that they adopt.

It would be wrong to get the impression that all businesses either retain all of their earnings or pay them all out as dividends. Where businesses pay dividends, and most of the larger ones do pay dividends, they typically pay no more than 50 per cent of the earnings, retaining the remainder to fund expansion or to return to lenders.

## Internal sources of short-term finance

The major internal forms of short-term finance are:

- tighter credit control
- reducing inventories levels
- delaying payments to trade payables.

These are shown in Figure 15.1.

We saw in Chapter 6, in the context of statements of cash flows, that increases and decreases in these working capital items will have a direct and immediate effect on cash. Having funds tied up in trade receivables and inventories and failing to take advantage of free credit from suppliers represents a financing opportunity cost. This is because those funds could be used for profit-generating activities or for returning funds to shareholders or lenders.

### Tighter credit control

By exerting tighter control over amounts owed by credit customers, a business may be able to reduce the funds tied up. It is important, however, to weigh the benefits of tighter credit control against the likely costs in the form of lost customer goodwill and lost sales.

Activity 15.2 involves weighing the costs of tighter credit control against the likely future benefits.

### Activity 15.2

Rusli Ltd provides a car valet service for car hire businesses when their cars are returned from hire. Details of the service costs are as follows:

|  | Per car |
| --- | --- |
|  | £ |
| Car valet charge | 20 |
| Variable costs | (14) |
| Fixed costs | (4) |
| Profit | 2 |

Sales revenue is £10 million a year and is all on credit. The average credit period taken by Rusli Ltd's customers is 45 days, although the terms of credit require payment within 30 days. Bad debts are currently £100,000 a year. Trade receivables are financed by a bank overdraft with an interest cost of 10 per cent a year.

The credit control department of Rusli Ltd believes it can eliminate bad debts and can reduce the average credit period to 30 days if new credit control procedures are implemented. These procedures will cost £50,000 a year and are likely to result in a reduction in sales of 5 per cent a year.

Should the business implement the new credit control procedures? (*Hint*: To answer this activity it is useful to compare the current cost of trade credit with the costs under the proposed approach.)

**Activity 15.2 (continued)**

The current cost of trade credit is:

| | £ |
|---|---|
| Bad debts | 100,000 |
| Overdraft interest [(£10m × 45/365) × 10%] | 123,288 |
| | 223,288 |

The annual cost of trade credit under the new policy will be:

| | £ |
|---|---|
| Overdraft interest [(95% × £10m) × (30/365) × 10%] | 78,082 |
| Cost of control procedures | 50,000 |
| Net cost of lost sales [(£10m/£20 × 5%)(20 − 14*)] | 150,000 |
| | 278,082 |

\* The loss will be the contribution from valeting the car, that is, the difference between the valet charge and the variable costs. The fixed costs are ignored as they do not vary with the decision.

These figures show that the business will be worse off if the new policies are adopted.

To remain competitive, a business must take account of the needs of its customers and the credit policies adopted by rival businesses within the industry. We consider this further in Chapter 16.

## Reducing inventories levels

This internal source of funds may prove attractive to a business. By reducing inventories, funds become available for other purposes. However, a business must ensure there are sufficient inventories available to meet likely future sales demand. Failure to do so will result in lost customer goodwill and lost sales revenue.

The nature and condition of the inventories held will determine whether it is possible to exploit this form of finance. A business may have excessive inventories as a result of poor buying decisions. This may mean that a significant proportion of inventories held is slow moving or obsolete and cannot, therefore, be reduced easily.

## Delaying payment to trade payables

By providing a period of credit, suppliers are in effect offering their customers interest-free loans. If the business delays payment, the period of the 'loan' is extended and funds are retained within the business. This can be a free form of finance for a business, although this is not always the case. If a business fails to pay within the agreed credit period, there may be significant costs: for example, the business may find it difficult to buy on credit when it has a reputation as a slow payer.

## Some final points

The so-called short-term sources just described are short term to the extent that they can be reversed at short notice. For example, a reduction in the level of trade receivables can be reversed within a couple of weeks. Typically, however, once a business has established a reduced receivable collection period, a reduced inventories holding period and/or an expanded payables payment period, it will tend to maintain these new levels.

In Chapter 16, we shall see how these three elements of working capital may be managed. We shall also see that, for many businesses, the funds invested in working capital items are vast and, in many cases, unnecessarily so. In many cases, there is considerable scope for generating funds through more efficient management of working capital.

# External sources of finance

The main external sources of long-term and short-term finance are summarised in Figure 15.2.

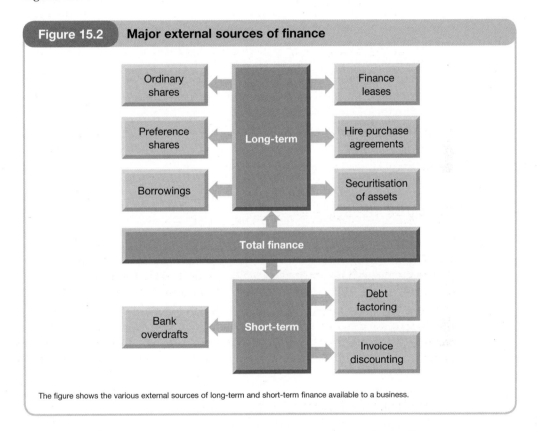

**Figure 15.2    Major external sources of finance**

The figure shows the various external sources of long-term and short-term finance available to a business.

# External sources of long-term finance

The major external sources of long-term finance are:

- ordinary shares
- preference shares
- borrowings
- finance leases (including sale-and-leaseback arrangements)
- hire purchase agreements
- securitisation of assets.

We shall now look at each of these sources in turn.

## Ordinary shares

Ordinary (equity) shares represent the risk capital of a business and form the backbone of a business's financial structure. There is no fixed rate of dividend, and ordinary shareholders will receive a dividend only if profits available for distribution still remain after other investors (preference shareholders and lenders) have received their dividend or interest payments. If the business is wound up, the ordinary shareholders will receive any proceeds from asset disposals only after lenders and creditors and, in some cases, preference shareholders, have received their entitlements. Because of the high risks associated with this form of investment, ordinary shareholders will normally expect a relatively high rate of return.

Although ordinary shareholders' potential losses are limited to the amount that they have invested or agreed to invest, the potential returns from their investment are unlimited. After preference shareholders and lenders have received their returns, all the remaining profits will accrue to the ordinary shareholders. Thus, while their 'downside' risk is limited, their 'upside' potential is not. Ordinary shareholders control the business through their voting rights, which give them the power to elect the directors and to remove them from office.

From the business's (the directors') perspective, ordinary shares can be a valuable form of financing compared to borrowing. It may be possible to avoid paying a dividend, whereas it is not usually possible to avoid interest payments.

**Activity 15.3**

Under what circumstances might a business wish to avoid paying a dividend?

Two possible circumstances are where a business is:

- expanding and wishes to retain funds in order to fuel future growth.
- in difficulties and needs the funds to meet its operating costs and debt obligations.

The two circumstances mentioned can have a quite different effect on shareholder confidence in the future, which will be reflected in share prices.

It is worth pointing out that the business does not obtain any tax relief on dividends paid to shareholders, whereas interest on borrowings is tax deductible. This makes it more expensive for the business to pay £1 of dividend than £1 of interest on borrowings.

## Preference shares

Preference shares offer investors a lower level of risk than ordinary shares. Provided there are sufficient profits available, preference shares will normally be given a fixed rate of dividend each year and preference dividends will be paid the first slice of any dividend paid. If the business is wound up, preference shareholders may be given priority over the claims of ordinary shareholders. (The business's own particular documents of incorporation will state the precise rights of preference shareholders in this respect.)

## Activity (15.4)

Would you expect the returns to preference shares to be higher or lower than those to ordinary shares?

Preference shareholders will be offered a lower level of return than those that ordinary shareholders expect to earn. This is because of the lower level of risk associated with this form of investment (preference shareholders have priority over ordinary shareholders regarding dividends and, perhaps, capital repayment).

Preference shareholders are not usually given voting rights, although these may be granted where the preference dividend is in arrears. Both preference shares and ordinary shares are, in effect, redeemable. The business is allowed to buy back the shares from shareholders at any time.

## Activity (15.5)

Would you expect the market price of ordinary shares or of preference shares to be the more volatile? Why?

The share price, which reflects the expected future returns from the share, will normally be less volatile for preference shares than for ordinary shares. The dividends of preference shares tend to be fairly stable over time, and there is usually an upper limit on the returns that can be received.

Preference shares are no longer an important source of new finance. A major reason for this is that dividends paid to preference shareholders, like those paid to ordinary shareholders, are not allowable against taxable profits, whereas loan interest is an allowable expense. From the business's point of view, preference shares and loans are quite similar, so the tax benefits of loan interest is an important issue.

## Borrowings

Most businesses rely on borrowings as well as share capital to finance operations. Lenders enter into a contract with the business in which the interest rate, dates of interest payments, capital repayments and security for the loan are clearly stated. If a business is successful, lenders will not benefit beyond the fact that their claim will become more secure. If, on the other hand, the business experiences financial difficulties, there is a risk that the agreed interest payments and capital repayments will not be made. To protect themselves against this risk, lenders often seek some form of **security** from the business. This may take the form of assets pledged either by a **fixed charge** on particular assets held by the business, or by a **floating charge**, which 'floats' over the whole of the business's assets. A floating charge will only fix on particular assets in the event that the business defaults on its obligations.

## Activity 15.6

What do you think is the advantage for the business of having a floating charge rather than a fixed charge on its assets?

A floating charge on assets will allow the managers of the business greater flexibility in their day-to-day operations than a fixed charge. Individual assets can be sold without reference to the lenders.

Not all assets are acceptable to lenders as security. They must normally be non-perishable, easy to sell and of high and stable value. (Property (land and buildings) normally meets these criteria and so is often favoured by lenders.) In the event of default, lenders have the right to seize the assets pledged and to sell them. Any surplus from the sale, after lenders have been paid, will be passed to the business. In some cases, security offered may take the form of a personal guarantee by the owners of the business or, perhaps, some third party. This tends to be particularly the case with small businesses.

Lenders may seek further protection through the use of **loan covenants**. These are obligations, or restrictions, on the business that form part of the loan contract. Covenants may impose:

● the right of lenders to receive regular financial reports concerning the business;
● an obligation to insure the assets being offered as security;
● a restriction on the right to issue further loan capital without prior permission of the existing lenders;
● a restriction on the right to sell certain assets held;
● a restriction on dividend payments and/or payments made to directors;
● minimum levels of liquidity and/or maximum levels of gearing.

Any breach of these covenants can have serious consequences. Lenders may demand immediate repayment of the loan in the event of a material breach.

**Real World 15.1** describes how one well-known retailer has recently struggled to generate profits, which, in turn, has led to the risk that it will breach its loan covenants.

## Real World 15.1

### Foxed HMV faces extinction                                               **FT**

If you want music, you will visit Amazon or iTunes online. But if you want profits warnings, look no further than HMV, which has just issued its third this year. Leaving behind a legacy business in high street entertainment retailing, the group has established itself as the UK's leading purveyor of earnings downgrades.

HMV faces extinction in its current form. In March, the struggling shopkeeper guided the City to cut pre-exceptional profits forecasts for the year to April 30 from some £45 million to below £40 million. HMV's latest advice to investors, who have seen shares plummet 86 per cent in a year, was that the figure will be closer to £30 million.

Operational gearing is digging remorselessly into profits as sales slump in response to weak consumer confidence and a secular decline in high street sales of CDs and DVDs.

Chief executive Simon Fox has exemplified courage in adversity but has plainly lost the ability to intuit the severity of both trends.

There is little comfort in the news that the group has extended the period over which loan covenants are measured. This suggests that banks now realise just how much trouble the group with the cute dog mascot is now in. HMV reported debt £60 million higher at £130 million in March, more than double its market capitalisation on Tuesday. With another £110 million of headroom in its facilities the figure may now be higher still. The half-year cash outflow from operations was a dispiriting £57 million.

Mr Fox hopes that lenders will reduce the stringency of profits covenants. For their part, they will pray that they do not end up as HMV's owners through a debt-for-equity swap. It is moot who would take up rights in any rescue share offering. Both digital and super-market competition threatens the company with obsolescence.

*Source*: 'Foxed HMV faces extinction', J. Guthrie, FT.com, 5 April 2011.

Loan covenants and the availability of security can lower the risk for lenders and can make the difference between a successful and an unsuccessful loan issue. They can also lower the cost of loan capital to the business as the rate of return that lenders require will depend on the perceived level of risk to which they are exposed.

It is possible for a business to issue loan capital that is subordinated to (that is, ranked below) other loan capital already in issue. Holders of subordinated loan capital will not receive interest payments or capital repayments until the claims of more senior loan holders (that is, lenders ranked above them) are met. Any restrictive covenants imposed by senior loan holders concerning the issue of further loan capital often ignore the issue of **subordinated loans** as it poses no real threat to their claims. Subordinated loan holders normally expect to receive a higher return than senior loan holders because of the higher risks.

### Activity (15.7)

Would you expect the returns to loan capital to be higher or lower than those to preference shares?

Investors are usually prepared to accept a lower rate of return from loan capital. This is because they normally view loans as being less risky than preference shares. Lenders have priority over any claims from preference shareholders and will usually have security for their loans.

The risk/return characteristics of loan, preference share and ordinary share finance are shown graphically in Figure 15.3. Note that, from the viewpoint of the business (the existing shareholders), the level of risk associated with each form of finance is in reverse order. Thus, borrowing is the most risky because it exposes shareholders to the legally enforceable obligation to make regular interest payments and, usually, repayment of the amount borrowed.

---

**Figure 15.3** | **The risk/return characteristics of sources of long-term finance**

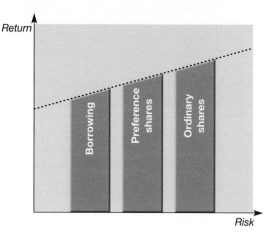

From an investor's perspective, borrowing is normally the least risky and ordinary shares the most risky.

---

**Activity (15.8)**

What factors might a business take into account when deciding between preference shares and loan capital as a means of raising new finance?

The main factors are as follows:

● Preference shares have a higher rate of return than loan capital. From the investors' point of view, preference shares are more risky. The amount invested cannot be secured and the return is paid after the returns paid to lenders.

● A business has a legal obligation to pay interest and make capital repayments on loan capital at the agreed dates. It will usually make every effort to meet its obligations, as failure to do so can have serious consequences. Failure to pay a preference dividend, on the other hand, is less important. There is no legal obligation to pay if profits are not available for distribution. Failure to pay a preference dividend may therefore prove to be an embarrassment and nothing more. It may, however, make it difficult to persuade investors to take up future preference share issues.

● Interest on loan capital can be deducted from profits for taxation purposes, whereas preference dividends cannot. As a result, the cost of servicing loan capital is, £ for £, usually much less for a business than the cost of servicing preference shares.

● The issue of loan capital may result in managers having to accept some restrictions on their freedom of action. Loan agreements often contain covenants that can be onerous. However, no such restrictions can be imposed by preference shareholders.

A further point is that any preference shares issued form part of the permanent capital base of the business. If they are redeemed, UK law requires that they be replaced, either by a new issue of shares or by a transfer from revenue reserves, so that the business's capital base stays intact. Loan capital, however, is not viewed, in law, as part of the business's permanent capital base and, therefore, there is no legal requirement to replace any loan capital that has been redeemed.

## Forms of borrowing

Borrowings may take various forms and we shall now consider some of the more important of these.

### Term loans

A **term loan** is a type of loan offered by banks and other financial institutions that can be tailored to the needs of the client business. The amount of the loan, time period, repayment terms and interest rate are all open to negotiation and agreement – which can be very useful. Where, for example, the whole amount borrowed is not required immediately, a business may agree with the lender that sums are drawn only when required. This means that interest will be paid only on amounts actually drawn and there is no need to pay interest on amounts borrowed that are not yet needed. Term loans tend to be cheap to set up (from the borrower's perspective) and can be quite flexible as to conditions. For these reasons, they tend to be popular in practice.

### Loan notes (or loan stock)

Another form of long-term borrowing is the **loan note** (or **loan stock**). Loan notes are frequently divided into units (rather like share capital), and investors are invited to purchase the number of units they require. Loan notes may be redeemable or irredeemable. The loan notes of public limited companies are often traded on the Stock Exchange. Their listed value will fluctuate according to the fortunes of the business, movements in interest rates, and so on.

Loan notes are usually referred to as **bonds** in the USA and, increasingly, in the UK. **Real World 15.2** describes how Manchester United made a bond issue that, though fully taken up by investors, lost them money within the first two weeks. There are fears that this may make it difficult for the club to raise future funds through a bond issue.

---

### Real World 15.2

#### Manchester United loses heavily                                      **FT**

Manchester United may be battling to retain the Premier League title but success on the pitch has worked little magic in the City. The club's first bond issue, launched barely two weeks ago, has become one of the market's worst performers this year.

While the club has secured the £500m funding that it needs to refinance its bank debt, the paper losses suffered by investors could affect its ability to return to bond markets.

If an investor had bought a £100,000 bond, he would have made a paper loss of £5,000. Analysts suggested the bonds had been priced too highly at launch and cited the lack of a credit rating.

Other recent issues that have fallen have not declined as heavily. 'In a benign credit market, Manchester United is one of the worst performing bonds since the beginning of 2009,' said Suki Mann, credit strategist at Société Générale.

While the club could issue more debt by increasing the size of the outstanding bond, people close to Manchester United said a return to the market was 'not on the agenda' and that the priority was to placate fans angered by the bond issue and plans by the Glazer family, United's US-based owners, to start paying down 'payment-in-kind' loans with club proceeds. The club declined to comment.

*Source*: Extracts from: 'Man Utd's first bond suffers from lack of support' A. Sakoui and R. Blitz, *Finanicial Times*, 3 February 2010.

## Eurobonds

**Eurobonds** are unsecured loan notes denominated in a currency other than the home currency of the business that issued them. They are issued by listed businesses (and other large organisations) in various countries, and the finance is raised on an international basis. They are often denominated in US dollars, but many are issued in other major currencies. They are bearer bonds (that is, the owner of the bond is not registered and the holder of the bond certificate is regarded as the owner) and interest is normally paid, without deduction of tax, on an annual basis.

Eurobonds are part of an international capital market that is not restricted by regulations imposed by authorities in particular countries. This partly explains why the cost of servicing eurobonds is usually lower than the cost of similar domestic bonds. Numerous banks and other financial institutions throughout the world have created a market for the purchase and sale of eurobonds. These bonds are made available to financial institutions, which may retain them as an investment or sell them to clients.

The extent of borrowing, by UK businesses, in currencies other than sterling has expanded greatly in recent years. Businesses are often attracted to eurobonds because of the size of the international capital market. Access to a wider pool of potential investors can increase the chances of a successful issue. As mentioned earlier, issuing eurobonds also allows national restrictions regarding loan issues to be overcome.

**Real World 15.3** provides an example of eurobond financing by a well-known business.

---

**Real World 15.3**

### Something worth watching?

ITV plc, the broadcasting and on-line business, has various Eurobonds in issue. As at 1 August 2011, Eurobonds with the following maturity dates and interest (coupon) rates were outstanding:

|  | Coupon |
|---|---|
| €86m Euro bond October 2011 | 6.0% |
| £110m Euro bond March 2013 | LIBOR plus 2.7% |
| €187.9m Euro bond June 2014 | 10% |
| £283m Euro bond due October 2015 | 5.375% |
| £100m Euro bond due October 2015 | 5.375% |
| £135m Convertible Euro bond due November 2016 | 4.0% |
| £250m Euro bond due January 2017 | 7.375% |

*Source*: ITVplc.com/investors/debt_ir. Accessed 1 August 2011.

---

## Deep discount bonds

A business may issue redeemable loan notes that offer a rate of interest below the market rate. In some cases, the loan notes may have a zero rate of interest. These loans are issued at a discount to their redeemable value and are referred to as **deep discount bonds**. Thus, loan notes may be issued at, say, £80 for every £100 of nominal value. Although lenders will receive little or no interest during the period of the loan, they will receive a £20 gain when it is finally redeemed at the full £100. The effective rate of return over the life of their loan (known as the redemption yield) can be quite high and often better than returns from other forms of lending with the same level of risk.

Deep discount bonds may have particular appeal to businesses with short-term cash flow problems. They receive an immediate injection of cash and there are no significant cash outflows associated with the loan notes until the maturity date. From an investment perspective, the situation is reversed. Deep discount bonds are likely to appeal to investors that do not have short-term cash flow needs since a large part of the return is received on maturity of the loan. However, deep discount bonds can often be traded on the London Stock Exchange, which will not affect the borrower but will enable the lender to sell the bonds and so obtain cash.

### Convertible loan notes

**Convertible loan notes** (or convertible bonds) give investors the right to convert loan notes into ordinary shares at a specified price and a given future date (or range of dates). The share price specified, which is known as the exercise price, will normally be higher than the market price of the ordinary shares at the time of the loan notes issue. In effect, the investor swaps the loan notes for a particular number of shares. The investor remains a lender to the business, and will receive interest on the amount of the loan notes, until such time as the conversion takes place. There is no obligation to convert to ordinary shares. This will be done only if the market price of the shares at the conversion date exceeds the agreed conversion price.

An investor may find this form of investment a useful 'hedge' against risk (that is, it can reduce the level of risk). This may be particularly useful when investment in a new business is being considered. Initially, the investment will be in the form of loan notes, and regular interest payments will be received. If the business is successful, the investor can then convert the investment into ordinary shares.

A business may also find this form of financing useful. If the business is successful, the loan notes become self-liquidating (that is, no cash outlay is required to redeem them) as investors will exercise their option to convert. It may also be possible to offer a lower rate of interest on the loan notes because of the expected future benefits arising from conversion. There will be, however, some dilution of control and possibly a dilution of earnings for existing shareholders if holders of convertible loan notes exercise their option to convert. (Dilution of earnings available to shareholders will not automatically occur as a result of the conversion of loan capital to share capital. There will be a saving in interest charges that will have an offsetting effect.)

**Real World 15.4** outlines a recent convertible loan notes (bonds) issue.

### Real World 15.4

### Business conversion

In November 2010, Misys plc, which provides IT solutions to the banking industry, issued £100,000,000 unsecured convertible bonds with a 2.5 per cent interest rate. They may be converted into fully paid-up ordinary shares at any time from 4 January 2011 until seven days before their maturity date in 2015. The conversion price is £3.7508 per ordinary share. The bonds were issued partly to finance the acquisition of another business.

This means that those investors who took up the bond issue will earn an interest rate of 2.5 per cent until either they convert their bonds to shares or the maturity date is reached in 2015. From 4 January 2011, these investors could choose to convert their bonds to ordinary shares. If they so choose, they will forfeit £3.7508 of the nominal value of their bonds for each ordinary share.

*Source:* Information taken from Mysis plc, 'Results for the year to 31 May 2011', p. 12; Listing particulars 11 April 2011, p. 59.

## Mortgages

A **mortgage** is a form of loan that is secured on an asset, typically land and property. Financial institutions such as banks, insurance businesses and pension funds are often prepared to lend to businesses on this basis. The mortgage may be over a long period (20 years or more).

## Interest rates

Interest rates on loan notes may be either floating or fixed. A **floating interest rate** means that the rate of return will rise and fall with market rates of interest. (But it is possible for a floating rate loan note to be issued that sets a maximum rate of interest and/or a minimum rate of interest payable.) The market value of the loan notes, however, is likely to remain fairly stable over time.

The converse will normally be true for loans with a **fixed interest rate**. Interest payments will remain unchanged with rises and falls in market rates of interest, but the value of the loan notes will fall when interest rates rise, and will rise when interest rates fall.

---

**Activity (15.9)**

Why do you think the value of fixed-interest loan notes will rise and fall with rises and falls in interest rates?

This is because investors will be prepared to pay less for loan notes that pay a rate of interest below the market rate of interest and will be prepared to pay more for loan notes that pay a rate of interest above the market rate of interest.

---

Movements in interest rates can be a significant issue for businesses that have high levels of borrowing. A business with a floating rate of interest may find that rate rises will place real strains on cash flows and profitability. Conversely, a business that has a fixed rate of interest will find that, when rates are falling, it will not enjoy the benefits of lower interest charges.

## Finance leases

When a business needs a particular asset, such as a piece of equipment, instead of buying it direct from a supplier, the business may arrange for a bank (or other business) to buy it and then lease it to the business. The bank that owns the asset, and then leases it the business, is known as a 'lessor'. The business that leases the asset from the bank and then uses it is known as the 'lessee'.

A **finance lease**, as such an arrangement is known, is in essence a form of lending. This is because, had the lessee borrowed the funds and then used them to buy the asset itself, the effect would be much the same. The lessee would have use of the asset but would also have a financial obligation to the lender – just as with a leasing arrangement.

With finance leasing, legal ownership of the asset remains with the lessor; however, the lease agreement transfers to the lessee virtually all the rewards and risks associated with the item being leased. The finance lease agreement will cover a substantial part of the life of the leased item and, often, cannot be cancelled. **Real World 15.5** gives an example of the use of finance leasing by a large international business.

### Real World 15.5

## Leased assets take off

Many airline businesses use finance leasing as a means of acquiring new aeroplanes. In July 2011 it was announced that Thai Airways had agreed to lease 22 aircraft from four different leasing companies. All were acquired under a standard 12-year leasing agreement with delivery of the new aircraft taking place between 2012 and 2017. The total value of the leased aircraft has been estimated at 69 billion baht (around £1.4 billion).

*Source*: Based on information in *Aviation News*, aviationnews-online.com, 6 July 2011.

A finance lease can be contrasted with an **operating lease** where the rewards and risks of ownership stay with the owner and where the lease is short term. An example of an operating lease is where a builder hires some earth-moving equipment for a week to carry out a particular job.

Over the years, some important benefits associated with finance leasing have disappeared. Changes in the tax laws no longer make it such a tax-efficient form of financing, and changes in accounting disclosure requirements no longer make it possible to conceal this form of 'borrowing' from investors. Nevertheless, the popularity of finance leases has continued. Other reasons must, therefore, exist for businesses to adopt this form of financing. These reasons are said to include the following:

- *Ease of borrowing.* Leasing may be obtained more easily than other forms of long-term finance. Lenders normally require some form of security and a profitable track record before making advances to a business. However, a lessor may be prepared to lease assets to a new business without a track record and to use the leased assets as security for the amounts owing.
- *Cost.* Leasing agreements may be offered at reasonable cost. As the asset leased is used as security, standard lease arrangements can be applied and detailed credit checking of lessees may be unnecessary. This can reduce administration costs for the lessor and, thereby, help in providing competitive lease rentals.
- *Flexibility.* Leasing can help provide flexibility where there are rapid changes in technology. If an option to cancel can be incorporated into the lease, the business may be able to exercise this option and invest in new technology as it becomes available. This will help the business to avoid the risk of obsolescence.
- *Cash flows.* Leasing, rather than buying an asset outright, means that large cash outflows can be avoided. The leasing option allows cash outflows to be smoothed out over the asset's life. In some cases, it is possible to arrange for low lease payments to be made in the early years of the asset's life, when cash inflows may be low, and for these to increase over time as the asset generates positive cash flows.

These benefits are summarised in diagrammatic form in Figure 15.4.

**Real World 15.6** provides some impression of the importance of finance leasing over recent years.

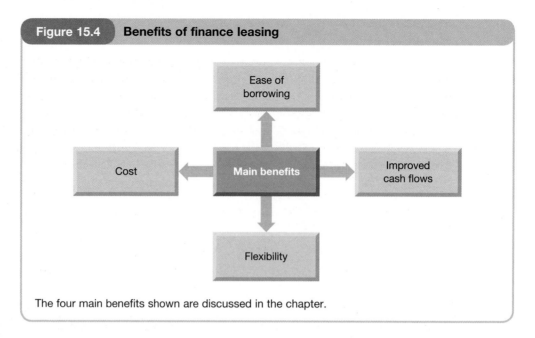

**Figure 15.4    Benefits of finance leasing**

The four main benefits shown are discussed in the chapter.

## Real World 15.6

### Finance leasing in the UK

Figure 15.5 charts the changes in the value of finance leasing in the UK over the years 2007 to 2010.

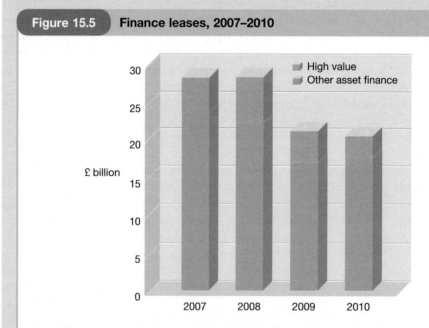

**Figure 15.5    Finance leases, 2007–2010**

Asset finance to businesses provided through finance leasing by FLA members has suffered a significant decline as a result of the economic recession. Business investment has fallen by more than 20 per cent, which was the worst fall for more than 40 years.

*Source*: FLA Annual Review 2011, p. 10, Finance and Leasing Association (www.fla.org.uk).

## Sale-and-leaseback arrangements

A **sale-and-leaseback** arrangement involves a business raising finance by selling an asset to a financial institution. The sale is accompanied by an agreement to lease the asset back to the business to allow it to continue to use the asset. The lease rental payment is a business expense that is allowable against profits for taxation purposes.

There are usually rental reviews at regular intervals throughout the period of the lease, and the amounts payable in future years may be difficult to predict. At the end of the lease agreement, the business must either try to renew the lease or find an alternative asset. Although the sale of the asset will result in an immediate injection of cash for the business, it will lose benefits from any future capital appreciation on the asset. Where a capital gain arises on the sale of the asset to the financial institution, a liability for taxation may also arise.

### Activity 15.10

Can you think which type of asset is often subject to a sale-and-leaseback arrangement?

Property is often the asset subject to such an arrangement.

Many of the well-known UK high-street retailers (for example, Boots, Debenhams, Marks and Spencer, Tesco and Sainsbury) have sold off their store sites under sale-and-leaseback arrangements.

Sale-and-leaseback agreements can be used to help a business focus on its core areas of competence. In recent years, for example, many hotel businesses have entered into sale-and-leaseback arrangements to enable them to become hotel operators rather than a combination of hotel operators and owners.

The terms of a sale-and-leaseback agreement may be vital to the future profitability and viability of a business. **Real World 15.7** explains how Woolworths' sale and leaseback arrangements contributed to the collapse of the business.

### Real World 15.7

#### The wonder of Woolworths' sale and leaseback arrangements

**FT**

At Woolworths' annual meeting this summer a perennially cheerful Trevor Bish-Jones cut a rather forlorn figure as he told his audience that making '£3 billion of [group] sales for £30 million of net profit is hard work this side of the fence'. The imperturbable chief executive could be forgiven for feeling a little sorry for himself: Mr Bish-Jones had just been ousted from the variety retailer having laboured for six-and-a-half years to keep Woolworths afloat under the weight of rising rents, shabby stores and an outdated business model.

This week the fight to save the much-loved but very under-shopped Woolworths chain finally drew to a close as the 800 stores and the wholesale distribution arm were placed into administration.

**Real World 15.7 (*continued*)**

Having limped along for seven years, with the profit line gradually shifting from black to red, the directors finally called it a day after the retailer, labouring under £385 million ($591 million) of debt, succumbed to a cash crisis. But how did it come to pass that the near 100-year-old chain, which in its heyday was opening a store a week and was still selling £1.7 billion of goods a year through its stores at the time of its collapse, should end up in such a dire predicament?

Those close to Woolworths place this week's collapse firmly at the feet of those who demerged the retailer from Kingfisher in August 2001. They argue that the decision to carry out a sale-and-leaseback deal for 182 Woolworths' stores in return for £614 million of cash – paid back to Kingfisher shareholders – crippled the chain. For in return for the princely price tag, Woolworths was saddled with onerous leases that guaranteed the landlords a rising income stream.

One person who knows Woolworths well says the rent bill rose from £70 million a decade ago to £160 million today. 'There is no doubt that back in 2001, with the de-merger and the sale of these stores, the company was saddled with a huge amount of quasi debt in terms of these leases,' says one former adviser. 'I think probably that is really where this goes back to. If Woolworths had more financial flexibility they might have been able to do more of the stuff they needed to. To build a sustainable business requires investment but they were not in a position to incur more costs,' the former adviser adds.

Tony Shiret, analyst at Credit Suisse, says Woolworths' lease-adjusted debt was the highest in the retail sector. 'They didn't really have enough cash flow to cover debt repayments.'

*Source*: 'Seeds of Woolworths' demise sown long ago', E. Rigby, *Financial Times*, 29 November 2008.

## Hire purchase

**Hire purchase** is a form of credit used to acquire an asset. Under the terms of a hire purchase (HP) agreement a customer pays for an asset by instalments over an agreed period. Normally, the customer will pay an initial deposit (down payment) and then make instalment payments at regular intervals, perhaps monthly, until the balance outstanding has been paid. The customer will usually take possession of the asset after payment of the initial deposit, although legal ownership of the asset will not be transferred until the final instalment has been paid.

HP agreements will often involve three parties:

● the supplier
● the customer
● a financial institution.

Although the supplier will deliver the asset to the customer, the financial institution will buy the asset from the supplier and then enter into an HP agreement with the customer. This intermediary role played by the financial institution enables the supplier to receive immediate payment for the asset but allows the customer a period of extended credit.

Figure 15.6 sets out the main steps in the hire-purchase process.

**Real World 15.8** describes how one well-known holiday operator uses hire purchase to help finance its assets.

**Figure 15.6    The hire-purchase process**

There are usually three parties to a hire-purchase agreement. The financial institution will buy the asset from the supplier, who will then deliver it to the customer. The customer will pay an initial deposit and will agree to pay the balance to the financial institution through a series of regular instalments.

**Real World 15.8**

## Paying by instalments

Holidaybreak plc has a camping division that includes well-known brands such as Eurocamp and Keycamp. The division provides mobile homes for holidaymakers, and the company's 2010 annual report revealed that the cost of mobile homes purchased during the year was £6.2 million. The company states that it has:

> . . . hire-purchase agreements with various UK financial institutions to finance the purchase of mobile homes. Just over half of expenditure on mobile homes is financed from this source.

*Source*: Holidaybreak plc Annual Report and Financial Statements 2010, p. 7.

HP agreements are similar to finance leases in so far as they allow a customer to obtain immediate possession of the asset without paying its full cost. Under the terms of an HP agreement, however, the customer will eventually become the legal owner of the asset, whereas under the terms of a finance lease, ownership will stay with the lessor.

## Securitisation

**Securitisation** involves bundling together illiquid financial or physical assets of the same type so as to provide financial backing for an issue of bonds. This financing method was first used by US banks, which bundled together residential mortgage loans to provide asset backing for bonds issued to investors. (Mortgage loans held by a bank are financial assets that provide future cash flows in the form of interest receivable.)

Securitisation has spread beyond the banking industry and has now become an important source of finance for businesses in a wide range of industries. Future cash flows from a variety of illiquid assets are now used as backing for bond issues, including:

● credit card receipts
● water industry charges
● rental income from university accommodation
● ticket sales for football matches
● royalties from music copyright
● consumer instalment contracts
● beer sales to pub tenants.

The effect of securitisation is to capitalise future cash flows arising from illiquid assets. This capitalised amount is sold to investors, through the financial markets, to raise finance for the business holding these assets.

Securitisation usually involves setting up a special-purpose vehicle (SPV) to acquire the assets from the business wishing to raise finance. This SPV will then arrange the issue of bonds to investors. Income generated from the securitised assets is received by the SPV and used to meet the interest payable on the bonds. When the bonds mature, the funds for repayment may come from either:

● receipts from the securitised assets (so long as the maturity dates are co-terminus); or
● the issue of new bonds, or from surplus income generated by the securitised assets.

To reassure investors about the quality of the bonds, the securitdised assets may be of a higher value than the value of the bonds (this is known as *overcollateralisation*). Alternatively, some form of credit insurance can be available from a third party, such as a bank.

The main elements of the securitisation process are set out in Figure 15.7.

**Figure 15.7** **The securitisation process**

A business will transfer assets to a special-purpose vehicle, which will then arrange for the issue of bonds to investors. Interest paid on the bonds will be met from income generated by the securitised assets.

Securitisation may also be used to help manage risk. Where, for example, a bank has lent heavily to a particular industry, its industry exposure can be reduced by bundling together some of the outstanding loan contracts and making a securitisation issue.

### Securitisation and the financial crisis

Securitising mortgage loan repayments became popular among US mortgage lenders during the early years of the 2000s. The monthly repayments due to be made by mortgage borrowers were 'securitised' and sold to many of the major banks, particularly in the USA. Unfortunately, many of the mortgage loans were made to people on low incomes who were not good credit risks (sub-prime loans). When the borrowers started to default on their obligations, it became clear that the securities, now owned by the banks, were worth much less than the banks had paid the mortgage lenders for them. This led to the so-called 'sub-prime' crisis that triggered the worldwide economic problems that emerged during 2008. There is, however, no inherent reason for securitisation to be a problem and it is unfortunate that the practice is linked with the sub-prime crisis. It can be a perfectly legitimate and practical way for a business to raise finance.

## External sources of short-term finance

Short term, in this context, is usually taken to mean up to one year. The major external sources of short-term finance (as were shown in Figure 15.2) are:

- bank overdrafts
- debt factoring
- invoice discounting.

Each of these sources is now discussed.

### Bank overdrafts

A **bank overdraft** enables a business to maintain a negative balance on its bank account. It represents a very flexible form of borrowing as the size of an overdraft can (subject to bank approval) be increased or decreased more or less instantaneously. It is relatively inexpensive to arrange and interest rates are often very competitive, though often higher than those for a term loan. As with all loans, the rate of interest charged will vary according to how creditworthy the customer is perceived to be by the bank. An overdraft is fairly easy to arrange – sometimes it can be agreed by a telephone call to the bank. In view of these advantages, it is not surprising that an overdraft is an extremely popular form of short-term finance.

Banks prefer to grant overdrafts that are self-liquidating, that is, the funds are used in such a way as to extinguish the overdraft balance by generating cash inflows. The banks may ask for projected cash flow statements from the business to see when the overdraft will be repaid and how much finance is required. They may also require some form of security on amounts advanced.

One potential drawback with this form of finance is that it is repayable on demand. This may pose problems for a business that is illiquid. However, many businesses operate for many years using an overdraft, simply because the bank remains confident of their ability to repay and the arrangement suits the business. Thus, bank overdrafts, though in theory regarded as short-term, can, in practice, become a source of long-term finance.

### Debt factoring

**Debt factoring** is a service offered by a financial institution (known as a factor). Many of the large factors are subsidiaries of commercial banks. Debt factoring involves the factor taking over the trade receivables collection for a business. In addition to operating normal credit control procedures, a factor may offer to undertake credit investigations and advise on the creditworthiness of the business. It may also offer protection for approved credit sales. Two main forms of factoring agreement exist:

● *Recourse factoring*, where the factor assumes no responsibility for bad debts arising from credit sales.
● *Non-recourse factoring*, where, for an additional fee, the factor assumes responsibility for bad debts up to an agreed amount.

The factor is usually prepared to make an advance to the business of up to around 80 per cent of approved trade receivables (although it can sometimes be as high as 90 per cent). This advance is usually paid immediately after the goods have been supplied to the customer. The balance of the debt, less any deductions for fees and interest, will be paid after an agreed period or when the debt is collected. The charge made for the factoring service is based on total sales revenue and is often around 2 or 3 per cent of sales revenue. Any advances made to the business by the factor will attract a rate of interest similar to the rate charged on bank overdrafts.

Debt factoring is, in effect, outsourcing trade receivables collection to a specialist subcontractor. Many businesses find a factoring arrangement very convenient. It can result in savings in credit management and can create more certain cash flows. It can also release the time of key personnel for more profitable ends. This may be extremely important for smaller businesses that rely on the talent and skills of a few key individuals. In addition, the level of finance available will rise 'spontaneously' with the level of sales. The business can decide how much of the finance available is required and can use only that which it needs. However, there is a possibility that some will see a factoring arrangement as an indication that the business is experiencing financial difficulties. This may have an adverse effect on the confidence of customers, suppliers and staff. For this reason, some businesses try to conceal the factoring arrangement by collecting outstanding debts on behalf of the factor.

Not all businesses will find factoring arrangements the answer to their financing problems. Factoring agreements may not be possible to arrange for very small businesses (those with total sales revenue of, say, less than £100,000) because of the high set-up costs. In addition, businesses engaged in certain sectors where trade disputes are part of the business culture, such as building contractors, may find that factoring arrangements are simply not available.

Figure 15.8 shows the factoring process diagrammatically.

When considering a factoring agreement, it is necessary to identify and carefully weigh the costs and likely benefits arising. Example 15.1 illustrates how this may be done.

### Example 15.1

Balkan Ltd has annual credit sales revenue of £50 million of which bad debts account for £0.2 million. The average settlement period for trade receivables is 80 days, which is causing some strain on the liquidity of the business.

Balkan Ltd is considering whether to use a factoring business to improve its liquidity position. The factor will advance an equivalent to 80 per cent of trade receivables (where the trade receivables figure is based on an average settlement period of 30 days) at an interest rate of 10 per cent. In addition, the factor will collect the trade receivables and will charge a fee of 3 per cent of total sales revenue for doing so. The remaining 20 per cent of the trade receivables will be paid to Balkan Ltd, when the factor receives the cash. If the factor service is used, it is expected that the average settlement period for trade receivables will be reduced to 30 days, bad debts will be eliminated and credit administration savings of £320,000 will be gained.

The business currently has an overdraft of £10.0 million at an interest rate of 11 per cent a year.

In evaluating the factoring arrangement, it is useful to begin by considering the cost of the existing arrangements:

*Existing arrangements*

|  | £000 |
|---|---|
| Bad debts written off each year | 200 |
| Interest cost of average receivables outstanding [(£50m × 80/365) × 11%] | 1,205 |
| Total cost | 1,405 |

The cost of the factoring arrangement can now be compared with this:

*Factoring arrangement*

|  | £000 |
|---|---|
| Factoring fee (£50m × 3%) | 1,500 |
| Interest on factor loan (assuming 80% advance and reduction in average credit period) [(£40m × 30/365) × 10%] | 329 |
| Interest on overdraft (remaining 20% of receivables financed in this way) [(£10m × 30/365) × 11%] | 90 |
|  | 1,919 |
| Savings in credit administration | (320) |
| Cost of factoring | 1,599 |

The net savings for the business from factoring would be £194,000 (£1,599,000 – £1,405,000).

---

**Figure 15.8    The debt-factoring process**

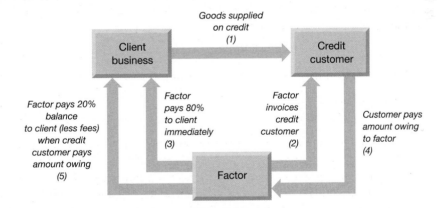

There are three main parties to the factoring agreement. The client business will sell goods on credit and the factor will take responsibility for invoicing the customer and collecting the amount owing. The factor will then pay the client business the invoice amount, less fees and interest, in two stages. The first stage typically represents 80 per cent of the invoice value and will be paid immediately after the goods have been delivered to the customer. The second stage will represent the balance outstanding and will usually be paid when the customer has paid the factor the amount owing.

## Invoice discounting

**Invoice discounting** involves a factor or other financial institution providing a loan based on a proportion of the face value of a business's credit sales outstanding. The amount advanced is usually 75 to 80 per cent of the value of the approved sales invoices outstanding. The business must agree to repay the advance within a relatively short period – perhaps 60 or 90 days. Responsibility for collecting the trade receivables outstanding remains with the business, and repayment of the advance is not dependent on the trade receivables being collected. Invoice discounting will not result in such a close relationship developing between the business and the financial institution as occurs with factoring. It may be a short-term arrangement whereas debt factoring usually involves a longer-term arrangement.

Invoice discounting is a much more important source of funds to businesses than factoring. There are three main reasons for this.

- It is a confidential form of financing which the business's customers will know nothing about.
- The service charge for invoice discounting is only about 0.2 to 0.3 per cent of sales revenue compared to 2.0 to 3.0 per cent for factoring.
- A debt factor may upset customers when collecting the amount due, which may damage the relationship between the business and its customers.

**Real World 15.9** shows the relative importance of invoice discounting and factoring.

### Real World 15.9

### The popularity of invoice discounting and factoring

Figure 15.9 charts the relative importance of invoice discounting and factoring in terms of the value of client sales revenue.

**Figure 15.9** **Client sales revenue: invoice discounting and factoring, 2006–2010**

Since 2006, client sales from invoice discounting have risen sharply. In 2009, however, there was a decline, which was probably due to the effects of the economic recession. Since 2006, client sales from debt factoring have declined.

*Source:* Chart constructed from data published by the Asset Based Finance Association (www.abfa.org.uk).

Factoring and invoice discounting are forms of **asset-based finance** as the assets of receivables are, in effect, used as security for the cash advances received by the business.

# Long-term versus short-term borrowing

Where it is clear that some form of borrowing is required to finance the business, a decision must be made as to whether long-term or short-term borrowing is more appropriate. There are many issues to be taken into account, which include the following:

- *Matching.* The business may attempt to match the type of borrowing with the nature of the assets held. Thus, long-term borrowing may be used to finance assets that form part of the permanent operating base of the business. These normally include non-current assets and a certain level of current assets. This leaves assets held for a short period, such as current assets used to meet seasonal increases in demand, to be financed by short-term borrowing, which tends to be more flexible in that funds can be raised and repaid at short notice. Figure 15.10 shows this funding division graphically.

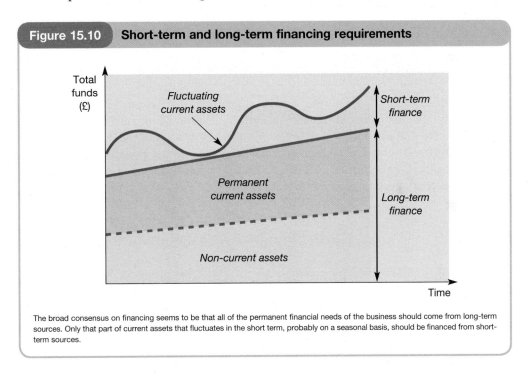

**Figure 15.10**  **Short-term and long-term financing requirements**

The broad consensus on financing seems to be that all of the permanent financial needs of the business should come from long-term sources. Only that part of current assets that fluctuates in the short term, probably on a seasonal basis, should be financed from short-term sources.

A business may wish to match the period of borrowing exactly with the asset life. This may not be possible, however, because of the difficulty of predicting the life of many assets.

- *Flexibility.* Short-term borrowing may be used as a means of postponing a commitment to long-term borrowing. This may be desirable if interest rates are high but are forecast to fall in the future. Short-term borrowing does not usually incur a financial penalty for early repayment, whereas a penalty may arise if long-term borrowing is repaid early.
- *Refunding risk.* Short-term borrowing has to be renewed more frequently than long-term borrowing. This may create problems for the business if it is in financial difficulties or if there is a shortage of funds available for borrowing.

● *Interest rates.* Interest payable on long-term borrowing is often higher than that for short-term borrowing, as lenders require a higher return where their funds are locked up for a long period. This fact may make short-term borrowing a more attractive source of finance for a business. However, there may be other costs associated with borrowing (arrangement fees, for example) to be taken into account. The more frequently borrowings are renewed, the higher these costs will be.

### Activity (15.11)

Some businesses may take up a less cautious financing position than that shown in Figure 15.10 and others may take up a more cautious one. How would the diagram differ under each of these options?

A less cautious position would mean relying on short-term finance to help fund part of the permanent capital base. A more cautious position would mean relying on long-term finance to help finance the fluctuating assets of the business.

## Gearing and the long-term financing decision

In Chapter 7 we saw that financial gearing (also known as 'leverage') occurs when a business is financed, at least in part, by contributions from fixed-charge capital (preference shares and borrowings). We also saw that the level of gearing associated with a business is often an important factor in assessing the risk and returns to ordinary shareholders. In Example 15.2, we consider the implications of making a choice between a geared and an ungeared approach to raising long-term finance.

### Example 15.2

The following are the summarised financial statements of Woodhall Engineers plc:

**Income statement for the year ended 31 December**

|  | Year 1 £m | Year 2 £m |
|---|---|---|
| Revenue | 47 | 50 |
| Operating costs | (42) | (48) |
| Operating profit | 5 | 2 |
| Interest payable | (1) | (1) |
| Profit before tax | 4 | 1 |
| Taxation | – | – |
| Profit for the year | 4 | 1 |

### Statement of financial position as at 31 December

|                                               | Year 1 £m | Year 2 £m |
|-----------------------------------------------|-----------|-----------|
| ASSETS                                        |           |           |
| Non-current assets                            | 21        | 20        |
| Current assets                                |           |           |
| Inventories                                   | 10        | 18        |
| Trade receivables                             | 16        | 17        |
| Cash at bank                                  | 3         | 1         |
|                                               | 29        | 36        |
| Total assets                                  | 50        | 56        |
| EQUITY AND LIABILITIES                        |           |           |
| Equity                                        |           |           |
| Called-up share capital (25p ordinary shares) | 16        | 16        |
| Retained earnings                             | 4         | 4         |
|                                               | 20        | 20        |
| Non-current liabilities                       |           |           |
| Borrowings – Long-term loans (secured)        | 15        | 15        |
| Current liabilities                           |           |           |
| Trade payables                                | 10        | 10        |
| Short-term borrowings                         | 5         | 11        |
|                                               | 15        | 21        |
| Total equity and liabilities                  | 50        | 56        |

The business is making plans to expand its premises. New plant will cost £8 million, and an expansion in output will increase working capital by £4 million. Over the 15 years' life of the project, incremental operating profit arising from the expansion will be £2 million a year. In addition, Year 3's operating profit from its existing activities is expected to return to Year 1 levels.

Two possible methods of financing the expansion have been discussed by Woodhall's directors. The first is the issue of £12 million of 10 per cent loan notes repayable in Year 18. The second is an issue of 40 million 25p ordinary shares, which will give the business cash of 30p per share after expenses.

The business has substantial tax losses, which can be offset against future profits, so taxation can be ignored in the calculations. The Year 3 total dividend is expected to be £1.0 million if the expansion is financed by loan notes, and £1.6 million if the share issue is made.

Prepare Woodhall's projected income statement (excluding revenue and operating costs) for the year ended 31 December Year 3, and a statement of its equity and number of shares in issue at that date, assuming that the business issues:

(a) loan notes
(b) ordinary shares.

The projected income statements under each financing option will be as follows:

**Projected income statements for the year ended 31 December Year 3**

| | Loan notes issue £m | Share issue £m |
|---|---|---|
| Operating profit (5.0 + 2.0) | 7.0 | 7.0 |
| Loan notes interest | (2.2) | (1.0) |
| Profit before tax | 4.8 | 6.0 |
| Taxation | – | – |
| Profit for the year | 4.8 | 6.0 |

The equity of the business and number of shares in issue under each option as at the end of Year 3 will be as follows:

| | Loan notes issue £m | Share issue £m |
|---|---|---|
| Equity | | |
| Share capital (25p ordinary shares) | 16.0 | 26.0 |
| Share premium account* | – | 2.0 |
| Retained earnings† | 7.8 | 8.4 |
| | 23.8 | 36.4 |
| Number of shares in issue (25p shares) | 64 million | 104 million |

*This represents the amount received from the issue of shares that is above the nominal value of the shares. The amount is calculated as follows:

$$40m \text{ shares} \times (30p - 25p) = £2m$$

† This is the retained profit figure after deducting the dividend paid.

## Activity (15.12)

Compute Woodhall's interest cover and earnings per share for the year ended 31 December Year 3 and its gearing on that date, assuming that the business issues:

(a) loan notes;
(b) ordinary shares.

Your answer should be as follows:

| | (a) Loan notes issue | (b) Share issue |
|---|---|---|
| **Interest cover ratio** | | |
| $\dfrac{\text{Operating profit}}{\text{Interest payable}}$ | $= \dfrac{7.2}{2.2}$ | $= \dfrac{7.0}{1.0}$ |
| | = 3.2 times | = 7.0 times |
| **Earnings per share** | | |
| $\dfrac{\text{Earning available to ordinary shareholders}}{\text{Number of ordinary shares}}$ | $= \dfrac{£4.8m}{64m}$ | $= \dfrac{£6.0m}{104m}$ |
| | = 7.5p | = 5.8p |
| **Gearing ratio** | | |
| $\dfrac{\text{Non-current liabilities}}{\text{Share capital + Reserves + Non-current liabilities}}$ | $= \dfrac{27m}{£23.8m + £27m}$ | $= \dfrac{£15m}{£36.4m + £15m}$ |
| | = 53.1% | = 29.2% |

**Activity (15.13)**

What would your views of the proposed schemes be in each of the following circumstances?

(a) If you were an investor who had been asked to take up some of the loan notes.

(b) If you were an ordinary shareholder in Woodhall and you were asked to subscribe to a share issue.

(a) Investors may be unenthusiastic about lending money to the business. The gearing ratio of 53.1 per cent is rather high, and would leave the loan notes holders in an exposed position. Their existing loan is already secured on the business's assets, and it is not clear whether the business is in a position to offer an attractive form of security for the new loan. The interest cover ratio of 3.2 times is also rather low. If the business is unable to achieve the expected returns from the new project, or if it is unable to restore profits from the remainder of its operations to Year 1 levels, this ratio would be even lower.

(b) Ordinary share investors may need some convincing that it would be worthwhile to make further investments in the business. The return on ordinary shareholders' funds in Year 1 was 20 per cent (£4 million/£20 million). The incremental profit from the new project is £2 million and the investment required is £12 million, which represents a return of 16.7 per cent. Thus, the returns from the project are expected to be lower than for existing operations. In making their decision, investors should discover whether the new investment is of a similar level of risk to their existing investment and how the returns from the investment compare with those available from other opportunities with similar levels of risk.

# Raising long-term finance

We shall now consider ways in which long-term finance may be raised by a business. We begin by looking at various forms of share issue and then go on to examine the role of capital markets.

# Share issues

A business may issue shares in a number of ways. These may involve direct appeals to investors or the use of financial intermediaries. The most common methods of share issues are set out in Figure 15.11.

We shall now discuss each of these methods in turn.

## Rights issues

As we saw in Chapter 4, **rights issues** can be made by established businesses that seek to raise additional funds by issuing new shares to their existing shareholders. Company law gives existing shareholders the first right of refusal to buy any new shares issued by a company, so the new shares would be offered to shareholders in proportion to their existing holding. Only where the existing shareholders agree to waive their right

**Figure 15.11**  **Common methods of share issue**

The figure sets out five methods of issuing shares. As explained in the chapter, bonus issues differ from the other methods in that they do not lead to an injection of cash for the business.

could the shares be offered to the investing public generally. Rights issues are a popular form of share issue. During 2010, they accounted for approximately 75 per cent of all finance raised from share issues by businesses already listed on the London Stock Exchange (see reference 1 at the end of the chapter). The business (in effect, the existing shareholders) would typically prefer that existing shareholders buy the shares through a rights issue, irrespective of the legal position. This is for two reasons:

● The ownership (and, therefore, control) of the business remains in the same hands; there is no 'dilution' of control.
● The costs of making the issue (advertising, complying with various company law requirements) tend to be less if the shares are to be offered to existing shareholders. It is estimated that the average cost of making a rights issue are 5.8 per cent of the funds raised. Since a lot of the cost is fixed, this percentage will be greater or lesser for smaller and larger rights issues, respectively (see reference 2 at the end of the chapter). This compares with up to 11 per cent for an issue to the public (see reference 3 at the end of the chapter).

To encourage existing shareholders to take up their 'rights' to buy some new shares, those shares are always offered at a price below the current market price of the existing ones. The evidence shows that shares are typically offered at 31 per cent below the current pre-rights price (see reference 2 at the end of the chapter).

**Activity (15.14)**

In Chapter 4 (Example 4.2, page 144) the point was made that issuing new shares at below their current worth was to the advantage of the new shareholders at the expense of the old ones. In view of this, does it matter that rights issues are always made at below the current value of the shares?

The answer is that it does not matter *in these particular circumstances*, because, in a rights issue, the existing shareholders and the new shareholders are exactly the same people. Moreover, the shareholders will hold the new shares in the same proportion as they currently hold the existing shares. Thus, shareholders will gain on the new shares exactly as much as they lose on the existing ones: in the end, no one is better or worse off as a result of the rights issue being made at a discount.

Calculating the value of the rights offer received by shareholders is quite straightforward, as shown in Example 15.3.

### Example 15.3

Shaw Holdings plc has 20 million ordinary shares of 50p in issue. These shares are currently valued on the Stock Exchange at £1.60 per share. The directors have decided to make a one-for-four issue (that is, one new share for every four shares held) at £1.30 per share.

The first step in the valuation process is to calculate the price of a share following the rights issue. This is known as the *ex-rights price* and is simply a weighted average of the price of shares before the issue of rights and the price of the rights shares. In this example, we have a one-for-four rights issue. The theoretical ex-rights price is therefore calculated as follows:

|  | £ |
|---|---|
| Price of four shares before the rights issue (4 × £1.60) | 6.40 |
| Price of taking up one rights share | 1.30 |
|  | 7.70 |

$$\text{Theoretical ex-rights price} = \frac{£7.70}{5} \qquad = £1.54$$

As the price of each share, in theory, should be £1.54 following the rights issue, and the price of a rights share is £1.30, the value of the rights offer will be the difference between the two:

$$£1.54 - £1.30 = £0.24 \text{ per share}$$

Market forces will usually ensure that the actual and theoretical price of rights shares will be fairly close.

### Activity (15.15)

An investor with 2,000 shares in Shaw Holdings plc (see Example 15.3) has contacted you for investment advice. She is undecided whether to take up the rights issue, sell the rights or allow the rights offer to lapse.

Calculate the effect on the net wealth of the investor of each of the options being considered.

Before the rights issue the position of the investor was:

|  | £ |
|---|---|
| Value of shares (2,000 × £1.60) | 3,200 |

If she takes up the rights issue, she will be in the following position:

|  | £ |
|---|---|
| Value of holding after rights issue ((2,000 + 500) × £1.54) | 3,850 |
| Cost of buying the rights shares (500 × £1.30) | (650) |
|  | 3,200 |

**Activity 15.15** (*continued*)

If the investor sells the rights, she will be in the following position:

|  | £ |
|---|---|
| Value of holding after rights issue (2,000 × £1.54) | 3,080 |
| Sale of rights (500 × £0.24) | 120 |
|  | 3,200 |

If the investor lets the rights offer lapse, she will be in the following position:

|  | £ |
|---|---|
| Value of holding after rights issue (2,000 × £1.54) | 3,080 |

As we can see, the first two options should leave her in the same position concerning net wealth as before the rights issue. Before the rights issue she had 2,000 shares worth £1.60 each, or £3,200 in total. However, she will be worse off if she allows the rights offer to lapse than under the other two options.

In practice, businesses will typically sell the rights on behalf of those investors who seem to be allowing them to lapse. It will then pass on the proceeds in order to ensure that they are not worse off as a result of the issue.

When considering a rights issue, the directors must first consider the amount of funds needing to be raised. This will depend on the future plans and needs of the business. The directors must then decide on the issue price of the rights shares. Normally, this decision is not critical. In Example 15.3, the business made a one-for-four issue with the price of the rights shares set at £1.30. However, it could have raised the same amount by making a one-for-two issue and setting the rights price at £0.65, a one-for-one issue and setting the price at £0.325, and so on. The issue price that is finally decided upon will not affect the value of the underlying assets of the business or the proportion of the underlying assets and earnings to which each shareholder is entitled. The directors must ensure that the issue price is not above the current market price of the shares, however, or the issue will be unsuccessful.

**Real World 15.10** describes how a major car dealer has used a rights issue to help to refinance its business.

---

**Real World 15.10**

### Repairing the statement of financial position          **FT**

Pendragon shares fell on Thursday as the car dealer moved to shore up its debt-laden statement of financial position with a £75.2 million ($121 million) rights issue. The fundraising is a condition of the banks agreeing to new three-year loan terms and will cut its £300 million debt burden to around £220 million by December, enabling a dividend to be paid next year. Existing investors will be offered new shares at 10p each, on the basis of nine new shares for every eight held.

Pendragon has also agreed to give pension trustees £36 million of security in 17 of its properties in exchange for wiping out the £40 million pension deficit.

Mike Allen, at Panmure Gordon stockbrokers, described the rights issue as 'good news'. 'It should allow the company to run the business on reduced gearing, allow a dividend to be paid in 2012 and also unlock significant cash flow through the reduction of its pension deficit,' he said. But the shares fell 2.3 per cent to close at 21.25p amid concerns that the slowdown in consumer spending would dent new car sales.

*Source*: Adapted from 'Pendragon launches rights issue', G. Plimmer, 14 July 2011, FT.com.

## Offers for sale and public issues

An **offer for sale** usually involves a business that trades as a public limited company selling a new issue of shares to a financial institution known as an *issuing house*. However, shares that are already in issue may also be sold to an issuing house. In this case, existing shareholders agree to sell all or some of their shares to the issuing house. The issuing house will, in turn, sell the shares, purchased from either the business or its shareholders, to the public. The issuing house will publish a prospectus that sets out details of the business and the type of shares to be sold, and investors will be invited to apply for shares. The advantage of this type of issue, from the business's viewpoint, is that the sale proceeds of the shares are certain.

A **public issue** involves the business making a direct invitation to the public to purchase its shares. Typically, this is done through a newspaper advertisement. The shares may, once again, be either a new issue or those already in issue. An offer for sale and a public issue will both result in a widening of share ownership in the business.

In practical terms, the net effect on the business is much the same whether there is an offer for sale or a public issue. As we have seen, the administrative costs of a public issue can be very large. Some share issues by Stock Exchange listed businesses arise from the initial listing of the business, often known as an *initial public offering (IPO)*. Other share issues are undertaken by businesses that are already listed and that are seeking additional finance from investors; usually such issues are known as a *seasoned equity offering (SEO)*. IPOs are very popular, but SEOs are rather less so.

## Setting a share price

When making an issue of shares, the business or the issuing house will usually set a price for the shares. Establishing this may not be an easy task, however, particularly where the market is volatile or where the business has unique characteristics. One way of dealing with this issue-price problem is to make a **tender issue** of shares. This involves the investors determining the price at which the shares are issued. Although the business (or issuing house) may publish a reserve price to help guide investors, it will be up to the individual investor to determine the number of shares to be purchased and the price the investor is prepared to pay. Once the offers from investors have all been received and recorded, a price at which all the shares can be sold will be established (known as the *striking price*). Investors who have made offers at, or above, the striking price will be issued shares at the striking price; offers received below the striking price will be rejected. Note that all of the shares will be issued at the same price irrespective of the prices actually offered by individual investors.

Although this form of issue is adopted occasionally, it is not popular with investors, and is therefore not in widespread use.

## Private placings

A **private placing** does not involve an invitation to the public to subscribe for shares. Instead the shares are 'placed' with selected investors, such as large financial institutions. This can be a quick and relatively cheap form of raising funds, because savings can be made in advertising and legal costs. However, it can result in the ownership of the business being concentrated in a few hands. Sometimes, unlisted businesses seeking relatively small amounts of cash will make this form of issue.

**Real World 15.11** describes how a placing was used by a high-technology business to fund the acquisition of other businesses.

**Real World 15.11**

## Well placed

**FT**

Oxford Instruments, the provider of high technology tools and systems for industrial and academic research, has placed shares worth nearly £40 million ($65 million) to fund the acquisition of two businesses which extends its involvement in the nanotechnology market. The company, the first commercial spin-out company from Oxford University, embarked on the placing which raised £39 million on the same day it modestly beat analysts' expectations with a 24 per cent jump in full-year revenue from £212 million to £262 million and a rise in pre-tax profits from £18 million to £27 million.

Its shares rose $18^{1}/_{2}$p to 800p as investors reacted positively to trading progress at Oxford Instruments, its placing and its expansion plans.

Jonathan Flint, chief executive, said the purchase of Frankfurt-based Omicron for €32 million ($46 million) in cash and Dallas-based Omniprobe for $19 million would strengthen Oxford Instruments position as the leading supplier of capital equipment for those involved in nanotechnology research.

Omicron produces microscopes capable of imaging and moving individual atoms while Omniprobe specialises in devices that can remove tiny pieces of silicon wafer for quality control testing in the semiconductor industry.

*Source*: 'Oxford Instruments to acquire two groups', M. Kavanagh, FT.com, 15 June 2011.

Placings are a popular way of issuing new shares for both newly listed and more seasoned listed businesses. During 2010, they accounted for more than 50 per cent of the total finance raised from shares issued by companies that were newly-listed on the London Stock Exchange (see reference 1 at the end of the chapter).

### Bonus issues

We should recall from Chapter 4 that a bonus issue is not a means of raising finance. It is simply converting one part of the equity (reserves) into another (ordinary shares). No cash changes hands; this benefits neither the business nor the shareholders.

## The role of the Stock Exchange

Earlier we considered the various forms of long-term capital that are available to a business. In this section we examine the role that the **Stock Exchange** plays in providing finance for businesses. The Stock Exchange acts as both an important *primary* and *secondary* capital market for businesses. As a primary market, its function is to enable businesses to raise new finance. As a secondary market, its function is to enable investors to sell their securities (including shares and loan notes) with ease. Thus, it provides a 'second-hand' market where shares and loan notes already in issue may be bought and sold.

To enable it to issue shares or loan notes through the Stock Exchange, a business must be 'listed'. Similarly, it must also be Stock Exchange listed before its existing shares and loan notes can be bought and sold there. Listing means that the business must meet fairly stringent requirements concerning size, profit history, information disclosure, and so on.

**Real World 15.12** suggests that IPOs may be a good investment for those taking up the shares.

### Real World 15.12

### Issues are not problems

It seems that taking up IPOs is profitable, relative to the returns available from investing in stock exchange listed shares generally. This emerged from a research exercise that examined 1,735 separate IPOs that took place through the London Stock Exchange during the period 1995 to 2006.

Among other things, the research looked at the performance (increase in share price and dividends, if any) during the 12 months following the date of the new issue. IPO shares fared about 13 per cent better than did the average stock exchange equity investment. In other words, an investor who took up all of the IPOs between 1995 and 2006 and held them for one year would be 13 per cent better off than one who bought shares in a range of other businesses listed on the stock exchange and held them for a year. This is not to say that all IPOs represented a profitable one-year investment. It simply means that the IPO investor would have lost less in those cases than the other investor.

*Source*: 'The London Markets and Private Equity-backed IPOs', M. Levis, Cass Business School, April 2008.

### Advantages of a listing

The secondary market role of the Stock Exchange means that shares and other financial claims are easily transferable. Furthermore, their prices are constantly under scrutiny by investors and skilled analysts. This helps to promote the tendency for the price quoted for a particular business's shares to reflect their true worth at that particular time. These factors can bring real benefits to a business.

### Activity 15.16

What kinds of benefits might a business gain from its shares being listed?

If it is generally accepted that shares can easily be sold for prices that tend to reflect their true worth, investors will have more confidence to invest. The business may benefit from this greater investor confidence by finding it easier to raise long-term finance and by obtaining this finance at a lower cost, as investors will view their investment as being less risky.

It is worth pointing out that investors are not obliged to use the Stock Exchange as the means of transferring shares in a listed business. However, it is usually the most convenient way of buying or selling shares.

The Stock Exchange can be a useful vehicle for a successful entrepreneur wishing to realise the value of the business that has been built up. By floating (listing) the shares on the Stock Exchange, and thereby making the shares available to the public, the entrepreneur will usually benefit from a gain in the value of the shares held and will be able to realise that gain easily, if required, by selling some shares.

## Disadvantages of a listing

A stock exchange listing can have certain disadvantages for a business. These include:

- Strict rules are imposed on listed businesses, including requirements for levels of financial disclosure additional to those already imposed by International Financial Reporting Standards (for example, the listing rules require that half-yearly financial reports are published).
- Financial analysts, financial journalists and others tend to monitor closely the activities of listed businesses, particularly larger ones. Such scrutiny may not be welcome, particularly if the business is dealing with sensitive issues or is experiencing operational problems.
- It is often suggested that listed businesses are under pressure to perform well over the short term. This pressure may detract from undertaking projects that will yield benefits only in the longer term. If the market becomes disenchanted with the business, and the price of its shares falls, this may make it vulnerable to a takeover bid from another business.
- The costs of obtaining and retaining a listing are huge and this may be a real deterrent for some businesses.

To make an initial public offering, a business will rely on the help of various specialists such as lawyers, accountants and bankers. As we have seen, this represents a significant cost to the business.

Although there are over 1,000 UK businesses listed on the London Stock Exchange, in terms of equity market value, the market is dominated by just a few large ones, as is shown in **Real World 15.13**.

### Real World 15.13

#### Listing to one side

At 31 July 2011, there were 1,009 businesses that had a London Stock Exchange listing. Just 121 of them (12.0 per cent) accounted for 86 per cent of their total equity market value.

A total of 201 businesses (19.9 per cent of listed businesses) accounted for 92.2 per cent of total equity market value.

*Source: Market Statistics, London Stock Exchange, June 2011, Table 8.*

**Real World 15.14** provides an analysis of the ownership of shares in UK listed businesses at the end of 2008.

THE ROLE OF THE STOCK EXCHANGE

**Real World 15.14**

## Ownership of UK listed shares

At the end of 2008, the proportion of shares of UK listed businesses held by UK investors was as shown in Figure 15.12.

**Figure 15.12    Ownership of UK listed shares by UK investors, end of 2008**

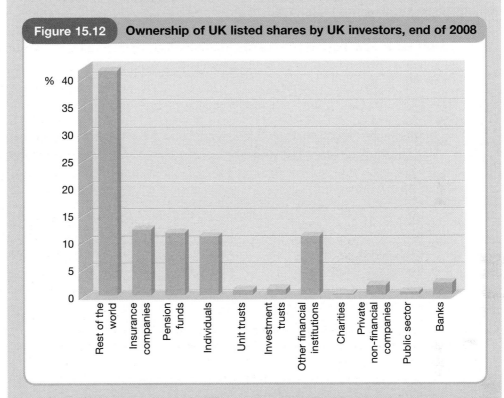

A striking feature of the ownership of UK shares is the extent of overseas ownership. At the end of 2008 this accounted for 42 per cent of the total; in 1963 it was 7 per cent and has grown fairly steadily ever since. This is broadly mirrored by the extent to which UK investors own shares of businesses based elsewhere in the world. It reflects increasing levels of globalisation of business.

Another striking feature is the extent to which large financial institutions now dominate the ownership of UK listed shares. In 1963, 58 per cent of those UK shares owned by UK investors were owned by individuals. At the end of 2008 it was only 10 per cent.

*Source: Financial Statistics*, Share Ownership Survey 2008, Office for National Statistics, p. 1. Copyright © 2010 Crown Copyright. Crown copyright material is reproduced with the permission of the Controller of HMSO.

### Going private

Such are the disadvantages of a stock market listing that many businesses have 'delisted'. This has obviously denied them the advantages of a listing, but it has avoided the disadvantages.

## The Alternative Investment Market

The **Alternative Investment Market (AIM)** was established in June 1995 by the London Stock Exchange for smaller, young and growing businesses. AIM is similar in style to the main London Stock Exchange but it is cheaper for the business to enter. Obtaining an AIM listing and raising funds costs the typical business about £500,000. Many AIM listed businesses are family-based ones. AIM has proved to be a very successful market where new equity finance can be raised and shares can be traded. Businesses listed on AIM tend to have market values in the range £1 million to £250 million, however, some of them have market values greater than £1,000 million, as is shown by **Real World 15.15**.

### Real World 15.15

#### Take AIM

At 30 June 2011, there were 1,136 businesses that had shares that were quoted on AIM. Their distribution according to market value is shown in Figure 15.13.

**Figure 15.13** Distribution of AIM listed companies by equity market value

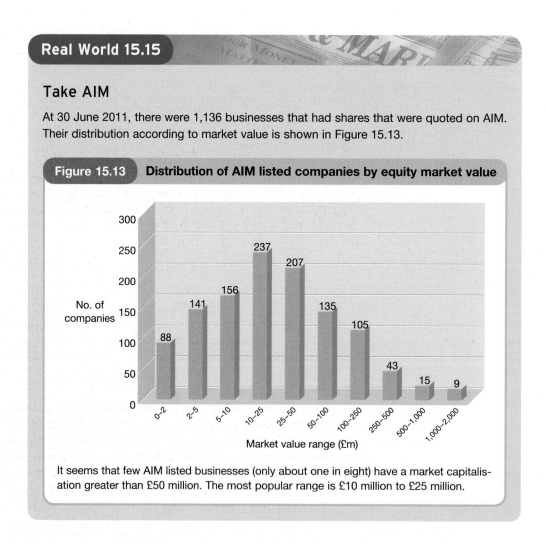

It seems that few AIM listed businesses (only about one in eight) have a market capitalisation greater than £50 million. The most popular range is £10 million to £25 million.

The listing requirements of AIM are less stringent than those of a full listing. AIM listed businesses tend to be more risky than fully listed ones, which can make AIM listed shares less attractive.

AIM listed companies include Majestic Wine plc, the wine retailer, and Millwall Football Club.

# Providing long-term finance for the small business

Although the Stock Exchange provides an important source of long-term finance for large businesses, it is not really suitable for small businesses. The aggregate market value of shares that are to be listed on the Stock Exchange must be at least £700,000 and, in practice, the amounts are much higher because of the high costs of listing. Thus, small businesses must look elsewhere for help in raising long-term finance. The more important sources of finance that are available to small businesses are venture capital, business angels and government assistance. We shall now consider these.

## Venture capital

**Venture capital** is long-term capital provided to small and medium-sized businesses that wish to grow but do not have ready access to stock markets because of the prohibitively large costs of obtaining a listing. The businesses of interest to the venture capitalist will have higher levels of risk than would normally be acceptable to traditional providers of finance, such as the major clearing banks. The attraction for the venture capitalist of investing in higher-risk businesses is the prospect of higher returns.

Many small businesses are designed to provide the owners with a particular lifestyle and with job satisfaction. These kinds of businesses are not of interest to venture capitalists, as they are unlikely to provide the desired financial returns. Instead, venture capitalists look for businesses where the owners are seeking significant sales revenue and profit growth and need some outside help in order to achieve this.

The risks associated with the business can vary in practice. They are often due to the nature of the products or the fact that it is a new business that either lacks a trading record or has new management or both of these.

Venture capitalists provide long-term capital in the form of share and loan finance for different situations, including:

- *Start-up capital.* This is available to businesses that are not fully developed. They may need finance to help refine the business concept or to engage in product development or initial marketing. They have not yet reached the stage where they are trading.
- *Early-stage capital.* This is available for businesses that are ready to start trading.
- *Expansion capital.* This is aimed at providing additional funding for existing, growing businesses.
- *Buy-out or buy-in capital.* This is used to fund the acquisition of a business either by the existing management team ('buy-out') or by a new management team ('buy-in'). Management buy-outs (MBOs) and buy-ins (MBIs) often occur where a large business wishes to divest itself of one of its operating units or where a family business wishes to sell out because of succession problems.
- *Rescue capital.* To help turn around businesses that are in difficulties.

The venture capitalist will often make a substantial investment in the business (usually more than £100,000), and this will often take the form of ordinary shares. However, some of the funding may be in the form of preference shares or loans. To keep an eye on the sum invested, the venture capitalist will usually require a representative on the board of directors as a condition of the investment.The venture capitalist may not be looking for a very quick return, and may well be prepared to invest in a business for five years or more. The return may take the form of a capital gain on the realisation of the investment (typically selling the shares).

Though venture capital is extremely important for some small businesses, the vast majority of small businesses obtain their finance from other sources. **Real World 15.16** shows the main sources of finance for small businesses in the UK.

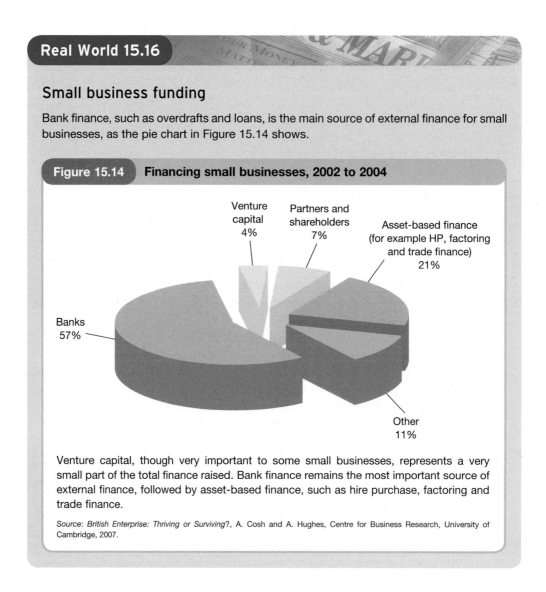

**Real World 15.16**

## Small business funding

Bank finance, such as overdrafts and loans, is the main source of external finance for small businesses, as the pie chart in Figure 15.14 shows.

**Figure 15.14**   **Financing small businesses, 2002 to 2004**

Venture capital, though very important to some small businesses, represents a very small part of the total finance raised. Bank finance remains the most important source of external finance, followed by asset-based finance, such as hire purchase, factoring and trade finance.

*Source: British Enterprise: Thriving or Surviving?*, A. Cosh and A. Hughes, Centre for Business Research, University of Cambridge, 2007.

## Business angels

**Business angels** are often wealthy individuals who have been successful in business. They are usually willing to invest, through a shareholding, between £10,000 and £750,000 in a start-up business or in a business that is wishing to expand. If larger amounts are required, a syndicate of business angels may be formed to raise the money. Business angels typically make one or two investments over a three-year period and will usually be prepared to invest for a period of between three and five years. They normally have a minority stake in the business, and although they do not usually become involved in its day-to-day management, they tend to take an interest, more generally, in the way that the business is managed.

Business angels fill an important gap in the market as the size and nature of investments they find appealing are often not so appealing to venture capitalists. They can be attractive to small businesses because they may:

- make investment decisions quickly, particularly if they are familiar with the industry in which the new business operates;
- offer useful skills, experience and business contacts;
- accept lower financial returns than those required from venture capitalists, in order to have the opportunity to become involved in a new and interesting project.

Business angels offer an informal source of share finance and it is not always easy for owners of small businesses to identify a suitable angel. However, numerous business angel networks have now developed to help owners of small businesses find their 'perfect partner'.

The panellists on the BBC TV programme *Dragons' Den* are business angels.

## Government assistance

One of the most effective ways in which the UK government assists small businesses is through the Enterprise Finance Guarantee Scheme (formerly the Small Firms Loan Guarantee Scheme). This aims to help small businesses that have viable business plans but lack the security to enable them to borrow. The scheme guarantees:

- 75 per cent of the amount borrowed, for which the borrower pays a premium of 2 per cent on the outstanding borrowing
- loans ranging from £1,000 to £1 million for a maximum period of ten years.

The scheme is available for businesses with annual sales revenue of up to £25 million.

In addition to other forms of financial assistance, such as government grants and tax incentives for investors to buy shares in small businesses, the government also helps by providing information concerning the sources of finance available.

### Self-assessment question (15.1)

Helsim Ltd is a wholesaler and distributor of electrical components. The most recent draft financial statements of the business revealed the following:

**Income statement for the year**

|  | £m | £m |
|---|---|---|
| Sales revenue |  | 14.2 |
| Opening inventories | 3.2 |  |
| Purchases | 8.4 |  |
|  | 11.6 |  |
| Closing inventories | (3.8) | (7.8) |
| Gross profit |  | 6.4 |
| Administration expenses |  | (3.0) |
| Distribution expenses |  | (2.1) |
| Operating profit |  | 1.3 |
| Finance costs |  | (0.8) |
| Profit before taxation |  | 0.5 |
| Tax |  | (0.2) |
| Profit for the period |  | 0.3 |

→

## Self-assessment question 15.1 (*continued*)

### Statement of financial position as at the end of the year

|  | £m |
|---|---|
| **ASSETS** | |
| **Non-current assets** | |
| *Property, plant and equipment* | |
| Land and buildings | 3.8 |
| Equipment | 0.9 |
| Motor vehicles | 0.5 |
|  | 5.2 |
| **Current assets** | |
| Inventories | 3.8 |
| Trade receivables | 3.6 |
| Cash at bank | 0.1 |
|  | 7.5 |
| **Total assets** | 12.7 |
| **EQUITY AND LIABILITIES** | |
| **Equity** | |
| Share capital | 2.0 |
| Retained earnings | 1.8 |
|  | 3.8 |
| **Non-current liabilities** | |
| Loan notes (secured on property) | 3.5 |
| **Current liabilities** | |
| Trade payables | 1.8 |
| Short-term borrowings | 3.6 |
|  | 5.4 |
| **Total equity and liabilities** | 12.7 |

*Notes:*

1  Land and buildings are shown at their current market value. Equipment and motor vehicles are shown at cost less accumulated depreciation.
2  No dividends have been paid to ordinary shareholders for the past three years.

In recent months, trade payables have been pressing for payment. The managing director has therefore decided to reduce the level of trade payables to an average of 40 days outstanding. To achieve this, he has decided to approach the bank with a view to increasing the overdraft (the short-term borrowings comprise only a bank overdraft). The business is currently paying 10 per cent a year interest on the overdraft.

*Required:*

(a) Comment on the liquidity position of the business.
(b) Calculate the amount of finance required to reduce trade payables, from the level shown on the balance sheet, to an average of 40 days outstanding.
(c) State, with reasons, how you consider the bank would react to the proposal to grant an additional overdraft facility.
(d) Identify four sources of finance (internal or external, but excluding a bank overdraft) that may be suitable to finance the reduction in trade payables, and state, with reasons, which of these you consider the most appropriate.

**The solution to this question may be found at the back of the book on pp. 742–743.**

## Summary

The main points in this chapter may be summarised as follows:

**Sources of finance**

- Long-term finance is for at least one year whereas short-term finance is for a shorter period.

- External sources of finance require the agreement of outside parties, whereas internal sources do not.

- The higher the risk associated with a source of finance, the higher the expected return from investors.

**Internal sources of finance**

- Retained earnings are by far the most important source of new long-term finance (internal or external) for UK businesses.

- Retained earnings are not a free source of finance, as investors will require returns similar to those from ordinary shares.

- Internal sources of short-term finance include tighter control of trade receivables, reducing inventories levels and delaying payments to trade payables.

**External sources of finance**

- External sources of long-term finance include ordinary shares, preference shares, borrowings, leases, hire-purchase agreements and securitisation.

- From an investor's perspective, ordinary shares are normally the most risky form of investment and provide the highest expected returns to investors. Borrowings (loans) are normally the least risky and provide the lowest expected returns to investors.

- Loans are relatively low risk because lenders usually have security for their loan. Loan covenants can further protect lenders.

- Types of loans include term loans, convertible loan notes, mortgages, eurobonds and deep discount bonds.

- Convertible loan notes offer the right of conversion to ordinary shares at a specified date and a specified price.

- Interest rates may be floating or fixed.

- A finance lease is really a form of lending that gives the lessee the use of an asset over most of its useful life in return for regular payments.

- A sale-and-leaseback arrangement involves the sale of an asset to a financial institution accompanied by an agreement to lease the asset back to the business.

- Securitisation involves bundling together similar, illiquid assets to provide backing for the issue of bonds.

- External sources of short-term finance include bank overdrafts, debt factoring and invoice discounting.

- Bank overdrafts are flexible and cheap but are repayable on demand.

- Debt factoring and invoice discounting use trade receivables as a basis for borrowing, with the latter more popular because of cost and flexibility.

- When choosing between long-term and short-term borrowing, important factors include matching the type of borrowing to the type of assets, flexibility, refunding risk, and interest rates.
- The level of gearing is often an important factor in assessing the risk and returns to ordinary shareholders.

**Share issues**

- Share issues that involve the payment of cash by investors can take the form of a rights issue, public issue, offer for sale or a private placing.
- A rights issue is made to existing shareholders. Most share issues are of this type as the law requires that shares that are to be issued for cash must first be offered to existing shareholders. Rights issue costs are relatively low.
- A public issue involves a direct issue to the public and an offer for sale involves an indirect issue to the public.
- A private placing is an issue of shares to selected investors.
- A bonus issue of shares does not involve the receipt of cash in exchange for the shares issued.

**The Stock Exchange**

- The Stock Exchange is an important primary and secondary market in capital for large businesses. However, obtaining a Stock Exchange listing can have certain drawbacks for a business.

**The Alternative Investment Market (AIM)**

- AIM is another important primary and secondary market managed by the London Stock Exchange for smaller, growing businesses. It tends to be a cheaper way for a business to become listed.

**Small businesses**

- Venture capital is long-term capital for small or medium-sized businesses that are not listed on the Stock Exchange. These businesses often have higher levels of risk but provide the venture capitalist with the prospect of higher levels of return.
- Business angels are wealthy individuals who are willing to invest in businesses at either an early stage or expansion stage of development.
- The government assists small businesses through guaranteeing loans and by providing grants and tax incentives.

## MyAccountingLab

Go to **www.myaccountinglab.com** to check your understanding of the chapter, create a personalised study plan, and maximise your revision time

## Key terms

| | |
|---|---|
| Security p. 599 | Sale and leaseback p. 609 |
| Fixed charge p. 599 | Hire purchase p. 610 |
| Floating charge p. 599 | Securitisation p. 611 |
| Loan covenants p. 600 | Bank overdraft p. 613 |
| Subordinated loans p. 601 | Debt factoring p. 613 |
| Term loan p. 603 | Invoice discounting p. 616 |
| Loan notes p. 603 | Asset-based finance p. 617 |
| Loan stock p. 603 | Rights issue p. 621 |
| Bonds p. 603 | Offer for sale p. 625 |
| Eurobonds p. 604 | Public issue p. 625 |
| Deep discount bonds p. 604 | Tender issue p. 625 |
| Convertible loan notes p. 605 | Private placing p. 625 |
| Mortgage p. 606 | Stock Exchange p. 626 |
| Floating interest rate p. 606 | Alternative Investment Market (AIM) |
| Fixed interest rate p. 606 | p. 630 |
| Finance lease p. 606 | Venture capital p. 631 |
| Operating lease p. 607 | Business angel p. 632 |

## References

1 *Market Statistics*, London Stock Exchange, December 2010, Table 3.

2 Armitage, S., 'The direct costs of UK rights issues and open offers', *European Financial Management*, March 2000.

3 *The Cost of Capital: An International Comparison*, London Stock Exchange, 2006.

## Further reading

If you wish to explore the topics discussed in this chapter in more depth, try the following books:

Arnold, G., *Corporate Financial Management*, 4th edn, Financial Times Prentice Hall, 2008, chapters 11 and 12.

Brealey, R., Myers, S. and Allen, F., *Corporate Finance*, 10th edn, McGraw-Hill International, 2010, chapters 14, 25 and 26.

Hillier, D., Ross, S., Westerfield, R., Jaffe, J. and Jordan, B., *Corporate Finance*, European edn, McGraw-Hill Higher Education, 2010, chapters 19 to 21.

Pike, R., Neale, B. and Linsley, P., *Corporate Finance and Investment*, 6th edn, Financial Times Prentice Hall, 2009, chapters 15 and 16.

## Review questions

**Solutions to these questions can be found at the back of the book on p. 758.**

**15.1** What are the potential disadvantages of raising finance through a sale-and-leaseback arrangement?

**15.2** Why might a business that has a Stock Exchange listing revert to being unlisted?

**15.3** Distinguish between an offer for sale and a public issue of shares.

**15.4** Distinguish between invoice discounting and factoring.

## Exercises

**Exercises 15.1 and 15.2 are basic level, 15.3 and 15.4 are intermediate level and 15.5, 15.6, and 15.7 are advanced level. Those with coloured numbers have solutions at the back of the book starting on page 796.**

**If you wish to try more exercises, visit the students' side of the Companion Website and MyAccountingLab.**

**15.1** Answer *all* parts of this question.

*Required:*
Provide reasons why a business may decide to:

(a) Lease rather than buy an asset which is to be held for long-term use.
(b) Use retained earning to finance growth rather than issue new shares.
(c) Repay long-term loan capital earlier than the specified repayment date.

**15.2** H. Brown (Portsmouth) Ltd produces a range of central heating systems for sale to builders' merchants. As a result of increasing demand for the business's products, the directors have decided to expand production. The cost of acquiring new plant and machinery and the increase in working capital requirements are planned to be financed by a mixture of long-term and short-term borrowing.

*Required:*
(a) Discuss the major factors that should be taken into account when deciding on the appropriate mix of long-term and short-term borrowing necessary to finance the expansion programme.
(b) Discuss the major factors that a lender should take into account when deciding whether to grant a long-term loan to the business.
(c) Identify three conditions that might be included in a long-term loan agreement.

**15.3** Devonian plc has the following equity as at 30 November Year 4:

|  | £m |
|---|---|
| Ordinary shares 25p fully paid | 50.0 |
| General reserve | 22.5 |
| Retained earnings | 25.5 |
|  | 98.0 |

The business has no long-term borrowings.

In the year to 30 November Year 4, the operating profit (profit before interest and taxation) was £40m and it is expected that this will increase by 25 per cent during the forthcoming year. The business is listed on the London Stock Exchange and the share price as at 30 November Year 4 was £2.10.

The business wishes to raise £72m in order to re-equip one of its factories and is considering two possible financing options. The first option is to make a 1-for-5 rights issue at a discount price of £1.80 per share. The second option is to borrow long-term at an interest rate of 10 per cent a year. If the first option is taken, it is expected that the price/earnings (P/E) ratio will remain the same for the forthcoming year. If the second option is taken, it is estimated that the P/E ratio will fall by 10 per cent by the end of the forthcoming year.

Assume a tax rate of 30 per cent.

*Required:*

(a) Assuming a rights issue of shares is made, calculate:
   (1) the theoretical ex-rights price of an ordinary share in Devonian plc; and
   (2) the value of the rights for each original ordinary share.
(b) Calculate the price of an ordinary share in Devonian plc in one year's time assuming:
   (1) a rights issue is made; and
   (2) the required funds are borrowed.
   Comment on your findings.
(c) Explain why rights issues are usually made at a discount.
(d) From the business's viewpoint, how critical is the pricing of a rights issue likely to be?

**15.4** Raphael Ltd is a small engineering business that has annual sales revenue of £2.4 million, all of which is on credit. In recent years, the business has experienced credit control problems. The average collection period for trade receivables has risen to 50 days even though the stated policy of the business is for payment to be made within 30 days. In addition, 1.5 per cent of sales are written off as bad debts each year.

The business has recently been in talks with a factor, which is prepared to make an advance to the business equivalent to 80 per cent of trade receivables, based on the assumption that customers will, in future, adhere to a 30-day payment period. The interest rate for the advance will be 11 per cent a year. The trade receivables are currently financed through a bank overdraft, which has an interest rate of 12 per cent a year. The factor will take over the credit control procedures of the business and this will result in a saving to the business of £18,000 a year. However, the factor will make a charge of 2 per cent of sales revenue for this service. The use of the factoring service is expected to eliminate the bad debts incurred by the business.

*Required:*

Calculate the net cost of the factor agreement to the business and state whether the business should take advantage of the opportunity to factor its trade receivables.

**15.5** Russell Ltd installs and services heating and ventilation systems for commercial premises. The business's most recent statement of financial position and income statement are as follows:

**Statement of financial position**

| | £000 |
|---|---|
| **ASSETS** | |
| **Non-current assets** | |
| Property, plant and equipment | 741.8 |
| **Current assets** | |
| Inventories at cost | 293.2 |
| Trade receivables | 510.3 |
| | 803.5 |
| **Total assets** | 1,545.3 |

**EQUITY AND LIABILITIES**

**Equity**

| | |
|---|---:|
| £1 ordinary shares | 400.0 |
| General reserve | 50.2 |
| Retained earnings | 382.2 |
| | 832.4 |

**Non-current liabilities**

| | |
|---|---:|
| Borrowings – 12% loan notes | 250.0 |
| (repayable in 5 years' time) | |

**Current liabilities**

| | |
|---|---:|
| Trade payables | 199.7 |
| Taxation | 128.0 |
| Borrowings – Bank overdraft | 135.2 |
| | 462.9 |
| **Total equity and liabilities** | 1,545.3 |

**Income statement for the year**

| | £000 |
|---|---:|
| Sales revenue | 5,207.8 |
| Operating profit | 542.0 |
| Interest payable | (30.0) |
| Profit before taxation | 512.0 |
| Taxation (25%) | (128.0) |
| Profit for the year | 384.0 |
| *Note*: | |
| Dividend paid during the year | 153.6 |

The business wishes to invest in more machinery and equipment in order to cope with an upsurge in demand for its services. An additional operating profit of £120,000 a year is expected if an investment of £600,000 is made in plant and machinery.

The directors are considering an offer from venture capitalists to finance the expansion programme. The finance will be made available immediately through either:

● an issue of £1 ordinary shares at a premium on par of £3 a share; or
● an issue of £600,000 10 per cent loan notes at par.

The directors wish to maintain the same dividend payout ratio in future years as in past years whichever method of finance is chosen.

*Required:*
(a) For each of the financing schemes:
  (1) prepare a projected income statement for next year;
  (2) calculate the projected earnings per share for next year;
  (3) calculate the projected level of gearing as at the end of next year.
(b) Briefly assess both of the financing schemes under consideration from the viewpoint of the existing shareholders.

**15.6** Carpets Direct plc wishes to increase the number of its retail outlets in the south of England. The board of directors has decided to finance this expansion programme by raising the funds from existing shareholders through a 1-for-4 rights issue. The most recent income statement of the business is as follows:

## Income statement for the year ended 30 April

|  | £m |
|---|---|
| Sales revenue | 164.5 |
| Operating profit | 12.6 |
| Interest | (6.2) |
| Profit before taxation | 6.4 |
| Taxation | (1.9) |
| Profit for the year | 4.5 |

A £2 million ordinary dividend had been paid in respect of the year.

The share capital consists of 120 million ordinary shares with a nominal value of £0.50 a share. These are currently being traded on the Stock Exchange at a price/earnings ratio of 22 times and the board of directors has decided to issue the new shares at a discount of 20 per cent on the current market value.

*Required:*
(a) Calculate the theoretical ex-rights price of an ordinary share in Carpets Direct plc.
(b) Calculate the price at which the rights in Carpets Direct plc are likely to be traded.
(c) Identify and evaluate, at the time of the rights issue, each of the options arising from the rights issue to an investor who holds 4,000 ordinary shares before the rights announcement.
(*Hint*: To answer part (a), first calculate the earnings per share and then use this and the P/E ratio to calculate the marker value per share.)

**15.7** Gainsborough Fashions Ltd operates a small chain of fashion shops in North Wales. In recent months the business has been under pressure from its suppliers to reduce the average credit period taken from three months to one month. As a result, the directors have approached the bank to ask for an increase in the existing overdraft for one year to be able to comply with the suppliers' demands. The most recent financial statements of the business are as follows:

### Statement of financial position as at 31 May

|  | £ |
|---|---|
| **ASSETS** | |
| **Non-current assets** | |
| Property, plant and equipment | 74,000 |
| **Current assets** | |
| Inventories at cost | 198,000 |
| Trade receivables | 3,000 |
|  | 201,000 |
| **Total assets** | 275,000 |
| **EQUITY AND LIABILITIES** | |
| **Equity** | |
| £1 ordinary shares | 20,000 |
| General reserve | 4,000 |
| Retained earnings | 17,000 |
|  | 41,000 |
| **Non-current liabilities** | |
| Borrowings – loan notes repayable in just over one year's time | 40,000 |
| **Current liabilities** | |
| Trade payables | 162,000 |
| Accrued expenses | 10,000 |
| Borrowings – bank overdraft | 17,000 |
| Taxation | 5,000 |
|  | 194,000 |
| **Total equity and liabilities** | 275,000 |

**Abbreviated income statement for the year ended 31 May**

|  | £ |
|---|---|
| Sales revenue | 740,000 |
| Operating profit | 38,000 |
| Interest charges | (5,000) |
| Profit before taxation | 33,000 |
| Taxation | (10,000) |
| Profit for the year | 23,000 |

A dividend of £23,000 was paid for the year.

*Notes:*
(1) The loan notes are secured by personal guarantees from the directors.
(2) The current overdraft bears an interest rate of 12 per cent a year.

*Required:*
(a) Identify and discuss the major factors that a bank would take into account before deciding whether to grant an increase in the overdraft of a business.
(b) State whether, in your opinion, the bank should grant the required increase in the overdraft for Gainsborough Fashions Ltd. You should provide reasoned arguments and supporting calculations where necessary.

# Managing working capital

## Introduction

This chapter considers the factors that must be taken into account when managing the working capital of a business. Each element of working capital will be identified and the major issues surrounding them will be discussed. Working capital represents a significant investment for many businesses and so its proper management and control can be vital. We saw in Chapter 14 that an investment in working capital is typically an important aspect of many new investment proposals.

## Learning outcomes

**When you have completed this chapter, you should be able to:**

- identify the main elements of working capital.

- discuss the purpose of working capital and the nature of the working capital cycle.

- explain the importance of establishing policies for the control of working capital.

- explain the factors that have to be taken into account when managing each element of working capital.

## MyAccountingLab

Visit **www.myaccountinglab.com** for practice and revision opportunities

## What is working capital?

**Working capital** is usually defined as current assets less current liabilities. The major elements of current assets are:

- inventories
- trade receivables
- cash (in hand and at bank).

The major elements of current liabilities are:

- trade payables
- bank overdrafts.

The size and composition of working capital can vary between industries. For some types of business, the investment in working capital can be substantial. A manufacturing business, for example, will often invest heavily in raw material, work in progress and finished goods. It will also normally sell its goods on credit, giving rise to trade receivables. A retailer, on the other hand, holds only one form of inventories (finished goods) and will normally sell its goods for cash rather than on credit. Many service businesses hold no inventories.

Most businesses buy goods and/or services on credit, giving rise to trade payables. Few, if any, businesses operate without a cash balance, although in some cases it is a negative one (a bank overdraft).

Working capital represents a net investment in short-term assets. These assets are continually flowing into and out of the business and are essential for day-to-day operations. The various elements of working capital are interrelated and can be seen as part of a short-term cycle. For a manufacturing business, the working capital cycle can be depicted as shown in Figure 16.1.

| Figure 16.1 | The working capital cycle |
| --- | --- |

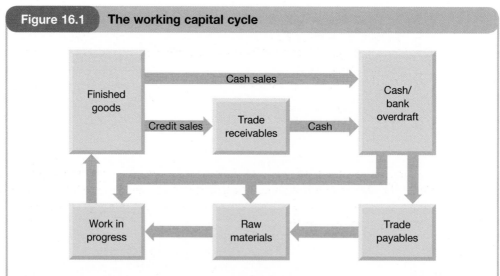

Cash is used to pay trade payables for raw materials, or raw materials are bought for immediate cash settlement. Cash is also spent on labour and other items that turn raw materials into work in progress and, finally, into finished goods. The finished goods are sold to customers either for cash or on credit. In the case of credit customers, there will be a delay before the cash is received from the sales. Receipt of cash completes the cycle.

For a retailer the situation would be as in Figure 16.1 except that there would be only inventories of finished goods and so no work in progress or raw materials. For a purely service business, the working capital cycle would also be similar to that depicted in Figure 16.1 except that there would be no inventories of finished goods or raw materials. There may well be work in progress, however, since many services, for example a case handled by a firm of solicitors, will take some time to complete and costs will build up before the client is billed for them.

## Managing working capital

The management of working capital is an essential part of the business's short-term planning process. Management must decide how much of each element should be held. As we shall see later, there are costs associated with holding either too much or too little of each element. Management must be aware of these costs, which include opportunity costs, in order to manage effectively. Potential benefits must be weighed against likely costs in order to achieve the optimum investment.

The working capital needs of a business are likely to vary over time as a result of changes in the business environment. Managers must monitor these changes to ensure an appropriate level of investment in working capital. Frequent working capital decisions may be necessary in order to adjust to the changed environment.

### Activity (16.1)

What kinds of changes in the business environment might lead to a decision to change the level of investment in working capital? Try to identify four possible changes that could affect the working capital needs of a business.

These may include the following:

- changes in interest rates
- changes in market demand for the business's output
- changes in the seasons
- changes in the state of the economy.

You may have thought of others.

Changes arising within the business could also alter working capital needs. These internal changes might include using different production methods (resulting, perhaps, in a need to hold a lower level of inventories) and changes in the level of risk that managers are prepared to take.

## The scale of working capital

It is tempting to think that, compared with the scale of investment in non-current assets, the amounts invested in working capital are trivial. However, this is not the case – the scale of investment in working capital for many businesses is vast.

**Real World 16.1** gives some impression of the working capital investment for five UK businesses that are either very well known by name, or whose products are everyday commodities for most of us. These businesses were randomly selected, except that each one is high profile and from a different industry. For each business, the major items appearing on the statement of financial position (balance sheet) are expressed as a percentage of the total investment by the providers of long-term finance (equity and non-current liabilities).

**Real World 16.1**

## A summary of the statements of financial position of five UK businesses

| Business: | Next plc | British Airways plc | Babcock Int Group plc | Tesco plc | Severn Trent plc |
|---|---|---|---|---|---|
| Statement of financial position date: | 30.1.10 | 31.3.10 | 31.3.10 | 27.2.10 | 31.3.10 |
| Non-current assets | 70 | 115 | 111 | 114 | 101 |
| Current assets | | | | | |
| Inventories | 33 | 1 | 11 | 9 | – |
| Trade and other receivables | 66 | 7 | 42 | 6 | 7 |
| Other current assets | 1 | 5 | – | 14 | – |
| Cash and near cash | 11 | 25 | 24 | 10 | 4 |
| | 111 | 38 | 77 | 39 | 11 |
| Total assets | 181 | 153 | 188 | 153 | 112 |
| Equity and non-current liabilities | 100 | 100 | 100 | 100 | 100 |
| Current liabilities | | | | | |
| Trade and other payables | 59 | 42 | 63 | 31 | 7 |
| Taxation | 12 | – | 1 | 2 | – |
| Other short-term liabilities | 10 | 11 | 4 | 15 | 1 |
| Overdrafts and short-term borrowings | – | – | 20 | 5 | 4 |
| | 81 | 53 | 88 | 53 | 12 |
| Total equity and liabilities | 181 | 153 | 188 | 153 | 112 |

The non-current assets, current assets and current liabilities are expressed as a percentage of the total net long-term investment (equity plus non-current liabilities) of the business concerned. Next plc is a major retail and home shopping business. British Airways plc (BA) is a leading airline. Babcock International Group plc is a large engineering and support business. Tesco plc is one of the UK's leading supermarkets. Severn Trent plc is an important supplier of water, sewerage services and waste management, mainly in the UK.

Source: Table constructed from information appearing in the financial statements for the year ended during 2010 for each of the five businesses concerned.

Real World 16.1 reveals quite striking differences in the make-up of the statement of financial position from one business to the next. Take, for example, the current assets and current liabilities. Although the totals for current assets are pretty large when compared with the total long-term investment, these percentages vary considerably between businesses. When looking at the mix of current assets, we can see that Next, Babcock and Tesco, which produce and/or sell goods, are the only ones that hold significant amounts of inventories. The other two businesses are service providers and so inventories are not a significant item. We can also see that Tesco does not sell much on credit and very few of BA's and Severn Trents's sales are on credit, as these businesses have little or nothing invested in trade receivables.

Note that Tesco's trade payables are much higher than its trade receivables. They are also high compared to its inventories. Since trade payables represent amounts due to suppliers of inventories, it means that Tesco receives the cash from a typical trolley load of groceries well in advance of paying for them.

In the sections that follow, we shall consider each element of working capital separately and how they might be properly managed. Before doing so, however, it is worth looking at **Real World 16.2**, which suggests that there is scope for improving working capital management among European businesses.

## Real World 16.2

### All tied up

According to a survey of 1,000 of Europe's largest businesses (excluding financial and auto manufacturing businesses), working capital is not as well managed as it could be. The survey, conducted in 2011 by Ernst and Young, suggests that larger European businesses had, in total, between €250 billion and €430 billion tied up in working capital that could be released through better management of inventories, trade receivables and trade payables. The potential for savings represents between 11 per cent and 19 per cent of the total working capital invested and between 4 per cent and 7 per cent of total sales. The lower figure of each range is calculated by comparing the results for each business with the results for the average for the industry, and the higher figure is calculated comparing the results for each business with the upper quartile of the industry within which that business operates.

The report suggests that the higher figure for each range probably represents an ambitious target for savings as there are wide variations in payment terms, customer types, discount practices, and so on across Europe.

The average investment (in days) for 2010 and 2009 by the largest 1,000 European countries for each of the main elements of working capital is set out in Figure 16.2:

The figure shows that there has been little variation in each element. In other words, the average performance, in terms of working capital management, has changed little over the two years. Within each average, however, some businesses have improved and some have deteriorated.

*Source:* Compiled from information in *All Tied Up: Working Capital Management Report 2011*, Ernst and Young, www.ey.com.

→

**Real World 16.2 (continued)**

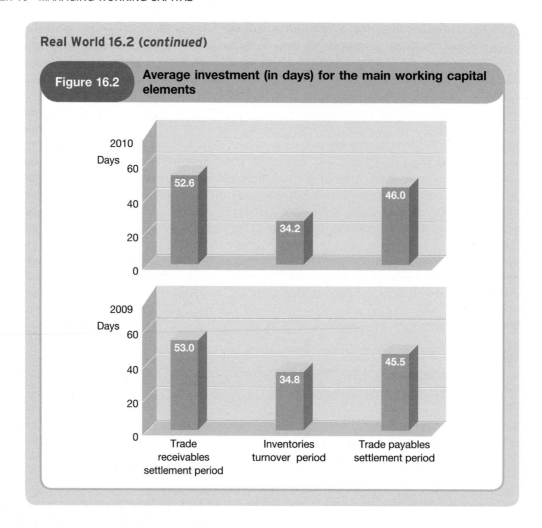

Figure 16.2 Average investment (in days) for the main working capital elements

## Managing inventories

A business may hold inventories for various reasons, the most common of which is to meet the immediate day-to-day requirements of customers and production. However, a business may hold more than is necessary for this purpose where there is a risk that future supplies may be interrupted or scarce. Similarly, if there is a risk that the cost of inventories will rise in the future, a business may decide to buy in large quantities.

For some types of business, inventories held may represent a substantial proportion of total assets held. For example, a car dealership that rents its premises may have nearly all of its total assets in the form of inventories. Inventories' levels of manufacturers tend to be higher than for other types of business as they need to hold three kinds of inventories: raw materials, work in progress and finished goods. Each form of inventories represents a particular stage in the production cycle.

For some types of business, the level of inventories held may vary substantially over the year owing to the seasonal nature of the industry. A greetings card manufacturer may provide an example of such a business. For other businesses, inventories levels may remain fairly stable throughout the year.

Businesses that hold inventories simply to meet the day-to-day requirements of their customers, and for production, will normally seek to minimise the amount of inventories held. This is because there are significant costs associated with holding inventories. These costs include:

- storage and handling costs
- the cost of financing the inventories
- the cost of pilferage and obsolescence
- the cost of opportunities forgone in tying up funds in this form of asset.

To gain some impression of the cost involved in holding inventories, **Real World 16.3** estimates the *financing* cost of inventories for four large businesses.

---

### Real World 16.3

### Inventories financing cost

The financing cost of inventories for each of four large businesses, based on their respective opportunity costs of capital, is calculated below.

| Business | Type of operations | Cost of capital | Average inventories held* | Cost of holding inventories | Operating profit/ (loss) | Cost as a % of operating profit/(loss) |
|---|---|---|---|---|---|---|
| | | (a) | (b) | (a) × (b) | | |
| | | % | £m | £m | £m | % |
| Associated British Foods | Food producer | 9.5 | 1,250 | 119 | 819 | 14.5 |
| British Airways | Airline | 8.9 | 113 | 10 | (231) | 4.3 |
| Kingfisher | Home improvement retailer | 8.1 | 1,668 | 135 | 698 | 19.3 |
| J Sainsbury | Supermarket | 10.0 | 757 | 76 | 851 | 8.9 |

\* Based on opening and closing inventories for the relevant financial period.

We can see that for all four businesses, inventories financing costs are significant in relation to their operating profit/(loss). This is particularly true for Associated British Foods and Kingfisher. The nature of the business for these two involves holding fairly large inventories. For the other two, BA and Sainsbury, inventories holding costs are less important. BA is a service provider and has very low levels of inventories. Sainsbury moves its inventories very fast. These figures do not take account of other costs of inventories' holding mentioned above, like the cost of providing secure storage.

These businesses were not selected because they have particularly high inventories costs but simply because they are among the relatively few that publish their costs of capital.

*Source*: Annual reports of the businesses for the years ending 2010 and 2011.

---

Given that the cost of holding inventories can be high, it may be tempting to think that a business should seek to hold few or no inventories. There are also, however, costs that can arise when the level of inventories is too low.

## Activity (16.2)

What costs might a business incur as a result of holding too low a level of inventories? Try to jot down at least three types of cost.

In answering this activity you may have thought of the following costs:

● loss of sales, from being unable to provide the goods required immediately;
● loss of customer goodwill, for being unable to satisfy customer demand;
● purchasing inventories at a higher price than might otherwise have been possible in order to replenish inventories quickly;
● high transport costs incurred to ensure that inventories are replenished quickly;
● lost production due to shortage of raw materials;
● inefficient production scheduling due to shortages of raw materials.

Before dealing with the various approaches that can be taken to managing inventories, let us consider **Real World 16.4**. It describes how one large international business has sought to reduce its inventories level.

## Real World 16.4

### Back to basics                                                            **FT**

Wal-Mart has said it will seek further reductions in the levels of backroom inventory it holds at its US stores, in a drive to improve its performance . . . John Menzer, vice chairman and head of Wal-Mart's US operations, made the retailer's efforts to cut inventory one of the key elements of remarks to reporters this week when he outlined current strategy. Wal-Mart, he said, currently 'has a real focus on reducing our inventory. Inventory that's on trailers behind our stores, in backrooms and on shelves in our stores.' Cutting back on inventory, he said, reduced 'clutter' in the retailer's stores, gave a better return on invested capital, reduced the need to cut prices on old merchandise, and increased the velocity at which goods moved through the stores.

Eduardo Castro-Wright, chief executive of Wal-Mart's US store network, said the inventory reduction marked a return to basics for the retailer, which would be 'getting more disciplined'. Earlier this year, he said Wal-Mart would link inventory reduction to incentive payments to its officers and managers. Wal-Mart is already regarded as one of the most efficient logistical operations in US retailing. It is currently rolling out to all its US stores and distribution centres a new parallel distribution system that speeds the delivery to stores of 5,000 high turnover (sale revenue) items. It is also discussing with its suppliers how new RFID radio frequency tagging could be used to further reduce the volume of goods in transit to its stores. But further reductions in its inventory turnover would release working capital that could fund investment in its ongoing initiatives to improve its stores.

Adrienne Shapira, retail analyst at Goldman Sachs, has estimated that the retailer could reduce its annual inventory by 18 per cent, which would lead to a $6 billion reduction in working capital needs on a trailing 12-month basis.

*Source*: 'Wal-Mart aims for further inventory cuts', J. Birchall, FT.com, 19 April 2006.

To try to ensure that the inventories are properly managed, a number of procedures and techniques may be used. We shall now consider the more important of these.

## Budgeting future demand

Preparing appropriate budgets is one of the best ways to ensure that inventories will be available to meet future production and sales requirements. These budgets should deal with each product that the business makes and/or sells. It is important that budgets are realistic as they will determine future ordering and production levels. The budgets may be derived in various ways. They may be developed using statistical techniques, such as time series analysis, or they may be based on the judgement of the sales and marketing staff. We considered inventories budgets and their link to production and sales budgets in Chapter 12.

## Financial ratios

One ratio that can be used to help monitor inventories levels is the average inventories turnover period. This ratio is calculated as follows:

$$\text{Average inventories turnover period} = \frac{\text{Average inventories held}}{\text{Cost of sales}} \times 365$$

The ratio provides a picture of the average period for which inventories are held. This can be useful as a basis for comparison. It is possible to calculate the average inventories turnover period for individual product lines as well as for inventories as a whole.

## Recording and reordering systems

A sound system of recording inventories movements is a key element in managing inventories. There must be proper procedures for recording inventories purchases and usages. Periodic checks would normally be made in an attempt to ensure that the amount of physical inventories actually held is consistent with what is indicated by the inventories records.

There should also be clear procedures for the reordering of inventories. Authorisation for both the purchase and the issue of inventories should be confined to a few nominated members of staff. This should avoid problems of duplication and lack of coordination. To determine the point at which inventories should be reordered, information will be required concerning the **lead time** (that is, the time between the placing of an order and the receipt of the goods) and the likely level of demand.

### Activity 16.3

An electrical retailer holds a particular type of light switch. The annual demand for the light switch is 10,400 units and the lead time for orders is four weeks. Demand for the light switch is steady throughout the year. At what level of inventories of the light switch should the business reorder, assuming that it is confident of the information given above?

The average weekly demand for the switch is 10,400/52 = 200 units. During the time between ordering new switches and receiving them, the quantity sold will be 4 × 200 units = 800 units. So the business should reorder no later than when the level held reaches 800 units. This should avoid running out of inventories.

In most businesses, there will be some uncertainty surrounding these factors (level of demand, pattern of demand and lead time). Here a buffer or safety inventories level may be maintained in case problems occur. The amount of the buffer to be held is really a matter of judgement. This judgement will depend on:

- the degree of uncertainty concerning these factors;
- the likely costs of running out of the item concerned;
- the cost of holding the buffer inventories.

The effect of holding a buffer will be to raise the inventories level at which an order for new inventories is placed (the reorder point).

## Activity 16.4

Assume the same facts as in Activity 16.3. However, we are also told that the business maintains buffer inventories of 300 units. At what level should the business reorder?

Reorder point = expected level of demand during the lead time *plus* the level of buffer
            inventories
           = 800 + 300
           = 1,100 units

Carrying a buffer will increase the cost of holding inventories. This must, however, be weighed against the cost of running out of inventories, in terms of lost sales, production problems, and so on.

## Activity 16.5

Hora plc holds inventories of a particular type of motor car tyre, which is ordered in batches of 1,200 units. The supply lead times and usage rates for the tyres are:

|  | Maximum | Average | Minimum |
|---|---|---|---|
| Supply lead times | 25 days | 15 days | 8 days |
| Daily usage | 30 units | 20 units | 12 units |

The business wishes to avoid the risk of running out of inventories.
    What will be the average number of buffer inventories held and the maximum number of inventories that could be held?

To be certain of avoiding running out of inventories, the business must assume a reorder point based on the maximum usage and lead time. This is 750 units (that is, 30 × 25). On average, usage during the lead time will only be 300 units (that is, 20 × 15). Thus, the buffer inventories based on average usage and lead time is 450 units (that is, 750 − 300).
    The maximum level of inventories occurs when a new order of 1,200 units is received, immediately following the minimum supply lead time and minimum daily usage during the lead time. Thus, it is 1,854 units (that is, 1,200 + 750 − (8 × 12)).

**Real World 16.5** provides an example of how small businesses can use technology in inventories reordering to help compete against their larger rivals.

## Real World 16.5

### Taking on the big boys                    FT

The use of technology in inventories recording and reordering may be of vital importance to the survival of small businesses that are being threatened by larger rivals. One such example is that of small independent bookshops. Technology can come to their rescue in two ways. First, electronic point-of-sale (EPOS) systems can record books as they are sold and can constantly update records of inventories held. Thus, books that need to be reordered can be quickly and easily identified. Second, the reordering process can be improved by using web-based technology, which allows books to be ordered in real time. Many large book wholesalers provide free web-based software to their customers for this purpose and try to deliver books ordered during the next working day. This means that a small bookseller, with limited shelf space, may keep one copy only of a particular book but maintain a range of books that competes with that of a large bookseller.

*Source*: Information taken from 'Small stores keep up with the big boys', *Financial Times*, FT.com, 5 February 2003.

## Levels of control

We have already seen that the proper management of inventories is an important issue. The cost of controlling inventories, however, must be weighed against the potential benefits. It may be possible to have different levels of control according to the nature of the inventories held. The **ABC system of inventories control** is based on the idea of selective levels of control.

A business may find it possible to divide its inventories into three broad categories: A, B and C. Each category will be based on the value of inventories held, as is illustrated in Example 16.1.

## Example 16.1

Alascan Products plc makes door handles and door fittings. It makes them in brass, in steel and in plastic. The business finds that brass fittings account for 10 per cent of the physical volume of the finished inventories that it holds, but these represent 65 per cent of the total value. These are treated as Category A inventories. There are sophisticated recording procedures, tight control is exerted over inventories movements and there is a high level of security where the brass inventories are stored. This is economically viable because these inventories represent a relatively small proportion of the total volume.

The business finds that steel fittings account for 30 per cent of the total volume of finished inventories and represent 25 per cent of the total value. These are treated as Category B inventories, with a lower level of recording and management control being applied.

The remaining 60 per cent of the volume of inventories is plastic fittings, which represent the least valuable items, that account for only 10 per cent of the total value of finished inventories held. These are treated as Category C inventories, so the level of recording and management control would be lower still. Applying to these inventories, the level of control that is applied to Category A or even Category B inventories would be uneconomic.

Categorising inventories in this way seeks to direct management effort to the most important areas. It also tries to ensure that the costs of controlling inventories are appropriate to their importance.

Figure 16.3 provides a graphical depiction of the ABC approach to inventories control.

| Figure 16.3 | ABC method of analysing and controlling inventories |

Category A contains inventories that, though relatively few in quantity, account for a large proportion of the total value. Category B inventories consists of those items that are less valuable, but more numerous. Category C comprises those inventories items that are very numerous, but relatively low in value. Different inventories' control rules would be applied to each category. For example, only Category A inventories would attract the more expensive and sophisticated controls.

## Inventories management models

### Economic order quantity

It is possible to use decision models to help manage inventories. The **economic order quantity (EOQ)** model is concerned with determining the quantity of a particular inventories item that should be ordered each time. In its simplest form, the EOQ model assumes that demand is constant. This implies that inventories will be depleted evenly over time to be replenished just at the point that they run out. These assumptions would lead to a 'saw-tooth' pattern to represent inventories' movements, as shown in Figure 16.4.

---

| Figure 16.4 | **Patterns of inventories movements over time** |

Here we assume that there is a constant rate of usage of the inventories item and that inventories are reduced to zero just as new inventories arrive. At time 0 there is a full level of inventories. This is steadily used as time passes; and just as it falls to zero it is replaced. This pattern is then repeated.

---

The EOQ model recognises that the key costs associated with inventories' management are the cost of holding the inventories and the cost of ordering them. The model can be used to calculate the optimum size of a purchase order by taking account of both of these cost elements. The cost of holding inventories can be substantial. Management may, therefore, try to minimise the average amount of inventories held. This will reduce the level of inventories held and, therefore the holding cost. It will, however, increase the number of orders placed during the period, and so ordering costs will rise.

Figure 16.5 shows how, as the level of inventories and the size of inventories orders increase, the annual costs of placing orders will decrease because fewer orders will be placed. However, the cost of holding inventories will increase, as there will be higher average inventories levels. The total costs curve, which is based on the sum of holding costs and ordering costs, will fall until the point E, which represents the minimum total cost. Thereafter, total costs begin to rise. The EOQ model seeks to identify point E, at which total costs are minimised. This will represent half of the optimum amount that should be ordered on each occasion. Assuming, as we are doing, that inventories are used evenly over time and that they fall to zero before being replaced, the average inventories level equals half of the order size.

The EOQ model, which can be used to derive the most economic order quantity, is:

$$EOQ = \sqrt{\frac{2DC}{H}}$$

where: $D$ = the annual demand for the inventories item (expressed in units of the inventories item);

$C$ = the cost of placing an order;

$H$ = the cost of holding one unit of the inventories item for one year.

**Figure 16.5** Inventories holding and order costs

Small inventories' levels imply frequent reordering and high annual ordering costs. Small inventories levels also imply relatively low inventories holding costs. High inventories levels imply exactly the opposite. There is, in theory, an optimum order size that will lead to the sum of ordering and holding costs (total costs) being at a minimum.

**Activity 16.6**

HLA Ltd sells 2,000 bags of cement each year. It has been estimated that the cost of holding one bag of cement for a year is £4. The cost of placing an order for new inventories is estimated at £250.

Calculate the EOQ for bags of cement.

Your answer to this activity should be as follows:

$$EOQ = \sqrt{\frac{2 \times 2,000 \times 250}{4}} = 500 \text{ bags}$$

This will mean that the business will have to order bags of cement four times each year (that is 2,000/500) in batches of 500 bags so that sales demand can be met.

Note that the cost of the inventories concerned, which is the price paid to the supplier, does not directly impact on the EOQ model. The EOQ model is concerned only with the administrative costs of placing and handling each order, on the one hand, and the costs of looking after the inventories, on the other. It will tend to be the case, however, that more expensive inventories items will have greater storage costs. Where the business operates an ABC system of inventories control, Category A inventories would tend to have a lower EOQ than Category B ones. Also, higher-cost inventories tie up more finance than cheaper ones, again leading to higher holding cost. So the cost of the inventories may have an indirect effect on the economic order size that the model recommends.

The basic EOQ model has a number of limiting assumptions. In particular, it assumes that:

- demand for an inventories item can be predicted with accuracy;
- demand is constant over the period and does not fluctuate through seasonality or for other reasons;
- no 'buffer' inventories are required;
- there are no discounts for bulk purchasing.

The model can be modified, however, to overcome each of these limiting assumptions. Many businesses use this model (or a development of it) to help in the management of inventories.

## Activity (16.7)

Petrov plc sells 10,000 tonnes of sand each year and demand is constant over time. The purchase cost of each tonne is £15 and the cost of placing and handling an order is estimated to be £32. The cost of holding one tonne of sand for one year is estimated to be £4. The business uses the EOQ model to determine the appropriate order quantity and holds no buffer inventories.

Calculate the total annual cost of trading in this product.

The total annual cost will be made up of three elements:

- the cost of purchases
- the cost of ordering
- the cost of holding this item in inventories

The annual cost of purchases is 10,000 × £15 = £150,000
The annual cost of ordering is calculated as follows:
The EOQ is:

$$EOQ = \sqrt{\frac{2 \times 10,000 \times 32}{4}} = 400 \text{ tonnes}$$

This will mean that 10,000/400 = 25 orders will be placed each year. The annual cost of ordering is therefore 25 × £32 = £800
The annual cost of holding inventories is calculated as follows:
The average quantity of inventories held will be half the optimum order size, as mentioned earlier. That is, 400/2 = 200 tonnes
The annual holding cost is, therefore 200 × £4 = £800
The total annual cost of trading in this product is therefore:

£150,000 + £800 + £800 = £151,600*

*Note that the annual ordering cost and annual holding cost are the same. This is no coincidence. If we look back at Figure 16.5 we can see that the economic order quantity represents the point at which total costs are minimised. At this point, annual order costs and annual holding costs are equal.

## Materials requirement planning systems

A **materials requirement planning (MRP) system** takes planned sales demand as its starting point. It then uses a computer package to help schedule the timing of deliveries of bought-in parts and materials to coincide with production requirements. It is a coordinated approach that links materials and parts deliveries to the scheduled time of their input to the production process. By ordering only those items that are necessary to ensure the flow of production, inventories levels are likely to be reduced. MRP is really a 'top-down' approach to inventories management, which recognises that inventories ordering decisions cannot be viewed as being independent of production decisions. In recent years, this approach has been extended to provide a fully integrated approach to production planning. The approach also takes account of other manufacturing resources such as labour and machine capacity.

## Just-in-time inventories management

In recent years, many businesses have tried to eliminate the need to hold inventories by adopting **just-in-time (JIT) inventories management**. This approach was originally used in the US defence industry during the Second World War, but was first used on a wide scale by Japanese manufacturing businesses. The essence of JIT is, as the name suggests, to have supplies delivered to the business just in time for them to be used in the production process or in a sale. By adopting this approach, the inventories holding cost rests with suppliers rather than with the business itself. A failure by a particular supplier to deliver on time, however, could cause enormous problems and costs to the business. Thus JIT may save cost, but it tends to increase risk.

For JIT to be successful, it is important that a business informs suppliers of its inventories requirements in advance. Suppliers must then deliver materials of the right quality at the agreed times. Any delivery failures could lead to a dislocation of production and could be very costly. This means a close relationship is required between a business and its suppliers. It may also tend to mean that suppliers have to be physically close to the business. A close relationship should enable suppliers to schedule their own production to that of the business. This should result in a net saving, between supplier and business, in the amount of inventories that need to be held.

Adopting JIT may well require re-engineering a business's production process. To ensure that orders are quickly fulfilled, factory production must be flexible and responsive. This may require changes to both the production layout and to working practices. Production flows may have to be redesigned and employees may have to be given greater responsibility to allow them to deal with unanticipated problems and to encourage greater commitment. Information systems must also be installed that facilitate an uninterrupted production flow.

Although a business that applies JIT will not have to hold inventories, there may be other costs associated with this approach. For example, the close relationship necessary between the business and its suppliers may prevent the business from taking advantage of cheaper sources of supply if they become available. Furthermore, suppliers may need to hold inventories for the customer and so may try to recoup this additional cost through increased prices. The close relationship between customer and supplier, however, should enable the supplier to predict its customers' inventories needs. This means that suppliers can tailor their own production to that of the customer.

Many people view JIT as more than simply an inventories control system. The philosophy underpinning this approach is that of *total quality management*, that we met in Chapter 11. This is concerned with eliminating waste and striving for excellence. There is an expectation that suppliers will always deliver inventories on time and that there will be no defects in the items supplied. There is also an expectation that, for manufacturers, the production process will operate at maximum efficiency. This means that there will be no production breakdowns and the queuing and storage times of products manufactured will be eliminated, as only time spent directly on processing the products is seen as adding value. While these expectations may be impossible to achieve, they can help to create a culture that is dedicated to the pursuit of excellence and quality.

**Real Worlds 16.6** and **16.7** show how two very well-known businesses operating in the UK (one a retailer, the other a manufacturer) use JIT to advantage.

---

### Real World 16.6

### JIT at Boots

Boots, the UK's largest healthcare retailer, has improved inventories management at its stores. The business is working towards a JIT system where delivery from its one central warehouse in Nottingham will be made every day to each retail branch, with nearly all of the inventories lines being placed directly on to the sales shelves, not into a store room at the branch. This is expected to bring major savings of stores staff time and lead to significantly lower levels of inventories being held, without any lessening of the service offered to customers. In fact, the need to hold little or no inventories in the stores, except on the shelves, liberates more space that can be used for selling. The new system is expected to lead to major economic benefits for the business.

*Source*: Information taken from 'Boots £60 million warehouse will improve supply chain', www.thisisnottingham.co.uk, 22 January 2009.

---

### Real World 16.7

### JIT at Nissan                                                           **FT**

Nissan Motors UK Limited, the UK manufacturing arm of the world famous Japanese car business has a plant in Sunderland in the north east of England. Here it operates a fairly well-developed JIT system. For example, Calsonic Kansei supplies car exhausts from a factory close to the Nissan plant. It makes deliveries to Nissan once every 30 minutes on average, so as to arrive exactly as they are needed in production. This is fairly typical of all of the 200 suppliers of components and materials to the Nissan plant.

The business used to have a complete JIT system. More recently, however, Nissan has drawn back from its total adherence to JIT. By using only local suppliers it had cut itself off from the opportunity to exploit low-cost suppliers, particularly some located in China. A change in policy has led the business to hold buffer inventories of certain items to guard against disruption of supply arising from sourcing parts from the Far East.

*Source*: Information taken from 'Planning for quality and productivity', *The Times* 100 Case Study, www.tt100.biz; 'Nissan reviews just-in-time parts policy', C. Tighe, *Financial Times*, 23 October 2006, and Sunderland Automotive Conference 2010, www.automotiveinternational.co.uk.

## Managing trade receivables

Selling goods or services on credit will result in costs being incurred by a business. These costs include credit administration costs, bad debts and opportunities forgone to use the funds for other purposes. However, these costs must be weighed against the benefits of increased sales resulting from the opportunity for customers to delay payment.

Selling on credit is very widespread and is the norm outside the retail industry. When a business offers to sell its goods or services on credit, it must have clear policies concerning:

- which customers should receive credit;
- how much credit should be offered;
- what length of credit it is prepared to offer;
- whether discounts will be offered for prompt payment;
- what collection policies should be adopted;
- how the risk of non-payment can be reduced.

In this section, we shall consider each of these issues.

### Which customers should receive credit and how much should they be offered?

A business offering credit runs the risk of not receiving payment for goods or services supplied. Thus, care must be taken over the type of customer to whom credit facilities are offered and how much credit is allowed. When considering a proposal from a customer for the supply of goods or services on credit, the business must take a number of factors into account. The following **five Cs of credit** provide a business with a useful checklist.

- *Capital.* The customer must appear to be financially sound before any credit is extended. Where the customer is a business, its financial statements should be examined. Particular regard should be given to the customer's likely future profitability and liquidity. In addition, any major financial commitments (such as outstanding borrowings, capital expenditure commitments and contracts with suppliers) should be taken into account.
- *Capacity.* The customer must appear to have the capacity to pay for the goods acquired on credit. The payment record of the customer to date should be examined to provide important clues. To help further assess capacity, the type of business and the amount of credit required in relation to the customer's total financial resources should be taken into account.
- *Collateral.* On occasions, it may be necessary to ask for some kind of security for goods supplied on credit. When this occurs, the business must be convinced that the customer is able to offer a satisfactory form of security.
- *Conditions.* The state of the industry in which the customer operates, as well as the general economic conditions of the particular region or country, should be taken into account. The sensitivity of the customer's business to changes in economic conditions can also have an important influence on the ability of the customer to pay on time.
- *Character.* It is important for a business to make some assessment of the customer's character. The willingness to pay will depend on the honesty and integrity of the individual with whom the business is dealing. Where the customer is a business, this

will mean assessing the characters of its senior managers as well as their reputation within the industry. The selling business must feel confident that the customer will make every effort to pay any amounts owing.

It is clear from this that a business will need to gather information concerning the ability and willingness of the customer to pay the amounts owing on or before the due dates.

## Activity 16.8

Assume that you are the credit manager of a business and that a limited company approaches you with a view to buying goods on credit. What sources of information might you decide to use to help assess the financial health of the potential customer?

There are various possibilities. You may have thought of some of the following:

- *Trade references*. Some businesses ask potential customers to supply them with references from other suppliers who have made sales on credit to them. This may be extremely useful provided that the references supplied are truly representative of the opinions of a customer's suppliers. There is a danger that a potential customer will be selective when giving details of other suppliers, in an attempt to create a more favourable impression than is deserved.
- *Bank references*. It is possible to ask the potential customer for a bank reference. Although banks are usually prepared to supply references, the contents of such references are not always very informative. If customers are in financial difficulties, the bank may be unwilling to add to their problems by supplying poor references. It is worth remembering that the bank's loyalty is likely to be with the customer rather than the enquirer. The bank will usually charge a fee for providing a reference.
- *Published financial statements*. A limited company is obliged by law to file a copy of its annual financial statements with the Registrar of Companies. These financial statements are available for public inspection and provide a useful source of information. Apart from the information contained in the financial statements, company law requires public limited companies to state (in the directors' report) the average time taken to pay suppliers. The annual reports of many companies are available on their own websites or on computer-based information systems.
- *The customer*. Interviews with the directors of the customer business and visits to its premises may be carried out to gain an impression of the way that the customer conducts its business. Where a significant amount of credit is required, the business may ask the customer for access to internal budgets and other unpublished financial information to help assess the level of risk involved.
- *Credit agencies*. Specialist agencies exist to provide information that can be used to assess the creditworthiness of a potential customer. The information that a credit agency supplies may be gleaned from various sources, including the financial statements of the customer and news items relating to the customer from both published and unpublished sources. The credit agencies may also provide a credit rating for the business. Agencies will charge a fee for their services.
- *Register of County Court Judgments*. Any money judgments given against the business or an individual in a county court will be maintained on the register for six years. This register is available for inspection by any member of the public for a small fee.
- *Other suppliers*. Similar businesses will often be prepared to exchange information concerning slow payers or defaulting customers through an industry credit circle. This can be a reliable and relatively cheap way of obtaining information.

Once a customer is considered creditworthy, credit limits for the customer should be established. When doing so, the business must take account of its own financial resources and risk appetite. Unfortunately, there are no theories or models to help a business decide on the appropriate credit limit to adopt; it is really a matter of judgement. Some businesses adopt simple 'rule of thumb' methods based on the amount of sales made to the customer (say, twice the monthly sales figure for the customer) or the maximum the business is prepared to be owed by all of its customers, say, a maximum of 20 per cent of the of its own (the seller's) working capital.

## Length of credit period

A business must determine what credit terms it is prepared to offer its customers. The length of credit offered to customers can vary significantly between businesses. It may be influenced by such factors as:

- the typical credit terms operating within the industry;
- the degree of competition within the industry;
- the bargaining power of particular customers;
- the risk of non-payment;
- the capacity of the business to offer credit;
- the marketing strategy of the business.

The last point identified may require some explanation. If, for example, a business wishes to increase its market share, it may decide to be more generous in its credit policy in an attempt to stimulate sales. Potential customers may be attracted by the offer of a longer credit period. However, any such change in policy must take account of the likely costs and benefits arising.

To illustrate this point, consider Example 16.2.

### Example 16.2

Torrance Ltd produces a new type of golf putter. The business sells the putter to wholesalers and retailers and has an annual sales revenue of £600,000. The following data relate to each putter produced.

|  | £ |
|---|---|
| Selling price | 40 |
| Variable cost | (20) |
| Fixed cost apportionment | (6) |
| Profit | 14 |

The business's cost of capital is estimated at 10 per cent a year.

Torrance Ltd wishes to expand the sales volume of the new putter. It believes that offering a longer credit period can achieve this. The business's average receivables collection period is currently 30 days. It is considering three options in an attempt to increase sales revenue. These are as follows:

|  | Option | | |
|---|---|---|---|
|  | 1 | 2 | 3 |
| Increase in average collection period (days) | 10 | 20 | 30 |
| Increase in sales revenue (£) | 30,000 | 45,000 | 50,000 |

To enable the business to decide on the best option to adopt, it must weigh the benefits of the options against their respective costs. The benefits arising will be represented by the increase in profit from the sale of additional putters. From the cost data supplied we can see that the contribution (that is, selling price (£40) less variable costs (£20)) is £20 a putter, that is, 50 per cent of the selling price. So, whatever increase there may be in sales revenue, the additional contributions will be half of that figure. The fixed costs can be ignored in our calculations, as they will remain the same whichever option is chosen.

The increase in contribution under each option will therefore be:

|  | Option 1 | Option 2 | Option 3 |
|---|---|---|---|
| 50% of the increase in sales revenue (£) | 15,000 | 22,500 | 25,000 |

The increase in trade receivables under each option will be as follows:

|  | Option 1 £ | Option 2 £ | Option 3 £ |
|---|---|---|---|
| Projected level of trade receivables |  |  |  |
| 40 × £630,000/365 (Note 1) | 69,041 |  |  |
| 50 × £645,000/365 |  | 88,356 |  |
| 60 × £650,000/365 |  |  | 106,849 |
| Current level of trade receivables |  |  |  |
| 30 × £600,000/365 | (49,315) | (49,315) | (49,315) |
| Increase in trade receivables | 19,726 | 39,041 | 57,534 |

The increase in receivables that results from each option will mean an additional finance cost to the business.

The net increase in the business's profit arising from the projected change is:

|  | Option 1 £ | Option 2 £ | Option 3 £ |
|---|---|---|---|
| Increase in contribution (see above) | 15,000 | 22,500 | 25,000 |
| Increase in finance cost (Note 2) | (1,973) | (3,904) | (5,753) |
| Net increase in profits | 13,027 | 18,596 | 19,247 |

The calculations show that Option 3 will be the most profitable one.

**Notes:**
1 If the annual sales revenue totals £630,000 and 40 days' credit is allowed (both of which will apply under Option 1), the average amount that will be owed to the business by its customers, at any point during the year, will be the daily sales revenue (that is, £630,000/365) multiplied by the number of days that the customers take to pay (that is 40).
   Exactly the same logic applies to Options 2 and 3 and to the current level of trade receivables.
2 The increase in the finance cost for Option 1 will be the increase in trade receivables (£19,726) × 10 per cent. The equivalent figures for the other options are derived in a similar way.

Example 16.2 illustrates the way that a business should assess changes in credit terms. However, if there is a risk that, by extending the length of credit, there will be an increase in bad debts, this should also be taken into account in the calculations, as should any additional trade receivable collection costs that will be incurred.

**Real World 16.8** shows how the length of credit taken varies greatly from one well-known UK business to the next.

---

### Real World 16.8

#### Credit where it's due

The following are the lengths of time taken on average for each business to pay its credit suppliers (trade payables).

|  | Days taken |
|---|---|
| Babcock International Group plc (engineering) | 32 |
| British Airways plc (airline) | 33 |
| British Telecommunications Group plc (telecommunications) | 49 |
| easyJet plc (airline) | 6 |
| Go-Ahead Group plc (transport) | 11 |
| J D Wetherspoon (pub operator) | 56 |
| Kingfisher plc (DIY retailer) | 45 |
| Marks and Spencer Group plc (retail) | 18 |
| Severn Trent Water Ltd (water) | 44 |
| Smith Group plc (manufacturer) | 31 |
| Tate and Lyle plc (sugar) | 53 |
| Thorntons plc (confectioner) | 39 |
| Tottenham Hotspur plc (football) | 56 |
| W H Smith plc (retail) | 51 |
| Wm Morrison Supermarkets plc (retail) | 29 |

These are all based on information in the financial statements of the businesses concerned for the year ended during 2010.

It is striking how much the days taken to pay suppliers vary from one business to another. Industry differences do not seem to explain this. British Airways takes more than five times longer to pay than easyJet. Marks and Spencer takes a little more than a third of the time taken by WH Smith to pay.

*Source*: The 2010 annual reports of the businesses concerned.

---

### An alternative approach to evaluating the credit decision

It is possible to view the credit decision as a capital investment decision. Granting trade credit involves an opportunity outlay of resources in the form of cash (which has been temporarily forgone) in the expectation that future cash flows will be increased (through higher sales) as a result. A business will usually have choices concerning the level of investment to be made in credit sales and the period over which credit is granted. These choices will result in different returns and different levels of risk. There is no reason in principle why the NPV investment appraisal method, which we considered in Chapter 14, should not be used to evaluate these choices. We have seen that the NPV method takes into account both the time value of money and the level of risk involved.

Approaching the problem as an NPV assessment is not different in principle from the way that we dealt with the decision in Example 16.2. In both approaches the time value of money is considered, but in Example 16.2 we did it by charging a financing cost on the outstanding trade receivables.

## Cash discounts

In an attempt to encourage prompt payment from its credit customers, a business may decide to offer a **cash discount** (or discount for prompt payment). The size of any discount will be an important influence on whether a customer decides to pay promptly.

From the business's viewpoint, the cost of offering discounts must be weighed against the likely benefits in the form of a reduction both in the cost of financing receivables and in the amount of bad debts. Example 16.3 shows how this may be done.

### Example 16.3

Williams Wholesalers Ltd currently asks its credit customers to pay by the end of the month after the month of delivery. In practice, customers take rather longer to pay; on average 70 days. Sales revenue amounts to £4 million a year and bad debts to £20,000 a year.

It is planned to offer customers a cash discount of 2 per cent for payment within 30 days. Williams estimates that 50 per cent of customers will accept this facility but that the remaining customers, who tend to be slow payers, will not pay until 80 days after the sale. At present the business has an overdraft facility at an interest rate of 13 per cent a year. If the plan goes ahead, bad debts will be reduced to £10,000 a year and there will be savings in credit administration expenses of £6,000 a year.

Should Williams Wholesalers Ltd offer the new credit terms to customers?

### Solution

The first step is to determine the reduction in trade receivables arising from the new policy.

|  |  | £ | £ |
|---|---|---:|---:|
| Existing level of trade receivables | (£4m × 70/365) |  | 767,123 |
| New level of trade receivables: | £2m × 80/365 | 438,356 |  |
|  | £2m × 30/365 | 164,384 | (602,740) |
| Reduction in trade receivables |  |  | 164,383 |

The costs and benefits of offering the discount can be set out as follows:

**Cost and benefits of policy**

| | | |
|---|---:|---:|
| Cost of discount (£2m × 2%) | | 40,000 |
| *Less* | | |
| Interest saved on the reduction in trade receivables (£164,383* × 13%) | 21,370 | |
| Administration cost saving | 6,000 | |
| Cost of bad debts saved (20,000 – 10,000) | 10,000 | (37,370) |
| Net cost of policy | | 2,630 |

These calculations show that the business will be worse off by offering the new credit terms.

* It could be argued that the interest should be based on the amount expected to be received; that is the value of the trade receivables *after* taking account of the discount. Basing it on the expected receipt figure would not, however, alter the conclusion that the business should not offer the new credit terms.

In practice, there is always the danger that a customer may be slow to pay and yet may still take the discount offered. Where the customer is important to the business, it may be difficult to insist on full payment. To overcome this problem, instead of allowing customers to deduct a discount, customers who pay promptly can be rewarded separately, say on a three-monthly basis. The reward could be a cash payment to the customer or, perhaps, a credit note. The value of the reward would be equal to the cash discounts earned by each customer during the three months.

## Debt factoring and invoice discounting

Trade receivables can, in effect, be turned into cash by either factoring them or having sales invoices discounted. Both are forms of asset-based finance, which involves a financial institution providing a business with an advance up to 80 per cent of the value of the trade receivables outstanding. These methods seem to be fairly popular approaches to managing receivables. Both were discussed in Chapter 15.

## Credit insurance

It is possible for a supplier to insure its entire trade receivables, individual accounts (customers) or the outstanding balance relating to a particular transaction.

## Collection policies and reducing the risk of non-payment

A business offering credit must ensure that receivables are collected as quickly as possible so that non-payment risk is minimised and operating cash flows are maximised. Various steps can be taken to achieve this, including the following.

### Develop customer relationships

For major customers it is often useful to cultivate a relationship with the key staff responsible for paying sales invoices. By so doing, the chances of prompt payment may be increased. For less important customers, the business should at least identify key staff responsible for paying invoices, who can be contacted in the event of a payment problem.

### Publicise credit terms

The credit terms of the business should be made clear in all relevant correspondence, such as order acknowledgements, invoices and statements. In early negotiations with the prospective customer, credit terms should be openly discussed and an agreement reached.

### Issue invoices promptly

An efficient collection policy requires an efficient accounting system. Invoices (bills) must be sent out promptly to customers, as must monthly statements. Reminders must also be despatched promptly to customers who are late in paying. If a customer fails to respond to a reminder, the accounting system should alert managers so that a stop can be placed on further deliveries.

### Monitor outstanding receivables

Management can monitor the effectiveness of collection policies in a number of ways. One method is to calculate the **average settlement period for trade receivables** ratio. This ratio, is calculated as follows:

$$\text{Average settlement period for trade receivables} = \frac{\text{Average trade receivables}}{\text{Credit sales}} \times 365$$

Although this ratio can be useful, it is important to remember that it produces an *average* figure for the number of days for which debts are outstanding. This average may be badly distorted by a few large customers who are very slow or very fast payers.

### Produce an ageing schedule of trade receivables

A more detailed and informative approach to monitoring receivables may be to produce an **ageing schedule of trade receivables**. Receivables are divided into categories according to the length of time they have been outstanding. An ageing schedule can be produced, on a regular basis, to help managers see the pattern of outstanding receivables. An example of an ageing schedule is set out in Example 16.4.

**Example 16.4**

**Ageing schedule of trade receivables at 31 December**

| Customer | Days outstanding | | | | Total |
|---|---|---|---|---|---|
| | 1 to 30 days | 31 to 60 days | 61 to 90 days | More than 90 days | |
| | £ | £ | £ | £ | £ |
| A Ltd | 20,000 | 10,000 | – | – | 30,000 |
| B Ltd | – | 24,000 | – | – | 24,000 |
| C Ltd | 12,000 | 13,000 | 14,000 | 18,000 | 57,000 |
| Total | 32,000 | 47,000 | 14,000 | 18,000 | 111,000 |

This shows a business's trade receivables figure at 31 December, which totals £111,000. Each customer's balance is analysed according to how long the amount has been outstanding. (This business has just three credit customers.)

Thus we can see from the schedule, for example, that A Ltd has £20,000 outstanding for 30 days or fewer (that is, arising from sales during December) and £10,000 outstanding for between 31 and 60 days (broadly, arising from November sales). This information can be very useful for credit control purposes.

Many accounting software packages now include this ageing schedule as one of the routine reports available to managers. Such packages often have the facility to put customers 'on hold' when they reach their credit limits. Putting a customer on hold means that no further credit sales will be made to that customer until amounts owing from past sales have been settled.

### Identify the pattern of receipts

A slightly different approach to exercising control over receivables is to identify the pattern of receipts from credit sales on a monthly basis. This involves monitoring the percentage of credit sales that are paid in the month of sale and the percentage that is paid in subsequent months. To do this, credit sales for each month must be examined separately. Example 16.5 illustrates this.

**Example 16.5**

A business made credit sales of £250,000 in June. It received 30 per cent of that amount during June, 40 per cent during July, 20 per cent during August and 10 per cent during September. The pattern of credit sales receipts and amounts owing is:

**Pattern of credit sales receipts**

|  | Receipts from June credit sales | Amounts received | Amount outstanding from June sales at month end | Amount outstanding |
|---|---|---|---|---|
|  | £ | % | £ | % |
| June | 75,000 | 30 | 175,000 | 70 |
| July | 100,000 | 40 | 75,000 | 30 |
| August | 50,000 | 20 | 25,000 | 10 |
| September | 25,000 | 10 | 0 | 0 |

This information can be used as a basis for control. The actual pattern of receipts can be compared with the expected (budgeted) pattern of receipts in order to see if there was any significant deviation (see Figure 16.6). If this pattern shows that customers are paying more slowly than expected, managers may decide to take corrective action.

**Figure 16.6** **Comparison of actual and expected (budgeted) receipts over time for Example 16.5**

It can be seen that 30 per cent of the sales income for June is received in that month; the remainder is received in the following three months. The expected (budgeted) pattern of cash receipts for June sales, which has been assumed, is also depicted. By comparing the actual and expected pattern of receipts, it is possible to see whether credit sales are being properly controlled and to decide whether corrective action is required.

### Answer queries quickly

It is important for relevant staff to deal with customer queries on goods and services supplied quickly and efficiently. Payment is unlikely to be made by customers until their queries have been dealt with.

### Deal with slow payers

A business making significant sales on credit will, almost inevitably, be faced with customers who do not pay. When this occurs, there should be agreed procedures for dealing with the situation. The cost of any action to be taken against delinquent credit customers, however, must be weighed against the likely returns. For example, there is little point in incurring large legal expenses to try to recoup amounts owing if there is evidence that the customer has no money. Where possible, an estimate of the cost of bad debts should be taken into account when setting prices for products or services.

As a footnote to our consideration of managing receivables, **Real World 16.9** outlines some of the excuses that long-suffering credit managers must listen to when chasing payment for outstanding debts.

---

**Real World 16.9**

### It's in the post

The Atradius Group provides trade credit insurance and trade receivables collections services worldwide. It has a presence in 40 countries. Its products and services aim to reduce its customers' exposure to buyers who cannot pay for the products and services customers purchase.

In a press release Atradius said:

> Although it happens rarely, some debtors (credit customers) still manage to surprise even us. These excuses have actually been used by credit customers:
>
> - It's not a valid debt as my vindictive ex-wife ran off with the company credit card
> - I just got back from my luxury holiday, it cost more than I thought so I no longer have the funds to pay
> - I wanted to pay but all the invoices were in my briefcase, which was stolen on the street
> - My wife has been kidnapped and I need the money to get her back.

*Source*: www.atradius.us/news/press-releases, 13 August 2008.

---

**Self-assessment question 16.1**

Corex plc produces a highly sophisticated thermostat that is sold to heating engineers. Financial data relating to the thermostat are as follows:

|  | Per thermostat | |
| --- | ---: | ---: |
|  | £ | £ |
| Sales price |  | 50.00 |
| Material costs | (10.00) |  |
| Labour (Note 1) | (12.00) |  |
| Overheads (Note 2) | (15.00) | (37.00) |
| Profit |  | 13.00 |

*Notes*
1. Labour cost is fixed.
2. Two-thirds of overhead cost incurred is fixed.

→

### Self-assessment question 16.1 (*continued*)

Sales of the thermostat have been stable at £20 million per year for several years. A new marketing director, however, has argued that sales revenue could be increased by 20 per cent if a marketing campaign costing £1.8 million a year is launched. Sales are made on credit, and customers are divided into three categories based on their payment characteristics. These are as follows:

| Category | Average collection period (Number of days) | Bad debts (%) |
|---|---|---|
| 1 | 30 | 1.0 |
| 2 | 40 | 3.0 |
| 3 | 50 | 5.0 |

Assuming the marketing campaign is launched and the sales increase is achieved, 20 per cent of additional sales would come from Category 1 customers, 30 per cent from Category 2 and 50 per cent from Category 3 customers. Corex plc will finance any expansion in its trade receivables using a bank overdraft, which will incur interest at 10 per cent a year.

*Required*:
Assuming the increase in sales is achieved, calculate the effect of launching the marketing campaign on annual profits before tax and comment on your findings. (All workings should be made to the nearest £000)

**The solution to this question can be found at the back of the book on pages 743–744.**

## Managing cash

### Why hold cash?

Most businesses hold a certain amount of cash. The amount of cash held tends to vary considerably between businesses.

### Activity (16.9)

**Why do you think a business may decide to hold at least some of its assets in the form of cash?** (*Hint*: There are broadly three reasons.)

The three reasons are:

1 To meet day-to-day commitments, a business requires a certain amount of cash. Payments for wages, overhead expenses, goods purchased, and so on must be made at the due dates. Cash has been described as the lifeblood of a business. Unless it circulates through the business, and is available for the payment of claims as they become due, the survival of the business will be at risk. Profitability is not enough; a business must have sufficient cash to pay its debts when they fall due.

2 If future cash flows are uncertain for any reason, it would be prudent to hold a balance of cash. For example, a major customer that owes a large sum to the business may be in financial difficulties. This could lead to an expected large receipt not arriving. Given

this situation, the business could retain its capacity to meet its obligations if it holds a cash balance. Similarly, if there is some uncertainty concerning future outlays, a cash balance will be required.

3 A business may decide to hold cash to put itself in a position to exploit profitable opportunities as and when they arise. For example, by holding cash, a business may be able to acquire a competitor's business that suddenly becomes available at an attractive price.

## How much cash should be held?

Although cash can be held for each of the reasons identified, doing so may not always be necessary. If a business is able to borrow quickly, the amount of cash it needs to hold can be reduced. Similarly, if the business holds assets that can easily be converted to cash (for example, marketable securities such as shares in Stock Exchange listed businesses or government bonds), the amount of cash held can be reduced.

The decision as to how much cash a particular business should hold is a difficult one. Different businesses will have different views on the subject.

### Activity (16.10)

**What do you think are the major factors that influence how much cash a particular business should hold? See if you can think of five possible factors.**

You may have thought of the following:

- *The nature of the business*. Some businesses, such as utilities (for example, water, electricity and gas suppliers), have cash flows that are both predictable and reasonably certain. This will enable them to hold lower cash balances. For some businesses, cash balances may vary greatly according to the time of year. A seasonal business may accumulate cash during the high season to enable it to meet commitments during the low season.
- *The opportunity cost of holding cash*. Where there are profitable opportunities it may not be wise to hold a large cash balance.
- *The level of inflation*. Holding cash during a period of rising prices will lead to a loss of purchasing power. The higher the level of inflation, the greater will be this loss.
- *The availability of near-liquid assets*. If a business has marketable securities or inventories that may easily be liquidated, high cash balances may not be necessary.
- *The availability of borrowing*. If a business can borrow easily (and quickly) there is less need to hold cash.
- *The cost of borrowing*. When interest rates are high, the option of borrowing becomes less attractive.
- *Economic conditions*. When the economy is in recession, businesses may prefer to hold cash so that they can be well placed to invest when the economy improves. In addition, during a recession, businesses may experience difficulties in collecting trade receivables. They may therefore hold higher cash balances than usual in order to meet commitments.
- *Relationships with suppliers*. Too little cash may hinder the ability of the business to pay suppliers promptly. This can lead to a loss of goodwill. It may also lead to discounts being forgone.

## Controlling the cash balance

Several models have been developed to help control the cash balance of the business. One such model proposes the use of upper and lower control limits for cash balances and the use of a target cash balance. The model assumes that the business will invest in marketable investments that can easily be liquidated. These investments will be purchased or sold, as necessary, in order to keep the cash balance within the control limits.

The model proposes two upper and two lower control limits (see Figure 16.7). If the business exceeds either of the *outer* limits, the managers must decide whether the cash balance is likely to return to a point within the *inner* control limits set, over the next few days. If this seems likely, then no action is required. If, on the other hand, it does not seem likely, management must change the cash position of the business by either buying or selling marketable investments.

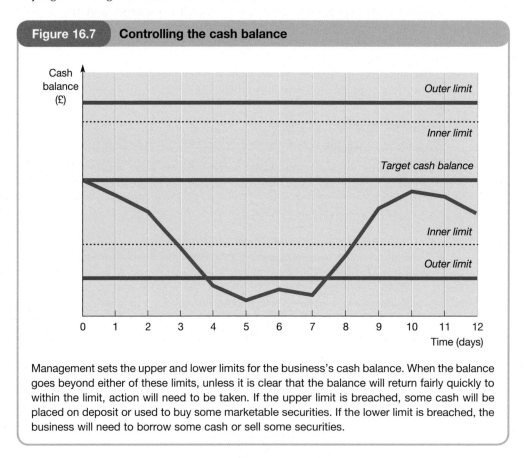

| Figure 16.7 | Controlling the cash balance |

Management sets the upper and lower limits for the business's cash balance. When the balance goes beyond either of these limits, unless it is clear that the balance will return fairly quickly to within the limit, action will need to be taken. If the upper limit is breached, some cash will be placed on deposit or used to buy some marketable securities. If the lower limit is breached, the business will need to borrow some cash or sell some securities.

In Figure 16.7 we can see that the lower outer control limit has been breached for four days. If a four-day period is unacceptable, managers must sell marketable investments to replenish the cash balance.

The model relies heavily on management judgement to determine where the control limits are set and the length of the period within which breaches of the control limits are acceptable. Past experience may be useful in helping managers decide on these issues. There are other models, however, that do not rely on management judgement. Instead, these use quantitative techniques to determine an optimal cash policy. One model proposed, for example, is the cash equivalent of the inventories economic order quantity model, discussed earlier in the chapter.

## Cash budgets and managing cash

To manage cash effectively, it is useful for a business to prepare a cash budget. This is a very important tool for both planning and control purposes. Cash budgets were considered in Chapter 12 and so we shall not consider them again in detail. However, it is worth repeating that these statements enable managers to see how planned events are expected to affect the cash balance. The cash budget will identify periods when cash surpluses and cash deficits are expected.

When a cash surplus is expected to arise, managers must decide on the best use of the surplus funds. When a cash deficit is expected, managers must make adequate provision by borrowing, liquidating assets or rescheduling cash payments or receipts to deal with this. Cash budgets are useful in helping to control the cash held. Actual cash flows can be compared with the planned cash flows for the period. If there is a significant divergence between the projected cash flows and the actual cash flows, explanations must be sought and corrective action taken where necessary.

To refresh your memory on cash budgets, it would probably be worth looking back at Chapter 12, pages 472–473.

## Operating cash cycle

When managing cash, it is important to be aware of the **operating cash cycle (OCC)** of the business. For a retailer, for example, this may be defined as the period between the outlay of cash necessary for the purchase of inventories and the ultimate receipt of cash from the sale of the goods. In the case of a business that purchases goods on credit for subsequent resale on credit, such as a wholesaler, the OCC is as shown in Figure 16.8.

**Figure 16.8** **The operating cash cycle**

The OCC is the time lapse between paying for goods and receiving the cash from the sale of those goods. The length of the OCC has a significant impact on the amount of funds that the business needs to apply to working capital.

Figure 16.8 shows that payment for inventories acquired on credit occurs some time after those inventories have been purchased. Therefore, no immediate cash outflow arises from the purchase. Similarly, cash receipts from credit customers will occur some time after the sale is made. There will be no immediate cash inflow as a result of the sale. The OCC is the period between the payment made to the supplier, for the goods concerned, and the cash received from the credit customer. Although Figure 16.8 depicts the position for a wholesaling business, the precise definition of the OCC can easily be adapted for other types of business.

The OCC is important because it has a significant influence on the financing requirements of the business. Broadly, the longer the cycle, the greater the financing requirements of the business and the greater the financial risks. For this reason, the business is likely to want to reduce the OCC to the minimum possible period.

For the type of business mentioned above, which buys and sells on credit, the OCC can be calculated from the financial statements by the use of certain ratios. It is calculated as shown in Figure 16.9.

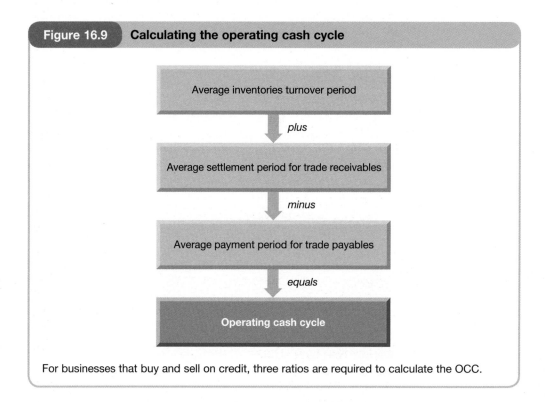

**Figure 16.9  Calculating the operating cash cycle**

For businesses that buy and sell on credit, three ratios are required to calculate the OCC.

## Activity 16.11

The financial statements of Freezeqwik Ltd, a distributor of frozen foods, for the year ended 31 December last year are:

### Income statement for the year ended 31 December last year

| | £000 | £000 |
|---|---|---|
| Sales revenue | | 820 |
| Cost of sales | | |
| Opening inventories | 142 | |
| Purchases | 568 | |
| | 710 | |
| Closing inventories | (166) | (544) |
| Gross profit | | 276 |
| Administration expenses | | (120) |
| Distribution expenses | | (95) |
| Operating profit | | 61 |
| Financial expenses | | (32) |
| Profit before taxation | | 29 |
| Taxation | | (7) |
| Profit for the year | | 22 |

### Statement of financial position as at 31 December last year

| | £000 |
|---|---|
| ASSETS | |
| Non-current assets | |
| *Property, plant and equipment* | |
| Property at valuation | 180 |
| Fixtures and fittings at cost less depreciation | 82 |
| Motor vans at cost less depreciation | 102 |
| | 364 |
| Current assets | |
| Inventories | 166 |
| Trade receivables | 264 |
| Cash | 24 |
| | 454 |
| Total assets | 818 |
| EQUITY AND LIABILITIES | |
| Equity | |
| Ordinary share capital | 300 |
| Retained earnings | 352 |
| | 652 |
| Current liabilities | |
| Trade payables | 159 |
| Taxation | 7 |
| | 166 |
| Total equity and liabilities | 818 |

All purchases and sales are on credit. There has been no change in the level of trade receivables or payables over the period.

Calculate the length of the OCC for the business and go on to suggest how the business may seek to reduce this period.

→

**Activity 16.11 (*continued*)**

The OCC may be calculated as follows:

*Number of days*

Average inventories turnover period:

$$\frac{(\text{Opening inventories} + \text{Closing inventories})/2}{\text{Cost of sales}} \times 365 = \frac{(142 + 166)/2}{544} \times 365 \qquad 103$$

Average settlement period for trade receivables:

$$\frac{\text{Trade receivables}}{\text{Credit sales}} \times 365 = \frac{264}{820} \times 365 \qquad 118$$

Average settlement period for trade payables:

$$\frac{\text{Trade payables}}{\text{Credit purchases}} \times 365 = \frac{159}{568} \times 365 \qquad \underline{(102)}$$

OCC $\qquad \underline{119}$

The business can reduce the length of the OCC in a number of ways. The average inventories turnover period seems quite long. At present, average inventories held represent more than three months' sales requirements. Lowering the level of inventories held will reduce this. Similarly, the average settlement period for trade receivables seems long, at nearly four months' sales. Imposing tighter credit control, offering discounts, charging interest on overdue accounts and so on may reduce this. However, any policy decisions concerning inventories and trade receivables must take account of current trading conditions.

Extending the period of credit taken to pay suppliers could also reduce the OCC. However, for reasons that will be explained later, this option must be approached with caution.

An objective of working capital management may be to maintain the OCC at a particular budgeted level or, at least, within cerain limits each side of the target. A problem with this is that not all days in the OCC are equally valuable. For example, in Activity 16.11, the operating cycle is 119 days. Were both trade receivables and trade payables to be increased by seven days (by allowing customers longer to pay and by Freezeqwik taking longer to pay for purchases), the OCC would be left exactly the same at 119 days. This would not leave the amount tied up in working capital the same, however. Trade receivables would have increased by £15,726 (that is, 7 × £820,000/365). Trade payables, however, would only have increased by £10,893 (that is, 7 × £568,000/365). This would be a net increase of £4,833 in working capital.

**Real World 16.10** shows the average operating cash cycle for large European businesses.

**Real World 16.10**

## Cycling along

The survey of working capital by Ernst and Young (see Real World 16.2, pages 647–648) calculates the average operating cash cycle for the top 1,000 European businesses (excluding financial and auto manufacturing businesses).

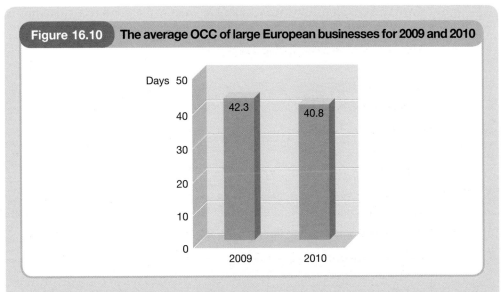

**Figure 16.10** The average OCC of large European businesses for 2009 and 2010

The average operating cycle has reduced by 16 per cent since 2002 with each element of working capital making a contribution to this improvement. Inventories have fallen by 9 per cent, trade receivables by 4 per cent while trade payable increased by 8 per cent over the period.

*Source*: Adapted from figure in *All Tied Up: Working Capital Management Survey 2011*, Ernst and Young, p. 2, www.ey.com.

## Cash transmission

A business will normally wish to benefit from receipts from customers at the earliest opportunity. Where cash is received, the benefit is immediate. Where, however, payment is made by cheque, there may be a delay before it is cleared through the banking system. The business must therefore wait before it can benefit from the amount paid in. In recent years, however, the CHAPS (Clearing House Automated Payments) system has helped to reduce the time that cheques spend in the banking system. It is now possible for cheques to be fast tracked so that they reach the recipient's bank account on the same day.

Another way for a business to receive money promptly is for the customer to pay by standing order or by direct debit. Both of these involve the transfer of an agreed sum from the customer's bank account to the business's bank account on an agreed date. Businesses providing services over time, such as insurance, satellite tevision and mobile phone services, often rely on this method of payment.

A final way in which a business may be paid promptly is through the use of a debit card. This allows the customer's bank account to be charged (debited) and the seller's bank account to be simultaneously increased (credited) with the sale price of the item. Many types of business, including retailers and restaurants, use this method. It is operated through computerised cash tills and is referred to as electronic funds transfer at point of sale (EFTPOS).

## Bank overdrafts

Bank overdrafts are simply bank current accounts that have a negative balance. They are a type of bank loan and can be a useful tool in managing the business's cash flow requirements.

**Real World 16.11** shows how Indesit, a large white-goods manufacturer, managed to improve its cash flows through better working capital management.

---

### Real World 16.11

## Dash for cash

Despite an impressive working capital track record, a 50% plunge in profit at Indesit in 2005 led to the creation of a new three-year plan that meant an even stronger emphasis on cash generation. Operating cash flow was added to the incentive scheme for senior and middle managers, who subsequently released more cash from Indesit's already lean processes by "attacking the areas that were somehow neglected," Crenna (the chief financial officer) says.

Hidden in the dark corners of the accounts-receivable department in the UK's after-sales service operation, for example, were a host of delinquent, albeit small, payments – in some cases overdue by a year or more. "If you don't put a specific focus on these receivables, it's very easy for them to become neglected," Crenna says. "In theory, nobody worries about collecting £20. In reality, we were sitting on a huge amount of receivables, though each individual bill was for a small amount."

More trapped cash was found in the company's spare-parts inventory. The inventory is worth around €30 million today compared with around €40 million three years ago. "This was a good result that came just from paying the same level of attention to spare parts as to finished products," Crenna says. In general, Indesit has been able to improve working capital performance through "fine-tuning rather than launching epic projects." Over the past two years, according to REL, Indesit has released €115 million from its working capital processes.

*Source*: 'Dash for Cash', J. Karaian, *CFO Europe Magazine*, 8 July 2008, www.CFO.com.

---

## Managing trade payables

Trade credit arises from the fact that most businesses buy their goods and service requirements on credit. In effect, suppliers are lending the business money, interest free, on a short-term basis. Trade payables are the other side of the coin from trade receivables. One business's trade payable is another one's trade receivable, in respect of a particular transaction. Trade payables are an important source of finance for most businesses. They have been described as a 'spontaneous' source, as they tend to increase in line with the increase in the level of activity achieved by a business. Trade credit is widely regarded as a 'free' source of finance and, therefore, a good thing for a business to use. There may be real costs, however, associated with taking trade credit.

First, customers who take credit may not be as well treated as those who pay immediately. For example, when goods are in short supply, credit customers may receive lower priority when allocating the goods available. In addition, credit customers may be less favoured in terms of delivery dates or the provision of technical support services. Sometimes, the goods or services provided may be more costly if credit is required. However, in most industries, trade credit is the norm. As a result, these disadvantages will not normally apply except, perhaps, to customers who abuse the credit facilities. A business that purchases supplies on credit will usually have to incur additional administration and accounting costs in dealing with the scrutiny and payment of invoices, maintaining and updating payables' accounts, and so on.

These points are not meant to imply that taking credit represents a net cost to a business. There are, of course, real benefits that can accrue. Provided that trade credit is not abused, it can represent a form of interest-free loan. It can be a much more convenient method of paying for goods and services than paying by cash and, during a period of inflation, there will be an economic gain by paying later rather than sooner for goods and services purchased. For most businesses, these benefits will vastly exceed the costs involved.

Sometimes delaying payment to suppliers can be a sign of financial problems. On occasions, however, it can reflect an imbalance in bargaining power. It is not unusual for large businesses to delay payment to small suppliers, which are reliant on them for continuing trade. The UK government has encouraged large businesses to sign up to a 'Prompt Payment Scheme' to help small suppliers. **Real World 16.12**, however, suggests that not all signatories have entered into the spirit of the scheme.

### Real World 16.12

## Two different definitions of prompt payment

Call me naive but I always thought there was only one meaning to the phrase "Prompt Payment". However, in the world of commercial "spin", this is apparently not true. It has been well documented in the press in recent years that many large organisations like Carlsberg , Matalan, Boots and Dell have unilaterally amended their invoice payment terms to suppliers, anticipating that most of them will just roll over and accept the newly imposed terms in order to keep the business.

If a supplier accepts 75 day terms, and the customer pays on day 75, the customer would call this prompt payment. On the other hand, most organisations outside that particular commercial arrangement would see it somewhat differently. Is a unilaterally imposed 75 days to pay a normal trade credit agreement prompt or is it slow?

Many suppliers to these large organisations that have flexed their commercial muscle to impose extended payment terms also consider them as bad payers, but those same large corporates would be quite in their rights to actually sign up to the government's "Prompt Payment Scheme" suggesting that they are fully supportive of attempts to get big companies to pay smaller ones in good time to help with their cash flows. It's quite ironic that the same organisation can appear on pro-SME (small and medium size enterprises) websites that publicise "Hall of Shame" poor payers, while appearing in the Government supported "Prompt Payer" list.

It's all about which angle you're coming from I suppose!

*Source*: 'The TWO different definitions of prompt payment', M. Williams, *Accountancy Age*, 28 June 2010, www.accountancyage.com.

## Taking advantage of cash discounts

Where a supplier offers a discount for prompt payment, the business should give careful consideration to the possibility of paying within the discount period. An example may be useful to illustrate the cost of forgoing possible discounts.

### Example 16.6

Hassan Ltd takes 70 days to pay for goods from its supplier. To encourage prompt payment, the supplier has offered the business a 2 per cent discount if payment for goods is made within 30 days.

Hassan Ltd is not sure whether it is worth taking the discount offered.

If the discount is taken, payment could be made on the last day of the discount period (that is, the 30th day). However, if the discount is not taken, payment will be made after 70 days. This means that, by not taking the discount, the business will receive an extra 40 days' (that is, 70 − 30) credit. The cost of this extra credit to the business will be the 2 per cent discount forgone. If we annualise the cost of this discount forgone, we have:

$$365/40 \times 2\% = 18.3\%^*$$

We can see that the annual cost of forgoing the discount is very high. It may, therefore, be profitable for the business to pay the supplier within the discount period, even if it means that it will have to borrow to enable it to do so.

\* This is an approximate annual rate. For the more mathematically minded, the precise rate is:

$$\{[(1 + 2/98)^{9.125}] - 1\} \times 100\% = 20.2\%$$

The key difference is that, in this calculation, compound interest is used whereas, in the first calculation, simple interest is used, which is not strictly correct.

## Controlling trade payables

To help monitor the level of trade credit taken, management can calculate the **average settlement period for trade payables**. This ratio is:

$$\text{Average settlement period for trade payables} = \frac{\text{Average trade payables}}{\text{Credit purchases}} \times 365$$

Once again, this provides an average figure, which could be misleading. A more informative approach would be to produce an ageing schedule for payables. This would look much the same as the ageing schedule for receivables described earlier in Example 16.4.

We saw earlier that delaying payment to suppliers may create problems for a business. **Real World 16.13**, however, describes how cash-strapped businesses may delay payments and still retain the support of its suppliers.

**Real World 16.13**

## Credit stretch

According to Gavin Swindell, European managing director of REL, a research and consulting firm, there are 'win-win' ways of extending credit terms. He states: "A lot of businesses aren't worried about getting paid in 40 or 45 days, but are more interested in the certainty of payment on a specific date."

Jas Sahota, a partner in Deloitte's UK restructuring practice, says that three-month extensions are common, "as long as the supplier can see that there is a plan." In times of stress, he says, it's important to negotiate with only a handful of the most important partners – squeezing suppliers large and small only generates grief and distracts employees with lots of calls.

More fundamentally, the benefits of pulling the payables lever in isolation is "questionable," notes Andrew Ashby, director of the working capital practice at KPMG in London, "especially as the impact on the receivables balance is typically a lot more than the payables balance."

Improving collections, such as achieving longer payment terms, relies on the strength of relationships built over time, notes Robert Hecht, a London-based managing director of turnaround consultancy AlixPartners. "You can't wait for a crisis and then expect suppliers to step up and be your best friends."

*Source*: 'Dash for Cash', J. Karaian, *CFO Europe Magazine*, 8 July 2008, www.CFO.com.

## Summary

The main points of this chapter may be summarised as follows.

**Working capital**

- Working capital is the difference between current assets and current liabilities.
- That is, working capital = inventories + trade receivables + cash – trade payables – bank overdrafts.
- An investment in working capital cannot be avoided in practice – typically large amounts are involved.

**Inventories**

- There are costs of holding inventories, which include:
  - lost interest
  - storage cost
  - insurance cost
  - obsolescence.
- There are also costs of not holding sufficient inventories, which include:
  - loss of sales and customer goodwill
  - production dislocation
  - loss of flexibility – cannot take advantage of opportunities
  - reorder costs – low inventories imply more frequent ordering.
- Practical points on inventories management include:
  - identify optimum order size – models can help with this
  - set inventories reorder levels
  - use budgets
  - keep reliable inventories records

- use accounting ratios (for example, inventories turnover period ratio)
- establish systems for security of inventories and authorisation
- consider just-in-time (JIT) inventories management.

### Trade receivables

- When assessing which customers should receive credit, the five Cs of credit can be used:
  - capital
  - capacity
  - collateral
  - condition
  - character.
- The costs of allowing credit include:
  - lost interest
  - lost purchasing power
  - costs of assessing customer creditworthiness
  - administration cost
  - bad debts
  - cash discounts (for prompt payment).
- The costs of denying credit include:
  - loss of customer goodwill.
- Practical points on receivables management:
  - establish a policy
  - assess and monitor customer creditworthiness
  - establish effective administration of receivables
  - establish a policy on bad debts
  - consider cash discounts
  - use financial ratios (for example, average settlement period for trade receivables ratio)
  - use ageing summaries.

### Cash

- The costs of holding cash include:
  - lost interest
  - lost purchasing power.
- The costs of holding insufficient cash include:
  - loss of supplier goodwill if unable to meet commitments on time
  - loss of opportunities
  - inability to claim cash discounts
  - costs of borrowing (should an obligation need to be met at short notice).
- Practical points on cash management:
  - establish a policy
  - plan cash flows
  - make judicious use of bank overdraft finance – it can be cheap and flexible
  - use short-term cash surpluses profitably
  - bank frequently
  - operating cash cycle (for a wholesaler) = length of time from buying inventories to receiving cash from receivables less payables' payment period (in days)
  - transmit cash promptly.
- An objective of working capital management is to limit the length of the operating cash cycle (OCC), subject to any risks that this may cause.

### Trade payables

- The costs of taking credit include:
  - higher price than purchases for immediate cash settlement
  - administrative costs
  - restrictions imposed by seller.
- The costs of not taking credit include:
  - lost interest-free borrowing
  - lost purchasing power
  - inconvenience – paying at the time of purchase can be inconvenient.
- Practical points on payables management:
  - establish a policy
  - exploit free credit as far as possible
  - use accounting ratios (for example, average settlement period for trade payables ratio).

## MyAccountingLab

Go to **www.myaccountinglab.com** to check your understanding of the chapter, create a personalised study plan, and maximise your revision time

## Key terms

**working capital**   p. 644
**lead time**   p. 651
**ABC system of inventories control**   p. 653
**economic order quantity (EOQ)**   p. 654
**materials requirement planning (MRP) system**   p. 658
**just-in-time (JIT) inventories management**   p. 658

**five Cs of credit**   p. 660
**cash discount**   p. 665
**average settlement period for trade receivables**   p. 666
**ageing schedule of trade receivables**   p. 667
**operating cash cycle (OCC)**   p. 673
**average settlement period for trade payables**   p. 680

## Further reading

If you would like to explore the topics covered in this chapter in more depth, try the following books:

Arnold, G., *Corporate Financial Management*, 4th edn, Financial Times Prentice Hall, 2008, chapter 13.

Hillier, D., Ross, S., Westerfield, R., Jaffe, J. and Jordan, B., *Corporate Finance,* European edn, McGraw-Hill Higher Education, 2010, chapters 26 to 28.

McLaney, E., *Business Finance: Theory and Practice*, 9th edn, Financial Times Prentice Hall, 2012, chapter 13.

Pike, R., Neale, B. and Linsley, P., *Corporate Finance and Investment*, 6th edn, Prentice Hall, 2009, chapters 13 and 14.

## Review questions

Solutions to these questions can be found at the back of the book on page 759.

**16.1** Tariq is the credit manager of Heltex plc. He is concerned that the pattern of monthly cash receipts from credit sales shows that credit collection is poor compared with budget. Heltex's sales director believes that Tariq is to blame for this situation, but Tariq insists that he is not. Why might Tariq not be to blame for the deterioration in the credit collection period?

**16.2** How might each of the following affect the level of inventories held by a business?

(a) An increase in the number of production bottlenecks experienced by the business.
(b) A rise in the business's cost of capital.
(c) A decision to offer customers a narrower range of products in the future.
(d) A switch of suppliers from an overseas business to a local business.
(e) A deterioration in the quality and reliability of bought-in components.

**16.3** What are the reasons for holding inventories? Are these reasons different from the reasons for holding cash?

**16.4** Identify the costs of holding:

(a) too little cash; and
(b) too much cash.

## Exercises

Exercises 16.1 and 16.2 are basic level, 16.3 and 16.4 are intermediate level and 16.5, 16.6 and 16.7 are advanced level. Those with coloured numbers have solutions at the back of the book starting on page 799.

If you wish to try more exercises, visit the students' side of the Companion Website.

**16.1** The chief executive officer of Sparkrite Ltd, a trading business, has just received summary sets of financial statements for last year and this year:

**Sparkrite Ltd**
**Income statements for years ended 30 September**

|  | Last year | | This year | |
|---|---|---|---|---|
|  | £000 | £000 | £000 | £000 |
| Sales revenue |  | 1,800 |  | 1,920 |
| Cost of sales |  |  |  |  |
| Opening inventories | 160 |  | 200 |  |
| Purchases | 1,120 |  | 1,175 |  |
|  | 1,280 |  | 1,375 |  |
| Closing inventories | (200) |  | (250) |  |
|  |  | (1,080) |  | (1,125) |
| Gross profit |  | 720 |  | 795 |
| Expenses |  | (680) |  | (750) |
| Profit for the year |  | 40 |  | 45 |

**Statements of financial position as at 30 September**

|  | Last year £000 | This year £000 |
|---|---|---|
| **ASSETS** | | |
| Non-current assets | 950 | 930 |
| **Current assets** | | |
| Inventories | 200 | 250 |
| Trade receivables | 375 | 480 |
| Bank | 4 | 2 |
|  | 579 | 732 |
| Total assets | 1,529 | 1,662 |
| **EQUITY AND LIABILITIES** | | |
| **Equity** | | |
| Fully paid £1 ordinary shares | 825 | 883 |
| Retained earnings | 509 | 554 |
|  | 1,334 | 1,437 |
| Current liabilities | 195 | 225 |
| Total equity and liabilities | 1,529 | 1,662 |

The chief financial officer has expressed concern at the increase in inventories and trade receivables levels.

*Required*:

(a) Show, by using the data given, how you would calculate ratios that could be used to measure inventories and trade receivables levels during last year and this year.

(b) Discuss the ways in which the management of Sparkrite Ltd could exercise control over:

(1) inventories levels; and

(2) trade receivables levels.

16.2 Hercules Wholesalers Ltd has been particularly concerned with its liquidity position in recent months. The most recent income statement and statement of financial position of the business are as follows:

**Income statement for the year ended 31 December last year**

|  | £000 | £000 |
|---|---|---|
| Sales revenue | | 452 |
| Cost of sales | | |
| Opening inventories | 125 | |
| Purchases | 341 | |
|  | 466 | |
| Closing inventories | (143) | (323) |
| Gross profit | | 129 |
| Expenses | | (132) |
| Loss for the year | | (3) |

## Statement of financial position as at 31 December last year

| | £000 |
|---|---:|
| ASSETS | |
| Non-current assets | |
| Property, plant and equipment | 357 |
| Current assets | |
| Inventories | 143 |
| Trade receivables | 163 |
| | 306 |
| Total assets | 663 |
| EQUITY AND LIABILITIES | |
| Equity | |
| Ordinary share capital | 100 |
| Retained earnings | 158 |
| | 258 |
| Non-current liabilities | |
| Borrowings – Loans | 120 |
| Current liabilities | |
| Trade payables | 145 |
| Borrowings – Bank overdraft | 140 |
| | 285 |
| Total equity and liabilities | 663 |

The trade receivables and payables were maintained at a constant level throughout the year.

*Required*:

(a)  Explain why Hercules Wholesalers Ltd is concerned about its liquidity position.

(b)  Calculate the operating cash cycle for Hercules Wholesalers Ltd.

(c)  State what steps may be taken to improve the operating cash cycle of the business.

**16.3**  International Electric plc at present offers its customers 30 days' credit. Half the customers, by value, pay on time. The other half takes an average of 70 days to pay. The business is considering offering a cash discount of 2 per cent to its customers for payment within 30 days.

The credit controller anticipates that half of the customers who now take an average of 70 days to pay (that is, a quarter of all customers) will pay in 30 days. The other half (the final quarter) will still take an average of 70 days to pay. The scheme will also reduce bad debts by £300,000 a year.

Annual sales revenue of £365 million is made evenly throughout the year. At present the business has a large overdraft (£60 million) with its bank at an interest cost of 12 per cent a year.

*Required*:

(a)  Calculate the approximate equivalent annual percentage cost of a discount of 2 per cent, which reduces the time taken by credit customers to pay from 70 days to 30 days. (*Hint*: This part can be answered without reference to the narrative above.)

(b)  Calculate the value of trade receivables outstanding under both the old and new schemes.

(c)  How much will the scheme cost the business in discounts?

(d)  Should the business go ahead with the scheme? State what other factors, if any, should be taken into account.

**16.4**  Your superior, the general manager of Plastics Manufacturers Limited, has recently been talking to the chief buyer of Plastic Toys Limited, which manufactures a wide range of toys for young children. At present, Plastic Toys is considering changing its supplier of plastic granules and has offered to buy its entire requirement of 2,000 kg a month from you at the going market rate, provided that you will grant it three months' credit on its purchases. The following information is available:

1 Plastic granules sell for £10 a kg, variable costs are £7 a kg, and fixed costs £2 a kg.
2 Your own business is financially strong, and has sales revenue of £15 million a year. For the foreseeable future it will have surplus capacity, and it is actively looking for new outlets.
3 Extracts from Plastic Toys' financial statements:

|  | Year 1 | Year 2 | Year 3 |
|---|---|---|---|
|  | £000 | £000 | £000 |
| Sales revenue | 800 | 980 | 640 |
| Profit before interest and tax | 100 | 110 | (150) |
| Capital employed | 600 | 650 | 575 |
| Current assets |  |  |  |
| Inventories | 200 | 220 | 320 |
| Trade receivables | 140 | 160 | 160 |
|  | 340 | 380 | 480 |
| Current liabilities |  |  |  |
| Trade payables | 180 | 190 | 220 |
| Overdraft | 100 | 150 | 310 |
|  | 280 | 340 | 530 |
| Working capital | 60 | 40 | (50) |

*Required*:
Advise your general manager on the acceptability of the proposal. You should give your reasons and do any calculations you consider necessary.

16.5 Mayo Computers Ltd has annual sales of £20 million. Bad debts amount to £0.1 million a year. All sales made by the business are on credit and, at present, credit terms are negotiable by the customer. On average, the settlement period for trade receivables is 60 days. Trade receivables are financed by an overdraft bearing a 14 per cent rate of interest per year. The business is currently reviewing its credit policies to see whether more efficient and profitable methods could be employed. Only one proposal has so far been put forward concerning the management of trade credit.

The credit control department has proposed that customers should be given a $2\frac{1}{2}$ per cent discount if they pay within 30 days. For those who do not pay within this period, a maximum of 50 days' credit should be given. The credit department believes that 60 per cent of customers will take advantage of the discount by paying at the end of the discount period. The remainder will pay at the end of 50 days. The credit department believes that bad debts can be effectively eliminated by adopting the proposed policies and by employing stricter credit investigation procedures, which will cost an additional £20,000 a year. The credit department is confident that these new policies will not result in any reduction in sales revenue.

*Required*:
Calculate the net annual cost (savings) to the business of abandoning its existing credit policies and adopting the proposals of the credit control department. (*Hint*: To answer this question you must weigh the costs of administration and cash discounts against the savings in bad debts and interest charges.)

16.6 Boswell Enterprises Ltd is reviewing its trade credit policy. The business, which sells all of its goods on credit, has estimated that sales revenue for the forthcoming year will be £3 million under the existing policy. Credit customers representing 30 per cent of trade receivables are expected to pay one month after being invoiced and 70 per cent are expected to pay two months after being invoiced. These estimates are in line with previous years' figures.

At present, no cash discounts are offered to customers. However, to encourage prompt payment, the business is considering giving a $2\frac{1}{2}$ per cent cash discount to credit customers who pay in one month or less. Given this incentive, the business expects that credit customers accounting for 60 per cent of trade receivables to pay one month after being invoiced and those accounting for 40 per cent of trade receivables to pay two months after being invoiced. The business believes that the introduction of a cash discount policy will prove attractive to some customers and will lead to a 5 per cent increase in total sales revenue.

Irrespective of the trade credit policy adopted, the gross profit margin of the business will be 20 per cent for the forthcoming year and three months' inventories will be held. Fixed monthly expenses of £15,000 and variable expenses (excluding discounts), equivalent to 10 per cent of sales revenue, will be incurred and will be paid one month in arrears. Trade payables will be paid in arrears and will be equal to two months' cost of sales. The business will hold a fixed cash balance of £140,000 throughout the year, whichever trade credit policy is adopted. Ignore taxation.

*Required*:
(a) Calculate the investment in working capital at the end of the forthcoming year under:
   (1) the existing policy; and
   (2) the proposed policy.
(b) Calculate the expected profit for the forthcoming year under:
   (1) the existing policy; and
   (2) the proposed policy.
(c) Advise the business as to whether it should implement the proposed policy.

(*Hint*: The investment in working capital will be made up of inventories, trade receivables and cash, *less* trade payables and any unpaid expenses at the year end.)

**16.7** Goliath plc is a food wholesaler. The most recent financial statements of the business are as follows:

### Income statement for the year to 31 May

|  | £000 | £000 |
|---|---|---|
| Sales revenue |  | 2,400.0 |
| Cost of sales |  |  |
| Opening inventories | 550.0 |  |
| Purchases | 1,450.0 |  |
|  | 2,000.0 |  |
| Closing inventories | (560.0) | (1,440.0) |
| Gross profit |  | 960.0 |
| Administration expenses |  | (300.0) |
| Selling expenses |  | (436.0) |
| Operating profit |  | 224.0 |
| Interest payable |  | (40.0) |
| Profit before taxation |  | 184.0 |
| Taxation (25%) |  | (46.0) |
| Profit for the period |  | 138.0 |

### Statement of financial position as at 31 May

|  | £000 |
|---|---|
| **Non-current assets** | |
| Property, plant and equipment | 456.4 |
| **Current assets** | |
| Inventories | 560.0 |
| Trade receivables | 565.0 |
| Cash at bank | 36.4 |
| | 1,161.4 |
| **Total assets** | 1,617.8 |
| **Equity** | |
| £1 ordinary shares | 200.0 |
| Retained earnings | 520.8 |
| | 720.8 |
| **Non-current liabilities** | |
| Borrowings – Loan notes | 400.0 |
| **Current liabilities** | |
| Trade payables | 451.0 |
| Taxation | 46.0 |
| | 497.0 |
| **Total equity and liabilities** | 1,617.8 |

All sales and purchases are made on credit.

The business is considering whether to grant extended credit facilities to its customers. It has been estimated that increasing the settlement period for trade receivables by a further 20 days will increase the sales revenue of the business by 10 per cent. However, inventories will have to be increased by 15 per cent to cope with the increased demand. It is estimated that purchases will have to rise to £1,668,000 during the next year as a result of these changes. To finance the increase in inventories and trade receivables, the business will increase the settlement period taken for suppliers by 15 days and use a loan facility bearing a 10 per cent rate of interest for the remaining balance.

If the policy is implemented, bad debts are likely to increase by £120,000 a year and administration costs will rise by 15 per cent.

*Required*:
(a) Calculate the increase or decrease to each of the following that will occur in the forthcoming year if the proposed policy is implemented:
  (1) operating cash cycle (based on year-end figures)
  (2) net investment in inventories, trade receivables and trade payables
  (3) profit for the period.
(b) Should the business implement the proposed policy? Give reasons for your conclusion.

# PART 4

# Supplementary information

Part 4 provides information that is supplementary to the main text of the book.

Appendix A takes the format of a normal textual chapter and describes the way in which financial transactions are recorded manually in books of account. Generally, this is by means of the 'double-entry' system, described in basic terms in the appendix.

Appendix B gives definitions of the key terms highlighted throughout the main text and listed at the end of each chapter. The aim of the appendix is to provide a single location to check on the meanings of the major accounting terms used in this book and in the world of finance.

Appendices C, D and E give answers to some of the questions set in the course of the main text. Appendix C gives answers to the self-assessment questions, Appendix D gives the answers to the review questions and Appendix E gives answers to those of the exercises that are marked as having their answers provided in the book.

Appendix F is a table of present value factors that can be used to discount future cash flows.

# Recording financial transactions

## Introduction

In Chapters 2 and 3, we saw how the financial transactions of a business may be recorded by making a series of entries on the statement of financial position (balance sheet) and/ or the income statement. Each of these entries had its corresponding 'double', meaning that both sides of the transaction were recorded. However, adjusting the financial statements, by hand, for each transaction can be very messy and confusing. With a reasonably large number of transactions it is pretty certain to result in mistakes.

For businesses whose accounting systems are on a computer, this problem is overcome because suitable software can deal with a series of 'plus' and 'minus' entries very reliably. Where the accounting system is not computerised, however, it would be helpful to have some more practical way of keeping accounting records. Such a system not only exists but, before the advent of the computer, was the routine way of keeping accounting records. In fact, the system had been in constant use for recording business transactions since medieval times. It is this system that is explained in this appendix. We should be clear that the system we are going to consider follows exactly the same rules as those that we have already met. Its distinguishing feature is its ability to provide those keeping accounting records by hand with a methodical approach that allows each transaction to be clearly identified and errors to be minimised.

## Learning outcomes

**When you have completed this appendix, you should be able to:**

- Explain the basic principles of double-entry bookkeeping.
- Write up a series of business transactions and balance the accounts.
- Extract a trial balance and explain its purpose.
- Prepare a set of financial statements from the underlying double-entry accounts.

## The basics of double-entry bookkeeping

When we record accounting transactions by hand, we use a recording system known as **double-entry bookkeeping**. This system does not use plus and minus entries on the face of a statement of financial position and income statement to record a particular transaction, in the way described in Chapters 2 and 3. Instead, these are recorded in accounts. An **account** is simply a record of one or more transactions relating to a particular item, such as:

- cash;
- property, plant and equipment;
- borrowings;
- sales revenue;
- rent payable; and
- equity.

A business may keep few or many accounts, depending on the size and complexity of its operations. Broadly, businesses tend to keep a separate account for each item that appears in either the income statement or the statement of financial position.

An example of an account, in this case the cash account, is as follows:

| **Cash** | | |
|---|---|---|
| £ | | £ |

We can see that an account has three main features:

- A title indicating the item to which it relates
- A left-hand side, known as the **debit** side
- A right-hand side, known as the **credit** side.

One side of an account will record increases in the particular item and the other will record decreases. This, of course, is slightly different from the approach we used when adjusting the financial statements. When adjusting the statement of financial position, for example, we put a reduction in an asset or claim in the same column as any increases, but with a minus sign against it. However, when accounts are used, a reduction is shown on the opposite side of the account.

The side on which an increase or decrease is shown will depend on the nature of the item to which the account relates. For example, an account for an asset, such as cash, will show increases on the left-hand (debit) side of the account and decreases on the right-hand (credit) side. However, for claims (that is, equity and liabilities) it is the other way around. An increase in the account for equity or for a liability will be shown on the right-hand (credit) side and a decrease will be shown on the left-hand (debit) side.

To understand why this difference exists, we should recall from Chapter 2 that the accounting equation is:

$$\text{Assets} = \text{Equity} + \text{Liabilities}$$

We can see that assets appear on one side of the equation and equity and liabilities appear on the other. Recording transactions in accounts simply expresses this difference in the recording process. Increases in assets are shown on the left-hand side of an account and increases in equity and liabilities are shown on the right-hand side of the account. We should recall the point made in Chapter 2 that each transaction has two aspects. Thus, when we record a particular transaction, two separate accounts will be affected. Recording transactions in this way is known as double-entry bookkeeping.

It is worth going through a simple example to see how transactions affecting statement of financial position items would be recorded under the double-entry bookkeeping system. Suppose a new business started on 1 January with the owner putting £5,000 into a newly opened business bank account, as initial equity. This entry would appear in the cash account as follows:

**Cash**

| | £ | | £ |
|---|---|---|---|
| 1 January Equity | 5,000 | | |

The corresponding entry would be made in the equity account as follows:

**Equity**

| | £ | | £ |
|---|---|---|---|
| | | 1 January Cash | 5,000 |

It is usual to show, in each account by way of note, where the other side of the entry will be found. Thus, someone looking at the equity account will know that the £5,000 arose from a receipt of cash. This provides potentially useful information, partly because it establishes a 'trail' that can be followed when checking for errors. Including the date of the transaction provides additional information to the reader of the accounts.

Now suppose that, on 2 January, £600 of the cash is used to buy some inventories. This would affect the cash account as follows:

**Cash**

| | £ | | £ |
|---|---|---|---|
| 1 January Equity | 5,000 | 2 January Inventories | 600 |

This cash account, in effect, shows 'positive' cash of £5,000 and 'negative' cash of £600, a net amount of £4,400.

## Activity A.1

As you know, we must somehow record the other side of the transaction involving the acquisition of the inventories for £600. See if you can work out what to do in respect of the inventories.

We must open an account for inventories. Since inventories are assets, an increase in it will appear on the left-hand side of the account, as follows:

**Inventories**

| | £ | | £ |
|---|---|---|---|
| 2 January Cash | 600 | | |

What we have seen so far highlights the key rule of double-entry bookkeeping: each left-hand entry must have a right-hand entry of equal size. Using the jargon, we can say that *every debit must have a credit.*

It might be helpful at this point to make clear that the words 'debit' and 'credit' are no more than accounting jargon for left and right, respectively. Generally, in English, (that is, when not referring to accounting), people tend to use credit to imply something good and debit something undesirable. Debit and credit have no such implication in accounting. Each transaction requires both a debit entry and a credit one. This is equally true whether the transaction is a 'good' one, like being paid by a credit customer, or a 'bad' one, like having to treat a credit customer's balance as worthless because that customer has gone bankrupt.

## Recording trading transactions

The rules of double entry also extend to 'trading' transactions, that is, making revenue (sales and so on) and incurring expenses. To understand how these transactions are recorded, we should recall that in Chapter 3 the extended accounting equation was set out as follows:

$$\text{Assets} = \text{Equity} + (\text{Revenues} - \text{Expenses}) + \text{Liabilities}$$

This equation can be rearranged so that:

$$\text{Assets} + \text{Expenses} = \text{Equity} + \text{Revenues} + \text{Liabilities}$$

We can see that increases in expenses are shown on the same side as assets and this means that they will be dealt with in the same way for recording purposes. Thus, an increase in an expense, such as wages, will be shown on the left-hand (debit) side of the wages account and a decrease will be shown on the right-hand (credit) side. Increases in revenues are shown on the same side as equity and liabilities and so will be dealt with in the same way as them. Thus, an increase in revenue, such as sales, will be shown on the right-hand (credit) side and a decrease will be shown on the left-hand (debit) side.

To summarise, therefore, we can say that:

● Debits (left-hand entries) represent increases in assets and expenses and decreases in claims and revenues.
● Credits (right-hand entries) represent increases in claims and revenues and decreases in assets and expenses.

Let us continue with our example by assuming that, on 3 January, the business paid £900 to rent business premises for the three months to 31 March. To record this transaction, we should normally open a 'rent account' and make entries in this account and in the cash account as follows:

| | Rent | |
|---|---|---|
| | £ | £ |
| 3 January Cash | 900 | |

### Cash

|  | £ |  | £ |
|---|---|---|---|
| 1 January Equity | 5,000 | 2 January Inventories | 600 |
|  |  | 3 January Rent | 900 |

The fact that assets and expenses are dealt with in the same way should not be altogether surprising since assets and expenses are closely linked. Assets transform into expenses as they are 'used up'. Rent, which, as here, is usually paid in advance, is an asset when it is first paid. It represents the value to the business of being entitled to occupy the premises for the forthcoming period (until 31 March in this case). As the three months progress, this asset becomes an expense; it is 'used up'. We need to remember that the debit entry in the rent account does not necessarily represent either an asset or an expense; it could be a mixture of the two. Strictly, by the end of the day on which it was paid (3 January), £30 would have represented an expense for the three days; the remaining £870 would have been an asset. As each day passes, an additional £10 (that is, £900/90 (there are 90 days in January, February and March altogether)) will transform from an asset into an expense. As we have already seen, it is not necessary for us to make any adjustment to the rent account as the days pass.

Assume, now, that on 5 January the business sold inventories costing £200 for £300 on credit. As usual, when we are able to identify the cost of the inventories sold at the time of sale, we need to deal with the sale and the cost of sales as two separate issues, each having its own set of debits and credits.

First, let us deal with the sale. We now need to open accounts for both 'sales revenue' and 'trade receivables' – which do not, as yet, exist. The sale gives rise to an increase in revenue and so there is a credit entry in the sales revenue account. The sale also creates an asset of trade receivables and so there is debit entry in trade receivables:

### Sales revenue

|  | £ |  | £ |
|---|---|---|---|
|  |  | 5 January Trade receivables | 300 |

### Trade receivables

|  | £ |  | £ |
|---|---|---|---|
| 5 January Sales revenue | 300 |  |  |

Let us now deal with the inventories sold. Since the inventories sold have become the expense 'cost of sales', we need to reduce the figure on the inventories account by making a credit entry and to make the corresponding debit in a 'cost of sales' account, opened for the purpose:

### Inventories

|  | £ |  | £ |
|---|---|---|---|
| 2 January Cash | 600 | 5 January Cost of sales | 200 |

### Cost of sales

|  | £ |  | £ |
|---|---|---|---|
| 5 January Inventories | 200 |  |  |

We shall now look at the other transactions for our hypothetical business for the remainder of January. These can be taken to be as follows:

| | |
|---|---|
| 8 January | Bought some inventories on credit costing £800 |
| 11 January | Bought some office furniture for £600 cash |
| 15 January | Sold inventories costing £600 for £900, on credit |
| 18 January | Received £800 from trade receivables |
| 21 January | Paid trade payables £500 |
| 24 January | Paid wages for the month £400 |
| 27 January | Bought inventories on credit for £800 |
| 31 January | Borrowed £2,000 from the Commercial Finance Company |

Naturally, we shall have to open several additional accounts to enable us to record all of these transactions in any meaningful way. By the end of January, the set of accounts would appear as follows:

### Cash

| | £ | | £ |
|---|---|---|---|
| 1 January Equity | 5,000 | 2 January Inventories | 600 |
| 18 January Trade receivables | 800 | 3 January Rent | 900 |
| 31 January Comm. Fin. Co. | 2,000 | 11 January Office furniture | 600 |
| | | 21 January Trade payables | 500 |
| | | 24 January Wages | 400 |

### Equity

| | £ | | £ |
|---|---|---|---|
| | | 1 January Cash | 5,000 |

### Inventories

| | £ | | £ |
|---|---|---|---|
| 2 January Cash | 600 | 5 January Cost of sales | 200 |
| 8 January Trade payables | 800 | 15 January Cost of sales | 600 |
| 27 January Trade payables | 800 | | |

### Rent

| | £ | | £ |
|---|---|---|---|
| 3 January Cash | 900 | | |

### Sales revenue

| | £ | | £ |
|---|---|---|---|
| | | 5 January Trade receivables | 300 |
| | | 15 January Trade receivables | 900 |

### Trade receivables

| | £ | | £ |
|---|---|---|---|
| 5 January Sales revenue | 300 | 18 January Cash | 800 |
| 15 January Sales revenue | 900 | | |

**Cost of sales**

| | £ | | £ |
|---|---|---|---|
| 5 January Inventories | 200 | | |
| 15 January Inventories | 600 | | |

**Trade payables**

| | £ | | £ |
|---|---|---|---|
| 21 January Cash | 500 | 8 January Inventories | 800 |
| | | 27 January Inventories | 800 |

**Office furniture**

| | £ | | £ |
|---|---|---|---|
| 11 January Cash | 600 | | |

**Wages**

| | £ | | £ |
|---|---|---|---|
| 24 January Cash | 400 | | |

**Borrowings – Commercial Finance Company**

| | £ | | £ |
|---|---|---|---|
| | | 31 January Cash | 2,000 |

All of the transactions from 8 January onwards are quite similar in nature to those up to that date, which we discussed in detail, and so we should be able to follow them using the date references as a guide.

## Balancing accounts and the trial balance

Businesses keeping their accounts in the way shown would find it helpful to summarise their individual accounts periodically – perhaps weekly or monthly – for two reasons:

- To be able to see at a glance how much is in each account (for example, to see how much cash the business has left).
- To help to check the accuracy of the bookkeeping so far.

Let us look at the cash account again:

**Cash**

| | £ | | £ |
|---|---|---|---|
| 1 January Equity | 5,000 | 2 January Inventories | 600 |
| 18 January Trade receivables | 800 | 3 January Rent | 900 |
| 31 January Comm. Fin. Co. | 2,000 | 11 January Office furniture | 600 |
| | | 21 January Trade payables | 500 |
| | | 24 January Wages | 400 |

Does this account tell us how much cash the business has at 31 January? The answer is partly yes and partly no.

We do not have a single figure showing the cash **balance** but we can fairly easily deduce this by adding up the debit (receipts) column and deducting the sum of the credit (payments) column. However, it would be better if the current cash balance were provided for us.

To summarise or 'balance' this account, we add up the column with the largest amount (in this case, the debit side) and put this total on *both* sides of the account. We then put in, on the credit side, the figure that will make that side add up to the total that appears in the account. We cannot put in this balancing figure only once, as the double-entry rule would be broken. Thus, to preserve the double entry, we also put it in on the other side of the same account below the totals, as follows:

**Cash**

|  |  |  |  |
|---|---|---|---|
|  |  |  | £ |
| 1 January Equity | 5,000 | 2 January Inventories | 600 |
| 18 January Trade receivables | 800 | 3 January Rent | 900 |
| 31 January Borrowings | 2,000 | 11 January Office furniture | 600 |
|  |  | 21 January Trade payables | 500 |
|  |  | 24 January Wages | 400 |
|  |  | 31 January Balance carried down | 4,800 |
|  | 7,800 |  | 7,800 |
| 1 February Balance brought down | 4,800 |  |  |

Note that the balance carried down (usually abbreviated to 'c/d') at the end of one period becomes the balance brought down ('b/d') at the beginning of the next. Now we can see at a glance what the present cash position is, without having to do any mental arithmetic.

**Activity A.2**

Try balancing the inventories account and then say what we know about the inventories position at the end of January.

The inventories account will be balanced as follows:

**Inventories**

|  |  |  |  |
|---|---|---|---|
|  | £ |  | £ |
| 2 January Cash | 600 | 5 January Cost of sales | 200 |
| 8 January Trade payables | 800 | 15 January Cost of sales | 600 |
| 27 January Trade payables | 800 | 31 January Balance c/d | 1,400 |
|  | 2,200 |  | 2,200 |
| 1 February Balance b/d | 1,400 |  |  |

We can see at a glance that the business held inventories that had cost £1,400 at the end of January. We can also see quite easily how this situation arose.

We can balance all of the other accounts in a similar fashion. However, there is no point in formally balancing accounts that have only one entry at the moment (for example, the equity account) because we cannot summarise one figure; it is already in as summarised a form as it can be. After balancing, the remaining accounts will be as follows:

### Equity

|  | £ |  | £ |
|---|---|---|---|
|  |  | 1 January Cash | 5,000 |

### Rent

|  | £ |  | £ |
|---|---|---|---|
| 3 January Cash | 900 |  |  |

### Sales revenue

|  | £ |  | £ |
|---|---|---|---|
| 31 January Balance c/d | 1,200 | 5 January Trade receivables | 300 |
|  |  | 15 January Trade receivables | 900 |
|  | 1,200 |  | 1,200 |
|  |  | 1 February Balance b/d | 1,200 |

### Trade receivables

|  | £ |  | £ |
|---|---|---|---|
| 5 January Sales revenue | 300 | 18 January Cash | 800 |
| 15 January Sales revenue | 900 | 31 January Balance c/d | 400 |
|  | 1,200 |  | 1,200 |
| 1 February Balance b/d | 400 |  |  |

### Cost of sales

|  | £ |  | £ |
|---|---|---|---|
| 5 January Inventories | 200 | 31 January Balance c/d | 800 |
| 15 January Inventories | 600 |  |  |
|  | 800 |  | 800 |
| 1 February Balance b/d | 800 |  |  |

### Trade payables

|  | £ |  | £ |
|---|---|---|---|
| 21 January Cash | 500 | 8 January Inventories | 800 |
| 31 January Balance c/d | 1,100 | 27 January Inventories | 800 |
|  | 1,600 |  | 1,600 |
|  |  | 1 February Balance b/d | 1,100 |

### Office furniture

|  | £ |  | £ |
|---|---|---|---|
| 11 January Cash | 600 |  |  |

### Wages

|  | £ |  | £ |
|---|---|---|---|
| 24 January Cash | 400 |  |  |

**Borrowings – Commercial Finance Company**

| £ | | | £ |
|---|---|---|---|
| | | 31 January Cash | 2,000 |

---

**Activity A.3**

If we now separately total the debit balances and the credit balances, what should we expect to find?

We should expect to find that these two totals are equal. This must, in theory be true since every debit entry was matched by an equally-sized credit entry.

---

Let us see if our expectation in Activity A.3 works in our example, by listing the debit and credit balances as follows:

| | Debits £ | Credits £ |
|---|---|---|
| Cash | 4,800 | |
| Inventories | 1,400 | |
| Equity | | 5,000 |
| Rent | 900 | |
| Sales revenue | | 1,200 |
| Trade receivables | 400 | |
| Cost of sales | 800 | |
| Trade payables | | 1,100 |
| Office furniture | 600 | |
| Wages | 400 | |
| Borrowings | | 2,000 |
| | 9,300 | 9,300 |

This statement is known as a **trial balance**. The fact that it agrees gives us *some* indication that we have not made bookkeeping errors.

This does not, however, give us total confidence that no error could have occurred. Consider, for example, the transaction that took place on 3 January (paid rent for the month of £900). In each of the following cases, all of which would be a wrong treatment of the transaction, the trial balance would still have agreed:

- The transaction was completely omitted from the accounts, that is, no entries were made at all.
- The amount was misread as £9,000 but then (correctly) debited to the rent account and credited to cash.
- The correct amount was (incorrectly) debited to cash and credited to rent.

Nevertheless, a trial balance that agrees does give some confidence that accounts have been correctly written up.

## Activity A.4

Why do you think the words 'debtor' and 'creditor' are used to describe those who owe money or are owed money by a business?

The answer simply is that debtors have a debit balance (that is, a balance brought down on the debit side) in the books of the business, whereas creditors have a credit balance.

# Preparing the financial statements (final accounts)

If the trial balance agrees and we are confident that there are no errors in recording, the next stage is to prepare the income statement and statement of financial position. Preparing the income statement is simply a matter of going through the individual accounts, identifying those amounts that represent revenue and expenses of the period, and transferring them to the income statement, which is itself also part of the double-entry system.

We shall now do this for the example we have been using. The situation is complicated slightly for three reasons:

- As we know, the £900 rent paid during January relates to the three months January, February and March.
- The business's owner estimates that the electricity used during January is about £110. There is no bill yet from the electricity supply business because it normally bills customers only at the end of each three-month period.
- The business's owner believes that the office furniture should be depreciated by 20% each year (straight-line).

These three factors need to be taken into account. As we shall see, however, the end-of-period adjustments of these types are very easily handled in double-entry accounts. Let us deal with these three areas first.

The rent account will appear as follow, after we have completed the transfer to the income statement:

**Rent**

|  | £ |  | £ |
|---|---|---|---|
| 3 January Cash | 900 | 31 January Income statement | 300 |
|  |  | Balance c/d | 600 |
|  | 900 |  | 900 |
| 1 February Balance b/d | 600 |  |  |

At 31 January, because two months' rent is still an asset, this is carried down as a debit balance. The remainder (representing January's rent) is credited to the rent account and debited to a newly opened income statement. As we shall see shortly, the £600 debit balance remaining will appear in the 31 January statement of financial position.

Now let us deal with the electricity. The electricity account will be as follows after the transfer to the income statement:

### Electricity

| | £ | | £ |
|---|---|---|---|
| | | 31 January Income statement | 110 |

Because there has been no cash payment or other transaction recorded so far for electricity, we do not already have an account for it. It is necessary to open one. We need to debit the income statement with the £110 of electricity used during January and credit the electricity account with the same amount. At 31 January, this credit balance reflects the amount owed by this business to the electricity supplier. Once again, we shall see shortly that this balance will appear on the statement of financial position.

Next we shall consider what is necessary regarding the office furniture. The depreciation for the month will be $20\% \times £600 \times \frac{1}{12}$, that is £10. Normal accounting practice is to charge (debit) this to the income statement, with the corresponding credit going to a 'provision for depreciation of office furniture' account. The latter entry will appear as follows:

### Provision for depreciation of office furniture account

| | £ | | £ |
|---|---|---|---|
| | | 31 January Income statement | 10 |

This £10 balance will be reflected in the statement of financial position at 31 January by being deducted from the office furniture itself, as we shall see shortly.

The balances on the following accounts represent straightforward revenue and expenses for the month of January:

- Sales revenue
- Cost of sales
- Wages.

The balances on these accounts will simply be transferred to the income statement.

To transfer balances to the income statement, we simply debit or credit the account concerned, such that any balance amount is eliminated, and make the corresponding credit or debit in the income statement. Take sales revenue, for example. This has a credit balance (because the balance represents a revenue). We must debit the sales revenue account with £1,200 and credit the income statement with the same amount. So a credit balance on the sales revenue account becomes a credit entry in the income statement. For the three accounts, then, we have the following:

### Sales revenue

| | £ | | £ |
|---|---|---|---|
| 31 January Balance c/d | 1,200 | 5 January Trade receivables | 300 |
| | | 15 January Trade receivables | 900 |
| | 1,200 | | 1,200 |
| 31 January Income statement | 1,200 | 1 February Balance b/d | 1,200 |

### Cost of sales

| | £ | | £ |
|---|---|---|---|
| 5 January Inventories | 200 | 31 January Balance c/d | 800 |
| 15 January Inventories | 600 | | |
| | 800 | | 800 |
| 1 February Balance b/d | 800 | 31 January Income statement | 800 |

**Wages**

| | £ | | £ |
|---|---|---|---|
| 24 January Cash | 400 | 31 January Income statement | 400 |

The income statement will now look as follows:

**Income statement**

| | £ | | £ |
|---|---|---|---|
| 31 January Cost of sales | 800 | 31 January Sales revenue | 1,200 |
| 31 January Rent | 300 | | |
| 31 January Wages | 400 | | |
| 31 January Electricity | 110 | | |
| 31 January Depreciation | 10 | | |

We must now transfer the balance on the income statement (a debit balance of £420).

## Activity A.5

**What does the balance on the income statement represent, and to where should it be transferred?**

The balance is either the profit or the loss for the period. In this case it is a loss as the total expenses exceed the total revenue. This loss must be borne by the owner, and it must therefore be transferred to the equity account.

The two accounts would now appear as follows:

**Income statement**

| | £ | | £ |
|---|---|---|---|
| 31 January Cost of sales | 800 | 31 January Sales revenue | 1,200 |
| 31 January Rent | 300 | | |
| 31 January Wages | 400 | | |
| 31 January Electricity | 110 | | |
| 31 January Depreciation | 10 | 31 January Equity (loss) | 420 |
| | 1,620 | | 1,620 |

**Equity**

| | £ | | £ |
|---|---|---|---|
| 31 January Income statement (loss) | 420 | 1 January Cash | 5,000 |
| 31 January Balance c/d | 4,580 | | |
| | 5,000 | | 5,000 |
| | | 1 February Balance b/d | 4,580 |

The last thing done was to balance the equity account.

Now all of the balances remaining on accounts represent either assets or claims as at 31 January. These balances can now be used to produce a statement of financial position, as follows:

**Statement of financial position as at 31 January**

|  | £ |
|---|---:|
| **ASSETS** | |
| **Non-current assets** | |
| *Property, plant and equipment* | |
| Office furniture: cost | 600 |
| depreciation | (10) |
| | 590 |
| **Current assets** | |
| Inventories | 1,400 |
| Prepaid expense | 600 |
| Trade receivables | 400 |
| Cash | 4,800 |
| | 7,200 |
| **Total assets** | 7,790 |
| **EQUITY AND LIABILITIES** | |
| Owners' equity | 4,580 |
| **Non-current liability** | |
| Borrowings | 2,000 |
| **Current liabilities** | |
| Accrued expense | 110 |
| Trade payables | 1,100 |
| | 1,210 |
| **Total equity and liabilities** | 7,790 |

The income statement could be written in a more stylish manner, for reporting to users, as follows:

**Income statement for the month ended 31 January**

|  | £ |
|---|---:|
| Sales revenue | 1,200 |
| Cost of sales | (800) |
| Gross profit | 400 |
| Rent | (300) |
| Wages | (400) |
| Electricity | (110) |
| Depreciation | (10) |
| Loss for the month | (420) |

## The ledger and its division

The book in which the accounts are traditionally kept is known as the **ledger**, and 'accounts' are sometimes referred to as 'ledger accounts', even where they are computerised.

In a handwritten accounting system, the ledger is often divided into various sections. This tends to be for three main reasons:

- Having all of the accounts in one book means that it is only possible for one person at a time to use the accounts, either to make entries or to extract useful information.
- Dividing the ledger along logical grounds can allow specialisation, so that various individual members of the accounts staff can look after their own part of the system. This can lead to more efficient record keeping.
- It can lead to greater security, that is, less risk of error and fraud, by limiting an individual's access to only part of the entire set of accounts.

There are no clear, universal rules on the division of the ledger, but the following division is fairly common:

- *The cash book*. This tends to be all of the accounts relating to cash either loose (often known as *petty cash*) or in the bank.
- *The sales (or trade receivables) ledger*. This contains the accounts of all of the business's individual trade receivables.
- *The purchases (or trade payables) ledger*. This consists of the accounts of all of the business's individual trade payables.
- *The nominal ledger*. These accounts tend to be those of expenses and revenue, for example, sales revenue, wages, rent, and so on.
- *The general ledger*. This contains the remainder of the business's accounts, mainly those to do with non-current assets and long-term finance.

## Summary

The main points in this appendix may be summarised as follows.

**Double-entry bookkeeping = a system for keeping accounting records by hand, such that a relatively large volume of transactions can be handled effectively and accurately.**

- There is a separate account for each asset, claim, expense and revenue that needs to be separately identified.
- Each account looks like a letter T.
- Left-hand (debit) side of the account records increases in assets and expenses and decreases in revenues and claims.
- Right-hand (credit) side records increases in revenues and claims and decreases in assets and expenses.
- There is an equal credit entry in one account for a debit entry in another.
- Double-entry bookkeeping can be used to record day-to-day transactions.
- It can also follow through to generate the income statement.
- The statement of financial position is a list of the net figure (the 'balance') on each of the accounts after appropriate transfers have been made to the income statement.
- The accounts are traditionally kept in a 'ledger', a term that persists even with computerised accounting.
- The ledger is traditionally broken down into several sections, each containing particular types of account.

## Key terms

**double-entry bookkeeping**  p. 694
**account**  p. 694
**debit**  p. 694
**credit**  p. 694

**balance**  p. 700
**trial balance**  p. 702
**ledger**  p. 706

## Further reading

If you would like to explore the topics covered in this appendix in more depth, we recommend the following books:

Bebbington, J., Gray, R. and Laughlin, R., *Financial Accounting*, 3rd edn, Thomson Learning, 2001, chapters 2 to 7.

Benedict, A. and Elliott, B., *Practical Accounting*, Financial Times Prentice Hall, 2008, chapters 2 to 5.

Thomas, A. and Ward, A., *An Introduction to Financial Accounting*, 6th edn, McGraw-Hill, 2009, chapters 3 to 8.

Wood, F. and Sangster, *A., Business Accounting, Volume 1*, 12th edn, Financial Times Prentice Hall, 2011, chapters 1 to 6.

## Exercises

The answers to all three of these exercises are at the back of the book, starting on page 802.

**A.1**  In respect of each of the following transactions, state in which two accounts an entry must be made and whether the entry is a debit or a credit. (For example, if the transaction were buying inventories for cash, the answer would be debit the inventories account and credit the cash account.)

(a) Bought inventories on credit.
(b) Owner made cash drawings.
(c) Paid interest on business borrowings.
(d) Bought inventories for cash.
(e) Received cash from a credit customer.
(f) Paid wages to employees.
(g) The owner received some cash from a credit customer, which was taken as drawings rather than being paid into the business's bank account.
(h) Paid a credit supplier.
(i) Paid electricity bill.
(j) Made cash sales.

**A.2**  (a) Record the following transactions in a set of double-entry accounts:

| | |
|---|---|
| 1 February | Lee (the owner) put £6,000 into a newly-opened business bank account to start a new business |
| 3 February | Bought inventories for £2,600 for cash |
| 5 February | Bought some equipment (non-current asset) for cash for £800 |
| 6 February | Bought inventories costing £3,000 on credit |
| 9 February | Paid rent for the month of £250 |
| 10 February | Paid fuel and electricity for the month of £240 |
| 11 February | Paid general expenses of £200 |
| 15 February | Sold inventories for £4,000 in cash; the inventories had cost £2,400 |
| 19 February | Sold inventories for £3,800 on credit; the inventories had cost 2,300 |
| 21 February | Lee withdrew £1,000 in cash for personal use |
| 25 February | Paid £2,000 to trade payables |
| 28 February | Received £2,500 from trade receivables |

(b) Balance the relevant accounts and prepare a trial balance (making sure that it agrees).
(c) Prepare an income statement for the month and a statement of financial position at the month end. Assume that there are no prepaid or accrued expenses at the end of the month and ignore any possible depreciation.

**A.3**  The following is the statement of financial position of David's business at 1 January of last year.

|  | £ | £ |
|---|---:|---:|
| **ASSETS** | | |
| **Non-current assets** | | |
| *Property, plant and equipment* | | |
| Buildings | | 25,000 |
| Fittings: cost | 10,000 | |
| dep'n | (2,000) | 8,000 |
| | | 33,000 |
| **Current assets** | | |
| Inventories of stationery | | 140 |
| Trading inventories | | 1,350 |
| Prepaid rent | | 500 |
| Trade receivables | | 1,840 |
| Cash | | 2,180 |
| | | 6,010 |
| **Total assets** | | 39,010 |
| **EQUITY AND LIABILITIES** | | |
| **Owners' equity** | | 25,050 |
| **Non-current liability** | | |
| Borrowings | | 12,000 |
| **Current liabilities** | | |
| Trade payables | | 1,690 |
| Accrued electricity | | 270 |
| | | 1,960 |
| **Total equity and liabilities** | | 39,010 |

The following is a summary of the transactions that took place during the year:

1 Inventories were bought on credit for £17,220.
2 Inventories were bought for £3,760 cash.
3 Credit sales revenue amounted to £33,100 (cost £15,220).
4 Cash sales revenue amounted to £10,360 (cost £4,900).
5 Wages of £3,770 were paid.
6 Rent of £3,000 was paid. The annual rental amounts to £3,000.
7 Electricity of £1,070 was paid.
8 General expenses of £580 were paid.
9 Additional fittings were purchased on 1 January for £2,000. The cash for this was raised from additional borrowings of this amount. The interest rate is 10% a year, the same as for the existing borrowings.
10 £1,000 of the borrowing was repaid on 30 June.
11 Cash received from trade receivables amounted to £32,810.
12 Cash paid to trade payables amounted to £18,150.
13 The owner withdrew £10,400 cash and £560 inventories for private use.

At the end of the year it was found that:

● The electricity bill for the last quarter of the year for £290 had not been paid.
● Trade receivables amounting to £260 were unlikely to be received.
● The value of stationery remaining was estimated at £150. Stationery is included in general expenses.
● The borrowings carried interest of 10% a year and were unpaid at the year end.

- Depreciation to be taken at 20% on the cost of the fittings owned at the year end. Buildings are not depreciated.

*Required*:

(a) Open ledger accounts and bring down all of the balances in the opening statement of financial position.

(b) Make entries to record the transactions 1 to 13 (above), opening any additional accounts as necessary.

(c) Open an income statement (part of the double entry, remember). Make the necessary entries for the bulleted list above and the appropriate transfers to the income statement.

(d) List the remaining balances in the same form as the opening statement of financial position (above).

# Glossary of key terms

**ABC system of inventories control**  A method of applying different levels of inventories control, based on the value of each category of inventories. *p. 653*

**Absorption costing**  A method of costing in which a 'fair share' of the total manufacturing/service provision overhead cost is included when calculating the cost of a particular product or service. *p. 365*

**Account**  A section of a double-entry bookkeeping system that deals with one particular asset, claim, expense or revenue. *p. 694*

**Accounting**  The process of identifying, measuring and communicating information to permit informed judgements and decisions by users of the information. *p. 2*

**Accounting conventions**  Generally accepted rules that accountants tend to follow when preparing financial statements. They have evolved over time to deal with practical problems rather than to reflect some theoretical ideal. *p. 60*

**Accounting information system**  The system used within a business to identify, record, analyse and report accounting information. *p. 8*

**Accounting rate of return (ARR)**  The average profit from an investment, expressed as a percentage of the average investment made. *p. 545*

**Accruals accounting**  The system of accounting that follows the accruals convention. This is the system followed in drawing up the statement of financial position and income statement. *p. 97*

**Accruals convention**  The convention of accounting that asserts that profit is the excess of revenue over expenses, not the excess of cash receipts over cash payments. *p. 97*

**Accrued expenses**  Expenses that are outstanding at the end of a reporting period. *p. 93*

**Acid test ratio**  A liquidity ratio that relates the liquid assets (usually defined as current assets less inventories) to the current liabilities. *p. 263*

**Activity-based budgeting (ABB)**  A system of budgeting based on the philosophy of activity-based costing (ABC). *p. 478*

**Activity-based costing (ABC)**  A technique for relating overheads to specific production or provision of a service. It is based on acceptance of the fact that overheads do not just occur but are caused by activities, such as holding products in stores, which 'drive' the costs. *p. 409*

**Adverse variance**    A difference between planned and actual performance, usually where the difference will cause the actual profit to be lower than the budgeted profit. *p. 502*

**Ageing schedule of trade receivables**    A report analysing receivables into categories, according to the length of time outstanding. *p. 667*

**Allotted share capital**    *See* Issued share capital. *p. 147*

**Allowance for trade receivables**    An amount set aside out of profit to provide for anticipated losses arising from debts (trade receivables) that may prove irrecoverable. *p. 113*

**Alternative Investment Market (AIM)**    A stock market for the shares of smaller businesses. AIM is a junior market to the main London Stock Exchange market. It is cheaper for a business to enter and has a lighter regulatory regime. *p. 630*

**Amortisation**    A measure of that portion of the cost (or fair value) of a non-current asset that has been consumed during a reporting period. The word 'amortisation' tends to be used where the particular non-current asset is an intangible one, whereas 'depreciation' is normally used with tangible assets. *p. 97*

**Assets**    Resources held by a business that have certain characteristics, such as the ability to provide future benefits. *p. 45*

**Asset-based finance**    A form of finance where assets are used as security for cash advances to the business. Factoring and invoice discounting, where the security is trade receivables, are examples of asset-based financing. *p. 617*

**Auditors**    Professionals whose main duty is to make a report to shareholders as to whether, in their opinion, the financial statements of a company show a true and fair view of performance and position and comply with statutory and financial reporting standard requirements. *p. 185*

**Average inventories turnover period ratio**    An efficiency ratio that measures the average period for which inventories are held by a business. *p. 255*

**Average settlement period for trade payables ratio**    An efficiency ratio that measures the average time taken for a business to pay its trade payables. *pp. 256, 680*

**Average settlement period for trade receivables ratio**    An efficiency ratio that measures the average time taken for trade receivables to pay the amounts owing. *pp. 257, 666*

**Bad debt**    An amount owed to the business that is considered to be irrecoverable. *p. 112*

**Balance**    The net of the debit and credit totals in an account in a double-entry book-keeping system. *p. 700*

**Balanced scorecard**    A framework for translating the aims and objectives of a business into a series of key performance measures and targets. *p. 431*

**Bank overdraft**    A flexible form of borrowing that allows an individual or business to have a negative current account balance. *p. 613*

**Batch costing**    A technique for identifying full cost, where the production of many types of goods and services, particularly goods, involves producing a batch of identical or nearly identical units of output, but where each batch is distinctly different from other batches. *p. 385*

**Behavioural aspects of budgetary control**    The effect on people's behaviour of the various aspects of using budgets as the basis for planning and controlling a business. *p. 522*

**Benchmarking**   Identifying a successful business, or part of a business, and measuring the effectiveness of one's own business by comparison with this standard. *p. 428*

**Bonds**   See Loan notes. *p. 603*

**Bonus shares**   Reserves that are converted into shares and issued 'free' to existing shareholders. *p. 145*

**Break-even analysis**   The activity of deducing the break-even point of some activity by analysing the relationship between cost, volume and revenue. *p. 325*

**Break-even chart**   A graphical representation of the cost and sales revenue of some activity, at various levels, that enables the break-even point to be identified. *p. 326*

**Break-even point (BEP)**   A level of activity where revenue will exactly equal total cost, so there is neither profit nor loss. *p. 326*

**Budget**   A financial plan for the short term, typically one year or less. *p. 454*

**Budget committee**   A group of managers formed to supervise and take responsibility for the budget-setting process. *p. 464*

**Budget holder**   An individual responsible for a particular budget. *p. 469*

**Budget officer**   An individual, often an accountant, appointed to carry out, or take immediate responsibility for having carried out, the tasks of the budget committee. *p. 464*

**Budgetary control**   Using the budget as a yardstick against which the effectiveness of actual performance may be assessed. *p. 519*

**Business angel**   An individual who supplies finance (usually equity finance) to a start-up business or a small business wishing to expand. Usually the amount of finance supplied falls between £10,000 and £750,000. *p. 632*

**Business entity convention**   The convention that holds that, for accounting purposes, the business and its owner(s) are treated as quite separate and distinct. *p. 60*

**Business review**   Part of the directors' report that helps shareholders to assess how well the directors have performed. It provides an analysis of financial performance, position and cash flows. It also sets out the principal risks and uncertainties facing the business. *p. 186*

**Called-up share capital**   That part of a company's share capital for which the shareholders have been asked to pay the agreed amount. It is part of the claim of the owners against the business. *p. 148*

**Capital rationing**   Where the amount of funds committed is insufficient for the investment opportunities available and decisions have to be made concerning the most profitable use of those funds. *p. 580*

**Capital reserves**   Reserves that arise from 'capital' profits or gains rather than from normal trading activities. They are not available for distribution to shareholders. *p. 143*

**Carrying amount**   The difference between the cost (or fair value) of a non-current asset and the accumulated depreciation relating to the asset. The carrying amount is also referred to as the written-down value (WDV) and the net book value (NBV). *p. 100*

**Cash discount**   A reduction in the amount due for goods or services sold on credit in return for prompt payment. *p. 665*

**Cash generated from operations per ordinary share ratio**   An investment ratio that relates the cash generated from operations and available to ordinary shareholders to the number of ordinary shares. *p. 275*

**Cash generated from operations to maturing obligations ratio**   A liquidity ratio that compares the cash generated from operations to the current liabilities of the business. *p. 264*

**Claims**   Obligations on the part of a business to provide cash or some other benefit to outside parties. *p. 45*

**Committed cost**   A cost incurred that has not yet been paid, but which must, under some existing contract or obligation, be paid. *p. 309*

**Common cost**   *See* Indirect cost. *p. 363*

**Comparability**   The quality that helps users to identify similarities and differences between items of information. It enhances the usefulness of accounting information. *p. 8*

**Compensating variances**   The situation where two variances, one adverse and the other favourable, are of equal size, and therefore cancel each other out. *p. 518*

**Conceptual framework**   The main concepts, or principles, that underpin accounting, which can help in identifying best practice and in developing accounting rules. *p. 183*

**Consistency convention**   The accounting convention that holds that, when a particular method of accounting is selected to deal with a transaction, this method should be applied consistently over time. *p. 112*

**Consolidated financial statements**   *See* Group financial statements. *p. 158*

**Consolidating**   Changing the nominal value of shares to a higher figure (from, say, £0.50 to £1.00) and then reducing the number of shares in issue so that each shareholder has the same total nominal value of shares as before. *p. 142*

**Continual budget**   A budgeting system that continually updates budgets so that there is always a budget for a full planning period. (Also known as a rolling budget.) *p. 458*

**Contribution margin ratio**   The contribution from an activity expressed as a percentage of the sales revenue. *p. 331*

**Contribution per unit**   Sales revenue per unit less variable cost per unit. *p. 331*

**Control**   Compelling events to conform to plan. *p. 455*

**Convertible loan notes**   Loan notes that give investors the right to convert loan notes into ordinary shares at a specified price and a given future date (or range of dates). *p. 605*

**Corporate governance**   Matters concerned with directing and controlling a company. *p. 133*

**Corporation tax**   Taxation that a limited company is liable to pay on its profits. *p. 132*

**Cost**   The amount of resources, usually measured in monetary terms, sacrificed to achieve a particular objective. *p. 302*

**Cost allocation**   Assigning cost to cost centres according to the amount of cost that has been incurred in each centre. *p. 378*

**Cost apportionment**   Dividing cost between cost centres on a basis that is considered to reflect fairly the cost incurred in each centre. *p. 378*

**Cost behaviour**   The manner in which cost alters with changes in the level of activity. *p. 366*

**Cost centre** Some area, object, person or activity for which elements of cost are separately collected. *p. 376*

**Cost drivers** Activities that cause cost. *p. 409*

**Cost of capital** The cost to a business of long-term finance needed to fund its investments. *p. 560*

**Cost of sales** The cost of the goods sold during a period. Cost of sales can be derived by adding the opening inventories held to the inventories purchases for the period and then deducting the closing inventories held. *p. 84*

**Cost pool** The sum of the overhead costs that are seen as being caused by the same cost driver. *p. 410*

**Cost unit** The objective for which the cost is being deduced, usually a product or service. *p. 362*

**Creative accounting** Adopting accounting policies to achieve a particular view of performance and position that preparers would like users to see rather than what is a true and fair view. *p. 197*

**Credit** An entry made in the right-hand side of an account in double-entry bookkeeping. *p. 694*

**Current assets** Assets that are held for the short term. They include cash itself and other assets that are held for sale or consumption in the normal course of a business's operating cycle. *p. 54*

**Current liabilities** Liabilities that are expected to be settled within the normal course of the business's operating cycle or within twelve months of the statement of financial position date, or which are held primarily for trading purposes, or for which the business does not have the right to defer settlement beyond twelve months of the statement of financial position date. *p. 56*

**Current ratio** A liquidity ratio that relates the current assets of the business to the current liabilities. *p. 262*

**Debit** An entry made in the left-hand side of an account in double-entry bookkeeping. *p. 694*

**Debt factoring** A service offered by a financial institution (a factor) that involves the factor taking over the management of the trade receivables of the business. The factor is often prepared to make an advance to the business, based on the amount of trade receivables outstanding. *p. 613*

**Deep discount bonds** Redeemable bonds (loan notes) offering a rate of interest below the market rate and issued at a discount to their redeemable value. *p. 604*

**Depreciation** A measure of that portion of the cost (or fair value) of a non-current asset that has been consumed during a reporting period. *p. 97*

**Direct cost** A cost that can be identified with a specific cost unit, to the extent that the effect of the cost can be measured in respect of that cost unit. *p. 363*

**Direct labour efficiency variance** The difference between the actual direct labour hours worked and the number of direct labour hours according to the flexed budget (budgeted direct labour hours for the actual output). This figure is multiplied by the budgeted direct labour rate for one hour. *p. 507*

**Direct labour rate variance**   The difference between the actual cost of the direct labour hours worked and the direct labour cost allowed (actual direct labour hours worked at the budgeted labour rate). *p. 507*

**Direct materials price variance**   The difference between the actual cost of the direct material used and the direct materials cost allowed (actual quantity of material used at the budgeted direct material cost). *p. 506*

**Direct materials usage variance**   The difference between the actual quantity of direct materials used and the quantity of direct materials according to the flexed budget (budgeted usage for actual output). This quantity is multiplied by the budgeted direct materials cost for one unit of the direct materials. *p. 505*

**Direct method**   An approach to deducing the cash flows from operating activities, in a statement of cash flows, by analysing the business's cash records. *p. 220*

**Directors**   Individuals who are appointed (normally by being elected by the shareholders) to act as the most senior level of management of a company. *p. 133*

**Directors' report**   A report containing information of a financial and non-financial nature that the directors must produce as part of the annual financial report to shareholders. *p. 186*

**Discount factor**   The rate applied to future cash flows to derive the present value of those cash flows. *p. 559*

**Discretionary budget**   A budget based on a sum allocated at the discretion of senior management. *p. 469*

**Discriminate function** (in financial distress assessment)   A boundary line, produced by multiple discriminate analysis, which can be used to identify those businesses that are likely to suffer financial distress and those that are not. *p. 283*

**Dividend**   The transfer of assets (usually cash) made by a company to its shareholders. *p. 141*

**Dividend cover ratio**   An investment ratio that relates the earnings available for dividends to the dividend announced, to indicate how many times the former covers the latter. *p. 272*

**Dividend payout ratio**   An investment ratio that relates the dividends announced for the period to the earnings available for dividends that were generated in that period. *p. 272*

**Dividend per share**   An investment ratio that relates the dividends announced for a period to the number of shares in issue. *p. 273*

**Dividend yield ratio**   An investment ratio that relates the cash return from a share to its current market value. *p. 273*

**Double-entry bookkeeping**   A system for recording financial transactions where each transaction is recorded twice, once as a debit and once as a credit. *p. 694*

**Dual aspect convention**   The accounting convention that holds that each transaction has two aspects and that each aspect must be recorded in the financial statements. *p. 63*

**Earnings per share**   An investment ratio that relates the earnings generated by the business during a period, and available to shareholders, to the number of shares in issue. *p. 274*

**Economic order quantity (EOQ)**   The quantity of inventories that should be bought with each order so as to minimise total inventories ordering and carrying costs. *p. 654*

**Economic value added (EVA®)** A measure of business performance that concentrates on wealth generation. It is based on economic profit rather than accounting profit and takes full account of the cost of financing. *p. 440*

**Economies of scale** Cost savings per unit that result from undertaking a large volume of activities; they are due to factors such as division and specialisation of labour and discounts from bulk buying. *p. 338*

**Equity** The owners' claim on the business. In the case of a limited company, it comprises the sum of shares and reserves. *p. 48*

**Eurobonds** A form of long-term borrowing where the finance is raised on an international basis. Eurobonds are issued in a currency that is not that of the country in which the bonds are issued. *p. 604*

**Expense** A measure of the outflow of assets (or increase in liabilities) incurred as a result of generating revenue. *p. 81*

**Fair values** The values ascribed to assets as an alternative to historic cost. They are usually the current market values (that is, the exchange values in an arm's-length transaction). *p. 68*

**Faithful representation** The ability of information to be relied on to represent what it purports to represent. This is regarded as a fundamental quality of useful accounting information. *p. 7*

**Favourable variance** The difference between planned and actual performance, usually where the difference will cause the actual profit to be higher than the budgeted profit. *p. 502*

**Feedback control** A form of control where actual performance is compared with planned performance and where action is taken to deal with any future divergences between the two. *p. 498*

**Feedforward control** A form of control where forecast future performance is compared with planned performance and where action is taken to deal with divergences between the two. *p. 498*

**Final accounts** The income statement, statement of cash flows and statement of financial position taken together. *p. 44*

**Finance** The study of how businesses raise funds and select appropriate investments. *p. 2*

**Finance lease** A financial arrangement where the asset title remains with the owner (the lessor) but the lease agreement transfers virtually all the rewards and risks to the business (the lessee). *p. 606*

**Financial accounting** The identification, measurement and communication of accounting information for external users (those users other than the managers of the business). *p. 13*

**Financial gearing** The existence of fixed payment-bearing sources of finance (for example, borrowings) in the capital structure of a business. *p. 265*

**Financial management** *See* Finance. *p. 2*

**First in, first out (FIFO)** A method of inventories costing which assumes that the earliest acquired inventories are used (in production or sales) first. *p. 107*

**Five Cs of credit** A checklist of factors to be taken into account when assessing the creditworthiness of a customer. *p. 660*

**Fixed charge** Where specific assets are pledged as security for a loan. *p. 599*

**Fixed costs** Costs that stay the same when changes occur to the volume of activity. *p. 320*

**Fixed interest rate** An interest rate on borrowings that will remain unchanged with rises and falls in market rates of interest. *p. 606*

**Fixed overhead spending variance** The difference between the actual fixed overhead cost and the fixed overhead cost, according to the flexed (and the original) budget. *p. 508*

**Flexible budget** A budget that is adjusted to reflect the actual level of output achieved. *p. 501*

**Flexing the budget** Revising a budget to what it would have been had the planned level of output been different. *p. 501*

**Floating charge** Where all a business's assets, rather than specific assets, are pledged as security for a loan. The charge will only fix on specific assets if the business defaults on its obligations. *p. 599*

**Floating interest rate** An interest rate on borrowings that will rise and fall with market rates of interest. *p. 606*

**Forecasts** Predictions of future outcomes or of the future state of the environment. *p. 458*

**Full cost** The total amount of resources, usually measured in monetary terms, sacrificed to achieve a particular objective. *pp. 361*

**Full costing** Deducing the total direct and indirect (overhead) costs of pursuing some activity or objective. *p. 362*

**Fully paid shares** Shares on which the shareholders have paid the full issue price. *p. 148*

**Gearing ratio** A ratio that relates the long-term, fixed-return, finance contributed (such as borrowings) to the total long-term finance of the business. *p. 268*

**Going concern convention** The accounting convention that holds a business is assumed to continue operations for the foreseeable future, unless there is reason to believe otherwise. In other words, it is assumed that there is no intention, or need, to liquidate the business. *p. 63*

**Gross profit** The amount remaining (if positive) after the cost of sales has been deducted from trading revenue. *p. 83*

**Gross profit margin ratio** A profitability ratio that expresses the gross profit as a percentage of the sales revenue for a period. *p. 252*

**Group financial statements** Financial accounting statements that combine the performance, position and cash flows of a group of companies under common control. Also known as consolidated financial statements. *p. 158*

**High-low method** An approach to distinguishing between the fixed and variable elements of a cost by looking at the highest and lowest figures in a set of past data. *p. 324*

**Hire purchase** A method of acquiring an asset by paying the purchase price by instalments over a period. Normally, control of the asset will pass as soon as the hire-purchase contract is signed and the first instalment is paid, whereas ownership will pass on payment of the final instalment. *p. 610*

**Historic cost**   What was paid for an asset when it was originally acquired. *p. 302*

**Historic cost convention**   The accounting convention that holds that assets should be recorded at their historic (acquisition) cost. *p. 61*

**Holding company**   *See* Parent company.

**Ideal standards**   Standards that assume perfect operating conditions where there is no inefficiency due to lost production time, defects, and so on. The objective of setting ideal standards is to encourage employees to strive towards excellence. *p. 526*

**Income statement**   A financial statement (also known as profit and loss account) that measures and reports the profit (or loss) the business has generated during a period. It is derived by deducting from total revenue for a period, the total expenses associated with that revenue. *p. 40*

**Incremental budgeting**   Constructing budgets on the basis of what happened in the previous period, with some adjustment for expected changes in the forthcoming budget period. *p. 469*

**Indirect cost (or common cost or overheads)**   The element of manufacturing cost that cannot be directly measured in respect of a particular cost unit – that is, all manufacturing cost except direct cost. *p. 363*

**Indirect method**   An approach to deducing the cash flows from operating activities, in a statement of cash flows, by analysing the business's other financial statements. *p. 220*

**Inflation**   An increase in the general price of goods and services resulting in a corresponding decline in the purchasing power of money. *p. 556*

**Intangible assets**   Assets that do not have a physical substance (for example, patents, goodwill and trade receivables). *p. 48*

**Interest cover ratio**   A gearing ratio that divides the operating profit (that is, profit before interest and taxation) by the interest payable for a period. *p. 268*

**Internal rate of return (IRR)**   The discount rate for an investment that will have the effect of producing a zero NPV. *p. 562*

**International Accounting Standards**   *See* International Financial Reporting Standards. *p. 174*

**International Financial Reporting Standards**   Transnational accounting rules that have been adopted, or developed, by the International Accounting Standards Board and which should be followed in preparing the published financial statements of listed limited companies. *p. 174*

**Invoice discounting**   Where a financial institution provides a loan based on a proportion of the face value of a business's credit sales outstanding. *p. 616*

**Irrelevant cost**   A cost that is not relevant to a particular decision. *p. 303*

**Issued share capital**   That part of the share capital that has been issued to shareholders. Also known as allotted share capital. *p. 147*

**Job costing**   A technique for identifying the full cost per cost unit, where each cost unit is not identical to other cost units produced. *p. 365*

**Just-in-time (JIT) inventories management**   A system of inventories management that aims to have supplies delivered just in time for their required use in production or sales. *p. 658*

**_Kaizen_ costing**  An approach to cost control where an attempt is made to control cost by trying continually to make cost savings, often only small ones, from one time period to the next during the production stage of the product life cycle. _p. 426_

**Last in, first out (LIFO)**  A method of inventories costing which assumes that the most recently acquired inventories are used (in production or sales) first. _p. 107_

**Lead time**  The time lag between placing an order for goods or services and their delivery to the required location. _p. 651_

**Learning curve**  The curved line on a graph that represents the tendency for people to carry out tasks more quickly as they become more experienced in doing them. _p. 527_

**Ledger**  The book in which accounts are traditionally kept. _p. 706_

**Liabilities**  Claims of individuals and organisations, apart from the owner(s), that have arisen from past transactions or events, such as supplying goods or lending money to the business. _p. 48_

**Limited company**  A form of business unit that is granted a separate legal existence from that of its owners. The owners of this type of business are liable for debts only up to the amount that they have agreed to invest. _p. 22_

**Limited liability**  The restriction of the legal obligation of shareholders to meet all of the company's debts. _p. 129_

**Limiting factor**  Some aspect of the business (for example, lack of sales demand) that will prevent it achieving its objectives to the maximum extent. _p. 458_

**Loan covenant**  A condition contained within a loan agreement that is designed to help protect the lenders. _p. 600_

**Loan notes**  Long-term borrowings usually made by limited companies. _pp. 148, 603_

**Loan stock**  _See_ Loan notes. _p. 603_

**Management accounting**  The identification, measurement and communication of accounting information for the managers of a business. _p. 13_

**Management by exception**  A system of control, based on a comparison of planned and actual performance, that allows managers to focus on areas of poor performance rather than dealing with areas where performance is satisfactory. _p. 462_

**Margin of safety**  The extent to which the planned level of output or sales lies above the break-even point. _p. 332_

**Marginal analysis**  The activity of decision making through analysing variable costs and revenues, ignoring fixed cost. _p. 344_

**Marginal cost**  The additional cost of producing one more unit. This is often the same as the variable cost _p. 344_

**Master budgets**  Summaries of individual budgets, usually consisting of a budgeted income statement, a budgeted statement of financial position and a cash budget. _p. 459_

**Matching convention**  The accounting convention that holds that, when measuring income, expenses should be matched to revenue which they helped generate in the same reporting period as that revenue was realised. _p. 92_

**Materiality**  Accounting information is material where its omission or misrepresentation will alter the decisions that users make. The threshold of materiality will vary from one business to the next. _p. 7_

**Materiality convention** The accounting convention that states that, where the amounts involved are immaterial, only what is expedient should be considered. *p. 96*

**Materials requirement planning (MRP) system** A computer-based system of inventories control that schedules the timing of deliveries of bought-in parts and materials to coincide with production requirements to meet demand. *p. 658*

**Mission statement** A brief statement setting out the essence of the business. *p. 454*

**Mortgage** A loan secured on property. *p. 606*

**Multiple discriminate analysis** A statistical technique that can be used to predict financial distress; it involves using an index based on a combination of financial ratios. *p. 283*

**Net book value** *See* Carrying amount. *p. 100*

**Net present value (NPV)** A method of investment appraisal based on the present value of all relevant cash flows associated with an investment. *p. 554*

**Nominal value** The face value of a share in a company. Also called par value. *p. 140*

**Non-controlling interests** That part of the net assets of a subsidiary company that is financed by shareholders other than the parent company. Also known as minority interests. *p. 158*

**Non-current assets** Assets held that do not meet the criteria of current assets. They are held for the long-term operations of the business rather than continuously circulating within the business. Non-current assets can be seen as the tools of the business. They are also known as fixed assets. *p. 55*

**Non-current liabilities** Liabilities of the business that are not current liabilities. *p. 57*

**Non-operating profit variances** Differences between budgeted and actual performance that do not lead directly to differences between budgeted and actual operating profit. *p. 515*

**Offer for sale** An issue of shares that involves a public limited company (or its shareholders) selling the shares to a financial institution that will, in turn, sell the shares to the public. *p. 625*

**Operating cash cycle (OCC)** The period between the outlay of cash to buy supplies and the ultimate receipt of cash from the sale of goods. *p. 673*

**Operating gearing (operational gearing)** The relationship between the total fixed and the total variable costs for some activity. *p. 335*

**Operating lease** An arrangement where a business hires an asset, usually for a short time. Hiring an asset under an operating lease tends to be seen as an operating, rather than a financing, decision. *p. 607*

**Operating profit** The profit achieved during a period after all operating expenses have been deducted from revenues from operations. Financing expenses are deducted after the calculation of operating profit. *p. 84*

**Operating profit margin ratio** A profitability ratio that expresses the operating profit as a percentage of the sales revenue for the period. *p. 251*

**Opportunity cost** The cost incurred when one course of action prevents an opportunity to derive some benefit from another course of action. *pp. 302, 567*

**Ordinary shares** Shares of a company owned by those who are due the benefits of the company's activities after all other stakeholders have been satisfied. *p. 141*

**Outlay costs** Costs that involve the spending of money or some other transfer of assets. *p. 304*

**Outsourcing**    Subcontracting activities to (sourcing goods or services from) organisations outside of the business. *p. 349*

**Overhead absorption (recovery) rate**    The rate at which overheads are charged to cost units (jobs), usually in a job costing system. *p. 368*

**Overheads**    *See* Indirect cost. *p. 363*

**Overtrading**    The situation arising where a business is operating at a level of activity that cannot be supported by the amount of finance that has been committed. *p. 279*

**Paid-up share capital**    That part of the share capital of a company that has been called and paid. *p. 148*

**Par value**    *See* Nominal value. *p. 140*

**Parent company**    A company that has a controlling interest in another company. *p. 157*

**Partnership**    A form of business unit where there are at least two individuals, but usually no more than twenty, carrying on a business with the intention of making a profit. *p. 21*

**Past costs**    Costs that have been incurred in the past. *p. 304*

**Payback period (PP)**    The time taken for the initial outlay for an investment to be repaid from its future net cash inflows. *p. 549*

**Periodic budget**    A budget developed on a one-off basis to cover a particular planning period. *p. 458*

**Post-completion audit**    A review of the performance of an investment project to see whether lessons can be drawn from the way in which the project was appraised and carried out. *p. 582*

**Practical standards**    Standards that do not assume perfect operating conditions. Although they demand a high level of efficiency, account is taken of possible lost production time, defects, and so on. They are designed to be challenging yet achievable. *p. 526*

**Preference shares**    Shares of a company that entitle their owners to the first part of any dividend that the company may pay. *p. 142*

**Prepaid expenses**    Expenses that have been paid in advance at the end of the reporting period. *p. 95*

**Price/earnings ratio**    An investment ratio that relates the market value of a share to the earnings per share. *p. 275*

**Private limited company**    A limited company for which the directors can restrict the ownership of its shares. *p. 131*

**Private placing**    An issue of shares that involves a limited company arranging for the shares to be sold to the clients of particular issuing houses or stockbrokers, rather than to the general investing public. *p. 625*

**Process costing**    A technique for deriving the full cost per unit of output where the units of output are the same, or it is reasonable to treat them as being so. *p. 363*

**Product cost centre**    Some area, object, person or activity for which cost is separately collected, in which cost units have cost added. *p. 378*

**Profit**    The increase in wealth attributable to the owners of a business that arises through business operations. *p. 80*

**Profit before taxation**   The result when all of the appropriately matched expenses of running a limited company have been deducted from the revenue for the year, but before the taxation charge is deducted. *p. 155*

**Profit for the period**   The result when all of the appropriately matched expenses of running a business have been deducted from the revenue for the year and then, in the case of a limited company, the taxation charge deducted. *p. 84*

**Profit–volume (PV) chart**   A graphical representation of the contributions (revenue less variable cost) of some activity, at various levels, which enables the break-even point, and the profit at various activity levels, to be identified. *p. 337*

**Property, plant and equipment**   Those non-current assets that have a physical substance (for example, plant and machinery, motor vehicles). *p. 53*

**Prudence convention**   The accounting convention that holds that caution should be exercised when making accounting judgements. It normally involves reporting actual and expected losses immediately but reporting profits when they arise. *p. 62*

**Public issue**   An issue of shares that involves a public limited company (plc) making a direct invitation to the public to buy shares in the company. *p. 625*

**Public limited company**   A limited company for which the directors cannot restrict the ownership of its shares. *p. 129*

**Quality costs**   The cost of establishing procedures which promote the quality of output, either by preventing quality problems in the first place or by dealing with them when they occur. *p. 424*

**Reducing-balance method**   A method of calculating depreciation that applies a fixed percentage rate of depreciation to the carrying amount of an asset in each period. *p. 100*

**Relevance**   The ability of accounting information to influence decisions. Relevance is regarded as a fundamental characteristic of useful accounting information. *p. 7*

**Relevant cost**   A cost that is relevant to a particular decision. *pp. 302, 567*

**Relevant range**   The range of output within which a particular business is expected to operate. *p. 339*

**Reporting period**   The time span for which a business prepares its financial statements. *p. 82*

**Reserves**   Part of the owners' claim (equity) of a limited company that has arisen from profits and gains, to the extent that these have not been distributed to the shareholders or reduced by losses. *p. 140*

**Residual value**   The amount for which a non-current asset is sold when the business has no further use for it. *p. 99*

**Return on capital employed ratio (ROCE)**   A profitability ratio that expresses the operating profit (that is, profit before interest and taxation) as a percentage of the long-term funds (equity and borrowings) invested in the business. *p. 249*

**Return on ordinary shareholders' funds ratio (ROSF)**   A profitability ratio that expresses the profit for the period available to ordinary shareholders as a percentage of the funds that they have invested. *p. 248*

**Revenue**   A measure of the inflow of assets (for example, cash or amounts owed to a business by credit customers), or a reduction in liabilities, arising as a result of trading operations. *p. 80*

**Revenue reserve**  Part of the owners' claim (equity) of a company that arises from realised profits and gains, including after-tax trading profits and gains from disposals of non-current assets. *p. 141*

**Rights issue**  An issue of shares for cash to existing shareholders on the basis of the number of shares already held. *p. 621*

**Risk**  The extent and likelihood that what is projected to occur will not actually occur. *p. 555*

**Risk premium**  The additional return required for investing in a risky project. *p. 555*

**Rolling budgets**  *See* Continual budget. *p. 459*

**Sale and leaseback**  An agreement to sell an asset (usually property) to another party and simultaneously to lease the asset back in order to continue using the asset. *p. 609*

**Sales price variance**  The difference between the actual sales revenue figure for the period and the sales revenue figure as shown in the flexed budget. *p. 504*

**Sales revenue per employee ratio**  An efficiency ratio that relates the sales revenue generated during a period to the average number of employees of the business. *p. 259*

**Sales revenue to capital employed ratio**  An efficiency ratio that relates the sales revenue generated during a period to the capital employed. *p. 258*

**Sales volume variance**  The difference between the operating profit as shown in the original budget, and the operating profit as shown in the flexed budget for the period. *p. 502*

**Scenario building**  Creating a model of a business decision, usually on a computer spreadsheet, enabling the decision maker to look at the effect of different assumptions on the decision outcome. *p. 579*

**Securitisation**  Bundling together illiquid physical or financial assets of the same type to provide backing for issuing interest-bearing securities, such as bonds. *p. 611*

**Security**  Assets pledged or guarantees given to provide lenders with some protection against default. *p. 599*

**Segmental financial reports**  Financial reports that break down the overall results of a business according to its different types of business operations. *p. 187*

**Semi-fixed (semi-variable) costs**  Costs that have an element of both fixed and variable cost. *p. 323*

**Sensitivity analysis**  An examination of the key variables affecting a decision (for example, an investment project) to see how changes in each input might influence the outcome. *p. 575*

**Service cost centre**  Some area, object, person or activity for which cost is collected separately, in which cost units do not have cost added, because service cost centres only render services to product cost centres and to other service cost centres. *p. 378*

**Shares**  Portions of an ownership, or equity, of a company. *p. 6*

**Share premium account**  A capital reserve reflecting any amount, above the nominal value of shares, that is paid for those shares when they are issued by a company. *p. 145*

**Sole proprietorship**  A form of business unit where an individual is operating a business on his or her own account. *p. 21*

**Splitting**  Changing the nominal value of shares to a lower figure (from, say, £1.00 to £0.50) and then issuing sufficient shares so that each shareholder has the same total nominal value of shares as before. *p. 142*

**Standard quantities and costs** Planned quantities and costs (or revenue) for individual units of input or output. Standards are the building blocks used to produce the budget. *p. 524*

**Statement of cash flows** A statement that shows a business's sources and uses of cash for a period. *p. 40*

**Statement of changes in equity** A financial statement, required by IAS 1, which shows the effect of gains/losses and capital injections/withdrawals on the equity base of a company. *p. 182*

**Statement of comprehensive income** A financial statement that extends the conventional income statement to include other gains and losses that affect shareholders' equity. *p. 179*

**Statement of financial position** A statement that shows the assets of a business and the claims on those assets. It is also known as a balance sheet. *p. 40*

**Stepped fixed costs** Fixed costs that do not remain fixed over all levels of output but which change in steps as a threshold level of output is reached. *p. 322*

**Stock exchange** A market where 'second-hand' shares may be bought and sold and new capital raised. *p. 626*

**Straight-line method** A method of accounting for depreciation that allocates the amount to be depreciated evenly over the useful life of the asset. *p. 99*

**Strategic management** Setting a course to achieve the business's objectives, taking account of the commercial and economic environment in which the business operates. *p. 27*

**Subordinated loans** Forms of loan where the lenders' claims are ranked below those of other loans already in use. *p. 601*

**Summary financial statements** A summarised version of the complete annual financial statements, which shareholders may choose to receive as an alternative to the complete statements. *p. 197*

**Sunk cost** A cost that has been incurred in the past; the same as a past cost. *p. 309*

**Takeover** The acquisition of control of one company by another, usually as a result of acquiring a majority of the ordinary shares of the former. *p. 159*

**Tangible assets** Those assets that have a physical substance (for example, plant and machinery, motor vehicles). *p. 48*

**Target costing** An approach to deriving product costs where the business starts with the projected selling price and from it deduces the target cost per unit that must be met to enable the business to meet its profit objectives. *p. 425*

**Tender issue** A public issue of shares or loan notes (by a public limited company) where potential investors are invited to state a bid price rather than the company setting the price for the securities. *p. 625*

**Term loan** Finance provided by financial institutions, like banks and insurance companies, under a contract with the borrowing business that indicates the interest rate and dates of payments of interest and repayment of the loan. The loan is not normally transferable from one lender to another. *p. 603*

**Timeliness** The provision of accounting information in time for users to make their decision. This quality enhances the usefulness of accounting information. *p. 8*

**Total cost** The sum of the variable and fixed costs of pursuing some activity. *p. 367*

**Total direct labour variance** The difference between the actual direct labour cost and the direct labour cost according to the flexed budget (budgeted direct labour hours for the actual output). *p. 507*

**Total direct materials variance** The difference between the actual direct materials cost and the direct materials cost according to the flexed budget. *p. 505*

**Total life-cycle costing** A form of costing that takes account of all the costs that will be incurred during the entire life of a product or service. *p. 420*

**Total quality management (TQM)** The TQM philosophy is concerned with providing products that meet, or exceed, customers' requirements all of the time. *p. 423*

**Transfer price** The price at which goods or services are sold, or transferred, between divisions of the same business. *p. 190*

**Trial balance** A totalled list of the balances on each of the accounts in a double-entry bookkeeping system. *p. 702*

**UK Corporate Governance Code** A code of practice for companies listed on the London Stock Exchange that deals with corporate governance matters. *p. 135*

**Understandability** The quality that enables accounting information to be understood by those for whom the information is primarily compiled. This quality enhances the usefulness of accounting information. *p. 8*

**Univariate analysis** A statistical technique that can be used to help predict financial distress, which involves the use of a single ratio as a predictor. *p. 283*

**Value chain analysis** Analysing each activity undertaken by a business to identify any that do not add value to the output of goods or services. *p. 427*

**Value drivers** Factors that create wealth, such as employee satisfaction, customer loyalty and the level of product innovation. *p. 430*

**Variable costs** Costs that vary according to the volume of activity. *p. 320*

**Variable (marginal) costing** An approach to costing in which only those costs that vary with the level of output are included in the product cost. *p. 394*

**Variance** The financial effect, usually on the budgeted profit, of the particular factor under consideration being more or less than budgeted. *p. 502*

**Venture capital** Long-term finance provided by certain institutions to small and medium-sized businesses in order to exploit relatively high-risk opportunities. *p. 631*

**Verifiability** The quality that provides assurance to users that the information provided faithfully represents what it is supposed to represent. It enhances the quality of accounting information. *p. 8*

**Weighted average cost (AVCO)** A method of inventories costing, which assumes that inventories entering the business lose their separate identity and any issues of inventories reflect the weighted average cost of the inventories held. *p. 107*

**Working capital** Current assets less current liabilities. *pp. 221, 644*

**Written-down value (WDV)** *See* Carrying amount. *p. 100*

**Zero-base budgeting (ZBB)** An approach to budgeting, based on the philosophy that all spending needs to be justified and that each budget should start as a clean sheet. *p. 470*

# Solutions to self-assessment questions

## Chapter 2

### 2.1 Simonson Engineering

The statement of financial position should be set out as follows:

**Simonson Engineering**
**Statement of financial position as at 30 September 2011**

|  | £ |
|---|---|
| **ASSETS** | |
| **Non-current assets** | |
| *Property, plant and equipment* | |
| Property | 72,000 |
| Plant and machinery | 25,000 |
| Fixtures and fittings | 9,000 |
| Motor vehicles | 15,000 |
|  | 121,000 |
| **Current assets** | |
| Inventories | 45,000 |
| Trade receivables | 48,000 |
| Cash in hand | 1,500 |
|  | 94,500 |
| **Total assets** | 215,500 |
| **EQUITY AND LIABILITIES** | |
| **Equity** | |
| Closing balance* | 120,500 |
| **Non-current liabilities** | |
| Long-term borrowings | 51,000 |
| **Current liabilities** | |
| Trade payables | 18,000 |
| Short-term borrowings | 26,000 |
|  | 44,000 |
| **Total equity and liabilities** | 215,500 |
| | |
| *The equity is calculated as follows: | |
| Opening balance | 117,500 |
| Profit | 18,000 |
|  | 135,500 |
| Drawings | (15,000) |
| Closing balance | 120,500 |

## Chapter 3

### 3.1   TT and Co.

**TT and Co.**
**Statement of financial position as at 31 December 2011**

|  | £ |
|---|---|
| **ASSETS** |  |
| Delivery van | 9,500 |
| (12,000 – 2,500) |  |
| Inventories (143,000 + | 65,000 |
| 12,000 – 74,000 – 16,000) |  |
| Trade receivables | 19,600 |
| (152,000 – 132,000 – 400) |  |
| Cash at bank (50,000 – 25,000 | 750 |
| – 500 – 1,200 – 12,000 |  |
| – 33,500 – 1,650 – 12,000 |  |
| + 35,000 + 132,000 |  |
| – 121,000 – 9,400) |  |
| Prepaid expenses |  |
| (5,000 + 300) | 5,300 |
| Total assets | 100,150 |
| **EQUITY AND LIABILITIES** |  |
| Equity (50,000 + 26,900) | 76,900 |
| Trade payables (143,000 – 121,000) | 22,000 |
| Accrued expenses (630 + 620) | 1,250 |
| **Total equity and liabilities** | 100,150 |

**Income statement for the year ended 31 December 2011**

|  | £ |
|---|---|
| Sales revenue (152,000 + 35,000) | 187,000 |
| Cost of goods sold (74,000 + 16,000) | (90,000) |
| Gross profit | 97,000 |
| Rent | (20,000) |
| Rates (500 + 900) | (1,400) |
| Wages (33,500 + 630) | (34,130) |
| Electricity (1,650 + 620) | (2,270) |
| Bad debts | (400) |
| Van depreciation ((12,000 – 2,000)/4) | (2,500) |
| Van expenses | (9,400) |
| Profit for the year | 26,900 |

The statement of financial position could now be rewritten in a more stylish form as follows:

**Statement of financial position as at 31 December 2011**

|  | £ |
|---|---:|
| **ASSETS** | |
| **Non-current assets** | |
| *Property, plant and equipment* | |
| Delivery van at cost | 12,000 |
| Accumulated depreciation | (2,500) |
|  | 9,500 |
| **Current assets** | |
| Inventories | 65,000 |
| Trade receivables | 19,600 |
| Prepaid expenses | 5,300 |
| Cash | 750 |
|  | 90,650 |
| **Total assets** | 100,150 |
| **EQUITY AND LIABILITIES** | |
| **Equity** | |
| Closing balance | 76,900 |
| **Current liabilities** | |
| Trade payables | 22,000 |
| Accrued expenses | 1,250 |
|  | 23,250 |
| **Total equity and liabilities** | 100,150 |

## Chapter 4

### 4.1 Dev Ltd

(a) The summarised statement of financial position of Dev Ltd, immediately following the rights and bonus issue, is as follows:

**Statement of financial position**

|  | £000 |
|---|---:|
| **Net assets** [235 + 40 (cash from the rights issue)] | 275 |
| **Equity** | |
| Share capital: 100,000 shares @ £1 [(100 + 20) + 60] | 180 |
| Share premium account (30 + 20 − 50) | – |
| Revaluation reserve (37 − 10) | 27 |
| Retained earnings | 68 |
|  | 275 |

Note that the bonus issue of £60,000 is taken from capital reserves (reserves unavailable for dividends) as follows:

|  | £000 |
|---|---:|
| Share premium account | 50 |
| Revaluation reserve | 10 |
|  | 60 |

More could have been taken from the revaluation reserve and less from the share premium account without making any difference to dividend payment possibilities.

(b) There may be pressure from a potential lender for the business to limit its ability to pay dividends or to undertake a share repurchase. This would place lenders in a more secure position because the maximum buffer or safety margin between the value of the assets and the amount owed by the business is maintained. It is not unusual for potential lenders to insist on some measure to lock up shareholders' funds in this way as a condition of granting the loan.

(c) The summarised statement of financial position of Dev Ltd, immediately following the rights and bonus issue, assuming a minimum dividend potential objective, is as follows:

**Statement of financial position**

|  | £000 |
|---|---|
| Net assets [235 + 40 (cash from the rights issue)] | 275 |
| **Equity** |  |
| Share capital: 100,000 shares @ £1 ((100 + 20) + 60) | 180 |
| Share premium account (30 + 20) | 50 |
| Revaluation reserve | 37 |
| Retained earnings (68 − 60) | 8 |
| **Total equity** | 275 |

(d) Before the bonus issue, the maximum dividend was £68,000. Now it is £8,000. Thus the bonus issue has had the effect of locking up an additional £60,000 of the business's assets in terms of the business's ability to pay dividends.

(e) Before the issues, Lee had 100 shares worth £2.35 (£235,000/100,000) each or £235 in total. Lee would be offered 20 shares in the rights issue at £2 each or £40 in total. After the rights issue, Lee would have 120 shares worth £2.2917 (£275,000/120,000) each or £275 in total.

The bonus issue would give Lee 60 additional shares. After the bonus issue, Lee would have 180 shares worth £1.5278 (£275,000/180,000) each or £275 in total.

None of this affects Lee's wealth. Before the issues, Lee had £235 worth of shares and £40 more in cash. After the issues, Lee has the same total wealth but all £275 is in the value of the shares.

(f) The things that we know about the company are as follows:

● It is a private (as opposed to a public) limited company, for it has 'Ltd' (limited) as part of its name, rather than plc (public limited company).

● It has made an issue of shares at a premium, almost certainly after it had traded successfully for a period. (There is a share premium account. It would be very unlikely that the original shares, issued when the company was first formed, would have been issued at a premium.)

● Certain of the assets in the statement of financial position have been upwardly revalued by at least £37,000. (There is a revaluation reserve of £37,000. This may just be what is left after a previous bonus issue had taken part of the balance.)

● The company has traded at an aggregate profit (though there could have been losses in some years), net of tax and any dividends paid. (There is a positive balance on retained earnings.)

## Chapter 5

### 5.1    Turner plc

We can see from the table below that the software segment generates the highest revenue, but also generates the lowest profit. We shall be considering financial ratios in detail in Chapter 7. However, we can use some simple ratios at this point to help evaluate segmental performance. We can start by considering the profit generated in relation to the sales revenue for each operating segment. The engineering segment generates the most profit in relation to sales revenue. Around 23%, or £0.23 in every £1, of profit is derived from the sales revenue generated. However, for the software segment, only 4%, or £0.04 in every £1, of profit is derived from the sales revenue generated.

We can also compare the profit generated with the net assets employed (that is, total assets – total liabilities) for each segment. We can see from the table below that the electronics segment produces the best return on net assets employed: around £0.65 for every £1 invested. Once again, the software segment produces the worst results.

The reasons for the relatively poor results from the software segment need further investigation. There may be valid reasons; for example, it may be experiencing severe competitive pressures. The results for this segment, however, are not disastrous: it is making a profit. Nevertheless, the business may wish to re-evaluate its long-term presence in this market.

It is interesting to note that the software segment benefited most from the investment in non-current assets during the period – as much as the other two segments combined. The reason for such a large investment in such a relatively poorly performing segment needs to be justified. It is possible that the business will reap rewards from the investment in the future; however, we do not have enough information to understand the reasons for the investment decision.

Depreciation charges in the software segment are significantly higher than for the other operating segments. This may be because the segment has more non-current assets, although we do not have a figure for the non-current assets held. The depreciation charge as a percentage of segment assets is also higher and the reasons for this should be investigated.

**Table of key results**

|                                                        | Software | Electronics | Engineering |
|--------------------------------------------------------|----------|-------------|-------------|
| Total revenue                                          | £250m    | £230m       | £52m        |
| Segment profit                                         | £10m     | £34m        | £12m        |
| Net assets (assets – liabilities)                      | £85m     | £52m        | £30m        |
| Segment profit as a percentage of sales revenue        | 4.0%     | 14.8%       | 23.1%       |
| Segment profit as a percentage of net assets employed  | 11.8%    | 65.4%       | 40.0%       |
| Expenditure on non-current assets                      | £22m     | £12m        | £10m        |
| Depreciation as a percentage of segment assets         | 42.9%    | 38.9%       | 29.4%       |

## Chapter 6

**6.1** Touchstone plc

**Touchstone plc**
**Statement of cash flows for the year ended 31 December 2011**

|  | £m |
|---|---|
| **Cash flows from operating activities** | |
| Profit before taxation (after interest) (see Note 1 below) | 60 |
| Adjustments for: | |
| Depreciation | 16 |
| Interest expense (Note 2) | 4 |
|  | 80 |
| Increase in trade receivables (26 – 16) | (10) |
| Decrease in trade payables (38 – 37) | (1) |
| Decrease in inventories (25 – 24) | 1 |
| *Cash generated from operations* | 70 |
| Interest paid | (4) |
| Taxation paid (Note 3) | (12) |
| Dividend paid | (18) |
| *Net cash from operating activities* | 36 |
| **Cash flows from investing activities** | |
| Payments to acquire tangible non-current assets (Note 4) | (41) |
| *Net cash used in investing activities* | (41) |
| **Cash flows from financing activities** | |
| Issue of loan notes (40 – 20) | 20 |
| *Net cash used in financing activities* | 20 |
| **Net increase in cash and cash equivalents** | 15 |
| Cash and cash equivalents at 1 January 2011 | |
| Cash | 4 |
| Cash and cash equivalents at 31 December 2011 | |
| Cash | 4 |
| Treasury bills | 15 |
|  | 19 |

To see how this relates to the cash of the business at the beginning and end of the year it can be useful to provide a reconciliation as follows:

**Analysis of cash and cash equivalents during the year ended 31 December 2011**

|  | £m |
|---|---|
| Cash and cash equivalents at 1 January 2011 | 4 |
| Net cash inflow | 15 |
| Cash and cash equivalents at 31 December 2011 | 19 |

**Notes:**
(1) This is simply taken from the income statement for the year.
(2) Interest payable expense must be taken out, by adding it back to the profit before taxation figure. We subsequently deduct the cash paid for interest payable during the year. In this case the two figures are identical.

(3) Companies pay 50% of their tax during their accounting year and the other 50% in the following year. Thus the 2011 payment would have been half the tax on the 2010 profit (that is, the figure that would have appeared in the current liabilities at the end of 2010), plus half of the 2011 tax charge (that is, $4 + (\frac{1}{2} \times 16) = 12$).

(4) Since there were no disposals, the depreciation charges must be the difference between the start and end of the year's non-current asset values, adjusted by the cost of any additions:

|  | £m |
|---|---|
| Carrying amount at 1 January 2011 | 147 |
| Additions (balancing figure) | 41 |
|  | 188 |
| Depreciation (6 + 10) | (16) |
| Carrying amount at 31 December 2011 | 172 |

## Chapter 7

### 7.1  Ali plc and Bhaskar plc

To answer this question, you may have used the following ratios:

|  | Ali plc | Bhaskar plc |
|---|---|---|
| Return on ordinary shareholders' funds ratio | $\dfrac{99.9}{687.6} \times 100 = 14.5\%$ | $\dfrac{104.6}{874.6} \times 100 = 12.0\%$ |
| Operating profit margin ratio | $\dfrac{151.3}{1{,}478.1} \times 100 = 10.2\%$ | $\dfrac{166.9}{1{,}790.4} \times 100 = 9.3\%$ |
| Average inventories turnover period ratio | $\dfrac{592.0}{1{,}018.3} \times 12 = 7.0$ months | $\dfrac{403.0}{1{,}214.9} \times 12 = 4.0$ months |
| Average settlement period for trade receivables ratio | $\dfrac{176.4}{1{,}478.1} \times 12 = 1.4$ months | $\dfrac{321.9}{1{,}790.4} \times 12 = 2.2$ months |
| Current ratio | $\dfrac{853.0}{422.4} = 2.0$ | $\dfrac{816.5}{293.1} = 2.8$ |
| Acid test ratio | $\dfrac{(853.0 - 592.0)}{422.4} = 0.6$ | $\dfrac{(816.5 - 403.0)}{293.1} = 1.4$ |
| Gearing ratio | $\dfrac{190}{(687.6 + 190)} \times 100 = 21.6\%$ | $\dfrac{250}{(874.6 + 250)} \times 100 = 22.2\%$ |
| Interest cover ratio | $\dfrac{151.3}{19.4} = 7.8$ times | $\dfrac{166.9}{27.5} = 6.1$ times |

(Note: It is not possible to use any average ratios because only the end-of-year figures are provided for each business)

Ali plc seems more effective than Bhaskar plc at generating returns for shareholders, indicated by the higher ROSF ratio. This is perhaps partly caused by Ali plc's higher operating profit margin.

Both businesses have a very high inventories turnover period; this probably needs to be investigated, particularly by Ali plc. Ali plc has a lower average settlement period for trade receivables than Bhaskar plc.

Ali plc has a much lower current ratio and acid test ratio than Bhaskar plc. The acid test ratio of Ali plc is substantially below 1.0: this may suggest a liquidity problem.

The gearing ratio of each business is quite similar. Neither business seems to have excessive borrowing. The interest cover ratio for each business is also similar. The ratios indicate that both businesses have good profit coverage for their interest charges.

To draw better comparisons between the two businesses, it would be useful to calculate other ratios from the financial statements. It would also be helpful to calculate ratios for both businesses over (say) five years as well as key ratios of other businesses operating in the same industry.

## Chapter 8

### 8.1 JB Limited

(a)

| | £ | |
|---|---|---|
| Material M1 | | |
| 400 × 3 @ £5.50 | 6,600 | The original cost is irrelevant since any inventories used will need to be replaced |
| Material P2 | | |
| 400 × 2 @ £2.00 (that is, £3.60 – £1.60) | 1,600 | The best alternative use of this material is as a substitute for P4 – an effective opportunity cost of £2.00/kg |
| Part number 678 | | |
| 400 × 1 @ £50 | 20,000 | |
| Labour | | |
| Skilled 400 × 5 @ £12 | 24,000 | The effective cost is £12/hour |
| Semi-skilled 400 × 5 @ £10 | 20,000 | |
| Overheads | 3,200 | It is only the additional cost which is relevant; the method of apportioning total overheads is not relevant |
| Total relevant cost | 75,400 | |
| Potential revenue | | |
| 400 @ £200 | 80,000 | |

Clearly, on the basis of the information available it would be beneficial for the business to undertake the contract.

(b) There are many possible answers to this part of the question, including:

- If material P2 had not already been held, it may be that it would not have been possible to buy it in and still leave the contract as a beneficial one. In this case the business may be unhappy about accepting a price under the particular conditions that apply, which could not be accepted under other conditions.
- Will the replacement for the skilled worker be able to do the normal work of that person to the necessary standard?
- Is JB Limited confident that the additional semi-skilled employee can be made redundant at the end of this contract without cost to the business?

## Chapter 9

### 9.1 Khan Ltd

(a) The break-even point, if only the Alpha service were rendered, would be:

$$\frac{\text{Fixed costs}}{\text{Sales revenue per unit} - \text{Variable cost per unit}} = \frac{£40,000}{£30 - £(15+6)} = 4,445 \text{ units (a year)}$$

(Strictly it is 4,444.44 but 4,445 is the smallest number of units of the service that must be rendered to avoid a loss.)

(b)

|  | Alpha | Beta | Gamma |
|---|---|---|---|
| Selling price (£/unit) | 30 | 39 | 20 |
| Variable materials (£/unit) | (15) | (18) | (10) |
| Variable production costs (£/unit) | (6) | (10) | (5) |
| Contribution (£/unit) | 9 | 11 | 5 |
| Staff time (hr/unit) | 2 | 3 | 1 |
| Contribution/staff hour | £4.50 | £3.67 | £5.00 |
| Order of priority | 2nd | 3rd | 1st |

(c)

| | Hours | | Contribution £ |
|---|---|---|---|
| Provide: | | | |
| 5,000 Gamma using | 5,000 | generating (that is, 5,000 × £5 =) | 25,000 |
| 2,500 Alpha using | 5,000 | generating (that is, 2,500 × £9 =) | 22,500 |
| | 10,000 | | 47,500 |
| | | Fixed costs | (40,000) |
| | | Profit | 7,500 |

This leaves a demand for 500 units of Alpha and 2,000 units of Beta unsatisfied.

## Chapter 10

### 10.1 Hector and Co. Ltd

(a) *Job-costing basis*

|  |  |  | £ |
|---|---|---|---|
| Materials: | Metal wire | 1,000 × 2 × £2.20* | 4,400 |
| | | Fabric 1,000 × 0.5 × £1.00* | 500 |
| Labour: | Skilled | 1,000 × (10/60) × £12.00 | 2,000 |
| | | Unskilled 1,000 × (5/60) × £7.50 | 625 |
| Indirect cost | | 1,000 × (15/60) × (50,000/12,500) | 1,000 |
| Total cost | | | 8,525 |
| *Add* Profit loading | | 12.5% thereof | 1,066 |
| Total tender price | | | 9,591 |

* In the traditional approach to full costing, the historic cost of materials tend to be used. It would not have been incorrect to used the 'relevant' (opportunity) costs here.

(b) *Minimum contract price (relevant cost basis)*

|  |  |  | £ |
|---|---|---|---|
| Materials: | Metal wire | 1,000 × 2 × £2.50 (replacement cost) | 5,000 |
|  | Fabric | 1,000 × 0.5 × £0.40 (scrap value) | 200 |
| Labour: | Skilled | (there is no effective cost of skilled staff) | – |
|  | Unskilled | 1,000 × 5/60 × £7.50 | 625 |
| Minimum tender price |  |  | 5,825 |

The difference between the two prices is partly that the relevant costing approach tends to look to the future, partly that it considers opportunity costs, and partly that the job-costing basis total has a profit loading.

# Chapter 11

## 11.1 Psilis Ltd

(a) **Full cost (present basis)**

|  | Basic | | Super | |
|---|---|---|---|---|
|  | £ | | £ | |
| Direct labour (all £10/hour) | 40.00 | (4 hours) | 60.00 | (6 hours) |
| Direct material | 15.00 | | 20.00 | |
| Overheads | 18.20 | (£4.55* × 4) | 27.30 | (£4.55* × 6) |
|  | 73.20 | | 107.30 | |

\* Total direct labour hours worked = (40,000 × 4) + (10,000 × 6) = 220,000 hours. Overhead recovery rate = £1,000,000/220,000 = £4.55 per direct labour hour.

Thus the selling prices are currently:

Basic:  £73.20 + 25% = £91.50
Super:  £107.30 + 25% = £134.13

(b) **Full cost (activity cost basis)**

Here, the cost of each cost-driving activity is apportioned between total production of the two products.

| Activity | Cost £000 | Basis of apportionment | Basic £000 | | Super £000 | |
|---|---|---|---|---|---|---|
| Machine set-ups | 280 | Number of set-ups | 56 | (20/100) | 224 | (80/100) |
| Quality inspection | 220 | Number of inspections | 55 | (500/2,000) | 165 | (1,500/2,000) |
| Sales order processing | 240 | Number of orders processed | 72 | (1,500/5,000) | 168 | (3,500/5,000) |
| General production | 260 | Machine hours | 182 | (350/500) | 78 | (150/500) |
| Total | 1,000 | | 365 | | 635 | |

The overheads per unit are:

$$\text{Basic:} \quad \frac{£365,000}{40,000} = £9.13$$

$$\text{Super:} \quad \frac{£635,000}{10,000} = £63.50$$

Thus, on an activity basis the full costs are as follows:

|  | Basic<br>£ | Super<br>£ |
|---|---|---|
| Direct labour (all £10/hour) | 40.00 (4 hours) | 60.00 (6 hours) |
| Direct material | 15.00 | 20.00 |
| Overheads | 9.13 | 63.50 |
| Full cost | 64.13 | 143.50 |
| Current selling price | £91.50 | £134.13 |

(c) It seems that the Supers are being sold for less than they cost to produce. If the price cannot be increased, there is a very strong case for abandoning this product. At the same time, the Basics are very profitable to the extent that it may be worth considering lowering the price to attract more sales revenue.

The fact that the overhead costs can be related to activities and, more specifically, to products does not mean that abandoning Super production would lead to immediate overhead cost savings. For example, it may not be possible or desirable to dismiss machine-setting staff overnight. It would certainly rarely be possible to release factory space occupied by machine setters and make immediate cost savings. Nevertheless, in the medium term these costs can be avoided and it may be sensible to do so.

## Chapter 12

### 12.1 Antonio Ltd

(a) (1) Raw materials inventories budget for the six months ending 31 December (physical quantities):

|  | July<br>Units | Aug<br>Units | Sept<br>Units | Oct<br>Units | Nov<br>Units | Dec<br>Units |
|---|---|---|---|---|---|---|
| Opening inventories (current month's production) | 500 | 600 | 600 | 700 | 750 | 750 |
| Purchases (balance figure) | 600 | 600 | 700 | 750 | 750 | 750 |
|  | 1,100 | 1,200 | 1,300 | 1,450 | 1,500 | 1,500 |
| Issues to production (from question) | (500) | (600) | (600) | (700) | (750) | (750) |
| Closing inventories (next month's production) | 600 | 600 | 700 | 750 | 750 | 750 |

Raw material inventories budget for the six months ending 31 December (in financial terms), that is, the physical quantities × £8:

|  | July<br>£ | Aug<br>£ | Sept<br>£ | Oct<br>£ | Nov<br>£ | Dec<br>£ |
|---|---|---|---|---|---|---|
| Opening inventories | 4,000 | 4,800 | 4,800 | 5,600 | 6,000 | 6,000 |
| Purchases | 4,800 | 4,800 | 5,600 | 6,000 | 6,000 | 6,000 |
|  | 8,800 | 9,600 | 10,400 | 11,600 | 12,000 | 12,000 |
| Issues to production | (4,000) | (4,800) | (4,800) | (5,600) | (6,000) | (6,000) |
| Closing inventories | 4,800 | 4,800 | 5,600 | 6,000 | 6,000 | 6,000 |

(2) Trade payables budget for the six months ending 31 December:

|  | July £ | Aug £ | Sept £ | Oct £ | Nov £ | Dec £ |
|---|---|---|---|---|---|---|
| Opening balance (current month's payment) | 4,000 | 4,800 | 4,800 | 5,600 | 6,000 | 6,000 |
| Purchases (from raw materials inventories budget) | 4,800 | 4,800 | 5,600 | 6,000 | 6,000 | 6,000 |
|  | 8,800 | 9,600 | 10,400 | 11,600 | 12,000 | 12,000 |
| Payments | (4,000) | (4,800) | (4,800) | (5,600) | (6,000) | (6,000) |
| Closing balance (next month's payment) | 4,800 | 4,800 | 5,600 | 6,000 | 6,000 | 6,000 |

(3) Cash budget for the six months ending 31 December:

|  | July £ | Aug £ | Sept £ | Oct £ | Nov £ | Dec £ |
|---|---|---|---|---|---|---|
| **Inflows** |  |  |  |  |  |  |
| Trade receivables (40% of sales revenue of two months previous) | 2,800 | 3,200 | 3,200 | 4,000 | 4,800 | 5,200 |
| Cash sales revenue (60% of current month's sales revenue) | 4,800 | 6,000 | 7,200 | 7,800 | 8,400 | 9,600 |
| Total inflows | 7,600 | 9,200 | 10,400 | 11,800 | 13,200 | 14,800 |
| **Outflows** |  |  |  |  |  |  |
| Payables (from payables budget) | (4,000) | (4,800) | (4,800) | (5,600) | (6,000) | (6,000) |
| Direct costs | (3,000) | (3,600) | (3,600) | (4,200) | (4,500) | (4,500) |
| Advertising | (1,000) | – | – | (1,500) | – | – |
| Overheads: 80% | (1,280) | (1,280) | (1,280) | (1,280) | (1,600) | (1,600) |
| 20% | (280) | (320) | (320) | (320) | (320) | (400) |
| New plant |  |  | (2,200) | (2,200) | (2,200) |  |
| Total outflows | (9,560) | (10,000) | (12,200) | (15,100) | (14,620) | (12,500) |
| Net inflows/(outflows) | (1,960) | (800) | (1,800) | (3,300) | (1,420) | 2,300 |
| Balance c/f | 5,540 | 4,740 | 2,940 | (360) | (1,780) | 520 |

The cash balances carried forward are deduced by subtracting the deficit (net outflows) for the month from (or adding the surplus for the month to) the previous month's balance.

Note how budgets are linked; in this case the inventories budget to the trade payables budget and the trade payables budget to the cash budget.

(b) The following are possible means of relieving the cash shortages revealed by the budget:

- Make a higher proportion of sales on a cash basis.
- Collect the money from credit customers more promptly, for example during the month following the sale.
- Hold lower inventories, both of raw materials and of finished goods.
- Increase the trade payables payment period.
- Delay the payments for advertising.
- Obtain more credit for the overhead costs; at present only 20 per cent are on credit.
- Delay the payments for the new plant.

A combination of two or more of these ways might be used.

## Chapter 13

### 13.1 Toscanini Ltd

(a)

|  | Budget | | Actual |
|---|---|---|---|
|  | Original | Flexed |  |
| Output (units) (production and sales) | 4,000 | 3,500 | 3,500 |
|  | £ | £ | £ |
| Sales revenue | 16,000 | 14,000 | 13,820 |
| Raw materials | (3,840) | (3,360) (1,400 kg) | (3,420) (1,425 kg) |
| Labour | (3,200) | (2,800) (350 hr) | (2,690) (345 hr) |
| Fixed overheads | (4,800) | (4,800) | (4,900) |
| Operating profit | 4,160 | 3,040 | 2,810 |

|  | £ | |
|---|---|---|
| Sales volume variance (4,160 − 3,040) | (1,120) | (A) |
| Sales price variance (14,000 − 13,820) | (180) | (A) |
| Materials price variance (1,425 × 2.40) − 3,420 | 0 | |
| Materials usage variance [(3,500 × 0.4) − 1,425] × £2.40 | (60) | (A) |
| Labour rate variance (345 × £8) − 2,690 | 70 | (F) |
| Labour efficiency variance [(3,500 × 0.10) − 345] × £8 | 40 | (F) |
| Fixed overhead spending variance (4,800 − 4,900) | (100) | (A) |
| Total net variances | (1,350) | (A) |
| Budgeted profit | 4,160 | |
| Less Total net variance | 1,350 | |
| Actual profit | 2,810 | |

(b) Sales volume variance: sales manager; sales price variance: sales manager; materials usage variance: production manager; labour rate variance: personnel manager; labour efficiency variance: production manager; fixed overhead spending variance: various, depending on the nature of the overheads.

(c) Feasible explanations include the following:

- Sales volume   Unanticipated fall in world demand would account for 400 × £2.24 = £896 of this variance (£2.24 is the budgeted contribution per unit). Ineffective marketing probably caused the remainder, though a lack of availability of the finished product to sell may be a reason.
- Sales price   Ineffective selling seems the only logical reason.
- Materials usage   Inefficient usage of material, perhaps because of poor performance by labour, or substandard materials.
- Labour rate   Less overtime worked or lower production bonuses paid as a result of lower volume of activity.
- Labour efficiency   More effective working.
- Overheads   Ineffective control of overheads.

(d) Clearly, not all of the sales volume variance can be attributed to poor marketing, given a 10 per cent reduction in demand.

It will probably be useful to distinguish between that part of the variance that arose from the shortfall in general demand (a planning variance) and a volume variance, which is more fairly attributable to the manager concerned. Thus accountability will be more fairly imposed.

|  | £ |
|---|---|
| Planning variance (10% × 4,000) × £2.24 | 896 |
| 'New' sales volume variance | |
| [4,000 − (10% × 4,000) − 3,500] × £2.24 | 224 |
| Original sales volume variance | 1,120 |

## Chapter 14

### 14.1 Beacon Chemicals plc

(a) Relevant cash flows are as follows:

|  | Year 0 £ million | Year 1 £ million | Year 2 £ million | Year 3 £ million | Year 4 £ million | Year 5 £ million |
|---|---|---|---|---|---|---|
| Sales revenue | | 80 | 120 | 144 | 100 | 64 |
| Loss of contribution | | (15) | (15) | (15) | (15) | (15) |
| Variable cost | | (40) | (50) | (48) | (30) | (32) |
| Fixed cost (Note 1) | | (8) | (8) | (8) | (8) | (8) |
| Operating cash flows | | 17 | 47 | 73 | 47 | 9 |
| Working capital | (30) | | | | | 30 |
| Capital cost | (100) | | | | | |
| Net relevant cash flows | (130) | 17 | 47 | 73 | 47 | 39 |

*Notes:*
1  Only the elements of fixed cost that are incremental to the project (only existing because of the project) are relevant. Depreciation is irrelevant because it is not a cash flow.
2  The research and development cost is irrelevant since it has been spent irrespective of the decision on X14 production.

(b) The payback period is as follows:

|  | Year 0 £ million | Year 1 £ million | Year 2 £ million | Year 3 £ million |
|---|---|---|---|---|
| Cumulative cash flows | (130) | (113) | (66) | 7 |

Thus the equipment will have repaid the initial investment by the end of the third year of operations. The payback period is, therefore, three years.

(c) The net present value is as follows:

|  | Year 0 £ million | Year 1 £ million | Year 2 £ million | Year 3 £ million | Year 4 £ million | Year 5 £ million |
|---|---|---|---|---|---|---|
| Discount factor | 1.00 | 0.926 | 0.857 | 0.794 | 0.735 | 0.681 |
| Present value | (130) | 15.74 | 40.28 | 57.96 | 34.55 | 26.56 |
| Net present value | 45.09 | (That is, the sum of the present values for years 0 to 5.) | | | | |

## Chapter 15

**15.1** **Helsim Ltd**

(a) The liquidity position may be assessed by using the liquidity ratios discussed in Chapter 7:

$$\text{Current ratio} = \frac{\text{Current assets}}{\text{Current liabilities}}$$

$$= \frac{£7.5\text{m}}{£5.4\text{m}}$$

$$= 1.4$$

$$\text{Acid test ratio} = \frac{\text{Current assets (excluding inventories)}}{\text{Current liabilities}}$$

$$= \frac{£3.7\text{m}}{£5.4\text{m}}$$

$$= 0.7$$

These ratios reveal a fairly weak liquidity position. The current ratio seems quite low and the acid test ratio very low. This latter ratio suggests that the business does not have sufficient liquid assets to meet its maturing obligations. It would, however, be useful to have details of the liquidity ratios of similar businesses in the same industry in order to make a more informed judgement. The bank overdraft represents 67% of the current liabilities and 40% of the total liabilities of the business. The continuing support of the bank is therefore important to the ability of the business to meet its commitments.

(b) The finance required to reduce trade payables to an average of 40 days outstanding is calculated as follows:

|  | £m |
|---|---|
| Trade payables at the date of the statement of financial position | 1.80 |
| Trade payables outstanding based on 40 days' credit | |
| 40/365 × £8.4m (that is, credit purchases) | (0.92) |
| Finance required | 0.88 (say £0.9m) |

(c) The bank may not wish to provide further finance to the business. The increase in overdraft will reduce the level of trade payables but will increase the risk exposure of the bank. The additional finance invested by the bank will not generate further funds (it will not increase profit) and will not therefore be self-liquidating. The question does not make it clear whether the business has sufficient security to offer the bank for the increase in overdraft facility. The profits of the business will be reduced and the interest cover ratio, based on the profits generated last year, would reduce to about 1.6* times if the additional overdraft were granted (based on interest charged at 10% each year). This is very low and means that only a small decline in profits would leave interest charges uncovered.

\* Existing bank overdraft (3.6) + extension of overdraft to cover reduction in trade payables (0.9) + loan notes (3.5) = £8.0m. Assuming a 10% interest rate means a yearly interest payment of £0.8m. The operating profit was £1.3m. Interest cover would be 1.63 (that is, 1.3/0.8).

(d) A number of possible sources of finance might be considered. Four possible sources are as follows:

- *Issue ordinary (equity) shares*. This option may be unattractive to investors. The return on equity is fairly low at 7.9% (that is, profit for the year (0.3)/equity (3.8)) and there is no evidence that the profitability of the business will improve. If profits remain at their current level the effect of issuing more equity will be to reduce further the returns to equity.

● *Make other borrowings*. This option may also prove unattractive to investors. The effect of making further borrowings will have a similar effect to that of increasing the overdraft. The profits of the business will be reduced and the interest cover ratio will decrease to a low level. The gearing ratio of the business is already quite high at 48% (that is, loan notes (3.5)/(loan notes + equity (3.5 + 3.8)) and it is not clear what security would be available for the loan. The gearing ratio would be much higher if the overdraft were to be included.

● *Chase trade receivables*. It may be possible to improve cash flows by reducing the level of credit outstanding from customers. At present, the average settlement period is 93 days (that is, (trade receivables (3.6)/sales revenue (14.2)) × 365), which seems quite high. A reduction in the average settlement period by approximately one-quarter would generate the funds required. However, it is not clear what effect this would have on sales.

● *Reduce inventories*. This appears to be the most attractive of the four options. At present, the average inventories holding period is 178 days (that is, (closing inventories (3.8)/cost of sales (7.8)) × 365), which seems very high. A reduction in this period by less than one-quarter would generate the funds required. However, if the business holds a large amount of slow-moving and obsolete items, it may be difficult to reduce inventories' levels.

## Chapter 16

### 16.1 Corex plc

The effect on profit (to nearest £000) is calculated as follows:

|  | £000 | £000 |
|---|---|---|
| *Sales increase per customer category* | | |
| Category 1 (20% × £4m) | | 800 |
| Category 2 (30% × £4m) | | 1,200 |
| Category 3 (50% × £4m) | | 2,000 |
| | | 4,000 |
| *Increase in variable costs* | | |
| Materials [(£4m/£50) × £10] | (800) | |
| Overheads [(£4m/£50) × £5] | (400) | (1,200) |
| Marketing campaign | | (1,800) |
| *Bad debts increase per customer category* | | |
| Category 1 (1.0% × £800) | (8) | |
| Category 2 (3.0% × £1,200) | (36) | |
| Category 3 (5.0% × £2,000) | (100) | (144) |
| *Increase in financing costs\** | | |
| Category 1 | (7) | |
| Category 2 | (13) | |
| Category 3 | (27) | (47) |
| *Profit* | | 809 |

\* Financing costs were calculated as follows:

|  | Customer category | | |
|---|---|---|---|
|  | 1 | 2 | 3 |
|  | £000 | £000 | £000 |
| Sales increase | 800,000 | 1,200,000 | 2,000,000 |
| Additional trade receivables (to nearest £000) | | | |
| (£800 × 30/365) | 66 | | |
| (£1,200 × 40/365) | | 132 | |
| (£2,000 × 50/365) | | | 274 |
| Interest charges (10%) (to nearest £000) | 7 | 13 | 27 |

Profits are predicted to increase by £809,000 following a successful marketing campaign. This represents a return on sales of slightly more than 20 per cent (£809/£4,000). Returns are fairly high because much of the production costs are fixed. Each thermostat sold makes a contribution of £35 (that is, £50 selling price less £15 variable costs) and so additional sales make a significant contribution to profit.

# APPENDIX  D

# Solutions to review questions

## Chapter 1

**1.1** The objective of providing accounting information is to enable users to make more informed decisions and judgements about the organisation concerned. Unless it fulfils this objective, there is no point in providing it.

**1.2** The main users of financial information for a university and the way in which they are likely to use this information may be summed up as follows:

| | |
|---|---|
| Students | Whether to enrol on a course of study. This would probably involve an assessment of the university's ability to continue to operate and to fulfil students' needs. |
| Other universities and colleges | How best to compete against the university. This might involve using the university's performance in various aspects as a 'benchmark' when evaluating their own performance. |
| Employees | Whether to take up or to continue in employment with the university. Employees might assess this by considering the ability of the university to continue to provide employment and to reward employees adequately for their labour. |
| Government/ funding authority | How efficient the university is in undertaking its various activities. Possible funding needs that the university may have. |
| Local community representatives | Whether to allow/encourage the university to expand its premises. To assess this, the university's ability to continue to provide employment for the community, to use community resources and to help fund environmental improvements might be considered. |
| Suppliers | Whether to continue to supply the university at all; also whether to supply on credit. This would involve an assessment of the university's ability to pay for any goods and services supplied. |
| Lenders | Whether to lend money to the university and/or whether to require repayment of any existing loans. To assess this, the university's ability to meet its obligations to pay interest and to repay the principal would be considered. |
| Board of governors and other managers (Faculty deans and so on) | Whether the performance of the university requires improvement. Here performance to date would be compared with earlier plans or some other 'benchmark' to decide whether action needs to be taken. Whether there should be a change in the university's future direction. In making such decisions, management will need to look at the university's ability to perform and at the opportunities available to it. |

We can see that the users of accounting information and their needs are similar to those of a private sector business.

**1.3** Most businesses are far too large and complex for managers to be able to see and assess everything that is going on in their own areas of responsibility merely by personal observation. Managers need information on all aspects within their control. Management accounting reports can provide them with this information, to a greater or lesser extent. These reports can be seen, therefore, as acting as the eyes and ears of the managers, providing insights not necessarily obvious without them.

**1.4** Since we can never be sure what is going to happen in the future, the best that we can do is to make judgements on the basis of past experience. Thus information concerning flows of cash and of wealth in the recent past is likely to be a useful source on which to base judgements about possible future outcomes.

## Chapter 2

**2.1** The confusion arises because the owner seems unaware of the business entity convention in accounting. This convention requires a separation of the business from the owner(s) of the business for accounting purposes. The business is regarded as a separate entity and the statement of financial position is prepared from the perspective of the business rather than that of the owner. As a result, funds invested in the business by the owner will be regarded as a claim that the owner has on the business. In the standard layout of the statement of financial position, this claim will be shown alongside other claims on the business from outsiders.

**2.2** A statement of financial position does not show what a business is worth, for two major reasons:

- Only those items that can be measured reliably in monetary terms are shown on the statement of financial position. Thus, things of value such as the reputation for product quality, skills of employees and so on will not normally appear in the statement of financial position.
- The historic cost convention results in assets often being recorded at their outlay cost rather than their current value. In the case of certain assets, the difference between historic cost and current value may be significant.

**2.3** The accounting equation is simply the relationship between a business's assets, liabilities and equity. For the standard layout, it is:

Assets (current and non-current) = Equity + Liabilities (current and non-current)

For the alternative layout mentioned in the chapter, the equation is:

Assets (current and non-current) – Liabilities (current and non-current) = Equity

**2.4** Some object to the idea of humans being treated as assets for inclusion on the statement of financial position. It can be seen as demeaning for humans to be listed alongside inventories, plant and machinery and other assets. However, others argue that humans are often the most valuable resource of a business and that placing a value on this resource will help bring to the attention of managers the importance of nurturing and developing this 'asset'. There is a saying in management that 'the things that count are the things that get counted'. As the value of the 'human assets' is not stated in the financial statements, there is a danger that managers will treat these 'assets' less favourably than other assets that are on the statement of financial position.

Humans are likely to meet the first criterion of an asset listed in the chapter, that is, that a probable future benefit exists. There would be little point in employing people if this were not the case. The second criterion concerning exclusive right of control is more problematic. Clearly a business cannot control humans in the same way as most other assets. However, a business can have the exclusive right to the employment services that a person provides. This distinction between control over the services provided and control over the person makes it possible to argue that the second criterion can be met.

Humans normally sign a contract of employment with the business, and so the third criterion is normally met. The difficulty, however, is with the fourth criterion, that is, whether the value of humans (or their services) can be properly measured. To date, none of the measurement methods proposed enjoy widespread acceptance.

## Chapter 3

**3.1**   At the time of preparing the income statement, it is not always possible to determine accurately the expenses that need to be matched to the sales revenue figure for the period. It will only be at some later point in time that the true position becomes clear. However, it is still necessary to try to include all relevant expenses in the income statement and so estimates of the future will have to be made. The income statement would lose much of its usefulness were the business to wait for all of the unkowns to become clear.

Examples of estimates that may have to be made include:

- expenses accrued at the end of the period such as the amount of telephone expenses incurred since the last quarter's bill
- the amount of depreciation based on estimates of the life of the non-current asset and future residual value
- the amount of bad and doubtful debts incurred.

**3.2**   Depreciation attempts to allocate the cost or fair value, less any residual value, of the asset over its useful life. Depreciation does not attempt to measure the fall in value of the asset during a particular accounting period. Thus, the carrying amount of the asset appearing on the statement of financial position normally represents the unexpired cost of the asset rather than its current market value.

**3.3**   The convention of consistency is designed to provide a degree of uniformity concerning the application of accounting policies. We have seen that, in certain areas, there may be more than one method of accounting for an item, for example inventories. The convention of consistency states that, having decided on a particular accounting policy, a business should continue to apply the policy in successive periods. While this approach helps to ensure that users can make valid comparisons concerning business performance *over time*, it does not ensure that valid comparisons can be made *between businesses*. This is because different businesses may consistently apply different accounting policies.

**3.4**   An expense is that element of the cost incurred that is used up during the accounting period. An asset is that element of cost which is carried forward on the statement of financial position and which will normally be used up in future periods. Thus, both assets and expenses arise from costs being incurred. The major difference between the two is the period over which the benefits (resulting from the costs incurred) accrue.

## Chapter 4

**4.1** It does not differ. In both cases they are required to meet their debts to the full extent that there are assets available. This means that they both have a liability that is limited to the extent of their assets. This is a particularly important fact for the shareholders of a limited company because they know that those owed money by the company cannot demand that the shareholders contribute additional funds to help meet debts. Thus the liability of the shareholders is limited to the amount that they have paid for their shares, or have agreed to pay in the case of partially unpaid shares. This contrasts with the position of the owner or part owner of an unincorporated (non-company) business. Here all of the individual's assets could be required to meet the unsatisfied liabilities of the business.

Thus, while there is a difference between the position of a shareholder (in a limited company) and that of a sole proprietor or partner, there is no difference between the position of the company itself and a sole proprietor or partner.

**4.2** A private limited company may place restrictions on the transfer of its shares, that is, the directors can veto an attempt by a shareholder to sell his or her shares to another person to whom the directors object. Thus, in effect, the majority can avoid having as a shareholder someone that they would prefer not to have. A public company cannot do this.

A public limited company must have authorised share capital of at least £50,000. There is no minimum for a private limited company.

The main advantage of being a public limited company is that the company may offer its shares and loan notes to the general public; a private company cannot make such an offer.

**4.3** A reserve is that part of the equity (owners' claim) of a company that is not share capital. Reserves represent gains or surpluses that enhance the claim of the shareholders above the nominal value of their shares. For example, the share premium account is a reserve that represents the excess over the nominal value of shares that is paid for them on a share issue. The retained earnings balance is a reserve that arises from ploughed-back profits earned by the company. Revenue reserves arise from realised profits and gains. Capital reserves arise from unrealised profits and gains (for example, the upward revaluation of a non-current asset) or from issuing shares at a premium (share premium).

**4.4** A preference share represents part of the ownership of a company. Preference shares entitle their owners to the first part of any dividend paid by the company, up to a maximum amount. The maximum is usually expressed as a percentage of the nominal or par value of the preference shares.

(a) They differ from ordinary shares to the extent that they only entitle their holders to dividends to a predetermined maximum value. Dividends to ordinary shareholders have no predetermined maximum. Were the company to be liquidated, the preference shareholders would normally receive a maximum of the nominal value of their shares, whereas the ordinary shareholders receive the residue after all other claimants, including the preference shareholders.

(b) They differ from loan notes in that these represent borrowings for the company, where normally holders have a contract with the company that specifies the rate of interest, interest payment dates and redemption date. They are often secured on the company's assets. Preference shareholders have no such contract.

## Chapter 5

**5.1**  Accounting is an evolving subject. It is not static and so the principles that are laid down at any particular point in time may become obsolete as a result of changes in our understanding of the nature of accounting information and its impact on users and changes in the economic environment within which accounting is employed. We must accept, therefore, that accounting principles will continue to evolve and that existing ones must be regularly reviewed.

**5.2**  Apart from increases in accounting regulation, financial reports have increased because of:

- increasing demands by influential user groups, such as shareholders and financial analysts, for financial information relating to the company;
- the increasing sophistication of influential user groups, such as financial analysts, to deal with financial information;
- the increasing complexity of business operations requiring greater explanation;
- increasing recognition of the need for greater accountability towards certain user groups (such as employees and community groups) requiring the need for additional reports, such as environmental reports and social reports.

**5.3**  There are various problems associated with the measurement of business segments. These include:

- the definition of a segment;
- the treatment of inter-segmental transactions, such as sales;
- the treatment of common costs.

There is no single correct method of dealing with these problems and variations will arise in practice. This, in turn, will hinder comparisons between businesses.

**5.4**  Preparing a business review may present a problem for accountants. For information to be credible to all interested parties, accountants should be as neutral as possible in measuring and reporting the financial performance and position of the business. The business review requires some interpretation of results and there is always a risk of bias, or at least the perception of bias among some users, in what items are reported and how they reflect on business performance. The business review is not normally audited and so comments made are not subject to independent scrutiny. The board of directors is charged with running the business and it is logical that the directors accept full responsibility for preparing the review. This should be made clear to users.

## Chapter 6

**6.1**  Cash is normally required in the settlement of claims. Thus, employees and contractors want to be paid for their work in cash. A supplier of non-current assets or inventories will normally expect to be paid in cash, perhaps after a short period of credit. When businesses fail, it is their inability to find the cash to pay claimants that actually drives them under. These factors lead to cash being the pre-eminent business asset and, therefore, the one that analysts and others watch carefully in trying to assess the ability of the business to survive and/or to take advantage of commercial opportunities.

**6.2**   With the direct method, the business's cash records are analysed for the period concerned. The analysis reveals the amounts of cash, in total, that have been paid and received in respect of each category of the statement of cash flows. This is not difficult in principle, or in practice if it is done by computer, as a matter of routine.

The indirect method takes the approach that, while the profit (loss) for the reporting period is not equal to the net inflow (outflow) of cash from operations, they are fairly closely linked to the extent that appropriate adjustment of the profit (loss) for the period figure will produce the correct cash flow one. The adjustment is concerned with the depreciation charge for, and movements in relevant working capital items over, the period.

**6.3**   (a) *Cash flows from operating activities.* This would normally be positive, even for a business with small profits or even losses. The fact that depreciation is not a cash flow tends to lead to positive cash flows in this area in most cases.

(b) *Cash flows from investing activities.* Normally this would be negative in cash flow terms since many non-current assets become less useful to the business and need to be replaced (or improved upon) in the normal course of business. This means that, typically, old non-current assets are generating less cash on their disposal than is having to be paid out to replace them.

(c) *Cash flows from financing activities.* There is a tendency for businesses either to expand or to fail. In either case, this is likely to mean that, over the years, more finance will be raised than will be redeemed or retired.

**6.4**   There are several possible reasons for this, including the following:

● Changes in inventories, trade receivables and trade payables. For example, an increase in trade receivables during a reporting period would mean that the cash received from credit sales would be less than the credit sales revenue for the same period.

● Cash may have been spent on new non-current assets or received from disposals of old ones; these would not directly affect profit.

● Cash may have been spent to redeem or repay a financial claim or received as a result of the creation or the increase of a claim. These would not directly affect profit.

● The taxation charged in the income statement would not normally be the same tax that is paid during the same reporting period.

## Chapter 7

**7.1**   The fact that a business operates on a low operating profit margin indicates that only a small operating profit is being produced for each £1 of sales revenue generated. However, this does not necessarily mean that the ROCE will be low. If the business is able to generate sufficient sales revenue during a period, the operating profit may be very high even though the operating profit per £1 of sales revenue is low. If the overall operating profit is high, this can lead, in turn, to a high ROCE, since it is the total operating profit that is used as the numerator (top part of the fraction) in this ratio. Many businesses (including supermarkets) pursue a strategy of 'low margin, high sales revenue'.

**7.2**   The statement of financial position is drawn up at a single point in time – the end of the financial period. As a result, the figures shown on the statement represent the position at that single point in time and may not be representative of the position during the period. Wherever possible, average figures (perhaps based on monthly figures) should be used.

However, an external user may only have access to the opening and closing statements of financial position for the year and so a simple average based on these figures may be all that it is possible to calculate. Where a business is seasonal in nature or is subject to cyclical changes, this simple averaging may not be sufficient.

**7.3** In view of the fact that Z-scores are derived from information that is published by the businesses themselves, it is difficult to say that Z-scores should not be made publicly available. Indeed, many of those connected with a business – shareholders, lenders, employees, and so on – may find this information extremely valuable for decision making. However, there is a risk that a poor Z-score will lead to a loss of confidence in the business among investors and suppliers, which will, in turn, prevent the business from taking corrective action as lines of credit and investment will be withdrawn.

**7.4** The P/E ratio may vary between businesses within the same industry for the following reasons:

- *Accounting policies* Differences in the methods used to compute profit (for example inventories valuation and depreciation) can lead to different profit figures and, therefore, different P/E ratios.
- *Different prospects* One business may be regarded as having a much brighter future due to factors such as the quality of management, the quality of products, location, and so on. This will affect the market price investors are prepared to pay for the share and, hence, it will also affect the P/E ratio.
- *Different asset structure* The business's underlying asset base may be much higher and this may affect the market price of the shares.

## Chapter 8

**8.1** The three attributes are:

1 They must relate to the objective(s) that the decision is intended to work towards. In most businesses this is taken to be wealth enhancement. This means that any information relating to the decision that does not impact on wealth enhancement is irrelevant, where wealth enhancement is the sole objective. In practice a business may have more than one objective.

2 They must relate to the future. Past costs cannot be relevant to decisions being made about the future.

3 They must differ between the options under consideration. Where a cost will be the same irrespective of the outcome of the decision that is to be taken it is irrelevant. It is only on the basis of things that differ from one outcome to another that decisions can be made.

**8.2** A sunk cost is a past and, therefore, an irrelevant cost in the context of any decision. Thus, for example, the cost of an item of inventories already bought is a sunk cost. It is irrelevant, in any decision involving the use of the inventories, because this cost will be the same irrespective of the decision made.

An opportunity cost is the cost of being deprived of the next best option to the one under consideration. For example, where using an hour of a worker's time on activity A deprives the business of the opportunity to use that time in a profitable activity B, the benefit lost from activity B is an opportunity cost of pursuing activity A.

**8.3** Cost may be defined as the amount of resources, usually measured in monetary terms, sacrificed to achieve a particular objective.

**8.4** A committed cost is like a past cost in that an irrevocable decision has been made to incur the cost. This might be because the business has entered into a binding contract, for example to rent some accommodation for the next two years. Thus it is effectively a past cost even though the payment (for rent, in our example) has yet to be made. Since the business cannot avoid a committed cost, committed costs cannot be relevant costs.

## Chapter 9

**9.1** A fixed cost is one that is the same irrespective of the level of activity or output. Typical examples of costs that are fixed, irrespective of the level of production or provision of a service, include rent of business accommodation, salaries of supervisory staff, and insurance.

A variable cost is one that varies with the level of activity or output. Examples include raw materials and labour, where labour is rewarded in proportion to the level of output.

Note particularly that it is relative to the level of activity that costs are fixed or variable. Fixed costs will be affected by inflation and they will be greater for a longer period than for a shorter one.

For a particular product or service, knowing which element of cost is fixed and which is variable enables managers to predict the total cost for any particular level of activity. It also enables them to concentrate only on the variable cost in circumstances where a decision will not alter the fixed cost.

**9.2** The BEP is the break-even point, that is, the level of activity, measured either in units of output or in value of sales revenue, at which the sales revenue exactly covers all of the costs, both fixed and variable.

Break-even point is calculated as

Fixed costs/(sales revenue per unit – variable costs per unit)

which may alternatively be expressed as

Fixed costs/Contribution per unit

Thus break-even will occur when the contributions for the period are sufficient to cover the fixed cost for the period.

Break-even point tends to be useful as a comparison with planned level of activity in an attempt to assess the riskiness of the activity.

**9.3** Operating gearing refers to the extent of fixed cost relative to variable cost in the total cost of some activity. Where the fixed cost forms a relatively high proportion of the total (at the business's normal level of activity), we say that the activity has high operating gearing.

Typically, high operating gearing is present in environments where there is a relatively high level of mechanisation (that is, capital-intensive environments). This is because such environments tend simultaneously to involve relatively high fixed cost of depreciation, maintenance, and so on and relatively low variable cost.

High operating gearing tends to mean that the effects of increases or decreases in the level of activity have an accentuated effect on operating profit. For example, a 20% decrease in output of a particular service will lead to a greater than 20% decrease in operating profit, assuming no cost or price changes.

**9.4**  In the face of a restricting scarce resource, profit will be maximised by using the scarce resource on output where the contribution per unit of the scarce resource is maximised.

This means that the contribution per unit of the scarce resource (for example, hour of scarce labour or unit of scarce raw material) for each competing product or service needs to be identified. It is then a question of allocating the scarce resource to the product or service that provides the highest contribution per unit of the particular scarce resource.

The logic of this approach is that the scarce resource is allocated to the activity that uses it most effectively, in terms of contribution and, therefore, profit.

## Chapter 10

**10.1**  In process costing, the total production cost for a period is divided by the number of completed units of output for the period to deduce the full cost per unit. Where there is work in progress at the beginning and/or the end of the period complications arise.

The problem is that some of the completed output incurred cost in the preceding period. Similarly, some of the cost incurred in the current period leads to completed production in the subsequent period. Account needs to be taken of these facts, if reliable full cost information is to be obtained. Making the necessary adjustment is not very complicated, however.

**10.2**  The only reason for distinguishing between direct and indirect costs is to help to deduce the full cost of a unit of output in a job-costing environment. In an environment where all units of output are identical, or can reasonably be regarded as being so, a process costing approach will be taken. This avoids the need for identifying direct and indirect costs separately.

Direct cost forms that part of the total cost of pursuing some activity that can, unequivocally, be associated with that particular activity. Examples of direct cost items in the typical job-costing environment include direct labour and direct materials.

Indirect cost is the remainder of the cost of pursuing some activity.

In practice, knowledge of the direct costs tends to provide the basis used to charge overheads to jobs.

The distinction between direct and indirect cost is irrelevant for any other purpose.

Directness and indirectness is dictated by the nature of that which is being costed, as much as the nature of the cost.

**10.3**  The notion of direct and indirect cost is concerned only with the extent to which particular elements of cost can unequivocally be related to, and measured in respect of, a particular cost unit, usually a product or service. The distinction between direct and indirect costs is made exclusively for the purpose of deducing the full cost of some cost unit, in an environment where each cost unit is not identical or close enough to being identical for it to be treated as such. Thus, it is typically in the context of job costing, or some variant of it, that the distinction between direct and indirect cost is usefully made.

The notion of variable and fixed cost is concerned entirely with how costs behave in the face of changes in the volume of output. The benefit of being able to distinguish between fixed and variable cost is that predictions can be made of what total cost will be at particular levels of volume and/or what reduction or addition to cost will occur if the volume of output is reduced or increased.

Thus the notion of direct and indirect cost, on the one hand, and that of variable and fixed cost, on the other, are not linked to one another, and, in most contexts, some elements of direct cost are variable, while some are fixed. Similarly, indirect cost might be fixed or variable.

**10.4**  The full cost includes all of the cost of pursuing the cost objective, including a 'fair' share of the overheads. Generally the full cost represents an average cost of the various elements, rather than a cost that arises because the business finds itself in a particular situation.

The fact that the full cost reflects all aspects of cost should mean that, were the business to sell its output at a price exactly equal to the full cost (manufacturing and non-manufacturing cost), the sales revenues for the period would exactly cover all of the cost and the business would break even, that is make neither profit nor loss.

## Chapter 11

**11.1**  ABC is a means of dealing with charging overheads to units of output to derive full cost in a multi-product (job or batch costing) environment.

The traditional approach tends to accept that once identifiable direct cost, normally labour and materials, has been taken out, all of the remaining cost (overheads) must be treated as a common cost and applied to jobs using the same formula, typically on the basis of direct labour hours.

ABC takes a much more enquiring approach to overheads. It follows the philosophy that overheads do not occur for no reason, but they must be driven by activities. For example, a particular type of product may take up a disproportionately large part of supervisors' time. If that product were not made, in the long run, the supervision cost could be cut (fewer supervisors would be needed). Whereas the traditional approach would just accept that supervisory salaries are an overhead, which needs to be apportioned along with other overheads, ABC would seek to charge that part of the supervisors' salaries which is driven by the particular type of product, to that product.

**11.2**  One criticism is on the issue of the cost/benefit balance. It is claimed that the work necessary to analyse activities and identify the cost drivers tends to be more expensive than is justified by the increased quality of the full cost information that emerges.

Linked to this is the belief of many that full cost information is of rather dubious value for most purposes, irrespective of how the full cost information is deduced. Many argue that full cost information is flawed by the fact that it takes no account of opportunity cost.

ABC enthusiasts would probably argue that deducing better quality full cost information is not the only benefit that is available, if the overhead cost drivers can be identified. Knowing what drives the costs can enable management to exercise more control over them. This benefit needs to be taken into account when assessing the cost/benefit of using ABC.

**11.3**  The four main areas in the balanced scorecard are:

1  *Finance*. Here targets for measures such as return on capital employed will be stated.
2  *Customer*. Here the market/customers that the business will aim for is established, as will be targets for such things as measures of customer satisfaction and rate of growth in customer numbers.
3  *Internal business process*. Here the processes that are vital to the business will be established. This might include levels of innovation, types of operation and after-sales service.
4  *Learning and growth*. In this area issues relating to growing the business and development of staff are identified and targets set.

**11.4** Three non-financial measures might include:

- Turnover of staff during the period.
- New clients obtained during the period.
- Level of client satisfaction during the period.

## Chapter 12

**12.1** A budget can be defined as a financial plan for a future period of time. Thus it sets out the intentions which management has for the period concerned. Achieving the budget plans should help to achieve the long-term plans of the business. Achievement of the long-term plans should mean that the business is successfully working towards its strategic objectives and mission.

A budget differs from a forecast in that a forecast is a statement of what is expected to happen without the intervention of management, perhaps because they cannot intervene (as with a weather forecast). A plan is an intention to achieve.

Normally management would take account of reliable forecasts when making its plans.

**12.2** The five uses of budget that have been identified are:

1 Budgets tend to promote forward thinking and the possible identification of short-term problems. Managers must plan and the budgeting process tends to force them to do so. In doing so, they are likely to encounter potential problems. If the potential problems can be identified early enough, solutions might be easily found.
2 Budgets can be used to help co-ordination between various sections of the business. It is important that the plans of one area of the business fit in with those of other areas; a lack of co-ordination could have disastrous consequences. Having formal statements of plans for each aspect of the business enables a check to be made that plans are complementary.
3 Budgets can motivate managers to better performance. It is believed that people are motivated by having a target to aim for. Provided that the inherent goals are achievable, budgets can provide an effective motivational device.
4 Budgets can provide a basis for a system of control. Having a plan against which actual performance can be measured provides a potentially useful tool of control.
5 Budgets can provide a system of authorisation. Many managers have 'spending' budgets such as research and development, staff training and so on. For these people, the size of their budget defines their authority to spend.

**12.3** Control can be defined as 'compelling things to occur as planned'. This implies that control can only be achieved if a plan exists. Budgets are financial plans. This means that, if actual performance can be compared with the budget (plan) for each aspect of the business, divergences from plan can be spotted. Steps can then be taken to bring matters back under control where they are going out of control.

**12.4** A budget committee is a group of senior staff that is responsible for the budget preparation process within an organisation. The existence of the committee places the budget responsibility clearly with an identifiable group of people. This group can focus on the tasks involved.

## Chapter 13

**13.1**  Feedforward controls try to anticipate what is likely to happen in the future and then assist in making the actual outcome match the desired outcome. They contrast with feedback controls, which simply compare actual to planned outcomes after the event. Feedforward controls are more pro-active and try to prevent things going out of control in the first place.

**13.2**  A variance is the effect on budgeted profit of the particular cost or revenue item being considered. It represents the difference between the budgeted profit and the actual profit assuming everything, except the item under consideration, had gone according to budget. From this it must be the case that

> Budgeted profit + favourable variances – unfavourable variances = actual profit.

The purpose of analysing variances is to identify whether, and if so where, things are not going according to plan. If this can be done, it may be possible to find out the cause of things going out of control. If this can be discovered, it may then be possible to put things right for the future.

**13.3**  Where the budgeted and actual volumes of output do not coincide it is impossible to make valid comparison of 'allowed' and actual costs and revenues. Flexing the original budget to reflect the actual output level enables a more informative comparison to be made.

Flexing certainly does not mean that output volume differences do not matter. Flexing will show (as the difference between flexed and original budget profits) the effect on profit of output volume differences.

**13.4**  Deciding whether variances should be investigated involves the use of judgement. Often management will set a threshold of significance, for example 5 per cent of the budgeted figure for each variance relating to revenue or cost items. All variances above this threshold would then be investigated. Even where variances are below the threshold, any sign of a systemic variance, shown, for example, by an increasing cumulative total for the factor, should be investigated.

Knowledge of the cause of a particular variance may well put management in a position to take actions that will be beneficial to the business in the future. Investigating variances, however, is likely to be relatively expensive in staff time. A judgement has to be made as to whether the value or benefit of knowing the cause of the variance will be justified by the cost of this knowledge. As with most investigations of this type, it is difficult to judge the value of the knowledge until after the variance has been investigated.

## Chapter 14

**14.1**  NPV is usually considered the best method of assessing investment opportunities because it takes account of:

- *The timing of the cash flows.* By *discounting* the various cash flows associated with each project according to when it is expected to arise, it recognises the fact that cash flows do not all occur simultaneously. Associated with this is the fact that, by discounting, using the opportunity cost of finance (that is, the return that the next best alternative opportunity would generate), the net benefit after financing costs have been met is identified (as the NPV).

● *The whole of the relevant cash flows.* NPV includes all of the relevant cash flows irrespective of when they are expected to occur. It treats them differently according to their date of occurrence, but they are all taken account of in the NPV and they all have, or can have, an influence on the decision.

● *The objectives of the business.* NPV is the only method of appraisal where the output of the analysis has a direct bearing on the wealth of the owners of the business. (Positive NPVs enhance wealth; negative ones reduce it.) Since most private-sector businesses seek to increase their owners' wealth, NPV clearly is the best approach to use.

NPV provides clear decision rules concerning acceptance/rejection of projects and the ranking of projects. It is fairly simple to use, particularly with the availability of modern computer software that takes away the need for routine calculations to be done manually.

**14.2**   The payback method, in its original form, does not take account of the time value of money. However, it would be possible to modify the payback method to accommodate this requirement. Cash flows arising from a project could be discounted, using the cost of finance as the appropriate discount rate, in the same way as in the NPV and IRR methods. The discounted payback approach is used by some businesses and represents an improvement on the original approach described in the chapter. However, it still retains the other flaws of the original payback approach that were discussed. For example, it ignores relevant data after the payback period. Thus, even in its modified form, the PP method cannot be regarded as superior to NPV.

**14.3**   The IRR method does appear to be preferred to the NPV method among practising managers. The main reasons for this appear to be as follows:

● A preference for a percentage return ratio rather than an absolute figure as a means of expressing the outcome of a project. This preference for a ratio may reflect the fact that other financial goals of the business are often set in terms of ratios, for example return on capital employed.

● A preference for ranking projects in terms of their percentage return. Managers feel it is easier to rank projects on the basis of percentage returns (though NPV outcomes should be just as easy for them). We saw in the chapter that the IRR method could provide misleading advice on the ranking of projects, and the NPV method was preferable for this purpose.

**14.4**   Cash flows are preferred to profit flows because cash is the ultimate measure of economic wealth. Cash is used to acquire resources and for distribution to shareholders. When cash is invested in a project, an opportunity cost is incurred, as the cash cannot be used in other investment projects. Similarly, when positive cash flows are generated by the project, the cash can be used to reinvest in other projects.

Profit, on the other hand, is relevant to reporting the productive effort for a relatively short period. This measure of effort may have only a tenuous relationship to cash flows for a period. The conventions of accounting may lead to the recognition of gains and losses in one period and the relevant cash inflows and outflows occurring in another period.

### Chapter 15

**15.1** A sale-and-leaseback arrangement may have the following disadvantages:

- There may be a tax liability arising on the sale of the asset.
- The future cost of the lease payments may be difficult to predict.
- Lease payments may become a burden over time as a result of upward reviews.
- Where property is being used in a sale-and-leaseback arrangement, the business may have to relocate its operations at the end of the lease period if a new lease agreement cannot be reached.
- The business will not benefit from any future increases in value of the asset.

**15.2** A listed business may wish to revert to unlisted status for a number of possible reasons. These include:

- *Cost.* A Stock Exchange listing can be costly, as the business must adhere to certain administrative regulations and financial disclosures.
- *Scrutiny.* Listed companies are subject to close scrutiny by analysts and this may not be welcome if the business is engaged in sensitive negotiations or controversial business activities.
- *Takeover risk.* The shares of the business may be purchased by an unwelcome bidder and this may result in a takeover.
- *Investor profile.* If the business is dominated by a few investors who wish to retain their interest in the business and do not wish to raise further equity by public issues, the benefits of a listing are few.

**15.3** An offer for sale involves an issuing house buying the shares in the business and then, in turn, selling the shares to the public. The issue will be advertised by the publication of a prospectus, which will set out details of the business and the issue price of the shares (or reserve price if a tender issue is being made). The shares issued by the issuing house may be either new shares or shares that have been purchased from existing shareholders. A public issue is where the business undertakes direct responsibility for issuing shares to the public. If an issuing house is employed it will usually be in the role of adviser and administrator of the issue. However, the issuing house may also underwrite the issue. A public issue runs the risk that the shares will not be taken up and is a less popular form of issue for businesses.

**15.4** Invoice discounting is a service offered to businesses by a financial institution whereby the institution is prepared to advance a sum equivalent to 80%, or so, of outstanding trade receivables. The amount advanced is usually repayable within 60 to 90 days. The business will retain responsibility for collecting the amounts owing from credit customers and the advance must be repaid irrespective of whether the trade receivables have been collected. Factoring is a service that is also offered to businesses by financial institutions. In this case, the factor will take over the business's sales and trade receivables records and will undertake to collect trade receivables on behalf of the client business. The factor will also be prepared to make an advance of 80%, or so, of approved trade receivables that is repayable from the amounts received from customers. The service charge for invoice discounting is up to 0.5% of sales revenue, whereas the service charge for factoring is up to 3% of sales revenue. This difference explains, in part, why businesses have shown a preference for invoice discounting rather than factoring in recent years. However, the factor provides additional services, as explained.

## Chapter 16

**16.1** Although the credit manager is responsible for ensuring that receivables pay on time, Tariq may be right in denying blame. Various factors may be responsible for the situation described which are beyond the control of the credit manager. These include:

- a downturn in the economy leading to financial difficulties among credit customers;
- decisions by other managers within the business to liberalise credit policy in order to stimulate sales;
- an increase in competition among suppliers offering credit, which is being exploited by customers;
- disputes with customers over the quality of goods or services supplied;
- problems in the delivery of goods leading to delays.

You may have thought of others.

**16.2** The level of inventories held will be affected in the following ways:

(a) An increase in production bottlenecks is likely to result in an increase in raw materials and work in progress being processed within the plant. Therefore, inventories levels should rise.

(b) A rise in the cost of capital will make holding inventories more expensive. This may, in turn, lead to a decision to reduce inventories levels.

(c) The decision to reduce the range of products should result in a lower level of inventories being held. It would no longer be necessary to hold certain items in order to meet customer demand.

(d) Switching to a local supplier may reduce the lead time between ordering an item and receiving it. This should, in turn, reduce the need to carry such high levels of the particular item.

(e) A deterioration in the quality of bought-in items may result in the purchase of higher quantities of inventories in order to take account of the defective element in inventories acquired. It may also lead to an increase in the inspection time for items received. This too would lead to a rise in inventories levels.

**16.3** Inventories are held:

- to meet customer demand,
- to avoid the problems of running out of inventories and
- to take advantage of profitable opportunities (for example, buying a product that is expected to rise steeply in price in the future).

The first reason may be described as transactionary, the second precautionary and the third speculative. They are, in essence, the same reasons why a business holds cash.

**16.4** (a) The costs of holding too little cash are:

- failure to meet obligations when they fall due which can damage the reputation of the business and may, in the extreme, lead to the business being wound up;
- having to borrow and thereby incur interest charges;
- an inability to take advantage of profitable opportunities.

(b) The costs of holding too much cash are:

- failure to use the funds available for more profitable purposes;
- loss of value during a period of inflation.

# APPENDIX E

# Solutions to selected Exercises

## Chapter 2

### 2.1 Paul

**Statement of cash flows for Thursday**

|  | £ |
|---|---|
| Opening balance (from Wednesday) | 59 |
| Cash from sale of wrapping paper | 47 |
| Cash paid to purchase wrapping paper | (53) |
| Closing balance | 53 |

**Income statement for Thursday**

|  | £ |
|---|---|
| Sales revenue | 47 |
| Cost of goods sold | (33) |
| Profit | 14 |

**Statement of financial position as at Thursday evening**

|  | £ |
|---|---|
| Cash | 53 |
| Inventories of goods for resale (23 + 53 − 33) | 43 |
| Total assets | 96 |
| Equity | 96 |

### 2.2 Paul (*continued*)

|  | £ |
|---|---|
| **Equity** | |
| Cash introduced by Paul on Monday | 40 |
| Profit for Monday | 15 |
| Profit for Tuesday | 18 |
| Profit for Wednesday | 9 |
| Profit for Thursday | 14 |
|  | 96 |

Thus the equity of the business, all of which belongs to Paul as sole owner, consists of the cash he invested to start the business plus the profit earned each day.

**2.3**    **Helen**

### Income statement for day 1

| | £ |
|---|---|
| Sales revenue (70 × £0.80) | 56 |
| Cost of sales (70 × £0.50) | (35) |
| Profit | 21 |

### Statement of cash flows for day 1

| | £ |
|---|---|
| Cash introduced by Helen | 40 |
| Cash from sales | 56 |
| Cash for purchases (80 × £0.50) | (40) |
| Closing balance | 56 |

### Statement of financial position as at end of day 1

| | £ |
|---|---|
| Cash balance | 56 |
| Inventories of unsold goods (10 × £0.50) | 5 |
| Total assets | 61 |
| Equity | 61 |

### Income statement for day 2

| | £ |
|---|---|
| Sales revenue (65 × £0.80) | 52.0 |
| Cost of sales (65 × £0.50) | (32.5) |
| Profit | 19.5 |

### Statement of cash flows for day 2

| | £ |
|---|---|
| Opening balance | 56.0 |
| Cash from sales | 52.0 |
| Cash for purchases (60 × £0.50) | (30.0) |
| Closing balance | 78.0 |

### Statement of financial position as at end of day 2

| | £ |
|---|---|
| Cash balance | 78.0 |
| Inventories of unsold goods (5 × £0.50) | 2.5 |
| Total assets | 80.5 |
| Equity | 80.5 |

### Income statement for day 3

| | £ |
|---|---|
| Sales revenue (20 × £0.80) + (45 × £0.40) | 34.0 |
| Cost of sales (65 × £0.50) | (32.5) |
| Profit | 1.5 |

### Statement of cash flows for day 3

|  | £ |
|---|---|
| Opening balance | 78.0 |
| Cash from sales | 34.0 |
| Cash for purchases (60 × £0.50) | (30.0) |
| Closing balance | 82.0 |

### Statement of financial position as at end of day 3

|  | £ |
|---|---|
| Cash balance | 82.0 |
| Inventories of unsold goods | – |
| Total assets | 82.0 |
| Equity | 82.0 |

---

**2.6   Crafty Engineering Ltd**

(a)

### Statement of financial position as at 30 June last year

|  | £000 |
|---|---|
| **ASSETS** | |
| **Non-current assets** | |
| *Property, plant and equipment* | |
| Property | 320 |
| Equipment and tools | 207 |
| Motor vehicles | 38 |
|  | 565 |
| **Current assets** | |
| Inventories | 153 |
| Trade receivables | 185 |
|  | 338 |
| Total assets | 903 |
| **EQUITY AND LIABILITIES** | |
| Equity (which is the missing figure) | 441 |
| **Non-current liabilities** | |
| Long-term borrowings (Loan Industrial Finance Co.) | 260 |
| **Current liabilities** | |
| Trade payables | 86 |
| Short-term borrowings | 116 |
|  | 202 |
| Total equity and liabilities | 903 |

(b) The statement of financial position reveals a high level of investment in non-current assets. In percentage terms, we can say that more than 60% of the total investment in assets (565/903) has been in non-current assets. The nature of the business may require a heavy investment in non-current assets. The investment in current assets exceeds the current liabilities by a large amount (approximately 1.7 times). As a result, there is no obvious sign of a liquidity problem. However, the statement of financial position reveals that the business has no cash balance and is therefore dependent on the continuing support of short-term borrowing in order to meet obligations when they fall due. When considering the long-term financing of the business, we can see that about 37% (that is, 260/(260 + 441)) of the total long-term finance for the business has been supplied by borrowings and about 63% (that is, 441/(260 + 441)) by the owners. This level of long-term borrowing seems quite high but not excessive. However, we would need to know more about the ability of the business to service the borrowing (that is, make interest payments and repayments of the amount borrowed) before a full assessment could be made.

## Chapter 3

**3.1**   (a) Equity does increase as a result of the owners introducing more cash into the business, but it will also increase as a result of introducing other assets (for example, a motor car) and by the business generating revenue by trading. Similarly, equity decreases not only as a result of withdrawals of cash by owners but also by withdrawals of other assets (for example, inventory for the owners' personal use) and through trading expenses being incurred. For the typical business in a typical accounting period, equity will alter much more as a result of trading activities than for any other reason.

(b) An accrued expense is not one that relates to next year. It is one that needs to be matched with the revenue of the accounting period under review, but that has yet to be met in terms of cash payment. As such, it will appear on the statement of financial position as a current liability.

(c) The purpose of depreciation is not to provide for asset replacement. Rather, it is an attempt to allocate the cost, or fair value, of the asset (less any residual value) over its useful life. Depreciation is an attempt to provide a measure of the amount of the non-current asset that has been consumed during the period. This amount will then be charged as an expense for the period in deriving the profit figure. Depreciation is a book entry (the outlay of cash occurs when the asset is purchased) and does not normally entail setting aside a separate amount of cash for asset replacement. Even if this were done, there would be no guarantee that sufficient funds would be available at the end of the asset's life for its replacement. Factors such as inflation and technological change may mean that the replacement cost is higher than the original cost of the asset.

(d) In the short term, it is possible for the current value of a non-current asset to exceed its original cost. However, nearly all non-current assets will wear out over time as a result of being used to generate wealth for the business. This will be the case for freehold buildings. As a result, some measure of depreciation should be calculated to take account of the fact that the asset is being consumed. Some businesses revalue their buildings where the current value is significantly different from the original cost. Where this occurs, the depreciation charged should be based on the revalued amount (fair value). This will normally result in higher depreciation charges than if the asset remained at its historic cost.

**3.3**   The existence of profit and downward movement in cash may be for various reasons, which include the following:

- the purchase of assets for cash during the period (for example, motor cars and inventories), which were not all consumed during the period and are therefore not having as great an effect on expenses as they are on cash;
- the payment of an outstanding liability (for example, borrowings), which will have an effect on cash but not on expenses in the income statement;
- the withdrawal of cash by the owners from the equity invested, which will not have an effect on the expenses in the income statement;
- the generation of revenue on credit where the cash has yet to be received. This will increase the sales revenue for the period but will not have a beneficial effect on the cash balance until a later period.

**3.5**

| | | |
|---|---|---:|
| (a) | Rent payable – expense for period | £9,000 |
| (b) | Rates and insurance – expense for period | £6,000 |
| (c) | General expenses – paid in period | £7,000 |
| (d) | Interest (on borrowings) payable – prepaid | £500 |
| (e) | Salaries – paid in period | £6,000 |
| (f) | Rent receivable – received during period | £3,000 |

**3.7** **Nikov and Co**

An examination of the income statements for the two years reveals a number of interesting points, which include:

- An increase in sales value and gross profit of 9.9% in 2011.
- The gross profit expressed as a percentage of sales revenue remaining at 70%.
- An increase in salaries of 7.2%.
- An increase in selling and distribution costs of 31.2%.
- An increase in bad debts of 392.5%.
- A decline in profit for the year of 39.3%.
- A decline in the profit for the year as a percentage of sales revenue from 13.3% to 7.4%.

Thus, the business has enjoyed an increase in sales revenue and gross profits, but this has failed to translate to an increase in profit for the year because of the significant rise in overheads. The increase in selling costs during 2011 suggests that the increase in sales revenue was achieved by greater marketing effort, and the huge increase in bad debts suggests that the increase in sales revenue may be attributable to selling to less creditworthy customers or to a weak debt-collection policy. There appears to have been a change of policy in 2011 towards sales, and this has not been successful overall as the profit for the year has shown a dramatic decline.

## Chapter 4

**4.1** Limited companies can no more set a limit on the amount of debts they will meet than can human beings. They must meet their debts up to the limit of their assets, just as we as individuals must. In the context of owners' claim, 'reserves' mean part of the owners' claim against the assets of the company. These assets may or may not include cash. The legal ability of the company to pay dividends is not related to the amount of cash that it has.

Preference shares do not carry a guaranteed dividend. They simply guarantee that the preference shareholders have a right to the first slice of any dividend that is paid. Shares of many companies can, in effect, be bought by one investor from another through the Stock Exchange. Such a transaction has no direct effect on the company, however. These are not new shares being offered by the company, but existing shares that are being sold 'second-hand'.

**4.2** (a) The first part of the quote is incorrect. Bonus shares should not, of themselves, increase the value of the shareholders' wealth. This is because reserves, belonging to the shareholders, are used to create bonus shares. Thus, each shareholder's stake in the company has not increased.

(b) This statement is incorrect. Shares can be issued at any price, provided that it is not below the nominal value of the shares. Once the company has been trading profitably for a period, the shares will not be worth the same as they were (the nominal value) when the company was first formed. In such circumstances, issuing shares at above their nominal value would not only be legal, but essential to preserve the wealth of the existing shareholders relative to any new ones.

(c) This statement is incorrect. From a legal perspective, the company is limited to a maximum dividend of the current extent of its revenue reserves. This amounts to any after-tax profits or gains realised that have not been eroded through, for example, payments of previous dividends. Legally, cash is not an issue; it would be perfectly legal for a company to borrow the funds to pay a dividend – although whether such an action would be commercially prudent is another question.

(d) This statement is partly incorrect. Companies do indeed have to pay tax on their profits. Depending on their circumstances, shareholders might also have to pay tax on their dividends.

**4.4** **Iqbal Ltd**

| Year | Maximum dividend £ | |
|------|------|------|
| 2007 | 0 | No profit exists out of which to pay a dividend |
| 2008 | 0 | There remains a cumulative loss of £7,000. Since the revaluation represents a gain that has not been realised, it cannot be used to justify a dividend |
| 2009 | 13,000 | The cumulative net realised gains are derived as (–£15,000 + £8,000 + £15,000 + £5,000) |
| 2010 | 14,000 | The realised profits and gains for the year |
| 2011 | 22,000 | The realised profits and gains for the year |

**4.6** **Pear Limited**

**Statement of financial position as at 30 September 2011**

| | £000 |
|------|------|
| **ASSETS** | |
| **Non-current assets** | |
| *Property, plant and equipment* | |
| Cost (1,570 + 30) | 1,600 |
| Depreciation (690 + 12) | (702) |
| | 898 |
| **Current assets** | |
| Inventories | 207 |
| Receivables (182 + 18 – 4) | 196 |
| Cash at bank | 21 |
| | 424 |
| **Total assets** | 1,322 |
| **EQUITY AND LIABILITIES** | |
| **Equity** | |
| Shares capital | 300 |
| Share premium account | 300 |
| Retained earnings (104 + 41 – 25) | 120 |
| | 720 |
| **Non-current liabilities** | |
| Borrowings 10% loan (repayable 2012) | 300 |
| **Current liabilities** | |
| Trade payables | 88 |
| Other payables (20 + 30 + 15 + 2) | 67 |
| Taxation | 17 |
| Dividend approved | 25 |
| Borrowings – Bank overdraft | 105 |
| | 302 |
| **Total equity and liabilities** | 1,322 |

**Income statement for the year ended 30 September 2011**

|  | £000 |
|---|---:|
| Revenue (1,456 + 18) | 1,474 |
| Cost of sales | (768) |
| Gross profit | 706 |
| Salaries | (220) |
| Depreciation (249 + 12) | (261) |
| Other operating costs (131 + (2% × 200) + 2) | (137) |
| Operating profit | 88 |
| Interest payable (15 + 15) | (30) |
| Profit before taxation | 58 |
| Taxation (58 × 30%) | (17) |
| Profit for the year | 41 |

## Chapter 5

### 5.1 The amount of published financial information

Some believe that the annual reports of companies are becoming too long and contain too much information. A few examples of the length of the 2011 accounts of large companies are as follows:

| Marks and Spencer plc | 116 pages |
|---|---|
| Tesco plc | 162 pages |
| National Grid plc | 185 pages |
| BT Group plc | 186 pages |

There is a danger that users will suffer from information overload if they are confronted with an excessive amount of information and that they will be unable to cope with it. This may, in turn, lead them to:

- fail to distinguish between important and less important information;
- fail to approach the analysis of information in a logical and systematic manner;
- feel a sense of confusion and avoid the task of analysing the information.

Lengthy annual reports are likely to be a particular problem for the less sophisticated user. This has been recognised and many companies publish summarised accounts for private investors, which include only the key points. For sophisticated users, however, the problem may be that the annual reports are still not long enough. They often wish to glean as much information as possible from the company in order to make investment decisions.

**5.3**  **I. Ching (Booksellers) plc**

### Statement of comprehensive income for the year ended 31 December 2011

|  | £000 |
|---|---|
| Revenue | 943 |
| Cost of sales | (460) |
| **Gross profit** | 483 |
| Distribution expenses | (110) |
| Administration expenses | (212) |
| Other expenses | (25) |
| **Operating profit** | 136 |
| Finance charges | (40) |
| **Profit before tax** | 96 |
| Taxation | (24) |
| **Profit for the period** | 72 |
| *Other comprehensive income* |  |
| Revaluation of property, plant and equipment | 20 |
| Foreign currency translation differences for foreign operations | (15) |
| Tax on other comprehensive income | (1) |
| Other comprehensive income for the year, net of tax | 4 |
| **Total comprehensive income for the year** | 76 |

**5.4**  **Manet plc**

### Statement of changes in equity for the year ended 31 December 2011

|  | Share capital £m | Share premium £m | Revaluation reserve £m | Translation reserve £m | Retained earnings £m | Total £m |
|---|---|---|---|---|---|---|
| Balance as at 1 January 2011 | 250 | 50 | 120 | 15 | 380 | 815 |
| Changes in equity for the year ended 31 December 2011 |  |  |  |  |  |  |
| Dividends (Note 1) |  |  |  |  | (80) | (80) |
| Total comprehensive income for the year (Note 2) |  |  | 30 | (5) | 160 | 185 |
| Balance at 31 December 2011 | 250 | 50 | 150 | 10 | 460 | 920 |

**Notes:**

(1) Dividends have been shown in the statement rather than in the notes. Either approach, however, is acceptable.

(2) The effect of each component of comprehensive income on each component of shareholder equity must be shown. The revaluation gain and loss on exchange translation are each transferred to a specific reserve and the profit for the year is transferred to retained earnings.

**5.7**  **Dali plc**

A striking feature of the segmental reports is that the car parts segment generates the highest revenue – more than the other two segments combined. Nevertheless, it is the aircr... parts segment that generates the highest profit. Although we shall be considering fina... ratios in detail in Chapter 7, we can use some simple ratios at this point to help e... performance.

We can start by considering the profit generated in relation to the sales revenue for each operating segment. We can see from the table below that the boat parts segment generates the most profit in relation to sales revenue. Around 21%, or £0.21 in every £1, of profit is derived from the sales revenue generated. The total revenue for this segment, however, is much lower than for the other two segments. Although the car parts segment generates the most revenue, less than 6%, or £0.06 in every £1, of profit is derived from the sales revenue generated. It is worth noting that the aircraft parts segment suffered a large impairment charge during the year, which had a significant effect on profits. The reasons for this impairment charge should be investigated.

We can also compare the profit generated with the net assets employed (that is, total assets – total liabilities) for each segment. We can see from the table below that the boat parts segment produces the best return on net assets employed by far: around 82%, that is, £0.82 for every £1 invested. Once again, the car parts segment produces the worst results with a return of less than 24%.

The relatively poor results from the car parts segment may simply reflect the nature of the market in which it operates. Compared with car parts segments of other businesses, it may be doing very well. Nevertheless, the business may still wish to consider whether future investment would not be better directed to those areas where greater profits can be found.

The investment in non-current assets during the period in relation to the total assets held is much higher for the boat parts segment. This may reflect the faith of the directors in the potential of this segment.

The depreciation charge as a percentage of segment assets seems to be high for all of the operating segments – but particularly for the car parts division. This should be investigated as it may suggest poor buying decisions.

### Table of key results

|  | Car | Aircraft | Boat |
|---|---|---|---|
| Total revenue | £360m | £210m | £85m |
| Segment profit | £20m | £24m | £18m |
| Net assets (assets – liabilities) | £85m | £58m | £22m |
| Segment profit as a percentage of sales revenue | 5.6% | 11.4% | 21.2% |
| Segment profit as a percentage of net assets employed | 23.5% | 41.4% | 81.8% |
| Expenditure on non-current assets | £28m | £23m | £26m |
| Depreciation as a percentage of segment assets | 47.1% | 44.0% | 34.1% |

## Chapter 6

(a) An increase in the level of inventories would, ultimately, have an adverse effect on cash.
rights issue of ordinary shares will give rise to a positive cash flow, which will be
the 'financing' section of the statement of cash flows.
f ordinary shares has no cash flow effect.
of the value of the inventories has no cash flow effect.
of a large number of shares by a major shareholder has no cash flow
business is concerned.
s not involve cash at all. Using the indirect method of deducing cash
ating activities involves the depreciation expense in the calculation, but
because we are trying to find out from the profit before taxation (after
igure what the profit before taxation *and* depreciation must have been.

**6.3**  **Torrent plc**

### Statement of cash flows for the year ended 31 December 2011

|  | £m |
|---|---:|
| **Cash flows from operating activities** | |
| Profit before taxation (after interest) (see Note 1 below) | 170 |
| Adjustments for: | |
| Depreciation (Note 2) | 78 |
| Interest expense (Note 3) | 26 |
|  | 274 |
| Decrease in inventories (41 – 35) | 6 |
| Increase in trade receivables (145 – 139) | (6) |
| Decrease in trade payables (54 – 41) | (13) |
| *Cash generated from operations* | 261 |
| Interest paid | (26) |
| Taxation paid (Note 4) | (41) |
| Dividend paid | (60) |
| *Net cash from operating activities* | 134 |
| **Cash flows from investing activities** | |
| Payments to acquire plant and machinery | (67) |
| *Net cash used in investing activities* | (67) |
| **Cash flows from financing activities** | |
| Redemption of loan notes (250 – 150) (Note 5) | (100) |
| *Net cash used in financing activities* | (100) |
| **Net decrease in cash and cash equivalents** | (33) |
| Cash and cash equivalents at 1 January 2011 | |
| Bank overdraft | (56) |
| Cash and cash equivalents at 31 December 2011 | |
| Bank overdraft | (89) |

To see how this relates to the cash of the business at the beginning and end of the year it can be useful to provide a reconciliation as follows:

### Analysis of cash and cash equivalents during the year ended 31 December 2011

|  | £m |
|---|---:|
| Cash and cash equivalents at 1 January 2011 | (56) |
| Net cash outflow | (33) |
| Cash and cash equivalents at 31 December 2011 | (89) |

**Notes:**

(1)  This is simply taken from the income statement for the year.

(2)  Since there were no disposals, the depreciation charges must be the difference between the start and end of the year's plant and machinery values, adjusted by the cost of any additions.

|  | £m |
|---|---:|
| Carrying amount at 1 January 2011 | 325 |
| Additions | 67 |
| Depreciation (balancing figure) | (78) |
| Carrying amount at 31 December 2011 | 314 |

(3)  Interest payable expense must be taken out, by adding it back to the profit before taxation fi[...] subsequently deduct the cash paid for interest payable during the year. In this case the two[...] identical.

(4)  Companies pay 50% of their tax during their accounting year and 50% in the following[...] 2011 payment would have been half the tax on the 2010 profit (that is, the figure[...]

appeared in the current liabilities at the end of 2010), plus half of the 2011 tax charge (that is, 23 + ($\frac{1}{2} \times 36$) = 41).

(5) It is assumed that the cash payment to redeem the loan notes was simply the difference between the two statement of financial position figures.

It seems that there was a bonus issue of ordinary shares during the year. These increased by £100m. At the same time, the share premium account balance reduced by £40m (to zero) and the revaluation reserve balance fell by £60m.

**6.6** **Blackstone plc**

### Statement of cash flows for the year ended 31 March 2011

|  | £m |
|---|---|
| **Cash flows from operating activities** | |
| Profit before taxation (after interest) (see Note 1 below) | 1,853 |
| Adjustments for: | |
| Depreciation (Note 2) | 1,289 |
| Interest expense (Note 3) | 456 |
|  | 3,598 |
| Increase in inventories (2,410 – 1,209) | (1,201) |
| Increase in trade receivables (1,173 – 641) | (532) |
| Increase in trade payables (1,507 – 931) | 576 |
| *Cash generated from operations* | 2,441 |
| Interest paid | (456) |
| Taxation paid (Note 4) | (300) |
| Dividend paid | (400) |
| *Net cash from operating activities* | 1,285 |
| **Cash flows from investing activities** | |
| Proceeds of disposals | 54 |
| Payment to acquire intangible non-current asset | (700) |
| Payments to acquire property, plant and equipment | (4,578) |
| *Net cash used in investing activities* | (5,224) |
| **Cash flows from financing activities** | |
| Bank borrowings | 2,000 |
| *Net cash from financing activities* | 2,000 |
| **Net decrease in cash and cash equivalents** | (1,939) |
| Cash and cash equivalents at 1 April 2010 | |
| Cash at bank | 123 |
| Cash and cash equivalents at 31 March 2011 | |
| Bank overdraft | (1,816) |

To see how this relates to the cash of the business at the beginning and end of the year it can be useful to provide a reconciliation as follows:

**~ash and cash equivalents during the year ended 31 March 2011**

|  | £m |
|---|---|
| cash equivalents at 1 April 2010 | 123 |
| tflow | (1,939) |
| h equivalents at 31 March 2011 | 1,816 |

m the income statement for the year.

charge was that stated in Note 2 to the question (£1,251m), plus the deficit on current assets. According to Note 2, these non-current assets had originally cost

£581m and had been depreciated by £489m, that is a net carrying amount of £92m. They were sold for £54m, leading to a deficit on disposal of £38m. Thus the full depreciation expense for the year was £1,289m (that is, £1,251m + £38m).

(3) Interest payable expense must be taken out, by adding it back to the profit before taxation figure. We subsequently deduct the cash paid for interest payable during the year. In this case the two figures are identical.

(4) Companies pay tax at 50% during their accounting year and the other 50% in the following year. Thus the 2011 payment would have been half the tax on the 2010 profit (that is, the figure that would have appeared in the current liabilities at 31 March 2010), plus half of the 2011 tax charge (that is, 105 + ($\frac{1}{2}$ × 390) = 300).

**6.7**  **York plc**

### Statement of cash flows for the year ended 30 September 2011

|  | £m |
|---|---|
| **Cash flows from operating activities** | |
| Profit before taxation (after interest) (see Note 1 below) | 10.0 |
| Adjustments for: | |
| Depreciation (Note 2) | 9.8 |
| Interest expense (Note 3) | 3.0 |
| | 22.8 |
| Increase in inventories and trade receivables (122.1 − 119.8) | (2.3) |
| Increase in trade payables (82.5 − 80.0) | 2.5 |
| *Cash generated from operations* | 23.0 |
| Interest paid | (3.0) |
| Taxation paid (Note 4) | (2.3) |
| Dividend paid | (3.5) |
| *Net cash from operating activities* | 14.2 |
| **Cash flows from investing activities** | |
| Proceeds of disposals (Note 2) | 5.2 |
| Payments to acquire non-current assets | (20.0) |
| *Net cash used in investing activities* | (14.8) |
| **Cash flows from financing activities** | |
| Increase in long-term borrowings | 3.0 |
| Share issue (Note 5) | 5.0 |
| *Net cash from financing activities* | 8.0 |
| **Net increase in cash and cash equivalents** | 7.4 |
| Cash and cash equivalents at 1 October 2010 | |
| Cash at bank | 9.2 |
| Cash and cash equivalents at 30 September 2011 | |
| Cash at bank | 16.6 |

To see how this relates to the cash of the business at the beginning and end of the year it can be useful to provide a reconciliation as follows:

### Analysis of cash and cash equivalents during the year ended 30 September 2011

|  | £m |
|---|---|
| Cash and cash equivalents at 1 October 2010 | 9.2 |
| Net cash inflow | 7.4 |
| Cash and cash equivalents at 30 September 2011 | 16.6 |

**Notes:**

(1) This is simply taken from the income statement for the year.

(2) The full depreciation charge was the £13.0m, less the surplus on disposal (£3.2m), both stated in Note 1 to the question. (According to the table in Note 4 to the question, the non-current assets disposed of had a net carrying value of £2.0m. To produce a surplus of £3.2m, they must have been sold for £5.2m.)

(3) Interest payable expense must be taken out, by adding it back to the profit before taxation figure. We subsequently deduct the cash paid for interest payable during the year. In this case the two figures are identical.

(4) Companies pay 50% of their tax during their accounting year and the other 50% in the following year. Thus the 2011 payment would have been half the tax on the 2010 profit (that is, the figure that would have appeared in the current liabilities at 30 September 2010), plus half of the 2011 tax charge (that is, $1.0 + (1/2 \times 2.6) = 2.3$).

(5) This issue must have been for cash since it could not have been a bonus issue – the share premium is untouched and 'Reserves' had altered over the year only by the amount of the 2011 retained earnings (profit for the year, less the dividend). The shares seem to have been issued at par (that is, at their nominal value). This is a little surprising since the business has assets that seem to be above that value. On the other hand, were this a rights issue, the low issue price would not have disadvantaged the existing shareholders since they were also the beneficiaries of the advantage of the low issue price.

## Chapter 7

### 7.1 Three businesses

A plc operates a supermarket chain. The grocery business is highly competitive and to generate high sales volumes it is usually necessary to accept low operating profit margins. Thus, we can see that the operating profit margin of A plc is the lowest of the three businesses. The inventories' turnover period of supermarket chains also tend to be quite low. They are often efficient in managing inventories, and most supermarket chains have invested heavily in inventories' control and logistical systems over the years. The average settlement period for receivables is very low as most sales are for cash: although where a customer pays by credit card, there is usually a small delay before the supermarket receives the amount due. A low inventories turnover period and a low average settlement period for receivables usually mean that the investment in current assets is low. Hence, the current ratio (current assets/ current liabilities) is also low.

B plc is the holiday tour operator. We can see that the sales to capital employed ratio is the highest of the three businesses. This is because tour operators do not usually require a large investment of capital: they do not need a large asset base in order to conduct their operations. The inventories' turnover period ratio does not apply to B plc. It is a service business, which does not hold inventories for resale. We can see that the average settlement period _____eivables is low. This may be because customers are invoiced near to the holiday date _____unts outstanding and must pay before going on holiday. The lack of inventories _____rage settlement period for receivables leads to a very low current ratio.

_____d manufacturing business. We can see that the sales to capital employed _____f the three businesses. This is because manufacturers tend to invest heav_____d non-current assets. The inventories turnover period is the highest of _____Three different kinds of inventories – raw materials, work in progress _____e held by manufacturers. The average receivables' settlement period _____e three businesses. Manufacturers tend to sell to other businesses _____and their customers will normally demand credit. A one-month _____rs is fairly common for manufacturing businesses, although _____iscount for prompt payment. The relatively high investment in _____es usually results in a high current ratio.

### 7.2  Amsterdam Ltd and Berlin Ltd

The ratios for Amsterdam Ltd and Berlin Ltd reveal that the average settlement period for trade receivables for Amsterdam Ltd is three times that for Berlin Ltd. Berlin Ltd is therefore much quicker in collecting amounts outstanding from customers. On the other hand, there is not much difference between the two businesses in the time taken to pay trade payables.

It is interesting to compare the difference in the trade receivables and payables settlement periods for each business. As Amsterdam Ltd allows an average of 63 days' credit to its customers, yet pays suppliers within 50 days, it will require greater investment in working capital than Berlin Ltd, which allows an average of only 21 days to its customers but takes 45 days to pay its suppliers.

Amsterdam Ltd has a much higher gross profit margin than Berlin Ltd. However, the operating profit margin for the two businesses is identical. This suggests that Amsterdam Ltd has much higher overheads (as a percentage of sales revenue) than Berlin Ltd. The average inventories turnover period for Amsterdam Ltd is more than twice that of Berlin Ltd. This may be due to the fact that Amsterdam Ltd maintains a wider range of inventories in an attempt to meet customer requirements. The evidence therefore suggests that Amsterdam Ltd is the one that prides itself on personal service. The higher average settlement period for trade receivables is consistent with a more relaxed attitude to credit collection (thereby maintaining customer goodwill) and the high overheads are consistent with incurring the additional costs of satisfying customers' requirements. Amsterdam Ltd's high inventories levels are consistent with maintaining a wide range of inventories, with the aim of satisfying a range of customer needs.

Berlin Ltd has the characteristics of a more price-competitive business. Its gross profit margin is much lower than that of Amsterdam Ltd, that is, a much lower gross profit for each £1 of sales revenue. However, overheads have been kept low, the effect being that the operating profit margin is the same as Amsterdam Ltd's. The low average inventories turnover period and average settlement period for trade receivables are consistent with a business that wishes to minimise investment in current assets, thereby reducing costs.

### 7.6  Ali plc and Bhaskar plc

(a)  The Altman model Z-score model is as follows:

$$Z = 0.717a + 0.847b + 3.107c + 0.420d + 0.998e$$

where    a = Working capital/Total assets
           b = Accumulated retained profits/Total assets
           c = Operating profit/Total assets
           d = Book (statement of financial position) value of ordinary and preference shares/Total liabilities at book (statement of financial position) value
           e = Sales revenue/Total assets

For Ali plc, the Z score is:

$$0.717[(853.0 - 422.4)/1,300.0] + 0.847(367.6/1,300.0) + 3.107(151.3/1,300.0)$$
$$+ 0.420[320.0/(190.0 + 422.4)] + 0.998(1,478.1/1,300.0) = \underline{2.193}$$

For Bhaskar plc, the Z score is:

$$0.717[(816.5 - 293.1)/1,417.7] + 0.847(624.6/1,417.7) + 3.107(166.9/1$$
$$+ 0.420[250.0/(250.0 + 293.1)] + 0.998(1,790.4/1,417.7) = \underline{2.4}$$

(b)  The Z scores for these two businesses are quite close, with Bhaskar look
They are both in the category of businesses in the 'zone of ignoran

difficult to classify (a Z score between 1.23 and 4.14). This is quite unusual in that the Altman model is able confidently to classify 91 per cent of businesses. Clearly, these two businesses fall into the remaining 9 per cent.

It is questionable whether the Altman model is strictly applicable to UK businesses, since it was derived from data relating to US businesses that had failed. On the other hand, it probably provides a useful insight.

**7.7 Genesis Ltd**

(a) and (b) Overtrading has been considered in the chapter and you are referred to the relevant section for a more detailed discussion. Briefly, it occurs where a business is trading at a level of activity that cannot be sustained by the finance available. It often results in liquidity problems, slow repayment of borrowings and payables, strained relations with suppliers and the inefficient use of managers' time for day-to-day crisis management.

(c)

$$\text{Current ratio} = \frac{232}{550} = 0.42$$

$$\text{Acid test ratio} = \frac{104}{550} = 0.19$$

$$\text{Inventories turnover period} = \frac{128}{1,248} \times 365 = 37 \text{ days}$$

$$\text{Average settlement period for trade receivables} = \frac{104}{1,640} \times 365 = 23 \text{ days}$$

$$\text{Average settlement period for trade payables} = \frac{184}{1,260} \times 365 = 53 \text{ days}$$

(d) Overtrading must be dealt with either by increasing the level of funding to match the level of activity or by reducing the level of activity to match the funds available. The latter option may result in a reduction in operating profit in the short term but may be necessary to ensure long-term survival.

**Chapter 8**

**8.1 Lombard Ltd**

Relevant costs of undertaking the contract are:

|  | £ |
|---|---|
| cost | 200,000 |
| X (20,000 × 4 × £5) | 400,000 |
| components used will need to be replaced. | |
| (20,000 × 3 × £8) | 480,000 |
| d units will come from inventories and this | |
| tive cost of the net realisable value. | |
| 000 × £8) | 160,000 |
| | 1,240,000 |
| ntract (20,000 × £80) | 1,600,000 |

ial point of view the project is acceptable. (Note that there is no the staff concerned will be paid irrespective of whether the con-

### 8.2 Andrews and Co. Ltd

Minimum contract price

|  |  |  | £ |
|---|---|---|---|
| *Materials* | Steel core: | 10,000 × £2.10 | 21,000 |
|  | Plastic: | 10,000 × 0.10 × £0.10 | 100 |
| *Labour* | Skilled: |  | – |
|  | Unskilled: | 10,000 × 5/60 × £7.50 | 6,250 |
| Minimum tender price |  |  | 27,350 |

### 8.5 The local education authority

(a) One-off financial net benefits of closing:

|  | D only | A and B | A and C |
|---|---|---|---|
| Capacity reduction | 800 | 700 | 800 |
|  | £m | £m | £m |
| Property developer (A) | – | 14.0 | 14.0 |
| Shopping complex (B) | – | 8.0 | – |
| Property developer (D) | 9.0 | – | – |
| Safety (C) | – | – | 3.0 |
| Adapt facilities | (1.8) | – | – |
| Total | 7.2 | 22.0 | 17.0 |
| Ranking based on total one-off benefits | 3 | 1 | 2 |

(Note that all of the past cost of buying and improving the schools are irrelevant.)

Recurrent financial net benefits of closing:

|  | D only £m | A and B £m | A and C £m |
|---|---|---|---|
| Rent (C) | – | – | 0.3 |
| Administrators | 0.2 | 0.4 | 0.4 |
| Total | 0.2 | 0.4 | 0.7 |
| Ranking based on total of recurrent benefits | 3 | 2 | 1 |

On the basis of the financial figures alone, closure of either A and B or A and C looks best. It is not possible to add the one-off and the recurring costs directly, but the large one-off cost saving associated with closing schools A and B makes this option look attractive. (In Chapter 14 we shall see that it is possible to combine one-off and recurring costs in a way that should lead to sensible conclusions.)

(b) The cost of acquiring and improving the schools in the past is a past cost or a sunk cost and, therefore, irrelevant. The cost of employing the chief education officer is a future cost, but irrelevant because it is not dependent on outcomes, it is a common cost.

(c) There are many other factors, some of a non-quantifiable nature. These include:

- Accuracy of projections of capacity requirements.
- Location of existing schools relative to where potential pupils live.
- Political acceptability of selling schools to property developers.
- Importance of purely financial issues in making the final decision.
- The quality of the replacement sporting facilities compared with the
- Political acceptability of staff redundancies.
- Possible savings/cost of employing fewer teachers, which might omies of scale are available by having fewer schools.
- Staff morale.

### 8.6  Rob Otics Ltd

(a) The minimum price for the proposed contract would be:

| | £ |
|---|---:|
| Materials | |
| Component X (2 × 8 × £180) | 2,880 |
| If the 16 units of this component are used on the proposed contract, the business will need to buy an additional 16 units at the new price | |
| Component Y | 0 |
| The history of the components held in inventories is irrelevant because it applies irrespective of the decision made on this contract. Since the alternative to using the units on this contract is to scrap them, the relevant cost is zero. | |
| Component Z [(75 + 32) × £20] − (75 × £25) | 265 |
| The relevant cost here is how much extra the business will pay the supplier as a result of undertaking the contract | |
| Other miscellaneous items | 250 |
| Labour | |
| Assembly (25 + 24 + 23 + 22 + 21 + 20 + 19 + 18) × £48 | 8,256 |
| The assembly labour cost is irrelevant because it will be incurred irrespective of which work the members of staff do. The relevant cost is based on the sales revenue per hour lost if the other orders are lost less the material cost per hour saved; that is £60 − £12 = £48 | |
| Inspection (8 × 6 × £12 × 150%) | 864 |
| Total | 12,515 |

Thus the minimum price is £12,515.

(b) Other factors include:

- Competitive state of the market.
- The fact that the above figure is unique to the particular circumstances at the time – for example, having Component Y available but having no use for it. Any subsequent order might have to take account of an outlay cost.
- Breaking even (that is, just covering the cost) on a contract will not fulfil the business's objective.
- Charging a low price may cause marketing problems. Other customers may resent the low price for this contract. The current enquirer may expect a similar price in future.

nter 9

int = fixed cost/contribution per unit

= (80,000 + 60,000)/[60 − (20 + 14 + 12 + 3)] = 12,727.27 radios.

usiness would need to sell 12,728 radios before it would break even.
e a sales value of £763,680 (that is, 12,728 × £60).
is 7,272 radios (that is, 20,000 − 12,728). This margin would have
320 (that is, 7,272 × £60).

### 9.3 Gandhi Ltd

(a) Given that the spare capacity could not be used by other services, the standard service should continue to be offered. This is because it renders a positive contribution.

(b) The standard service renders a contribution per unit of £15 (that is, £80 – £65), or £30 during the time it would take to render one unit of the nova service. The nova service would provide a contribution of only £25 (that is, £75 – £50).

　　The nova service should, therefore, not replace the standard service.

(c) Under the original plans, the following contributions would be rendered by the basic and standard services:

|  |  | £ |
|---|---|---|
| Basic | 11,000 × (£50 – £25) = | 275,000 |
| Standard | 6,000 × (£80 – £65) = | 90,000 |
|  |  | 365,000 |

If the basic were to take the standard's place, 17,000 units (that is, 11,000 + 6,000) of them could be produced in total. To generate the same total contribution, each unit of the standard service would need to provide £21.47 (that is, £365,000/17,000) of contribution. Given the basic's variable cost of £25, this would mean a selling price of £46.47 each (that is £21.47 + £25.00).

### 9.6 Products A, B and C

(a) Total time required on cutting machines is:

$$(2{,}500 \times 1.0) + (3{,}400 \times 1.0) + (5{,}100 \times 0.5) = 8{,}450 \text{ hours}$$

Total time available on cutting machines is 5,000 hours. Therefore, this is a limiting factor.

　　Total time required on assembling machines is:

$$(2{,}500 \times 0.5) + (3{,}400 \times 1.0) + (5{,}100 \times 0.5) = 7{,}200 \text{ hours}$$

Total time available on assembling machines is 8,000 hours. Therefore, this is not a limiting factor.

|  | A (per unit) £ | B (per unit) £ | C (per unit) £ |
|---|---|---|---|
| Selling price | 25 | 30 | 18 |
| Variable materials | (12) | (13) | (10) |
| Variable production cost | (7) | (4) | (3) |
| Contribution | 6 | 13 | 5 |
| Time on cutting machines | 1.0 hour | 1.0 hour | 0.5 hour |
| Contribution per hour on cutting machines | £6 | £13 | £10 |
| Order of priority | 3rd | 1st | 2nd |

Therefore, produce:

| 3,400 product B using | 3,400 hours |
|---|---|
| 3,200 product C using | 1,600 hours |
|  | 5,000 hours |

(b) Assuming that the business would make no saving in variable production cost by sub-contracting, it would be worth paying up to the contribution per unit (£5) for product C, which would therefore be £5 × (5,100 – 3,200) = £9,500 in total.

　　Similarly it would be worth paying up to £6 per unit for product A – that is, £6 × 2,500 = £15,000 in total.

**9.7** **Darmor Ltd**

(a) Contribution per hour of skilled labour of product X is:

$$\frac{£(30 - 6 - 2 - 12 - 3)}{\left(\dfrac{6}{12}\right)} = £14$$

Given the scarcity of skilled labour, if the management is to be indifferent between the products, the contribution per skilled-labour-hour must be the same. Thus for product Y the selling price must be:

$$[£(14 \times (9/12)) + 9 + 4 + 25 + 7] = £55.50$$

(that is, the contribution plus the variable cost), and for product Z the selling price must be:

$$[£(14 \times (3/12)) + 3 + 10 + 14 + 7] = £37.50$$

(b) The business could pay up to £26 an hour (£12 + £14) for additional hours of skilled labour. This is the potential contribution per hour, before taking account of the labour rate of £12 an hour.

# Chapter 10

**10.1** **Offending phrases and explanations**

| Offending phrase | Explanation |
| --- | --- |
| 'Necessary to divide up the business into departments' | This can be done but it will not always be of much benefit. Only in quite restricted circumstances will it give a significantly different job cost. |
| 'Fixed costs (or overheads)' | This implies that fixed cost and overheads are the same thing. They are not really connected with one another. 'Fixed' is to do with how cost behaves as the level of output is raised or lowered; 'overheads' are to do with the extent to which cost can be directly measured in respect of a particular unit of output. Though it is true that many overheads are fixed, not all are. Also, direct labour is usually a fixed cost. |
| | All of the other references to fixed and variable costs are wrong. The person should have referred to indirect and direct costs. |
| 'Usually this is done on the basis of area' | Where overheads are apportioned to departments, they will be apportioned on some logical basis. For certain elements of cost – for example, rent – the floor area may be the most logical; for others, such as machine maintenance cost, the floor area would be totally inappropriate. |
| 'When the total fixed costs for each department have been identified, this will be divided by the number of hours that were worked' | Where overheads are dealt with on a departmental basis, they may be divided by the number of direct labour hours to deduce a recovery rate. However, this is only one basis of applying overheads to jobs. For example, machine hours or some other basis may be more appropriate to the particular circumstances involved. |
| 'It is essential that this approach is taken in order to deduce a selling price' | It is relatively unusual for the 'job cost' to be able to dictate the price at which the manufacturer can price its output. For many businesses, the market dictates the price. |

**10.4** **Promptprint Ltd**

(a) The plan (budget) may be summarised as:

|  | £ |
|---|---|
| Sales revenue | 196,000 |
| Direct materials | (38,000) |
| Direct labour | (32,000) |
| Total indirect cost | (77,000) |
| Profit | 49,000 |

(2,400 + 3,000 + 27,600 + 36,000 + 8,000)

The job may be priced on the basis that both indirect cost and profit should be apportioned to it on the basis of direct labour cost, as follows:

|  | £ |  |
|---|---|---|
| Direct materials | 4,000 |  |
| Direct labour | 3,600 |  |
| Overheads | 8,663 | (£77,000 × 3,600/32,000) |
| Profit | 5,513 | (£49,000 × 3,600/32,000) |
|  | 21,776 |  |

This answer assumes that variable overheads vary in proportion to direct labour cost.

Various other bases of charging overheads and profit loading the job could have been adopted. For example, materials cost could have been included (with direct labour) as the basis for profit loading, or even apportioning overheads.

(b) This part of the question is, in effect, asking for comments on the validity of 'full cost-plus' pricing. This approach can be useful as an indicator of the effective long-run cost of doing the job. On the other hand, it fails to take account of relevant opportunity cost as well as the state of the market and other external factors. For example, it ignores the price that a competitor printing business may quote.

(c) Revised estimates of direct material cost for the job:

|  | £ |  |
|---|---|---|
| Paper grade 1 | 1,500 | (£1,200 × 125%) This item of inventories needs to be replaced |
| Paper grade 2 | 0 | It has no opportunity cost value |
| Card | 510 | (£640 – £130: using the card on another job would save £640, but cost £130 to achieve that saving) |
| Inks and so on | 300 | This item of inventories needs to be replaced |
|  | 2,310 |  |

**10.5** (a) Charging overheads to jobs on a departmental basis means that overheads are collected 'product' cost centre (department) by 'product' cost centre. This involves picking up the overheads that are direct to each department and adding to them a share of overheads that are general to the business as a whole. The overheads of 'service' cost centres must then be apportioned to the product cost centres. At this point, all of the overheads for the whole business are divided between the 'product' cost centres, such that the sum of the 'product' cost centre overheads equals those for the whole business.

Dealing with overheads departmentally is believed to provide more fair and useful information to decision makers, because different departments may have rather different overheads, and applying overheads departmentally can take account of that and reflect it in the job costs derived.

In theory, dealing with overheads on a departmental basis is more costly than on a business-wide basis. In practice, it possibly does not make too much difference to the cost of collecting the information. This is because, normally, businesses are divided into departments, and the costs are collected departmentally, as part of the normal routine for exercising control over the business.

(b) In order to make any difference to the job cost that will emerge as a result of dealing with overheads departmentally, as compared with a business-wide basis, the following *both* need to be the case:

- the overheads per unit of the basis of charging (for example direct labour hours) need to be different from one department to the next; and
- the proportion (but not the actual amounts) of total overheads that are charged to jobs must differ from one job to the next.

Assume, for the sake of argument, that direct labour hours are used as the basis of charging overheads in all departments. Also assume that there are three departments, A, B and C.

There will be no difference to the overheads charged to a particular job if the rate of overheads per direct labour hour is the same for all departments. Obviously, if the charging rate is the same in all departments, that same rate must also apply to the business taken as a whole.

Also, even where overheads per direct labour hour differ significantly from one department to another – if all jobs spend, say, about 20 per cent of their time in Department A, 50 per cent in Department B and 30 per cent in Department C – it will not make any difference whether overheads are charged departmentally or overall.

These conclusions are not in any way dependent on the basis of charging overheads or even whether overheads are charged on the same basis in each department.

The statements above combine to mean that, probably in many cases in practice, departmentalising overheads is not providing information that is significantly different from that which would be provided by charging overheads to jobs on a business-wide basis.

## 10.7   Bookdon plc

(a) To answer this question, we need first to allocate and apportion the overheads to product cost centres, as follows:

| Cost | Basis of apportionment | Total | Machine shop | Fitting section | Canteen | Machine main'ce section |
|---|---|---|---|---|---|---|
| | | £ | £ | £ | £ | £ |
| Allocated items: | Specific | 90,380 | 27,660 | 19,470 | 16,600 | 26,650 |
| Rent, rates, heat, light | Floor area | 17,000 | 9,000 | 3,500 | 2,500 | 2,000 |
| | | | (3,600/ 6,800) | (1,400/ 6,800) | (1,000/ 6,800) | (800/ 6,800) |
| Dep'n and insurance | Book value | 25,000 | 12,500 | 6,250 | 2,500 | 3,750 |
| | | | (150/300) | (75/300) | (30/300) | (45/300) |
| | | 132,380 | 49,160 | 29,220 | 21,600 | 32,400 |
| Canteen | Number of employees | – | 10,800 | 8,400 | (21,600) | 2,400 |
| | | | (18/36) | (14/36) | | (4/36) |
| | | 132,380 | 59,960 | 37,620 | – | 34,800 |
| Machine maintenance section | Specified % | – | 24,360 | 10,440 | – | (34,800) |
| | | | (70%) | (30%) | | |
| | | 132,380 | 84,320 | 48,060 | – | – |

Note that the canteen overheads were reapportioned to the other cost centres first because the canteen renders a service to the machine maintenance section but does not receive a service from it.

Calculation of the overhead absorption (recovery) rates can now proceed:

(1) Total budgeted machine hours are:

|  | Hours |
|---|---|
| Product X (4,200 × 6) | 25,200 |
| Product Y (6,900 × 3) | 20,700 |
| Product Z (1,700 × 4) | 6,800 |
|  | 52,700 |

Overhead absorption rate for the machine shop is:

$$\frac{£84,320}{52,700} = £1.60/\text{machine hour}$$

(2) Total budgeted direct labour cost for the fitting section is:

|  | £ |
|---|---|
| Product X (4,200 × £12) | 50,400 |
| Product Y (6,900 × £3) | 20,700 |
| Product Z (1,700 × £21) | 35,700 |
|  | 106,800 |

Overhead absorption rate for the fitting section is:

$$\frac{£48,060}{£106,800} \times 100\% = 45\% \text{ or } £0.45 \text{ per £ of direct labour cost.}$$

(b) The cost of one unit of product X is calculated as follows:

|  | £ |
|---|---|
| Direct materials | 11.00 |
| Direct labour |  |
| Machine shop | 6.00 |
| Fitting section | 12.00 |
| Overheads |  |
| Machine shop (6 × £1.60) | 9.60 |
| Fitting section (£12 × 45%) | 5.40 |
|  | 44.00 |

Therefore, the cost of one unit of product X is £44.00.

## Chapter 11

### 11.1 Aires plc

The EVA® approach to determining shareholder value will be as follows:

| Year | Opening capital invested (C) £m | Capital charge (12% × C) £m | Operating profit after tax £m | EVA® £m |
|---|---|---|---|---|
| 1 | 64.0 | 7.7 | 12.0 | 4.3 |
| 2 | 48.0 | 5.8 | 12.0 | 6.2 |
| 3 | 32.0 | 3.8 | 12.0 | 8.2 |
| 4 | 16.0 | 1.9 | 12.0 | 10.1 |

### 11.2 The balanced scorecard

(a) The balanced scorecard has nothing to do with the statement of financial position. The former is a framework that translates the aims and objectives of a business into a series of key performance measures and targets. The latter is a statement of the assets of a business and the claims against it; it is sometimes known as the 'balance sheet'.

(b) The finance area of the balanced scorecard specifies financial targets for the future and is usually expressed in terms of financial ratios, such as return on capital employed. The income statement is a historic statement of revenues, the expenses matched against them and the resulting profit or loss.

(c) The balanced scorecard approach does not prescribe a particular set of objectives and targets. It is up to the business concerned to establish its own set of parameters.

(d) The balanced scorecard in no way downplays financial objectives and measures. Financial aspects are key issues in all areas of the balanced scorecard.

### 11.3 Kaplan plc

(a) The business makes each model of suitcase in a batch. The direct cost (materials and labour) will be recorded in respect of each batch. To this cost will be added a share of the overheads of the business for the period in which production of the batch takes place. The basis of the batch absorbing overheads is a matter of managerial judgement. A popular method is direct labour hours spent working on the batch, relative to total direct labour hours worked during the period. This is not the 'correct' way, however. There is no correct way. If the activity is capital intensive, some machine-hour basis of dealing with overheads might be more appropriate, though still not 'correct'. Overheads might be collected, cost centre by cost centre (department by department), and charged to the batch as it passes through each product cost centre. Alternatively, all of the overheads for the entire production facility might be totalled and the overheads dealt with more globally. It is only in restricted circumstances that overheads charged to batches will be affected by a decision to deal with them by cost centres, rather than globally.

Once the 'full cost' (direct cost plus a share of indirect cost) has been ascertained for the batch, the cost per suitcase can be established by dividing the batch cost by the number in the batch.

(b) Whereas the traditional approach to dealing with overheads is just to accept that they exist, and deal with them in a fairly broad manner, ABC takes a much more enquiring approach. ABC takes the view that overheads do not just 'occur', but that they are caused or 'driven' by 'activities'. It is a matter of finding out which activities are driving the cost and how much cost they are driving.

For example, a significant part of the cost of making suitcases of different sizes might be resetting machinery to cope with a batch of a different size from its predecessor batch. Where a particular model is made in very small batches, because it has only a small market, ABC would advocate that this model is charged directly with its machine-setting cost. The traditional approach would be to treat machine setting as a general overhead that the individual suitcases (irrespective of the model) might bear equally. ABC, it is claimed, leads to more accurate costing and thus to more accurate assessment of profitability.

(c) The other advantage of pursuing an ABC philosophy and identifying cost drivers is that, once the drivers have been identified, they are likely to become much more susceptible to being controlled. Thus the ability of management to assess the benefit of certain activities against their cost becomes more feasible.

## 11.5   Badger Ltd

(a) *Price using absorption costing*

Overhead absorption rate = total overheads/total direct labour hours = £280,000/4,000 = £70 per direct labour hour.

|                          | Largeflo | Smallflo |
|--------------------------|:--------:|:--------:|
|                          | £        | £        |
| Direct materials         | 16.00    | 15.00    |
| Direct labour            | 8.00     | 8.00     |
| Overheads: 1/2 × £70     | 35.00    | 35.00    |
| Total cost               | 59.00    | 58.00    |
| Mark up at 35%           | 20.65    | 20.30    |
| Price                    | 79.65    | 78.30    |

(b) *Price using activity based costing*

Cost driver rates:

| | | |
|---|---|---|
| Large machine   | £96,000/480    | = £200 per hour |
| Small machine   | £44,800/1,280  | = £35 per hour |
| Set ups         | £32,500/260    | = £125 per set up |
| Ordering        | £10,800/120    | = £90 per part |
| Handling        | £45,600/380    | = £120 per movement |
| Other overheads | £50,300/4,000  | = £12.58 per direct labour hour |

Prices for the two products

|                  |                     | Largeflo |                   | Smallflo |
|------------------|---------------------|:--------:|-------------------|:--------:|
|                  |                     | £        |                   | £        |
| Direct materials |                     | 16.00    |                   | 16.00    |
| Direct labour    |                     | 8.00     |                   | 8.00     |
| Large machine    | (100 × £200)/1,000  | 20.00    |                   | –        |
| Small machine    |                     |          | (25 × £35)/50     | 17.50    |
| Set ups          | £125/1,000          | 0.13     | (2 × £125)/50     | 5.00     |
| Ordering         |                     | –        | (3 × £90)/50      | 5.40     |
| Handling         | £120/1,000          | 0.12     | (5 × £120)/50     | 12.00    |
| Other overheads  | 1/2 × £12.58        | 6.29     | 1/2 × £12.58      | 6.29     |
| Total cost       |                     | 50.54    |                   | 70.19    |
| 35% mark up      |                     | 17.69    |                   | 24.57    |
| Price            |                     | 68.23    |                   | 94.76    |

(c) *Points for the management*

- Under the traditional approach, the prices are quite similar because the direct costs are quite similar, which also leads to a similar allocation of overheads (because these are absorbed on the basis of direct labour hours).
- With ABC the prices are quite different between the products. This is because the Smallflo product causes much more overhead cost than the Largeflo one and ABC reflects this fact.
- Management must seriously consider its pricing policy. If the traditionally based price is, in fact, the current selling price, the Smallflo product is earning only a small margin.
- If the market will not bear a higher price for Smallflo products, management may consider dropping them and concentrating its efforts on the Largeflo ones. Projected market demand for the two products will obviously have a major bearing on these considerations.

(d) *Practical problems of using ABC*

- Identifying the cost-driving activities and determining cost-driver rates can be difficult and expensive. It is sometimes necessary to use arbitrary approaches to certain parts of the overheads, as with 'other overheads' in the Largeflo/Smallflo example above.
- The costs of introducing ABC may outweigh the benefits.
- Changing the culture necessary to introduce ABC may pose difficulties. There may be resistance to a new approach.
- On a positive note, ABC may have benefits beyond cost determination and pricing. Careful analysis of costs and what drives them can provide a basis for exercising better control over costs.

## Chapter 12

### 12.1 Prolog Ltd

(a) Cash budget for the six months to 30 June

|  | Jan. £000 | Feb. £000 | Mar. £000 | Apr. £000 | May £000 | June £000 |
|---|---|---|---|---|---|---|
| **Receipts** |  |  |  |  |  |  |
| Credit sales revenue (Note 1) | 100 | 100 | 140 | 180 | 220 | 260 |
| **Payments** |  |  |  |  |  |  |
| Trade payables (Note 2) | 112 | 144 | 176 | 208 | 240 | 272 |
| Operating expenses | 4 | 6 | 8 | 10 | 10 | 10 |
| Shelving |  |  |  | 12 |  |  |
| Taxation |  |  | 25 |  |  |  |
|  | 116 | 150 | 209 | 230 | 250 | 282 |
| Cash flow | (16) | (50) | (69) | (50) | (30) | (22) |
| Opening balance | (68) | (84) | (134) | (203) | (253) | (283) |
| Closing balance | (84) | (134) | (203) | (253) | (283) | (305) |

**Notes:**

(1) Sales receipts will equal the month's sales revenue, but be received two months later. For example, the January sales revenue = £2,000 × (50 + 20) = £140,000, to be received in March.

(2) Payments to suppliers will equal the next month's sales requirements, payable the next month. For example, January purchases = £1,600 × (50 + 40) = £144,000, payable in February.

(b) A banker may require various pieces of information before granting additional overdraft facilities. These may include:

- Security available for the loan.
- Details of past profit performance.
- Profit projections for the next 12 months.
- Cash projections beyond the next six months to help assess the prospects of repayment.
- Details of the assumptions underlying projected figures supplied.
- Details of the contractual commitment between Prolog Ltd and its supplier.
- Details of management expertise. Can they manage the expansion programme?
- Details of the new machine and its performance in relation to competing models.
- Details of funds available from owners to finance the expansion.

## 12.3  Nursing Home

(a) The rates per patient for the variable overheads, on the basis of experience during months 1 to 6, are as follows:

| Expense | Amount for 2,700 patients | Amount per patient |
|---|---|---|
| | £ | £ |
| Staffing | 59,400 | 22 |
| Power | 27,000 | 10 |
| Supplies | 54,000 | 20 |
| Other | 8,100 | 3 |
| | 148,500 | 55 |

Since the expected level of activity for the full year is 6,000, the expected level of activity for the second six months is 3,300 (that is, 6,000 − 2,700).

Thus the budget for the second six months will be:

| Variable element: | £ | |
|---|---|---|
| Staffing | 72,600 | (3,300 × £22) |
| Power | 33,000 | (3,300 × £10) |
| Supplies | 66,000 | (3,300 × £20) |
| Other | 9,900 | (3,300 × £3) |
| | 181,500 | (3,300 × £55) |
| | | |
| Fixed element: | | |
| Supervision | 60,000 | 6/12 of the annual figure |
| Depreciation/finance | 93,600 | ditto |
| Other | 32,400 | ditto |
| | 186,000 | (per patient = £56.36 (that is, £186,000/3,300)) |
| Total (second six months) | 367,500 | (per patient = £111.36 (that is, £56.36 + £55.00)) |

(b) For the second six months the actual activity was 3,800 patients. For a valid comparison with the actual outcome, the budget will need to be revised to reflect this activity.

| | Actual cost | Budget (3,800 patients) | Difference |
|---|---|---|---|
| | £ | £ | £ |
| Variable element | 203,300 | 209,000 (3,800 × £55) | 5,700 (saving) |
| Fixed element | 190,000 | 186,000 | 4,000 (overspend) |
| Total | 393,300 | 395,000 | 1,700 (saving) |

(c) Relative to the budget, there was a saving of nearly 3 per cent on the variable element and an overspend of about 2 per cent on fixed cost. Without further information, it is impossible to deduce much more than this.

The differences between the budget and the actual may be caused by some assumptions made in framing the budget for 3,800 patients in the second part of the year. There may be some element of economies of scale in the variable cost; that is, the cost may not be strictly linear. If this were the case, basing a relatively large activity budget on the experience of a relatively small activity period would tend to overstate the large activity budget. The fixed-cost budget was deduced by dividing the budget for 12 months by two. In fact, there could be seasonal factors or inflationary pressures at work that might make such a crude division of the fixed cost element unfair.

### 12.4 Linpet Ltd

(a) Cash budgets are extremely useful for decision-making purposes. They allow managers to see the likely effect on the cash balance of the plans that they have set in place. Cash is an important asset and it is necessary to ensure that it is properly managed. Failure to do so can have disastrous consequences for the business. Where the cash budget indicates a surplus balance, managers must decide whether this balance should be reinvested in the business or distributed to the owners. Where the cash budget indicates a deficit balance, managers must decide how this deficit should be financed or how it might be avoided.

(b) Cash budget for the six months to 30 November

|  | June £ | July £ | Aug. £ | Sept. £ | Oct. £ | Nov. £ |
|---|---|---|---|---|---|---|
| **Receipts** |  |  |  |  |  |  |
| Cash sales revenue (Note 1) | 4,000 | 5,500 | 7,000 | 8,500 | 11,000 | 11,000 |
| Credit sales revenue (Note 2) | – | – | 4,000 | 5,500 | 7,000 | 8,500 |
|  | 4,000 | 5,500 | 11,000 | 14,000 | 18,000 | 19,500 |
| **Payments** |  |  |  |  |  |  |
| Purchases (Note 3) | – | 29,000 | 9,250 | 11,500 | 13,750 | 17,500 |
| Overheads | 500 | 500 | 500 | 500 | 650 | 650 |
| Wages | 900 | 900 | 900 | 900 | 900 | 900 |
| Commission (Note 4) | – | 320 | 440 | 560 | 680 | 880 |
| Equipment | 10,000 |  |  |  |  | 7,000 |
| Motor vehicle | 6,000 |  |  |  |  |  |
| Leasehold | 40,000 |  |  |  |  |  |
|  | 57,400 | 30,720 | 11,090 | 13,460 | 15,980 | 26,930 |
| Cash flow | (53,400) | (25,220) | (90) | 540 | 2,020 | (7,430) |
| Opening balance | 60,000 | 6,600 | (18,620) | (18,710) | (18,170) | (16,150) |
| Closing balance | 6,600 | (18,620) | (18,710) | (18,170) | (16,150) | (23,580) |

**Notes:**

(1) 50 per cent of the current month's sales revenue.

(2) 50 per cent of sales revenue of two months previous.

(3) To have sufficient inventories to meet each month's sales will require purchases of 75 per cent of the month's sales inventories figures (25 per cent is profit). In addition, each month the business will buy £1,000 more inventories than it will sell. In June, the business will also buy its initial inventories of £22,000. This will be paid for in the following month. For example, June's purchases will be (75% × £8,000) + £1,000 + £22,000 = £29,000, paid for in July.

(4) This is 5% of 80% of the month's sales revenue, paid in the following month. For example, June's commission will be 5% × 80% × £8,000 = £320, payable in July.

**12.5  Lewisham Ltd**

(a) The finished goods inventories budget for the three months ending 30 September (in units of production) is:

|  | July '000 units | Aug. '000 units | Sept '000 units |
|---|---|---|---|
| Opening inventories (Note 1) | 40 | 48 | 40 |
| Production (Note 2) | 188 | 232 | 196 |
|  | 228 | 280 | 236 |
| Inventories sold (Note 3) | (180) | (240) | (200) |
| Closing inventories | 48 | 40 | 36 |

(b) The raw materials inventories budget for the two months ending 31 August (in kg) is:

|  | July '000 kg | Aug. '000 kg |
|---|---|---|
| Opening inventories (Note 1) | 40 | 58 |
| Purchases (Note 2) | 112 | 107 |
|  | 152 | 165 |
| Production (Note 4) | (94) | (116) |
| Closing inventories | 58 | 49 |

(c) The cash budget for the two months ending 30 September is:

|  | Aug. £ | Sept £ |
|---|---|---|
| Inflows |  |  |
|   Receivables – Current month (Note 5) | 493,920 | 411,600 |
| Preceding month (Note 6) | 151,200 | 201,600 |
|   Total inflows | 645,120 | 613,200 |
| Outflows |  |  |
|   Payments to trade payables (Note 7) | 168,000 | 160,500 |
|   Labour and overheads (Note 8) | 185,600 | 156,800 |
|   Fixed overheads | 22,000 | 22,000 |
|   Total outflows | 375,600 | 339,300 |
| Net inflows/(outflows) | 269,520 | 273,900 |
| Balance carried forward | 289,520 | 563,420 |

**Notes:**
(1) The opening balance is the same as the closing balance from the previous month.
(2) This is a balancing figure.
(3) This figure is given in the question.
(4) This figure derives from the finished inventories budget (July, 188,000 × 0.5 = 94,000).
(5) This is 98 per cent of 70 per cent of the current month's sales revenue.
(6) This is 28 per cent of the previous month's sales revenue.
(7) This figure derives from the raw materials inventories budget (July, 112,000 × £1.50 = 168,000).
(8) This figure derives from the finished inventories budget (August, 232,000 × £0.80 = £185,600).

## Chapter 13

### 13.1 True or false

(a) A favourable direct labour rate variance can only be caused by something that leads to the rate per hour paid being less than standard. Normally, this would not be linked to efficient working. Where, however, the standard envisaged some overtime working, at premium rates, the actual labour rate may be below standard if efficiency has removed the need for the overtime.

(b) The statement is true. The action will lead to an adverse sales price variance and may well lead to problems elsewhere, but the sales volume variance must be favourable.

(c) It is true that below-standard materials could lead to adverse materials usage variances because there may be more than a standard amount of scrap. This could also cause adverse labour efficiency variances because working on materials that would not form part of the output would waste labour time.

(d) Higher-than-budgeted sales revenue could well lead to an adverse labour rate variance because producing the additional work may require overtime working at premium rates.

(e) The statement is true. Nothing else could cause such a variance.

### 13.2 Overheard remarks

(a) Flexing the budget identifies what the profit would have been, had the volume of output been the only difference between the original budget and the actual figures. Thus, comparing the flexed budget profit figure with that in the original budget reveals the profit difference (variance) arising solely from the volume difference (sales volume variance). Flexing the budget does not mean that volume differences do not matter. It is simply a way of discovering the effect on profit of the volume difference.

In one sense, all variances are 'water under the bridge'. The past cannot be undone, and we cannot go back to the last control period and put in a better performance. Identifying variances can, however, be useful in identifying where things went wrong. This should help managers to ensure that the same things do not to go wrong in the future.

(b) Variances will not tell us why things went wrong. They do not identify underlying causes. Rather they identify relevant questions that the manager, within whose sphere of responsibility things went wrong, should be able to answer.

(c) Identifying the reason for variances may well cost money, usually in terms of staff time. It is a matter of judgement in any particular situation, of balancing the cost of investigation against the potential benefits. As is usual in such judgements, it is difficult, before undertaking the investigation, to know either the cost or the likely benefit.

In general, significant variances, particularly adverse ones, should be investigated. Persistent (over a period of months) smaller variances should also be investigated. It should not automatically be assumed that favourable variances can be ignored. They indicate that things are not going according to plan, possibly because the plans (budgets) are flawed.

(d) Research evidence does not show this. Demanding, yet achievable, budget targets tend to motivate better than less demanding targets. However, unrealistically demanding targets tend to have an adverse effect on managers' performance. Once managers begin to view the budget targets as being too difficult to achieve, their level of motivation and performance declines.

(e) Budgets may provide the basis of both feedforward and feedback control. For feedforward control, budgets may be compared with forecast outcomes. Where there is a divergence, steps can be taken to revise the plans in order to avoid the potential problem. Thus, potential problems are anticipated and eliminated before they can occur.

For feedback control, budgets may be compared against actual outcomes. This can help to identify where something has gone wrong, and corrective action can then be taken to avoid this occurring in the future.

### 13.3 Pilot Ltd

(a)

| | Budget | | |
|---|---|---|---|
| | Original | Flexed | Actual |
| Output (units) | | | |
| (production and sales) | 5,000 | 5,400 | 5,400 |
| | £ | £ | £ |
| Sales revenue | 25,000 | 27,000 | 26,460 |
| Raw materials | (7,500) | (8,100) (2,700 kg) | (8,770) (2,830 kg) |
| Labour | (6,250) | (6,750) (675 hr) | (6,885) (650 hr) |
| Fixed overheads | (6,000) | (6,000) | (6,350) |
| Operating profit | 5,250 | 6,150 | 4,455 |

| | £ | |
|---|---|---|
| Sales volume variance (5,250 − 6,150) | 900 | (F) |
| Sales price variance (27,000 − 26,460) | (540) | (A) |
| Materials price variance (2,830 × 3) − 8,770 | (280) | (A) |
| Materials usage variance [(5,400 × 0.5) − 2,830] × £3 | (390) | (A) |
| Labour rate variance (650 × £10) − 6,885 | (385) | (A) |
| Labour efficiency variance [(5,400 × 7.5/60) − 650] × £10 | 250 | (F) |
| Fixed overhead spending variance (6,000 − 6,350) | (350) | (A) |
| Total net variances | (795) | (A) |

| | £ |
|---|---|
| Budgeted profit | 5,250 |
| Less Total net variance | (795) |
| Actual profit | 4,455 |

(b) Sales volume variance: sales manager; sales price variance: sales manager; materials price variance: buyer; materials usage variance: production manager; labour rate variance: personnel manager; labour efficiency variance: production manager; fixed overhead spending variance: various, depending on the nature of the overheads.

**13.5 Bradley-Allen Ltd**

(a)

| | Original | Flexed | Actual |
|---|---|---|---|
| | **Budget** | | |
| Output (units) (production and sales) | 800 | 950 | 950 |
| | £ | £ | £ |
| Sales revenue | 64,000 | 76,000 | 73,000 |
| Raw materials – A | (12,000) | (14,250) (285 kg) | (15,200) (310 kg) |
| – B | (16,000) | (19,000) (950 m) | (18,900) (920 m) |
| Labour – skilled | (4,000) | (4,750) (475 hr) | (4,628) (445 hr) |
| – unskilled | (10,000) | (11,875) (1,484.375 hr) | (11,275) (1,375 hr) |
| Fixed overheads | (12,000) | (12,000) | (11,960) |
| Operating profit | 10,000 | 14,125 | 11,037 |

Sales variances

Volume: $10,000 - 14,125 = £4,125$ (F)

Price: $76,000 - 73,000 = £3,000$ (A)

Direct materials A variances

Usage: $[(950 \times 0.3) - 310] \times £50 = £1,250$ (A)

Price: $(310 \times £50) - £15,200 = £300$ (F)

Direct materials B variances

Usage: $[(950 \times 1) - 920] \times £20 = £600$ (F)

Price: $(920 \times £20) - £18,900 = £500$ (A)

Skilled direct labour variances

Efficiency: $[(950 \times 0.5) - 445] \times £10 = £300$ (F)

Rate: $(445 \times £10) - £4,628 = £178$ (A)

Unskilled direct labour variances

Efficiency: $[(950 \times 1.5625) - 1,375] \times £8 = £875$ (F)

Rate: $(1,375 \times £8) - £11,275 = £275$ (A)

Fixed overhead variances

Spending: $(12,000 - 11,960) = £40$ (F)

| | | | | £ |
|---|---|---|---|---|
| **Budgeted profit** | | | | 10,000 |
| Sales: | Volume | 4,125 | (F) | |
| | Price | (3,000) | (A) | 1,125 |
| Direct material A: | Usage | (1,250) | (A) | |
| | Price | 300 | (F) | (950) |
| Direct material B: | Usage | 600 | (F) | |
| | Price | (500) | (A) | 100 |
| Skilled labour: | Efficiency | 300 | (F) | |
| | Rate | (178) | (A) | 122 |
| Unskilled labour: | Efficiency | 875 | (F) | |
| | Rate | (275) | (A) | 600 |
| Fixed overheads: | Expenditure | | | 40 |
| **Actual profit** | | | | 11,037 |

(b) The statement in (a) is useful to management because it enables them to see where there have been failures to meet the original budget and to quantify the extent of such failures. This means that junior managers can be held accountable for the performance of their particular area of responsibility.

## Chapter 14

### 14.1  Mylo Ltd

(a) The annual depreciation of the two projects is:

$$\text{Project 1: } \frac{(£100,000 - £7,000)}{3} = £31,000$$

$$\text{Project 2: } \frac{(£60,000 - £6,000)}{3} = £18,000$$

**Project 1**

(1)

|  | Year 0 £000 | Year 1 £000 | Year 2 £000 | Year 3 £000 |
|---|---|---|---|---|
| Operating profit/(loss) |  | 29 | (1) | 2 |
| Depreciation |  | 31 | 31 | 31 |
| Capital cost | (100) |  |  |  |
| Residual value |  |  |  | 7 |
| Net cash flows | (100) | 60 | 30 | 40 |
| 10% discount factor | 1.000 | 0.909 | 0.826 | 0.751 |
| Present value | (100.00) | 54.54 | 24.78 | 30.04 |
| Net present value | 9.36 | (That is, the sum of the present values for years 0 to 3) |  |  |

(2) Clearly the IRR lies above 10%. Try 15%:

|  |  |  |  |  |
|---|---|---|---|---|
| 15% discount factor | 1.000 | 0.870 | 0.756 | 0.658 |
| Present value | (100.00) | 52.20 | 22.68 | 26.32 |
| Net present value | 1.20 |  |  |  |

Thus the IRR lies a little above 15%, perhaps around 16%.

(3) To find the payback period, the cumulative cash flows are calculated:

|  |  |  |  |  |
|---|---|---|---|---|
| Cumulative cash flows | (100) | (40) | (10) | 30 |

Thus the payback will occur after three years if we assume year-end cash flows.

### Project 2

(1)

|  | Year 0 £000 | Year 1 £000 | Year 2 £000 | Year 3 £000 |
|---|---|---|---|---|
| Operating profit/(loss) |  | 18 | (2) | 4 |
| Depreciation |  | 18 | 18 | 18 |
| Capital cost | (60) |  |  |  |
| Residual value |  |  |  | 6 |
| Net cash flows | (60) | 36 | 16 | 28 |
| 10% discount factor | 1.000 | 0.909 | 0.826 | 0.751 |
| Present value | (60.00) | 32.72 | 13.22 | 21.03 |
| Net present value | 6.97 |  |  |  |

(2) Clearly the IRR lies above 10%. Try 15%:

|  |  |  |  |  |
|---|---|---|---|---|
| 15% discount factor | 1.000 | 0.870 | 0.756 | 0.658 |
| Present value | (60.00) | 31.32 | 12.10 | 18.42 |
| Net present value | 1.84 |  |  |  |

Thus the IRR lies a little above 15%, perhaps around 17%.

(3) The cumulative cash flows are:

|  |  |  |  |  |
|---|---|---|---|---|
| Cumulative cash flows | (60) | (24) | (8) | 20 |

Thus, the payback will occur after three years (assuming year-end cash flows).

(b) Assuming that Mylo Ltd is pursuing a shareholder wealth-enhancement objective, Project 1 is preferable since it has the higher net present value. The difference between the two net present values is not, however, significant.

### 14.3 Dirk plc

(a) (1) Net relevant cash flows are:

|  | Year 0 £m | Year 1 £m | Year 2 £m | Year 3 £m | Year 4 £m |
|---|---|---|---|---|---|
| Sales revenue | – | 9.0 | 9.6 | 7.2 | 3.0 |
| Loss of contribution |  | (0.8) | (0.8) | (0.8) |  |
| Variable cost |  | (1.0) | (1.2) | (1.2) | (0.7) |
| Fixed cost (Note 2) |  | (1.7) | (1.7) | (1.7) | (1.7) |
| Operating cash flows |  | 5.5 | 5.9 | 3.5 | 0.6 |
| Working capital | (1.8) |  |  |  | 1.8 |
| Capital cost (Note 3) | (10.5) |  |  |  | 0.5 |
| Net relevant cash flows | (12.3) | 5.5 | 5.9 | 3.5 | 2.9 |

The NPV is:

|  | Year 0 £m | Year 1 £m | Year 2 £m | Year 3 £m | Year 4 £m |
|---|---|---|---|---|---|
| Net relevant cash flows | (12.3) | 5.5 | 5.9 | 3.5 | 2.9 |
| Discount rate (8%) | 1.0 | 0.93 | 0.86 | 0.79 | 0.74 |
| Present value | (12.3) | 5.1 | 5.1 | 2.8 | 2.1 |
| NPV | 2.8 | (That is, the sum of the present values for years 0 to 4.) | | | |

**Notes:**
(1) The development cost of £0.4 million is irrelevant as it is a past cost.
(2) Only that part of the fixed cost that arises as a direct result of the project is relevant. Depreciation is irrelevant as it is not a cash flow.
(3) The residual value of the equipment is [£10.5m – (4 × £2.5m)] = £0.5m

(2) To calculate the IRR, a higher discount figure (12%) will be applied.

|  | Year 0 £m | Year 1 £m | Year 2 £m | Year 3 £m | Year 4 £m |
|---|---|---|---|---|---|
| Net relevant cash flows | (12.3) | 5.5 | 5.9 | 3.5 | 2.9 |
| Discount rate (12%) | 1.0 | 0.89 | 0.80 | 0.71 | 0.64 |
| Present value | (12.3) | 4.9 | 4.7 | 2.5 | 1.9 |
| NPV | (1.7) | | | | |

| Trial | Discount factor % | Net present value £000 |
|---|---|---|
| 1 | 8 | 2.8 |
| 2 | 12 | (1.7) |
| Difference | 4 | 4.5 |

For every 1 per cent change in the discount rate, the change in NPV will be:

$$4.5/4 = 1.125$$

Increase in the 8% discount rate necessary to achieve a zero NPV will be:

$$2.8/1.125 = 2\% \text{ (to nearest per cent)}$$

Thus the approximate IRR is:

$$8.0 + 2.0 = \underline{10.00}\%$$

(b) The NPV of the project is positive and the IRR of the project exceeds the cost of capital. Acceptance of the project will therefore enhance shareholder wealth. The NPV, however, is not very high and an analysis of the sensitivity of the key inputs to the decision may be useful to help assess the riskiness of the project.

**14.4** **Newton Electronics Ltd**

(a) **Option 1**

|  | Year 0 £m | Year 1 £m | Year 2 £m | Year 3 £m | Year 4 £m | Year 5 £m |
|---|---|---|---|---|---|---|
| Plant and equipment | (9.0) |  |  |  |  | 1.0 |
| Sales revenue |  | 24.0 | 30.8 | 39.6 | 26.4 | 10.0 |
| Variable cost |  | (11.2) | (19.6) | (25.2) | (16.8) | (7.0) |
| Fixed cost (ex. dep'n) |  | (0.8) | (0.8) | (0.8) | (0.8) | (0.8) |
| Working capital | (3.0) |  |  |  |  | 3.0 |
| Marketing cost |  | (2.0) | (2.0) | (2.0) | (2.0) | (2.0) |
| Opportunity cost |  | (0.1) | (0.1) | (0.1) | (0.1) | (0.1) |
|  | (12.0) | 9.9 | 8.3 | 11.5 | 6.7 | 4.1 |
| Discount factor 10% | 1.000 | 0.909 | 0.826 | 0.751 | 0.683 | 0.621 |
| Present value | (12.0) | 9.0 | 6.9 | 8.6 | 4.6 | 2.5 |
| Net present value | 19.6 | (That is, the sum of the present values for years 0 to 5.) | | | | |

**Option 2**

|  | Year 0 £m | Year 1 £m | Year 2 £m | Year 3 £m | Year 4 £m | Year 5 £m |
|---|---|---|---|---|---|---|
| Royalties | – | 4.4 | 7.7 | 9.9 | 6.6 | 2.8 |
| Discount factor 10% | 1.000 | 0.909 | 0.826 | 0.751 | 0.683 | 0.621 |
| Present value | – | 4.0 | 6.4 | 7.4 | 4.5 | 1.7 |
| Net present value | 24.0 |  |  |  |  |  |

**Option 3**

|  | Year 0 | Year 2 |
|---|---|---|
| Instalments | 12.0 | 12.0 |
| Discount factor 10% | 1.000 | 0.826 |
| Present value | 12.0 | 9.9 |
| Net present value | 21.9 |  |

(b) Before making a final decision, the board should consider the following factors:

- The long-term competitiveness of the business may be affected by the sale of the patents.
- At present, the business is not involved in manufacturing and marketing products. Would a change in direction be desirable?
- The business will probably have to buy in the skills necessary to produce the product itself. This will involve costs, and problems will be incurred. Has this been taken into account?
- How accurate are the forecasts made and how valid are the assumptions on which they are based?

(c) Option 2 has the highest net present value and is therefore the most attractive to shareholders. However, the accuracy of the forecasts should be checked before a final decision is made.

**14.7** **Simtex Ltd**

(a) Net operating cash flows each year will be:

|  | £000 |
|---|---|
| Sales revenue (160 × £6) | 960 |
| Variable cost (160 × £4) | (640) |
| Relevant fixed costs | (170) |
|  | 150 |

The estimated net present value of the new product can then be calculated:

|  | £000 |
|---|---|
| Annual cash flows (150 × 3.038*) | 456 |
| Residual value of equipment (100 × 0.636) | 64 |
|  | 520 |
| Initial outlay | (480) |
| Net present value | 40 |

\* This is the sum of the discount factors over four years (that is 0.893 + 0.797 + 0.712 + 0.636 = 3.038). Where the cash flows are constant, it is a quicker procedure than working out the present value of cash flows for each year and then adding them together.

(b) (1) Assume the discount rate is 18%. The net present value of the project would be:

|  | £000 |
|---|---|
| Annual cash flows (150 × 2.690*) | 404 |
| Residual value of equipment (100 × 0.516) | 52 |
|  | 456 |
| Initial outlay | (480) |
| Net present value | (24) |

\* That is 0.847 + 0.718 + 0.609 + 0.516 = 2.690.

Thus an increase of 6%, from 12% to 18%, in the discount rate causes a fall from +40 to –24 in the net present value: a fall of 64, or 10.67 (that is, 64/6) for each 1% rise in the discount rate. So a zero net present value will occur with a discount rate approximately equal to 12 + (40/10.67) = 15.75%. (This is, of course, the internal rate of return.)

This higher discount rate represents an increase of about 31% on the existing cost of capital figure.

(2) The initial outlay on equipment is already expressed in present-value terms and so, to make the project no longer viable, the outlay will have to increase by an amount equal to the net present value of the project (that is, £40,000) – an increase of 8.3% on the stated initial outlay.

(3) The change necessary in the annual net cash flows to make the project no longer profitable can be calculated as follows.

Let $Y$ = change in the annual operating cash flows. Then ($Y$ × cumulative discount rates for a four-year period) – NPV = 0. This can be rearranged as:

$$Y \times \text{cumulative discount rates for a four-year period} = \text{NPV}$$

$$Y \times 3.038 = £40,000$$
$$Y = £40,000/3.038$$
$$= £13,167$$

In percentage terms, this is a decrease of 8.8% on the estimated cash flows.

(4) The change in the residual value required to make the new product no longer profitable can be calculated as follows.

Let $V$ = change in the residual value. Then ($V$ × discount factor at end of four years) – NPV of product = 0. This can be rearranged as:

$$V \times \text{discount factor at end of four years} = \text{NPV of product}$$

$$V \times 0.636 = £40,000$$
$$V = £40,000/0.636$$
$$= £62,893$$

This is a decrease of 62.9% in the residual value of the equipment.

(c) The net present value of the product is positive and so it will increase shareholder wealth. Thus, it should be produced. The sensitivity analysis suggests the initial outlay and the annual cash flows are the most sensitive variables for managers to consider.

## Chapter 15

### 15.1 Financing issues

(a) This topic is dealt with in the chapter. The main benefits of leasing include ease of borrowing, reasonable cost, flexibility and avoidance of large cash outflows (which normally occurs where an asset is purchased).

(b) This topic is also dealt with in the chapter. The main benefits of using retained profits include no dilution of control, no share issue costs, no delay in receiving funds and the tax benefits of capital appreciation over dividends.

(c) A business may decide to repay a loan earlier than required for various reasons including:

- A fall in interest rates may make the existing loan interest rates higher than current loan interest rates. Thus, the business may decide to repay the existing loan using finance from a cheaper loan.
- A rise in interest rates or changes in taxation policy may make loan financing more expensive than other forms of financing. This may make the business decide to repay the loan using another form of finance.
- The business may have surplus cash and may have no other profitable uses for the cash.
- The business may wish to reduce the level of financial risk by reducing the level of gearing.

### 15.2 H. Brown (Portsmouth) Ltd

(a) The main factors to take into account are:

- *Risk.* If a business borrows, there is a risk that at the maturity date for the repayment of the funds the business will not have sufficient funds to repay the amount owing and will be unable to find a suitable form of replacement borrowing. With short-term borrowings, the maturity dates will arrive more quickly and the type of risk outlined will occur at more frequent intervals.
- *Matching.* A business may wish to match the life of an asset with the maturity date of the borrowing. In other words, long-term assets will be purchased with long-term borrowed funds. A certain level of current assets, which form part of the long-term asset base of the business, may also be funded by long-term borrowing. Those current

assets that fluctuate owing to seasonality and so on will be funded by short-term borrowing. This approach to funding assets will help reduce risks for the business.

- *Cost.* Interest rates for long-term borrowings may be higher than for short-term ones as investors may seek extra compensation for having their funds locked up for a long period. However, issue costs may be higher for short-term borrowings as there will be a need to refund at more frequent intervals.
- *Flexibility.* Short-term borrowings may be more flexible. It may be difficult to repay long-term ones before the maturity period.

(b) When deciding to grant a loan, a lender should consider the following factors:

- security
- purpose of the loan
- ability of the borrower to repay
- loan period
- availability of funds
- character and integrity of the senior managers.

(c) Loan conditions may include:

- the need to obtain permission before issuing further loans
- the need to maintain a certain level of liquidity during the loan period
- a restriction on the level of dividends and directors' pay.

### 15.3  Devonian plc

(a) (1)  *Ex-rights price*

|  | £ |
|---|---|
| 5 original shares @ £2.10 per share | 10.50 |
| 1 rights share @ £1.80 | 1.80 |
|  | 12.30 |
| Theoretical ex-rights price (£12.30/6) | £2.05 |

(2)  *Value of rights*

|  | £ |
|---|---|
| Value of a share after the rights issue | 2.05 |
| Cost of a rights share | 1.80 |
| Value of rights | 0.25 |
| Value of rights attached to each original share = £0.25/5 = | £0.05 |

(b) (1)  *Share price in one year's time*

*Rights issue*
We must first calculate the existing P/E ratio in order to determine the share price in one year's time. This can be done as follows:

|  | £m |
|---|---|
| Operating profit (Year 4) | 40.0 |
| Taxation (30%) | (12.0) |
| Profit for the year (available to shareholders) | 28.0 |
| Earnings per share (EPS) (£28.0m/200m) | = £0.14 |
| P/E ratio | $= \dfrac{\text{Share price}}{\text{EPS}}$ |
|  | = £2.10/£0.14 |
|  | = 15 times |

|  | £m |
|---|---|
| Operating profit (Year 5) | 50.0 |
| Taxation (30%) | (15.0) |
| Profit for the year (available to ordinary shareholders) | 35.0 |
| Earnings per share (£35m/240m) | = £0.146 |
| Share price (Year 5) | = EPS × P/E ratio |
|  | = £0.146 × 15 |
|  | = £2.19 |

(2) *Borrowing*

|  | £m |
|---|---|
| Operating profit (Year 5) | 50.0 |
| Interest payable (£72m @ 10%) | (7.2) |
|  | 42.8 |
| Taxation (30%) | (12.8) |
| Profit for the year (available to ordinary shareholders) | 30.0 |
| Earnings per share (£30m/200m) | = £0.15 |
| Share price (Year 5) | = EPS × P/E ratio |
|  | = £0.15 × 13.5 |
|  | = £2.03 |

These calculations reveal that in one year's time the share price is expected to rise by more than 4% above the current share price if a rights issue is made, whereas the share price will fall by more than 3% if the business borrows the money. Given the additional financial risks attached to borrowing, it seems that a rights issue offers the better option – at least in the short term.

(c) By issuing rights shares at a discount, shareholders are encouraged to either take up the shares or to sell the right to someone who will. Failure to do one of these will lead to a loss of wealth for the shareholder. (Since the discount offered on rights shares does not represent a real bonus to the shareholders, it can be quite large.)

(d) The price at which rights issues are made is not normally critical. It should, however, be low enough to ensure that, between setting the rights price and the date of the rights issue, the market price of existing shares will not fall below the rights issue price.

### 15.6  Carpets Direct plc

(a) The earnings per share (EPS) is:

$$\frac{\text{Profit after taxation}}{\text{Number of ordinary shares}} = \frac{£4.5m}{120m} = £0.0375$$

The current market value per share is:

$$\text{Earnings per share} \times \text{P/E} = £0.0375 \times 22 = £0.825$$

The rights issue price will be £0.825, less 20% discount = £0.66.
The theoretical ex-rights price is:

|  | £ |
|---|---|
| Original shares (4 @ £0.825) | 3.30 |
| Rights share (1 @ £0.66) | 0.66 |
| Value of five shares following rights issue | 3.96 |

Therefore, the value of one share following the rights issue is:

$$\frac{£3.96}{5} = 79.2\text{p}$$

(b)

| | |
|---|---:|
| Value of one share after rights issue | 79.2p |
| Cost of a rights share | (66.0p) |
| Value of rights to shareholder | 13.2p |

(c)  (1)  *Taking up rights issue*

| | £ |
|---|---:|
| Shareholding following rights issue [(4,000 + 1,000) × 79.2p] | 3,960 |
| *Less* Cost of rights shares (1,000 × 66p) | (660) |
| Shareholder wealth | 3,300 |

(2)  *Selling the rights*

| | |
|---|---:|
| Shareholding following rights issue (4,000 × 79.2p) | 3,168 |
| *Add* Proceeds from sale of rights (1,000 × 13.2p) | 132 |
| Shareholder wealth | 3,300 |

(3)  *Doing nothing*

As the rights are neither purchased nor sold, the shareholder wealth following the rights issue will be:

| | |
|---|---:|
| Shareholding (4,000 × 79.2p) | 3,168 |

We can see that the investor will have the same wealth under the first two options. However, by the investor doing nothing, the rights offer will lapse and so the investor will lose the value of the rights and will be worse off.

## Chapter 16

### 16.2  Hercules Wholesalers Ltd

(a)  The business is probably concerned about its liquidity position because:

- it has a substantial overdraft, which together with its non-current borrowings means that it has borrowed an amount roughly equal to its equity (according to statement of financial position values);
- it has increased its investment in inventories during the past year (as shown by the income statement); and
- it has a low current ratio of 1.1:1 (that is, 306/285) and a low acid-test ratio of 0.6:1 (that is, 162/285).

(b)  The operating cash cycle can be calculated as follows:

*Number of days*

Average inventories holding period:

$$\frac{[(\text{Opening inventories} + \text{Closing inventories})/2] \times 365}{\text{Cost of inventories}} = \frac{[(125 + 143/2)] \times 365}{323} \qquad = 151$$

*Add* Average settlement period for receivables:

$$\frac{\text{Trade receivables} \times 365}{\text{Credit sales revenue}} = \frac{163}{452} \times 365 \qquad = \underline{132}$$

$$283$$

*Less* Average settlement period for payables:

$$\frac{\text{Trade payables} \times 365}{\text{Credit purchases}} = \frac{145}{341} \times 365 \qquad = \underline{155}$$

Operating cash cycle $\qquad\qquad$ 128

(c) The business can reduce the operating cash cycle in a number of ways. The average inventories holding period seems quite long. At present, average inventories held represent about five months' inventories usage. Reducing the level of inventories held can reduce this period. Similarly, the average settlement period for receivables seems long at more than four months' sales revenue. Imposing tighter credit control, offering discounts, charging interest on overdue accounts, and so on may reduce this. However, any policy decisions concerning inventories and receivables must take account of current trading conditions.

Extending the period of credit taken to pay suppliers would also reduce the operating cash cycle. For the reasons mentioned in the chapter, however, this option must be given careful consideration.

**16.4** Plastics Manufacturers Ltd

*Ratio analysis – Plastic Toys Ltd*

|  | Year 1 | Year 2 | Year 3 |
|---|---|---|---|
| ROCE | 16.7% | 16.9% | (26.1%) |
| Operating profit margin | 12.5% | 11.2% | (23.4%) |
| Current ratio | 1.2 | 1.1 | 0.9 |
| Acid test ratio | 0.5 | 0.5 | 0.3 |
| Inventories' turnover period* | 91 days | 82 days | 183 days |
| Average settlement period for trade receivables | 64 days | 60 days | 91 days |

\* Using sales revenue figure rather than cost of sales, which is unavailable

The above figures reveal that Year 3 was a disastrous year for Plastic Toys Ltd (PT). Sales revenue and profitability fell dramatically. The fall in sales revenue does not appear to have been anticipated as inventories levels have risen dramatically in Year 3. The fall in profitability and increase in inventories has created a strain on liquidity that should cause acute concern. The liquidity ratios are very low and it seems the business is in a dangerous state. Extreme caution must therefore be exercised in any dealings with the business.

Before considering the proposal to supply, Plastics Manufacturers Ltd (PM) should establish why Plastic Toys Ltd wishes to change its suppliers. In view of the problems that it faces, there may well be problems with current suppliers. If three months' credit were to be granted, PM will be committed to supplying 6,000 kilos before payment is due. At a marginal cost of £7 a kilo, this means an exposure of £42,000. The risks of non-payment seem to be very high unless there is information concerning PT that indicates that its fortunes will improve in the near future. If PM is determined to supply the goods to PT, then some kind of security should be required in order to reduce the risk to PM.

**16.5** **Mayo Computers Ltd**

**New proposals from credit control department**

|  | £000 | £000 |
|---|---|---|
| Current level of investment in receivables |  |  |
| (£20m × (60/365)) |  | 3,288 |
| Proposed level of investment in receivables |  |  |
| ((£20m × 60%) × (30/365)) | (986) |  |
| ((£20m × 40%) × (50/365)) | (1,096) | (2,082) |
| Reduction in level of investment |  | 1,206 |

The reduction in overdraft interest as a result of the reduction in the level of investment will be £1,206,000 ×14% = £169,000.

|  | £000 | £000 |
|---|---|---|
| Cost of cash discounts offered (£20m × 60% × 2.5%) |  | 300 |
| Additional cost of credit administration |  | 20 |
|  |  | 320 |
| Bad debt savings | (100) |  |
| Interest charge savings (see above) | (169) | (269) |
| Net cost of policy each year |  | 51 |

These calculations show that the business would incur additional annual cost if it implemented this proposal. It would therefore be cheaper to stay with the existing credit policy.

**16.6  Boswell Enterprises Ltd**

(a) The investment in working capital will be:

|  | Current policy | | New policy | |
|---|---|---|---|---|
|  | £000 | £000 | £000 | £000 |
| Trade receivables |  |  |  |  |
| [(£3m × 1/12 × 30%) + (£3m × 2/12 × 70%)] |  | 425.0 |  |  |
| [(£3.15m × 1/12 × 60%) + (£3.15m × 2/12 × 40%)] |  |  |  | 367.5 |
| Inventories |  |  |  |  |
| [£3m − (£3m × 20%)] × 3/12 |  | 600.0 |  |  |
| {[£3.15m − (£3.15m × 20%)] × 3/12} |  |  |  | 630.0 |
| Cash (fixed) |  | 140.0 |  | 140.0 |
|  |  | 1,165.0 |  | 1,137.5 |
| Trade payables |  |  |  |  |
| [£3m − (£3m × 20%)] × 2/12] | (400.0) |  |  |  |
| {[£3.15m − (£3.15m × 20%)] × 2/12} |  |  | (420.0) |  |
| Accrued variable expenses |  |  |  |  |
| [£3m × 1/12 × 10%] | (25.0) |  |  |  |
| [£3.15m × 1/12 × 10%] |  |  | (26.3) |  |
| Accrued fixed expenses | (15.0) | (440.0) | (15.0) | (461.3) |
| Investment in working capital |  | 725.0 |  | 676.2 |

(b) The expected profit for the year

|  | Current policy | | New policy | |
|---|---|---|---|---|
|  | £000 | £000 | £000 | £000 |
| Sales revenue |  | 3,000.0 |  | 3,150.0 |
| Cost of goods sold |  | (2,400.0) |  | (2,520.0) |
| Gross profit (20%) |  | 600.0 |  | 630.0 |
| Variable expenses (10%) | (300.0) |  | (315.0) |  |
| Fixed expenses | (180.0) |  | (180.0) |  |
| Discounts (£3.15m × 60% × 2.5%) | – | (480.0) | (47.3) | (542.3) |
| Profit for the year |  | 120.0 |  | 87.7 |

(c) Under the proposed policy we can see that the investment in working capital will be slightly lower than under the current policy. However, profits will be substantially lower as a result of offering discounts. The increase in sales revenue resulting from the discounts will not be sufficient to offset the additional cost of making the discounts to customers. It seems that the business should, therefore, stick with its current policy.

## Appendix A

### A.1

| Account to be debited | Account to be credited |
|---|---|
| (a) Inventories | Trade payables |
| (b) Equity (or a separate drawings account) | Cash |
| (c) Interest on borrowings | Cash |
| (d) Inventories | Cash |
| (e) Cash | Trade receivables |
| (f) Wages | Cash |
| (g) Equity (or a separate drawings account) | Trade receivables |
| (h) Trade payables | Cash |
| (i) Electricity (or heat and light) | Cash |
| (j) Cash | Sales revenue |

Note that the precise name given to an account is not crucial so long as it is clear to those who are using the information what each account deals with.

### A.2 (a) and (b)

**Cash**

| | | £ | | | £ |
|---|---|---|---|---|---|
| 1 Feb. | Equity | 6,000 | 3 Feb. | Inventories | 2,600 |
| 15 Feb. | Sales revenue | 4,000 | 5 Feb. | Equipment | 800 |
| 28 Feb. | Trade receivables | 2,500 | 9 Feb. | Rent | 250 |
| | | | 10 Feb. | Fuel and electricity | 240 |
| | | | 11 Feb. | General expenses | 200 |
| | | | 21 Feb. | Equity | 1,000 |
| | | | 25 Feb. | Trade payables | 2,000 |
| | | | 28 Feb. | Balance c/d | 5,410 |
| | | 12,500 | | | 12,500 |
| 1 Mar. | Balance b/d | 5,410 | | | |

**Equity**

| | | £ | | | £ |
|---|---|---|---|---|---|
| 21 Feb. | Cash | 1,000 | 1 Feb. | Cash | 6,000 |
| 28 Feb. | Balance c/d | 5,000 | | | |
| | | 6,000 | | | 6,000 |
| | | | 28 Feb. | Balance b/d | 5,000 |
| 28 Feb. | Balance c/d | 7,410 | 28 Feb. | Income statement | 2,410 |
| | | 7,410 | | | 7,410 |
| | | | 1 Mar. | Balance b/d | 7,410 |

## Inventories

|  |  | £ |  |  | £ |
|---|---|---|---|---|---|
| 3 Feb. | Cash | 2,600 | 15 Feb. Cost of sales | | 2,400 |
| 6 Feb. | Trade payables | 3,000 | 19 Feb. Cost of sales | | 2,300 |
| | | | 28 Feb. Balance c/d | | 900 |
| | | 5,600 | | | 5,600 |
| 1 Mar. | Balance b/d | 900 | | | |

## Equipment

|  |  | £ |  | £ |
|---|---|---|---|---|
| 5 Feb. | Cash | 800 | | |

## Trade payables

|  |  | £ |  |  | £ |
|---|---|---|---|---|---|
| 25 Feb. | Cash | 2,000 | 6 Feb. | Inventories | 3,000 |
| 28 Feb. | Balance c/d | 1,000 | | | |
| | | 3,000 | | | 3,000 |
| | | | 1 Mar. | Balance b/d | 1,000 |

## Rent

|  |  | £ |  | £ |
|---|---|---|---|---|
| 9 Feb. | Cash | 250 | 28 Feb. Income statement | 250 |

## Fuel and electricity

|  |  | £ |  | £ |
|---|---|---|---|---|
| 10 Feb. | Cash | 240 | 28 Feb. Income statement | 240 |

## General expenses

|  |  | £ |  | £ |
|---|---|---|---|---|
| 11 Feb. | Cash | 200 | 28 Feb. Income statement | 200 |

## Sales revenue

|  |  | £ |  | £ |
|---|---|---|---|---|
| 28 Feb. Balance c/d | | 7,800 | 15 Feb. Cash | 4,000 |
| | | | 19 Feb. Trade receivables | 3,800 |
| | | 7,800 | | 7,800 |
| 28 Feb. Income statement | | 7,800 | 28 Feb. Balance b/d | 7,800 |

## Cost of sales

|  |  | £ |  | £ |
|---|---|---|---|---|
| 15 Feb. Inventories | | 2,400 | 28 Feb. Balance c/d | 4,700 |
| 19 Feb. Inventories | | 2,300 | | |
| | | 4,700 | | 4,700 |
| 28 Feb. Balance b/d | | 4,700 | 28 Feb. Income statement | 4,700 |

**Trade receivables**

| | £ | | £ |
|---|---|---|---|
| 19 Feb. Sales revenue | 3,800 | 28 Feb. Cash | 2,500 |
| | | 28 Feb. Balance c/d | 1,300 |
| | 3,800 | | 3,800 |
| 1 Mar. Balance b/d | 1,300 | | |

**Trial balance as at 28 February**

| | Debits | Credits |
|---|---|---|
| | £ | £ |
| Cash | 5,410 | |
| Equity | | 5,000 |
| Inventories | 900 | |
| Equipment | 800 | |
| Trade payables | | 1,000 |
| Rent | 250 | |
| Fuel and electricity | 240 | |
| General expenses | 200 | |
| Sales revenue | | 7,800 |
| Cost of sales | 4,700 | |
| Trade receivables | 1,300 | |
| | 13,800 | 13,800 |

**(c)** **Income statement**

| | £ | | £ |
|---|---|---|---|
| 28 Feb Cost of sales | 4,700 | 28 February Sales revenue | 7,800 |
| 28 Feb Rent | 250 | | |
| 28 Feb Fuel and electricity | 240 | | |
| 28 Feb General expenses | 200 | | |
| 28 Feb Equity (profit) | 2,410 | | |
| | 7,800 | | 7,800 |

**Statement of financial position as at 28 February**

| | £ |
|---|---|
| ASSETS | |
| Non-current assets | |
| Equipment | 800 |
| Current assets | |
| Inventories | 900 |
| Trade receivables | 1,300 |
| Cash | 5,410 |
| | 7,610 |
| Total assets | 8,410 |
| EQUITY AND LIABILITIES | |
| Equity (owners' claim) | 7,410 |
| Current liabilities | |
| Trade payables | 1,000 |
| Total equity and liabilities | 8,410 |

### Income statement for the month ended 28 February

| | £ |
|---|---|
| Sales revenue | 7,800 |
| Cost of sales | (4,700) |
| Gross profit | 3,100 |
| Rent | (250) |
| Fuel and electricity | (240) |
| General expenses | (200) |
| Profit for the month | 2,410 |

**A.3**

### Buildings

| | | £ | | £ |
|---|---|---|---|---|
| 1 Jan. | Balance brought down | 25,000 | | |

### Fittings – cost

| | | £ | | £ |
|---|---|---|---|---|
| 1 Jan. | Balance brought down | 10,000 | 31 Dec. Balance carried down | 12,000 |
| | Cash | 2,000 | | |
| | | 12,000 | | 12,000 |
| 1 Jan. | Balance brought down | 12,000 | | |

### Fittings – depreciation

| | £ | | £ |
|---|---|---|---|
| 31 Dec. Balance carried down | 4,400 | 1 Jan. Balance brought down | 2,000 |
| | | 31 Dec. Income statement | |
| | | (£12,000 × 20%) | 2,400 |
| | 4,400 | | 4,400 |
| | | 1 Jan. Balance brought down | 4,400 |

### General expenses

| | | £ | | £ |
|---|---|---|---|---|
| 1 Jan. | Balance brought down | 140 | 31 Dec. Income statement | 570 |
| | Cash | 580 | Balance carried down | 150 |
| | | 720 | | 720 |
| 1 Jan. | Balance brought down | 150 | | |

### Inventories

| | | £ | | | £ |
|---|---|---|---|---|---|
| 1 Jan. | Balance brought down | 1,350 | 31 Dec. | Cost of sales | 15,220 |
| 31 Dec. | Trade payables | 17,220 | | Cost of sales | 4,900 |
| | Cash | 3,760 | | Capital | 560 |
| | | | | Balance carried down | 1,650 |
| | | 22,330 | | | 22,330 |
| 1 Jan. | Balance brought down | 1,650 | | | |

### Cost of sales

| | £ | | £ |
|---|---|---|---|
| 31 Dec. Inventories | 15,220 | 31 Dec. Income statement | 20,120 |
| Inventories | 4,900 | | |
| | 20,120 | | 20,120 |

### Rent

| | £ | | £ |
|---|---|---|---|
| 1 Jan. Balance brought down | 500 | 31 Dec. Income statement | 3,000 |
| 31 Dec. Cash | 3,000 | Balance carried down | 500 |
| | 3,500 | | 3,500 |
| 1 Jan. Balance brought down | 500 | | |

### Trade receivables

| | £ | | £ |
|---|---|---|---|
| 1 Jan. Balance brought down | 1,840 | 31 Dec. Cash | 32,810 |
| 31 Dec. Sales revenue | 33,100 | Income statement (bad debt) | 260 |
| | | Balance carried down | 1,870 |
| | 34,940 | | 34,940 |
| 1 Jan. Balance brought down | 1,870 | | |

### Cash

| | £ | | £ |
|---|---|---|---|
| 1 Jan. Balance brought down | 2,180 | 31 Dec. Inventories | 3,760 |
| 31 Dec. Sales revenue | 10,360 | Wages | 3,770 |
| Borrowings | 2,000 | Rent | 3,000 |
| Trade receivables | 32,810 | Electricity | 1,070 |
| | | General expenses | 580 |
| | | Fittings | 2,000 |
| | | Borrowings | 1,000 |
| | | Trade payables | 18,150 |
| | | Capital | 10,400 |
| | | Balance carried down | 3,620 |
| | 47,350 | | 47,350 |
| 1 Jan. Balance brought down | 3,620 | | |

### Equity

| | £ | | £ |
|---|---|---|---|
| 31 Dec. Inventories | 560 | 1 Jan. Balance brought down | 25,050 |
| Cash | 10,400 | Income statement (profit) | 10,900 |
| Balance carried down | 24,990 | | |
| | 35,950 | | 35,950 |
| | | 1 Jan. Balance brought down | 24,990 |

### Borrowings

| | £ | | £ |
|---|---|---|---|
| 30 Jun. Cash | 1,000 | 1 Jan. Balance brought down | 12,000 |
| 31 Dec. Balance carried down | 13,000 | Cash | 2,000 |
| | 14,000 | | 14,000 |
| | | 1 Jan. Balance brought down | 13,000 |

### Trade payables

| | £ | | £ |
|---|---|---|---|
| 31 Dec.  Cash | 18,150 | 1 Jan.  Balance brought down | 1,690 |
| Balance carried down | 760 | 31 Dec. Inventories | 17,220 |
| | 18,910 | | 18,910 |
| | | 1 Jan.   Balance brought down | 760 |

### Electricity

| | £ | | £ |
|---|---|---|---|
| 31 Dec.  Cash | 1,070 | 1 Jan.  Balance brought down | 270 |
| 31 Dec.  Balance carried down | 290 | 31 Dec. Income statement | 1,090 |
| | 1,360 | | 1,360 |
| | | 1 Jan.   Balance brought down | 290 |

### Sales revenue

| | £ | | £ |
|---|---|---|---|
| 31 Dec.  Income statement | 43,460 | 31 Dec. Trade receivables | 33,100 |
| | | Cash | 10,360 |
| | 43,460 | | 43,460 |

### Wages

| | £ | | £ |
|---|---|---|---|
| 31 Dec. Cash | 3,770 | 31 Dec. Income statement | 3,770 |

### Interest on borrowings

| | £ | | £ |
|---|---|---|---|
| | | 31 Dec. Income statement | 1,350 |
| | | [(6/12 × 14,000) + | |
| | | (6/12 × 13,000)] × 10% | |

### Income statement for the year to 31 December

| | £ | | £ |
|---|---|---|---|
| 31 Dec. Cost of sales | 20,120 | 31 Dec. Sales revenue | 43,460 |
| Depreciation | 2,400 | | |
| General expenses | 570 | | |
| Rent | 3,000 | | |
| Bad debts (Trade receivables) | 260 | | |
| Electricity | 1,090 | | |
| Wages | 3,770 | | |
| Interest on borrowings | 1,350 | | |
| Profit (Capital) | 10,900 | | |
| | 43,460 | | 43,460 |

## Statement of financial position as at 31 December last year

|  |  | £ |
|---|---:|---:|
| **ASSETS** | | |
| **Non-current assets** | | |
| *Property, plant and equipment* | | |
| Buildings | | 25,000 |
| Fittings: cost | 12,000 | |
| depreciation | (4,400) | 7,600 |
| | | 32,600 |
| **Current assets** | | |
| Inventories of stationery | | 150 |
| Inventories | | 1,650 |
| Prepaid rent | | 500 |
| Trade receivables | | 1,870 |
| Cash | | 3,620 |
| | | 7,790 |
| **Total assets** | | 40,390 |
| **EQUITY AND LIABILITIES** | | |
| Equity (owners' claim) | | 24,990 |
| **Non-current liabilities** | | |
| Borrowings | | 13,000 |
| **Current liabilities** | | |
| Trade payables | | 760 |
| Accrued electricity | | 290 |
| Accrued interest on borrowings | | 1,350 |
| | | 2,400 |
| **Total equity and liabilities** | | 40,390 |

# Present value table

Present value of £1, that is, $1/(1 + r)^n$

where $r$ = discount rate
$n$ = number of periods until payment

| Periods (n) | | | | | Discount rates (r) | | | | | | |
|---|---|---|---|---|---|---|---|---|---|---|---|
| | 1% | 2% | 3% | 4% | 5% | 6% | 7% | 8% | 9% | 10% | |
| 1 | 0.990 | 0.980 | 0.971 | 0.962 | 0.952 | 0.943 | 0.935 | 0.926 | 0.917 | 0.909 | 1 |
| 2 | 0.980 | 0.961 | 0.943 | 0.925 | 0.907 | 0.890 | 0.873 | 0.857 | 0.842 | 0.826 | 2 |
| 3 | 0.971 | 0.942 | 0.915 | 0.889 | 0.864 | 0.840 | 0.816 | 0.794 | 0.772 | 0.751 | 3 |
| 4 | 0.961 | 0.924 | 0.888 | 0.855 | 0.823 | 0.792 | 0.763 | 0.735 | 0.708 | 0.683 | 4 |
| 5 | 0.951 | 0.906 | 0.863 | 0.822 | 0.784 | 0.747 | 0.713 | 0.681 | 0.650 | 0.621 | 5 |
| 6 | 0.942 | 0.888 | 0.837 | 0.790 | 0.746 | 0.705 | 0.666 | 0.630 | 0.596 | 0.564 | 6 |
| 7 | 0.933 | 0.871 | 0.813 | 0.760 | 0.711 | 0.665 | 0.623 | 0.583 | 0.547 | 0.513 | 7 |
| 8 | 0.923 | 0.853 | 0.789 | 0.731 | 0.677 | 0.627 | 0.582 | 0.540 | 0.502 | 0.467 | 8 |
| 9 | 0.914 | 0.837 | 0.766 | 0.703 | 0.645 | 0.592 | 0.544 | 0.500 | 0.460 | 0.424 | 9 |
| 10 | 0.905 | 0.820 | 0.744 | 0.676 | 0.614 | 0.558 | 0.508 | 0.463 | 0.422 | 0.386 | 10 |
| 11 | 0.896 | 0.804 | 0.722 | 0.650 | 0.585 | 0.527 | 0.475 | 0.429 | 0.388 | 0.350 | 11 |
| 12 | 0.887 | 0.788 | 0.701 | 0.625 | 0.557 | 0.497 | 0.444 | 0.397 | 0.356 | 0.319 | 12 |
| 13 | 0.879 | 0.773 | 0.681 | 0.601 | 0.530 | 0.469 | 0.415 | 0.368 | 0.326 | 0.290 | 13 |
| 14 | 0.870 | 0.758 | 0.661 | 0.577 | 0.505 | 0.442 | 0.388 | 0.340 | 0.299 | 0.263 | 14 |
| 15 | 0.861 | 0.743 | 0.642 | 0.555 | 0.481 | 0.417 | 0.362 | 0.315 | 0.275 | 0.239 | 15 |

*(continued over)*

| Periods (n) | Discount rates (r) | | | | | | | | | | |
|---|---|---|---|---|---|---|---|---|---|---|---|
| | 11% | 12% | 13% | 14% | 15% | 16% | 17% | 18% | 19% | 20% | |
| 1 | 0.901 | 0.893 | 0.885 | 0.877 | 0.870 | 0.862 | 0.855 | 0.847 | 0.840 | 0.833 | 1 |
| 2 | 0.812 | 0.797 | 0.783 | 0.769 | 0.756 | 0.743 | 0.731 | 0.718 | 0.706 | 0.694 | 2 |
| 3 | 0.731 | 0.712 | 0.693 | 0.675 | 0.658 | 0.641 | 0.624 | 0.609 | 0.593 | 0.579 | 3 |
| 4 | 0.659 | 0.636 | 0.613 | 0.592 | 0.572 | 0.552 | 0.534 | 0.516 | 0.499 | 0.482 | 4 |
| 5 | 0.593 | 0.567 | 0.543 | 0.519 | 0.497 | 0.476 | 0.456 | 0.437 | 0.419 | 0.402 | 5 |
| 6 | 0.535 | 0.507 | 0.480 | 0.456 | 0.432 | 0.410 | 0.390 | 0.370 | 0.352 | 0.335 | 6 |
| 7 | 0.482 | 0.452 | 0.425 | 0.400 | 0.376 | 0.354 | 0.333 | 0.314 | 0.296 | 0.279 | 7 |
| 8 | 0.434 | 0.404 | 0.376 | 0.351 | 0.327 | 0.305 | 0.285 | 0.266 | 0.249 | 0.233 | 8 |
| 9 | 0.391 | 0.361 | 0.333 | 0.308 | 0.284 | 0.263 | 0.243 | 0.225 | 0.209 | 0.194 | 9 |
| 10 | 0.352 | 0.322 | 0.295 | 0.270 | 0.247 | 0.227 | 0.208 | 0.191 | 0.176 | 0.162 | 10 |
| 11 | 0.317 | 0.287 | 0.261 | 0.237 | 0.215 | 0.195 | 0.178 | 0.162 | 0.148 | 0.135 | 11 |
| 12 | 0.286 | 0.257 | 0.231 | 0.208 | 0.187 | 0.168 | 0.152 | 0.137 | 0.124 | 0.112 | 12 |
| 13 | 0.258 | 0.229 | 0.204 | 0.182 | 0.163 | 0.145 | 0.130 | 0.116 | 0.104 | 0.093 | 13 |
| 14 | 0.232 | 0.205 | 0.181 | 0.160 | 0.141 | 0.125 | 0.111 | 0.099 | 0.088 | 0.078 | 14 |
| 15 | 0.209 | 0.183 | 0.160 | 0.140 | 0.123 | 0.108 | 0.095 | 0.084 | 0.074 | 0.065 | 15 |

# Index